Chronicle of Progress

TRIDENT
PRESS

Published by Trident Press Ltd
Text copyright © 1996: Trident Press Ltd
Additional text copyright © 1996: Contributing authors
Pictures copyright: Mediatec LLC. & Ministry of Information & Culture, UAE
Additional pictures copyright of individual photographers and respective sources.
Layout & Design © 1996: Trident Press Ltd

Editors: Ibrahim Al Abed, Paula Vine, Abdullah Al Jabali

Photographs: The publishers are pleased to acknowledge and thank Al Ittihad
newspaper for complete access to their extensive collection of historical
photographs on the UAE (unless otherwise credited, pictures are from this source).
In addition the publishers are grateful to the British Petroleum Company which
offered access to its own fascinating archive of pictures taken prior to formation of
the Federation. The following additional photographic sources are also
acknowledged and thanked: Mohammed Badr; Nour Ali Rashid; Christine
Osborne; Aspect Picture Library; Hutchison Picture Library; Helen Rodgers;
Mediatec: Adam Woolfitt, Charles Crowell, Hanne & Jens Eriksen; and the UAE
government who retain respective copyrights.

Photographic Research: Jane Lewis.
Photographic laboratory services: Hussein Rasheed
Research: Abbas Al Zubair, Fakhri Wadha, Martin Harrison

English edition typesetting: Johan Hofsteenge
Arabic edition typing: Omar Abeedo
Arabic translator: Clyde Leamaster

The editors and publishers wish to acknowledge the cooperation and assistance of
the Emirates News Agency - WAM.

Published with the cooperation of the Higher Committee for the UAE Silver Jubilee
and the Ministry of Information and Culture, PO Box 17, Abu Dhabi, United Arab
Emirates. Tel: (971 2) 453000; Fax: (971 2) 450458. E-mail: mininfex@emirates.net.ae

Trident Press Ltd., 2-5 Old Bond Street, London W1X3TB

British Library Cataloguing in Publication Data
A CIP catalogue record for this book is available from the British Library.
ISBN: 1-900724-03-0

Contents

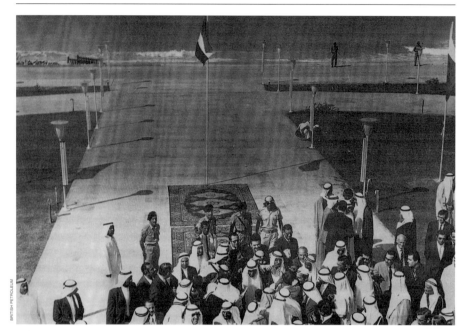

The above historic picture was taken on 2 December 1971, after the first hoisting of the flag of the United Arab Emirates.

First meeting of the Federal Supreme Council after Ras al-Khaimah joined, in February 1972.

Foreword

Whilst the pages of this book span a relatively brief period of time, a little over a quarter of a century, they record the numerous achievements and milestones which together form the building blocks of the United Arab Emirates. They take the reader on a literary excursion from the period prior to formation of the Federation, when a journey from Abu Dhabi to Dubai or Al-Ain was a time-consuming and quite arduous adventure, to the present day in which such trips are undertaken in air-conditioned comfort over fast, smooth multi-laned highways or by intercity air-link.

Progress has taken place in all aspects of development, from the burgeoning economic sector, through social, cultural, environmental fields, to that of international relations. The physical evidence of this rapid growth is prominent and impressive, involving massive infrastructural projects such as dams, ports, roads, airports, power stations and desalination plants; together with key social amenities such as comfortable modern housing, purpose built educational institutions, efficiently equipped hospitals, and a wide range of sporting and leisure facilities - in short, a complete infrastructure - extending throughout the country from east to west, from north to south, from coast to mountains to desert.

Whilst any visitor to the UAE can easily recognize that paramount attention has been directed towards the well-being of the UAE's people, together with its natural environment and its culture, the pace at which these goals have been achieved is less apparent. Just as the people of the

Emirates could hardly have imagined, 25 years ago, that they would experience such rapid growth in their lives, so the visitor today finds it hard to believe just how much has changed in such a short period of time. This book is therefore a unique record, both for those who have lived through the changes, and for those who have only known the modern UAE with all its sophisticated facilities.

Behind every major success story there is inevitably another tale of human endeavour, of perseverance and, most importantly, of leadership. In the case of this particular story the strong guiding hand of H.H. Sheikh Zayed, President of the UAE since its formation, is clearly portrayed on every page of this book. He has led by personal example, providing a consistency, level of commitment and coherence of thought that few political leaders can match. His initial views on the United Arab Emirates itself, on solidarity, Arab unity, on the youth of the country, on the role of women, on culture, the environment and greening of the desert are as much in evidence today as they were at the start of his mission. This genuine and natural wisdom has been a vital guiding force behind the development of the country through this crucial period of establishment and growth.

It is a story which needs to be told in all its detail and this book will provide fascinating reading for all who delve into its pages. The research, writing and editorial team has worked for over a year in order to create this unique record which maps out the country's evolution, from that of a fledgling state to one of the most successful and highly respected, worldwide.

With these thoughts in mind, it is indeed a pleasure to introduce this *Chronicle of Progress* in the certain knowledge that it will highlight for its readers the main developments in the United Arab Emirates from the period since its establishment in 1971 to its Silver Jubilee celebrated on 2 December 1996.

Hamdan bin Zayed Al Nahyan
Chairman
Higher Committee for the Silver Jubilee Celebrations of the UAE

Abu Dhabi's foreshore in 1953.

The town of Abu Dhabi in 1953.

Abu Dhabi's main fort in 1954.

An Abu Dhabi fort guard with falcon in October 1954.

BRITISH PETROLEUM

Commander Jacques Yves Cousteau was commissioned by BP to carry out an underwater survey in Abu Dhabi in 1954. Here he is seen on board Calypso, and in a shark protection cage, preparing to dive. The team dived to almost 80 metres and brought up bottom samples.

Abu Dhabi fort in 1957.

Abu Dhabi citizens in 1957.

Aerial view of Das island in 1957.

Aerial view of Abu Dhabi in 1958.

Dove aircraft of Gulf Airways preparing to leave Das Island for the mainland. In the background is 'Adma Enterprise' being towed to the site of Umm Shaif No 1 well in 1958.

A scene in Dubai harbour in 1960.

Dhows in Dubai harbour in 1960.

First section of the well head tower suspended from the draw works of Adma Enterprise at the site of Umm Shaif no.3 well. 1960. Adma Enterprise changed hands in 1966 and was subsequently known as Offshore Enterprise.

Aerial view of Abu Dhabi town in 1960.

Abu Dhabi "Customs Point" in September 1961.

Buraimi, with Jebel Hafit in background. March 1962.

Aerial view of Das island in September 1962.

Asab oasis in the Liwa, March 1962.

BRITISH PETROLEUM

Airstrip on Das island in 1962, with Gulf Aviation Dakota in the foreground.

The Beach Hotel, Abu Dhabi in October 1962.

*Two aerial views of Abu Dhabi in 1963,
showing new roads and buildings and Abu
Dhabi fort.*

*Aerial view of tugs manoeuvring BP's
35,000 ton British Signal away from the
loading berth off Das island, after she loaded
the first cargo of crude oil from the Umm
Shaif field in 1962.*

Camel caravan on trek in the Liwa district of Abu Dhabi, 1962.

Mosque and minaret in Abu Dha

Girls dance before Sheikh Zayed during Eid festivities at Hili village in March 1962.

Windtowers in Dubai in March 1962.

wn in March 1962.   *A golf match being played on Das island in October 1962.*

A scene in Al-Ain - Buraimi in March 1962.

Main street of Al-Ain, Buraimi oasis, showing the Eastern Bank, in 1963.

The first Jersey bull to

Al-Ain in 1963.

Water distillation pla
Aquachem in Abu Dh

e imported from England in 1963.

The state of the "road" between Abu Dhabi and Al Ain in 1963.

*upplied by UK company
n December 1963.*

*In 1966 most people in Abu Dhabi were still drawing water
from points such as this. The water was piped from Al-Ain.*

In 1970 Sheikh Zayed visited Cairo where he held a series of high level meetings. He is seen here with the late President Sadat of Egypt, President Asad of Syria and President Nimeiri of Sudan.

Sheikh Zayed and the late President Sadat in Cairo in 1970.

Prologue

EVENTS LEADING TO THE ESTABLISHMENT OF THE FEDERATION

February 1968: At a meeting in Dubai, His Highness Sheikh Zayed bin Sultan Al Nahyan, Ruler of Abu Dhabi, and His Highness Sheikh Rashid bin Saeed Al Maktoum, Ruler of Dubai, discussed setting-up a federation which would undertake the supervision of foreign affairs, defence, internal security, health and educational services on behalf of the individual emirates. They agreed to invite the Rulers of other emirates in the region to a meeting in Dubai to discuss federating nine Arab emirates.

25-27 February 1968: The Rulers of the emirates of Abu Dhabi, Dubai, Sharjah, Ras al-Khaimah, Ajman, Umm al-Qaiwain, Qatar and Bahrain met in Dubai. At this meeting, an agreement, to be known as the Dubai Agreement, was reached to set-up a union of Arab emirates. Work on the federation was scheduled to begin on 30 March 1968.

25-27 March 1968: The first meeting of the Rulers' Council of the nine emirates took place in Abu Dhabi to resume discussions on the implementation of the Dubai Agreement.

6 July 1968: His Highness Sheikh Zayed bin Sultan Al Nahyan was nominated as President of the proposed federation of Arab emirates in a meeting convened by the Rulers in Abu Dhabi. It was decided to hold the third meeting of the Rulers' Council in Doha on 20 October 1968.

11-15 October 1969: The Rulers of the emirates of Abu Dhabi, Dubai, Sharjah, Ras al-Khaimah, Ajman, Umm al-Qaiwain and Fujairah held continuous meetings after which it was formally agreed to establish a federal State to be known as the United Arab Emirates. Sheikh Zayed bin Sultan Al Nahyan was elected President of the federation for a period of two years and the late Sheikh Rashid bin Saeed Al Maktoum was elected as Vice President for the same period.

18 July 1971: The seven Rulers held a meeting in Dubai in which they affirmed their commitment to establish the federal State with a provisional constitution. Ras al-Khaimah, however, did not announce its adherence to the federation at this meeting.

2 December 1971: The Rulers of the six remaining emirates held an important meeting after which they issued an historic proclamation announcing the establishment of the State of the United Arab Emirates.

10 February 1972: The inclusion of the emirate of Ras al-Khaimah as the seventh member of the federation was unanimously approved by the United Arab Emirates' Supreme Council.

Nineteen Seventy One

2 January: A meeting was held in Ras al-Khaimah to study the latest developments connected to the establishment of the United Arab Emirates. Attending the meeting were Sheikh Saqr bin Mohammad Al Qassimi, Sheikh Rashid bin Humaid Al Nuaimi, Sheikh Rashid bin Ahmed Al Mualla and Sheikh Humaid bin Rashid Al Nuaimi.

19 January: Sheikh Zayed bin Sultan Al Nahyan held discussions with a joint Saudi-Kuwaiti delegation which included Prince Nawwaf bin Abdulaziz and Sheikh Sabah Al Ahmed Al Sabah. They dealt with ways to establish a federation of coastal emirates. When the talks were concluded the delegation went to Sharjah.

28 January: Sheikh Khalid bin Mohammad Al Qassimi, Ruler of Sharjah, confirmed his wish for the complete unity of the emirates. At the conclusion of the discussions, he called on the joint Saudi-Kuwaiti delegation to overcome impediments in the way of a strong federation.

The annual budget for the emirate of Abu Dhabi for 1971 was almost 45 million Bahraini dinars.

15 February: An agreement signed in Tehran by Abu Dhabi, Iran, Iraq, Kuwait, Saudi Arabia, Qatar and the oil companies operating in these countries included an increase in the price of oil exported from the Gulf. Estimates indicated that Abu Dhabi's annual revenues would rise to nearly 40 million Bahraini dinars as a result of this agreement.

16 February: Sheikh Khalifa bin Zayed Al Nahyan opened the new head-quarters building for the Abu Dhabi Telephone and Telegraph Company.

25 February: Sheikh Khalifa bin Zayed Al Nahyan attended celebrations by the Abu Dhabi Broadcasting Station to mark the passage of two years since it began transmission.

Sheikh Hamdan bin Mohammad Al Nahyan signed a 4 million Bahraini dinar agreement for a sewage treatment project in the city of Abu Dhabi.

1 March: In the House of Commons, the British Foreign Secretary, Sir Alec Douglas-Home, announced that treaties between Britain and nine Arab emirates would be terminated at the end of 1971.

9 March: Rulers of the seven emirates attended a dinner in Dubai given by Sheikh Rashid bin Saeed Al Maktoum on the occasion of his son Maktoum bin Rashid Al Maktoum's marriage, during which they discussed the next steps to be taken to establish the federation in light of the British announcement of its intention to withdraw from the region at the end of the year.

13-14 March: At the end of their meetings in Dubai, the Rulers Council, composed of the Rulers of the seven emirates, issued a statement in which they affirmed a 2.75 million Bahraini dinar budget for the Development Board for 1971. Sheikh Saqr bin Mohammad Al Qassimi was elected Chairman of the Council and it was decided to reconvene the Council in three months and to postpone the adoption of any decrees governing membership of the emirates in any agencies until the proposed federation had been formally established.

21 March: Renewed efforts were made toward federation at both local and Arab levels. Sheikh Zayed bin Sultan Al Nahyan met with Sheikh Rashid bin Saeed Al Maktoum to exchange points of view regarding federal affairs. Hassan Sabri Al Kholi, the personal representative of the Egyptian President, Anwar Sadat, visited the emirates as did Sayyid Ahmed Al Tarawna, Chief of the Royal Jordanian Diwan. In addition, the Governments of Kuwait and Saudi Arabia formed a joint committee to hold discussions concerning the federation with the Rulers of the emirates. Sheikh Mohammad bin Mubarak Al Khalifa, Bahrain's Minister of Foreign Affairs also made telephone contact with officials in Abu Dhabi.

22 March: Sheikh Zayed bin Sultan Al Nahyan returned to Abu Dhabi from Dubai having participated in the meetings of the Council of Rulers. He held discussions with the Rulers of the coastal emirates and Sheikh Ahmed bin Ali Al Thani, Ruler of Qatar, concerning the latest developments in the federation.

7 April: Sheikh Zayed bin Sultan Al Nahyan arrived in Rabat on a visit to the Moroccan kingdom at the beginning of a tour which included the United Arab Republic. In an interview with the Egyptian newspaper, *Al Ahram*, he stated that team spirit and honest co-operation were the key to success in efforts leading towards federation, that everyone believed in one goal and that the ties of brotherhood would overcome all problems. Sheikh Zayed, expressing his optimism regarding the establishment of the federation, pointed out that there was no federal state in the world that did not encompass conflicting points of view.

12 April: Sheikh Zayed arrived in Cairo where he immediately held a meeting with the Egyptian President, Anwar Sadat. He also met with Syrian President Hafez Al Asad and with the Sudanese President, Jaafar Al Numeiri, who were in the Egyptian capital .

A joint communiqué was issued on the outcome of Sheikh Zayed's visit to Morocco and his talks with King Hassan the Second. The statement confirmed support for the establishment of a federation of united Arab emirates to ensure security and stability in the region and achieve prosperity and a good life for its people.

29 April: Sheikh Zayed bin Sultan Al Nahyan attended the last function to be given by the British Political Agency in Abu Dhabi which took place on the occasion of the Queen's birthday. The British Political Agent announced that the agreement on relations between the British Government and the Government of Abu Dhabi would cease to be operative at the end of 1971.

Following discussions with the joint Saudi-Kuwait mission, Sheikh Rashid bin Saeed Al Maktoum announced that there was optimism concerning the posibility of forming a federation of nine emirates.

5 May: The first census to be taken in the city of Abu Dhabi commenced.

11 May: Ceremonies marking the shipment of the 100 millionth barrel of oil to be exported from Jebel al-Dhanna were attended by Mana Said Al Otaiba, Director of the Oil and Industry Office. The first tanker carrying oil from Jebel al-Dhanna had sailed on 13 December 1963.

15 May: Sheikh Rashid bin Saeed Al Maktoum opened the new Dubai International Airport: the old Dubai airport was built in 1959.

30 May: Sheikh Ahmed bin Hamid, Director of the Office of Social Affairs, Labour, Information, Tourism and the Civil Service, issued a decree forming the first Football Federation in Abu Dhabi.

10 June: Sheikh Zayed donated 50,000 dollars to support UNICEF activities.

The Amiri Diwan of Abu Dhabi directed that the Hegira date be affixed to all correspondence issued by government offices.

The Al-Ahli Club won the first football match to be held in Abu Dhabi.

17 June: Sheikh Khalifa bin Zayed Al Nahyan announced that the Government of Abu Dhabi donated 20,000 Bahraini dinars to support Gaza's defiant stand against Zionist occupation.

22 June: Thousands of people from Abu Dhabi and the other emirates converged on Sheikh Zayed when he returned from a medical visit to London. Ahmed Khalifa Al Suweidi announced that Sheikh Zayed had taken the opportunity while he was in Europe to hold discussions with important officials regarding efforts being made to set-up a federation of emirates.

23 June: The Shah of Iran threatened to forcibly take the three islands of Abu Musa and the Greater and Lesser Tunbs which belonged to the emirates of Ras al-Khaimah and Sharjah but were under British protection as a result of treaties concluded in the last century.

1 July: Abu Dhabi was the scene of important political activity regarding the creation of a federation of emirates. Sheikh Zayed bin Sultan Al Nahyan received the Rulers of Dubai, Ras al-Khaimah, Sharjah and the Deputy Rulers of Ajman and Umm al-Qaiwain. He assured them that Abu Dhabi was still attempting to achieve a federation of Arab Gulf emirates.

Sheikh Mubarak bin Mohammad Al Nahyan, the Commander of the Police and Public Security, gave orders to ensure that passports issued by Arab Gulf emirates would retain their validity and that the passage of these passport holders would be facilitated irrespective of their country of origin or their place of residence.

8 July: Abu Dhabi emirate was the object of great interest on the part of the media following the formation of the first Council of Ministers and the first National Consultative Council. The Executive Council of Ministers held a meeting in which it expressed its pleasure at the steps being taken by Sheikh Zayed to make the federation a reality.

13 July: The Council of Rulers held a special meeting in Dubai under the chairmanship of Sheikh Saqr bin Mohammad Al Qassimi to discuss questions regarding the federation. Sheikh Zayed, having discussed the proposed federation with the Rulers present at the meeting, announced that they had no choice but to form a federation and that no time must be lost. He said that the federation would prosper and that he had devoted his life to achieving this goal.

19 July: The establishment of the State of the United Arab Emirates was announced in Dubai, six emirates having joined the federation: Abu Dhabi, Dubai, Sharjah, Ajman, Umm al-Qaiwain and Fujairah.

Sheikh Zayed bin Sultan Al Nahyan ordered that all facilities and administrative/technical experience of the Government of Abu Dhabi be placed at the disposal of the federation until its constituent elements were put in place and it had begun to exercise its responsibilities. He expressed the hope that Ras al-Khaimah, Qatar and Bahrain would also join the United Arab Emirates.

16 July: Sheikh Zayed bin Sultan Al Nahyan issued a law establishing the Abu Dhabi Fund for Arab Economic Development (ADFAED) with a capital of 50 million Bahraini dinars.

26 July: Sheikh Zayed issued a decree appointing Sheikh Tahnoun bin Mohammad Al Nahyan as Ruler's Representative in the Eastern Region of Abu Dhabi.

The representatives of the Rulers of the emirates ended their series of meetings in Abu Dhabi where they drafted a number of laws concerning the new institutions of the State.

9 September: Mana Said Al Otaiba announced that he had initialled an agreement delimiting the continental shelf between Abu Dhabi and Iran during a recent visit to Iran.

30 October: Abu Dhabi's National Consultative Council held its first meeting during which Sheikh Zayed stressed that the federation of nine emirates was a national imperative. He said that federation was the destiny of the region and the destiny of the Arab nation.

14 October: A meeting of representatives of the constituent members of the United Arab Emirates was held in Abu Dhabi to choose the national anthem, the national emblem and the national flag from entries submitted in competition.

4 November: Ahmed Khalifa Al Suweidi, the Minister for Presidential Affairs, opened a training course for diplomatic personnel. Forty students from Abu Dhabi and the other emirates took part.

29 November: Ruler of Sharjah, Sheikh Khaled bin Mohammad Al Qassimi, announced that Iran would accept Sharjah's sovereignty over the island of Abu Musa, but Sharjah agreed to permit

Iranian toops to be stationed on half the island according to a Memorandum of Understanding concluded between the parties.

30 November: Preparations began in Dubai for a meeting of the Rulers of the six emirates to agree on steps leading toward the formal declaration of the federal State of the United Arab Emirates.

The Government of Ras al-Khaimah submitted a complaint to the British Government following the Iranian occupation of the two islands of Greater and Lesser Tunb on the grounds that the British Government was responsible for protecting the islands according to existing treaties.

The Abu Dhabi Government, in rejection of the Iranian move, announced its regret at Iran's occupation of the islands belonging to Ras al-Khaimah.

2 December: The historic first meeting of the Supreme Council of the Federation of the United Arab Emirates was convened. During the meeting His Highness Sheikh Zayed bin Sultan Al Nahyan was elected as President of the State with His Late Highness, Sheikh Rashid bin Saeed Al Maktoum, the Ruler of Dubai, as Vice President.

The flag of the United Arab Emirates was decided upon and it was announced that work on a provisional constitution had begun and that a prime minister had been appointed.

Issuing from the meeting was the declaration establishing the State of the United Arab Emirates. The declaration reads as follows:

On this Thursday, the fifteenth of the Month of Shawwal 1391 A.H. which corresponds to the second of December 1971 A.D., in the emirate of Dubai the Rulers of the following emirates met: Abu Dhabi, Dubai, Sharjah, Ajman, Umm al-Qaiwain and Fujairah. At the meeting, they signed the provisional constitution of the United Arab Emirates in an atmosphere of sincere fraternal feeling, mutual confidence and a deep concern to achieve the will of the people of these emirates. The provisions of the above-mentioned constitution become effective from this date.

The Rulers then continued their meeting as the Supreme Council of the Federation. With the help of the Almighty, in this meeting His Highness Sheikh Zayed bin Sultan Al Nahyan, the Ruler of Abu Dhabi, was elected as President of the State of the United Arab Emirates for the period of five Gregorian years and His Highness Sheikh Rashid bin Saeed, the Ruler of the emirate of Dubai, was elected as Deputy to the President for the same period. Both of them took the constitutional oath of office according to the provisions of the constitution. Sheikh Maktoum bin Rashid Al Maktoum, the Crown Prince of the emirate of Dubai, was appointed as Chairman of the Council of Ministers. The Council will convene its second meeting in Abu Dhabi on Tuesday, the seventh of the month of December 1971.

The Supreme Council brings glad tidings to the people of the United Arab Emirates, to all fraternal Arab nations, to friendly nations and to the world in general, announcing the establishment of the State of the United Arab Emirates as an independent fully sovereign State which is a part of the greater Arab nation. It aims to maintain its independence, sovereignty, security and stability and to repel all aggression against its being or the being of an emirate who is a member thereof. It also aims to protect the rights and freedoms of its people and to achieve firm co-operation among the emirates in their best mutual interests. For the sake of these objectives and for the sake of prosperity and progress in all fields it further aims to provide a better life for all citizens, to provide aid for Arab and Islamic causes and interests and to strengthen the bonds of friendship and co-operation with all countries and peoples on the basis of the principles of the Charter of the Arab League, the Charter of the United Nations and exemplary international norms. The Federation condemns the principle of the use of force and it regrets that Iran has recently occupied part of the Arab nation and it therefore deems it necessary to honour legal rights and to resolve disputes between nations by means which are internationally recognized.

The Supreme Council of the Federation on this blessed historic occasion turns to Allah, the High and Mighty, with praise and thanks for His granting of a happy outcome and for His help. It also turns to the people of the Federation with congratulations and blessings on the achievement of security having faith with the Council that any unity or unification in any part of the Arab world is a step on the way to the true call for complete Arab unity. The Council emphasizes that it is keen to welcome other countries to join the United Arab Emirates and especially the brother emirates who signed the Agreement of the Federation of the Arab Emirates in Dubai on the 28th of February 1968 A.D.

Allah is the Giver of success which is a blessings from the Lord, a blessing from the Defender.

Issued in Dubai on 15 Shawwal 1391, A.H. corresponding to 2 December 1971 A.D.

A Treaty of Friendship, valid for ten years, was signed between the UAE and the United Kingdom, replacing earlier treaties between Britain and the individual emirates. H.H. President Sheikh Zayed signed the Treaty on behalf of the UAE, Geoffrey Arthur, British Political Resident in the Gulf, on behalf of the UK.

A number of federal decrees and edicts were issued relating to the declaration of the founding and organization of the State of the United Arab Emirates.

The committee representing the Rulers of the six emirates met with Sheikh Saqr bin Mohammad Al Qassimi, Ruler of Ras al-Khaimah and listened to his report on Iran's invasion of the Greater Tunb and the Lesser Tunb islands.

Sheikh Khalifa bin Zayed Al Nahyan witnessed the Emirates' flag-raising ceremony at Al-Manhal Palace.

Ahmed Khalifa Al Suweidi announced that the subject of the islands occupied by Iran would be the most important topic to be discussed by the Federal Council of Ministers.

3 December: H. H. Sheikh Zayed bin Sultan Al Nahyan, President of the UAE, informed U Thant, Secretary General of the United Nations, of the announcement which established the United Arab Emirates as a State.

4 December: A delegation from the UAE under the chairmanship of Mohammad Al Habroush presented a request that the UAE be included in the Arab League and attended an emergency meeting of the Arab League's Council in Cairo to discuss Iran's occupation of the three Arab islands in the Gulf.

6 December: The United Arab Emirates

became the eighteenth member of the Arab League.

A request to join the United Nations was presented.

8 December: The emirate of Ras al-Khaimah requested membership in the Federation of the United Arab Emirates.

The United Nations Security Council announced that it had accepted the United Arab Emirates as a member of the United Nations.

The number of states, both Arab and foreign, which recognized the UAE rose to twenty nine.

Abu Dhabi National Consultative Council expressed its strong condemnation of the occupation by Iranian forces of the Arab islands.

H. H. President Sheikh Zayed bin Sultan Al Nahyan met with Sheikh Maktoum bin Rashid Al Maktoum who gave him a list of the members of the new cabinet.

9 December: The United Arab Emirates took its seat in the United Nations as the 132nd member of the international organization following its acceptance by a majority of 93 votes in the General Assembly.

President Sheikh Zayed bin Sultan Al Nahyan issued a federal decree formally appointing the first Council of Ministers and its Deputy Chairman.

10 December: The Chairman of the Council of Ministers took the constitutional oath of office before the President. The Council of Ministers subsequently held its first meeting under the chairmanship of the President.

11 December: Ceremonies were held at the United Nations Headquarters in New York on the occasion of the raising of the UAE's flag following its acceptance for membership.

13 December: Mana Said Al Otaiba paid a visit to Mubarraz island where he observed the Abu Dhabi National Oil Company's plans to develop the island.

19 December: H. H. President Sheikh Zayed bin Sultan Al Nahyan was presented with a letter from US President Richard Nixon by the American Assistant Secretary of State for Middle East and South Asian Affairs.

The Government of Sharjah announced that British forces had evacuated the British base in the emirate.

22 December: Sheikh Zayed signed an agreement with Britain placing the Trucial Oman Scouts at the disposal of the UAE Government.

Mohammad Al Habroush announced that the first federal budget would be between 10 and 20 million dinars.

The Supreme Council approved four new federal laws concerning the flag, the official gazette, diplomatic relations and the Federal Defence Forces.

The emirate of Sharjah celebrated the raising of its flag on the British military base following British withdrawal.

23 December: Britain officially surrendered control over the Trucial Oman Scouts to the Federation's Ministry of Defence.

24 December: The emirate of Ras al-Khaimah joined the State of the United Arab Emirates and announced that its membership was effective from 2 December 1971.

Nineteen Seventy Two

2 January: A symbolic review of the Federation Defence Forces took place in Dubai with units of the Infantry, Tank Corps, Airforce and Navy participating.

3 January: Sheikh Khaled bin Saqr Al Qassimi, Ruler of Sharjah, attended the first exercises of the Abu Dhabi Defence Forces in Al-Falaj district and renamed the former British base 'Al Qassimi'.

4 January: The world boxing champion, Mohammad Ali (Cassius) Clay, was received by Sheikh Zayed.

The Council of Ministers agreed on a draft law defining the areas of competence of the federal ministries and the authority of the ministers. It also approved the percentage participation of the individual emirates in the federal budget.

5 January: Sheikh Zayed received the successful graduates of the first diplomatic course organized by the Ministry of Foreign Affairs.

The emirate of Abu Dhabi exported 43.8 million tons of oil during 1971, having exported 32.8 million tons in 1970.

Mohammad Al Habroush announced that federal expenditure during the year would amount to 115.5 million dinars.

The National Consultative Council recommended that the telephone system in the country be subject to Government administration similar to other public utilities such as water, electricity and communications.

12 January: President Sheikh Zayed issued the nation's Police and Public Security Law.

The Council of Ministers approved the organizational structure of the federal ministries.

The Ministry of Petroleum and Industry in Abu Dhabi announced that annual oil production had reached 34.977 million barrels.

17 January: Sheikh Mohammad bin Hamad Al Sharqi, Ruler of Fujairah, issued a decree appointing Sheikh Suhail bin Hamdan as Deputy Ruler of Fujairah and Sheikh Surour bin Saif as Assistant Deputy Ruler.

19 January: The Council of Ministers approved the draft of the Federation's Civil Service Law.

Sheikh Khalifa bin Zayed Al Nahyan ordered that a search-and-rescue unit be set up in the Ministry of Defence in Abu Dhabi.

Abu Dhabi Executive Council began discussions on a new 150 million dinar budget, the largest in the history of the emirate.

20 January: Sheikh Khalifa bin Mohammad Al Nahyan signed a 700 million dinar contract for the construction of a water pipeline network for Abu Dhabi.

25 January: Sheikh Khaled bin Mohammad Al Qassimi, Ruler of Sharjah, was murdered during a failed coup attempt led by Saqr bin Sultan, the former ruler who was deposed in 1965. Sheikh Zayed ordered Sheikh Mohammad bin Rashid Al Maktoum, Minister of Defence, to re-establish security and stability in Sharjah. All the conspirators were arrested, information channels in all parts of the country were closed down and a 40-day period of mourning was announced.

The Supreme Council of the Federation, at an extraordinary meeting held in Dubai, chose Sheikh Sultan bin Mohammad Al Qassimi, the federal Minister of Education and former director of the office of the ruler of Sharjah, as Ruler of Sharjah.

2 February: Sheikh Zayed received the first Soviet delegation under the leadership of Simon Eshkin, Deputy Chairman of the Middle East Section of the Soviet Foreign Ministry who confirmed that Moscow was working toward strengthening the UAE's independence. The Council of Ministers approved the formation of the first three units of police dogs in the Police Department and Public Security and decided to send 20 nationals to international police academies for training.

6 February: The Council of Ministers approved a draft federal decree inviting the Federal National Council to convene on 12 February. It also approved a draft federal law regarding the appointment of the members of the diplomatic and consular corps in the Ministry of Foreign Affairs and the organization of the federal ministries and their departments.

7 February: Sheikh Zayed, at the invitation of the Federal National Council, issued a federal decree convening the eleventh session of the first legislative group.

The Yemeni Government received an offer by the President to establish a broadcasting station in Sana'a as a gift to the Yemen from the UAE.

9 February: Sheikh Rashid bin Saeed Al Maktoum visited Dubai broadcasting studios which had begun transmission on 23 January.

The Ministry of Petroleum and Industry announced a tender for an oil refinery project in Abu Dhabi.

10 February: The Supreme Council of the Federation met in extraordinary session under the Presidency of Sheikh Zayed to unanimously approve the inclusion of the emirate of Ras al-Khaimah in the Federation. Sheikh Saqr bin Mohammad Al Qassimi, Ruler of Ras al-Khaimah, subsequently participated in the meeting.

12 February: The Federal National Council held the first meeting of its first ordinary session in which the members took the constitutional oath. Thani bin Abdulla was elected Speaker of the Council.

15 February: The UAE and the Soviet Union agreed to set up diplomatic relations at ambassadorial level.

19 February: Sheikh Zayed issued a federal decree appointing ministers to the Federal Council of Ministers.

The Council of Ministers confirmed the federal budget for 1972 and also approved the draft law regarding nationality, passports and immigration.

21 February: Sheikh Zayed arrived in Khartoum on his first visit to Sudan.

23 February: The Voice of the Emirates began broadcasting in Abu Dhabi, extending transmission for the first time on a waveband which covered half the globe.

The Ministry of Petroleum announced a tender for onshore oil exploration in Abu Dhabi.

1 March: Sheikh Zayed donated 50,000 dinars towards the establishment of the Nasser College and Hospital in the Sudanese city of Wadi Madani as a perpetual memorial to the late President Gamal Abdul Nasser.

Sheikh Zayed arrived in Tripoli from Khartoum on his first visit to Libya during which he held talks with Colonel Muammar Al Gadhafi.

4 March: Sheikh Zayed arrived in Damascus on his first official visit to Syria.

10 March: Sheikh Zayed donated 3 million dollars to help solve the drought problem in Sudan. He also received a delegation from the Egyptian Ministry of Foreign Affairs after it had completed a mission concerned with organizing the UAE's Ministry of Foreign Affairs.

17 March: Sheikh Zayed inaugurated the largest agricultural exhibition in the history of the region in which all the emirates of the UAE participated, along with 200 local and foreign companies

working in agriculture in the country.

Sheikh Zayed and Sheikh Khalifa bin Zayed Al Nahyan, Crown Prince and Prime Minister, visited the Eastern Region to inspect conditions after the heavy rainstorms which hit the country, the like of which had not been experienced for many years.

21 March: The President issued an order appointing Sheikh Tahnoun bin Mohammad Al Nahyan as Chairman of the Administrative Council of the Agricultural Experimental Project in Al-Ain.

22 March: Abu Dhabi Executive Council approved the establishment of a College of Petroleum in the country to train nationals in this field.

23 March: The Council of Ministers, under the chairmanship of Sheikh Maktoum bin Rashid Al Maktoum, confirmed federal development projects amounting to 6 million dinars; including the building of 1200 public housing units and development of utilities such as water, electricity, roads and other services. The Council also approved the expenditure of 1 million dinars on electricity following the President's decision to reduce the price of electricity for nationals to 7.5 fils per kilowatt in an attempt to reduce the cost of living.

The Ministry of Public Works announced the establishment of two secondary schools for boys and a secondary school for girls in Abu Dhabi, as well as two secondary schools for boys in Al-Ain.

Mana Said Al Otaiba announced that the Abu Dhabi Petroleum Company and the Abu Dhabi Marine Areas Company (ADMA) had agreed to a 20 per cent shareholding by the emirate of Abu Dhabi.

29 March: Sheikh Zayed received the first federal ambassadors to be sent abroad: Dr Ali Humaidan (UAE Representative to the United Nations), Saif bin Ghobash (Lebanon), and Taryam Omran Taryam (Cairo).

The National Football Team was placed first in the Third Division in the Second Arab Gulf Games which were held in Saudi Arabia.

The Ministry of Higher Education of the Egyptian Arab Republic approved the equivalency of the General Secondary Certificate of Abu Dhabi emirate to the General Secondary Certificate in Egypt, considering it to be an acceptable qualification for enrolling in Egyptian university colleges and higher institutes.

1 April: Sheikh Zayed inspected operations in the Ministry of Municipalities and Agriculture in Al-Ain.

2 April: The Council of Ministers, under the chairmanship of Sheikh Maktoum bin Rashid Al Maktoum, debated the federal budget which amounted to approximately 19.5 million dinars.

3 April: Abu Dhabi Executive Council ordered the publication of the Commercial Registration Law.

4 April: Sheikh Zayed inspected the streets of the capital.

The Council of Ministers gave their approval for the UAE to join a number of international organizations.

A special office of the Federal National Council was opened in Dubai.

Sheikh Saif bin Mohammad Al Nahyan, Minister of Health in Abu Dhabi, confirmed that the country was free of smallpox and that strong measures had been taken to protect the country against the entry of this disease. Fourteen inoculation centres were opened.

12 April: Sheikh Zayed made his first round of inspection tours of the emirates comprising the Federation. Meeing with Rulers and citizens, he issued instructions to provide services and rapidly set up agricultural and building projects.

Sheikh Zayed and Sheikh Rashid inspected samples of the Federation's new currency in 5 dirham, 100 dirham and 1000 dirham denominations. The Federation had made representations to join the International Currency Board.

The Council of Ministers approved the Federation's draft budget for 1972-73. It also approved the draft of the federal decree establishing the UAE's embassies in Kuwait, Egypt, Lebanon and the United Kingdom.

The Federal National Council approved a draft law governing the incorporation of the official emblem of the State into its official stamp.

18 April: Sheikh Zayed received a number of the Rulers of the emirates and senior officials at Al-Khawaneej Palace. He subsequently undertook his first inspection tour of the Northern Emirates.

23 April: Jaafar Mohammad Numeiri, the Sudanese President, arrived in Abu Dhabi on the first visit of an Arab head of state to the Emirates.

Sheikh Zayed continued his round of field visits to inspect the ministries in Abu Dhabi. He also examined the plans produced by the Ministry of Public Works for new houses which he had ordered for UAE citizens.

26 April: Heavy rains and floods which hit Ras al-Khaimah, Ajman and Umm al-Qaiwain caused the death of four people and the destruction of the main bridge on the road between Sharjah and Ras al-Khaimah.

27 April: His Holiness the Pope presented the Vatican's *Cavalieri* decoration to Sheikh Zayed in appreciation of the assistance and care which had been given to the Christian community in Abu Dhabi.

A joint communiqué issued following the visit to the Emirates of Sudanese President, Jaafar Mohammad Numeiri, emphasized the necessity of solving the problem of the islands occupied by Iran. Right and justice should prevail, it was declared.

Mohammad Khalifa Al Kindi, Minister of Education, opened the Living Language Laboratory which was donated by Abu Dhabi Petroleum Company to the ministry.

29 April: At a meeting of the Council of Ministers presided over by Sheikh Maktoum bin Rashid Al Maktoum it was agreed that five new UAE embassies would be established in Pakistan, India, Sudan and the Yemen Arab Republic. It also confirmed payment of compensation to nationals hit by the floods.

1 May: Sheikh Mohammad bin Rashid Al Maktoum, Minister of Defence, announced that national volunteers were to become the core of the army. He also confirmed that the Federation would provide the army with the latest weaponry.

2 May: Sheikh Zayed paid a brief visit to the Sultanate of Oman where he met His Majesty Sultan Qaboos bin Said.

Sheikh Khallifa bin Zayed Al Nahyan inaugurated a military base in Al-Ain.

The Federation's Ministry of Education approved the construction of 51 new schools at a cost of 6 million dinars.

3 May: Sheikh Rashid bin Saeed Al Maktoum signed a contract with a British company to establish the largest dry dock in the Middle East in Dubai.

The Ministry of Communications prepared a draft law unifying postage stamps and services in the Federation, thus cancelling all previous stamps in use in the various emirates.

The Federal National Council held its first secret session since it was established during which it debated the draft federal law concerning nationality and passports.

General Sheikh Mubarak bin Mohammad Al Nahyan, Minister of the Interior, ordered the setting-up of traffic lights and the construction of pavements for pedestrians on major streets.

4 May: Sheikh Zayed issued a federal decree appointing Hamouda bin Ali as Minister of State for the Interior.

7 May: Sheikh Zayed began an official visit to Pakistan.

8 May: A law imposing fees and port charges on oil tankers was issued by Sheikh Khalifa bin Zayed Al Nahyan.

General Sheikh Mubarak bin Mohammad Al Nahyan, Minister of the Interior, ordered the purchase of equipment for measuring the speed of automobiles in Abu Dhabi and Al-Ain.

9 May: Sheikh Rashid issued an order for the erection of a water storage tank at Jebel Hatta.

10 May: A communiqué was issued detailing the outcome of Sheikh Zayed's visit to Pakistan.

The Higher Appeals Court for *Sharia* law was established in Ras al-Khaimah.

11 May: Sheikh Zayed issued two decrees appointing Said Sultan Al Darmaki as Chief Secretary and Humaid bin Bishr as Director of the Office of the Presidency.

13 May: Sheikh Maktoum bin Rashid Al Maktoum confirmed the internal rules and regulations of the Council of Ministers.

Abu Dhabi Executive Council, at an extraordinary meeting under the chairmanship of Sheikh Khalifa bin Zayed Al Nahyan, approved the formation of a purchasing committee for the Ministries of Defence and Interior under the chairmanship of Sheikh Khalifa bin Zayed Al Nahyan. It was also decided to build 100 new houses for distribution to nationals.

15 May: Sheikh Zayed met with UAE university students studying in Pakistan. The Ministry of Works announced the construction of 240 housing units in both the capital and desert regions.

The Embassy of the United States of America was opened in Abu Dhabi.

16 May: Meeting under the Chairmanship of Sheikh Khalifa bin Zayed Al Nahyan, Abu Dhabi Executive Council confirmed new facilities for national companies whereby bank guarantees would be reduced by 50 per cent for contracts.

18 May: Abu Dhabi Executive Council discussed the establishment of the new port of Mubarraz.

20 May: The Indian oil tanker, *Jawaharlal Nehru*, left Jebel Dhanna port carrying the billionth barrel of oil produced by the fields attached to Abu Dhabi Petroleum Company. The first barrel of oil was exported from the same port on 14 December 1963.

21 May: General Sheikh Mubarak bin Mohammad Al Nahyan, Minister of the Interior, issued the rules and regulations governing traffic for 1972.

Work began on the dredging of 11 million sq. m of earth from the tidal flats around Abu Dhabi island.

22 May: Sheikh Zayed returned to the country from a 15-day visit to Pakistan.

24 May: Sheikh Khalifa bin Zayed Al Nahyan began visits to Sudan, Egypt and Syria.

25 May: The details of Abu Dhabi's budget for 1972 were published. Expenditure was estimated at around 63 million dinars with 77 million dinars earmarked for development projects and 40 million dinars allocated to cover Abu Dhabi's share of the federal budget and international aid.

28 May: Sheikh Khalifa bin Zayed Al Nahyan arrived in Cairo from Khartoum on an official visit to Egypt.

29 May: The Pakistani President, Zulfikar Ali Bhutto arrived in Abu Dhabi for discussions with Sheikh Zayed before departing for Kuwait.

The Council of Ministers, under the chairmanship of Sheikh Maktoum bin Rashid Al Maktoum, approved the donation of 200,000 dollars to the Palestine refugee relief agency.

31 May: Dubai's Al-Ahli Club were victorious in the football championship.

1 June: Sheikh Zayed stressed to new ambassadors accredited to the UAE from Kuwait, Pakistan, Iraq and Yemen, that the riches with which Allah had blessed the country would always be at the service of the people.

4 June: It was confirmed that the new port of Abu Dhabi would be named 'Zayed'.

Sheikh Khalifa bin Zayed Al Nahyan began an official visit to Syria.

5 June: The Council of Ministers granted approval for Arab and foreign news agencies to open offices in the UAE. It also approved the inclusion of the Ajman Electricity Company in the federal Ministry of Electricity.

7 June: Mana Said Al Otaiba signed an agreement pertaining to the establishment of a share company for drilling operations under the name of the National Drilling Company.

9 June: Abu Dhabi Executive Council approved the construction of the TV building. It also agreed to increase the funds designated for housing construction: the total sum stood at more than 2286 million dinars for the year.

13 June: The Khalidiyya football team won the President's Cup, having defeated Al-Ain by three goals.

15 June: Sheikh Zayed issued a federal decree establishing a General Directorate for Information attached to the federal Ministry of Information to take over planning and overseeing of federal information affairs.

The Federal National Council approved the draft law organizing the entry to and residence of foreigners in the UAE.

18 June: Sheikh Zayed met the federal Ministers after the weekly meeting of the Council. He expressed his complete confidence in the ministers and said:'I place myself at the service of this country and I am prepared to continue to co-operate with you in performing your duties with all my energies'. The Council approved the draft law concerning compulsory education.

20 June: It was decided that the Federal Council of Ministers would be the authority for issuing licences for newspapers and magazines published abroad carrying the name of individual members of the Federation.

21 June: Sheikh Zayed decided to open three new UAE embassies in Rabat, Paris and Tokyo.

Ahmed Khalifa Al Suweidi, federal Minister of Foreign Affairs, began a tour of Qatar and Bahrain.

22 June: Sheikh Zayed ordered the construction of 30 new housing units in the Abu Samra area at a cost of 137,000 Bahraini dinars.

23 June: The President issued a federal law unifying the postal services in the State.

At this stage 15 countries had opened embassies in the Emirates: the United Kingdom, Pakistan, the United States, Kuwait, India, Sudan, Lebanon, Libya, Holland, the Yemen Arab Republic, France, Egypt, Iraq, Jordan and Tunisia.

27 June: The Council of Ministers issued a decree attaching the Passports, Nationality and Immigration Departments in the Emirates to the federal Ministry of the Interior. It also issued a decree assigning the points of entry and exit to and from the Emirates at airports, seaports and land border posts.

28 June: Sheikh Zayed inaugurated Port Zayed's 18 million dinar first phase at an elaborate official ceremony attended by Sheikh Rashid.

Abdulla Omran Taryam, Minister of Education, announced at the National Council that 20 new centres for combating illiteracy would be completed in all the emirates and that classes would commence on 1 October.

30 June: Hamouda bin Ali, Minister of State for Internal Affairs, stated that Sheikh Zayed had ordered that federal police be provided with all possible means to ensure adequate coastal surveillance in order to combat illegal entry into the country.

2 July: The first anniversary of the formation of the first Abu Dhabi cabinet under the chairmanship of Sheikh Khalifa bin Zayed was celebrated.

Sheikh Khalifa bin Zayed Al Nahyan issued a statement in support of the Bahrain Government's decision not to devalue the dinar, ordering all banks and traders in dinars to abide by this decision.

3 July: Sheikh Zayed attended a meeting of the Abu Dhabi Executive Council where he spoke about the ministers' responsibility towards the people who were looking forward to improved services. He told the ministers that wrong and right were attributes of humankind .... 'and we will not look for un-intentional wrong-doing and we will excuse the wrong doer if he was sincere...' and he advised the ministers to work in co-operation and solidarity with each other.

4 July: Sheikh Khaled bin Saqr Al Qassimi, Crown Prince of Ras al-Khaimah, signed an agreement with a Japanese company in Abu Dhabi to construct a cement factory in Ras al-Khaimah with a capital of 6 million dinars.

5 July: Sheikh Zayed issued an Amiri decree laying down the bases for payment of compensation for workers in the event of death or injury during or because of service.

Mana Said Al Otaiba, Minister of Petroleum, withdrew from a meeting of the Board of Directors of the Abu Dhabi Petroleum Company in London in protest at the slowness of company production and the drop in exports during the previous few months.

9 July: Sheikh Zayed issued an Amiri decree appointing Sheikh Khalifa bin Zayed Al Nahyan as Chairman of the board of directors of the Abu Dhabi Fund for Arab Economic Development (ADFAED).

Work began on the construction of the 300,000 dinars headquarters building for the General Directorate of Police in the capital.

10 July: Sheikh Zayed received King Hussain of Jordan who was in Abu Dhabi on a private visit.

11 July: Abu Dhabi state television produced three documentary films; *Abu Dhabi: Yesterday and Today, Pearl Fishing and Pearls.*

12 July: Abu Dhabi Executive Council approved the formation of a supreme committee for eliminating illiteracy.

13 July: Sheikh Zayed issued instructions for the naming of streets, squares and roundabouts in Abu Dhabi. Abu Dhabi Executive Council requested that the oil companies operating in the area reply immediately to Gulf States' demands to realize the principle of partnership between governments and private companies and it warned the companies against any attempt to bargain. It confirmed that Abu Dhabi unequivocally supported the position of Saudi Arabia and OPEC member states as regards partnership.

15 July: Sheikh Mubarak bin Mohammad Al Nahyan, in his capacity as Interior Minister of Abu Dhabi, issued rules and regulations relating to the weapons law for 1972.

Mohammad Khalifa Al Kindi commissioned an Arab expert to prepare a comprehensive educational plan for Abu Dhabi which would include curricula, school building administration, the establishment of higher institutes and student and teacher training.

Dubai Municipality began work on a study for the Shindagha Tunnel to connect Deira with Bur Dubai.

17 July: The Supreme Council of the Federation, at a meeting under the Presidency of Sheikh Zayed, considered federal policy in a number of fields as well as the achievements which had been made since the establishment of the United Arab Emirates. The members of the Supreme Council in a spirit of brotherhood also discussed the conflict which had erupted between the two emirates of Sharjah and Al-Fujairah. The dispute was finally settled and the two parties undertook to prevent the occurrence of any further conflict. The Council approved the following laws:

(1) Federal Law No. 291 for 1972 governing private schools which set out the basis for the establishment of such schools and put them under the supervision of the Ministry of Education.

(2) Federal Law No. 10 for 1972 governing educational missions abroad, laying down the rules for sending UAE nationals abroad for study at the expense of the State.

(3) Federal Law No. 11 for 1972 governing compulsory free education.

(4) Federal Law No. 12 for 1972 regarding rules and regulations governing clubs and societies operating in the field of youth welfare.

(5) Federal Law No. 13 for 1972 on social assistance, establishing the rules and regulations governing payments to deserving persons.

Sheikh Khalifa bin Zayed Al Nahyan began an official visit to France at the invitation of Michel Debre, French Minister of Defence.

Sheikh Tahnoun bin Mohammad Al Nahyan, Minister of Municipalities and Agriculture, issued Order No. 1 for providing model fire-fighting systems to buildings.

18 July: Sheikh Rashid bin Saeed Al Maktoum of Dubai earmarked 8 million riyals for housing, including the building of 808 new housing units.

19 July: Sheikh Zayed spoke to the members of the National Council at the conclusion of its first session. He said: that '...your Council is the Council of the nation and you must study matters which are clearly in the public interest... I ask of you that you always give your opinion frankly in all matters which are presented to you. It should not matter whether the person is powerful or not'.

A new 1.25 million dinar electricity station became operational in Abu Dhabi. Initially generating 18,000 kilowatts, the capacity of the generating station will eventually rise to 92,000 kilowatts.

The decree transferring the Office of Passports, Residence and Nationality from the Abu Dhabi Ministry of Interior to the federal Ministry of the Interior was implemented.

20 July: Sheikh Zayed ordered the construction of 1600 new housing units in various parts of the UAE as well as nine model villages supplied with all services. The villages were named: Al-Wathba, Dahhan, Al-Khaznah, Rimah, Abu Samra, Al-Ehar, Zakhir, Al-Heer and Sweihan. Each village was to have 80 houses.

Sheikh Zayed visited the island of Mubarraz where he inspected the projects established on the island to prepare it as a centre for oil export. He also inspected the new oil field on the island.

23 July: The Council of Ministers approved the draft law forming the Supreme Defence of the United Arab Emirates in application of the provisions of Article 141 of the Constitution. The Council also approved the draft law regarding the boycott of Israel and allotted funds for a plan to distribute 1200 houses in the member emirates at a cost of 3.6 million dinars.

Sheikh Ahmed bin Sultan Al Qassimi, Minister of Justice, and Counsellor Adel Younis, the first President of the Supreme Court, took the oath of office before Sheikh Zayed in Al-Manhal Palace.

24 July: The federal Ministries accepted responsibility for supervising and maintaining educational and health institutions belonging to Saudi Arabia, Kuwait, Qatar and Bahrain which were located in some of the emirates of the Federation.

Abu Dhabi Executive Council approved the internal rules and regulations of the National Consultative Council.

25 July: The Council of Ministers issued a decree organizing the Ministry of the Interior and defining its responsibilities.

26 July: Sheikh Rashid issued orders for the town planning of Bur Dubai and the establishment of parks in new districts.

Abu Dhabi Executive Council approved the importation of modern cranes, trailers and launches for Port Zayed at a cost of 320,000 dinars.

29 July: Sheikh Zayed issued the law governing educational missions abroad for UAE nationals.

30 July: The Council of Ministers ordered the federal Ministry of Electricity and Water to supervise the power station in Umm al-Qaiwain.

5 August: Sheikh Surour bin Mohammad Al Nahyan, Minister of Justice, and Ahmed Khalifa Al Suweidi, Minister of Foreign Affairs, inaugurated the first programme for administrative leaders in which 40 federal ministerial under-secretaries participated as well as under-secretaries from Abu Dhabi. The aim was to raise the standard of government administration.

7 August: Sheikh Zayed received Ali Al Shorafa on the occasion of his appointment as the first UAE ambassador to Sudan.

Abu Dhabi Executive Council approved the secondment of 198 teachers (male and female) from other Arab countries.

8 August: Abdulla Omran Taryam, Minister of Education, announced the opening of seven new schools and 20 centres for eradicating illiteracy in remote areas of the country this year.

9 August: The foreign ministers of the Conference of Non-Aligned Nations approved the membership of the United Arab Emirates at its opening session in the city of Georgetown.

10 August: Sheikh Zayed issued Federal Law No. 12 for 1972 regarding the management of clubs and societies working in the field of youth welfare.

It was announced that the production of crude oil in Abu Dhabi during July had risen to 966,000 barrels or 550 barrels daily.

12 August: Sheikh Rashid visited the Ministry of Defence building in Dubai and met with the engineers responsible for planning the Deira-Dubai tunnel. Later in London he signed the contract for its construction.

13 August: Sheikh Zayed visited Umm an-Nar Island and ordered that an oil refinery be set up there.

The Council of Ministers approved the concessions agreement and the provisions for granting diplomatic immunity to United Nations agencies.

14 August: Sheikh Zayed, accompanied by Sheikh Sultan bin Zayed, paid a surprise visit to Port Zayed.

Sheikh Zayed selected the names for new schools to be opened in Abu Dhabi in September.

15 August: Sheikh Zayed ordered that construction-work on the new half a million Bahraini dinar Maternity and Gynaecology Hospital in Abu Dhabi be speeded-up.

Sheikh Hamdan bin Mohammad Al Nahyan, Vice President of the Council of Ministers and Minister of Works, inspected the Abu Dhabi sewage treatment project.

Abdulmalik Al Hamar, Deputy Minister of Education, announced that special launches would be provided for transporting students from Saadiyyat island to Abu Dhabi to meet school timetables.

16 August: Mana Said Al Otaiba, Minister of Petroleum and Industry, announced details of the country's industrialization plan, including the setting-up of a petrochemical factory as well as a gas liquefaction plant which would make the gas available for local consumption. Two other factories were designated for export production, in addition to a number of factories for building materials and foodstuffs.

20 August: The Council of Ministers approved the payment of its 6 per cent contribution to the budget of the Arab League for the year 1972-73.

21 August: Sheikh Hamdan bin Mohammad Al Nahyan, Deputy President of the Council of Ministers and Minister of Works, issued a new price schedule for electricity and water in Abu Dhabi. Water was to be free to houses occupied by nationals: non-nationals would be charged 70 fils for each 1000 gallons. The price of electricity was pegged at 2 fils per kilowatt for national and 7 fils per kilowatt for non-national commercial and industrial establishments.

22 August: Sheikh Hamdan bin Mohammad Al Nahyan signed a contract for the construction of the police headquarters and 65 housing units in Al-Saad and Al-Hili.

Abu Dhabi Executive Council approved the payment of 400,000 Bahraini dinars to purchase a number of school buses. A sum of 87,000 dinars was allotted for the purchase of two pilot boats for the port.

Khalaf Al Otaiba, Minister of Economy and Trade, issued a directive for the setting-up of a business registry in the ministry.

23 August: It was decided to work around the clock on the Abu Dhabi port, electric lights having been set-up on the port's pavements.

24 August: Mahmoud Riyadh, Secretary General of the Arab League, was received by Sheikh Zayed in Al-Ain.

Sheikh Zayed visited Ain al-Fayidha to inspect the tourist project.

The Temporary Project Committee agreed to the setting-up of the 660,000 Bahraini dinar gas liquefaction plant to fill gas bottles for household use throughout the entire country.

28 August: Sheikh Zayed, presiding over a four-hour meeting of Abu Dhabi Executive Council, directed the ministers to provide more services to citizens and requested that the nation's youth be trained for administrative works in the new ministries and Government offices.

The Ministry of Works decided to expand the road connecting Dubai and Sharjah into a dual carriage way.

Abu Dhabi Television began broadcasting the Twentieth Olympic Games from Munich.

30 August: Sheikh Surour bin Mohammad Al Nahyan, Minister of Justice, distributed certificates to graduates of the first session of the Administrative Leadership Course at the deputy ministerial level.

It was decided to register all fishing boats working in Abu Dhabi and to define mooring sites.

The decision was made to form a High Council for Scouting in the UAE in order to encourage the scouting movement.

1 September: At the end of July 1972, the number of Government employees in Abu Dhabi stood at 6691, 1867 of whom were nationals.

It was decided that Abu Dhabi Municipality would supervise the setting-up of all commercial establishments in the capital according to new rules and regulations for granting building permits.

2 September: Sheikh Zayed met groups of citizens at Al-Khawaneej Palace in Dubai.

Sheikh Sultan, Ruler of Sharjah, attended the passing-out ceremony of the first batch of National Guard graduates.

Abu Dhabi Executive Council approved a draft law for the formation of the Abu Dhabi National Insurance Company with a capital of 500,000 Bahraini dinars, the Government subscribing for 25 per cent of the company shares.

Abu Dhabi Municipality issued 1546 commercial licences in 1972.

2 September: The Ministry of Finance decided to pay employees' salaries in excess of 160 dinars directly into their bank accounts.

It was decided to build four bridges in the Eastern Province to alleviate traffic problems caused by flooding.

4 September: A new programme for administrative development included 75 participants from executive and leadership posts in the Government, as well as office directors and heads of departments in the federal Government and the Abu Dhabi Ministries. The programme was enacted in response to Sheikh Zayed's directive to raise the competence of Government personnel and improve the level of administrative performance.

The Ministry of Foreign Affairs issued identity cards bearing the official emblem of the State to members of diplomatic missions in the UAE.

The building of breakwaters was completed at Port Zayed.

The Office of the Abu Dhabi Government in Bombay was changed to a Consulate General of the UAE.

7 September: Sheikh Zayed arrived in London on his first visit to Britain since he became Head of State.

Sheikh Zayed ordered that a new comprehensive map of the city of Abu Dhabi be prepared.

It was decided to establish six new UAE embassies in Syria, Jordan, Tunisia, Algeria and Morocco.

9 September: The Civil Service Council, under the Presidency of Sheikh Surour bin Mohammad Al Nahyan, Minister of Justice and Chairman of the Council for Granting Preferential Employment, decided that preference in hiring would be given firstly to UAE citizens and then to nationals of other Arab countries.

10 September: The Council of Ministers decided to dispense with the stamping of passports for travel between individual emirates.

12 September: The UAE condemned Israeli aggression against Palestinian refugee camps in Syria and Lebanon in the wake of the Munich operation which killed a large number of Israeli olympic athletes.

Sheikh Rashid bin Saeed Al Maktoum inspected offshore petroleum projects in Dubai and ordered the establishment of technical training centres for UAE nationals.

13 September: Sheikh Zayed held talks with Sir Alec Douglas-Home, the British Foreign Secretary, concerning developments in the Gulf and the Middle East.

Ahmed Khalifa Al Suweidi, UAE Minister of Foreign Affairs, criticized the positions of some of the members of the Security Council, particularly their use of the veto to block condemnation of Israel for its aggression against Syria and Lebanon.

Two branch post offices were opened in Khalidiya and the Industrial Area in Abu Dhabi.

14 September: Sheikh Khalifa issued a law establishing the Abu Dhabi National Insurance Company.

16 September: Sheikh Khalifa issued an Amiri decree establishing a Diwan for the Governor of the Eastern Region.

17 September: The Government of Dubai announced the commencement of work on the establishment of the dry dock and ship repair workshop.

18 September: Sheikh Zayed issued a federal law by which the UAE joined the International Monetary Fund (IMF) and the International Bank for Reconstruction and Development (World Bank). The law stipulated that the National Bank of Abu Dhabi would be in charge of all the State's dealings with these two organizations.

Sheikh Khalifa bin Mohammad Al Nahyan, Minister of Water and Electricity, announced that the capacity of the water desalination plant in the capital had been raised to 10 million gallons per day.

Abu Dhabi Municipality announced the establishment of three fire stations in residential and industrial areas of the capital.

20 September: Sheikh Zayed donated 1 million dollars to the victims of Israeli aggression in the south of Lebanon.

21 September: Abdulla Omran Taryam, Minister of Education, signed the executive protocol accepting responsibility for the educational institutions and health centres which had been set up by the Government of Kuwait in the UAE.

23 September: The UAE became the 124th member of the IMF and the World Bank.

Sheikh Saif bin Mohammad Al Nahyan, Minister of Health, announced the construction of a new 15 million dinar hospital in Abu Dhabi within two years.

Work began on the first drinking water network in the capital.

Harib bin Sultan, Deputy Minister of Public Works, said that work on the Abu Dhabi highway would be completed by March 1973.

Dubai Municipality fixed the price of meat to 3 riyals per kilo.

24 September: The Council of Ministers approved a study for the development of the electrical grid in the UAE.

25 September: Abu Dhabi Executive Council approved new rules and regulations governing the employment of foreigners and the contractual conditions for employment.

A decree from Sheikh Abdulla bin Humaid Al Qassimi, Minister of Water and Electricity, prohibited the drilling of wells without special permission from the federal Ministry in order to regulate the use of groundwater.

Five Abu Dhabi nationals travelled to London for training in the oil industry.

26 September: Sheikh Khalifa bin Zayed Al Nahyan issued a decree formally establishing the internal rules and regulations for the National Consultative Council.

Abdulla Omran Taryam, Minister of Education, announced that a special ministerial division for adult education had been created by directive of the President of the Federation.

28 September: Ahmed Khalifa Al Suweidi, delivering the UAE speech in the General Assembly of the United Nations, outlined the UAE's position on various Arab, regional and international issues.

Abu Dhabi Executive Council decided to set-up centres for marketing vegetables to protect farmers' produce.

30 September: The Ruler of Sharjah inaugurated the UAE Broadcasting Station in Sharjah.

Abu Dhabi Executive Council decided to cancel customs duties between Abu Dhabi and the other emirates.

1 October: Sheikh Khalifa bin Zayed Al Nahyan opened the new session of the National Consultative Council and delivered the Government's statement in which he dealt with its internal and external policies and the progress which had been achieved in the country.

The first elections in the history of the National Consultative Council were held: Sheikh Sultan bin Surour Al Dhahiri was elected as Chairman and Ahmed Al Masoud as Vice Chairman.

Sheikh Sultan announced the cancellation of customs duties between the emirate of Sharjah and the other members of the Federation, effective from 1 October 1972.

Al-Ain Municipal Council decided to plant trees on the Abu Dhabi - Al-Ain highway.

2 October: Sheikh Khalifa bin Zayed Al Nahyan signed rules and regulations governing housing allowances for national Government employees. He also signed the rules and regulations governing the employment of foreigners working in the Abu Dhabi Government.

3 October: Dubai celebrated the commencement of work on the 7.5 million sterling pound Shindagha tunnel connecting Deira with Dubai.

4 October: Sheikh Rashid established the first dry dock for ship repairs in the region.

5 October: Sheikh Rashid inaugurated Dubai's new Port Rashid which had cost 25 million sterling pounds to construct.

The Higher Committee for Eradicating Illiteracy held its first meeting under the chairmanship of Mohammad Khalifa Al Kindi, Minister of Education.

9 October: Sheikh Sultan bin Mohammad Al Qassimi announced that oil had been discovered in the offshore area of Sharjah. The oil was in sufficient quantity for production at Mubarak Well No. 1.

10 October: Abu Dhabi Executive Council approved implementation of the traffic signal project in the streets of the capital.

11 October: Sheikh Zayed issued a federal decree regarding the boycott of Israel, including the confiscation of Israeli commodities entering the country or passing through it.

The UAE was chosen as a member of the committee of nine states which was formed by the Islamic States' Ministers of Foreign Affairs at their meeting held in New York to investigate the Israeli transformation of monuments in Jerusalem.

12 October: It was announced that oil production in Abu Dhabi rose in September, reaching 36 million barrels.

On average, 182,000 barrels of oil were exported daily.

15 October: Sheikh Zayed having instructed that sufficient meat be available to citizens during the month of Ramadan, the price of 1 kg of lamb was set at 700 fils for the month.

18 October: Abu Dhabi was included in the agreement on the formation of an Arab fleet of oil tankers.

Mana Said Al Otaiba, Minister of Petroleum and Industry, announced that Abu Dhabi supported the Participation Agreement which was arrived at in New York on 5 October between five Arab Gulf oil-producing states and foreign oil companies holding concessions on their territories. The agreement stated that Gulf state participation would be pegged at 25 per cent, gradually increasing to a level of 51 per cent in 1983.

21 October: Abu Dhabi Executive Council approved the formation of a higher committee for administrative development in the country under the chairmanship of Sheikh Surour bin Mohammad Al Nahyan, Minister of Justice and Chairman of the Civil Service Commission.

Fifteen UAE nationals left Abu Dhabi to study in Bahrain's industrial colleges having been sent by ADMA-OPCO to study engineering and administrative sciences.

It was announced that 238 students were studying abroad funded by the Abu Dhabi Government.

24 October: Abu Dhabi Executive Council approved the formation of a company to improve ground services at Abu Dhabi International Airport.

26 October: Sheikh Khalifa bin Zayed Al

Nahyan confirmed the rules and regulations for Zayed Military College.

28 October: The Governments of the United Arab Emirates and the Iranian Empire decided to establish diplomatic relations at ambassadorial level.

31 October: Abu Dhabi Executive Council approved a draft law concerning oil terminals.

2 November: The United Arab Emirates condemned an Israeli attack on Syrian territory and the Ministry of Foreign Affairs called on the nations of the world to use their best efforts to stop Israeli aggression against civilians.

4 November: Abu Dhabi Executive Council held an emergency session to discuss a number of important petroleum matters.

The United Arab Emirates and Romania signed an agreement to strengthen technical co-operation in industry.

Work began in Al-Ain on the construction of the largest market in the area for fruit, vegetables, meat and fish.

12 November: The Syrian President, Hafez Al Asad, arrived in Abu Dhabi on an official four-day visit to the UAE.

15 November: The joint communiqué issued following discussions between Zayed and Al Asad underlined the necessity of concentrating and channelling Arab energies while strengthening the armed struggle by all means possible.

Abu Dhabi and Pakistan signed a protocol for setting-up joint petroleum and industrial projects which would include the building of a 41 million dollar oil refinery in Pakistan with a capacity of 1 million tons and a 540-mile,

37 million dollar pipeline to transport crude oil to the refinery.

16 November: Sheikh Zayed ordered the payment of 5 million Bahraini dinars compensation to nearly 1600 citizens whose homes were destroyed during the period 1968 to 1970 to make way for the development and re-planning of the two cities of Abu Dhabi and Al-Ain.

18 November: Sheikh Zayed said in an interview with *Petroleum Intelligence* : 'It is my duty to provide the basics of a decent life for every citizen in the country ... our goal is to prepare the next generation to carry the responsibility for building the future'.

19 November: Sharjah celebrated the beginning of work on Mubarak Well No. 2.

20 November: Sheikh Zayed delivered a speech at the opening of the new session of the Federal National Council in which he gave some important guidance for the next phase of economic and social development. He said: 'We are looking forward to a shining future with much work and effort'. He also announced the issuance of the Nationality and Passport Law for federal citizens and he said that strengthening and protecting the Federation was one of their highest goals. 'The future of the country depends on our sincerity, efforts, sacrifice and faith in our spiritual values and cultural heritage', he claimed.

22 November: Sheikh Zayed arrived in Sana'a to an enthusiastic welcome from the people. He was received by Judge Abdulrahman Al Iryani, President of the Yemeni Republican Council, who decorated him with the Marib Medal, First Class, the Yemen's highest decoration.

The UAE was accepted as a member of

the International Police Organization (INTERPOL).

Technical studies were prepared for the international airport project in Al-Ain.

A passport post was opened at Khatm Malaaha between Al-Fujairah and the Sultanate of Oman.

23 November: A joint communiqué was issued in both Abu Dhabi and Sana'a following Sheikh Zayed's visit to Yemen. To foster mutual relations, it was agreed that the UAE would offer assistance to Yemen to build new schools and housing and to open regular air service between Sana'a and Abu Dhabi.

Sheikh Zayed arrived in Mogadishu to a crowded official and popular welcome which was led by the Somali President, Mohammad Siyad Barre.

26 November: Sheikh Zayed confirmed to the Egyptian magazine *Rose Al-Yousif* that the progress which has been achieved in the UAE was brought about by its citizens. He said that the UAE did not need to import rules and regulations from abroad since the ideas of justice and progress were inherent in Islam.

The Council of Ministers approved a draft law establishing the nation's Supreme Court.

27 November: Sheikh Khalifa bin Zayed Al Nahyan raised the United Nations flag on the regional office of UNICEF in Abu Dhabi.

Abu Dhabi Executive Council studied the draft law on the Abu Dhabi Defence Forces.

The UAE contracted to contribute to the budget of the aid agency for Palestinian refugees to the amount of 220,000 dollars.

29 November: A joint communiqué was issued following the visit of Sheikh Zayed to Somalia in which the two countries announced the opening of embassies and the inauguration of an air connection between them.

Mr William Fulbright, Chairman of the Foreign Relations Committee of the US Senate, arrived in Abu Dhabi on a two-day visit at the invitation of Ahmed Khalifa Al Suweidi, Minister of Foreign Affairs.

30 November: Sheikh Zayed received Mr Abdulaziz Butaflika, Algerian Foreign Minister, and Mr William Fulbright. The visitors commented on the great progress being made by the UAE under the leadership of Sheikh Zayed.

The first phase of the 70-km internal road network in Al-Ain was opened by Sheikh Tahnoun bin Mohammad Al Nahyan.

2 December: Celebrations for the first UAE National Day began. Flags were raised on all houses and the Federal Forces participated in a large military parade for the first time. This was followed by an impressive procession of young men from all the emirates. The President, the Rulers of the emirates, Sheikhs, Ministers and numerous guests were in attendance. Among the latter was Dr Aziz Sidqi, the Egyptian Prime Minister, and Mr Abdulaziz Butaflika, Algerian Foreign Minister. On the occasion of the first UAE National Day, Sheikh Zayed confirmed that the Federation was the starting point on the way to a more extensive Federation in the region as well as a step towards complete Arab unity. VIP's attended a concert given by the Ministry of Information and Tourism in which the famous singer Najat Al Saghira sang the new national anthem written by Maestro Mohammad Abdulwahhab.

3 December: Sheikh Zayed inaugurated five new projects in Abu Dhabi; the vocational training centre, an automatic landing system at Abu Dhabi Airport, the Tourist Club, a 250-km road project in the capital and a 2.5 million Bahraini dinar desalination plant.

5 December: Sheikh Abdulaziz bin Rashid Al Nuaimi, Minister of Communications, issued a decree establishing the new postal fees for internal mail.

6 December: The Minister of the Interior prepared a draft federal law governing traffic and transport on federal roads.

7 December: The first cultural season began following preparations by the Ministry of Presidential Affairs under the patronage of Ahmed Khalifa Al Suweidi.

9 December: Abu Dhabi Executive Council formed a committee of six ministers to study bids for the construction of the oil refinery.

10 December: The Council of Ministers under the chairmanship of Sheikh Hamdan bin Mohammad Al Nahyan, Deputy Prime Minister, discussed the federal budget for 1973.

Abu Dhabi Executive Council approved the appropriation of 1790 million Bahraini dinars to equip and transform the Shaheen Hotel into a 196-bed maternity hospital.

Mana Said Al Otaiba, Minister of Petroleum and Industry, journeyed to Riyadh to continue discussions with the oil companies operating in Abu Dhabi as to how work would be carried out when the Participation Agreement came into effect. The largest steam turbine in the world

arrived at Port Zayed destined for the power generating plant.

12 December: Sheikh Khalifa bin Zayed Al Nahyan issued the Nationality and Passport Law for UAE citizens.

14 December: The German savant, Herbert Richard, declared his Islam before Sheikh Zayed at Al-Manhal Palace.

Discussions were concluded between a delegation from Abu Dhabi and representatives of international companies regarding the setting-up of a 500 million dollar natural gas plant on Das Island in Abu Dhabi.

Rashid bin Humaid, Minister of Youth and Sports, issued a ministerial decree governing the organization of clubs in the UAE. Each club was obliged to maintain a register of members as well as a register of club activities.

16 December: Sheikh Khalifa bin Zayed Al Nahyan opened a branch of the Bank of Cairo in Abu Dhabi, raising the number of banks operating in Abu Dhabi to fourteen.

Sheikh Khalifa bin Zayed paid the expenses of 500 nationals to perform the *Hajj* rites.

Sheikh Mubarak bin Mohammad Al Nahyan accompanied by Hamouda bin Ali, attended the passing-out ceremony of the first batch of 26 police trainees who completed a course on record-keeping and fingerprinting.

17 December: The Council of Ministers approved nominations put forth to complete the selection of legal personnel and members of the Federal Supreme Court.

18 December: Prime Minister, Sheikh Maktoum bin Rashid Al Maktoum, opened the First Arab Police and Security

Conference in Al-Ain which was attended by Arab leaders in these fields.

The Al-Arouba Secondary School in Sharjah was opened by Sheikh Sultan bin Mohammad Al Qassimi.

Abu Dhabi Executive Council approved a draft law for the protection of Government funds.

Sheikh Ahmed bin Hamid, Minister of Information, signed an information protocol with Kuwait whereby it was agreed that the TV station in Dubai would be handed over to the State.

21 December: The Participation Agreement was signed between Abu Dhabi and foreign oil companies operating in its territory. Mana Said Al Otaiba stated that in the following three years Abu Dhabi would get 220 million dollars as a result of the application of this agreement which would come into effect at the beginning of 1973.

Sheikh Khaled bin Saqr Al Qassimi, Ahmed Khalifa Al Suweidi and Mohammad Al Habroush signed a 6 million Bahraini dinar contract with a Japanese company to set up the first cement plant in Ras al-Khaimah, Abu Dhabi providing 25 per cent of the capital.

23 December: The Iranian Government agreed to accept Sheikh Hasher bin Maktoum bin Juma Al Maktoum as UAE Ambassador to Iran.

26 December: Sheikh Sultan bin Mohammad Al Qassimi issued a law organizing the Real Estate Registry in the emirate of Sharjah.

27 December: Japan purchased 45 per cent of the shares of the British Petroleum Company's operations in Abu Dhabi's offshore areas at a cost of 780 million dollars.

The Abu Dhabi Telephone and Telegraph Company announced the opening of a direct telephone line with Beirut.

Nineteen Seventy Three

2 January: Discussions began in Abu Dhabi regarding implementation of the Participation Agreement which Abu Dhabi had signed with foreign oil companies operating in its territory.

Abdulmalik Al Hamar, Deputy Minister of Education, informed the National Consultative Council that the number of students in Abu Dhabi had risen to 15,000 whereas five years previously the number was only 800.

The federal Ministry of Posts celebrated the opening of new post offices in Deira and Dubai.

4 January: The Supreme Committee for Adult Education, under the chairmanship of Mohammad Khalifa Al Kindi, Minister of Education, discussed the draft law on adult education.

There was a huge leap in oil production and exports in Abu Dhabi in 1972 with some 4,665,533 tons of oil exported from land-based and offshore fields.

6 January: It was decided to send a number of federal Government employees to Washington to attend training sessions organized by the International Monetary Fund in financial analysis, general finance and budgeting.

7 January: The Council of Ministers studied the personnel policy of the State, including personnel requirements and opportunities for employing nationals.

Sheikh Khalifa bin Zayed Al Nahyan issued rules and regulations for Municipal Councils.

The Ministry of Defence decided to grant incentives to individuals studying at its adult education centres.

8 January: Sheikh Rashid bin Saeed Al Maktoum signed a 100 million Qatari riyal contract for a new cement factory.

Abu Dhabi Executive Council approved the Participation Agreement which Abu Dhabi had signed with foreign oil companies operating on its territory.

Mana Said Al Otaiba, Minister of Petroleum and Industry, said that Abu Dhabi was keeping track of the proposed sale by the British Petroleum Company of part of its shares in ADMA-OPCO (45 per cent) to a Japanese company. He confirmed that the sale could not go ahead without Abu Dhabi's approval.

The Dubai Broadcasting Station, formerly known as the Voice of the Coast, celebrated its first anniversary.

10 January: Sheikh Abdulaziz bin Rashid Al Nuaimi, Minister of Posts, authorized new charges for domestic and international mail.

17 January: The Ministry of Communications announced the first draft law governing the country's wireless communications systems, including rules for granting licences.

The first athletic society was established with the aim of training leaders in athletics under the direction of Nasser Saif, Director General of the Ministry of Youth and Sport.

18 January: Sheikh Zayed received the credentials of Manucher Bahnam, the first ambassador of the Iranian Empire to the UAE.

21 January: The Council of Ministers approved a draft Press and Publications law. It also approved membership of the UAE in the Arab Organization for Agricultural Development and the International Union of Tourism Boards.

The Council of Ministers condemned an Israeli plan to transform the Hebron Mosque into a Jewish temple.

Ahmed Khalifa Al Suweidi, Minister of Foreign Affairs, opened the first diplomatic study session to be organized by the Ministry of Foreign Affairs for UAE and Gulf diplomats.

22 January: Abu Dhabi Executive Council decreed the formation of a committee to speed-up the establishment of a number of hospitals and eight new schools in Abu Dhabi and Al-Ain.

23 January: Sheikh Hamdan bin Mohammad Al Nahyan signed a 3120 million Bahraini dinar contract for the execution of the third phase of the Abu Dhabi to Sila highway, a distance of 113 kms.

24 January: Mana Said Al Otaiba announced the setting-up of a new oil company (Abu al-Bukoush Oil Company Ltd) in Abu Dhabi to develop the Abu al-Bukoush offshore field.

25 January: Sheikh Zayed issued a federal decree whereby the UAE took on board the laws of the individual emirates in the Federation.

Sheikh Zayed inspected the Military College in Al-Ain and witnessed manoeuvres with live ammunition.

It was decided to replan the Fareeq al-Khor area which occupies an important position at the entrance to the capital from Port Zayed in Abu Dhabi.

29 January: The UAE welcomed the announcement of the ceasefire in Vietnam, the Ministry of Foreign Affairs expressing the hope of the UAE people that the people of Vietnam would find stability and peace.

3 February: It was announced in Dubai that the first satellite station would be set up at Jebel Ali at a cost of 3 million sterling pounds .

5 February: Approximately 5526 students sat examinations in Abu Dhabi and Al-Ain schools.

6 February: The Ministry of Water and Electricity completed a new 12-km water pipeline network in Al-Fujairah.

Abu Dhabi oil export figures for January of 37 million barrels showed an increase of 15 per cent.

7 February: The Ministry of Works announced a tender for the construction of 70 new housing units in Al-Saad and Abu Samra.

8 February: UAE First Lady, Sheikha Fatima bint Mubarak, opened the Abu

Dhabi Women's Association, the first of its kind in the country.

The executive committee of the Federation of Chambers of Commerce and Industry in the Emirates held its first meeting in Abu Dhabi to prepare draft rules and regulations for the organization.

13 February: Sheikh Zayed received Mr Robert MacNamara, President of the World Bank.

14 February: Sheikh Zayed, receiving participants from the diplomatic training course organized by the Ministry of Foreign Affairs, said: 'Your country is looking to you to help build a nation based on firm modern foundations'.

Sheikh Hamdan bin Mohammad Al Nahyan signed a 3.57 million Bahraini dinar contract to implement the fourth stage of the Abu Dhabi to Sila highway covering the 109 kms between Jebel Dhanna and Sila.

The Federal National Council approved the draft Printing and Publishing Law.

The Ministry of Works completed delineation of the road between Khor Fakkan and Sharjah.

15 February: The new Hassa School in the Zabeel district was opened by Sheikh Rashid bin Saeed Al Maktoum opened.

17 February: Sheikh Zayed in an interview with the Egyptian newspaper, *Al-Ahram*, confirmed that security and stability in the Arab Gulf area were the main goals which the UAE was attempting to achieve and protect.

Abu Dhabi Executive Council approved the formation of the National Petroleum Construction Company, the Abu Dhabi National Oil Company owning 60 per cent of the shares.

The Ministry of the Interior stated that the permissible speed for automobiles within city limits would be 45 kms per hour; outside the city the speed limit would range between 80 and 100 kms per hour.

18 February: Sheikh Zayed made an inspection tour of development and tourism projects and the new highways in the Eastern Region.

It was decided to show the first colour film prepared by the Ministry of Information and Tourism in the Dag Hammerskjold Hall at the United Nations.

21 February: Sheikh Zayed inspected the first annual scout encampment which was set-up by the Ministry of Education in the Abu Samra area.

It was decided to establish 15 new schools for boys and girls in all parts of the country in order to accommodate the increase in the number of students.

23 February: The Brazilian Santos Football Team, which included the Brazilian football hero Pele, defeated the Al-Nasr Team by four goals to one in Dubai.

24 February: Sheikh Zayed visited a new drilling site in Jarn Yaphour some 25 kms from the Al-Maqta Bridge in Abu Dhabi where a search for oil was underway.

The City of Al-Ain hosted an international meeting of radio and television educationalists who discussed the introduction of satellite television to Arab countries.

25 February: The Council of Ministers approved the 1973 federal draft budget.

Abu Dhabi Executive Council approved participation in the Arab Marine Oil Transportation Company which was capitalized at 100 million dollars.

26 February: Sheikh Rashid issued the executive draft UAE Nationality and Passports Law.

27 February: Sheikh Khalifa visited the new oil exploration site in Jarn Yaphour.

28 February: Sheikh Zayed, continuing his tour of various parts of the country, arrived in Dubai's Al-Awir region where he met the local people. He also inspected settlement and land reclamation projects in remote areas.

Air traffic at Abu Dhabi International airport stopped for one hour as part of a general strike at all Arab airports and sea ports in protest at the downing by Israel of a Libyan passenger airplane which resulted in 107 fatalities.

1 March: Sheikh Zayed, meeting with citizens in Dubai, announced that the 1973 federal budget would be approximately 51 million dinars, three times the budget for 1972. The budget encompassed many development projects among which were health and educational services and 1700 new housing units.

Sheikh Zayed, on the fifth day of his tour of the country, inspected work on the dual carriageway between Sharjah and Dubai. He ordered that essential services be provided to citizens in the Al-Khan region.

3 March: During a visit to the first scout encampment in Al-Hamriyya, Sheikh Zayed delivered a speech in which he addressed the responsibilities of youth in building the future and the opportunities available to the State to foster the young generation. He said: 'The fortunes of all the people and the riches of petroleum will lay the foundation for the future'.

Sheikh Zayed received His Eminence Al Imam Musa as-Sadr, Chairman of the Higher Shia Islamic Council in Lebanon. His Highness spoke of the meaning of development and the fundamentals of religion, saying: 'The building of a righteous man and the building of a nation is our goal ... we were brought up on the morals of our religion and were taught by our ancestors and the Sunnah of our Prophet'. Al Imam as-Sadr replied: 'I ask Allah to give us more Muslim leaders like you'.

The British Petroleum Company replied to proposals put by the Government of Abu Dhabi as relations between them rapidly deteriorated. Government employees working on Das Island withdrew. Mana Said Al Otaiba announced that the Abu Dhabi Government approved the deal in which the British Petroleum Company relinquished part of its share in ADMA to a Japanese company. British Petroleum also agreed to pay 36 million dollars of the oil refinery project costs at Umm an-Nar, to provide interest-free loans of 50 million dollars, and to help raise the production capacity of the ADMA oil fields.

4 March: Sheikh Zayed visited the Zaid region where he inspected agricultural installations and projects as well as the conditions of farmers in the area.

5 March: Sheikh Zayed inspected new housing sites in Zaid and Falaj al-Mualla.

Mana Said Al Otaiba signed a 36.7 million dollar contact for the oil refinery project in Umm an-Nar with a completion date of 25 months.

6 March: Sheikh Zayed inspected the Al-Mleiha archaeological region in Sharjah where he discussed ancient civilizations with the Iraqi archeological mission. He remarked that: 'The Arabs were always victorious because of their links with Islam and the teachings of the Book of Allah'. Zayed also inspected the Al-Mleiha agricultural area and instructed that agricultural land be distributed to 70 families living in the area. He later visited Ras al-Khaimah hospital where he ordered that the capacity of the hospital be doubled from 60 to 120 beds. He also inaugurated the third phase of the new 9000 kilowatt per hour electrical power plant.

The Council of Ministers approved the draft federal law governing the importation of agricultural plants and seeds to assist in agricultural development in the country.

7 March: Sheikh Zayed laid the foundation stone for the federal cement factory in Ras al-Khaimah, the first factory to be set up under federal auspices. He also visited a number of schools and spoke to the students, encouraging them to equip themselves with knowledge in order to face the challenges of the future.

The Federal National Council approved the draft law organizing the federal judiciary and the Federal Supreme Court.

10 March: Mana Said Al Otaiba signed contracts with four large companies for a gas liquefaction plant on Das Island. He said that the Abu Dhabi Government's share of the profit from this project over the first 20 years would be around 50 million dollars. This would be in addition to income received from the Abu Dhabi National Oil Company's participation in the capital of the project which amounted to 700 million dollars.

Ahmed Khalifa Al Suweidi confirmed that discussions were taking place between the UAE, Qatar and Bahrain to achieve the wishes of the peoples for unity and progress.

It was announced in Sharjah that the Sharjah Women's Society had been formed under the chairmanship of the wife of the late Sheikh Khaled bin Mohammad Al Qassimi.

11 March: Sheikh Zayed agreed to the establishment of a national trading company for importing basic necessities to be marketed at relatively low prices in order to reduce the cost of living. He also ordered a 2 million dinar increase in the capital of the Development Loan Establishment and he raised the amount of building loans to 90 per cent in order to solve the housing crisis.

Sheikh Zayed, in the course of a tour of various regions of the country, ordered that immediate steps be taken to complete the construction and commissioning of the Khaled Hospital in Sharjah.

Sheikh Khalifa visited the first fuel depot handed over to the Abu Dhabi National Oil Company by British Petroleum - part of a programme to integrate oil distribution into a network throughout the country.

It was decided that 27 March would be an annual national holiday for UAE youth.

12 March: The giant Japanese automobile transport ship *Jean Tsomaru* docked at Port Zayed for the first time.

14 March: Sheikh Zayed, accompanied by Sheikh Rashid, inspected living conditions in the villages of Al-Manama, Musafi and Idhn Wadi Showka in the Eastern Region.

Sheikh Zayed visited the UAE television studios in Dubai where he spoke to the employees and advised them to focus on opportunities for expanding and encouraging national talent. He said: 'We must welcome constructive and well-intentioned criticism because criticism is in the public interest'.

Following four hours of debate, the Council of Ministers approved the budget for 1973.

15 March: Sheikh Zayed met with members of the National Guard in Sharjah and expressed his pride in this newly-formed force. He also attended the passing out parade of the first batch of 250 graduates from the Reserve Police School in Sharjah.

17 March: Sheikh Zayed announced at the conclusion of his tour to various parts of the Emirates that numerous signs of progress were creating a new-found confidence and a feeling of well-being.

18 March: The Al-Khaleej Football Club won championship matches in the Sharjah and Ajman clubs having defeated Al-Arouba by two goals to nil.

19 March: Abu Dhabi Executive Council studied electrical and water requirements for the country until the year 1985.

The Khalidiya Football Club won the championship in Abu Dhabi.

20 March: Sheikh Zayed received Judge Abdulla Al Hajri, Prime Minister of the Arab Republic of Yemen.

21 March: Sheikh Zayed received a letter from His Highness Sheikh Sabah Salim as Sabah, Ruler of Kuwait, outlining the situation following the crossing of Kuwaiti borders by Iraqi forces. Sheikh Zayed communicated his extreme embarrassment concerning the trouble between two brother Arab countries, at the same time expressing his readiness to exert all his efforts to mediate in the conflict. He asked that the situation return to the *status quo ante*.

24 March: Sheikh Zayed and Sheikh Rashid received His Majesty Sultan Qaboos bin Said, Sultan of Oman, who arrived in Abu Dhabi on his first visit to the UAE.

Sheikh Zayed accompanied Sultan Qaboos on a tour of the capital, visiting the electricity plant and Port Zayed. The Omani Ruler welcomed the exchange of experience between the two countries in the field of marine works and port administration and he said that the impressive electricity station in Abu Dhabi was a sign of the vast development programme which was taking place in the country.

Al-Nasr Football Club defeated Al-Ahli in Dubai by one goal to nil.

25 March: Sheikh Zayed and Sultan Qaboos visited the Zayed Military College in Al-Ain. His Majesty praised the level of training in the college.

26 March: Sheikh Zayed and Sultan Qaboos visited Dubai where they inspected the Federal Defence Force and various development projects. Sultan Qaboos, meeting the Rulers of the emirates in Dubai, confirmed that stability and progress in the UAE supported Oman in its own development efforts. Sheikh Zayed replied: 'We are as one with our brothers in Oman and we will remain so... we will help strengthen each other and co-operate to the fullest extent'.

27 March: A joint communiqué was issued regarding the discussions between Sheikh Zayed and Sultan Qaboos who had completed his visit to the UAE.

UAE youth celebrated the holiday set-up in their honour for the first time.

29 March: Sheikh Rashid bin Saeed Al Maktoum opened the Rashid Hospital in Dubai.

31 March: Mana Said Al Otaiba requested that Abu Dhabi's share in the Abu Dhabi Oil Company Ltd (Japan) be raised to 51 per cent. The delegation from the Japanese company asked for time to study the request.

2 April: Mana Said Al Otaiba signed an agreement with the International Union of Contractors forming the National Petroleum Construction Company. The Abu Dhabi Government will own 60 per cent of the shares of this company which will specialize in constructing offshore towers and laying oil pipelines.

The country's first Federation of Chambers of Industry, Commerce and Agriculture was established with Ahmed Al Masoud as President of the founding committee and Saif Ahmed Al Ghurair as Vice President.

4 April: Sheikh Zayed issued a law creating the Abu Dhabi National Trade Company with a capital of 250 million dinars, the Government owning 25 per cent of the shares with the remainder open to public purchase. The purpose of the company was to import and trade in consumer food items in accordance with the measures which had been adopted to reduce the cost of living and put an end to the spiralling rise in prices.

7 April: Sheikh Zayed received the members of delegations participating in the Conference of Arab Chambers of Commerce, Industry and Agriculture which was held in Abu Dhabi. He confirmed that the UAE was striving to co-operate with its fellow Arabs in all areas.

Sheikh Zayed made a tour of the capital accompanied by Sheikh Mubarak bin Mohammad Al Nahyan, during which he inspected the measures which had been taken by the Ministry of Interior for Traffic Week.

The first society for women in Umm al-Qaiwain was formed under the chairmanship of the wife of Sheikh Sultan bin Ahmed Al Mualla, Minister of Health.

10 April: Sheikh Zayed attended the passing-out parade of the first batch of officers from the Zayed Military College in Al-Ain. He said that the college is a force for the Arab nation and that 'our concern for it derives from our concern for the defence of the nation at the same time as we are building up the country'.

11 April: The first shipment of oil, totalling 167,000 tons, was despatched from Das Island. The shipment to Japan, representing Abu Dhabi's share in the 'Petroleum Participation Agreement', was considered to be a huge step forward in the UAE's plans for running its own oil affairs.

Sheikh Zayed issued a decree establishing a committee to follow-up on the activities of the federal ministries and to uncover faults in administrative, technical and financial systems. The committee, which will also study the complaints of citizens, is composed of the Chairman of the National Federal Council, two ministers and three members of the National Council.

15 April: Sheikh Zayed laid the

foundation stone for the refinery on Umm an-Nar. He also ordered that a bridge be constructed to the mainland, that a deep water navigational passage be opened and that fill be used to reclaim land so that the island of Umm an-Nar would be connected to the neighbouring island. He emphasized that the refinery was only the first structure in the country's future industrial complex.

16 April: Sheikh Zayed held an international press conference at Al-Bahr Palace in which he confirmed that unity was the way to victory and that the reason for the despair through which the nation was living was the division between brothers. He said: 'Our goal is to raise the level of the human individual in the UAE because that is the basis for raising the standard of the nation'.

18 April: Abu Dhabi Executive Council approved the construction of 90 housing units in various parts of Al-Ain.

22 April: Sheikh Hamdan Al Nahyan signed a 2 million dinar contract to construct the Al-Shati (Al-Corniche) Hospital which will specialize in obstetrics, gynaecology and pediatrics.

24 April: Sheikh Zayed emphasized during his visit to the second General Exhibition of Abu Dhabi Schools that the State would encourage all opportunities for the expansion of education in the country.

25 April: The Federal National Council approved membership of the Arab Parliamentary Union.

29 April: Sheikh Zayed received the President of Chad, Francois Tomblaye, who arrived in Abu Dhabi on an official visit.

3 May: Sheikh Zayed in an interview with the Jordanian newspaper *At-Rai*, expressed his complete optimism about the future of the Federation and emphasized that the enormous success of the federal experiment had come about because of the efforts of the people of the Emirates. He said that discussions with Qatar and Bahrain had not yet concluded with regard to joining the Federation.

The Governments of Abu Dhabi and Japan reached agreement on Japan's involvement in the Das Island gas liquefaction project. Five companies were now involved in the execution of the 300 million dollar project, Abu Dhabi holding 20 per cent of the shares. It was also agreed to form a company for the transport of the gas to Japan.

5 May: Sheikh Zayed informed a visiting Japanese delegation under the leadership of Yasuhiro Nakasone, Minister of External Trade, that UAE oil policy was based on the principle of exploitation of this resource in order to diversify the sources of national income and industrialize the country. He said that the oil consuming countries must take a fair stand with regard to Arab issues.

6 May: Sheikh Mohammad Al Qassimi, Minister of Public Works, signed contracts for the construction of a 75-km highway between Dhaid and Fujairah.

The Higher Scouting Council of the UAE held its first meetings under the chairmanship of Sheikh Hamdan bin Rashid Al Maktoum. Two headquarters were chosen for the council, one in Abu Dhabi and the other in Dubai.

It was agreed to establish a group of Girl Scouts in the UAE.

8 May: The new budget for the Government of Abu Dhabi for the year 1973 was published. Estimated income was 253 million dinars and expenditure was calculated at 281,271 million dinars: 44 million dinars was allocated for the federal budget.

9 May: Sheikh Zayed sent Ahmed Khalifa Al Suweidi, Minister of Foreign Affairs, to Beirut to make contact with the parties concerned in order to end clashes between the Lebanese Army and the Palestinian Resistance.

The Society for the Preparation of Athletic Leadership was inaugurated with graduation ceremonies for the first batch of youth leaders.

10 May: The Monetary Council announced that the UAE's new national currency would begin circulation on Saturday, 19 May, replacing the Bahraini dinar and the Qatari Riyal. The latter would continue to be legal tender for the acquittal of debts until further notice.

It was decided that the Abu Dhabi National Bank would be the executive agency for the new UAE Currency Board.

16 May: The Federal National Council approved a draft law to set up the Currency Board.

Sheikh Rashid ordered the construction of 300 housing units in Dubai to assist citizens in countering development expansion in the city.

17 May: Commencing from this date, UAE banks stopped paying out dinars and riyals to the public in preparation for issuing of the new national currency.

18 May: Sheikh Khalifa issued an order that the Arabic language must replace English in all correspondence in Abu Dhabi.

19 May: First payments in the new federal currency commenced. People queued at banks to change Bahraini dinars and Qatari riyals into the new currency.

20 May: The Council of Ministers approved a federal law imposing a liberation tax on all Palestinians working in the UAE Government.

22 May: Sheikh Zayed announced UAE agreement for the holding of an Arab summit conference.

Rashid bin Humaid, Minister of Youth and Sports in Abu Dhabi, opened the first Youth House in the UAE.

23 May: Sheikh Zayed attended the opening of the Hilton Hotel in Abu Dhabi which was constructed at a cost of 38 million dirhams.

24 May: Sheikh Zayed accompanied by Sheikh Rashid opened the Ministry of Education's art exhibition in Dubai. Sheikh Zayed delivered a speech in which he confirmed his belief that education is the foundation on which the future is to be built and that with education the status of the country could be enhanced while ensuring progress for the future.

26 May: Sheikh Hamdan Al Nahyan signed a design contract for the television studios in Abu Dhabi.

27 May: Sheikh Zayed told West German television that the UAE was playing an effective role in Arab affairs. He said that the federal budget for 1973 represented an increase of 120 per cent over the previous year. He continued '... we have used all our wealth in raising the standard of living because we believe that the people have the right to their wealth'.

Sheikh Zayed made a tour of Dubai during which he witnessed the progress being made on the Shindagha tunnel, the fishing and tourism boat harbour in Hamriya and the new popular housing project on the road between the airport and Al-Khawaneej.

28 May: Sheikh Zayed made an inspection tour of important projects in Sharjah including Khaled Port and Sharjah Creek.

The UAE signed an agreement with the Yemen Arab Republic in which the latter was given 8 million dirhams as its share of World Bank programmes for the improvement and development of education in Yemen.

30 May: Sheikh Zayed returned to Abu Dhabi after a seven-day inspection tour of the Northern Emirates.

1 June: Sheikh Zayed delegated Sheikh Surour Al Nahyan to attend the handover ceremony whereby foreign companies granted the Abu Dhabi National Oil Company (ADNOC) the right to distribute and market oil products in the country.

3 June: Sheikh Zayed began an inspection tour of the Northern Emirates, including Ras al-Khaimah, Rams, Dibba, Khor Fakkan, Fujairah and Musafi.

4 June: Sheikh Khalifa arrived in Salalah on an official visit to the Sultanate of Oman at the invitation of His Majesty Sultan Qaboos bin Said.

Preparations were completed in all parts of the country to begin registration of citizens in the Nationality Registry in accordance with the new federal law.

5 June: Sheikh Zayed attended the ceremonies surrounding the first shipment of oil from the Mubarraz offshore field. He said that the wealth must be directed toward the service of citizens in the present and also to build the future of the nation, the goal being to provide the basic requirements of every individual in order to compensate for the deprivations of the past.

Sheikh Sultan Al Qassimi announced that drilling operations and testing at the Mubarak well in Sharjah confirmed the existence of oil in large quantities. Estimated daily oil production of the well would be around 59,500 barrels with 52,350,000 cubic feet of gas.

7 June: Sheikh Mubarak Al Nahyan issued a decree inviting citizens to register their names in the Nationality Register in application of the federal law and in preparation for the issuance of identity cards and federal passports.

9 June: Sheikh Zayed approved the federal Printing and Publishing Law which regulates the establishment of printing presses, the issuance of permits to establish newspapers, the importation of printed material and films and the right to pursue the profession of journalism.

Sheikh Rashid opened the first radar station at Dubai airport.

10 June: Sheikh Zayed confirmed in talks with a number of foreign journalists and a Spanish television delegation that justice is the road to democracy. He said: 'We are not afraid of rapid progress so long as we adhere to the teachings of the Holy Islamic religion. We are now prepared to face the situation when the oil wells run dry'.

11 June: Sheikh Zayed arrived in Washington on a three-week visit to the United States of America.

Sheikh Mubarak announced that the Ministry of the Interior would study the purchase of special vehicles to provide immediate emergency services to the victims of traffic accidents.

12 June: Sheikh Rashid confirmed to foreign journalists that oil revenues were being spent in executing developmental projects for the benefit of citizens. 'We are investing all our wealth inside the country and we are not thinking about investing it abroad'. He also said that democracy was in the service of the people and would give them an opportunity to participate in building up their country.

13 June: Sheikh Khalifa attended the ceremonies which were held for the first time in Al-Ain on the occasion of Al-Madfa'iya Day.

16 June: Sheikh Sultan bin Mohammad met Kurt Waldheim, Secretary General of the United Nations, in New York.

18 June: Grape-growing proved to be successful in Muleiha and other parts of the Eastern Region after a successful experiment undertaken by the Ministry of Agriculture and Fisheries.

20 June: Sheikh Khalifa was present at the graduation ceremony for the new batch of young cadets, the acceptance ceremony for the second term in the Zayed Military College, and training of the first battalion of commando officers.

26 June: Sheikh Zayed informed a delegation from the World Muslim League which he received at Al-Bahr Palace that freedom of opinion was a necessity for the progress of Muslims. Youth requires convincing by opinion and proof and not by terrorism, he said.

30 June: The UAE and Kuwait signed an economic co-operation agreement. Ahmed Khalifa Al Suweidi, who signed the agreement on behalf of the UAE, welcomed the holding of a Gulf Arab States Summit Conference to discuss regional issues.

3 July: Sheikh Rashid Al Maktoum made an inspection tour of the Fatah No. 1 and Fatah Southwest oil wells located in the emirate of Dubai, during which he watched the operation of the electronic equipment controlling the underwater pumping of oil.

4 July: Sheikh Zayed travelled to the Eastern Region to investigate development projects and the circumstances of the citizens.

The number of telephone lines in Abu Dhabi rose to 7700 and 149,000 external calls were made during 1972.

7 July: Sheikh Zayed stipulated during a meeting with the Minister of Justice and the members of the Supreme Court that the Islamic *Sharia* should be the principle source of new legislation in the Federation. He emphasized his desire to establish a firm base for justice and the sovereignty of the law.

9 July: Sheikh Saqr Al Qassimi, Ruler of Ras al-Khaimah and Sheikh Mohammad Al Maktoum, Minister of Defence, attended the passing out parade of the new batch of soldiers of the Federal Forces in Ras al-Khaimah.

11 July: It was decided to attach the Labour Office in Ras al-Khaimah to the Federal Ministry of Labour and Social Affairs.

12 July: It was announced that production in the Mubarak oil field in Sharjah would commence in *Rabi Al-Awwal* of next year.

16 July: A training course on information systems was organized by the Ministry of Information and Tourism for a number of employees.

18 July: Sheikh Zayed issued four decrees: the Board of the Abu Dhabi National Oil Company was re-formed with the appointment of Sheikh Tahnoun Al Nahyan as Chairman of the Board; the UAE joined the Arab Establishment for the Guarantee of Investments and Shares with a capital of 500,000 Kuwait dinars; the appointment of Sheikh Surour Al Nahyan as Vice Chairman of the Board of the Abu Dhabi Fund for Arab Economic Development (ADFAED); and the appointment of Mohammad Al Habroush as a member of Board of the National Bank of Abu Dhabi.

21 July: The Supreme Council of the Federation began meetings in Al-Manhal Palace in Abu Dhabi under the chairmanship of Sheikh Zayed. However, the evening meeting was postponed because a hijacked Japanese aircraft landed at Dubai airport and Sheikh Zayed went to Dubai to oversee developments.

23 July: Sheikh Zayed remained in contact with Sheikh Mohammad Al Maktoum and Colonel Hamouda regarding the hijacked Japanese aircraft which took off for Damascus after spending 70 hours at Dubai airport. The aircraft was subsequently blown up at Benghazi airport after its passengers were freed.

Sheikh Hamdan Al Nahyan signed a 24.59 million dirham contract to construct the Bida to Zayed highway a distance of 52 kms - the second phase of the Abu Dhabi to Sila highway.

25 July: The Supreme Council of the Federation held two sessions under the chairmanship of Sheikh Zayed during which subjects relating to the development of the country and its citizens were debated and a report from the Prime Minister was heard regarding achievements during the Federation's first year.

26 July: The Supreme Council of the Federation, at the conclusion of its meetings in Abu Dhabi, issued a statement in which the State's general policy was outlined as were the achievements made under the aegis of the Federation. It was decided to form a committee under the chairmanship of the Ruler of Sharjah to study ways and means for achieving the goals of the Federation and supporting its institutions. One hundred million dirhams was also set aside for constructing public housing.

27 July: Sheikh Zayed issued a federal decree forming an administration board for the UAE Currency Board under the chairmanship of Sheikh Hamdan bin Rashid Al Maktoum.

29 July: The UAE Currency Board announced that the UAE dirham would be tied to gold and that the rate would be the equivalent of 186621 grams of pure gold.

30 July: Sheikh Zayed received a piece of moon rock as a present from US President, Richard Nixon.

31 July: Sheikh Zayed issued the first federal Civil Service Law.

Mana Said Al Otaiba announced the discovery of oil in Marzouq No. 3 well south-west of Jebel Dhanna.

1 August: Sheikh Zayed issued a federal law establishing the Federal Supreme Court, the highest judicial body in the Federation.

6 August: The newspaper *Al-Wahida* was issued; a daily newspaper, it was the second to be published in Abu Dhabi.

7 August: Sheikh Zayed issued a federal law controlling the use of public housing units.

Members of the Federal Supreme Court took the legal oath of office before the President who advised them to exert their utmost efforts to achieve justice in the Federation.

8 August: Sheikh Zayed undertook a tour of the capital which included the corniche districts, Al-Bateen and Airport Street. He instructed that work should begin on the Sports City project opposite Abu Dhabi Airport. He also set aside areas for new housing complexes for low income families and a new headquarters for the Abu Dhabi Women's Association.

Sheikh Zayed received a UAE sports delegation before it left for Libya to participate in the championship competition for the Palestine Cup. He told the young men that: 'You are the hope of the future and the nation places all its facilities at your disposal'.

It was decided to set up a helicopter pad inside Abu Dhabi hospital in order to receive emergency cases.

11 August: Sheikh Zayed issued a federal law relating to telecommunications installations.

13 August: Sheikh Sultan Al Qassimi ordered the importation and installation of new electrical generators in Sharjah and Khor Fakkan as well as the extension of additional freshwater pipelines to connect all regions of the emirate of Sharjah.

15 August: Sheikh Zayed bin Sultan Al Nahyan issued a federal law stipulating that all immigration, nationality,

passport and residence offices in the Emirates were branches of the federal administration in Abu Dhabi.

18 August: Sheikh Khalifa, on behalf of the President, attended graduation ceremonies for the first batch of 100 trainees in the Abu Dhabi Defence Forces.

19 August: Sheikh Zayed passed a federal law regarding the organization of judicial relations between members of the Federation, including provisions governing reciprocal execution of judgments and judicial secondments.

The Council of Ministers approved the formation of the Civil Aviation Board to conceive and implement a general civil aeronautics policy and develop air transport services for the Federation.

20 August: Sheikh Zayed, visiting the headquarters of the Ministry of Agriculture and Fisheries, asked the responsible officials to improve their methods of irrigation and to work towards an increase in production in order to meet the nation's requirements.

23 August: Abu Dhabi Executive Council decided to form a general projects committee to prepare construction, development and industrial plans and to follow-up on their execution.

29 August: Sheikh Khalifa attended the graduation of the first batch of cadets at the Zayed Military College in Al-Ain.

1 September: Sheikh Zayed arrived in Qatar at the beginning of a tour which would include a visit to Bahrain.

The Abu Dhabi Telephone and Telegraph Company contracted with an international company to construct and install a new 400-line automatic electronic switchboard, the first of its kind in the Gulf region. This would augment the Abu Dhabi telex service from which 125 subscribers benefited.

3 September: Sheikh Zayed arrived in Bahrain from Qatar in the course of his tour of the region. A joint statement was issued on his visit to Bahrain in which the two parties confirmed their desire to deepen and develop relations. The statement emphasized that mutual assistance between the brother States of the Arab Gulf would guarantee the creation of a suitable climate for progress of its peoples, removed from international struggles and foreign avarice.

Sheikh Zayed met with UAE students attending the training centre in Doha, Qatar. He encouraged them to exert their utmost efforts to acquire knowledge in order to achieve national progress.

4 September: Sheikh Zayed arrived in Algeria to attend the summit meetings of the non-aligned nations.

A joint communiqué issued following the visit of Sheikh Zayed to Bahrain focused on an agreement to support co-operation between the two countries in various fields.

5 September: Sheikh Zayed participated in the opening session of the Non - aligned Summit in Algeria where the UAE was elected for membership of the drafting committee.

8 September: Sheikh Zayed made an important speech to the Non-aligned Summit in which he emphasized the faith of the UAE in the principles of non-alignment and its support of national liberation movements. He condemned foreign interference in the internal affairs of States.

The Algerian President, Houari Boumedienne, announced that Zayed had donated 3.5 million dollars for drought stricken regions in Africa and aid for national liberation movements. Boumedienne said that he wished that those who indulged in endless discussion would follow Zayed's practical example.

10 September: Abu Dhabi Executive Council approved draft rules and regulations governing vocational training centres and the construction of a sports stadium in Abu Dhabi. It also approved invitations to specialized international companies to submit bids for the execution of three projects: a microwave network in Abu Dhabi-Al-Ain, an FM broadcasting station, and the equipping of a vehicle for mobile external television transmission.

13 September: Sheikh Hamdan Al Maktoum signed a 91 million sterling pound contract for the building of a dry dock in Dubai.

17 September: Sheikh Mohammad Al Maktoum attended the graduation of a new batch of cadets in the Federal Defence Forces in Dubai.

Ten thousand students were accepted during the academic year and 23 new schools were established throughout the Federation.

19 September: Sheikh Maktoum donated 216,000 dirhams to construct houses for young people and a building for the Society for Training Sports Leaders in Dubai.

Sheikh Rashid bin Humaid, Minister of Youth and Sports, issued three important decrees relating to the distribution of 1 million dirhams as aid to clubs in the Federation; the merging of a number of these clubs; the formation of a General Sports Union at the Federation level and the dissolution of local branch unions.

20 September: Sheikh Zayed met with the British Prime Minister Edward Heath in London, and the Foreign Secretary, Sir Alec Douglas-Home.

Sheikh Khalifa opened the Infantry School attached to the Abu Dhabi Defence Forces in Al-Qassimiya, Sharjah.

26 September: Traffic lights came into operation in Abu Dhabi.

28 September: Mana Said Al Otaiba, Minister of Petroleum and Industry, signed a 27.7 million dirham contract with a Japanese company to establish the first cement factory with an annual capacity of 200 tons.

1 October: Kurt Waldheim, Secretary General of the United Nations, announced that the UAE donated 1 million dollars to support the international organization.

3 October: Sheikh Khalifa issued a law establishing the Abu Dhabi National Petroleum Construction Company with a capital of 30 million dirhams.

4 October: Sheikh Ahmed bin Hamid, Minister of Information and Tourism, opened the Sheikh Khalifa Guest House in the Rimah area on the Abu Dhabi Al-Ain highway.

6 October: As the war of liberation commenced, Sheikh Zayed informed both Anwar Sadat and President Hafez Al Asad that the UAE pledged all its resources in support of Egyptian and Syrian efforts for the return of occupied Arab territory.

Sheikh Khalifa issued a law organizing commercial agencies.

8 October: In London, Sheikh Zayed discussed developments in the Middle East with Edward Heath, the British Prime Minister. He asked Mr Heath to clarify the British position on the situation.

Sheikh Khalifa, in a meeting with the Syrian ambassador and Egyptian Chargé d'Affaires, informed them of the orders of the President, that all the resources of the UAE would be placed at the service of the armed conflict.

9 October: Sheikh Khalifa, in a speech at the opening of the new session of the National Consultative Council, emphasized once again that all the country's resources were at the disposal of Egypt and Syria. The Council elected Sheikh Sultan bin Surour Al Dhahiri as Chairman and Ahmed Al Masoud as Vice Chairman.

10 October: The UAE decided to send an official medical mission to the war fronts in Egypt and Syria.

11 October: Sheikh Rashid announced that the UAE would place all its energies at the service of the armed conflict.

Sheikh Khalifa opened a blood donation drive. He also issued a decree forming a committee for collecting donations for the war effort under the chairmanship of Sheikh Tahnoun Al Nahyan.

12 October: Sheikh Maktoum opened a centre for blood donations in the UAE embassy in London.

13 October: Sheikh Rashid and Sheikh Khalifa received Sayyid Marei, Assistant to the Egyptian President, Anwar Sadat, who briefed them on developments on the military and political fronts.

14 October: Sheikh Mohammad Al Maktoum announced that the Federal Defence Forces had been placed on high alert in preparation for immediate despatch to the battle zones.

A medical mission composed of 83 doctors and nurses proceeded to Cairo and Damascus to participate in the war effort.

15 October: Sheikh Zayed returned to Abu Dhabi and advised the Egyptian President, Anwar Sadat, and the Syrian President, Hafez Al Asad by telephone that all the UAE's resources, not just oil, had been placed at the conflict's disposal.

16 October: Mana Said Al Otaiba said that he had concluded an agreement between Abu Dhabi and oil companies operating on its territory whereby the price of oil would be increased by 70 per cent. He also obtained a sulphur allowance retroactive to 1971.

17 October: The Ministers of Oil of the Arab Oil Producing States (OAPEC), the UAE taking the lead, decided on an immediate 5 per cent decrease in Arab oil exports to America and other pro-Israeli countries and threatened to accumulate the same percentage decrease on a monthly basis until occupied territory had been liberated.

18 October: The UAE decided to cut oil supplies to the United States. Mana Said Al Otaiba said that the President issued a decree placing an embargo on all oil exports to America because of US support for Israeli aggression against the Arab nation. He added that Abu Dhabi had been supplying between 15 and 20 per cent of America's oil requirements from the Arabian Gulf.

Mana Said Al Otaiba said that Abu Dhabi's oil income would increase in the coming year by about 1500 million dollars as a result of the adjustment of the price of Abu Dhabi petroleum and obtaining the sulphur allowance in addition to a world increase in the price of petroleum.

19 October: Sheikh Zayed received a cable from the Iraqi President, Ahmed Hassan Al Bakr in which he declared: 'Your courageous decision to cut off petroleum from the United States is a token of your pure and noble Arabism'.

20 October: Sheikh Zayed announced in an international news conference that the decision to place an embargo on oil supplies to the United States because of their assistance to Israel was part of a phased process of measures against the US for its Middle East policy. He said: 'This battle has united us and given us the hope that we needed. We call on Allah to increase our unity so we can achieve a great victory'.

Mana Said Al Otaiba said that practical steps had been taken to ensure that the UAE's petroleum would not reach America. The oil companies were obliged to sign a commitment to abide by this decision.

21 October: Sheikh Rashid bin Saeed Al Maktoum issued a decree prohibiting the export of petroleum to America. He ordered that this decree be applied to any country aiding Israel, either morally or materially.

22 October: The Federal National Council held an emergency session in which it supported the Government's policies and positions regarding the armed conflict and asked that the oil embargo on America be continued.

23 October: Sheikh Zayed announced the banning of oil exports to Holland in response to its inimical stand against the Arab nation. Holland had imported 4 million tons of Abu Dhabi oil annually.

28 October: Sheikh Zayed and Sheikh Rashid made a tour of the capital including Port Zayed.

31 October: The UAE Currency Board issued a statement in which it announced that the period of circulation of Bahraini dinars and Qatari riyals had ended. The final period for withdrawing these currencies from the markets and exchanging them for UAE dirhams was also defined.

1 November: Sheikh Tahnoun Al Nahyan signed the agreement for the first foreign investment project in which Abu Dhabi participated. The project included the creation of an Arab-Pakistan company to establish a fertilizer factory in Pakistan at a cost of 92 million dollars for which Abu Dhabi would provide 30 per cent of the capital.

6 November: Sheikh Zayed discussed the Arab situation with King Hussain of Jordan who arrived in Abu Dhabi on a short visit.

The Syrian President, Hafez Al Asad, awarded medals to all the members of the UAE medical mission in appreciation of their efforts in giving first aid treatment to the wounded during the war.

Abu Dhabi began implementation of the OAPEC decision to reduce oil production by 25 per cent.

11 November: Sheikh Zayed visited the tourist centre at Ain al-Fayidha.

12 November: Said Al Ghaith, Director of the Political Department of the Ministry of Foreign Affairs, delivered a cheque for 2 million Egyptian pounds to the Egyptian Foreign Minister, the first payment to be made from donations by UAE citizens in support of the armed conflict.

13 November: Abu Dhabi Executive Council approved the project for establishing flour mills in the country.

14 November: Sheikh Zayed said in an interview with German television that the oil embargo would continue until America had fulfilled her promises. He confirmed that future relations with Europe would be determined in the light of its stand on the Arab question.

15 November: It was decided to cancel celebrations for the second anniversary of the formation of the United Arab Emirates because of the difficulties being experienced by the Arab nation.

17 November: Mana Said Al Otaiba signed a 120 million dollar contract for the construction of the oil refinery and pipeline in Pakistan, the UAE providing one third of the cost.

18 November: The Council of Ministers approved the establishment of a Housing, Construction and Planning Institute at a cost of 220,000 dollars in order to improve technical and administrative competence and to develop ways of using building materials.

20 November: Sheikh Zayed announced in a comprehensive speech on the occasion of the opening of the new session of the Federal National Council that the next phase would centre on strengthening the Federation, supporting its foundations, shaping it into a well-known entity and making the hopes and well-being of the people a reality by providing a better life for its citizens. With regard to the Arab situation, he confirmed the UAE's support for the confrontation states. He said that Arab oil was not dearer than Arab blood and that the people of the UAE would not spare either their souls or their wealth in the face of the battle.

Sheikh Rashid opened a 18 million dirham cement pipe factory in Dubai with an annual production capacity of 30,000 pipes.

21 November: Sheikh Zayed, in talks with the Egyptian newspaper, *Al Jumhouriya,* said that complete Arab unity was the only cure for all that ailed the Arab nation. He said that the experiment in union on the two sides of the Gulf had confirmed this fact. With regard to oil, he said that if the entire cessation of pumping would help the political situation, the UAE would not hesitate for one minute to take that decision.

24 November: Sheikh Zayed, accompanied by Syrian President Hafez Al Asad, visited civilian targets bombarded by Israeli aircraft in Damascus during the Ramadan War. Zayed was in Damascus on his way from Cairo to Algeria to attend the Arab Summit Conference.

25 November: The Ministry of Electricity and Water decided to establish the first central water desalination plant at a cost of 100,000 dirhams.

26 November: Sheikh Zayed, attending the Arab Summit Conference in Algeria, held a series of important meetings with Arab leaders.

27 November: A hijacked Dutch jumbo jet landed at Dubai airport and took off three hours later. The hijackers demanded the closure of Jewish immigration centres in Holland and the freeing of their companions in Cypriot prisons.

28 November: The hijacked Dutch aircraft returned to Dubai airport where the hijackers surrendered themselves to the authorities and released all hostages.

2 December: Sheikh Zayed congratulated citizens on the occasion of the second anniversary of the formation of the Federation. He called on them to work hard and to examine their consciences. He also emphasized that what had been accomplished was done through the solidarity of the Rulers.

3 December: Sheikh Zayed laid the foundation stone for the cement factory in the Al-Ain region.

4 December: Sheikh Zayed performed the opening ceremony of the gas liquefaction plant on Das Island. He said that the plant was important to the Federation's economy and to its future and that Allah gave riches to the nation and not to the individual.

Elections for the new Board of the Abu Dhabi Chamber of Commerce and Industry resulted in Ahmed Al Masoud becoming Chairman, and Hamil bin Khadim Al Ghaith and Salim Ibrahim Al Saman, Deputy Chairmen.

5 December: Mana Said Al Otaiba, Minister of Petroleum and Industry, explained the UAE's oil policy at a press conference. He said that the UAE did not wish to exchange its petroleum in return for money only. The industrial countries were required to participate in the industrialization of the country in return for oil.

Abdulla Omran Taryam, Minister of Education, announced that a five-year educational plan for the UAE had been prepared. He said that there were 110 schools in existence in which 40,000 students were being educated.

8 December: Sheikh Zayed was present at boat races organized by the Ministry of Information and Tourism at Abu Dhabi Tourism Club.

Sixteen UAE students travelled to Khartoum to join the Sudanese Military College.

10 December: Sheikh Tahnoun signed an agreement with Pakistan to set up a joint oil refinery in Multan Province with a refining capacity of 40,000 barrels per day, as well as an 800 km pipeline.

11 December: Sheikh Zayed held talks with the Pakistan Prime Minister Zulfikar Ali Bhutto regarding the Islamic Summit Conference which was scheduled for the following month in Lahore. Mr Bhutto said that Sheikh Zayed's participation would help to support Islamic solidarity.

Sheikh Zayed informed a Japanese delegation, under the chairmanship of the Deputy Prime Minister, Takio Miki, that co-operation with Japan was tied to achievement of Arab objectives.

13 December: Sheikh Zayed accepted the resignation of Abu Dhabi Executive Council and the Federal Council of Ministers in preparation for a cabinet change aimed at stabilizing support for the Federation. Abu Dhabi Executive Council, the first in the history of the country, was formed at the beginning of July 1971. The first Federal Council of Ministers had been formed early in December 1971, shortly after the Federation of the United Arab Emirates was established.

15 December: Sheikh Zayed commissioned Sheikh Maktoum to form the new cabinet.

20 December: The Armed Forces celebrated Federal Army Day.

22 December: The Jabir bin Hayyan Secondary School in Abu Dhabi formed the first Parents Council to facilitate parental participation in school administration.

23 December: Sheikh Zayed issued a federal decree forming the new cabinet under the Prime Ministership of Sheikh Maktoum bin Rashid Al Maktoum with Sheikh Khalifa bin Zayed Al Nahyan as Deputy Prime Minister.

24 December: Sheikh Zayed chaired the first meeting of the new cabinet after which the ministers took the oath of office before the President who said: 'We have begun a new phase which demands from us all that we co-operate for the good of the Federation. Our goal is to eliminate what is negative and support the Federation. There must be equal treatment for all citizens of the Federation with regard to both rights and duties. We have become a single State and we must clearly and completely understand this fact'.

25 December: The Council of Ministers at its first meeting confirmed the draft law bringing some government offices within the federal system and also defined the responsibilites of the new ministries.

26 December: Mana Said Al Otaiba announced the discovery of a new crude oil and gas field 10 kms south of Arzhana Island and 60 kms north of Jebel al-Dhanna.

30 December: Sheikh Rashid signed a 95 million sterling pound contract relating to the dry dock project in Dubai.

Nineteen Seventy Four

3 January: Sheikh Zayed ordered the preparation of an urgent study on methods of benefiting from floodwater in order to raise the groundwater level.

5 January: Hamouda bin Ali in a meeting with the UAE Chiefs of Police in the Al-Qassimi Camp in Sharjah discussed the unification of the emirates'police forces under the Ministry of the Interior.

6 January: Sheikh Zayed held talks in Abu Dhabi with the Somali President Mohammad Siyad Barre and President Omar Bongo of Gabon. The talks were part of a drive by UAE to strengthen ties with African States.

8 January: Hamil bin Khadim was chosen as Chairman of the Abu Dhabi Municipal Council and Salim Ibrahim Al Saman as Vice Chairman in elections which were held in the Ministry of Municipalities and Agriculture.

9 January: The Organization of Oil Exporting Countries (OPEC) approved the transfer of Abu Dhabi's membership in the organization to the United Arab Emirates.

10 January: The Supreme Council of the Federation held a meeting under the chairmanship of Sheikh Zayed in which a number of matters relating to the future progress of the Federation were debated. The Council discussed a report on Government works and confirmed the fixed principles of the foreign policy of the country. At the end of its meetings it issued a number of decrees among which was the formation of a committee to follow up on the execution of projects.

12 January: Lord Balniol, the British Minister of State for Foreign Affairs, arrived in Abu Dhabi on the first visit of a Minister from the British Ministry of Foreign Affairs to the Gulf States since the withdrawal of Britain from the region at the end of 1971.

14 January: The Council of Ministers studied steps for the execution of Supreme Council of the Federation decrees dealing with improving the standard of living and ensuring the provision of public utilities and services. Sheikh Zayed issued an Amiri decree appointing Sheikh Khalifa bin Zayed Al Nahyan as the Commander in Chief of the Abu Dhabi Defence Forces.

Sheikh Khalifa issued Amiri decrees re-organizing the Abu Dhabi governmental structure and creating an Executive Council under his chairmanship. He also appointed directors for the 11 local council departments.

Sheikh Sultan bin Ahmed Al Mualla, Minister of Economy & Trade, opened the Boycott of Israel Conference which began its meetings in Abu Dhabi at a secret session with a debate on the stance of the airlines and shipping companies during the October War.

17 January: Sheikh Rashid issued a decree establishing a new company to be jointly owned by Dubai and Australia which would import, store and market food products from Western Australia.

20 January: President Anwar Sadat arrived in Abu Dhabi as part of a tour of the Gulf. He was received by Sheikh Zayed who cut short a private visit to Pakistan to discuss developments in Arab affairs with the Egyptian President.

22 January: The Council of Ministers decided to set-up a group to receive citizen's complaints and suggestions, as well as analyse public trends, in order to speed up progress.

Sharjah granted the American Crystal Oil Company oil exploration rights in its territories.

26 January: Sheikh Sultan bin Mohammad Al Qassimi announced in an interview with the *New York Times* that oil production in Sharjah would begin in a few months with a production target of 80,000 barrels for this year.

Abu Dhabi was hit by heavy rain storms which continued for three days, leading to the collapse of parts of the Corniche and the destruction of goods in Port Zayed.

27 January: The Board of Abu Dhabi Fund for Arab Economic Development (ADFAED) decided to grant loans

totalling more than 30 million dollars to five Arab countries, Jordan, Egypt, Syria, Yemen and Tunisia, to execute a number of vital developmental and infra-structural projects.

Sheikh Ahmed bin Hamid issued rules and regulations governing the profession of journalism in the UAE.

18 January: Sheikh Hamdan bin Mohammad Al Nahyan signed a 5 million dirham contract for the construction of the Islamic Studies Institute in Al-Ain.

The first airline connecting Abu Dhabi and Cairo was inaugurated.

31 January: The first direct telephone line between Abu Dhabi and Dubai was completed. Sheikh Maktoum bin Rashid Al Maktoum talked from his office in Dubai with Sheikh Hamdan bin Mohammad Al Nahyan in his office in Abu Dhabi.

Sheikh Mubarak bin Mohammad Al Nahyan issued an order changing the name of the Ministry of the Interior in Abu Dhabi to the General Police Directorate.

2 February: Direct telephone contact between Abu Dhabi, Dubai, Umm al-Qaiwain and Ajman was instituted on this date.

5 February: Abu Dhabi Ministry of Works announced that it had decided to build a new village on the Abu Dhabi Al-Ain highway in which there would be 170 public housing units, schools, clinics, mosques, and public markets located at Al-Mafraq roundabout, Al-Haffar, Ghayathi and Al-Samha.

A direct telephone connection was completed between Sharjah, Abu Dhabi and Al-Ain.

H.H.Sheikh Zayed bin Sultan Al Nahyan and H.H. Sheikh Rashid bin Saeed Al Maktoum,
founding fathers of the United Arab Emirates, photographed in 1972.

Sheikh Zayed with Sheikh Rashid bin Saeed Al Maktoum and Sheikh Saqr bin Mohammed Al Qassimi, ruler of Ras al-Khaimah in 1972.

Inauguration of Al Ain Cen

Sheikh Zayed with fellow dignitaries and council members at the first meeting of the Federal National Council on 1 March 1972.

Sheikh Zayed opens Abu D

Sheikh Zayed inspects a generator engine at Sadiyat island on 1 January 1972.

...ctory on 3 December 1972.

Sheikh Zayed on a visit to Dubai, 1972.

...ist Club on 3 January 1972.

Sheikh Zayed visits Fujairah in 1972.

Inauguration of Port Zayed on 28 June 1972.

Sheikh Zayed has been a keen supporter of the Boy Scout movement. This picture was taken in 1972.

Sheikh Zayed with President Assad of Syria in 1972.

Sheikh Zayed with Kurt V Countries Summit Conferenc

Sheikh Zayed personall Abu Dhabi in 1973.

The Abu Dhabi corniche in 1974.

...n at the non-Aligned
...iers on 1 January 1973.

Sheikh Zayed at the Non-Aligned Countries Summit Conference in
Algiers on 1 January 1973.

...vs development plans for

Meeting of the Supreme Council on 10 February 1974.

Sheikh Zayed played a constructive role in friendly discussions
between Colonel Gadhafi and President Sadat at a meeting held in
Alexandria, 1974.

Attending a school exhibition in 1974.

Sheikh Zayed presides over a distribution of houses to local people in Al-Ain in 1974.

A representative of His Holiness the Pope, presents a medal to H.H. Sheikh Zayed on 1 November 1974.

Sheikh Zayed and King Faisal sign a border agreement on 18 August, 1974.

Sheikh Zayed with King Faisal in 1975.

Sheikh Zayed with Indira Gandhi during his visit to India in 1975.

H.H. Sheikh Zayed with the Shah of Iran in 1975.

Archbishop Makarios, President of Cyprus, visiting Abu Dhabi in June 1975.

The Dubai World Trade Centre in 1975.

New Umm an-Nar refinery in 1975.

The first bedouin resettlement village at Abu Samrah, close to the Abu Dhabi – Al-Ain highway, in 1975.

Abu Dhabi's first Liquid Natural Gas plant in 1975.

Sheikh Zayed visited Jordan on 1 January 1975. He is seen here with King Hussein.

A meeting held in Jordan with Yasser Arafat, Leader of the Palestinian people, on 1 January 1975.

Inaugurating Abu Dhabi Television on 3 January 1975.

With President Zulfikar Ali Bhutto on 18 February 1975.

Sheikh Zayed with one of his falcons in 1975.

Local falconers attend a falconry meeting.

A bedouin waters his camels in a resettlement village in Abu Dhabi, in 1975.

With Indira Gandhi during a visit to India on 13 January 1975.

A traditional meeting with local people, held in 1975.

Inaugurating the Second Exhibition of the Abu Dhabi Womens Association in 1975.

Sheikh Zayed, Sheikh Rashid and other members of the Supreme Council inaugurating Jebel Ali Satellite station on 8 November 1975.

Sheikh Zayed, Sheikh Rashid and other dignitaries celebrate the opening of the Shindagha tunnel on 21 December 1975.

A 'modern' Spinney's supermarket was opened in Abu Dhabi in 1975.

6 February: Sheikh Khalifa bin Zayed opened a branch of the Paribas Bank in Abu Dhabi and welcomed the strengthening of relations between the Federation and France.

The Federal National Council recommended that a draft law be prepared encouraging UAE men to marry UAE women and to increase the number of children.

7 February: Sheikh Khalifa bin Zayed issued an Amiri decree establishing the Abu Dhabi National Company for Building Materials with a capital of 2 million dirhams.

11 February: Sheikh Zayed issued a federal decree re-organizing the Federal National Council on the expiry of the Council formed two years previously.

The Council of Ministers formed a permanent projects committee under the chairmanship of the Minister of Planning, Mohammad Khalifa Al Kindi, to oversee development projects and award development contracts.

12 February: The new Federal National Council at its first session elected Thani bin Abdulla as Chairman, Rahma Mohammad Al Masoud as the first Vice Chairman, and Mohammad Rahma Al Ameri second Vice Chairman. Salim Ibrahim Darwish and Hamad Bu Shihab were elected as Council observers.

The National Planning Board advised that steps be taken to undertake a general census before the end of the current year.

13 February: A lecture series organized by the Ministry of Foreign Affairs commenced, its aim being to upgrade the Ministry's young diplomats.

The Ministry of Education announced that there were 155 schools with 51,000 students in the Federation.

14 February: Sheikh Khalifa bin Zayed witnessed the graduation of Troop No. 1 officers from their course at the Al-Qassimiya Camp in Sharjah.

18 February: It was officially announced that Sheikh Zayed would lead the federal delegation to the Islamic Conference Summit in Lahore accompanied by Sheikh Rashid bin Saeed Al Maktoum, Vice President of the Federation.

Dubai Municipal Council announced that commercial signs must be written in Arabic as a condition for granting and renewing commercial licences.

18 February: Together with 11 other Arab countries, the UAE signed an agreement in Cairo establishing the Arab Bank for African Development.

19 February: Sheikh Mohammad bin Rashid Al Maktoum attended the graduation of the new batch of Armed Forces cadets at Al-Mirqaab Camp.

21 February: Sheikh Zayed confirmed that the UAE was committed to fulfill its duty toward the Islamic Community and to participate with it in raising high the Word of Justice and Truth. In an announcement upon arrival in Lahore to participate in the Islamic Summit he said that the Conference represented a new phase of Islamic co-operation aimed at achieving security and justice as well as strengthening international stability.

Abu Dhabi Municipality announced that it had decided not to permit citizens to rent houses given to them by the State.

23 February: Sheikh Zayed and Sheikh Rashid attended two working sessions held by the Islamic Summit Conference in Lahore in which they considered the granting of practical aid to the confrontation States.

24 February: Sheikh Zayed said that discussions at the Islamic Summit Conference centred on the hopes of Muslims to free occupied territories.

An agreement was reached with the International Currency Fund on the initial official equivalent price of the UAE dirham which was fixed at 186621 grams of gold.

Sheikh Mohammad bin Rashid Al Maktoum attended the opening ceremonies at the flour mills in Dubai, considered to be the largest of their kind in the UAE. Costing 25 million dirhams, the mills could produce 100 tons daily.

25 February: The UAE broadcasting station in Abu Dhabi celebrated the fifth anniversary of its establishment.

26 February: Sheikh Zayed praised the solidarity of the Islamic community which was clearly manifest at the Lahore Summit. He said that the conference re-established the Islamic community in its rightful place among the nations and rekindled its cohesion with its brothers in the Arab nation.

28 February: Sheikh Khalifa bin Zayed Al Nahyan received Yasser Arafat, Chairman of the Executive Committee of the Palestine Liberation Organization.

2 March: Abu Dhabi Executive Council under the chairmanship of Sheikh Khalifa bin Zayed Al Nahyan decided to form an executive committee to prepare a comprehensive plan for sewerage system projects and to follow-up on their execution.

Executive regulations were issued organizing the distribution of public housing units. It was decided to form a housing distribution committee under the chairmanship of the Minister of Housing.

In Abu Dhabi, the Wahda Club was merged with the Ittihad Club to form the Abu Dhabi Athletic and Cultural Club.

4 March: Sheikh Zayed received the President of Zaire, Mobutu Sesiko, who arrived in Abu Dhabi on his first official visit to the Emirates.

5 March: The Council of Ministers debated the draft law regulating the establishment of co-operative societies for farmers and fishermen and it approved in principle that the State would bear 50 per cent of the loans to farmers and fishermen. The Council also approved the plan to train a core group of UAE personnel in transport.

6 March: Sheikh Zayed and President Mobutu, in a joint statement at the conclusion of their discussions, emphasized the necessity of Israel withdrawing from occupied territories and guaranteeing the full rights of the Palestinian people. The two Presidents agreed to set up diplomatic relations and economic co-operation between their countries.

Sheikh Zayed signed a new agreement with a group representing five Canadian companies for oil exploration in two of Abu Dhabi's offshore regions: ADMA had relinquished these concession in 1972 by mutual agreement.

The Syrian President, Hafez Al Asad, in remarks published in Beirut, praised the stance taken by the UAE during the October War: he said that the UAE had contributed 100 million dollars during the war.

Sheikh Zayed received the famous American boxer, Mohammad Ali

(Cassius) Clay, who arrived in Abu Dhabi on his second visit to the UAE.

9 March: Official discussions began in Islamabad between Sheikh Zayed and the President of Pakistan, Zulfikar Ali Bhutto. An agreement was concluded on strengthening co-operation between the two countries in all fields with a strong emphasis on achieving security and stability in the region.

The UAE recognized the Republic of Bangladesh and decided to exchange diplomatic relations with it at ambassadorial level.

The UAE began withdrawing local passports which were issued by each emirate and issuing new passports in the name of the United Arab Emirates.

11 March: Sheikh Zayed approved the allocation of an extra sum amounting to 710,000 dollars to complete the Yemen TV and broadcasting studios.

The Council of Ministers approved the executive programme for public housing prepared by the Ministry of Housing at a cost of 100 million dirhams. Phase One of the project was scheduled to begin in April.

The municipalities of Sharjah, Ras al-Khaimah, Ajman, Umm al-Qaiwain and Fujairah began distributing requests for the 1720 public housing units costing 96 million dirhams which were built by the State in cities and villages of these emirates.

12 March: Sheikh Zayed and Zulfikar Ali Bhutto signed the co-operation agreement between the UAE and Pakistan and the two leaders decided to form a joint ministerial committee which would meet every six months to follow up on the execution of projects agreed by the parties.

Sheikh Rashid bin Saeed Al Maktoum signed a 9.5 million dirham contract for the construction of a second bridge connecting Deira and Bur Dubai.

14 March: One billion one hundred million dirhams was allocated for development in Abu Dhabi.

18 March: The Council of Ministers approved the formation of a joint bank by the UAE, Libya and Algeria. Headquartered in Abu Dhabi, it was formed to support financial and banking relations between the three countries.

The UAE Football Team defeated the Bahrain team by four goals to nil in the Third Gulf Games held in Kuwait.

20 March: Sheikh Zayed and Sheikh Rashid witnessed military manoeuvres by the Air Division of the Abu Dhabi Defence Forces in which Mirage aircraft and helicopters equipped with air/ground missiles participated.

22 March: Sheikh Zayed opened the Sixth Agricultural Exhibition in Al-Ain in which 420 UAE farmers participated.

27 March: The Federal National Council approved the draft law organizing the federal security forces and subjecting them to the authority of the Minister of the Interior.

28 March: Sheikh Zayed received Saddam Hussein, Vice President of the Revolutionary Council in Iraq. Saddam emphasized Iraq's great concern for the Arab character of the Gulf Region.

31 March: The Ministry of Information decided to establish a national news agency.

1 April: Construction of the first oil tanker built by the UAE was completed in Singapore. The tanker had a capacity of 650, 000 barrels of oil.

Abu Dhabi airport began receiving jumbo jets.

2 April: Sheikh Zayed, meeting representatives of the Abu Dhabi National Oil Company, announced that Abu Dhabi's oil policy was not to increase its production except in reasonable quantities which would be in line with its national interest and in accordance with development requirements.

Sheikh Hamdan bin Mohammad Al Nahyan signed a 9.157 million dirham contract for the construction of harbour walls required to limit the extent of silting in the port at Khor Ajman.

6 April: The Council of Ministers confirmed that the draft budget of the State for 1974 amounted to 850 million dirhams in comparison with the 1973 budget of 510 million dirhams.

7 April: Sheikh Zayed issued a federal decree substituting Abu Dhabi's OPEC membership with that of the UAE.

8 April: Sheikh Rashid opened a branch of the UAE Currency Board in Dubai.

13 April: The UAE gave 100,000 dollars to the Arab League as a first payment in support of Arab information in the international arena.

14 April: Sheikh Zayed and Sheikh Rashid toured the Agricultural Experimental Station in Al-Ain.

15 April: In Abu Dhabi, Sheikh Ahmed bin Hamid opened the conference of heads of broadcasting and television establishments in the Gulf countries and the Arabian Peninsula. The conference studied the UAE proposal to set-up the Gulf Establishment for Joint Radio and Television Production.

17 April: ADFAED decided to grant long term loans of more than 120 million dirhams to five countries; Bahrain, Egypt, Somalia, Tunisia and Mauritania.

20 April: At the conclusion of his inspection tour of Fujairah, Sheikh Zayed confirmed that the Federation had made real progress in providing the highest standard of services to citizens in the fields of education, health, communications and labour and that the Federation was a guarantee for a dignified standard of living for all of its citizens. The Sheikh also laid the foundation stone for the Musafi electricity plant and opened the main Fujairah highway.

21 April: Sheikh Zayed and Sheikh Sultan Al Qassimi toured the Khor Fakkan region, including the port, housing projects, the Corniche Road, the hospital and two schools for boys and girls in the region. Sheikh Zayed also opened the Marbah Camp for the Federal Defence Forces.

22 April: Sheikh Zayed ordered an immediate feasibility study on developing Khor Fakkan port to accommodate big ships.

24 April: Sheikh Zayed laid the foundation stone for the Falaj al-Mualla electricity plant and inspected work on the health clinic in Al-Manama as well as public housing in Falaj al-Mualla, Al-Manama and Al-Zaid, at the same time distributing title deeds for these houses to a number of citizens.

In Abu Dhabi, the UAE, Algeria and Libya signed the agreement for the establishment of the Arab Bank for Foreign Investment and Trade with a capital of 70 million dirhams.

25 April: Sheikh Zayed, at the end of the first phase of his tour of the UAE, said that the Federation had achieved much in a short space of time and that the future would be bright. He visited Ras al-Khaimah where he inaugurated the water project at Idhna, laid the foundation stone for the development of Al-Nakheel Hospital and set up the nursing hospital. He also visited a number of educational institutions and distributed title deeds for public housing to the people of Tubb.

29 April: Sheikh Zayed and the Mauritanian President, Ould Dada, in Abu Dhabi on his first official visit, went on a tour of development projects in the Eastern Region. Zayed, in the presence of his guest, opened the main offices of the Abu Dhabi National Bank in Abu Dhabi.

30 April: ADFAED signed an agreement for a loan of 17 million dirhams to finance an iron smelter in Mauritania.

2 May: Sheikh Hamdan bin Mohammad Al Nahyan signed three new contracts for the construction of a highway between Umm al-Qaiwain and Falaj al-Mualla and a road bridge connecting the island of Umm al-Nar to the mainland.

4 May: Sheikh Zayed, in a meeting with citizens in Ras al-Khaimah in the presence of Sheikh Saqr bin Mohammad Al Qassimi, confirmed that the future looked very promising. Zayed and Saqr inspected the cement factory, housing, water and educational projects.

5 May: Sheikh Zayed visited Umm al-Qaiwain where he met with citizens and opened the Umm al-Qaiwain electricity plant. He also laid the foundation stone for the second phase of the Umm al-Qaiwain hospital and inspected work on a number of development projects.

6 May: Sheikh Zayed announced at a huge rally in the Al-Rams Club of Ras al-

Khaimah that he was totally committed to continue his policy of providing public utilities to every citizen.

Sheikh Surour bin Mohammad Al Nahyan signed a 48.5 million dirham contract with an international company to supply pipelines for the transport of gas from Habshan to the Maqta'a region.

7 May: Sheikh Rashid bin Saeed Al Maktoum witnessed the graduation of the new batch of soldiers from Al-Mirqaab Camp. Sheikh Mohammad bin Rashid Al Maktoum, Minister of Defence, announced that this group had joined the Federal Forces.

8 May: Sheikh Zayed expressed his appreciation for the efforts made by responsible people in the various sectors in achieving progress at the end of his inspection tour of a number of new projects in Ajman in the company of Sheikh Rashid bin Humaid Al Nuaimi. He said: 'I am very proud of the sons of this country who have taken their responsibilities seriously'.

9 May: Sheikh Zayed inaugurated the National Youth Theatre in Dubai, a gift from Sheikh Rashid to the youth of the Emirates.

11 May: Sheikh Rashid bin Saeed Al Maktoum raised the flag of the UAE on the oil tanker *Said*, the first ship in the national commercial fleet. The tanker had a capacity of 20,000 tons.

ADFAED gave a loan of 5 million dirhams to Syria to help establish two farms for cattle breeding. Sheikh Zayed also announced a fourfold increase in ADFAED's capital available to 500 million dollars to loan to less developed countries including non-Arab Islamic States. Hassan Abbas Zaki, director of ADFAED said: 'It is the expressed policy of the UAE to play its role in helping other countries to surmount their problems of energy and development.'

UAE doubled its African drought relief contribution to 6 million dollars; doubled its contribution to liberation movements to 1 million dollars; and pledged 2 million dollars to an African technical development fund.

12 May: The Council of Ministers approved the formation of an executive committee to oversee events in the Federation. It also approved the creation of a national company (Abu Dhabi National Company for Oil Product Distribution) to take over the distribution of petroleum products in all the Emirates.

13 May: Sheikh Zayed and Sheikh Sultan bin Mohammad Al Qassimi inspected a number of important projects in Sharjah, including the new Industrial School, the Creek, popular housing projects and the Sharjah - Dubai highway.

14 May: Sheikh Zayed took a number of important steps to improve the standard of living after his wide-ranging tour of the Emirates, during which he had experienced at first hand the hardship brought about by rocketing food prices. Zayed allocated 27 million dirhams to subsidize principal food commodities and to change the Abu Dhabi Trade Company into a federal company with branches in all the Emirates.

Sheikh Sultan bin Mohammad Al Qassimi arrived in Tehran on an official two-day visit to Iran.

Sheikh Tahnoun bin Mohammad Al Nahyan opened the new vegetable market in Al-Ain.

15 May: Sheikh Zayed and Sheikh Rashid inspected three schools in Dubai.

During his meeting with the students of the Industrial School, Sheikh Zayed said that more attention should be paid to the training of technicians for the service of the nation.

Sheikh Khalifa bin Zayed Al Nahyan signed an agreement between Abu Dhabi and the World Bank whereby the bank could issue bonds in UAE dirhams, up to 300 million dirhams, to be paid off over a ten year period at an interest rate of 8 per cent. The loan marked the first occasion in which the UAE's currency was used in an international transaction.

21 May: Sheikh Zayed issued a decision to establish a national bank for investment and development with a capital of 500 million dirhams, with the aim of granting loans to citizens for projects in industrial, agricultural and real estate fields.

Sheikh Zayed inspected the marble quarries in Masfoot and in the Hadhaf and Al-Hamraniya areas.

Sheikh Hamdan bin Mohammad Al Nahyan signed three contracts valued at 10 million dirhams for the second stage of the Umm al-Qaiwain hospital, the health centre in the Shaam region of Ras al-Khaimah, and three clinics in various regions of the emirate.

22 May: Sheikh Zayed completed his month-long tour of the Emirates.

The Ministry of Justice prepared a draft law regulating the legal profession in the country.

25 May: Sheikh Zayed witnessed the huge celebrations which were launched by the Umm Ammar Secondary School in Abu Dhabi on the occasion of the first Flag Day. Sheikh Zayed honoured outstanding students.

The Minister of Education said Sheikh Zayed had ordered the payment of grants to all students in the UAE beginning from 1975.

Sheikh Sultan bin Mohammad Al Qassimi opened the Bank of Sharjah with a capital of 15 million dirhams.

29 May: The Conference of Women's Societies in the UAE announced the formation of the UAE's Women's Federation which would amalgamate all women's societies in the UAE. The Conference elected Sheikha Fatima bint Mubarak, wife of Sheikh Zayed as the president of the Women's Federation.

1 June: The Supreme Council of the Federation under the chairmanship of Sheikh Zayed confirmed the federal budget for 1974. It was decided to subsidize basic commodities in order that they might be sold to citizens at prices 35 per cent below cost. It was also decided to hold a general census of residents and to amalgamate the Awqaf Departments of the Emirates with the Ministry of Islamic Affairs and Awqaf.

The federal flag was raised by itself for the first time over the Saray Presidential Palace in Abu Dhabi. Formerly, all the individual flags of the emirates were raised with it.

3 June: Sheikh Khalifa bin Zayed Al Nahyan arrived in Amman on an official visit to Jordan.

4 June: In Cairo, Sultan bin Ahmed Al Mualla, Minister for Economy & Trade, signed an agreement concerning the inclusion of the UAE in the Arab Economic Unity Agreement and membership in the Economic Unity Council.

5 June: Sheikh Zayed issued a federal law approving the federal budget for 1974. Estimated at 1692 million dirhams, the budget focused on raising the standard of living, the realization of high growth averages, and the provision of 2499 new work opportunities.

The Federal National Council approved a draft law regarding firearms, ammunitions and explosives, authorizing stiff penalties for violators of this law.

It was announced officially in Damascus that the UAE had transferred 50 million dollars to the Central Bank of Syria in support of the Syrian war effort.

11 June: Sheikh Zayed issued a federal decree defining the responsibilities of the Ministry of Planning. The decree stipulated that the ministry would take charge of supervising the country's economic and social development plan.

14 June: Sheikh Rashid ordered the commencement of the third phase of the Port Rashid project in which 30 new berths would be built.

16 June: Sheikh Zayed issued a federal decree establishing a nursing school to provide the UAE with trained nurses.

17 June: Sheikh Zayed visited Bida Zayed region where he chose new public housing sites. He said that the aim of establishing this city was to settle the bedouin and provide them with all the services they required.

Sheikh Tahnoun bin Mohammad Al Nahyan signed an agreement with the French Petroleum Institute to make a study of investment in Abu Dhabi gas and the international marketing of the gas.

19 June: Shaikh Khaled bin Saqr Al Qassimi opened the first centre in Ras al-

Khaimah for the distribution of commodities to citizens at reduced prices. Sheikh Surour bin Mohammad Al Nahyan and Sheikh Ahmed bin Hamid opened the first exhibition mounted by the UAE in Western Europe in the German city of Hamburg.

Rules and regulations were issued governing work visas. The regulations defined conditions for the employment of labourers and transfer from one sponsor to another.

20 June: During a visit to the Western Region, Sheikh Zayed issued directions for establishing a new city and port in Al-Marfa.

22 June: The UAE condemned renewed Israeli aggression against the south of Lebanon and Palestinian refugee camps. The Ministry of Foreign Affairs announced that the State would give 4 million dollars to mitigate the damage done to Lebanese and Palestinians.

23 June: At the conference of Ministers of Foreign Affairs of Islamic countries held in Kuala Lumpur, Ahmed Khalifa Al Suweidi announced the donation by the UAE of 1 million dollars to set-up an Islamic news agency and another million dollars to support the General Secretariat of the Islamic Conference.

27 June: Sheikh Zayed issued directions for the construction of a new port on Delma Island with the aim of reviving the island which was once an important centre for pearl fishing and trading.

29 June: Sheikh Hamdan bin Mohammad Al Nahyan signed agreements valued at 45 million dirhams, among which was a 25 million dirham contract for the design and construction of the Ministry of the Interior building in Abu Dhabi.

3 July: Sheikh Zayed received a delegation from the oil companies operating in Abu Dhabi at Al-Maqam Palace in Al-Ain. Talks were held regarding partnership with the Ministry of Petroleum and Mineral Resources. Mana Said Al Otaiba announced that experts from both sides would complete technical studies after which the two delegations would resume their discussions.

A statistical study by the Ministry of Petroleum revealed that the rise in the average consumption of oil products in Abu Dhabi had exceeded all expectations, rising to 25 million gallons in the previous six months.

5 July: Sheikh Zayed issued an Amiri decree organizing the Abu Dhabi Planning Office. The office was given the task of assessing the needs of the country in relation to development plans, the preparation of development plans and budgets, supervision of the execution of the plans, and the dissemination of development awareness in the country.

6 July: Sheikh Zayed and King Hussein of Jordan held talks covering Arab affairs and bilateral relations in the VIP lounge of Abu Dhabi airport. King Hussein had arrived in Abu Dhabi from Muscat for a brief visit to the UAE.

Sheikh Sultan bin Mohammad Al Qassimi signed an oil exploration concessions agreement with the American Rezeef Oil and Gas Company for the offshore waters of Sharjah. Sheikh Mohammad bin Hamad Al Sharqi signed a similar agreement with the same company for oil exploration in Fujairah.

7 July: Mana Said Al Otaiba announced the postponement of negotiations on the Partnership Agreement between Abu Dhabi and a delegation of the major oil companies operating in the country after discussions reached a deadlock. He said that Abu Dhabi had set a time limit for studying the recommendations which the Government had put forth and he emphasized his commitment to obtaining the maximum returns possible from the UAE's oil wealth.

7 July: Sheikh Zayed issued an Amiri decree establishing the posted price of crude oil exported from the Abu al-Bukhoush field at 11.656 dollars per barrel.

Sheikh Zayed issued an Amiri decree establishing the law regarding pensions and retirement gratuities for Abu Dhabi's civil servants (UAE nationals as well as citizens of the Sultanate of Oman, Qatar and Bahrain). Two per cent of the basic salary was to be deducted monthly and applied towards retirement.

9 July: Sheikh Zayed issued a federal decree modifying the articles dealing with royalties on all oil concession agreements: as of 1 July 1974, royalty payments rose from 12.5 to 14.5 per cent.

10 July: Sheikh Rashid issued an Amiri decree appointing Sheikh Hamdan bin Rashid Al Maktoum as Chairman of Dubai Municipality Council. A second decree appointed 35 members to the new Municipality Council.

Sheikh Hamdan bin Mohammad Al Nahyan signed a 150 million dirham contract for the construction of the 102 km Al-Ain - Sahar highway.

12 July: Sheikh Zayed issued a federal decree establishing the law governing the practice of the profession of pharmacist and trading in medicines.

Sheikh Humaid bin Rashid Al Nuaimi announced that the emirate of Ajman signed an oil exploration agreement covering all the territory of Ajman with the British company, United Refinex Oil Company.

14 July: Sheikh Zayed inspected a class at the Centre for the Memorization of the Holy Qur'an in Al-Ain. He said that the Book of Allah is sufficient foundation for all knowledge and the source of morality and virtue and that all Muslims must hold fast to it and make it the basis of their life in both thought and practice.

15 July: Sheikh Zayed approved the construction of an oil refinery in Jebel al-Dhanna with a capacity of 200,000 barrels per day.

Sheikh Sultan signed a 36 million dollar contract for the dredging of Sharjah port. The contract was facilitated by the participation of a group of 20 international banks.

16 July: The UAE Government granted approval to join the Arab Investment Company headquartered in Riyadh, which was capitalized at 200 million dollars.

18 July: Sheikh Sultan announced the commencement of oil exports from the Mubarak Field in Abu Musa island.

22 July: The first batch of 46 public housing units for low income citizens in Abu Dhabi was distributed. The units were located on Airport Street.

24 July: Sheikh Zayed ordered that rice be sold at a reduced price to all citizens in the UAE in the same manner as other commodities such as flour and sugar. He allocated 44 million dirhams to meet the difference in prices and it was decided to apply this order in the 1975 budget.

The Ministry of Economy and Commerce decided that a 91-kilo sack of rice should be sold to the public for only 185 dirhams.

25 July: Sheikh Zayed made an inspection tour of Abu Dhabi Hospital and ordered that the hospital be supplied with the latest medical equipment. He also ordered that financial assistance be given to 421 patients in the hospital.

27 July: Sheikh Zayed inspected the new housing complexes which had been built near the Abu Dhabi Traffic Office. He ordered that priority in assigning these houses which could accommodate 400 families be given to families who live in wooden houses inside the capital, and especially those living near the Al-Zuaab district.

28 July: Sheikh Zayed allocated 7 million dirhams to meet the expenses of the Qur'an Memorization Centres. These allocations include the payment of 200 dirhams per month to the students.

29 July: In Abu Dhabi, Sheikh Zayed and Prince Fahad bin Abdulaziz, Second Deputy Prime Minister and Minister of the Interior of Saudi Arabia, initialled an agreement relating to the borders between the two countries. A joint communiqué was issued which indicated that the discussions were aimed at the future security and stability of the region and an increase in co-operation between the two countries and all Gulf countries, so that the region could avoid influences foreign to their Islamic beliefs.

Sheikh Zayed began official talks with the Iraqi President, Ahmed Hassan Al Bakr, after his arrival in Baghdad at the beginning of an Arab tour which was to include Tunisia, Algeria, Morocco, Mauritania and Libya.

1 August: Sheikh Zayed held discussions in Tunis with the Tunisian President, Al Habib Bourgiba.

The UAE donated 15 million dirhams to promote stability in Jordan.

4 August: Sheikh Zayed signed an agreement to establish the Abu Dhabi National Company for Plastic Pipe Manufacture with the Japanese company, See Ito. The first factory of its kind in Abu Dhabi, it would have an annual capacity of 3000 tons.

6 August: Sheikh Zayed arrived in Tripoli and met with the Libyan President, Muammar Al Gadhafi.

For the first time, Abu Dhabi television carried live the departure ceremonies of Sheikh Zayed from the Tunisian capital over the satellite station in Kuwait.

7 August: Sheikh Zayed visited Algeria on his way back from Libya. Ahmed Khalifa Al Suweidi was instructed by Sheikh Zayed to remain behind in Tripoli for further discussions with Libyan officials regarding the UAE's efforts to mediate between Libya and Egypt.

Sheikh Khalifa bin Zayed Al Nahyan issued the Abu Dhabi Defence Force Law.

8 August: Sheikh Zayed held important discussions with the Algerian President, Houari Boumedienne, concerning Arab and international issues as well as bilateral relations.

Police Chiefs of the emirates agreed in a meeting under the chairmanship of Colonel Khalfan Khamis to unify vehicle number plates in all the emirates. The new plates will carry the name of the Federation along with a letter symbolizing the emirate.

9 August: The UAE signed an agreement with India to set up a steel mill in Dubai.

11 August: Sheikh Zayed held discussions with King Hassan II of Morocco. The two leaders attended the opening of the Abu al-Niqraq dam in the Moroccan kingdom.

Sheikh Rashid arrived in Tehran on an official visit, meeting with the Shah, Mohammad Rida Pahlavi, immediately after his arrival.

Sheikh Khalifa bin Zayed Al Nahyan issued a decree concerning the organization of the Social Services Department and its objectives.

Sheikh Surour bin Mohammad Al Nahyan signed an agreement to extend water services to the villages of Al-Wathba, Al-Khatm and Al-Khazna.

13 August: Sheikh Zayed arrived in Nouakchott to a warm reception in which more than 100 Mauritanians participated, led by President Mukhtar Ould Dada.

14 August: Sheikh Rashid returned to the country after an official three-day visit to Tehran in which he signed an agreement demarcating the continental shelf between the Emirates and Iran.

15 August: Sheikh Sultan Al Qassimi was present at the commencement of the export of oil from the Mubarak Field.

17 August: Mediation between two Arab leaders, Anwar Sadat and Muammar Al Gadhafi, was successfully undertaken by Sheikh Zayed. Al Gadhafi arrived in Alexandria to participate in important talks between the three leaders.

The name *Zayed* was given to a huge quarter of Alexandria.

18 August: The three leaders, Zayed, Sadat and Gadhafi, held important discussions in an atmosphere of frankness and concern for brotherly relations between Egypt and Libya. Zayed spoke about the importance of Arab solidarity and the necessity of putting an end to conflicts between Arab counties.

19 August: Sheikh Zayed arrived in Jeddah where he was received by His Majesty King Faisal bin Abdulaziz Al Saud.

A communiqué was issued on the discussions between Zayed and Sadat which confirmed the agreement between the two countries to increase co-operation in all fields.

20 August: Official discussions between Zayed and Faisal began in Jeddah. Zayed said that a new era of continuing co-operation between the UAE and Saudi Arabia was commencing which would enhance Arab dignity and help the stability of the Gulf region.

21 August: In Jeddah, Sheikh Zayed and King Faisal signed an agreement which defined the border between the two countries, with a joint technical committee established to set about mapping the border according to the agreement. A communiqué was issued in which the two leaders expressed their complete readiness to co-operate to keep foreign influences out of the Gulf region. They called on the leaders of the Arab nation to work toward the unification of their efforts until final victory.

22 August: In London, Sheikh Zayed met with Mr David Ennals, the British Minister of State for Foreign Affairs, who congratulated him on the border agreement with Saudi Arabia.

24 August: Sheikh Zayed sent Mana Said Al Otaiba to Qatar, Bahrain and Kuwait and Saif bin Ghobash to the Sultanate of Oman, Iran and Iraq carrying letters outlining the border agreement with Saudi Arabia.

25 August: Sheikh Zayed ordered the construction of a new residential city at Al-Mafraq and, in the first phase, the building of 1000 prefabricated houses.

29 August: Mana Said Al Otaiba signed a 55 million dirham contract for the construction of a flour mill in Abu Dhabi.

The Asian Games Federation accepted the UAE as a member.

Concorde, the fastest passenger aircraft in the world, successfully landed at Dubai airport. The plane had left Abu Dhabi on a one-hour trial flight.

31 August: Sheikh Zayed approved the establishment of the new industrial zone in Musaffah.

Discussions recommenced in Abu Dhabi regarding alterations to the Partnership Agreement between the Government of Abu Dhabi and the oil companies operating in the country. The talks had been in abeyance since June.

2 September: Mana Said Al Otaiba and negotiators from the oil companies operating in Abu Dhabi signed a new Partnership Agreement granting Abu Dhabi 60 per cent ownership in the companies retroactive to 1 January 1974. Al Otaiba announced that, according to the agreement, the companies would pay Abu Dhabi 500 million dollars covering the previous nine months.

3 September: Abdulla Omran Taryam, Minister for Education, confirmed that equal treatment would be given to children of residents and children of UAE nationals in the proposed payment of school grants. He also said that studies regarding the establishment of a university for the UAE would be completed within a year.

4 September: Sheikh Surour bin Mohammad Al Nahyan signed an agreement relating to the design of the new Abu Dhabi international airport. The Paris Airport Authority were the consultants for the project.

7 September: Abdulla Omran Taryam announced on the occasion of the World Day for the Elimination of Illiteracy that 7797 citizens were studying in 91 Adult Education Centres.

10 September: Sheikh Zayed held a meeting with students pursuing higher studies in Britain. He directed them to persevere until they could join in building their country.

Mohammad Khalifa Al Kindi signed a 52 million dirham contract for the construction and surfacing of the road between Khor Fakkan and Dibba.

11 September: Sheikh Rashid bin Saeed Al Maktoum witnessed inaugural ceremonies at the new telex station in Dubai.

14 September: Abu Dhabi Executive Council approved the relinquishment by the Middle East Oil Company (Japan) of its onshore concessions in Abu Dhabi, according to an agreement arrived at between the Abu Dhabi Government and the company on the 31 January 1970.

16 September: Abdulla Omran Taryam announced that Sheikh Zayed had decided to pay monthly grants totalling 30 million dirhams to students from October. Sixty thousand students were enrolled in UAE schools, an increase of 25 per cent over 1973.

17 September: Sheikh Zayed announced the death of Sheikh Mohammad bin Hamad Al Sharqi, Ruler of Fujairah, who passed away after a full life of service to his people and country.

Sheikh Rashid signed a new agreement with the Texas Pacific Company (Dubai) for a period of 35 years for oil exploration in Dubai's offshore areas.

18 September: The Supreme Council of the Federation announced that Sheikh Hamad bin Mohammad Al Sharqi had succeeded his father, the late Sheikh Mohammad bin Hamad Al Sharqi, as Ruler of Fujairah.

19 September: Sheikh Surour bin Mohammad Al Nahyan dedicated the new 13,500- ton ship Al-Dhafra, part of the fleet of the Abu Dhabi National Shipping Company, in a ceremony at Karachi Port.

21 September: The Government of Abu Dhabi decided to support the UAE dirham in international financial markets and to encourage Governments and banks, including Spanish, Austrian, Finnish and Swedish banks, to issue bonds in dirhams.

Sheikh Surour bin Mohammad Al Nahyan signed a 266 million dirham contract for a major expansion of the capital's electrical power plant, including the installation of six new turbines with a total output of 140,000 kilowatts.

Omar Khalifa Al Kindi signed a 30 million dirham contract for the construction of a road from Umm al-Qaiwain to Falaj al-Mualla.

24 September: Sheikh Hamdan bin Rashid Al Maktoum signed a 33 million dirham contract to construct the new municipality building in Dubai.

25 September: Mana Said Al Otaiba signed an agreement establishing the Arab Company for Petroleum Investments in which the UAE will own shares amounting to 20 per cent of the 3.6 million Saudi riyal capitalization .

26 September: The Council of Ministers approved the principal strategic planning goals for the development of the country which could be summarized as follows: personal growth of the individual, development of the national labour force, supporting the national economy and investing the nation's wealth.

28 September: Kurt Waldheim, Secretary General of the United Nations, announced that the UAE had allocated 117 million dollars to support the Regional Arab Funds.

Sheikh Surour bin Mohammad Al Nahyan signed a 158 million dirham contract for the importation and installation in the capital of four new waterworks producing 12 million gallons daily.

30 September: Sheikh Rashid approved plans for the second phase of the Dubai Creek project, including the construction of tourist islands, hotels, markets and sports playgrounds at a cost of 300 million dirhams.

The law establishing the Abu Dhabi National Company for Plastic Pipe Manufacture (capital 2 million dirhams) was promulgated.

Sheikh Mohammad bin Butti Al Hamid took over chairmanship of the Board of the Development Bank.

1 October: The Ministry of Defence celebrated the first anniversary of the founding of the Air Wing.

A football competition under floodlighting was staged for the first time in Abu Dhabi.

2 October: Sheikh Zayed examined the proofs of the Holy Qur'an which he had ordered to be printed in varying sizes for distribution to the country's guests and to mosques.

8 October: The Council of Ministers decided to recruit and encourage Arab workers and to provide them with facilities so that they could share in the country's economic and social renaissance.

10 September: UAE and Somalia signed an economic and trade agreement in Dubai.

11 October: Abu Dhabi had become a great centre for engineering accomplishments, not least of which was the completion of the world's largest barge. Weighing 750 tons, it was designed to transport equipment to Das Island.

14 October: Sheikh Surour bin Mohammad Al Nahyan announced that Sheikh Zayed had approved the designs for 5000 houses in New Al-Mafraq.

15 October: Sheikh Rashid approved plans prepared by an international company for the construction of the Dubai International Trade Centre at a cost of 56 million sterling pounds.

21 October: Sheikh Rashid approved the establishment of the first poultry farm in Dubai which would cover local requirements for poultry meat and eggs.

25 October: Sheikh Zayed arrived in Rabat to attend the Seventh Arab Summit Conference, having made a short visit to Doha on his way.

29 October: Abu Dhabi Executive Council approved the establishment of the National Hotel Company in the UAE.

1 November: Sheikh Zayed reviewed the military parade which was mounted by Algeria to celebrate the twentieth anniversary of the Algerian revolution.

2 November: Sheikh Zayed arrived in Damascus on a three-day official visit and announced that all the UAE's resources were at Syria's disposal.

3 November: Sheikh Zayed and the Syrian President, Hafez Al Asad, studied the results of the Arab Summit Conference and relations between the two countries, as well as visiting the liberated city of Qunaitra.

4 November: Whilst in Syria, Sheikh Zayed visited Aleppo and Revolution City and he inspected the Euphrates Dam which, he said, added a new dimension to Arab power.

5 November: Sheikh Zayed visited Latakia in the course of his tour of a number of cities and important institutions in Syria.

6 November: The UAE paid a 10 million Islamic dinar installment to the Islamic Development Bank, raising the UAE's total pledge to the bank to 110 million dinars.

8 November: Sheikh Zayed returned to the UAE after a short visit to Bahrain where he held discussions with His Highness Sheikh Essa bin Salman Al Khalifa during which it was agreed that the UAE would participate in development projects in Bahrain.

9 November: Sheikh Zayed received the oil ministers of the Gulf States attending the first day of the emergency conference called by the UAE in order to co-ordinate positions regarding the price of oil before the OPEC meeting in December. Saudi Arabia proposed a tax increase on oil companies and a reduction in the posted price of oil.

10 November: Mana Said Al Otaiba announced the decision by the UAE, Qatar and Saudi Arabia to increase taxes on oil companies and reduce the price of a barrel of oil by 40 cents. Kuwait, Iraq and Iran had reservations concerning the Saudi project and requested that it be presented to the next OPEC Conference. Sheikh Mubarak bin Mohammad Al Nahyan dedicated the barge *Pearl of the Sea*. Built in Abu Dhabi, it was considered to be the largest sea barge in the world.

17 November: Sheikh Mubarak bin Mohammad Al Nahyan issued the decision to cancel the inspection of automobiles and travellers at the Seeh Shuaib in order to reassure people concerning the unity of the territories of the Federation.

19 November: Mana Said Al Otaiba signed a 6 million dirham contract for the construction of a steel factory in Abu Dhabi with a capacity of 25 tons per year.

20 November: Sheikh Zayed delivered a speech before the Federal National Council in which he defined the most important aspects of the national work plan in the next phase. Projects highlighted included preparation of the permanent constitution, the speeding up of development, the promulgation of important legislation, establishment of the UAE university, the broadening of information services and the strengthening of utilities and services, especially in the fields of health and education.

26 November: ADFAED gave a 40-million dirham loan to Bahrain to jointly finance an electricity and water desalination project.

Abu Dhabi Government gave a loan of 33 million dollars to finance the expansion and development of the Suez Canal.

27 November: Shaikh Tahnoun bin Mohammad Al Nahyan laid the foundation stone for a fertilizer factory in the Pakistani city of Multan. He described the project as a basis for co-operation between the two countries.

2 December: On the occasion of the Third National Day, Sheikh Zayed renewed his commitment to work untiringly to lay down the foundation of the Federation and support the institutions of the State in order to realize the hopes of the people. A large military parade was mounted on this occasion which was witnessed by the Sudanese President, Jaafar Numeiri, and delegations from brotherly and friendly countries. A number of chiefs of staff of Arab armies were also present.

UAE television in Abu Dhabi began experimental colour transmission at 8 a.m. with a broadcast of the National Day parade.

3 December: Sheikh Zayed with His Majesty King Faisal bin Abdulaziz attended the graduation ceremonies for the fourth batch from the Technical Institute of the Saudi Air Force in Dhahran. Also viewing the ceremonies were the Amirs of Bahrain and Qatar. Sheikh Rashid bin Saeed Al Maktoum and the Sudanese President Jaafar Numeiri were present at military manoeuvres in the Muqatara region in which tanks, rockets and Mirage aircraft were used.

Sheikh Ahmed bin Hamid signed an agreement establishing a microwave network to transmit television programmes to all parts of the country.

4 December: Sheikh Zayed returned to the country after a one-day visit to Saudi Arabia.

7 December: Sheikh Khalifa bin Zayed Al Nahyan was present at the official ceremonies for the commencement of oil exportation from the offshore Abu al-Bukoush area.

Mana Said Al Otaiba signed a 21 million dirham contract for construction of the first organic fertilizer factory using waste products as raw material. Having an annual capacity of 27,000 tons, the factory would, at the same time, supply the requirements of agricultural regions and remove a source of pollution

9 December: At the headquarters of the Naval Forces in Abu Dhabi, Sheikh Sultan bin Zayed Al Nahyan witnessed the graduation of the first batch of naval recruits.

10 December: King Faisal met a large delegation under the chairmanship of Ahmed Khalifa Al Suweidi visiting Saudi Arabia to look into co-ordination and co-operation between the two countries in the political, economic, educational, informational and agricultural fields. This visit was intended to complete the discussions held between Sheikh Zayed and the Saudi monarch.

The first official UAE *Hajj* delegation travelled to the Holy Land under the chairmanship of Thani Essa Harib, Minister of Islamic Affairs and Awqaf.

14 December: Ahmed Khalifa Al Suweidi opened the sixteenth session of the Board of Trustees of the Palestinian Studies Institute which began its deliberations in Abu Dhabi. He confirmed the UAE's readiness to support this cultural institute.

17 December: Mohammad Said Al Mulla, Minister of Communications, announced that it had been decided to merge the telephone and telegraph companies operating in the UAE into a unified company with 60 per cent stateholding. This was to be accomplished during the first half of 1975.

18 December: Sheikh Zayed greeted Sheikh Mujiburrahman, President of the Bangladesh Republic, who was on an official three-day visit to Abu Dhabi.

21 December: Large crowds turned out on Army Day in Dubai and Sharjah to greet the troops of the Federal Army during a military parade which proceeded from the Al-Mirqaab Camp. Sheikh Mohammad bin Rashid Al Maktoum, Minister of Defence, praised the great role of His Highness, the President, and his brothers, the Rulers, in supporting and building the Army.

Sheikh Rashid signed the contract for construction of the 33-storey International Trade Centre in Dubai.

22 December: Sheikh Zayed issued an Amiri decree exempting a large number of commodities and materials from customs duties in a concerted effort to combat inflation. The decree was effective for 90 per cent of Abu Dhabi's imports and this included the reduction of fees on goods in transit to 25 per cent. During a meeting with representatives of Abu Dhabi fishermen, Sheikh Zayed ordered that the marketing of fish be organized in all parts of the Federation and he issued his directions to the Investment and Development Bank to extend loans to fishermen to buy modern fishing boats.

23 December: Sheikh Zayed having ordered that the number of mosques be increased, it was decided that the Ministry of Islamic Affairs and Awqaf would undertake the construction of 70 new mosques in all parts of the Federation.

The Bottle Gas Factory, the first of its kind in the country, began production.

29 December: James Abrobey, the astronaut who led the first space craft on the surface of the moon, arrived in Abu Dhabi to deliver a lecture on the experiment as part of the cultural season organized by the Ministry of Information and Tourism.

30 December: Sheikh Zayed issued a federal decree forming the first board of directors for the Emirates Development Bank under the chairmanship of the Minister of Economy & Trade. He also issued a number of decisions which included the payment of monthly grants to students in UAE schools, an increase in the percentage of public participation in the Trade Company from 25 to 50 per cent, and the laying down of urgent programmes for the industrialization of the Northern Emirates, as well as development in remote areas.

Nineteen Seventy Five

2 January: During his trip to India, Sheikh Zayed visited Indian arms factories and met with Arab ambassadors in New Delhi to whom he emphasized the importance of uniting Arab efforts.

3 January: Sheikh Zayed and Mrs Indira Ghandi attended ceremonies for the signing of a cultural agreement between the UAE and India.

Sheikh Zayed issued two federal laws changing the name of the Abu Dhabi National Trade Company to the Emirates Trade Company and that of the National Investment and Development Bank to the Emirates Development Bank.

4 January: Sheikh Zayed donated the cost of establishing the Petroleum Studies College at the Aligarh Islamic University in India. The name 'Zayed' was given to the college.

The UAE became a member of the Arab Union of Historians.

6 January: A joint communiqué issued following discussions between Sheikh Zayed and Mrs Indira Ghandi affirmed the importance of establishing more secure technical and economic co-operation between all developing countries, demanded total demilitarization and stressed the need to use atomic energy for peaceful purposes.

Sheikh Zayed, in remarks made to Radio Monte Carlo, confirmed that oil revenues would, first of all, be used for local development and, secondly, to assist Arab and Islamic countries.

7 January: Sheikh Zayed signed a 50 million dollar contract for construction of the Intercontinental Hotel.

Sheikh Khalifa inaugurated the new military hospital in the Al Nahyan camp.

10 January: Chiefs of Police in the UAE decided, following a meeting in the Al-Qassimiya camp in Sharjah, to fit security alarms to banks and large commercial establishments. They also agreed to unify police uniforms in the entire UAE as well as to standarize measures for deporting foreigners.

11 January: Sheikh Hamdan Al Nahyan signed a number of agreements, including the setting-up of the first artificial limb centre in the Arab Gulf area, the expansion of Al-Ain Hospital at a cost of 31 million dirhams and the establishment of new departments in Al-Asima Hospital.

14 January: Sheikh Zayed ordered the construction of a new dock in Port Zayed, the expansion of 16 deep berths and the building of flour mills.

15 January: Abu Dhabi Executive Council approved the formation of a national oil tanker company in which the public would be permitted to buy shares.

16 January: Said Ghaith signed an agreement creating a new film unit to take charge of film production.

19 January: Sheikh Khalifa signed a 23 million dollar contract with Gulf Air to build the Abu Dhabi Al-Khaleej Hotel.

20 January: Mana Said Al Otaiba signed a 2 million dirham contract for the first all-UAE minerals survey.

26 January: Sheikh Khalifa bin Zayed Al Nahyan signed a 30 million dollar contract for the construction of the Al-Ain Intercontinental Hotel.

27 January: The Council of Ministers approved the draft law changing the name of the Ministry of Information and Tourism to the Ministry of Information and Culture and broadening its responsibilities. It also approved a project to protect the fishing rights of UAE nationals.

30 January: The UAE Currency Board decided to stop issuing the 1 dirham bank note for a period of one month in order to facilitate circulation of dirham coins.

1 February: Sheikh Khalifa issued a new civil service law for Abu Dhabi emirate.

The Council of Ministers approved a draft federal law whereby births and deaths had to be registered with the Preventive Medicine Offices in the UAE and at UAE consulates for UAE nationals residing abroad.

3 February: Sheikh Saqr bin Mohammad Al Qassimi signed a 17 million pound sterling contract for the construction of the first phase of a deepwater port at Khor al-Khwair in Ras al-Khaimah.

The Board of Directors of the Emirates Development Bank in its first meeting decided to give loan priority to industrial, agricultural and tourism projects in the Northern Emirates and to give loans to fishermen to buy modern fishing boats.

6 February: Sheikh Ahmed bin Hamid signed an agreement with the British firm, Marconi, to set up a 750-kilohertz broadcasting transmission station on Sadiyyat Island which would enable transmission to all parts of the UAE, the Gulf States and the Middle East, in addition to Pakistan and Iran.

8 February: Sheikh Rashid signed a contract with a Canadian company for a gas liquefaction plant in Dubai to supply the domestic market.

Sheikh Mubarak bin Mohammad Al Nahyan received the first batch of trainee helicopter pilots, the nucleus of the Ministry of the Interior Air Wing Unit.

Abu Dhabi Executive Council decided to transfer responsibility for public housing in Abu Dhabi to the Social Service Administration.

10 February: The Council of Ministers approved the Ministry of Information and Culture's plan to set up cultural centres in the Emirates.

13 February: Sheikh Saqr bin Mohammad Al Qassimi announced that exploration for oil in Ras al-Khaimah would begin in about three months.

14 February: Sheikh Rashid received Kurt Waldheim, Secretary-General of the

United Nations, who arrived in the country on an official two-day visit. He discussed with Ahmed Khalifa Al Suweidi the current situation in the Gulf and the Middle East.

It was decided to set up 77 telephone booths in Abu Dhabi, 45 in Al-Ain and ten on the highway between the two cities.

15 February: Sheikh Tahnoun bin Mohammad Al Nahyan contracted to buy the giant oil tanker *Al-Dhafra* to be added to the fleet of Abu Dhabi tankers at the end of February.

18 February: Sheikh Zayed, who was on a private visit to Pakistan, held discussions with Pakistani President, Zulfikar Ali Bhutto concerning situations in the Gulf, the Middle East and the Indian subcontinent.

Mohammad Said Al Mulla discussed with the UAE telephone and telegraph companies implementation of the Supreme Council of the Federation decision to amalgamate them into one company with 60 per cent State ownership.

20 February: Sheikh Rashid approved plans for the construction of the Dubai Sheraton Hotel at a cost of 15 million dollars.

22 February: Sheikh Rashid signed a 259 million dirham contract for the dredging of Dubai creek.

24 February: Sheikh Zayed gave his approval for a number of important Abu Dhabi projects, including the Sports City and the construction of 2000 prefabricated houses for government employees.

26 February: Sheikh Zayed ordered the doubling of monthly grants paid to students in the Federation's schools, religious and technical institutes in the hope of encouraging them to continue their studies, education being the conerstone of future development.

Sheikh Rashid issued an Amiri decree setting-up a Development Council in Dubai which would take charge of granting loans to low income citizens for development and construction on their own land. The sum of 200 million dirhams was allocated for this purpose.

1 March: Sheikh Zayed, in an interview with the German economic magazine *Capital,* said that the idea of oil-producing states cutting oil prices without a corresponding reduction in industrialized countries' export prices was unjust.

2 March: Sheikh Zayed stopped at Tripoli International Airport on his way to Algeria. In Tripoli he held discussions with Colonel Abdusalam Jalloud concerning relations between the two countries. Zayed later arrived in Algiers to participate in the OPEC summit meeting.

4 March: Sheikh Zayed held consultations with the heads of the delegations of participating countries at the OPEC Summit in Algeria. In an interview with *Newsweek* he emphasized that foreign oil companies were trying to break OPEC, and he confirmed his belief that the United States was undermining relations between Egypt and Syria to disrupt the confrontation front with Israel.

5 March: Sheikh Rashid inaugurated the Intercontinental Hotel in Dubai.

6 March: Sheikh Rashid reviewed the passing-out parade of the twelfth batch of graduates of the Federal Forces.

7 March: Sheikh Zayed confirmed that the agreement which was signed between Iraq and Iran in Algeria would help realize security and stability in the Arab Gulf region. He considered this an important accomplishment for OPEC and he said that it would help strengthen the unity of the organization and consolidate its achievements.

8 March: Sheikh Rashid opened Dubai Museum.

9 March: Sheikh Zayed issued a decree appointing Sheikh Mohammad bin Butti Al Hamid as chairman of the Abu Dhabi Municipality and Town Planning Council.

10 March Sheikh Rashid opened the ninth petroleum conference in which 21 Arab and 35 other states, as well as Arab and foreign petroleum organizations, were participating.

12 March: Sheikh Zayed visited Delma Island and inspected progress on development projects. He ordered the expansion of marine berthing and the construction of 50 houses as well as water and electricity plants.

Sheikh Rashid issued an Amiri decree establishing the Dubai Islamic Bank with a capital of 50 million dirhams.

Mana Said Al Otaiba confirmed in a press conference that oil companies operating in Abu Dhabi who were assigning their production were committing an illegal act, and that the UAE would not be lenient with any one who attempted to influence its political or oil decisions. He further stated that the State was determined to protect its natural resources.

15 March: Sheikh Zayed ordered the construction of 3000 houses for distribution to citizens in all parts of the Federation as part of his plan to provide healthy housing for every family.

Sheikh Zayed, Ahmed Khalifa Al Suweidi, Sheikh Surour bin Mohammad Al Nahyan and Saif bin Ghobash held talks with Robert MacNamara, Chairman of the World Bank, who was visiting Abu Dhabi. Discussions focused on the possibility of increasing the voting rights of oil exporting countries in conformity with their increase in the share capital of the Bank.

16 March: Sheikh Ahmed bin Rashid Al Mualla issued decrees establishing the Umm al-Qaiwain Municipality and forming the first Municipal Council. The Council Chairman and the Municipality Director were appointed.

17 March: Sheikh Zayed arrived in Dubai as part of his tour of the Northern Emirates.

The Currency Board, chaired by Sheikh Hamdan bin Rashid Al Maktoum, debated unstable conditions in international currency markets but decided not to make any changes in the price equivalency of the UAE dirham.

18 March: Sheikh Rashid signed an agreement with a group of offshore companies to explore for oil on-land in Dubai. He also inspected work on Dubai's third bridge, the largest in the Arab Gulf region.

19 March: Sheikh Zayed made a tour of Sharjah, Ajman and Umm al-Qaiwain where he met with the the Rulers and the people and inspected progress on development projects. He proclaimed to the people: 'The wealth is yours, all of it. There is no barrier between you and me.'

20 March: Sheikh Zayed visited Ras al-Khaimah and met with Sheikh Saqr bin Mohammad Al Qassimi and citizens of the emirate.

Sheikh Tahnoun bin Mohammad Al Nahyan witnessed the completion of the first phase of the water pumping project from the Ghashayah fields to Hilli, estimated to be nearly 20 million gallons of water per day.

It was announced that imports for the Federation in the previous year (1974) amounted to nearly 5536 million dirhams, an increase of 60 per cent over 1973.

21 March: Sheikh Zayed continued his tour of the Northern Emirates and opened the Al-Rams - Shaam highway which cost 10 million dirhams.

22 March: Sheikh Zayed ordered the allocation of 10 million dirhams for the payment of grants to students who were successful in the Holy Qur'an Memorization Centres. He also ordered that students should not be employed in Government offices during summer holidays.

24 March: Sheikh Zayed mourned the late King Faisal bin Abdulaziz, the King of Saudi Arabia, who had been assassinated.

26 March: Sheikh Zayed and the Rulers of the Emirates returned to the country having attended the funeral of King Faisal.

27 March: Abu Dhabi Executive Council decided to attach the task of supervising housing and new village services included in this year's annual programme for development to the Office of the President instead of the Department of Works.

2 April: Sheikh Rashid opened the Al Maktoum Bridge II which was built at a cost of 1 million sterling pounds.

3 April: The Ministry of Education began a study aimed at revising the curriculum for all levels of study to take account of local circumstances and environment.

4 April: The Ministry of Justice completed the preparation of a draft law prescribing Arabic as the official language to be used in all governmental transactions.

6 April: Sheikh Saqr bin Mohammad Al Qassimi led the first meeting of the new Municipal Council for Ras al-Khaimah in which he announced the allocation of 15 million dirhams for the development of the emirate.

7 April: Sheikh Hamdan bin Mohammad Al Nahyan signed a 38.45 million dirham contract for the construction and maintenance of the Abu Dhabi - Sweihan highway.

The Council of Ministers approved the UAE's adherence to the International Atomic Energy Authority.

10 April: Sheikh Rashid issued instructions to set up a sports city in Dubai conforming to the latest international standards.

The Al-Ahli Football Club won the President's Cup after defeating Al-Nasr by two goals to nil.

12 April: Sheikh Tahnoun bin Mohammad Al Nahyan signed a contract to purchase a new oil tanker to be named *Lama*, having a load capacity of 260,000 tons.

13 April: Sheikh Zayed issued laws governing the establishment of the Abu Dhabi National Tanker Company and the Abu Dhabi National Hotels Company; the provisions of the federal pension law for employees in Abu Dhabi; and exemptions for shareholders in the Abu Dhabi National Company for Plastic Pipe Manufacture from taxes imposed on shareholders' profits.

Sheikh Khalifa witnessed the ceremonies which were held on Das Island for the dedication of the oil tanker *al-Dhafra*, the first tanker in the Abu Dhabi National Tanker Company fleet. He also inspected the gas liquefaction plant on the island.

14 April: The Council of Ministers decided to exempt Arab nationals from entry visa fees.

Mana Said Al Otaiba announced that Abu Dhabi would definitely not surrender the principle of maintaining complete control over its oil production and mineral resources. He called for the training of nationals to take the place of foreign oil-sector employees.

15 April: Sheikh Zayed called on the Lebanese President, Suleiman Frangieh and the Palestinian Leader, Yasser Arafat, to put an end to the current fighting in Lebanon and to save the spilling of Arab blood.

16 April: Sheikh Saif bin Mohammad Al Nahyan issued a decree forming a committee to prepare a price list for the marketing of medicines in private pharmacies throughout the Emirates.

19 April: Three hundred and forty three tons of food valued at 639 million dirhams were imported into the UAE in 1974.

20 April: The Indian President, Fakhrudddin Ali Ahmad, attended the opening of Sheikh Zayed's office in Bombay.

23 April: The National Consultative Council recommended a reconsideration of the agreement with CCC Company, owners of 40 per cent of the capital of the Abu Dhabi National Oil Installation Company, so that that the shares could be offered to the public for general subscription.

26 April: The Supreme Council of the Federation chaired by Sheikh Zayed, decided to take additional measures aimed at supporting and strengthening the federal nature of the State. A committee was formed to liase with the Rulers of the emirates on this issue and report back to the Supreme Council at the next meeting on 12 May 1975.

27 April: Sheikh Zayed examined progress on the first model cattle-breeding farm and instructed that the 100 hectare project be speeded up.

28 April: Sheikh Zayed chaired a meeting of the Council of Ministers and delivered a speech in which he emphasized the vital importance of the next phase in the context of supporting the federal nature of the State and realization of the peoples' expectations in all regions of the Federation. He issued instructions that students be attached to the Armed Forces training camps during the summer holiday.

29 April: Sheikh Zayed, in a meeting with the members of the Federal National Council, underlined his commitment to building up the State. He expressed his hope that positive results would be achieved in supporting the Federation at the next meeting of the Supreme Council.

Sheikh Rashid bin Ahmed Al Mualla chaired the committee which was formed by the Supreme Council of the Federation to look into ways of bolstering the federal nature of the State.

30 April: Ahmed Khalifa Al Suweidi, Minister for Foreign Affairs, held important discussions in Tehran with his Iranian counterpart, Abbas Khalatbari.

1 May: Emperor Mohammad Rida Pahlavi and the visiting UAE delegation under the chairmanship of Ahmed Khalifa Al Suweidi considered relations between the two countries and the other States in the region. Al Suweidi underlined the necessity of co-operation among all the States of the region in order to solve disputes in a peaceful manner.

3 May: Sheikh Zayed paid an inspection visit to the Ministry of Public Works during which he examined the plans for the Presidential Diwan building.

4 May: Sheikh Zayed issued instructions to build 40 new houses in Al-Wathba model village.

Eighty-six public housing units were distributed to citizens in Ras al-Khaimah.

6 May: Sheikh Zayed attended the closed five-hour meeting which was held by the National Federal Council to debate matters concerned with the development of federal work and to evaluate the current phase from a political, economic and social standpoint.

Shaikh Rashid signed 150 million pound sterling contract for setting-up an aluminum smelter in Dubai with a annual production capacity of 150,000 tons.

11 May: Sheikh Zayed signed an agreement between the UAE, Saudi Arabia, Egypt and Qatar establishing the Arab Military Industrialization Corporation capitalized at 1040 million dollars. Sheikh Khalifa bin Zayed Al Nahyan described the agreement as a great event in the history of the Arab nation.

12 May: Sheikh Zayed chaired the meeting of the Supreme Council of the Federation in which firm steps were taken to support the federal nature of the State: the unification of the defence forces of the emirates was approved; the Ministry of the Interior was authorized to supervise immigration facilities and set-up and unify internal security installations; the federal authorities were granted the appropriate power to co-ordinate oil policy through the Ministry of Petroleum and Minerals; and steps were taken to ensure that all communications with foreign Governments would be made through the Ministry of Foreign Affairs. The Supreme Council delegated the task of forming a committee to oversee the drafting of the permanent constitution to the President of the Federation. The Council of Ministers was also directed to give special attention to the development of the Eastern Region.

13 May: Sheikh Zayed inspected the Police College in Abu Dhabi.

15 May: Sheikh Zayed issued an Amiri decree regarding Abu Dhabi's general budget for 1975. Revenue was estimated at more than 13 billion dirhams and expenditure at approximately 13 billion dirhams.

18 May: Sheikh Rashid signed a 300 million dirham contract to construct 1710 housing units in Dubai.

Sheikh Rashid bin Humaid Al Nuaimi opened the headquarters of the Arab Bank of Ajman.

Mohammad Said Al Mulla chaired a meeting in the Ministry of Communications to study proposals made by the Ministry and the telecommunications companies operating in the country concerning implementation of the Supreme Council of the Federation's decree incorporating them into a single public company with a 60 per cent Government shareholding.

19 May: Sheikh Zayed accompanied Sheikh Jabir Al Ahmad Al Sabah, Heir Apparent of Kuwait, on an inspection tour of the capital.

Sheikh Tahnoun signed an agreement with a French company to plant 400 hectares of forest in the Western Region of Abu Dhabi.

The Ministry of the Interior received helicopters representing the first unit of the air arm of the Ministry.

22 May: Sheikh Saqr bin Mohammad Al Qassimi witnessed the installation of a new rig for underwater oil exploration in the Gulf in an area 32 nautical miles from the city of Ras al-Khaimah.

23 May: Sheikh Zayed inspected Zayed Military College in Al-Ain.

24 May: Sheikh Zayed received Archbishop Makarios, the President of Cyprus, on his first official visit to the UAE.

25 May: Sheikh Zayed ordered the planting of 300 dunams of wheat in the Al-Saad region following the successful experimental planting of 300 dunams in Al-Ain by the Department of Agriculture.

27 May: Sheikh Zayed issued a federal decree permitting Tunisian judges to be seconded to the UAE and for extradition to and from each country. This was considered to be the first agreement of this kind entered into by the UAE with an Arab country.

29 May: Sheikh Zayed ordered that a permanent headquarters be established in Abu Dhabi for the UAE Women's Federation. He opened the second exhibition of the Abu Dhabi Women's Association.

31 May: Sheikh Khalifa bin Zayed Al Nahyan visited the Suez canal front and Ismailiya to view the results of Zionist aggression against the city. He also inspected progress in constructing the Zayed Quarter of the city of Ismailiya.

Sheikh Sultan bin Zayed Al Nahyan attended the graduation ceremonies for eight UAE Air Force officers who had completed their training in the Pakistani Air Academy.

1 June: Sheikh Zayed during his reception of the American Senator, James Abu Rizk, emphasized that the United States, in her capacity as a great power, had an effective role to play in the Arab-Israeli conflict and must therefore be acquainted with the Arab point of view. He said that the American voter was more deserving of the funds being spent by the US Government in support of Israeli aggression against Arab states.

2 June: Sheikh Khalifa led the UAE delegation to the first meeting of the Arab Military Industrialization Corporation which was held in the Republican Palace in Cairo.

The Council of Ministers approved a childrens allowance of 100 to 140 dirhams per child, payable to employees who were citizens of the UAE.

5 June: Sheikh Zayed paid a visit to the headquarters of the Abu Dhabi Naval Forces during which he inspected the naval unit *Arzana* .

Sheikh Mohammad bin Rashid Al Maktoum led the UAE delegation to the ceremonies for the re-opening of the Suez Canal.

7 June: The Ministry of Labour and Social Affairs completed the draft law governing the care and treatment of delinquents.

8 June: The Minister of Education announced that all this year's secondary school graduates, who so desired, were being sent to universities in Arab and foreign countries in order to fill the State's requirements for specializations, especially in the field of science.

9 June: The Ministry of Communications in a memorandum asked the Supreme Council of the Federation for the authority to supervise transportation, the control of air space in all airports, and all agreements made with airline companies in all the emirates.

The Council of Ministers approved the construction of the highway between Dibba and Musafi at a cost of 94.5 million dirhams.

10 June: Sheikh Surour bin Mohammad Al Nahyan signed a 45 million dirham contract with the British company, John Brown, to install two electrical generating units on Umm al-Nar island.

12 June: An agreement was signed between the Ministry of Communications and telecommunications companies operating in the country with a view to amalgamating the larger companies.

The Boycott of Israel Office in the Federation decided to prohibit the activities of the Bahai Society on the grounds that it was believed to be a Zionist organization.

12 June: The UAE Women's Federation participated in the World Conference of Women which was held in Mexico.

14 June: Sheikh Zayed made a tour of Al-Ain during which he inspected the Agricultural Experimental Station, the Municipality Office, agricultural projects

and the new designs for expansion projects in Al-Ain.

18 June: Sheikh Rashid bin Ahmed Al Mualla chaired a meeting of the follow-up committee which was formed by the Supreme Council of the Federation. During the meeting, there was a debate on co-ordination between information offices in the Federation, especially in the fields of broadcasting and television. The unification of communications facilities in the Federation was also discussed.

19 June: Sheikh Surour bin Mohammad Al Nahyan signed an agreement for construction of the first sand brick factory in the Federation.

20 June: Sheikh Zayed witnessed the championship match of the second Gulf swimming competition in Abu Dhabi. Participating in the competition were the UAE, Saudi Arabia, Kuwait, Bahrain, the Sultanate of Oman and Palestine.

21 June: Sheikh Zayed reviewed developments in Arab and international affairs as well as bilateral relations with King Hussein of Jordan who was on a one-day visit to the country.

22 June: Sheikh Hamdan bin Mohammad Al Nahyan signed an agreement to construct Al-Maqta bridge connecting the island of Abu Dhabi to the mainland.

24 June: Sheikh Zayed received the Arab Technical Military Committee which visited the country based on a decision of the Supreme Council of the Federation to make a study of the unification of the military forces in the Emirates.

25 June: Sheikh Rashid bin Saeed Al Maktoum received the committee of Arab military experts studying the unification of the military forces in the country.

26 June: Sheikh Zayed issued a decree forming a drafting committee, comprising 28 members representing all the emirates in the Federation, to prepare a draft of the permanent federal constitution under the chairmanship of Sheikh Surour bin Mohammad Al Nahyan.

Sheikh Rashid bin Ahmed Al Mualla received the Arab military experts who were examining issues surrounding the unification of the military forces.

28 June: Sheikh Zayed and Colonel Ibrahim Al Hamdi, the visiting President of the Leadership Council of the Yemen Arab Republic, examined ways of strengthening relations between the two countries.

30 June: Sheikh Surour bin Mohammad Al Nahyan chaired a meeting of the constitutional drafting committee who said that they favoured granting citizens the opportunity to express their opinion and make suggestions for changes to the provisional constitution. Ahmed Khalifa Al Suweidi explained that the goal of adopting a constitution was to strengthen and support the Federation.

UAE food import prices trebled betwen 1973 to 1974 - the result of global inflation and increased traffic costs, poor warehouse capacity, and demand far outstripping supply levels.

1 July: Sheikh Khalifa bin Zayed Al Nahyan received the delegation of Arab military experts visiting the UAE to study the unification of the military forces in the country.

Sheikh Ahmed bin Hamid issued a decree regarding the protection of scientific, literary and technical works in the Federation.

2 July: Sheikh Zayed and Sheikh Rashid held discussions on a number of subjects of vital importance to both the nation and its citizens.

3 July: Sheikh Zayed arrived in Paris on an official three-day visit to France. He met with the French President, Giscard d'Estaing, and Arab ambassadors in the French capital.

July 4: Sheikh Zayed ended his official visit to France and began a private four-day visit. Both the French News Agency and Radio Monte Carlo aired interviews with Sheikh Zayed in which he expressed his satifaction at the outcome of his visit to France.

6 July: Sheikh Rashid bin Ahmed Al Mualla signed an agreement with an American company for onshore oil exploration in Umm al-Qaiwain.

7 July: The Council of Ministers approved the recommendations of the ministerial committee for education, culture and information regarding plans for co-ordination between broadcasting and television stations in the Federation.

8 July: Sheikh Zayed issued instructions to the Ministry of Justice to apply the provisions of the Islamic *Sharia* to crimes of morality and indecency. These cases will be considered by the *Sharia* Courts for the application of *Sharia* penalties.

9 July: The French magazine, *L'Express*, reported that the UAE allocated 4 per cent of its GNP to assisting developing nations whereas industrialized countries allocated less than 1 per cent of GNP to aid developing countries.

Khalfan ar-Rumi announced that the Ministry of Education had decided to open 23 new centres for adult education in various parts of the Emirates.

10 July: Sheikh Rashid signed an 100 per cent Participation Agreement copperfastening Dubai's ownership of oil and gas concerns in Dubai, having paid 110 million dollars to the oil companies operating there.

12 July: Traffic Police Chiefs studied the unification of traffic operations in the country.

13 July: Sheikh Tahnoun bin Moham-med Al Nahyan distributed title deeds for 200 commercial buildings, built by the Development Loan Establishment, to citizens in Abu Dhabi and Al-Ain.

14 July: Sheikh Surour bin Mohammad Al Nahyan issued a decree imposing fines of 100,000 dirhams, plus payment of the cost of repairs and losses, following conviction by the courts for interference with electrical supplies in Abu Dhabi.

Sheikha Fatima bint Mubarak, President of the UAE Women's Federation, arrived in Cairo on an official visit to observe aspects of women's activities in Egypt.

15 July: Hamouda bin Ali received the committee of Arab police and public security experts visiting the country to study the unification of police and public security institutions in the Emirates.

16 July: Sheikh Rashid signed a 60 million dollar contract to construct a road bridge to Port Rashid in Dubai.

19 July: Sheikh Hamdan bin Moham-med Al Nahyan signed two contracts for the construction of the airport and sea port in Fujairah.

21 July: The Ministry of Justice com-pleted the preparation of the federal draft law governing proceedings to be followed in summary justice courts in the Federation.

23 July: Sheikh Khalifa bin Zayed Al Nahyan issued an Amiri decree regarding the protection of privileged statistical information.

24 July: Sheikh Saqr bin Mohammad Al Qassimi received General Othman Al Hamdi, chairman of the committee of Arab military experts which was preparing a study on the integration of the armed forces in the Emirates.

26 July: The first underwater oil explo-ration equipment owned by the National Drilling Company arrived at Abu Dhabi port from England.

27 July: The Council of Ministers approved the law governing co-operative societies.

30 July: The cement factory in Ras al-Khaimah, the first of four planned for the UAE, began operations. Sheikh Saqr bin Mohammad Al Qassimi was presented with the first bag of cement produced by the factory.

31 July: The first administrative divisions in the UAE were authorized, having been confirmed by the Members of the Supreme Council of the Federation. There were 56 control posts in these divisions, covering 368 villages.

1 August: Sheikh Zayed arrived in Casablanca on a private visit to Morocco.

5 August: Sheikh Khalifa bin Zayed Al Nahyan issued a decree reducing the price of sugar for citizens by 30 per cent in order to relieve hardships caused by the rise in the cost of living.

8 August: The Council of Ministers approved the Federation's broadcasting and television co-ordination plan which unified both internal and external information policy.

10 August: There were 16,534 employees and labourers in the ministries and other departments of the Federal Government in July 1975.

11 August: The Council of Ministers studied the Ministry of Electricity and Water's plan for connecting the emirates through a unified electrical grid network.

12 August: A meeting of the traffic and driving licence directors studied measures for issuing unified driving licences at the federal level.

18 August: The Diwan of the Ruler of Ras al-Khaimah announced that sulphur had been discovered in the rocks of Wadi Ham in the emirate.

24 August: Phillips (Abu Dhabi) relinquished all its concession rights, granted in 1967, to the Government of Abu Dhabi.

25 August: The Abu Dhabi National Oil Company signed a four-year contract with the British company, Minholm Overseas, to operate the oil tankers belonging to the company and to train UAE nationals for work on the tankers.

30 August: Sheikh Hamad bin Mohammad Al Sharqi announced that exploration for oil in the territorial waters of Fujairah would begin in January 1976.

9 September: Mohammad Khalifa Al Kindi signed a 100 million dirham contract for the construction of the final phase of the Abu Dhabi - Qatar highway.

15 September: Sheikh Rashid was present at the inauguration ceremonies of the Islamic Bank of Dubai.

16 September: Sheikh Tahnoun bin Mohammad Al Nahyan signed an agreement for setting-up dairy and poultry production projects in Al-Ain.

17 September: Abdulaziz bin Rashid Al Nuami issued a decree recognizing the registration of the UAE Women's Federation which was formed under the chairmanship of Sheikha Fatima bint Mubarak, wife of Sheikh Zayed.

23 September: Sheikh Hamdan bin Rashid Al Maktoum signed a 25 million dirham contract for the construction of the Deira Corniche.

30 September: Sheikh Saqr bin Mohammed Al Qassimi inspected progress on the drilling of the first oil well in the concession zones granted to the American company, Netoil.

UAE plans for 1975 aid allocations totalled nearly 1.25 billion dollars, with 1 billion dollars going to Arab states, 185 million dollars to African and Asian countries and 53 million dollars to international agencies for development.

1 October: Sheikh Zayed issued instructions to the Abu Dhabi Development Bank to give financial support to newspaper organizations in the country as a token of his appreciation of the role played by the press in the service of society. He also issued similar instructions to the Abu Dhabi Municipality to set aside a plot of land on which to build local presses.

4 October: Sheikh Zayed, on the occasion of the third anniversary of the October War, sent greetings to the Arab nation in which he called for the Arabs to protect the solidarity which they achieved during the war until the liberation of all occupied Arab territory. It was decided to name the Grand Mosque in Abu Dhabi, 'Zayed', in honour of the President.

8 October: Sheikh Zayed emphasized at a reception for the President and members of the Federal Supreme Court his deep concern that the provisions of the Islamic *Sharia* law would be applied in the Federation.

11 October: Sheikh Zayed issued two Amiri decrees, one forming the National Consultative Council and the other inviting it to convene on the first day of November.

Sheikh Hamdan bin Rashid Al Maktoum announced that the assets of the Currency Board in March 1975 stood at 3645 million dirhams. Total assets in June 1973 stood at 216.1 million dirhams.

14 October: Sheikh Zayed issued a law establishing the Al-Ain vegetable production company capitalized at 10,137,000 dirhams, with 60 per cent Abu Dhabi Government shareholding, the French company Finlo owning the remaining 40 per cent.

15 October: Sheikh Rashid laid the foundation stone for the 150 million pound sterling aluminum smelter, the first in the country.

Sheikh Khalifa opened the petroleum exhibition which was mounted by the Abu Dhabi National Oil Company (ADNOC) and the Abu Dhabi Marine Areas Company (ADMA).

16 October: It was announced that Abu Dhabi had so far exported 2 billion barrels of oil from Jebel al-Dhanna.

17 October: Sheikh Zayed, in talks with a visiting Egyptian information mission, stressed that the establishment of the UAE Federation would serve to make the Arab nation more powerful. He also called for the strengthening of Arab solidarity in confronting the Zionist enemy.

The Permanent Projects Committee approved the establishment of the Emirates News Agency.

18 October: Sheikh Zayed and the visiting Ugandan President, Idi Amin, discussed bilateral relations.

Mana Said Al Otaiba signed an agreement with 'Sea Bathinol', an advisory company, to prepare a feasibility study on sulphur and sulphuric acid production in Abu Dhabi.

19 October: Sheikh Saqr laid the foundation stone for the satellite station in Ras al-Khaimah.

Abu Dhabi Executive Council discussed a project to establish the largest electricity generating plant in the Gulf region in order to provide Abu Dhabi's future electricity and water requirements. The decision was made to set-up the plant on the Al-Dhab'iyya peninsula.

20 October: ADFAED extended a 40 million dirham loan to finance rural development projects in Yemen.

21 October: Sheikh Zayed held talks with local information officials covering a variety of domestic matters. He stressed his own responsibility along with that of the members of the Supreme Council of the Federation, and the people, to overcome all obstacles and advance the Federation. He said that stability can only be achieved through unification of defence and security.

Hamouda bin Ali, at a meeting of the Federation's Marriage and Dowry Committee, encouraged UAE nationals to marry UAE women instead of foreigners. He also stressed the importance of finding secure ways for establishing limits to the rise in dowries.

22 October: Sheikh Zayed received the delegation of Arab military experts who presented him with their study on the unification of the Federation's Armed Forces.

The Council of Ministers approved the setting-up of a supreme council for the environment which would be part of the Manpower Planning Council.

26 October: Abu Dhabi Executive Council approved the setting-up of a new television transmission station as well as completion of the broadcasting transmission station on Al-Sadiyyat Island.

27 October: Sheikh Rashid opened the conference of Arab housing ministers in Dubai.

28 October: ADFAED extended a 120 million dirham loan towards financing of the Abukir electricity project in Egypt.

29 October: Sheikh Ahmed bin Hamid issued a decree separating the broadcasting unit from the television unit. Both will become independent entities under separate administrations.

An agreement was signed between the Abu Dhabi Helicopter Company and the 'World Helicopter Company', a Bahamian company.

30 October: Mohammad Al Habroush and Mamoun Awad Abu Zaid, an adviser to the Sudanese President for Arab Affairs, signed an agreement for establishing a 20-million dollar company to be owned by the UAE and Sudan.

31 October: The members of the National Consultative Council took the oath of office before Sheikh Zayed who told them that he did not want a council who would act as a rubber-stamping institution: 'I want from you positive partnership in the service of the nation,' he said 'and I will not be lenient with those who dally with the nation's money'.

1 November: Sheikh Khalifa bin Zayed Al Nahyan opened a new session of the National Consultative Council and delivered a speech in which he stressed the necessity of supporting the federal entity. He announced that 25 per cent of Abu Dhabi's budget was allocated in support of the confrontation states.

Sheikh Ahmed bin Hamad and local newspaper editors studied ways in which to organize the profession of journalism in the Federation.

2 November: Sheikh Zayed issued a federal law prohibiting begging in the UAE. He also issued a law establishing the Abu Dhabi Drilling Chemicals and Products Company capitalized at 200 million dirhams of which the Government of Abu Dhabi would have a 60 per cent shareholding and the American company, N. L. Andestreen, 40 per cent.

The UAE and Tunisia signed an agreement for economic co-operation which included the establishment of a company to produce phosphate and fertilizer.

3 November: Sheikh Zayed issued one law establishing the Al-Ain Insurance Company and another setting-up the Abu Dhabi Helicopter Company Ltd.

Sheikh Rashid opened the first paint factory in the Rashidiya area of Dubai.

4 November: Sheikh Zayed issued the law organizing the registration of births and deaths in the Federation.

Sheikh Sultan bin Mohammad Al Qassimi, attending opening ceremonies for the new Sharjah Police Headquarters building, delivered a speech in which he announced the amalgamation of Sharjah's national guard, police, courts, broadcasting station, and telecommunications office with federal institutions.

Sheikh Khalifa witnessed graduation ceremonies for the first batch of helicopter pilots. Ceremonies were held at the Air Force Headquarters in Abu Dhabi.

The UAE donated 3 million dollars to international food and agriculture programmes in order to increase assistance to developing countries.

5 November: Sheikh Zayed and Sheikh Rashid studied a number of subjects concerned with support for federal integration.

Sheikh Sultan bin Mohammad Al Qassimi received a large group of citizens congratulating him for the measures he adopted in strengthening and supporting the federal entity.

Sheikh Mubarak bin Mohammad Al Nahyan chaired a meeting of the chiefs of police and public security in the Federation at which ways and means to implement the Ruler of Sharjah's decision to amalgamate the Sharjah Police and Public Security department with the Ministry of the Interior were studied.

6 November: Sheikh Sultan bin Mohammad Al Qassimi delivered a speech to crowds of citizens who came out in support of his decisions to facilitate federal integration. Sheikh Sultan announced that the UAE flag would replace the flag of Sharjah.

7 November: Sheikh Zayed led the UAE delegation in official discussions with the visiting Senegalese delegation under the leadership of Leopold Senghor.

Seventy thousand students were registered in all stages of education in the Federation during this academic year.

8 November: Sheikh Zayed opened the Arab Bank for Investments and External Trade in the presence of the Senegalese President. Partners in the bank were the UAE, Algeria and Libya. He also opened the ground satellite communications station at Jebel Ali in the presence of Sheikh Rashid and the members of the Supreme Council of the Federation. Sheikh Zayed praised Sheikh Sultan's decrees in favour of federal unity and called for others to support the Federation in like manner.

9 November: The Abu Dhabi Government decided to undertake a project for the exploitation of onshore natural gas areas following negotiations between the Abu Dhabi National Company and representatives of foreign companies in control of the Abu Dhabi Oil Company, Ltd.

10 November: Sheikh Zayed issued a federal decree calling the Federal National Council to convene for its third session of the second legislative term on 18 November 1975.

The Council of Ministers praised the federal decrees which were adopted by the Ruler of Sharjah.

11 November: Sheikh Hamad bin Mohammad Al Sharqi announced that the UAE flag would take the place of the flag of Fujairah.

12 November: The UAE donated 2 million dirhams as its share in the financing of education programmes for the United Nations Relief & Works Agency for Palestine Refugees (UNWRA).

13 November: Mohammad Al Habroush returned from Manama after signing on behalf of the UAE the agreement establishing the Gulf International Bank, for which six Gulf states would provide capital of 40 million Bahraini dinars.

14 November: Sheikh Zayed ordered that permanent centres be set up in larger mosques for the Memorization of the Holy Qur'an.

15 November: The Supreme Council of the Federation, at a meeting chaired by Sheikh Zayed, adopted a number of decrees in support of federal integration, including the unification of a number of local institutions with ministries and federal institutions.

Sheikh Zayed confirmed the recommendations which were adopted by the experts from the Arab League military committee concerning unification of the defence and security forces in the UAE.

16 November: Sheikh Zayed issued important decrees governing the replacement of the Abu Dhabi flag with the UAE flag; the allocation of 50 per cent of the emirate's revenues to the Federation's annual budget; the establishment of the first university in the UAE during the following academic year; and the setting-up of an auditors department.

17 November: Sheikh Zayed issued a federal law changing some of the provisions of the Nationality and Passport Law in order to grant nationality to Arabs from Oman, Qatar, Bahrain and members of Arab tribes after three years residence in the Federation. Arabs from other Arab countries would be granted nationality after seven years of continuous residence in the Emirates. The law governing the practice of medicine in the Federation was also issued.

18 November: Sheikh Rashid opened the new session of the Federal National Council.

Sheikh Maktoum bin Rashid Al Maktoum issued a decree setting-up a supreme committee for the environment in the UAE.

21 November: The Ministry of Electricity and Water signed a 32 million dirham contract for the construction of an electrical network connecting the cities and villages of the Northern Emirates.

22 November: Abu Dhabi Executive Council approved the construction of flour mills in Abu Dhabi at a cost of 102 million dirhams.

25 November: Sheikh Zayed instructed that 34 permanent Centres for the Memorization of the Holy Qur'an be established throughout the Emirates, the moneys to be provided from his private purse.

Sheikh Rashid opened the new headquarters of the Chamber of Commerce and Industry in Dubai. He also opened the industrial and commercial exhibition mounted at the Chamber's headquarters.

28 November: There were 23 diplomatic missions abroad and three consulates general on this date.

29 November: Sheikh Surour bin Mohammad Al Nahyan signed an agreement for setting-up an electrical station.

Mana Said Al Otaiba signed a 48 million dirham contract with a Swiss company to execute the mechanical and electrical works for the flour mills project in Abu Dhabi. He also signed a 55 million sterling pound contract with a British company to set up a block factory in the Al-Saad region.

1 December: The Council of Ministers approved new rules and regulations for unifying the federal civil service.

2 December: Sheikh Zayed and the

members of the Supreme Council of the Federation reviewed the military exhibition which was mounted in Abu Dhabi on the occasion of the fourth National Day.

3 December: Sheikh Zayed opened the colour television transmission station in Abu Dhabi.

Sheikh Rashid opened Al-Mushref Gardens in Dubai.

5 December: The UAE donated 2 million dollars to help flood victims in Sudan.

6 December: Sheikh Zayed arrived in Tehran on a three-day official visit. At the head of the reception committee was the Emperor Mohammad Rida Pahlavi. Sheikh Zayed issued a statement in which he emphasized the indispensability of co-operation between Gulf States in order to achieve security and stability for the peoples of the strategically important area.

Sheikh Rashid laid the foundation stone for the 70 million dirham Sheraton Hotel in Dubai.

7 December: Sheikh Zayed held discussions with the Emperor Mohammad Rida Pahlavi concerning bilateral as well as international relations.

10 December: Sheikh Rashid bin Humaid Al Nuaimi laid the foundation stone for the Al-Zowra Shipbuilding and Repair Workshop in Ajman.

Mana Said Al Otaiba signed a contract with a Swedish company for a technical and economic feasibility study of the steel pipe manufacturing project.

17 December: Sheikh Zayed chaired the first meeting of the Supreme Defence Council in the Federation. The Council confirmed the armed forces development plan, including the provision of sophisticated weapons. It was decided to establish a Secretariat General for the Council which would meet regularly every two months.

21 December: Sheikh Zayed received His Highness Sheikh Khalifa bin Hamad Al Thani, Amir of Qatar, who arrived in the country on a visit lasting several days.

A World Bank publication confirmed that the average income in the UAE during 1974 year was the highest in the world.

Mana Said Al Otaiba condemned the kidnapping of a number of oil ministers from OPEC member states. A group led by the international terrorist, Carlos was responsible for the seizure.

23 December: Sheikh Zayed and Sheikh Khalifa bin Hamad Al Thani, Amir of Qatar, paid a visit to Dubai where they were received by Sheikh Rashid. During the visit, the Deira - Dubai tunnel was inaugurated.

The Currency Board decided to issue a new 1000-dirham bank note to come into circulation in January '76.

The National Council confirmed the draft law governing co-operative societies in the UAE. The Government decided to provide start-up assistance of around 250,000 dirhams for each co-operative society.

30 December: The first general census of the UAE population began.

James Callaghan, who visited in December, became the first British Foreign Secretary to visit the UAE since independence.

Nineteen Seventy Six

5 January: The UAE decided to contribute 45 million dollars to the formation of the Arab Monetary Fund.

12 January: The Council of Ministers approved the allocation of 35 million dirhams in the budget for 1976 to cover the costs of establishing the UAE University.

13 January: Sheikh Hamad bin Mohammad Al Sharqi and Sheikh Ahmed bin Hamid studied preparatory arrangements for the microwave station being set up in Fujairah in order to strengthen radio and television transmission in the Eastern Region.

18 January: Sheikh Zayed issued an Amiri decree establishing the Board of the National Hotel Company under the chairmanship of Mohammad Al Habroush.

24 January: Mana Said Al Otaiba commissioned Swiss consultants to study the feasibility of setting-up a local tyre factory for both the export and domestic markets.

25 January: Sheikh Sultan bin Mohammed Al Qassimi, at the conclusion of his visit to Somalia, announced that an agreement had been reached whereby the UAE would take over the 40 million dollar financing of a sugar factory and a large dam. The UAE also agreed to set-up joint projects between the two countries.

26 January: Sheikh Rashid bin Ahmed Al Mualla announced that oil exploration would begin on 1 February on both land and offshore areas of Umm al-Qaiwain. The oil to be extracted would be placed at the service of the Federation.

28 January: ADFAED granted a loan of 40 million dirhams to the Ministry of Islamic Affairs and Awqaf in Morocco.

The founding committee of the Red Crescent Society held a meeting to discuss its draft rules and regulations and to adopt the necessary legal measures in order to serve notice of the founding of the institution.

29 January: Sheikh Zayed spoke by telephone with the Algerian President, Houari Boumedienne, and King Hassan the Second of Morocco, calling on them to exercise restraint and not to shed Arab blood in the dispute between the two countries.

Mana Said Al Otaiba signed a three-year contract with a Swiss company for the operation and management of a cement factory in Al-Ain.

30 January: Sheikh Sultan bin Mohammed Al Qassimi made an inspection tour during which he observed progress on the new Sharjah International Airport.

31 January: Sheikh Zayed made telephone calls to the Moroccan King and the Algerian President in his efforts to control the crisis and arrive at a peaceful solution.

1 February: Sheikh Zayed, who was visiting Pakistan, inaugurated the 100-bed Zayed hospital in the presence of Zulfikar Ali Bhutto.

Sheikh Mohammad bin Rashid Al Maktoum received the new batch of UAE officers who graduated from the Egyptian Military College.

2 February: Abu Dhabi Executive Council approved the draft law for setting-up the Abu Dhabi Investment Authority to take the place of the Financial Investments Council. The Authority will be responsible for managing the emirate's investments abroad.

3 February: Official celebrations were held for the commencement of production in the Al-Bunduq oil well which is jointly owned by the UAE and Qatar.

4 February: The Ministry of Foreign Affairs warned the Belgian Government of the consequences of holding a Zionist conference in Brussels to study the immigration of Soviet Jews to Israel.

5 February: Mohammad Khalifa Al Kindi published preliminary results of the first population census in the UAE which showed that at the end of December 1975 the population of the UAE stood at 655,937.

8 February: Sheikh Zayed received a delegation from the television network CBS which was visiting the country to make a documentary film about the UAE. Zayed talked about developmental and economic advances which the country had experienced and he advised the mission to take a close look at the country's archaeological remains yielding evidence of a 4000-year old civilization.

9 February: Sheikh Zayed inspected some of the new towns on the Abu Dhabi - Al-Ain highway and ordered the construction of a new suburb in Al-Wathba.

The Council of Ministers approved the construction of 285 new housing units in various parts of the Federation.

11 February: Sheikh Zayed issued a decree creating a supreme committee for preserving the cultural inheritance, history and documentation of the Federation.

ADFAED extended two loans amounting to 160 million dirhams to Bahrain to finance electrical and industrial projects.

12 February: Sheikh Zayed received a delegation of American astronauts visiting the country. He praised their space discoveries and confirmed that he would help in launching an Arab satellite to study the desert.

16 February: Sheikh Zayed in a statement to *Manar al-Islam* magazine, on the occasion of the publication of its first issue, confirmed that the new constitution of the UAE would have Islam as its foundation and that officials in the Federation would exert all their efforts to preserve the Islamic creed and to stand firm in face of all deviation.

The Council of Ministers decided to give 100,000 dollars to help earthquake victims in Guatemala.

17 February: The first batch of documents, part of a collection dealing with the region which the British Foreign Office had agreed to return, arrived at the Document and Studies Centre in Abu Dhabi. Among the documents were a number of manuscripts concerning the Al Nahyan Rulers and their correspondence with neighbouring Rulers.

Mohammad Said Al Mulla and telecommunications companies operating in the country signed an agreement amalgamating the companies under the name Emirates Telecommunications Corporation (EMIRTEL).

18 February: The Ministry of Information and Culture announced its intention to form an arts group in order to revive and develop popular art.

25 February: Sheikh Zayed and the members the Council witnessed the fifth round of the international shooting competition finals which was organized by the Ministry of Defence in the Al-Manama region.

26 February: Sheikh Zayed and Anwar Sadat, who was visiting the country in the course of a tour of the region, discussed bilateral relations and the Arab situation, agreeing on the necessity of continuing to support Arab solidarity.

27 February: A joint communiqué was issued in both Abu Dhabi and Cairo following the visit of President Mohammad Anwar Sadat to the UAE. Among the most important results of the visit was the decision by Sheikh Zayed to offer 150 million dollars of direct financial assistance to Egypt to meet its current needs.

The Ministry of Works entrusted supervision of the building of 8000 housing units in Ras al-Khaimah and surrounding areas to the Engineering Studies and Works Company (Abu Dhabi - Tunisia).

29 February: The UAE gave a 2.4 million dollars interest free loan to UNESCO.

1 March: Sheikh Zayed issued a federal decree appointing Major General Awwad Al Khalidi as Chief of Staff of the Federal Armed Forces.

The Council of Ministers approved the law governing the new UAE University.

Ahmed Khalifa Al Suweidi issued a decree forming a technical committee to study demarcation of the territorial waters of the UAE.

2 March: Sheikh Zayed decreed that all gas reserves extracted with or without oil in Abu Dhabi were the sole property of the emirate.

Sheikh Hamdan bin Rashid Al Maktoum declared that in the coming days positive measures would be announced concerning the amalgamation of the Armed Forces

3 March: Sheikh Sultan bin Mohammad Al Qassimi opened a new branch of the Currency Board in Sharjah.

6 March: Ahmed bin Sultan bin Sulayyem, Minister of State, chaired the first meeting of the Committee for Heritage and History of the UAE.

10 March: Sheikh Zayed, accompanied by Sheikh Saqr bin Mohammad Al Qassimi, opened the new international airport in Ras al-Khaimah.

14 March: Abu Dhabi Executive Council approved the Ministry of Information and Culture's plan for setting-up television relay stations in Turaif, Al-

Qada, Liwa and the neighbouring coastal areas.

17 March: Mana Said Al Otaiba announced that work was being done on establishing a comprehensive petro-chemical plant at a cost of 1 billion dirhams.

20 March: Sheikh Zayed made a tour of the dam area in the Eastern Region where he inspected progress on work which had commenced under his instructions.

Sheikh Rashid inspected progress on the 350 million dirham project to dredge Dubai Creek

21 March: Sheikh Zayed received the Austrian Chancellor, Bruno Kreisky, in Al-Ain, stressing that there would be no peace in the Middle East without the return of the Palestinian people to their land.

23 March: Sheikh Zayed and the members of Supreme Council of the Federation were present at the gradua-tion of a new batch of officers from Zayed Military College in Al-Ain.

27 March: Sheikh Zayed and the members of the Supreme Council of the Federation received His Majesty King Khalid bin Abdulaziz of Saudi Arabia who arrived in the country on his first visit.

29 March: Sheikh Zayed and King Khaled issued a call to the Security Council in which they asked that the Council and the international community take steps to bring a halt to despotic Israeli measures

2 April: The UAE won a gold medal at the Cairo International Market where its stand was much admired.

4 April: Sheikh Zayed issued an Amiri decree establishing the Board of the Abu Dhabi Investment Authority.

5 April: Sheikh Zayed and the members of the Supreme Council of the Federation were present at the ceremonies commemorating the Third Science Day in the Federation.

8 April: Sheikh Tahnoun bin Moham-med Al Nahyan and the Vice President of the Tokyo Electric Company signed a memorandum amending the price of liquid gas, which Abu Dhabi had agreed to export to Japan for a period of 20 years, from 2 to 7 billion dollars.

11 April: The Ministerial Committee for Financial Affairs completed its debate on the 4 billion dirham draft budget for 1976 which will include the creation of 5400 new civil service posts.

14 April: Sheikh Khalifa bin Zayed Al Nahyan opened the French Cultural Centre in Abu Dhabi.

Sheikh Saif bin Mohammad Al Nahyan announced that he had decided to build three hospitals with 185 beds in the UAE.

15 April: Sheikh Sultan opened the first rope factory in Sharjah.

18 April: Sheikh Zayed, in a statement to the Kuwaiti newspaper *Al-Rai Al-Aam*, stressed that the unity which must be established among the States of the region should be a unity between peoples and not just Rulers. He also emphasized that unifying the sources of weapons supplied to Arab Gulf military forces would serve to weaken these armies since it would place them under the control of a monoply.

19 April: Sheikh Surour bin Mohammad Al Nahyan signed the contract to build the Sana'a - Marib highway, the con-struction costs of which were donated by Sheikh Zayed.

22 April: Sheikh Zayed met with Colonel Ibrahim Al Hamdi who arrived in the country on a one-day visit.

23 April: UAE's Currency Board agreed to allow Offshore Banking Units (OBU's) in the country. Initial numbers of OBU were to be restricted.

24 April: Sheikh Zayed ordered the planting and distribution to UAE farmers of 30 hectares in Ghiyathi.

Sheikh Rashid allocated a budget of 635 million dirhams for the Municipality of Dubai for 1976, 20 times the budget for the previous year.

Sheikh Mohammad bin Butti Al Hamid signed the contract to establish a major fire station in the capital.

27 April: Sheikh Zayed in the presence of the members of the Supreme Council of the Federation opened the refinery at Umm al-Nar.

Sheikh Tahnoun bin Mohammad Al Nahyan announced that Sheikh Zayed had fixed the retail price of fuel.

The Arab Ministers of Finance, meeting in Rabat, agreed to set up the Arab Currency Fund with a capital of 250 million Arab account dinars. Abu Dhabi was designated as the headquarters for the fund.

29 April: ADFAED gave a 70 million dirham loan to Morocco to finance two cotton spinning factories.

30 April: The UAE and 11 Arab states signed an agreement establishing the Arab Board for Investment and Agricultural Development with a capital of 150 million dinars.

1 May: Sheikh Zayed, in a statement to the Egyptian newspaper *Al-Jumhouriya,* said that the UAE was endeavouring to keep the Arab Gulf region removed from international power struggles. He conceded that no region can expect to exist in a political or military vacuum, however he stressed that the Gulf was not there for the taking.

Sheikh Hamdan bin Mohammad Al Nahyan signed a 474 million dirham contract for the construction of 5000 houses throughout the UAE.

2 May: Sheikh Zayed inspected health, tourism and development projects in Abu Dhabi.

3 May: The Council of Ministers approved the proposed development of Ajman Creek and the construction of houses in a number of the villages in that emirate.

6 May: The Supreme Defence Council, chaired by Sheikh Zayed, announced the merging of all the emirates' armed forces under one flag and one leadership. Sheikh Zayed issued a federal decree appointing General Sheikh Khalifa bin Zayed Al Nahyan as the Deputy Supreme Commander of the Federal Defence Forces and a member in the Supreme Defence Council.

8 May: Sheikh Rashid bin Saeed Al Maktoum began an official visit to Kuwait where he met with Sheikh Sabah Al Salim Al Sabah, the Amir of Kuwait.

12 May: Sheikh Zayed paid a surprise visit to a number of projects undertaken by the Department of Works in Abu Dhabi and inspected progress on the Abu Dhabi - Sila road and the housing complex in Ghiyathi. Sheikh Zayed also ordered the construction of 50 housing units at his own expense in the Sila Region, to be distributed amongst the people to help them achieve stability and to free them from fishing and herding in the desert.

Abu Dhabi Executive Council exempted private schools from paying for electricity.

16 May: Sheikh Saqr bin Mohammad Al Qassimi opened power stations in the Shaam, Ghalila and Al-Jeer regions of Ras al-Khaimah.

Sheikh Hamdan bin Rashid Al Maktoum, in his capacity as chairman of the Board of Dubai Aluminum Company (DUBAL), signed four contracts worth 476 dirhams for the construction and management of an aluminium smelter at Jebel Ali, considered to be the foundation for the production of aluminium in the region.

The Committee of Saudi Police Experts arrived in Abu Dhabi having been invited by the Supreme Council of the Federation in order to provide assistance in amalgamating the police forces in the emirates.

17 May: Sheikh Hamdan bin Moham-med Al Nahyan signed an agreement for the importation and installation of three electrical generators in Al-Ain at a cost of 129 million dirhams.

18 May: Sheikh Sultan bin Mohammad Al Qassimi signed an agreement with two American companies to explore for oil on-land in Sharjah.

20 May: Sheikh Zayed delivered a speech dealing with a number of important domestic matters including the participation of individual emirates in the federal budget and the proposal to draft a permanent constitution. He said that Abu Dhabi's participation should not be considered as a favour since it was only doing its rightful duty as a member of the Federation. He stressed the necessity of encouraging the Federal National Council to enter into the democratic experiment in order to guarantee its success.

22 May: Sheikh Zayed chaired a meeting at the general headquarters of the Armed Forces. He spoke about the dimensions and incentives of the decision to amalgamate the Armed Forces and about the nature and scope of the duties of the Armed Forces in the coming phase. Sheikh Zayed asked that General Khalifa bin Zayed Al Nahyan, Sheikh Mohammad bin Rashid Al Maktoum and General Awwad Al Khalidi meet weekly on a continuing basis to make managerial decisions concerning the Armed Forces.

26 May: Sheikh Rashid bin Saeed Al Maktoum reviewed military manoeuvres undertaken by the First Yarmouk Division for the first time since the decision to amalgamate the Federation's Armed Forces.

28 May: ADFAED decided to join with a number of other Arab funds in financing the 141 million dollar Salanji Dam project in the Mali Republic.

1 June: Sheikh Zayed and Sheikh Suhaim bin Hamad Al Thani, the Foreign Minister of Qatar who was visiting the country, inspected dredging of navigation channels around Abu Dhabi island and the vegetable growing projects on Al-Sadiyyat Island.

3 June: Sheikh Zayed informed a Palestinian delegation under the chairmanship of Hani Al Hassan, political consultant to the Chairman of the Palestine Liberation Organization, of his readiness to mediate in solving the dispute with Lebanon, if there was an honest desire on the part of all parties to accept mediation. Zayed requested a comprehensive solution to the Lebanese crisis within the framework of the Arab League and he announced the UAE's support for the holding of an Arab summit to deal with the crisis.

The Ministry of Education was allocated 570 million dirhams from the budget for 1976, as opposed to 63.5 million dirhams in 1972.

5 June: Sheikh Zayed ordered that 500 million dirhams be set aside for interest-free, long-term loans to UAE nationals who were federal government employees for the purpose of building houses in order to help ease the housing crisis.

The Board of Administration of the Federal Union of Journalists and Publishers held its first meeting under the chairmanship of Ahmed bin Hamid.

12 June: Sheikh Zayed donated 2 million dollars to the Palestine Liberation Organization to help those wounded and maimed during the bloody incidents in Lebanon.

13 June: Sheikh Zayed issued a federal decree organizing land grants and building loans for Government employees.

19 June: The Arab Bank for Investment and Foreign Trade granted a 100 million dirham loan to the Algerian Navigation Company.

20 June: Sheikh Zayed and the members of the Supreme Council of the Federation received Sheikh Essa bin Salman Al Khalifa, Amir of Bahrain, on his arrival in the country on an official three-day visit.

Abu Dhabi Executive Council approved the allocation of the necessary funds to plant 1200 hectares of forests in the Western Region.

21 June: Sheikh Zayed in the presence of Sheikh Essa opened the cement factory in Al-Ain.

The National Consultative Council approved Abu Dhabi's budget for 1976. Revenues were forecast at 18.401 billion dirhams and expenditure was estimated to be 18.25 billion dirhams.

23 June: Sheikh Zayed greeted the Egyptian President, Mohammad Anwar Sadat, on his arrival in the country from Doha.

25 June: Sheikh Sultan bin Mohammad Al Qassimi issued a decree incorporating the Al Qassimi Hospital with the Federal Ministry of Health.

Sheikh Rashid bin Ahmed Al Mualla announced the commencement of drilling at Al Ali Oil Well No. 1 on-land in Umm Al-Qaiwain.

It was decided to prepare a 3 billion dirham plan for a sewage project in Abu Dhabi.

26 June: ADFAED gave a loan of 40 million dirhams to finance development projects in Bangladesh.

28 June: Sheikh Hamad bin Mohammad Al Sharqi signed a contract to construct a Hilton Hotel in Fujairah.

The Ministry of the Interior decided to begin standardization of car licence plates on a State-wide level from the middle of next October.

29 June: State income in 1975 was approximately 10.241 billion dirhams compared with 8.83 billion dirhams in 1974.

4 July: The Oil and Minerals Office in Umm al-Qaiwain confirmed that oil and natural gas had been found in the offshore area of the emirate.

5 July: Sheikh Zayed issued a decree

allocating 11 million dirhams to assist cattle production and the development of animal resources in the country.

6 July: The Chiefs of Police in the Emirates decided to establish a full-time office to combat drugs in each police directorate. The central drugs office would give technical support to these sub-offices and co-ordinate their activities.

ADFAED extended a 68 million dirham loan to India to finance an electricity generatiing project.

7 July: The Supreme Council of the Federation, under the Presidency of Sheikh Zayed, ratified the federal budget of approximately 4.152 billion dirhams, an increase of 33 per cent over the previous year. It also ratified the law establishing the UAE University and a number of other federal decrees, including the agreement for setting-up the special OPEC fund.

The Council of Ministers approved the extension of the axisline connecting the Buraimi region in the Sultanate of Oman with Al-Ain.This project was agreed upon by the two countries as a part of the plan facilitating cable and wireless communications.

8 July: The federal budget for 1976 included funds for the construction of 5000 houses, 43 water and electricity projects, support for the highway network, 134 new schools, the setting-up of 90 hospitals and health centres and the building of 97 mosques. The allocations for investments and services amounted to 1797 million dirhams whereas the total for 1975 was 1971 million dirhams.

12 July: The Supreme Council of the Federation under the Presidency of Sheikh Zayed decided to extend the provisional constitution for a five-year period and the Council was invited to convene in an extraordinary session to consider the measures for constitutional change.

The Council approved a number of recommendations whereby the Ministry of the Interior assumed responsibility for direct supervision and complete control of immigration, including control of coasts, land border posts, sea ports and airports.

13 July: Sheikh Zayed paid an inspection visit to the Ministry of Public Works and issued instructions to establish a new city of 8000 houses at the Al-Mafraq roundabout on the road leading to Dubai and Al-Ain in order to alleviate the housing crisis in the capital. The new city, which is to be supplied with all utilities and services, including gardens and sports clubs, will be called Bani Yas.

Sheikh Khalifa bin Zayed Al Nahyan and Sheikh Mohammad bin Rashid Al Maktoum studied progress towards unification of the armed forces and arrangements for the handover.

14 July: Sheikh Rashid ordered the immediate commencement of construction on the 320 million dirham Sports City project in Dubai.

15 July: Ahmed Khalifa Al Suweidi announced during his short visit to Saudi Arabia that the UAE welcomed the holding of an Arab Gulf States Summit Conference.

20 July: ADFAED granted an 80 million dirham loan to Sudan to finance a cotton-spinning project in the Al-Haat Abdulla region of Sudan.

21 July: Sheikh Zayed, presiding over an extraordinary meeting of the Board of the Emirates Development Bank, stressed the need for concentrating on projects which would guarantee a good standard of living for the people of the UAE, as well as the extension of loans which would strengthen the ties of unity between them.

Sheikh Zayed arrived in the Al-Khawaneej region of Dubai at the beginning of a tour of the Northern Emirates.

22 July: Sheikh Zayed toured development projects in Sharjah.

23 July: Sheikh Zayed visited Fujairah. He also inspected the new Dibba - Khor Fakkan highway project and visited Falaj al-Mualla village.

25 July: Sheikh Zayed presided over a meeting of the Federation's Heritage and History Committee. He told the members of the committee that they must pursue accuracy and objectivity in their work.

Sheikh Zayed authorized Abu Dhabi's budget for 1976.

26 July: The Council of Ministers approved the terms for organizing the Fifth Gulf Games Cup Football Competition to be held in the UAE in March 1978.

28 July: Sheikh Zayed, during a visit to the Ministry of Petroleum and Minerals, inspected rock samples confirming the existence of important minerals in the country.

Sheikh Rashid bin Ahmed Al Mualla signed an agreement for the construction of an asbestos pipe and board factory in Umm al-Qaiwain.

The Veedol Company announced that it had discovered oil in its offshore concessions in Ras al-Khaimah. Production was estimated to be 4000 barrels per day.

30 July: A 500 million dollar contract was concluded between the UAE and Japan for the establishment of an iron and steel factory in Al-Ruwais.

31 July: Sheikh Sultan bin Zayed Al Nahyan agreed to take over the chairmanship of the UAE Football Federation.

1 August: Sheikh Zayed, in remarks to the Bahraini newspaper *Akhbar al-Khaleej,* confirmed that he would not accept a second term of office as President of the Federation when his present term expired in December.

Sheikh Rashid bin Ahmed Al Mualla signed an agreement to set up a new broadcasting station in Umm al-Qaiwain.

2 August: Sheikh Zayed, accompanied by Sheikh Rashid and members of the Supreme Council of the Federation, attended ceremonies marking the laying of the foundation stone for the 3 billion dirham, 74-berth Jebel Ali marine port.

Sheikh Zayed's announcement that he did not wish to renew his presidential term of office prompted a huge reaction at both official and popular levels. The Rulers of the emirates and important Government officials expressed their support for the leadership of Sheikh Zayed as well as their desire that he should continue as President of the Federation.

5 August: Sheikh Zayed left for Somalia on a week-long private visit. Telegrams flooding the Diwan of Sheikh Sultan bin Mohammad Al Qassimi asked that the factors which had led to Sheikh Zayed's decision to resign be addressed. Sheikh Mohammad bin Rashid Al Maktoum declared that since Zayed was instrumental in building the Federation it was vital that he reconsidered his resignation.

6 August: A procession of students and young people flowed into the streets of Al-Ain demanding that Sheikh Zayed remain on as President. The procession proceeded to the house of Ahmed Khalifa Al Suweidi who discussed the circumstances which had led to Sheikh Zayed's decision and his hope that all obstactles hindering full federal integration might be removed.

7 August: Sheikh Zayed held a press conference in Mogadishu. In reply to questions about his proposed resignation, he outlined the conditions under which he might reverse his decision. He stressed that the population of the UAE had become better-educated and aware and accordingly that the demands of the people had become more difficult to meet but that these demands must be responded to.

10 August: Sheikh Hamdan bin Mohammed Al Nahyan signed contracts worth 54 million dirhams to construct Government buildings and roads in Ras al-Khaimah, Ajman and Fujairah.

The Union of Journalists and Publishers began distributing the daily newspapers, *Al-Ittihad*, and the English language *Emirates News*, by taxi to all cities in the Federation.

11 August: The Municipal Council of Fujairah, at a meeting held under the Presidency of Sheikh Hamad bin Mohammad Al Sharqi, asked that Sheikh Zayed withdraw his resignation and remain as leader of the Federation.

12 August: Sheikh Saqr bin Mohammad Al Qassimi declared in remarks to the Kuwaiti newspapers *Al-Watn* and *Al-*

Siyasa that he and the Rulers of the Emirates were committed to the leadership of Zayed. He confirmed that the armed forces of Ras al-Khaimah were a part of the Federal Forces and he said that internal differences, including the border problems, must be solved in a brotherly spirit of mutual understanding.

Sheikh Surour bin Mohammad Al Nahyan signed a 46 million dirham contract for a satellite station in Abu Dhabi.

14 August: ADFAED granted two loans to the Maldive Republic to finance the purchase of two fishing boats and the setting-up of a telecommunications station at a cost of 80 million dirhams.

15 August: Sheikh Zayed arrived in Columbo to attend the Summit Conference of the Non-aligned Nations.

Sheikh Zayed received a flood of telegrams from Rulers, citizens, and officials, stressing their support for his wise leadership and requesting that he withdraw his decision to resign from the Presidency of the Federation.

17 August: ADFAED granted a 60 million dirham loan to the Sultanate of Oman to finance the development and exploitation of natural gas fields in the Ebat Region and to lay pipes for the transport of the gas to Muscat.

18 August: Sheikh Zayed met with Colonel Ibrahim Al Hamdi in Columbo. Al Hamdi asked that Zayed remain as President of the Federation in order to guarantee its continuation.

19 August: Sheikh Zayed arrived in Bombay on a private visit to India.

20 August: Sheikh Ahmed bin Rashid Al Mualla stressed the commitment of all the members of the Supreme Council of the Federation and the people of the Emirates to Zayed's Presidency. He said that it was Sheikh Zayed who had laid the foundations of the Federation, made most of the effort and provided much of the money and that his resignation was a deep shock.

The Executive Council decided to allocate 226 million dirhams from the Abu Dhabi budget to support the Ministry of Education.

Sheikh Khalifa bin Zayed Al Nahyan issued an Amiri decree forming a 28 member Al-Ain Municipal Council.

21 August: Sheikh Zayed issued a federal decree recognizing the formation of EMIRTEL and transferring the ownership of all telephone and telegraph companies in the State to the new establishment.

22 August: Sheikh Zayed arrived in London on a private visit to Britain.

Abu Dhabi Executive Council approved the construction of 300 new houses in Jarn Yaphour.

29 August: It was announced that ADFAED had committed 584 million dirhams to Arab, African and Asian countries in the eight-month period from 1 January, more than in all the years put together since the founding of ADFAED.

1 September: UAE, Bahrain and Qatar agreed to make their currencies legal tender in each of the three States from 1 September.

3 September: Sheikh Khalifa bin Zayed Al Nahyan stressed to the Syrian newspaper, *Tishreen*, the commitment of the people of the Emirates to the leadership of Sheikh Zayed. He said that his father really had no choice but to

remain in office because of fears for the future of the nation.

9 September: Sheikh Zayed returned to the country after a one-month tour abroad. The members of the Supreme Council of the Federation, Crown Princes, sheikhs and crowds of citizens took part in a popular demonstration and requested that Sheikh Zayed stay on as President of the Federation. Sheikh Zayed ordered that the gates of Al-Bateen Palace be opened to the thousands of citizens who gathered in front of the palace. The crowd proceeded to renew their allegiance to him. Sheikh Sultan bin Mohammad Al Qassimi stressed that the people of the Emirates were absolutely determined that Zayed should remain on as their leader.

10 September: Sheikh Zayed sent a letter of thanks to the people of the Emirates for their historic stand and for all their love and appreciation. He also thanked them for their enthusiastic concern for the unity of the federal entity.

Sheikh Khalifa bin Zayed Al Nahyan issued an Amiri decree setting up the Diwan of the Heir Apparent. He appointed Ali bin Ahmed Al Dhahiri as the Deputy of the Diwan.

11 September: The UAE and the Sultanate of Oman were connected directly by telephone for the very first time.

12 September: It was decided to construct a huge 500 million dollar oil refinery in Al-Ruwais with a capacity of 120,000 barrels per day.

13 September: Sheikh Zayed issued a decree establishing the Ruler's Diwan in the Western Province.

Sheikh Sultan bin Mohammad Al Qassimi announced that he would do his best to convince Sheikh Zayed to remain as leader of the Federation. He confirmed that he would take direct charge of contacts with the Rulers of the Emirates urging them to adopt measures which would guarantee the removal of the underlying reasons for the President's decision to resign.

14 September: Sheikh Zayed approved the choice of a unified emblem for the Armed Forces.

19 September: Sheikh Zayed issued a federal decree inviting the Supreme Council of the Federation to convene in an extraordinary session to discuss the possibility of extending the provisional federal constitution for a period of five years. Sheikh Zayed stressed that what concerned him most was the security of the country and its citizens since he believed that security was the guarantee of stability. He stressed that the border problems were not the only difficuties that had arisen and that the security of the interior of the country was even more important.

The Executive Council approved the establishment of the first steel pipe factory in the country to fill the requirements of the domestic market.

21 September: King Khalid bin Abdulaziz of Saudi Arabia called on Sheikh Zayed to revoke his decision to resign, expressing the hope that he would continue as President of the UAE.

22 September: Sheikh Zayed received Sheikh Rashid who informed him that the Supreme Council of the Federation members were unanimously determined that he would remain as President of the Federation.

Sheikh Zayed ordered the construction of 2350 residences for Abu Dhabi policemen, 2000 of which would be built near the Al-Mafraq roundabout, forming the core of Police City.

29 September: Sheikh Sultan bin Zayed Al Nahyan attended ceremonies surrounding the laying of the foundation stone for the Sana'a - Marib highway. Costing 187 million Yemeni riyals, the road was constructed with money donated by the UAE.

30 September: Sheikh Zayed called on those from all parts of the Federation who were preparing to march to the Ruler's Palace in Al-Ain the next morning in a huge popular demonstration endorsing Sheikh Zayed's Presidency, to cancel the march. Sheikh Zayed requested the cancellation in order to give him an opportunity to complete on-going discussions with regard to achieving the progress which everyone wished for the Federation. He stressed that the wishes and hopes of the people would be paramount as far as he was concerned.

Mohammad Khalifa Al Kindi signed a 359 dirham contract for the construction of the new international airport building.

1 October: Sheikh Zayed at his palace in Al-Ain greeted demonstrators from the huge march in support of his Presidency. Sheikh Zayed stressed that his decision to resign did not mean that he would abandon his responsibilities to the Federation. He said that every one of them was a soldier in the service of the country and each was responsible in his own way.

2 October: Sheikh Zayed made an inspection tour of the Eastern Region where he paid a visit to Al-Khazna Village to observe progress on land reclamation.

3 October: The UAE awarded 400 scholarships to Eritrean students for Arab schools, institutes and universities.

4 October: Sheikh Zayed met with Sheikh Rashid during which they contacted the Rulers of the other emirates. It was decided to convene a meeting of the Supreme Council of the Federation on 16 October.

Petroleum Minister, Mana Said Al Otaiba said that the Federation would support any rise in oil price that OPEC considered 'necessary'.

8 October: Sheikh Khalifa bin Zayed Al Nahyan presided over a meeting at the General Headquarters of the Armed Forces. He approved the final organization of the Armed Forces and ordered that a unified defence budget be prepared for 1977.

12 October: The Federal National Council at an extraordinary meeting approved the extension of the provisional constitution for another five years, beginning next December. The members of the Council called on Sheikh Zayed to remain in his post and they sent him a petition from the people asking him to renew his mission as President of the Federation.

14 October: Sheikh Zayed toured Port Zayed and observed how sand was being dredged from the bottom of the sea and used for land reclamation in other parts of the port.

Contacts were made between the members of the Supreme Council of the Federation, as a result of which the date for the next meeting of the Council was fixed as 26 October instead of 16 October, to allow for additional contacts and consultations.

The Somali President, Mohammad Siyad Barre, called on Sheikh Zayed to withdraw his decision to resign.

15 October: Sheikh Zayed received a letter from the Egyptian President, Mohammad Anwar Sadat, calling on him to remain as leader of the UAE.

17 October: Sheikh Zayed met with Sheikh Saqr bin Mohammad Al Qassimi within the framework of continuing contacts between the members of the Supreme Council of the Federation in support of federal continuity.

24 October: Sheikh Zayed arrived in Cairo at the head of the UAE delegation to the Eighth Arab Summit Conference.

26 October: Mahmoud Riyadh, Secretary General of the Arab League, announced that the UAE had decided to pay 15 per cent of the expenses of the Arab Deterrent Force in Lebanon.

27 October: Sheikh Zayed cut the ribbon opening Zayed City donated by him to the Egyptian city of Ismailiya.

1 November: Sheikh Khalifa bin Zayed Al Nahyan delivered a speech at the opening of the second ordinary meeting of the National Consultative Council where he announced that 25 per cent of Abu Dhabi's budget was allocated for support of the Arab confrontation states against Israel.

2 November: Mana Said Al Otaiba signed a 30 million dirham contract for the construction of a new fertilizer factory in Al-Ain.

5 November: Sheikh Zayed issued a decree setting-up the Federation of Chambers of Commerce and Industry with headqurters in Abu Dhabi.

6 November: The Supreme Council of the Federation held a meeting under the Presidency of Sheikh Zayed in which it was decided to amend the provisional constitution by adding the clause that only the Federation had the right to establish Armed Forces. It was also decided to set-up an internal security system in the Federation which would report directly to the President. The President of the Federation was granted supreme control over immigration, residence, keeping the peace, preventing illegal entry and ensuring the security of the Federation. The Council also decided to unify the authority to supervise all information in the Federation.

7 November: Hamouda bin Ali, the Minister of State for Internal Affairs, took office as head of the Federation's internal security .

Abu Dhabi Executive Council approved the establishment of a civil airport in Al-Ain.

11 November: The UAE was elected for a two-year term as President of the Financial Solidarity Fund of the Islamic Conference Organization.

12 November: ADFAED extended a 20 million dirham loan to the Fisheries Resources Establishment in Sri Lanka.

17 November: Sheikh Zayed arrived in Muscat to participate in celebrations for Oman's National Day. In a meeting with His Majesty Sultan Qaboos bin Said he discussed ways of supporting co-operation between the two countries and developments in the Arab Gulf region in general.

18 November: Sheikh Saqr bin Mohammad Al Qassimi announced that the Rulers of the emirates had agreed to renew Sheikh Zayed's Presidency of the UAE for the next phase and that, in accordance with the public interest, the members of the Supreme Council of the

Federation granted complete freedom to Sheikh Maktoum bin Rashid Al Maktoum to form the new Council of Ministers.

22 November: Abu Dhabi Executive Council allocated the necessary sums for constructing 5000 prefabricated houses in Abu Dhabi.

Sheikh Sultan bin Zayed was elected by acclamation as president of the UAE Football Federation at a general meeting of the Federation held at the head-quarters of the Ministry of Youth and Sports in Dubai.

24 November: Sheikh Sultan bin Mohammad Al Qassimi presided over the meeting of the Supreme Committee which was formed by the Supreme Council of the Federation to define the general scope of the Federation's budget for 1977 and the percentage participation of the various emirates.

25 November: Abdulmalik Kayid Al Qassimi, Minister of State for the Affairs of the Supreme Council of the Federation, announced that the Council would convene on 29 November under the Presidency of Sheikh Zayed to elect a President of the Federation and his deputy for the coming period.

26 November: Sheikh Hamad bin Mohammad Al Sharqi issued an Amiri decree establishing the Fujairah National Insurance Company.

28 November: Sheikh Zayed issued a decision accepting the resignation of the cabinet and empowering the ministers to remain in their posts until the formation of the new cabinet. He also issued a decree whereby the provisional consti-tution would be renewed for another five years beginning on 2 December 1976.

H.H.Sheikh Zayed bin Sultan Al Nahyan.

Sheikh Zayed with Sheikh Rashid discussing the first plans of Jebel Ali's new man-made deepwater port, on 2 August 1976.

Maktoum bridge and approach roads in 1976.

Highway construction in Dubai during 1976.

Al Garhoud bridge under construction .

Hamdan Street in Abu Dhabi during its early construction phase in 1976.

Looking at plans for new housing to be distributed to local people. 21 October 1976.

Traditional fishing boats at dawn in the old harbour of Abu Dhabi, 1976.

President Zayed with the late President Anwar Sadat of Egypt on 26 February 1976.

Sheikh Rashid of Dubai and Sheikh Saqr of Ras al-Khaimah in 1976.

A rally to support Sheikh Zayed, calling for him to remain on as President of the UAE.
1 October 1976.

Inauguration of Umm an-Nar refinery on 27 April 1976.

Aerial view of Dubai creek in 1976.

Sheikh Zayed and colleagues at the opening of a falconry conference in Abu Dhabi.

Sheikh Zayed attends the International Falconry Conference in Abu Dhabi on 11 December 1976.

Sheikh Zayed viewing plans, in 1976, for a falconry clinic.

Despite the rapid pace of modernization, the people of the UAE have remained close to their traditions through activities such as falconry.

Chartered Bank building in 1976, on Dubai creek.

*A Rolls Royce sales promotion
in Abu Dhabi in 1976.*

Dubai Dry Dock under construction.   *Sheikh Zayed on a visit to India in 1976.*

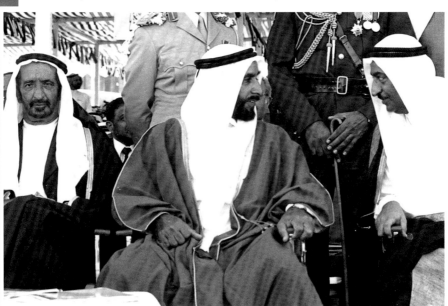

*Sheikh Zayed, President of the UAE and ruler of Abu Dhabi with Sheikh
Rashid, Vice-President of the UAE and ruler of Dubai, together with
Sheikh Sultan, ruler of Sharjah, on 12 December 1976, in Abu Dhabi.*

Inauguration of the Ras al-Khaimah satellite station on 28 April 1977.

An agricultural exhibition on 25 March 1977.

Sheikh Rashid, ruler of Dubai, in 1977.

The UAE President, Sheikh Zayed, on a visit to North Yemen in 1977.

Burning of gas at the Das Island oil refinery in 1977.

The new bridge under construction in Ras al-Khaimah, 1977.

New Earth satellite station at Ras al-Khaimah in 1977.

Sheikh Zayed admires the results of agricultural development in the Emirates, during a visit to an agricultural exhibition on 5 March 1977.

Tribesmen celebrate the opening of
the Fujairah Hilton hotel in 1978.

New means of transport in the Gulf. Goods leave
Abu Dhabi by road whilst a jet passes overhead.

Construction of the ADNOC offices
and residences in Abu Dhabi, 1978.

The corniche mosque in Abu Dhabi, together with
the first clock-tower in 1978.

The new Nasser Stadium, Abu
Dhabi versus Dubai in 1978.

The new Sheikh Mohammad building, one of the
oldest mosques in the city area of Abu Dhabi, in 1978.

Sheikh Sultan bin Mohammad Al Qassimi opened the National Lubricating Oil Factory in Sharjah. The first of its kind in the Federation, it was built at a cost of 20 million dirhams.

29 November: The Supreme Council held a meeting under the Presidency of Sheikh Zayed.

2 December: Sheikh Zayed issued a statement on the occasion of the fifth anniversary of the establishment of the UAE. In it he confirmed that he would renew the vow he had taken to shoulder the responsibilities of Presidency with the commitment and deep concern demanded of a parent for his children and with the sincerity of a leader for his people.

9 December: Sheikh Zayed issued a decree commissioning Sheikh Maktoum bin Rashid Al Maktoum to preside over the new cabinet and to choose its members.

12 December: Sheikh Zayed and the Members of the Supreme Council of the Federation reviewed the military parade mounted on the occasion of the fifth National Day. Zayed delivered a speech in which he confirmed that Federation was the only means of providing a stable internal existence and a distinguished international presence for the country. He called on everyone to co-operate in unification in order to build a better future for the UAE and he spoke in glowing terms about the confidence shown in him by the members of the Supreme Council in renewing his election as President of the Federation.

14 December: Sheikh Rashid opened the Al-Garhoud Bridge in Dubai, considered to be the largest and longest bridge in the Federation.

10 December: Sheikh Sultan bin Mohammad Al Qassimi opened the cement bag factory in Sharjah which cost 12 million dirhams to build.

Sheikh Surour bin Mohammad Al Nahyan opened the Abu Dhabi National Commercial Bank, capitalized at 50 million dirhams.

16 December: Sheikh Zayed was present at the competition mounted between Arab and foreign falconers in Abu Dhabi as part of the International Conference of Falconers held in the Federation.

UAE Ministers of Finance, and Foreign Affairs and the Iranian Minister of Economy, Hushang Ansary, signed agreements to increase co-operation in capital investment, agriculture and industry, along with the creation of a joint investment bank with capitalization of 100 million dollars, and a joint commission to meet twice a year. Another agreement on agriculture enabled Iran to export 120,000 live sheep and carcasses into UAE in 1977.

17 December: Sheikh Surour bin Mohammad Al Nahyan signed a 238 million dirham contract to construct a general hospital in Al-Ain.

18 December: Sheikh Rashid opened the National Flour Mills in Dubai. He also made a round of inspection visits to work sites at Dubai Dry Dock.

22 December: Sheikh Sultan bin Mohammad Al Qassimi opened the Islamic Centre in Sharjah.

ADFAED gave a loan of 16.5 million dirhams for rural development projects in Darfur in the west of Sudan.

24 December: Sheikh Hamad bin Mohammad Al Sharqi opened the Fujairah Beach Hotel, the first hotel in the region.

25 December: Sheikh Zayed issued a decree awarding the Federation's Armed Forces Unity Medal to all military men who were in service in the Armed Forces or in the Defence Forces of one of the member emirates of the Federation on 6 May 1976.

Sheikh Rashid bin Humaid Al Nuaimi ordered the replacement of the Ajman flag by the flag of the UAE.

It was announced that loans granted by ADFAED up to 1976 amounted to 1,100 million dirhams.

27 December: Sheikh Khalifa bin Zayed Al Nahyan opened the Abu Dhabi National Oil Company Plastic Pipe Factory. He also opened the Emirates Commercial Bank in Abu Dhabi.

28 December: Sheikh Surour bin Mohammad Al Nahyan signed a 500 million dirham contract for the construction of the principal stadium for Zayed Sports City in Abu Dhabi.

30 December: The Ministry of Electricity and Water signed contracts worth 200 million dirhams to set up new electricity stations in Al-Dhaid, Falaj al-Mualla, Musafi, Idhna and Al-Manama.

Nineteen Seventy Seven

3 January: Sheikh Zayed issued a federal decree forming the new cabinet with Sheikh Maktoum bin Rashid Al Maktoum as Prime Minister and Sheikh Hamdan bin Mohammad Al Nahyan as his Deputy. Six ministers joined the new cabinet for the first time; five from the previous cabinet were given new responsibilities and a number of ministries were merged, resulting in 22 ministerial posts as opposed to 28 in the previous cabinet. Cabinet members took the constitutional oath before Sheikh Zayed.

4 January: Sheikh Zayed, having praised the efforts of the previous cabinet, directed the new Government to shoulder the burdens of the coming phase, to continue the Federation's forward momentum, to accomplish more and provide better services.

7 January: It was decided to set up the first Department of Forensic (*Shar'i*) Medicine in the Federation.

8 January: Sheikh Zayed visited the Duraid, Zubaida and Umm Ammar schools where he observed study and teaching methods. During a discussion with female students at the Umm Ammar School, Zayed renewed his invitation to Gulf unity. He said that: 'At all times we welcome the inclusion of our brothers in Qatar and Bahrain'.

Sheikh Zayed issued an Amiri decree appointing Sheikh Mohammad bin Butti Al Hamid as the Ruler's Representative in the Western Region.

Sheikh Hamdan bin Mohammad Al Nahyan signed a contract to construct a tarred road between Eiri and Nizwa in the Sultanate of Oman, to be paid for by the UAE at a cost of 126 million dirhams.

Sheikh Zayed issued a federal decree promoting Sheikh Mohammad bin Rashid Al Maktoum to the rank of General, effective from December 1976.

9 January: Sheikh Zayed issued an Amiri decree reconstituting the Abu Dhabi Executive Council under the Presidency of Sheikh Khalifa bin Zayed Al Nahyan.

10 January: Sheikh Rashid bin Saeed Al Maktoum opened the first floating hotel in the Gulf region in Dubai.

The new federal cabinet held its first meeting under the Presidency of Sheikh Maktoum bin Rashid Al Maktoum. The work plan for the coming phase was studied as well as efforts to support the Federation.

The Executive Council approved the granting of loans to farmers for introducing hydroponic irrigation onto their private farms.

11 January: Sheikh Rashid bin Saeed Al Maktoum issued a decree establishing the Federal Company of Dubai for Public Investments Ltd, with a capital of 1 billion dirhams.

The Executive Council approved a 5500 million dirham budget for Abu Dhabi's annual development programme, an increase of 10 per cent over last year. The amount of 456 million dirhams was appropriated for constructing 10,000 new houses. It was also decided to build 145 schools and 370 health units.

13 January: Sheikh Sultan bin Zayed Al Nahyan issued an Amiri decree establishing the National Real Estate Investment Company with a capital of 1 billion dirhams.

Sheikh Rashid bin Saeed Al Maktoum signed a contract with Lloyds International Bank, under the terms of which an account in the amount of 202.4 million sterling pounds would be opened to finance the importation of equipment for the aluminum complex at Jebel Ali.

15 January: Sheikh Tahnoun bin Mohammad Al Nahyan signed an 83 million dirham contract to purchase two giant dredgers to aid in construction of the new port and deepen the old ports.

16 January: EMIRTEL decided to allocate 800 million dirhams to upgrade telephone services in the Federation.

The Development Bank granted 33 million dirhams worth of loans to middle-income citizens.

17 January: The Federal Council of Ministers approved a number of projects costing 56 million dirhams, including the expansion of the Kuwait Hospital in Dubai, the construction of the Masfoot-Hatta Road, water distribution in Ajman and Dibba and the erection of electrical lines between Ajman and Umm al-Qaiwain.

19 January: To construct the new Abu Dhabi port, 2400 million dirhams was allocated. In addition, 326 million dirhams was set aside to build a breakwater in the new port.

21 January: Sheikh Zayed issued a law organizing the country's Police and Security Forces.

Sheikh Hamad bin Mohammad Al Sharqi inspected development projects in Fujairah, Dibba, Badiyya and the Murbah and Qadfa'a areas.

22 January: Sheikh Hamad bin Mohammed Al Sharqi signed an agreement with a Japanese company to establish fish-canning factories in Fujairah.

23 January: Seventy million dirhams was allocated from the current federal budget to establish the UAE University.

31 January: Sheikh Rashid bin Humaid Al Nuaimi ratified the formation of the 300 million dirham UAE-Kuwaiti Gulf Real Estate Investment Company.

13 February: Sheikh Khalifa bin Zayed Al Nahyan conferred with Sheikh Mohammad bin Rashid Al Maktoum and General Awwad Al Khalidi on the steps to be taken to develop the Armed Forces.

The Executive Council approved the building of a number of roads in Abu Dhabi at a cost of 38 million dirhams.

15 February: Sheikh Zayed issued two federal decrees: one reconstituted the Federal National Council and the other invited it to convene on 1 March. The Council was composed of 40 members, 24 of which were new, representing all the emirates in the Federation.

16 February: Sheikh Rashid bin Ahmed Al Mualla signed a 15 million dirham contract to dredge Umm al-Qaiwain creek and construct a corniche.

17 February: Sheikh Khalifa bin Zayed Al Nahyan issued an Amiri decree bringing employees salaries and allowances in Abu Dhabi General Police Directorate in line with those of the Armed Forces, with effect from 1 August 1976.

18 February: Sheikh Zayed inspected dredging by the Abu Dhabi Oil Company near Al-Sadiyyat Island.

Sheikh Mubarak bin Mohammad Al Nahyan approved the setting-up of a comprehensive crime laboratory for the Ministry of the Interior, with its headquarters to be located in Sharjah.

Sheikh Zayed made a tour of the Al-Shuwaib Dam region north of Al-Ain.

The number of government employees on 31 January 1977 stood at 24,352, an increase of 808 employees over the previous December.

20 February: Sheikh Zayed met with the heads of delegations to the second Conference of Gulf and Arabian Peninsula Agriculture Ministers which was held in Dubai. He urged them to diversify the sources of national income and stop depending entirely on oil.

Sheikh Saqr bin Mohammad Al Qassimi opened a branch of the Currency Board in Ras al-Khaimah. He also inaugurated four new electrical generators at the main station in Ras al-Khaimah.

23 February: Sheikh Tahnoun bin Mohammad Al Nahyan signed an agreement with the French Petroleum Company to establish a new oil company for exploiting the offshore oil fields in Zakum and to construct a new port for exporting oil on the island of Zarkuwa.

Dr Mana Said Al Otaiba called for a summit meeting of OPEC members to examine pricing problems. He said that the dangers threatening the organization were greater than those which led to the first summit meeting in Algeria.

25 February: Abu Dhabi finalized a three-year development plan for the emirate - the first of the seven to do so. Spending was set at 23.8 billion dirhams between 1977-79: 37 per cent of the funds were earmarked for industrial development, 39 per cent for the services sector and 24 per cent for the public utilities and agricultural sector.

26 February: Sheikh Zayed toured Khatm al-Oha, Seeh Ghashaba and Seeh Jarf Juan during which he observed progress on agricultural projects in the Al-Ain district of Al-Oha.

Sheikh Zayed issued a law establishing the Abu Dhabi Investments Company with a capital of 200 million dirhams. He also issued a decree forming the seven-member Company Board.

27 February: Sheikh Zayed, in remarks made to the Lebanese newspaper *Al-Anwar*, emphasized the continuing co-ordination between the UAE and Saudi Arabia with regard to oil-pricing. He said that the Gulf region in the next few years would see greater steps toward unity.

Sheikh Zayed made a tour of Al-Shuwaib Dam north of Al-Ain where he inspected building and agricultural projects underway in the Al-Heer region. He ordered that the road between Al-Ain and Dubai be asphalted and the building of 45 public housing units in Al-Shuwaib area.

Abu Dhabi Executive Council approved the draft law establishing the Abu Dhabi Gas Liquefaction Co., Ltd, and granted licences to citizens to set-up factories for producing school chairs.

28 February: Sheikh Khalifa bin Zayed Al Nahyan witnessed the annual military manoeuvres mounted by the Western Military Region Headquarters in the Jebel al-Dhanna and Al-Hamra region.

1 March: Sheikh Zayed opened the first session of the Federal National Council's third legislative period, during which he outlined the achievements of the previous phase. Taryam Omran Taryam was chosen as President of the Council.

4 March: Sheikh Saqr bin Mohammad Al Qassimi opened the Mineral Water Company in the Musafi region of Ras al-Khaimah.

6 March: Sheikh Rashid bin Saeed Al Maktoum planted the first tree as part of the ceremonies which were mounted by the Dubai Municipality on the occasion of Tree Day.

7 March: Sheikh Zayed, who was attending the first Afro-Arab Summit Conference in Cairo in which 60 Arab and African states participated, held detailed discussions with a number of Arab and African leaders.

7 March: Sheikh Zayed announced the UAE's 137 million dollar contribution for the development of Africa, expressing the hope before the Afro-Arab Summit in Cairo that this would be a step towards greater co-operation.

9 March: Mohammad Khalifa Al Kindi signed contracts for establishing a number of post offices in the Northern Emirates.

12 March: Arriving in Sana'a on an official visit, Sheikh Zayed visited the Girls Secondary School, one of the establishments given to the Yemen by the UAE. He also laid the foundation stone for the new UAE embassy building, opened Sharia Zayed, and cut the ribbon for an extension to the Sana'a television building.

13 March: During the course of his visit to Yemen, Sheikh Zayed witnessed military manoeuvres with live ammunition in the Dhamar region, after which he travelled by land to the city of Taizz.

14 March: Sheikh Zayed, accompanied by Colonel Ibrahim Al Hamdi, attended a huge sports festival in his honour in the Taizz Sports City. Zayed announced that the UAE would build two teachers' institutes (one each for men and women), a vocational training centre for young men and a public library. He subsequently visited Jebel Sabr and Taizz Museum.

15 March: Sheikh Zayed, accompanied by Colonel Ibrahim Al Hamdi, visited the Khalid ibn Al Waleed Camp where a new batch of soldiers was graduating. It was decided to give the name 'Zayed' to the Yemeni battalion.

Sheikh Rashid bin Saeed Al Maktoum opened the first pipe factory to be established in the Federation.

Sheikh Saqr bin Mohammad Al Qassimi laid the foundation stone for the new 120 million dirham Saqr hospital in Ras al-Khaimah.

Sheikh Sultan bin Zayed Al Nahyan

inspected UAE positions in the Arab Deterrent Forces in Lebanon.

Sheikh Ahmed bin Hamid opened the new rest house on Al-Sadiyyat Island.

16 March: At a meeting under the chairmanship of Sheikh Sultan bin Mohammad Al Qassimi, the Federal Higher Budget Committee ratified the Ministry of Health's 828 million dirham budget for 1977, an increase of 447 million dirhams over the previous year.

Sheikh Humaid bin Rashid Al Nuaimi opened the first Chamber of Commerce and Industry in Ajman.

17 March: Sheikh Zayed arrived in Aden from Sana'a on his first visit to the Democratic Republic of Yemen. A series of discussions was held between the UAE delegation, under Zayed's leadership, and the Yemeni delegation, under the chairmanship of Salim Rubei, Chairman of the Presidency Council. Sheikh Zayed stressed the UAE's readiness to extend all possible support to Yemen and he said: 'We and the Yemen are one body'.

21 March: Sheikh Zayed ordered the construction of 200 villas at various sites in the capital to help solve the housing crisis.

22 March: Sheikh Zayed witnessed the finals of the Sixth International Weapons Competition which was organized by the Defence Forces in the Al-Zaid region.

27 March: The Executive Council approved the establishment of three factories for producing building materials, furniture, sweets and biscuits.

29 March: The Dubai Carlton Towers hotel, built at a cost of 100 million dirhams, was inaugurated.

Sheikh Surour bin Mohammad Al Nahyan signed a 232 dirham contract for the construction of Al-Mafraq Hospital.

A slight earthquake hit Abu Dhabi during the evening. Tremors were felt by the residents but they did not cause any damage.

30 March: Sheikh Zayed ordered the reclamation of 1000 hectares of land in the region located 50 kms east of Al-Ain.

31 March: Khalfan Al Roumi issued a decree setting up the Health Office in Dubai.

3 April: Sheikh Zayed made a tour by boat of the new marine channels surrounding the city of Abu Dhabi. During the tour, he observed dredging in the Al-Siyayeef and Al-Hadariya regions which were being joined to become an island connected to the city of Abu Dhabi by bridge.

5 April: Sheikh Surour bin Mohammad Al Nahyan signed a 165 million dirham contract for the construction of a huge hotel near the Al-Maqta bridge, as well as a 246 million dirham contract to build a new sewage treatment plant in Al-Mafraq.

Sheikh Zayed ordered the creation of a charity fund for orphans and widows.

9 April: Sheikh Zayed received the new UAE ambassadors to Kuwait, Iraq, Spain and Chad. Zayed praised the role of young people in building the State and he said that they must accept their responsibilities toward their country and its citizens.

Sheikh Zayed approved construction plans for 100 villas in the capital and 100 villas in Bani Yas.

Sheikh Tahnoun bin Mohammad Al Nahyan signed two contracts totalling 1000 million dollars for a huge gas exploitation project centred on the oil fields of Bu Hassa, Asab and Bab Sahil. The project should result in an annual income of 600 million dollars.

11 April: Sheikh Zayed and the members of the Supreme Council of the Federation witnessed the Flag Day ceremonies which were mounted by the Abu Dhabi Secondary Schools. Sheikh Zayed made an inspection tour of housing projects in the Jarn Yaphour region.

The Council of Ministers approved the paving of playgrounds in all school yards in the State and the construction of two secondary schools, one in Zabeel in Dubai and the other in Sharjah.

16 April: Sheikh Tahnoun bin Mohammad Al Nahyan, the Ruler's Representative in the Eastern Region, opened the Japanese Desert Development Institute in the Al-Sulaimaat area of Al-Ain.

17 April: Sheikh Zayed, arriving in Doha on a visit to Qatar, held discussions with Sheikh Khalifa bin Hamad Al Thani, which centred on strengthening relations between the two countries as well as Gulf and Arab affairs.

19 April: ADFAED granted a 57 million dirham loan to finance an electrical project in Bandung, Indonesia.

21 April: Sheikh Saqr bin Mohammad Al Qassimi opened the new EMIRTEL Headquarters in Ras al-Khaimah. The telephone exchange with 2500 lines replaced the old one which had only 750 lines.

23 April: Sheikh Tahnoun bin Mohammed Al Nahyan signed a 35 million dirham contract to construct 50 kms of new roads in Al-Ain.

24 April: Sheikh Mubarak bin Mohammed Al Nahyan issued a ministerial decree regarding the rules and regulations governing firearms, ammunition and explosives.

25 April: Sheikh Zayed presided over a meeting of the Council of Ministers in which he stressed that the interests of the State were paramount. The Council studied the report from the ministerial committee, set up under the chairmanship of Hamouda bin Ali, which dealt with various questions touching on the vital interests of the country and its stability and security. The Council will present a report to the Supreme Council of the Federation on immigration, land ownership, commercial licences and manpower.

26 April: Sheikh Zayed visited the Public Works Office in Abu Dhabi where he observed models of some of the vital projects which the Office was undertaking, including the Abu Dhabi International Airport.

Sheikh Khalifa bin Zayed Al Nahyan arrived in France on an official three-day visit.

Sheikh Tahnoun signed an agreement to set up a 68 million dirham cattle-farm in the Al-Khadr area of Al-Ain.

Abdulla Omran, Minister of Education and Chancellor of the UAE University, announced that it had been decided to admit all female students graduating from the UAE's secondary schools this year to the four new colleges at the University in which study will begin in 1978.

27 April: Sheikh Mohammad bin Rashid Al Maktoum announced that all necessary steps had been completed for co-ordinating and unifying weapons and training of the Defence Forces.

28 April: Sheikh Zayed inaugurated the

earth satellite station in Ras al-Khaimah in the presence of Sheikh Rashid and Sheikh Saqr.

29 April: UAE and France signed a defence pact which will enable UAE to receive French military hardware, weapons and training facilities. After the signing, the French President, Giscard d'Estaing received Sheikh Khalifa and the accompanying delegation.

Sheikh Ahmed bin Hamid issued a ministerial decree setting-up an information documentation centre for the Federation as part of the Ministry of Information and Culture.

30 April: It was decided to give Sheikh Zayed's name to a number of municipal projects in Bethlehem as a sign of appreciation for Zayed's support for Palestinian rights.

1 May: Sheikh Zayed and the Venezuelan President, Carlos Perez, who was on an official visit to the country, discussed the oil market. Zayed clarified the UAE position regarding oil prices and its adherence to a unified stance by OPEC members.

Ahmed Khalifa Al Suweidi, returning to the country after an official visit to Pakistan, announced that Pakistani Government officials and opposition leaders hailed the role played by the UAE in helping to find a peaceful political settlement in Pakistan.

2 May: The Federal Council of Ministers approved the 1977 draft budget for the State, which included an allocation for the merger of the Armed Forces.

3 May: Sheikh Zayed visited the Corniche Maternity Hospital.

Mohammad Khalifa Al Kindi signed agreements for setting-up a station for

boosting television transmission in Fujairah and opening a post office at Shaam in Ras al-Khaimah.

4 May: Sheikh Zayed visited Saudi Arabia where he held talks with King Khalid bin Abdulaziz. He confirmed that his discussions were successful and that they took place in a positive spirit of mutual understanding.

7 May: Sheikh Zayed, on a visit to the boat-building district in Al-Bateen, ordered that equipment for the repair and building of boats be made available.

Sheikh Rashid bin Saeed Al Maktoum opened the 20 million dirham Gulf Iron and Steel Plant in Dubai.

Sheikh Sultan bin Mohammad Al Qassimi issued an Amiri decree creating the Industries and Development Company, Ltd with a capital of 200 million dirhams.

8 May: Sheikh Zayed issued an order raising the salaries of *Sharia* judges according to their rank.

Abu Dhabi Executive Council approved the allocation of the necessary funds in the budget for running the flour mills project in Port Zayed and the cement bag factory in Musaffah.

9 May: Sheikh Rashid bin Saeed Al Maktoum arrived in Tehran where he met with Emperor Mohammad Rida Pahlavi for discussions on the security and stability of the Gulf region.

12 May: Sheikh Zayed issued a federal decree adhering to the agreement for settling investment disputes between Arab host countries and nationals of other Arab States.

ADFAED extended a 5.4 million dirham loan for the financing of the international airport at Banjul in the Republic of Gambia.

14 May: Sheikh Zayed in a statement to the Kuwaiti magazine, *Al-Majalis al-Musawwara*, called for co-ordination between Gulf States in matters concerning arms policy and military training. He stressed that the regional armies should have the capacity to unite in defence against external aggression.

Sheikh Sultan bin Mohammad Al Qassimi inaugurated a new 24 million dirham electricity generator at the Sharjah plant.

15 May: The Council of Ministers approved a draft law for the elimination of fraud in commercial transactions.

17 May: In Cairo, the Egyptian President, Anwar Sadat, received Sheikh Khalifa bin Zayed Al Nahyan and the heads of the delegations participating in the meetings of the Arab Military Industrialization Corporation.

18 May: Sheikh Zayed made an inspection tour of Al-Khazna where he examined land reclamation operations, the boring of wells and agricultural projects.

22 May: Sheikh Zayed ordered the construction of a road connecting the capital with the Northern Emirates. Commencing at Al-Maqta Bridge, it will meet the Dubai highway at Abu Marikha without crossing Al-Mafraq. He also ordered, during his visit to the Works Office in Abu Dhabi, that projects be completed on time, stressing that questions would be asked about delays.

Abu Dhabi Executive Council approved the allocation of an additional 50 million dirhams for dredging Umm al-Nar channel.

Dr Mana Said Al Otaiba signed an 85 million dirham contract to expand the production capacity of the Abu Dhabi fertilizer factory to 600 tons per day.

23 May: Sheikh Sultan bin Mohammad Al Qassimi opened a new 130 million dirham cement factory in Sharjah with an annual production capacity of 220,000 tons.

26 May: Sheikh Zayed, in a statement to *Hawadith* magazine, called for the convening of an Arab oil ministers conference to study prices and co-ordinate their positions before the next OPEC conference.

Mohammad Said Al Mulla, Minister of Communications and Chairman of the Board of Administration of Dubai Electricity Company, signed a 280 million dirham contract with five Japanese companies to set-up two electricity generating stations and one desalination plant in Jebel Ali.

Sultan bin Ahmed Al Mualla, Minister of Economy and Commerce and Director of the Oil Office in Umm al-Qaiwain, confirmed the discovery of large amounts of gas in the oil fields of the emirate.

29 May: Sheikh Zayed made an inspection tour of Abu al-Abyad island to determine projects suitable for the island, at the same time calling for the development of all the islands, including supply of the fundamental necessities of modern life.

30 May: Sheikh Zayed issued a federal decree extending the period of the Board of Administration of the Currency Board and asking it to meet immediately. He also ordered the appointment of a national committee to take over the responsibilities of the Director General of the Currency Board commencing from this date. Sheikh Zayed commented that the Currency Board had

'... Failed to fulfil its functions lately and should therefore be replaced by a Central Bank which would be set up to supervise the activities of banks in the UAE.'

Sheikh Zayed visited islands in the Al-Marfa region where he issued instructions for the building of a modern fishing port and 40 houses on the island.

31 May: Sheikh Saqr bin Mohammad Al Qassimi opened a fish factory in Ras al-Khaimah in the Khor Khwair area with a daily production capacity of 250 tons of dried fish.

2 June: Sheikh Zayed visited Sir Bani Yas Island and inspected ongoing development projects on the island.

3 June: Sheikh Zayed toured Delma Island and examined the feasibility of exploiting the vast tracts of land on the island. He ordered an increase in the amount of freshwater on Delma to 150,000 gallons per day, the building of 50 houses and expansion of the hospital. He also instructed that efforts to develop remote islands be redoubled.

5 June: Sheikh Khalifa bin Zayed Al Nahyan announced that the merger of the Armed Forces had been completed and that the UAE Army was now united, thus embodying the unity of the Federation. He said in a statement to the Kuwaiti magazine, *Al-Yaqdha*, that the UAE was now developing its forces and supplying them with the latest weapons.

6 June: Sheikh Zayed visited the Sila region during which he observed progress on house-building. Some 45 farms, two schools and a hospital had been completed in the region and Sheikh Zayed ordered the distribution of 80 houses to the people.

8 June: ADFAED signed an agreement for a 100 million dirham loan to finance Al-Hisaab phosphates project in Jordan.

10 June: It was announced that the total amount of loans extended by ADFAED to Arab, African and Asian countries since it was founded three year ago amounted to 1628 million dirhams.

11 June: The Supreme Council of the Federation, convened under the Presidency of Sheikh Zayed, listened to reports on the foreign and domestic policies of the Federation and sanctioned a number of federal laws and decrees.

12 June: Sheikh Zayed visited the Ministry of Public Works and Housing where he viewed models of the Federal National Council and the Council of Ministers buildings. He ordered that the completion of delayed projects be given priority over the commencement of new projects.

12 June: Sheikh Zayed instructed the Currency Board to cancel his decree concerning a mandatory bank deposit by importers of 25 per cent of the value of an order, so as to encourage trade and to support the private sector.

Sheikh Zayed ordered the publication of the law regulating the legal profession in the country and stressed that the formulation of current laws must be re-examined to ensure that they were in agreement with the provisions of Islamic *Sharia*.

15 June: Sheikh Khalifa bin Zayed Al Nahyan opened an iron bar reinforcing plant and a fertilizer factory in the Musaffah Industrial Area.

18 June: The Supreme Council of the Federation convened a meeting under the Presidency of Sheikh Zayed, during which they approved the federal budget of 13 billion dirhams for 1977. The Council debated the President's proposal whereby 50 per cent of each emirate's revenues would be allocated to the federal budget. This was deemed to be absolutely essential. The Council also studied a number of other domestic issues.

The Emirates News Agency began an experimental transmission.

19 June: Sheikh Zayed held discussions with President Zulfikar Ali Bhutto who arrived in the country on an official visit. Dubai Municipality budget for this year was 1174 million dirhams, of which 200 million dirhams was earmarked for road projects.

20 June: The Higher Budget Committee held a meeting under the chairmanship of Sheikh Sultan bin Mohammad Al Qassimi in which additional funds were distributed to cover the budgets of the ministries and completion costs for a number of projects facing a deficit in financing.

21 June: Sheikh Sultan bin Mohammad Al Qassimi delivered a speech before the Federal National Council in which he highlighted the negative factors which had hindered unity since the announcement of the Federation. He said that it was necessary to be practical in planning federal projects.

22 June: Sheikh Rashid bin Ahmed Al Mualla signed an 8 million dirham contract to deepen and expand Umm al-Qaiwain port.

23 June: Sheikh Zayed held a meeting with the Somali President, Mohammad Siyad Barre, who arrived in the country on an official visit.

Sheikh Rashid bin Saeed Al Maktoum issued a decree giving ownership of six apartments to each of the participants in the Development Council. Each of them may benefit from the property which can also be inherited by their children.

Sheikh Tahnoun bin Mohammad Al Nahyan signed an agreement setting-up and establishing a company to be jointly owned by ADNOC and the French Petroleum Company for the development of Zakum oil field.

25 June: Sheikh Hamdan bin Rashid Al Maktoum distributed title deeds for 732 apartments to limited income citizens in Dubai.

26 June: Abu Dhabi Executive Council approved the construction of a new 17 million dirham building for the Amiri Diwan in Al-Ain.

Shaikh Hamdan bin Mohammad Al Nahyan, during a meeting with local newspaper editors, stressed the State's whole-hearted appreciation of the press and its concern to lend it support so that it would be able to perform its duty.

3 July: Sheikh Zayed made a tour of Al-Ain in which he inspected the Agricultural Experimental Farm and the new tourist hotel.

In the Ramoul area of Al-Rashidiya, Sheikh Rashid opened a 25 million dirham factory for manufacturing pre-fabricated buildings which could produce four dwellings per day.

5 July: Sultan bin Ahmed Al Mualla, Minister of Economy and Commerce, opened the first consumers co-operative society in Umm al-Qaiwain and the first such society in the Federation.

6 July: Sheikh Sultan bin Mohammad Al Qassimi directed that the ownership of 1000 new houses be given to citizens whose dwellings were torn down in Al-Ghissa area.

8 July: Sheikh Zayed continued his inspection tour of road and agriculture projects in the Zakhir region. He ordered the speeding-up of existing projects and he set aside 100 hectares for further land reclamation in the area.

Sheikh Rashid bin Saeed Al Maktoum issued an order designating 80 apartments for distribution to elderly citizens without family or means of support.

12 July: Sheikh Zayed inspected the Al-Ain vegetable farm in Al-Oha and housing units in the Al-Manasir region to which he added 40 houses.

18 July: The Executive Council approved the setting-up of a national public library and cultural centre in Abu Dhabi costing 117 million dirhams.

22 July: Sheikh Zayed issued a federal decree forming an advisory committee under the chairmanship of Ahmed Khalifa Al Suweidi to focus on issues relating to border demarcation.

25 July: Sheikh Zayed presided over a meeting of the Council of Ministers in which the dispute between Egypt and Libya was discussed. Sheikh Zayed called on both the Egyptian and the Libyan Presidents to put a stop to the clashes between the two countries for the sake of Arab interests.

31 July: Sheikh Zayed personally financed two new roads in Sana'a

Abu Dhabi Executive Council approved the appointment of an American consultant to assist in the regulation of traffic in the capital.

1 August: The Council of Ministers decided to set up a computer centre to serve the ministries and other government offices.

8 August: The Council of Ministers approved the draft labour law.

9 August: Sheikh Zayed ordered the widening of the highway connecting the UAE with Qatar.

10 August: A draft law was prepared to establish the first Central Bank in the UAE.

The first Board of Administration of the Abu Dhabi Marine Areas Operating Company (ADMA-OPCO) was formed, State ownership in the company amounting to 60 per cent with foreign companies owning 40 per cent. This signalled the UAE's move into a new phase in its policy of controlling exploitation of its oil resources.

12 August: Sheikh Zayed commented, in remarks made to the Lebanese magazine *Al-Hawadith,* that if a new war broke out in the area, it would not be limited to the Middle East and the United States would bear the responsibility. He called on Washington not to sacrifice its interests in the Arab world for the sake of Israel.

15 August: ADFAED granted a loan of 10 million dirhams for the Bakwash - Arada highway in Uganda.

16 August: Sheikh Hamdan bin Rashid Al Maktoum signed a 500 million dirham contract establishing the new Dubai Hospital.

19 August: Work began on the construction of the most modern central laboratory in the Middle East. Located in the UAE on the Abu Dhabi - Al-Ain highway, it will cost 24 million dirhams.

23 August: Abdulla Omran Taryam announced that the UAE University would accept all State employees holding the General Secondary School Certificate or its equivalent. Children of faculty members would also be accepted on the same basis.

24 August: Sheikh Sultan bin Mohammed Al Qassimi witnessed Concorde's first landing at Sharjah International Airport.

25 August: Sheikh Zayed renewed the UAE's support for the struggle of the Eritrean people during his meeting with a delegation from the Popular Front for the Liberation of Eritrea.

Sheikh Rashid bin Saeed Al Maktoum ordered the formation of a committee under the chairmanship of Sheikh Mohammed bin Rashid Al Maktoum to take over the administration of Dubai Airport and its technical and administrative development.

21 August: Sheikh Rashid bin Saeed Al Maktoum issued an order lowering the cost of electricity to the public. Sheikh Rashid will bear the difference between the actual cost and the selling price in order to relieve the burden on citizens and to give a boost to construction and industrialization in the emirate of Dubai.

4 September: Sheikh Rashid ordered the construction and distribution of 1060 houses in various districts of Dubai.

During the previous August the quantity of oil produced from the Zakum and Umm al-Shaif fields amounted to 14,911,507 barrels.

6 September: Sheikh Zayed issued a federal law applying new conditions of employment for State employees, including a retroactive 40 per cent salary increase.

12 September: Sheikh Tahnoun bin Mohammed Al Nahyan signed an agreement setting up the Al-Ruwais refinery at a cost of 500 million dollars.

ADFAED extended a 30 million dirham loan to finance the sugar project in Gilan in Afghanistan.

17 September: Sheikh Saqr bin Mohammad Al Qassimi opened Ras al-Khaimah's new port Mina Saqr in Khor Khwair.

18 September: Sheikh Zayed inspected progress on the new bridge connecting the capital with the mainland. He also ordered the construction of the new Abu Dhabi - Dubai highway.

Sheikh Saqr bin Mohammad Al Qassimi attended ceremonies mounted in the Khor Khwair region to celebrate the export of 5 million tons of rock from the Ras al-Khaimah mountains.

19 September: Sheikh Zayed discussed developments in the crisis between Somalia and Eritrea with the visiting Somali President, Mohammad Siyad Barre.

20 September: Sheikh Sultan bin Mohammad Al Qassimi issued an Amiri decree establishing the Gulf Agricultural Development Company with a capital of 200 million dirhams.

The Federal National Council was accepted as a full member in the International Parliamentary Union.

24 September: The Supreme Council of the Federation decided at its meeting under the Presidency of Sheikh Zayed to re-organize the Armed Forces. It also commissioned the Council of Ministers to prepare a draft law regulating land ownership by foreigners and to form a ministerial committee to study the labour and commercial licensing laws, the studies to be presented to the Supreme Council at its next meeting.

Sheikh Zayed instructed the Ministry of Petroleum, the Coast Guard and the

Defence Forces to co-ordinate efforts to mount surveillance on ships polluting the State's territorial waters and to apply the laws which prohibit marine pollution.

25 September: The Executive Council approved the setting-up of two factories for the production of cement blocks in Abu Dhabi and Al-Ain at a cost of 31 million dirhams.

26 September: Sheikh Zayed inspected work on the dredging project in Ras al-Akhdar, the sea wall and repair of the Corniche walls. He ordered the rapid completion of rural hospitals in Sweihan, Ramah, Badii Zayed and Ghiyathi, in addition to the construction of more than 50,000 houses in Al-Wathba and Al-Mafraq. He also instructed the Minister of Awqaf and Islamic Affairs to ensure that the official *Hajj* delegation provided medical services free to all pilgrims without discrimination.

Sheikh Abdulaziz bin Humaid Al Qassimi announced that the Supreme Council of the Federation had decided at its last meeting to commission the Ministry of Defence to prepare a draft law concerning compulsory military service.

28 September: Sheikh Rashid bin Saeed Al Maktoum signed a 45 million dirham contract to set-up a dry-dock for ship repairs in Dubai.

The Permanent Projects Committee approved a number of development projects including the establishment of a hospital for mental illness in Jumairah, Dubai, at a cost of more than 66 million dirhams.

28 September: Sultan bin Mohammad Al Qassimi issued an Amiri decree

establishing the Arabian Industrial Gas Company with a capital of 20 million dirhams.

30 September: Sheikh Hamad bin Mohammad Al Sharqi opened the Fujairah and Safa Refrigeration Company.

1 October: Sheikh Tahnoun bin Mohammad Al Nahyan signed a 20 million dollar contract with the Japanese Oil Development Company, *Nudico*, to set-up a joint company for the development and operation of the Umm al-Dalkh Field.

Mohammad Said Al Mulla inaugurated the direct dialling system with Kuwait and Iran.

4 October: Sheikh Zayed opened the gas liquefaction plant on Das Island, representing a huge step forward in the development of the oil industry in the country. The Japanese Company, *Teko*, purchased the total production of the factory for a period of 20 years. Dr Mana Said Al Otaiba also announced that the gas plant in Al-Ruwais, with 77 per cent Government participation, would begin construction next year.

8 October: Sheikh Zayed held discussions with General Zia Al Haq, Military Governor of Pakistan, after his arrival in the UAE on his first official visit to the country.

9 October: Sheikh Sultan bin Mohammad Al Qassimi inspected progress on Sharjah International Airport.

Sheikh Humaid bin Rashid Al Nuaimi signed a contract to establish a factory for transforming waste materials into glass and fertilizer products.

Abu Dhabi Executive Council formed a high level committee charged with implementing petroleum resource conservation measures.

Sheikh Mohammad bin Rashid Al Maktoum paid a field visit to the headquarters of the UAE's Armed Forces in Shtoura, Lebanon, where they were participating in the Arab Deterrent Force.

It was announced that 12 international companies were involved in oil exploration in the waters around Ras al-Khaimah.

10 October: Sheikh Sultan bin Mohammed Al Qassimi issued a decree establishing the joint stock Sharjah Heavy Industry Company with a capital of 200 million dirhams. The Company will build steel structures for ships, bridges and storage tanks.

12 October: Sheikh Zayed inspected progress on the first children's park in Al-Khalidiya.

13 October: Sheikh Zayed met with the Indonesian President, Ahmed Suharto, who was in the country on an official visit.

14 October: The UAE, for humanitarian reasons, allowed a hijacked German aeroplane to land at Dubai Airport with 91 passengers aboard. Sheikh Mohammad bin Rashid Al Maktoum spoke to the hijackers to bring an end to the operation.

15 October: Sheikh Zayed followed the hijacking events with great concern and instructed that all the necessary facilities be placed at the disposal of the Minister of Defence to deal with the matter in a peaceful way.

16 October: Sheikh Humaid bin Rashid Al Nuaimi issued a decree forming a jointly-owned Kuwaiti and UAE cattle-raising company with a capital of 100 million dirhams.

Sheikh Mohammad bin Rashid Al Maktoum announced after the take-off of the hijacked German aeroplane from Dubai airport that the UAE was opposed to terrorism and hijack operations and that in the future hijacked aeroplanes would be refused permission to land in the UAE.

18 October: Sheikh Zayed issued strict instructions confirming that no hijacked aeroplanes would be permitted to land at UAE airports.

Sheikh Rashid laid the foundation stone for Jebel Ali Hotel.

ADFAED granted two loans of 67.8 million dirhams for financing the electrical network in Lebanon and the fourth dock at Beirut port.

19 October: Sheikh Sultan bin Mohammed Al Qassimi issued an order creating the Archaeology Department in Sharjah.

21 October: Sheikh Rashid bin Humaid Al Nuaimi issued an Amiri decree permitting a national company to construct a 200-room hotel on the beach by Ajman city, the first in the emirate.

A 24 million dirham agreement was signed between ADFAED and the Government of Tanzania to finance the Kajeera Sugar Project.

22 October: Sheikh Sultan bin Mohammed Al Qassimi arrived in Khartoum on an official visit to Sudan.

UAE and Kuwait rejected US Energy Secretary James Schlesinger's comments that the US might need at some point to ensure the security of Middle East oil supplies. Dr Mana Said Al Otaiba stressed that the UAE rejected any threats or foreign intervention regarding the protection of oilfields in the area. He said that the President had insisted more than once that Arab solidarity was the guarantee against any danger to the oil wells.

The production of fruits and vegetables in the UAE during the previous ten months reached 86,000 tons.

24 October: The Council of Ministers approved a donation of 50 million dollars by the UAE to the International Committee of the Red Cross.

25 October: Sheikh Zayed condemned the vile attack in which Saif bin Ghobash, Minister of State for Foreign Affairs, lost his life. Saif Ghobash died from a bullet wound inflicted at Abu Dhabi airport while he was accompanying Abdul Halim Khaddam, Syria's Foreign Minister, to the VIP lounge before his departure from the country. The killer was apprehended as he attempted to take refuge in an aircraft on the airport tarmac.

The Council of Ministers decided to declare a seven-day official mourning period for Saif bin Ghobash who was a great loss to the country.

29 October: The Supreme Council of the Federation, having held a joint emergency meeting with the Council of Ministers to study the results of the investigation into the circumstances of the fatal attack on Saif bin Ghobash, condemned the attack and decided to adopt measures to strengthen internal security and confront elements who were attempting to disrupt the peace.

1 November: Sheikh Zayed, in a statement on his arrival in Tehran for an official visit, stressed the UAE's fundamental belief in the importance of renewing efforts to guarantee stability and peace in the region. Sheikh Zayed also met with the visiting Egyptian President, Anwar Sadat in the Iranian capital.

Sheikh Khalifa bin Zayed Al Nahyan opened the new session of the National Consultative Council with a speech in which he stressed that the Federation would retaliate against criminal attempts to disturb the integrity and security of the country. At the same time, he stressed the determination to continue to support matters of great import.

2 November: Official discussions took place between the UAE delegation, headed by Sheikh Zayed, and the Iranian delegation, led by the Emperor Mohammad Rida Pahlavi. The President in a speech broadcast on television referred to threats against the safety of the oil fields and he stressed that the Federation was not frightened by these threats and would protect its wealth. He described relations with Iran as good.

3 November: Sheikh Zayed ended his official visit to Iran during which an agreement was reached to establish a UAE-Iranian joint-venture bank with a capital of 100 million dirhams. Sheikh Zayed began a private visit to Isfahan.

5 November: Following Sheikh Zayed's return after his official visit to Iran, a joint communiqué was broadcast from both Abu Dhabi and Tehran in which the two countries stressed the necessity of preserving the security and stability of the region without any foreign interference.

7 November: Sheikh Zayed made a tour of the Al-Wathba region where he ordered the planning of a new residential area and that houses be built for the families of officers and soldiers of the Armed Forces.

Sheikh Zayed issued a federal decree appointing Ambassador Abdulmalik Al Hamar to the Currency Board.

Sheikh Zayed opened the Arab Education and Planning Conference with an invitation to the convention to formulate an Arab strategy for education which would comply with development requirements and achieve scientific progress for Arab peoples.

8 November: Saudi Oil Minister, Ahmed Zaki Al Yamani, visited UAE where he had talks with Sheikh Zayed and UAE Petroleum Minister, Mana Said Al Otaiba in the run up to the OPEC price-fixing summit in Caracas in December. After the talks, it was announced that the two countries had reached agreement on a common approach to oil pricing. A week earlier, Sheikh Zayed had said that whatever decision regarding OPEC pricing was reached, this would be supported by UAE: '... UAE will abide by any pricing decision approved by all the other members, whether it be for raising the price of oil or leaving it unchanged, even if the decision runs against our own interests'.

9 November: Sheikh Zayed issued a federal decree appointing Rashid Abdulla Al Nuaimi as Minister of State for Foreign Affairs.

10 November: Sheikh Zayed inaugurated the University of the United Arab Emirates. He announced that the best investment of all is the investment towards the creation of educated and cultured future generations.

12 November: Sheikh Mubarak bin Mohammad Al Nahyan issued a decree whereby the Security Forces and the Police adopted the President's motto and emblem.

Abu Dhabi Executive Council decided to construct a new road between Al-Ain and Abu Dhabi in addition to widening the present road between the two cities.

15 November: The Supreme Council of the Federation met under the Presidency of Sheikh Zayed, however the meeting was adjourned until a later date.

Sheikh Zayed opened the new session of the Federal National Council with a speech in which he requested that everyone work towards strengthening the pillars of the Federation.

18 November: Sheikh Sultan bin Mohammad Al Qassimi opened the Expo 77 exhibition in which 300 local and international companies participated.

28 November: Sheikh Zayed called for all nations to take a common stance against terrorism. He announced in an interview with the Iranian newspaper, *Rast Khabar,* that important steps had been taken and that there were continuing contacts for co-operation to maintain stability and security in the Gulf region.

ADFAED extended a 17 million dirham loan to finance an iron smelting project in Mauritania.

28 November: Sheikh Saqr bin Mohammed Al Qassimi opened a factory belonging to the Rayda Ras al-Khaimah Company, the first factory in the Arab Gulf region to assemble and maintain electromagnetic pumps used in pumping oil and groundwater.

30 November: It was decided to cancel the ceremonies, including the military parade, for the sixth National Day as an expression of the State's appreciation of the delicate and decisive phase which the Arab nation was passing through.

3 December: Discussions were held between Sheikh Zayed and the visiting Somali President, Mohammad Siyad Barre, covering developments in the Middle East and relations between the two countries.

5 December: The Supreme Council of the Federation reconvened under the Presidency of Sheikh Zayed and a number of important decisions were adopted which would ensure the Federation's progress and strengthen internal security. The Council also debated the current Arab situation.

6 December: Sheikh Zayed and the members of the Supreme Council of the Federation attended graduation ceremonies for the fourth batch of students from the Zayed Military Academy in Al-Ain.

Sheikh Zayed issued a law increasing salaries of judges, members of the Federal Supreme Court and the Public Prosecutor by 40 per cent.

8 December: ADFAED granted a loan amounting to 70 million dirhams to help finance dredging and clearing of the Suez Canal channel.

10 December: The Government of Ajman signed a contract with a German company to set-up a huge factory for producing cement and manufacturing cement products: it will also mine gypsum on Jebel Masfoot.

11 December: Sheikh Zayed held a closed session of discussions with the visiting Syrian President, Hafez Al Asad, focusing on developments in the Arab situation and relations between the two countries. The UAE emphasized its firm position on the importance of Arab solidarity and holding firm to the decisions of the Arab summit conference.

13 December: Sheikh Rashid bin Saeed Al Maktoum signed a contract to establish a cable factory in Jebel Ali for which Dubai will contribute 60 per cent of the costs.

14 December: Sheikh Rashid bin Saeed Al Maktoum and Sheikh Rashid bin Ahmed Al Mualla signed an agreement by which Dubai will utilize the natural gas produced in the Umm al-Qaiwain fields to meet its requirements.

Sheikh Rashid bin Saeed Al Maktoum opened the Emirates National Bank in Dubai.

Sheikh Rashid bin Ahmed Al Mualla opened the second navigational channel in Umm al-Qaiwain port, which was constructed at a cost of 22 million dirhams.

15 December: Sheikh Rashid bin Saeed Al Maktoum was present at the inauguration of Bahrain's dry dock which was established with Arab capital, including UAE funds.

18 December: The Executive Council approved a number of vital projects in the emirate of Abu Dhabi, among which was the erection of traffic lights, construction of overpasses, the establishment of a mineral water project in Al-Ain and the building of 5000 prefabricated houses.

20 December: ADFAED issued a 56 million dirham loan towards the financing of an electrical project in Banias, Syria.

21 December: Sheikh Zayed met with King Hussein bin Talal of Jordan who arrived in the country on a short official visit.

Sheikh Mubarak bin Mohammad Al Nahyan issued a decree forming a consultative committee for implementing the Supreme Council of the Federation decree governing the granting of UAE nationality.

ADFAED gave a 40 million dirham loan to Sudan.

24 December: The Higher Budget Committee chaired by Sheikh Sultan bin Mohammad Al Qassimi decided to allot 1600 million dirhams for investment projects in the coming financial year, an increase of 200 million dirhams.

ADFAED granted a 20 million dirham loan to finance an electrical project in Bahrain and a 16 million dirham loan to finance a cement factory in Guinea.

25 December: Sheikh Mubarak bin Mohammad al Nahyan issued a decree merging the Dubai Coast Guard Unit with the General Directorate of Border Guards in the Ministry of the Interior, thus implementing the Supreme Council of the Federation decree.

26 December: The Council of Ministers studied the Hamouda bin Ali report on the general security situation in the country and the results of the landmine explosion in front of the Egypt Air office in Sharjah.

27 December: Sheikh Sultan bin Mohammad Al Qassimi issued an Amiri decree which terminated the concession contract enjoyed by the Sharjah Insurance Company limiting its work to selling insurance in the emirate.

29 December: Sheikh Zayed arrived in Muscat where he held discussions with Sultan Qaboos bin Said which centred on supporting brotherly relations between the two countries.

Nineteen Seventy Eight

2 January: A census on 31 December 1977 showed that the population of the UAE was 862,000; 613,700 men and 248,300 women.

3 January: Sheikh Sultan bin Mohammed Al Qassimi decided to merge the Sharjah broadcasting station with the Voice of the UAE in Abu Dhabi and transfer it to the Federation's official relay station.

4 January: Sheikh Zayed decreed that non-citizens convicted of drug-related crimes would be expelled from the country following judicial punishment.

The Executive Council approved the allotment of 21 million dirhams to set up the first veterinarian/agricultural hospitals in the Federation.

5 January: It was decided to merge the Ajman Courts with the federal court system.

6 January: Sheikh Zayed held discussions with the Algerian President, Houari Boumedienne, who arrived in the country on an official visit.

7 January: From 1 February, it was decided to reduce telephone charges by 60 per cent for internal calls with the State bearing the difference in cost which was expected to amount to 18 million dirhams per year.

8 January: ADFAED loaned Senegal 4 million dirhams to finance a dam feasibility survey.

9 January: Sheikh Zayed issued an Amiri decree prohibiting the hunting of birds and wild animals in the Federation.

10 January: Sheikh Sultan bin Mohammed Al Qassimi opened the wharf at Dibba which can accommodate 80 fishing boats. Part of the port will be used as ships berths.

ADNOC announced the formation of a joint company with Japan Oil Company to develop the offshore Umm al-Dalkh oilfield near Abu Dhabi.

16 January: Sheikh Zayed ordered the establishment of 110 farms in the Al-Wajn area and 24 farms in Al-Saad to be distributed among farmers.

17 January: The UAE donated a broadcasting station to the Eritrean Liberation Front.

18 January: It was decided to sink a new well in the Jarn Yaphour area after samples taken from Well No. 4 revealed the presence of oil and gas.

24 January: Sheikh Sultan bin Mohammed Al Qassimi signed a 450 million dirham contract with an Italian company to expand the new power station in Layya.

25 January: The total value of loans granted by ADFAED during the four years since its establishment stood at nearly 1600 million dirhams.

31 January: Sheikh Zayed issued a decree finalizing the restructuring of the Federal Armed Forces. The decree merged land, air and naval forces into one organization, cancelled regional headquarters, and transformed the regional forces into regular military formations. A federal decree also appointed Colonel Sheikh Sultan bin Zayed Al Nahyan as a Brigadier and Commander-in-Chief of the Armed Forces.

Sheikh Khalid bin Saqr Al Qassimi, Heir Apparent of Ras al-Khaimah, signed an agreement to set up a refinery to be jointly owned by the Governments of Ras al-Khaimah and Kuwait.

2 February: Abu Dhabi Executive Council ruled that contracts, legal documents and correspondence connected with Government projects must be in Arabic.

Direct telephone communication began between the UAE and USA, Italy and a number of other European countries.

Work began on the construction of a 11.5 million dirham oil and adhesive materials plant in the Al-Saja area of Sharjah.

The first shipment of 28,000 tons of Australian wheat arrived at Abu Dhabi port for the new Abu Dhabi silos and flour mills.

3 February: It was decided to construct two rainwater dams, one at Wadi al-

Beeh in Ras al-Khaimah and the second at Wadi Ham in Fujairah.

The 30 million dirham cement bag factory in Abu Dhabi began experimental production.

5 February: Sheikh Rashid signed an agreement with representatives of the Hilton International Hotel Company and the International Exhibition Company for the administration of the Dubai World Trade Centre.

The Executive Council approved the Abu Dhabi draft budget of 7.249 billion, an increase of 1.949 billion on 1977.

12 February: The annual report of the American State Department lauded the UAE's human rights policy as enshrined in the UAE Constitution

13 February: Sheikh Zayed held talks with General Zia Al Haq at his residence in Pakistan.

14 February: The Ministry of the Interior decided to launch the first female police unit.

Direct telephone links commenced between Fujairah and the rest of the emirates in the Federation.

15 February: Sheikh Sultan bin Mohammad Al Qassimi signed the draft federal budget of 10.5 billion dirhams for 1978.

Dr Mana Said Al Otaiba signed a contract for the construction of a plastic pipe and storage tank factory in Abu Dhabi.

Mohammad Khalifa Al Kindi witnessed the first trial use of sulphur in paving public highways: the experiment terminated at kilo. 46 of the Umm al-Qaiwain - Ras al-Khaimah road.

17 February: Sheikh Khalifa bin Zayed Al Nahyan announced at a meeting of the Higher Committee of the Arab

Military Industrialization Corporation in Abu Dhabi that the establishment of the board would free the Arab nation from foreign control and the arms monopoly.

The Ministry of Water and Electricity announced that the east coast from Dibba to Fujairah had been connected through an electrical feeder station.

18 February: Sheikh Tahnoun bin Mohammed Al Nahyan signed two contracts, one for construction of a desalination plant and the other for an electricity generating station in Al-Ruwais.

The daily newspaper, *Al-Wathba*, was published for the first time in Abu Dhabi.

20 February: Sheikh Zayed praised the role of the Arab Military Industrialization Corporation in breaking the arms monopoly. During his reception of heads of delegations participating in Corporation meetings in Abu Dhabi he stressed that Arab solidarity would provide the means to confront challenges.

Sheikh Sultan bin Zayed Al Nahyan resigned from the chairmanship of the Football Federation.

24 February: It was decided to establish an internal department for female students at the UAE University, comprising around 560 female students.

27 February: Sheikh Zayed ordered the distribution of 100 new farms to citizens in the Al-Khazna and Dahhan areas. The United Arab Emirates deposited the documents of adherence to the Joint Arab Defence Treaty at the Arab League in Cairo.

28 February: ADFAED agreed to finance the project linking the electricity grids of East and West Bangladesh at a cost of 60 million dirhams.

1 March: Sheikh Zayed visited Wadi al-Hinoo north of the Al-Hili region and instructed that the wadi be deepened and widened so that agricultural and fish stocking projects could benefit from the rainwater.

The Higher Budget committee under the chairmanship Sheikh Sultan bin Mohammad Al Qassimi approved the creation of 3028 new civil service jobs in 1978, including 50 posts for national university graduates.

Personnel structures for all State ministries and establishments were authorized.

Sheikh Rashid bin Ahmed Al Nuaimi opened the Umm al-Qaiwain broadcasting station.

2 March: Sheikh Zayed inspected wheat farms in Al-Oha as part of his tour of agricultural, development and tourism projects in the Al-Ain district.

5 March: Sheikh Zayed ordered the establishment of an airport on the island of Delma.

Sheikh Sultan bin Mohammad Al Qassimi opened Al-Jabir Journalism, Printing and Publishing Establishment which will publish a daily newspaper, *Sawt al-Umma*, beginning from 6 March.

6 March: Sheikh Zayed and President Ziaurrahman, the President of the Bangladesh Republic, explored ways of strengthening relations between the two countries.

Sheikh Zayed issued a decree re-organizing ADFAED's Board under the Presidency of Sheikh Zayed, with Sheikh Surour bin Mohammad Al Nahyan as Vice President.

7 March: UAE Petroleum Minister, Mana Said Al Otaiba, proposed using a basket of currencies and the value of gold in order to calculate oil prices. This proposal came at a time of decline in the value of the dollar - the currency in which all oil sales were paid for.

12 March: The formation of an inter-ministerial committee to assess the impact of the dollar's fall on the UAE's economy was announced. Later in the month it was announced that the dirham was to be linked to the IMF Special Drawing Right (SDR).

10 March: A law was introduced stating that in all industrial ventures set up in the Federation, a UAE national must have a 51 per cent stake.

11 March: Oil produc-tion from the Abu Dhabi offshore fields amounted to nearly 190 million barrels.

12 March: Abu Dhabi Executive Council approved the construction of a new building for *Shari* judges in Abu Dhabi.

13 March: Sheikh Zayed received the Mauritanian President, Al-Mukhtar Ould Dada, the Senegalese President, Leopold Senghor and the Mali President, Mousa Tarawari following their arrival in the country on an official visit. The four presidents held discussions during which they dealt with international issues, the problem of the Middle East and Afro-Arab co-operation between the UAE and the three countries in a number of fields.

14 March: Sheikh Zayed held talks with the Djibouti President, Hassan Gouled, who was visiting the country.

15 March: Sheikh Zayed sent a cable to General Zia Al Haq calling on him to commute the death sentence passed on the former Pakistani Prime Minister, Zulfikar Ali Bhutto.

The UAE agreed to hold an emergency Arab summit meeting to discuss Israeli aggression against the south of Lebanon.

23 March: Sheikh Zayed arrived in Saudi Arabia on an official visit during which he held talks with His Majesty, King Khalid bin Abdulaziz, regarding Arab affairs, including mobilizing power to confront the Israeli enemy.

25 March: Sheikh Zayed met with Ali Nasser Mohammad, Prime Minister of the Democratic Republic of Yemen, who was visiting the country.

26 March: Sheikh Rashid bin Saeed Al Maktoum opened the Al-Ittihad Private School in Al-Hamriya district. He had personally contributed 15 million dirhams towards the first phase of the school.

Abu Dhabi Executive Council authori-zed the payment of 220 million dirhams compensation for citizens whose property was razed for re-planning purposes in Medinat Zayed.

28 March: Sheikh Rashid bin Saeed Al Maktoum opened the Excelsior Hotel in Deira.

ADFAED extended a 28 million dirham loan for financing the first phase of Shulook port in Malta.

29 March: Mohammad bin Khalifa Al Kindi signed contacts for the con-struction of 47 new schools in various parts of the Federation.

30 March: ADNOC announced that its production from onshore oil fields amounted to 980,723 barrels in 1977.

31 March: Taryam Omran Taryam, Vice Chairman of the Federal National Council, assumed the chairmanship of the Arab Parliamentary Union.

2 April: Sheikh Rashid bin Saeed Al Maktoum paid a short visit to the Sultanate of Oman during which he held discussions with Sultan Qaboos bin Said.

Abu Dhabi Executive Council approved a contract with a Pakistani company to plant 100 hectares of forests in the Fasasa area.

Dr Mana Said Al Otaiba signed a 5 million dirham contract for setting-up a lime factory in Al-Ain, the first in the Federation.

Sharjah Municipality proposed the creation of a general secretariat for co-ordination among all municipalities in the Federation.

3 April: Sheikh Zayed arrived in the Al-Khawaneej region at the beginning of a tour of the Northern Emirates.

4 April: Sheikh Zayed met with the members of the Supreme Council of the Federation during his inspection tour of the Al-Khawaneej region and discussed with them domestic affairs and work requirements for the coming phase.

5 April: Sheikh Khalifa bin Zayed Al Nahyan approved the final design for an 80 million dirham equestrian centre in Abu Dhabi.

Direct telephone links commenced between Fujairah and Sharjah.

6 April: Sheikh Zayed opened new highway projects in Ajman and inspected progress on development projects at Khor Ajman.

7 April: Sheikh Zayed inspected work on the Dry Dock in Dubai's Port Rashid.

10 April: Sheikh Zayed concluded his tour of the Northern Emirates. He also announced that the UAE would always support a unified Arab stance, at all times channelling its capabilities to assist the Arab nation in maintaining its position in a world which only respects strength.

11 April: Sheikh Khalifa bin Zayed Al Nahyan announced at the opening ceremonies of the new radar station at Abu Dhabi International Airport that the Federation was continuing its well-defined plan to establish ties with other Arab countries and the world in general in the field of land, sea and air communications.

12 April: The Red Crescent Society was officially established in the Federation, in co-operation with the Secretariat General of the Arab Hilal Al-Ahmar Societies.

13 April: Sultan bin Ahmed Al Mualla issued a decree prohibiting Masonic activity or the establishment of Masonic centres in the country.

15 April: Sheikh Rashid bin Saeed Al Maktoum opened the *Khaleej Times* newspaper office in Dubai.

18 April: Sheikh Rashid witnessed graduation ceremonies for 12 new groups of policewomen, officer candidates and various police units.

19 July: The Pepsi Cola factory in Dubai was opened by Sheikh Rashid.

20 April: Sheikh Zayed meeting with Sheikh Sultan bin Mohammad Al Qassimi, Chairman of the Higher Budget Committee, approved the federal budget and the budgets for both the Federal National Council and UAE University.

23 April: Sheikh Zayed bin Sultan Al Nahyan ratified the 10.5 billion dirham federal budget to which Abu Dhabi pledged to contribute 50 per cent of its oil revenue.

Abu Dhabi announced that no new projects would begin in 1979 in order to limit spending in the emirate to 6 billion dirhams. Projects in 1980 would only be permissible up to 300 million dirhams.

Sheikh Sultan bin Mohammad Al Qassimi ordered the construction of 289 houses in various parts of Sharjah for distribution to low income families.

26 April: Sheikh Rashid opened the Dubai Sheraton Hotel.

27 April: Sheikh Zayed attended the secondary-level military schools' cultural festival which was mounted in the Medinat Zayed Military School, thus commencing his tour of the Western Region.

28 April: Sheikh Mohammad bin Butti Al Hamid issued a decree prohibiting the manufacture of any food items containing pork products.

29 April: Sheikh Zayed inspected development projects and services in the Zayed Cities, Ghiyathi and Liwa in the Western Region.

30 April: Sheikh Rashid bin Saeed Al Maktoum signed an agreement with two companies for oil exploration in Dubai, both offshore and onshore.

The Ministry of Planning announced that last year the Federation's trade surplus was 21.3 billion dirhams.

1 May: The Council of Ministers decided to form a ministerial committee to implement presidential orders to study the service needs of the Northern Emirates.

Direct telephone lines were opened between Dubai and nine European countries.

2 May: Sheikh Tahnoun issued a decree forming a committee for the development of tourism in the Ain al-Fayidha area, as instructed by Sheikh Zayed.

3 May: Sheikh Zayed ordered the immediate commencement of housing and agricultural development in Ghiyathi.

The ground communications station in Bada' Hamama began operations.

7 May: Sheikh Rashid bin Saeed Al Maktoum opened the Gulf Caltex plant in Dubai.

Said Al Rikabi signed an agreement with a French company to carry-out a 7 million dirham water and soil survey throughout the Federation.

A decree was issued founding the first co-operative society in Ajman with a capital of 400,000 dirhams.

8 May: Sheikh Zayed inspected afforestation and dam projects on Sir Bani Yas Island.

Abu Dhabi Executive Council approved a 78 million dirham agreement with Iran for the afforestation of 3000 hectares in the Federation.

The questions for the General Secondary Certificate Examination were set for the first time in the Federation in co-operation with university professors and curriculum advisers in the Ministry of Education.

9 May: Sheikh Zayed donated 11 million dirhams for the establishment of the Gulf and Arabian Peninsula Social and Humanitarian Services City to be set-up in Sharjah. Sheikh Sultan bin Mohammed Al Qassimi also donated 1 million sq. ms of land for the institution.

Sheikh Mubarak bin Mohammad Al Nahyan issued a decree opening the police post in the border area with Saudi Arabia.

10 May: Sheikh Zayed donated a new headquarters building for Dubai Women's Society. Sheikh Rashid also donated land for the headquarters and money for equipment.

11 May: Discussions on the Palestinian question were held at the rest house on Sir

Bani Yas Island between Sheikh Zayed and the Palestinian leader Yasser Arafat.

13 May: The Ministry of Labour and Social Affairs decided to begin opening social centres immediately in various parts of the Federation.

14 May: Sheikh Sultan bin Mohammad Al Qassimi laid the foundation stone for the Noora Factory, stessing that the project would generate 10 million dirhams annual profit in the first years of operation, rising to 25 million dollars thereafter.

15 May: Sheikh Rashid bin Saeed Al Maktoum issued a Council of Ministers decree establishing the first National Housing Council in the country under the chairmanship of the Minister of Public Works and Housing.

Sheikh Ahmed bin Hamid signed a contract for construction of the UAE's External Television Department in Abu Dhabi.

UAE University declared that that they would accept 1000 students for the next academic year.

17 May: Sheikh Zayed issued a decree allocating 50 million dirhams to subsidize principal food commodities. He also ordered the payment of a housing allowance to citizens living in public housing, from which 1500 employees would benefit.

22 May: The Council of Ministers formed a committee with multiple ministry involvement to review the Federation's foreign investments with the aim of achieving a better return and greater security.

23 May: Mohammad Khalifa Al Kindi announced that, in 1978, 1183 million dirhams was allocated to implement federal development and service projects

supervised by the Ministry of Public Works and Housing.

25 May: Sheikh Zayed issued a decree awarding the Accession Day medal to all military men who were in service in the Police and Security Forces in Abu Dhabi emirate on 6 August 1966.

26 May: Sheikh Zayed ordered the revitalization of Al-Marfa Port in the Western Region.

Sheikh Rashid attended the opening of the 42 million dirham Al-Nasr Club stadium in Dubai.

Imports into the Federation rose in 1977 to 17.4 billion dirhams, as opposed to 10.9 billion dirhams in 1975.

27 May: In Dubai, Sheikh Rashid opened a UAE - Indian co-operative venture for producing barrels and containers.

A 162 million dirham contract to set up a major sewage treatment plant in Al-Ain was signed by Sheikh Tahnoun bin Mohammad Al Nahyan.

29 May: The UAE's financial participation in the Arab Military Industrialization Corporation amounted to 284 million dirhams.

Sheikh Tahnoun bin Mohammad Al Nahyan opened the 3 million dirham oil distribution plant at Al-Mafraq, considered to be the largest in the Middle East.

30 May: Sheikh Sultan bin Mohammad Al Qassimi adopted the financing of an irrigation water network and the establishment of a secondary school in the Palestinian city of Jericho.

3 June: Sheikh Zayed held talks with the visiting Sudanese President, Jaafar Al Numeiri, in which he stressed the need to re-establish Arab solidarity as quickly as possible.

The new Abu Dhabi hospital was inspected by Sheikh Zayed.

Sheikh Rashid bin Saeed Al Maktoum opened the National Refreshment Company's new 18 million dirham factory in Al-Safa.

6 June: The UAE University announced that it would open the College of Law and *Sharia* and the College of Agriculture in the next academic year.

9 June: The French newspaper *Le Figaro* published a special supplement on the Arab Gulf, the first page of which was devoted to the future of the United Arab Emirates and its accomplishments under the leadership of Zayed.

The value of oil exports in 1977 reached 35.3 million dirhams while the value of imports was 17.4 million dirhams. The trade surplus was 21.335 million dirhams.

Arable land in the emirate of Abu Dhabi, aside from cultivated areas, amounted to around 14.8 sq. kms or the equivalent of 2 per cent of the total area of the emirate (67,250 sq.kms).

10 June: Sheikh Zayed toured Al-Ain where he ordered the construction of 500 model housing units for citizens and the construction of 700 dwellings for non-national Government employees and workers. He also ordered that ten tunnels be built to ease traffic in the city.

11 June: Commercial bank assets in the Federation at the end of December 1977 reached 33.5 billion dirhams as opposed to 28 billion at the end of 1976.

Sheikh Tahnoun bin Mohammad Al Nahyan signed an agreement for setting-up a gas transportation project from the Zakum field to Umm al-Shaif.

12 June: Sheikh Sultan bin Mohammad Al Qassimi issued a decree forming the Gulf Islamic Investment Company in Sharjah.

The Council of Ministers empowered the Minister of Agriculture and Fisheries to sign a construction contract for two huge dams in Ras al-Khaimah and Fujairah to collect rainwater.

14 June: Sheikh Rashid bin Saeed Al Maktoum signed a contract with the American Sealand Company to manage the Jebel Ali Port for a period of ten years.

Sheikh Sultan bin Mohammad Al Qassimi signed an Amiri decree establishing a share company for the development of hotels and tourism in Sharjah with a capital of 400 million dirhams.

Sheikh Khalifa bin Zayed Al Nahyan approved projects to construct the main ring road around the capital, to excavate a tunnel at the Grand Mosque roundabout and to construct a flyover at the Defence Headquarters roundabout in Abu Dhabi.

16 June: A conglomerate of 41 international banks approved a 100 million dollar loan to EMIRTEL to finance its projects for the coming four years.

19 June: Sheikh Rashid bin Saeed Al Maktoum opened a steel frame factory in Dubai.

20 June: Sheikha Fatima bint Mubarak distributed certificates to the first graduates from the anti-illiteracy classes organized by the Abu Dhabi Women's Association.

22 June: Sheikh Zayed inspected progress on the 70-hectare land reclamation project in the Dahhan area, in preparation for planting palm trees.

23 June: Sheikh Zayed and the visiting Somali President, Mohammad Siyad

Barre, discussed the situation in the Horn of Africa.

A number of freshwater areas were discovered in Falaj al-Mualla.

24 June: A 260 million dirham bank guarantee for the Federal Cement Company in Ras al-Khaimah was signed by Sheikh Saqr bin Mohammad Al Qassimi.

26 June: Sheikh Zayed issued a decree making 300,000 EMIRTEL shares available for purchase by the public.

27 June: The Federal National Council, at an historic meeting attended by Sheikh Hamdan bin Mohammad Al Nahyan, demanded that the problems facing the progress of the nation be confronted sincerely and responsibly. It warned of external dangers which had begun to surround the region. The Council decided to form a joint committee to meet with the Rulers after studying matters concerned with the higher interests of the country. It was also decided to give the name Al-Jazira Hospital to the new Abu Dhabi Hospital which had opened recently.

28 June: Sheikh Zayed donated 2 million dollars in aid to Burmese Muslims expelled by the Government of their country.

Sheikh Hamad bin Mohammad Al Sharqi laid the foundation stone of the 8 million dirham Fujairah National Insurance Company building.

1 July: Sheikh Saqr bin Mohammad Al Qassimi issued an Amiri decree establishing the Gulf Petroleum Products Marketing Company. Jointly-owned by Ras al-Khaimah and the Kuwait National Oil Company, it was formed with a capital of 50 million dirhams.

4 July: The Executive Council approved the formation of two national companies for marine and navigational services in Port Zayed.

8 July: Sheikh Rashid bin Saeed Al Maktoum expressed his support for the joint committee which was formed by the Council of Ministers and the Federal National Council to study matters of public interest.

9 July: Abu Dhabi Executive Council approved the establishment of a national share company to import and market food products.

A delegation from the Ministry of Information and Culture paid a visit to Abu Musa Island where they listened to the people's requirements, including the need for informational services.

13 July: Sheikh Saqr bin Mohammad Al Qassimi opened the first session of Ras al-Khaimah's new Municipal Council, calling on the members of the Council to serve the people well.

15 July: Sheikh Zayed published a law forbidding the the burning-off of gas in the emirate of Abu Dhabi, directing that it be employed in production operations.

17 July: As instructed by the President, the Council of Ministers approved the decree which offered for public sale 20 per cent of the Government's shares in EMIRTEL and 49 per cent of its shares in the Arab Navigation Company.

23 July: The joint committee of the Council of Ministers and the Federal National Council decided to present its recommendations and the results of its contacts with the Rulers of the emirates to the Supreme Council of the Federation. It also decided to form an inner committee under the chairmanship of Sheikh Hamdan bin Mohammad Al Nahyan to follow up the recommendations.

Sheikh Tahnoun bin Mohammad Al Nahyan signed an agreement to participate in the establishment of the Abu Dhabi Gas Company, Ltd, (Gasco), formed to exploit the gas in the oil fields of Bu Hassa, Asab and Bab Sahil.

Mohammad Khalifa Al Kindi signed contracts to construct five schools in the Northern Emirates which were expected to cost nearly 35.5 million dirhams.

24 July: The Council of Ministers approved the establishment of the Federal Industrial Bank, the first Industrial Development Bank in the Federation, with the aim of supporting and developing industry in the country.

25 July: ADFAED issued a 25 million dirham loan to finance the refurbishment and expansion of a spinning and weaving factory in Uganda.

26 July: Sheikh Rashid opened the 45 million dirham Dubai Dry Dock for ship repair and maintenance.

31 July: Sheikh Zayed ordered the construction of a 30-bed hospital on Delma Island to provide the inhabitants with comprehensive health care.

1 August: Sheikh Zayed ordered that immediate aid amounting to 1.5 million dollars be given to those stricken by floods in Sudan.

Graduation ceremonies for the first group of policewomen were attended by Sheikh Mubarak bin Mohammad Al Nahyan.

5 August: The annual report of the US State Department confirmed that the UAE respected human rights and was endeavouring to provide for the well-being of its citizens.

8 August: The Executive Council decided to prepare a comprehensive plan to fulfil the water and electrical requirements of the capital in the coming years.

9 August: The Office of Agriculture and Forestry in Al-Ain reclaimed 400 hectares of land in Al-Oha district for agriculture, half of which, according to Sheikh Zayed's instructions, will be planted with wheat.

14 August: Sheikh Mubarak bin Mohammed Al Nahyan confirmed Police Directorate recommendations that all foreign residents be registered; that the streets and quarters of the city be named; that housing units be repaired, and that rental contracts between renter and owner be studied.

15 August: The Council of Ministers approved the principle that maternity leave would be 45 days with full pay which could be taken either before or after delivery.

16 August: The UAE agreed to transfer its share in the profits in the International Monetary Fund to the Secretariat of the Fund for re-submission as loans to developing nations.

18 August: Statistics issued by the Ministry of Information and Culture revealed that more than 7000 daily Arabic newspapers entered the country as did some 12,700 Arabic weekly and monthly magazines.

19 August: ADNOC began sinking an exploratory well in the waters around Al-Dhahlain in the Al-Shuwaihat area west of Jebel al-Dhanna.

22 August: It was decided to establish five youth welfare centres in Abu Dhabi,

Al-Ain, Dubai, Ajman and Umm al-Qaiwain at a cost of 50 million dirhams.

24 August: Sheikh Rashid opened the new 50 million dirham National Cement Company plant at Jebel Ali.

26 August: Sheikh Zayed ordered the distribution of 200,000 dirhams in prizes to outstanding pupils in the Zayed Project for the Memorization of the Holy Qur'an.

Sheikh Maktoum bin Rashid Al Maktoum donated 100 million dirhams for the setting-up of an institute for the handicapped.

29 August: Sheikh Rashid donated 1 million dirhams for families of the Palestinian martyrs, as well as some equipment, to the Palestine Liberation Organization.

1 September: The average daily export of oil had risen by 27 per cent in five years. In 1977 the average daily export was more than 1.5 million barrels.

10 September: Sheikh Zayed led the UAE delegation in discussions with a visiting Japanese delegation under the chairmanship of Takeo Fukuda, the Prime Minister. A joint communiqué at the end of the talks confirmed that there was agreement between their points of view regarding the Palestinian issue and the development of bilateral relations.

Sheikh Tahnoun bin Mohammad Al Nahyan signed an agreement between ADNOC and JODCO to develop the Umm al-Dalkh oil field.

14 September: Mohammad Khalifa Al Kindi signed two contracts worth 19.864 million dirhams: the first established a central laboratory in Al-Ain and the second set-up the first internal department in the University of the UAE.

UAE, Bahrain and Qatar made a co-ordinated 0.5 per cent revaluation of their currencies against the dollar.

17 September: Abu Dhabi Executive Council approved a 40 per cent increase in local government employees' salaries, in line with the increase granted to federal government employees.

Sheikh Tahnoun bin Mohammad Al Nahyan signed a 315 million dirham contract for setting-up a salt, chlorine and other related chemical products factory on Umm al-Nar island.

18 September: Sheikh Zayed arrived in Cairo on a three-day visit to Egypt, his first official visit to the country.

19 September: Sheikh Rashid bin Saeed Al Maktoum visited the headquarters of the Second Field Army of Egypt in the city of Ismailiya and the Barlev Line. He announced that the October victories had restored the Arabs to their rightful place.

20 September: Sheikh Sultan bin Mohammad Al Qassimi allocated temporary premises to the Arab Family Organization.

An agreement to establish the Abu Dhabi Petroleum Company for Onshore Oil Operations (ADCO) was signed by Sheikh Tahnoun bin Mohammad Al Nahyan.

Ahmed Khalifa Al Suweidi chaired an important meeting at the Ministry of Foreign Affairs to study the provisions of the two Camp David agreements between Israel and Egypt in order to crystallize the Federation's position regarding the agreements.

21 September: An extraordinary session was convened by the Council of Ministers during which the UAE's position with regard to the two Camp David Agreements was defined. It was stressed that the two agreements did not oblige Israel to withdraw totally from all occupied land and restore Palestinian rights. The agreements furthermore ignored the Palestinian Liberation Organization. The Council announced that the UAE confirmed that its hopes lay in Arab solidarity and the implementation of decisions taken at the con-ferences in Algeria and Rabat.

28 September: Sheikh Zayed ordered that 6 million dollars of humanitarian aid be given immediately to earthquake victims in Iran.

29 September: During 1972-77, there were nearly 395 housing units either constructed or under construction in the emirates of Ras al-Khaimah, Sharjah, Ajman, Umm al-Qaiwain and Fujairah.

30 September: Sheikh Zayed issued two laws establishing the Abu Dhabi Gas Industry, Ltd (ADGIL), with a capital of 1600 million dirhams, and the Abu Dhabi Company for Pipeline Construction with a capital of 16 million dirhams.

1 October: Sheikh Khalifa bin Zayed Al Nahyan issued a decree imposing a fine as a penalty for damage to public buses.
The Dubai Police College of Technology was opened by Sheikh Mohammad bin Rashid Al Maktoum.

2 October: Sheikh Rashid bin Ahmed Al Mualla signed a contract for constructing jetties at Umm al-Qaiwain port. The Council of Ministers approved the draft law governing obligatory military service. It also approved the memorandum forbidding the export of fish.

3 October: The President's Office issued a statement in which he confirmed the UAE's support for an Iraqi initiative to convene an Arab summit in Baghdad in November in order to discuss the Camp David agreements.

5 October: A marble factory in Fujairah was opened by Sheikh Hamad bin Mohammad Al Sharqi.

7 October: An elevated walkway connecting the old and the new souks on Sheikh Khalifa Street in Abu Dhabi was opened.

8 October: Sheikh Zayed issued instructions to extend the land survey in the Musaffah industrial area with a view to establishing more factories and companies to provide services for ships.

9 October: Sheikh Khalifa bin Zayed Al Nahyan issued decrees forming two new companies: Abu Dhabi Company for Onshore Oil Operations (ADCO) - with a capital of 1 million dirhams, and the Abu Dhabi Marine Areas Operating Company (ADMA-OPCO) with 60 million dirhams capital.

He also confirmed during his meeting with an Italian press delegation that the UAE was concentrating on building a vigilant naval force to ensure the safety of oil installations and protect its extensive coastline.

10 October: The UAE agreed to attend the meeting of foreign ministers from countries participating in the Arab Deterrent Force in Lebanon following talks between Sheikh Zayed and the visiting Lebanese President, Elias Sarkis.

11 October: ADFAED granted a 623 million dirham loan to finance an oil-drilling project in the south of the Sultanate of Oman.

14 October: Sheikh Saqr bin Mohammad Al Qassimi opened the head office of the United Insurance Company in Ras al-Khaimah, which was capitalized at 10 million dirhams.

17 October: Sheikh Khalifa issued two

decrees: one established the Umm al-Dalkh Development Company and the other amended some of the provisions of the law establishing the Abu Dhabi National Oil Company (ADNOC).

Documents were signed for the issuance of a 40 million dollar loan granted by the Abu Dhabi National Bank to the Algerian External Bank to finance a number of industrial projects in Algeria.

The Oil Technology Conference began its deliberations in Abu Dhabi with the participation of nearly 100 engineers and experts from 25 oil companies in the Gulf.

19 October: Sheikh Zayed returned to the country after a European tour which lasted a number of weeks.

20 October: A Dubai Petroleum Company report stated that by 1977 the company's production had increased nine times over what it was in 1969 when it produced 319,028 barrels daily.

22 October: The Executive Council approved the creation of an iron and steel plant in Abu Dhabi and ordered the preparation of a feasibility study.

Twenty million dirhams was allocated to construct a hospital in Sweihan.

23 October: Sheikh Zayed received a letter from the Saudi Crown Prince, Fahad bin Abdulaziz, concerning the Arab Summit Conference which was to be held in Baghdad in November to discuss the Camp David Agreements.

Sheikh Tahnoun bin Mohammad Al Nahyan signed an agreement to establish Abu Dhabi Petroleum Ports Operating Company (ADPPOC) with a capital of 25 million dirhams.

24 October: A decree forming the Federation's Heritage and History Committee was issued by Sheikh Zayed.

25 October: Sheikh Zayed received envoys from the King of Saudi Arabia and the Egyptian and Yemeni Presidents.

29 October: Sheikh Zayed issued a decree declaring equality between men and women in respect to blood money amounting to 35,000 dirhams.

Sheikh Hamdan bin Rashid Al Maktoum signed a 23 million dirham agreement to set-up eight operating theatres in the Mohammad Ali Jinnah Hospital in the Bahawlior Province of Pakistan to be built at Sheikh Rashid's expense.

Dubai's new trade centre hosted its first trade fair, Middle East Construction Exhibition, with around 300 companies represented.

1 November: Sheikh Zayed ordered that the construction of separate medical clinics for women be speeded up in order to maintain the teachings, values and traditions of the Islamic religion in the country.

Khalid bin Humaid Al Qassimi, Chairman of the Civil Aviation Office in Ras al-Khaimah, opened the first two direct routes from Ras al-Khaimah airport to London and Bombay.

2 November: Sheikh Zayed arrived in Baghdad to attend the ninth Arab Summit Conference. He stated that the UAE hoped that this conference would result in greater Arab unity

3 November: Sheikh Zayed held in-depth consultations with the leaders attending the Arab Summit Conference in Baghdad.

4 November: The UAE's *Sharia* courts were instructed by Sheikh Zayed to apply the provisions of *Sharia* law, including that agreed by the doctors of the four schools of law on the question of blood money for women.

6 November: Sheikh Zayed, on his return from Baghdad, expressed satisfaction at the outcome of the ninth Arab Summit Conference.

13 November: Sheikh Sultan bin Mohammad Al Qassimi signed agreements with two American companies to explore for oil in Sharjah.

17 November: There were 2280 students (male and female) studying abroad at the expense of the State during the 1977-78 academic year: 1424 were nationals, the remainder students from neighbouring countries.

24 November: Sheikh Tahnoun bin Mohammad Al Nahyan approved the setting-up in Al-Ain of the first permanent exhibition by the Palestinian Samid Establishment in the country.

29 November: Sheikh Tahnoun bin Mohammad Al Nahyan signed a 56 million dirham contract for the construction and expansion of the Al-Ain - Abu Dhabi highway.

30 November: Sheikh Zayed convened the third session of the Federal National Council where he outlined the State's accomplishments and the work plan for the future.

1 December: Sheikh General Khalifa bin Zayed Al Nahyan encouraged the officers and soldiers of the Armed Forces to make great efforts to protect the Federation's achievements. He said in a remarks made on the occasion of the seventh National Day that the establishment of the Federation was an historic event which gave concrete form to the hopes of the people for a system of government which would provide a good standard of living for every citizen.

2 December: Sheikh Sultan bin Mohammad Al Qassimi opened Sharjah's new souk, airport passenger terminal, flyover at the Al-Khan roundabout and container terminal at Khor Fakkan.

Brigadier Sheikh Sultan bin Zayed confirmed that the army command was composed of nationals and that the Armed Forces were supplied with the latest weapons.

5 December: Sheikh Zayed, meeting with the directors and members of the Chambers of Commerce and Industry and the Chairman of the UAE Currency Board, stressed the need to join forces in making an effort to revitalize the economy. He ordered the formation of a committee to formulate a long-term economic strategy.

Sheikh Brigadier Sultan bin Zayed Al Nahyan opened the earth satellite station in Abu Dhabi.

6 December: Sheikh Zayed held discussions in Abu Dhabi with the Yemeni President, Ali Abdulla Saleh.

7 December: ADMA's crude oil production from 1 January to the end of October 1978 amounted to 150,441,787 barrels.

8 December: Liquid gas exported to Japan from Das Island from 1 January to end of October 1978 was more than 78,460,000 metric tons.

9 December: The Telephone Exchange in the eastern district of the capital was opened by Sheikh Mohammad bin Butti Al Hamid.

10 December: The Executive Council approved exemption from electricity payments for people in receipt of social assistance.

Thani bin Essa Harib, Minister of Water

and Electricity, signed a contract for sinking 45 drinking water wells in the Northern Emirates.

12 December: Sheikh Zayed led the UAE's delegation in discussions with the visiting Kuwaiti delegation under the Presidency of Sheikh Saad Al Abdulla Al Sabah.

13 December: As a result of Sheikh Zayed's meeting with the recently-formed economic committee, a number of decrees were issued to assist in reversing the current economic slump. These included the creation of the first real estate bank in the Federation with a capital of 1 billion dirhams; that all building work for real estate investment purposes should cease; that commercial banks be forbidden to finance such building work; and an industrial bank be set-up for financing projects which would help achieve an economic renaissance in the country.

17 December: Sheikh Sultan bin Mohammad Al Qassimi opened the new EMIRTEL building in Sharjah.

OPEC Oil Ministers meeting in Abu Dhabi approved a 20 per cent increase in the price of oil to be phased in from 1 January 1979.

18 December: Sheikh Rashid bin Saeed Al Maktoum opened the central EMIRTEL complex in Dubai.

19 December: Sheikh Hamad bin Mohammad Al Sharqi opened a marble tile factory in the Al-Sharba region of Fujairah.

20 December: The UAE officially received the Supreme Committee of the Arab Military Industrialization Corporation's decree appointing Sheikh Faisal Al Qassimi, the UAE member of the Board of Administration, as the temporary Chairman of the Board from 16 December, following the resignation of Dr Ashraf Marwan.

25 December: Sheikh Zayed ordered that a 14-hectare park for women and children located in the Al-Mushrif area be reserved and provided with all amusement facilities.

30 December: An agreement to construct a television transmittal station in Al-Ain was signed by Sheikh Ahmed bin Hamid.

It was decided to computerize traffic lights in Dubai.

Nineteen Seventy Nine

7 January: Abu Dhabi Executive Council decreed that primary industrial materials would be exempted from customs duties as an encouragement to the private sector.

11 January: The 14 million dirham electrical plant in Dibba was opened by Sheikh Hamad bin Mohammad Al Sharqi.

12 January: The Monetary Council report stated that in 1979 commercial bank deposits in the Federation amounted to 18.7 billion dirhams while credit stood at 31.2 billion dirhams, resulting in a commercial trade balance of 21 billion dirhams.

The UAE occupied fifth place of the 12 oil producing countries in the Middle East in relation to oil reserves which were estimated to be nearly 22.6 billion barrels.

13 January: According to a recent statistical report, at the end of 1978 the population of the UAE was 877,340.

15 January: Decrees issued by Sheikh Khalifa bin Zayed Al Nahyan established the Abu Dhabi Petroleum Ports Operating (ADPPOC) Company with a capital of 100 million dirhams and the

Abu Dhabi Foodstuffs Company with a capital of 10 million dirhams.

The Al-Ahli Club stadium in Dubai was opened by Sheikh Rashid.

16 January: The electro-biochemistry laboratory and the health education department in Al-Ain municipality were opened by Sheikh Tahnoun bin Mohammed Al Nahyan.

18 January: Sheikh Rashid bin Humaid Al Nuaimi opened the gas powered electricity generating station in Ajman.

22 January: Sheikh Sultan bin Mohammed Al Qassimi, meeting with General Sheikh Khalifa bin Zayed Al Nahyan, discussed ways of supporting the federal structure and a number of other domestic matters.

21 January: Talks between Sheikh Hamad bin Mohammad Al Sharqi and General Sheikh Khalifa bin Zayed Al Nahyan focused on ways of supporting the federal structure and providing a high standard of living for citizens.

23 January: The Federal National Council debated domestic and security issues, support for the future of the Federation and developments in the area. It was decided to hold a closed emergency meeting of the Ministers of Interior, Defence and Foreign Affairs for further discussion on these matters.

26 January: The Council of Ministers approved the formation of the Supreme Planning Board in the Federation.

28 January: The emergency meeting of the Federal National Council attended by the Ministers of Foreign Affairs, Defence and Interior discussed a number of important domestic matters.

30 January: Dr Mana Said Al Otaiba announced that the UAE had plans to spend 20 billion dollars by 1985 to develop the petrochemical industry.

31 January: The total amount of loans granted by ADFAED for financial development projects in Arab, Asian and African states was said to be nearly 1560 million dirhams.

4 February: The Executive Council decreed that citizens living in housing provided by the State in seven remote regions of Abu Dhabi emirate would be exempted from electricity payments.

5 February: The Council of Ministers formed a committee of ministers to study urgent requirements for services in the Northern Emirates.

6 February: The first joint session of the Council of Ministers and the Federal National Council was held, during which a number of recommendations and suggestions were adopted in support of the Federation's future on both domestic and external levels.

UAE Planning Minister, Said Al Ghobash revealed that *per capita* income in the Federation had risen from 20,200 dirhams in 1972 to 60,800 dirhams in 1978. (The UAE had the world's highest *per capita* income in 1977.) GDP rose

from 6.4 billion dirhams to 53.4 billion dirhams in the same period. GDP dependency on oil also declined from 80 per cent of GDP in 1972 to 57 per cent in 1978.

The Gulf News Agency in Bahrain stated that the UAE occupied first place among the news agencies in the area from the point of view of news outflow during 1978.

8 February: A new oil well was discovered in Abu Dhabi some 8 kms north of Delma Island.

9 February: Sheikh Zayed, returning to the UAE after a private visit to Pakistan, renewed his call to General Zia Al Haq to commute the death sentence on the former Prime Minister Zulfikar Ali Bhutto.

11 February: Abu Dhabi Executive Council approved the first draft law for creating a public body for regulating and developing the industrial sector in Abu Dhabi. Abu Dhabi's cabinet also approved a 6900 million dirham development budget for 1979 which was destined to fund 1222 projects in various sectors.

The Ministerial Committee formed to debate Company Law decreed that there must be 51 per cent public shareholding in commercial companies.

12 February: The Ministry of Education, based on instructions from the President, decreed that 64 university level scholarships be granted to Palestinians working in the Federation.

The Council of Ministers decreed that the national education curriculum would be based on the glorious history of the people of the UAE.

13 February: Sheikh Zayed, during his meeting with the joint committee of the

Ministers and the Federal National Council, received a ten-point memorandum containing comprehensive proposals for dealing with internal difficulties and ensuring the future of the Federation. He expressed the hope that the effect of the proposals would be positive and that they would be adopted by the responsible officials, not only for the sake of firmly anchoring the Federation, but also to achieve a high standard of living for its people and all the peoples of the region.

The UAE recognized the new Iranian Government under the Prime Minister Mehdi Bazargan.

16 February: The annual report of the US State Department praised the UAE's respect for the dignity of the individual and its attention to the socio-economic needs of its citizens. It also confirmed that the UAE's judicial system was based on fair procedures.

18 February: The Executive Council officially directed companies operating in the emirate of Abu Dhabi to purchase all their material requirements from local markets or to import them through local companies.

21 February: Sheikh Zayed and Sheikh Rashid toured Abu al-Abyad island in the Western Region. The visit took place following the third meeting between them in four days to study ways of supporting the Federation and strengthening its institutions.

24 February: Sheikh Zayed greeted Queen Elizabeth II who was on an official visit to the UAE.

Sheikha Fatima bint Mubarak, wife of Sheikh Zayed, outlined for the Queen the activities of women in the Federation and their achievements in various fields.

25 February: Sheikh Zayed and Queen Elizabeth went on a tour which included Jebel al-Dhanna and Al-Ain. The Queen subsequently visited Dubai where she was received by Sheikh Rashid.

26 February: Sheikh Zayed urged the two Yemeni Presidents to put an end to the armed conflict between them and to resolve their differences in a spirit of sincere brotherhood.

Sheikh Rashid and Queen Elizabeth officially opened Jebel Ali Port. The Queen, in remarks directed at His Highness, said: 'Your dreams in transforming the desert to a green land have been achieved'.

Khalfan Al Roumi visited the Abu Dhabi Central Hospital in which an operation for re-attaching a severed hand was successfully completed, the first of its kind in the Federation.

27 February: Sheikh Rashid bin Humaid Al Nuaimi opened the new telephone exchange in Ajman.

1 March: Taryam Omran Taryam was elected Chairman of the Federal National Council in its fourth legislative term: Hamad Bu Shihab and Hilal Lootah were chosen as his deputies.

2 March: UAE revenue for the first nine months of 1978 was 4.139 billion dirhams, an increase of 16 per cent over 1977.

4 March: Petroleum Minister, Mana Said Al Otaiba, said he would advocate to the OPEC Summit on 26 March imposing sanctions on oil companies that made excessive profits by exploiting the current state of the oil market and selling oil at prices above the posted OPEC rate. If the warnings were ignored, Otaiba recommended that such oil companies should be blacklisted and

OPEC States impose a ban on selling oil to them.

5 March: Sheikh Zayed held talks with the Guinean President, Ahmed Sekou Toure, who arrived in the country on an official visit.

The Council of Ministers approved a memorandum from the Ministry of Health prohibiting doctors working in the Ministry from opening private clinics.

Sheikh Surour bin Mohammad Al Nahyan opened the first exhibition mounted by the Abu Dhabi Chamber of Commerce and Industry in which products from 134 local and foreign companies were exhibited.

7 March: The first issue of the magazine *Al-Azmina al-Arabiya*, edited by Mohammad Obaid Ghobash, was published.

8 March: The Paving Stone and Block factory, established with national capital and expertise, was opened by Sheikh Tahnoun bin Mohammad Al Nahyan.

9 March: Legal formations in the federal and appeal courts were completed for the first time.

10 March: The Executive Council approved the formation of the Public Corporation for Industry under the chairmanship of Dr Mana Said Al Otaiba.

13 March: Sheikh Zayed allocated an additional 100 million dollars to be deposited with the Currency Board to serve the national economy and to strengthen the position of the UAE dirham

18 March: The Executive Council allocated 3.8 million dirhams to the UAE's Supreme Heritage and History Committee.

19 March: Sheikh Zayed presided over a meeting of the Supreme Council of the Federation (from which the emirate of Dubai was absent) called to discuss a UAE cabinet and Federal National Council memorandum to unify emirate boundaries, create a central bank and unite the Armed Forces.

The meeting was set against a back-drop of huge pro-unity demonstrations, during which Sheikh Zayed made a statement to the crowds outlining the steps taken in support of unity and the reinforcement of the Federation. As the demonstrations came to an end, Zayed and the members of the Supreme Council received a testament of allegiance from the people.

Sheikh Abdulaziz bin Humaid Al Qassimi, Minister of State for Supreme Council Affairs, subsequently announced that the Council had decided to leave the session open until the following Tuesday in order to deal with all the items on its agenda.

Sheikh Zayed, in a statement to the Lebanese magazine *Al-Kifah al-Arabi* stressed that the Egyptian-Israeli settlement would not bring real peace and that it may again lead to the outbreak of war in the region, because the United States, which was overseeing the agreement, could not guarantee peace to anyone.

21 March: Public demonstrations continued in many parts of the country for the third straight day with the participants demanding that complete unity be achieved between the emirates.

22 March: The first all-female demonstration took place in Fujairah. Participants stressed the determination of women that full unity, the common destiny and highest goal of each citizen, male and female, be achieved.

24 March: Sheikh Zayed ordered that annual grants of 16 million dirhams be paid for 1978 to rural cattle breeders in the Northern Emirates.

Dr Mana Said Al Otaiba signed a 50 million dirham contract for the construction of an animal feed factory in Abu Dhabi.

25 March: Sheikh Zayed, in a statement published by his office, appealed to employees to suspend public demonstrations for the sake of public order, security and stability. He stressed his desire and that of the Members of the Supreme Council, to achieve full unity for the sake of the UAE's citizens.

The Fatwa and Legislation Office issued a *fatwa* allowing the demolition and rebuilding of mosques.

26 March: The Federal National Council, in an emergency meeting, acknowledged the public demonstrations and Sheikh Zayed's statements concerning the protests. The Council issued a statement emphasizing their faith in the role of the people in building their history while directing their lives and their future.

28 March: Sheikh Zayed, presiding over a meeting of the Supreme Council of the Federation (from which Dubai and Ras al-Khaimah were absent), stressed to groups of citizens who had gathered that their demands for unity required unending work and that this work would continue for the sake of strengthening the structure of the Federation and achieving the nation's and the citizen's best interests.

Sheikh Zayed and the visiting President of the Comoros Islands, Ahmed Abdulla, examined ways of strengthening relations between the two countries.

29 March: Sheikh Zayed paid a one-day visit to Saudi Arabia during which he and King Khalid bin Abdulaziz discussed political developments.

Sheikh Saqr bin Mohammad Al Qassimi, in talks with demonstrators in Ras al-Khaimah, stressed that he supported their demands for the development of the Federation, especially the drafting of a permanent constitution. He said that the fact that he did not participate in the recent meeting of the Supreme Council did not mean that he opposed these demands.

The Government of Dubai sent a memorandum to the Ministry of State for Supreme Council Affairs to be presented to the Supreme Council of the Federation.

30 March: Sheikh Zayed sent a cable to the Pakistani President Mohammad Zia Al Haq calling on him again to exercise mercy in the case of the former Pakistani prime minister, Zulfikar Ali Bhutto, and commute the death sentence which had been passed on him, in appreciation of his past services and efforts to strengthen ties between Arab and Islamic countries.

Sheikh Khalifa bin Zayed Al Nahyan approved plans to extend New Airport Street in Abu Dhabi.

31 March: Rashid Abdulla, Minister of State for Foreign Affairs, announced the UAE's concurrence with the move to sever economic ties and place an oil embargo on the Egyptian authorities following their signature of the Camp David Agreement with Israel.

1 April: Sheikh Zayed and the visiting Mobutu Sesi Seko, President of Zaire, discussed co-operation between the two countries.

Sheikh Rashid bin Saeed Al Maktoum, meeting with the Committee formed by the Supreme Council of the Federation to unite the different points of view, told them that he supported the Committee in their efforts to find common ground. He also said that he strongly supported the continuation of the federal structure since it was a matter of national destiny. Sheikh Rashid bin Ahmed Al Mualla, Chairman of the Committee, stressed that Sheikh Rashid bin Saeed Al Maktoum's point of view was identical with Sheikh Zayed's concerning the necessity of providing the people with a good standard of living and advancing the nation: the only dispute was about the best way of achieving this aim.

Rashid Abdulla recalled the UAE Ambassador to Egypt, Saif al-Jarwan, in accordance with the resolutions of the Conference of Arab Ministers of Foreign Affairs and Economy in Baghdad which had called for the severance of diplomatic relations with Egypt following its signature of the peace treaty with Israel.

The total amount of loans granted to developing countries by ADFAED since it was established was declared to be 2 billion dollars.

2 April: Sheikh Zayed met with the Supreme Council of the Federation Committee. Sheikh Rashid bin Ahmed Al Mualla confirmed that Sheikh Zayed would set a date very shortly for convening a meeting of the Supreme Council of the Federation.

The Executive Council approved an agreement with the Australian Government which would guarantee the delivery of Abu Dhabi's wheat requirements for three years.

3 April: Sheikh Zayed allotted 50 million dirhams to subsidize food commodities in all parts of the Federation.

Sheikh Zayed congratulated Ayatollah Al Khomeini on the occasion of the establishment of the Islamic Republic of Iran.

4 April: The Ministry of Labour and Social Affairs issued a decree announcing the formation of the first Society of Engineers in the Federation. The Society's headquarters will be in Sharjah.

5 April: Sheikh Zayed sent his condolences and those of the UAE to the widow of the executed former Pakistani Prime Minister, Zulfikar Ali Bhutto. He regretted that he had not received any response from the Pakistan authorities to his repeated calls for mercy. Sheikh Zayed's Office issued a statement in which it was stressed that the Islamic nation had lost one of its most distinguished leaders.

9 April: The UAE announced that its troops serving with the Arab Deterrent Force based in Lebanon would be withdrawn when the Force's existing mandate expired on 27 April.

11 April: Sheikh Surour bin Mohammad Al Nahyan signed a 418 million dirham contract with an American company to administer the Towam Hospital in Al-Ain.

ADFAED extended a 40 million dirham loan to finance an agricultural project in the Moroccan Sahel.

12 April: Sheikh Zayed, in a statement made to *Al-Watn Al-Arabi* magazine, announced that his decision to withdraw

UAE troops from Lebanon was a direct consequence of the signing of the peace treaty between Egypt and the Zionist enemy, which he described as a great loss to all Arabs and to the Egyptians themselves.

12 April: The Ministry of Health decided to construct four new medical clinics in Abu Dhabi in order that the entire country should be covered by the health services.

16 April: Sheikh Zayed, during a meeting with the chairman of the Federal National Council, emphasized his faith in the Federation and his hope that efforts to support the Federation's future would be successful.

20 April: Sheikh Zayed, who was visiting France, gave a statement to *Al-Mostaqbal* magazine in which he stressed his support for progress towards unity in the Gulf and Arabian Peninsula and his readiness to attend any summit conference to discuss this issue.

21 April: Sheikh Zayed received a letter from the Ruler of Kuwait, delivered by Sheikh Sabah Al Ahmed Al Sabah, Minister of Foreign Affairs, concerning Kuwait's attempts to mediate between the different points of view in the Federation.

Sheikh Sultan bin Mohammad Al Qassimi opened Sharjah International Airport.

A statistical study revealed that production from the Federation's oil reserves would last for 45 years at 1979's average daily production which was less than 2 million barrels daily.

22 April: Sheikh Zayed, Sheikh Rashid bin Saeed Al Maktoum and Sheikh Sultan bin Mohammad Al Qassimi received Sheikh Sabah Al Ahmed Al Sabah. The meeting took place within the framework of Kuwaiti mediation efforts.

The Supreme Council of the Federation sanctioned a special decree forming a committee to distribute public housing.

23 April: The Rulers of Ras al-Khaimah, Fujairah and Ajman, along with the Heir Apparent of Umm al-Qaiwain, met with Sheikh Sabah Al Ahmed Al Sabah. Sheikh Saqr bin Mohammad Al Qassimi announced that Kuwait's efforts had been successful in erasing all differences of opinion between the members of the Supreme Council of the Federation.

The Council of Ministers approved a comprehensive project for bringing electricity to all the villages in the eastern region of the Northern Emirates.

24 April: Sheikh Zayed and Sheikh Rashid met Sheikh Sabah Al Ahmed Al Sabah who announced after the meeting that all disputes had been resolved and that a new federal Government would shortly be formed.

25 April: The Government submitted its resignation to the President in preparation for the formation of a new Government.

The Ministry of Foreign Affairs announced the severance of diplomatic relations with Egypt.

27 April: Sheikh Zayed ordered the payment of special prizes to students who achieved a 'Superior with Honours' evaluation in the first semester at the UAE University.

28 April: Sheikh Zayed issued a Civil Defence Law.

29 April: The President accepted the Government's resignation and asked that the Ministers remain in their posts to deal with urgent matters until the formation of a new Government.

30 April: The Supreme Council of the Federation met in session under the Presidency of Sheikh Zayed during which it was decided to charge Sheikh Rashid bin Saeed Al Maktoum with the formation of a new Government. Sheikh Rashid stated that he considered this assignment to be a huge responsibility requiring full co-operation in order to realize the hopes of the nation and the aspirations of its citizens.

1 May: Sheikh Zayed visited the Police Academy during which he witnessed the second training session for female recruits for the women's police force. He commended the competence of the women trainees.

Sheikh Zayed issued two federal laws regarding agricultural and veterinarian restrictions.

Sheikh Rashid bin Saeed Al Maktoum began consultations with the members of the Federal National Council with a view to forming the new Government.

4 May: Currency Board statistics revealed that the Federation's per capita income during 1978 was 18,022 dirhams.

5 May: The Council of Ministers approved the formation of the Federation's Secretariat General for Municipalities.

9 May: Sheikh Sultan bin Mohammad Al Qassimi opened the first Arabic Book Fair in Sharjah.

12 May: The British Royal College of Surgeons recognized Abu Dhabi Central Hospital as the first university hospital in the Federation and the second in the Gulf.

13 May: Sheikh Sultan bin Mohammad Al Qassimi authorized the formation of the Sharjah Cement and Industrial Development Company with a capital of 200 million dirhams.

15 May: A Ministry of Economy and Trade report announced that the net general trade balance was 17.4 million dirhams in the Federation's favour. Oil exports reached 33.7 million dirhams and non-oil exports amounted to 4.2 million dirhams.

19 May: ADFAED signed agreements whereby it would contribute 11 million Tunisian dinars to the Arab Fertilizer and Nitro-Phosphate Company in Tunis as well as grant a 5.5 million Tunisian dinar loan to the Tunisian Government.

20 May: Sheikh Rashid opened the headquarters of the Dubai Islamic Bank.

Minister of Electricity and Water Resources, Thani bin Essa, signed two contracts worth 27.3 million dirhams to supply 28 villages in the Northern Emirates with electricity.

21 May: Minister of Information, Sheikh Ahmed bin Hamid, signed an agreement setting-up a broadcasting centre.

24 May: Sheikh Khalifa bin Zayed Al Nahyan decided to set up a benevolent Islamic *waqf* in Kenya with a value of 20 million dirhams.

Thani bin Essa signed a 57 million dirham contract to execute a new electrical project in Ajman

28 May: Sheikh Khalifa bin Zayed Al Nahyan issued regulations covering indemnification for the death of non-national Abu Dhabi Government employees, which was set at 35,000 dirhams.

Sheikh Ahmed bin Hamid signed three agreements for boosting television transmission in the Eastern Region.

30 May: Sheikh Zayed and the members of the Supreme Council of the Federation, attended the graduation of the fifth batch of officers from Zayed Military College in Al-Ain.

2 June: Dr Mana Said Al Otaiba signed a contact with a German consulting firm to establish a vocational training centre in Abu Dhabi.

Crude oil production in the country reached 668 million barrels in 1979, as opposed to 730 million barrels in 1977, representing a decrease of 8.5 per cent which was in line with the Federation's policy of protecting its oil reserves and implementing OPEC decisions on production programming.

9 June: Sheikh Zayed visited Al-Jazira Hospital, inspected the conditions of the patients and observed the standard of services.

10 June: The new 80 million dirham asbestos factory in Umm al-Qaiwain was opened by Sheikh Zayed and the members of the Supreme Council.

12 June: Sheikh Zayed issued Amiri decrees forming the Public Industry Corporation with a board of administration chaired by Dr Mana Said Al Otaiba.

13 June: Princess Alexandra opened the Zayed Centre for Liver Studies in London.

25 June: Graduating ceremonies were held for the first batch of students from the Civil Defence Academy.

26 June: Sheikh Zayed, with King Khalid bin Abdulaziz and a number of other leaders from the region, viewed annual military manoeuvres in Abha, Saudi Arabia

28 June: Sheikh Zayed confirmed that King Khalid had talks with leaders of the Gulf States and the Arabian Peninsula concerning mutual relations and important regional matters.

30 June: Sheikh Zayed issued a statement in which he confirmed that

Arab Gulf leaders were completely aware of their historic responsibility to create a self-reliant Arab force to confront the challenges faced by the region. He said that quiet determined efforts to build such a force was the most eloquent reply to the spate of attacks which enemies were mounting.

1 July: Sheikh Zayed issued a decree ratifying the new Government under the Prime Ministership of Sheikh Rashid bin Saeed Al Maktoum. Sheikh Rashid announced that the aim of his Government, which included two Deputy Prime Ministers and 21 ministers, would be to revive the economy, raise the standard of services and strengthen administrative organization.

3 July: Sheikh Zayed and the Libyan President, Muammar Al Gadhafi, who arrived in the country on an official visit, discussed the current Arab situation in the Gulf and relations between the two countries.

Jebel Ali's new electrical power generating station and desalination plant were opened by Sheikh Rashid.

7 July: Sheikh Surour bin Mohammad Al Nahyan witnessed trial operations at the Western Umm al-Nar power plant.

8 July: Sheikh Zayed, meeting the members of the new Government after they took the oath of office, reassured them that they would have his support but that they must re-double their efforts to provide better services to citizens in all parts of the Emirates.

Sheikh Rashid spoke of the necessity of mutual support for the good of the nation and its citizens.

ADFAED granted a 4 million dirham loan to the Government of Mauritania.

10 July: The Council of Ministers, presided over by Sheikh Rashid, decided to form a ministerial committee under the chairmanship of the Minister of Finance and Industry to prepare the federal budget for the rest of the current year and to begin immediate work on next year's budget.

12 July: Statistics from the Ministry of Planning revealed that 2287 million dirhams was spent on industrial consultancy.

16 July: Sheikh Zayed held talks with visiting French President Giscard d'Estaing on the Middle East and energy.

The Council of Ministers approved the federal budget for 1979, estimated at around 9.7 billion dirhams.

17 July: Sheikh Khalifa bin Zayed Al Nahyan ordered the housing at Government expense of all Abu Dhabi Government employees working on local contracts. He also ordered both the Finance Office and the local banks to lower the interest on buildings guaranteed by him from 7 per cent to 4 per cent and to grant owners 10 per cent of the annual income from their properties.

18 July: Sheikh Zayed arrived in Liwa after an inspection visit to development projects on Delma Island where he determined the site of the new airport.

The UAE donated 10 million dollars to the Lebanese Government to assist those stricken by the events in the south and as aid to Lebanese benevolent societies.

21 July: Sheikh Zayed ordered the sinking of 120 wells in Liwa, to be followed by another 700 wells, to provide water and increase the area under cultivation. He also ordered the

establishment of certain industrial installations in the region

Sheikh Saqr bin Mohammad Al Qassimi ordered that the Saqr Hospital in Ras al-Khaimah be merged with the Ministry of Health.

22 July: Sheikh Rashid bin Saeed Al Maktoum opened the Emirates Macaroni Factory, the first of its kind in the Federation.

23 July: The Council of Ministers discussed the formulation of an overall plan for industrialization in the country which would take relevant circumstances as well as development requirements into account. This would be accomplished through effective coordination between the Federal Government and local offices.

30 July: The Council of Ministers decided to form a committee to study the real estate situation in the Federation and another to prepare regulations for granting loans to citizens to build private dwellings for which 200 million dirhams had been allocated.

1 August: Real estate investments from 1972 to the end of 1978 were valued at 15.236 billion dirhams.

3 August: Sheikh Zayed issued a federal decree ratifying the agreement on economic co-operation between the UAE and Saudi Arabia which permitted free movement of nationals betwen the two countries and reciprocal residence facilities. It also sought to encourage public and private joint ventures and included customs and transit agreements.

4 August: First Lady Sheikha Fatima bint Mubarak opened the first Islamic book exhibition to be mounted by the Abu Dhabi Women's Association.

5 August: The Supreme Council of the Federation sanctioned the basic principles of the Federation's Fifth Development Plan covering the years 1981-85.

6 August: Chairman of Abu Dhabi National Oil Company (ADNOC), Sheikh Tahnoun bin Mohammad Al Nahyan, announced the discovery of a huge natural gas field in the Al-Kahaif Region of Umm al-Shaif. He confirmed that ADNOC had 100 per cent ownership of the companies in its group.

The Council of Ministers decided to prepare a comprehensive study for the creation of a central power station network in the Northern Emirates. It also decided to construct 2000 prefabricated dwellings in the Northern Emirates.

7 August: Sheikh Zayed, during his visit to the first Islamic Book Exhibition mounted by the Abu Dhabi Women's Association, stressed the necessity of encouraging young people to become aware of Islamic thought and to help them hold fast to the principles and goals of the Islamic creed and *Sharia* law.

9 August: Digging of 50 wells to bring water to every house in Al-Ain was completed.

11 August: At the end of July, there were 31,595 employees in the federal ministries.

18 August: The UAE's diplomatic missions abroad numbered 32.

27 August: A 45 million dirham contact to construct the new municipality building in Al-Ain was signed by Tahnoun bin Mohammad Al Nahyan.

28 August: An agreement was concluded for laying down submarine cables between the UAE, Qatar and Bahrain at a cost of 44 million dollars of which the UAE would pay 41.9 per cent. Said Al Raqbani signed an agreement to dig 120 irrigation wells in the Northern Emirates.

29 August: An Amiri decree setting up the Al-Dhafra Insurance Company with a capital of 10 million dirhams was issued by Sheikh Zayed.

31 August: Sheikh Zayed arrived in Tripoli to participate in the celebrations of the tenth anniversary of the Libyan revolution. President Gadhafi presented His Highness with the 'Great Conqueror' decoration during the grand celebrations.

1 September: Sheikh Zayed attended the military parade mounted in Tripoli on the occasion of the anniversary of the Libyan revolution in which the UAE's Armed Forces participated. The Libyan Leader, Muammar Al Gadhafi, commended Zayed for the role he played in achieving unity in the Emirates and for the role he was playing in the movement towards Arab unity.

3 September: Sheikh Rashid bin Saeed Al Maktoum and Sheikh Saqr bin Mohammad Al Qassimi inspected water, electricity and housing projects in the emirate of Ras al-Khaimah.

10 September: The Council of Ministers approved an increase in funds available to sports clubs to 38 million dirhams. The Executive Council granted subsidies of 40 million dirhams to the National Food Company.

11 September: The construction of 145 housing units in the emirate of Fujairah and the paving of 52 kms of highway was ordered by Sheikh Maktoum bin Rashid Al Maktoum.

15 September: Sheikh Rashid bin Saeed Al Maktoum arrived in Salalah where he held discussions with Sultan Qaboos bin Said regarding the situation in the Arabian Gulf region.

16 September: Work began on the first phase of Sharjah's Humanitarian Services City.

17 September: Sheikh Rashid bin Saeed Al Maktoum returned to the country following a visit to the Sultanate of Oman where his discussions with Sultan Qaboos had resulted in the settlement of border problems between the UAE and Oman.

20 September: Sheikh Zayed, on a private visit to Lausanne in Switzerland, met with Saudi Arabia's King Khalid bin Abdulaziz.

25 September: Sheikh Zayed donated two mosques and 400 dwellings to limited income families in Morocco.

26 September: Sheikh Khalifa bin Zayed Al Nahyan issued a local order prohibiting building on agricultural lands in Al-Ain.

28 September: Sheikh Tahnoun bin Mohammad Al Nahayan attended ceremonies for the first class of policemen graduating from the Police School in Al-Oha.

1 October: Direct telephone links between the UAE and Saudi Arabia, Hong Kong and Singapore were inaugurated.

2 October: Sheikh Rashid bin Saeed Al Maktoum and the Omani Interior, Minister Badr bin Saud, completed discussions with regard to the demarcation of borders between the two countries.

8 October: Sheikh Khalifa bin Zayed al Nahyan passed a local law forming the National Maritime Dredging Company (NMDC) with a capital of 60 million dirhams.

13 October: Contracts for the construction of two overpasses in Al-Ain were signed by Sheikh Tahnoun bin Mohammad Al Nahyan.

14 October: Sheikh Zayed began an one-week inspection tour of agricultural and development projects in the Western Region.

15 October: Sheikh Rashid donated 20 million dirhams to the Palestine National Fund.

20 October: Sheikh Sultan bin Mohammed Al Qassimi opened Sharjah's Humanitarian Services City.

21 October: Construction of 1200 prefabricated houses in Al-Ain and Abu Dhabi was approved by the Executive Council. ADFAED signed an agreement for a loan of 16 million dirhams to finance a hydroelectric project in Madagascar.

22 October: The Council of Ministers, to assist with accommodation problems, approved the allocation of 200 million dirhams for the immediate start of a project to grant loans to citizens to build private villas. The Council also decided to allocate other funds annually for granting interest-free loans to citizens to be paid back over a period of 30 years. Sheikh Zayed received Said Ahmed Said, a UAE youth who had won the World Chess Championships for beginners which was held in Mexico.

24 October: Sheikh Saqr bin Mohammad Al Qassimi sent a letter to Sheikh Khalifa bin Zayed Al Nahyan setting out his agreement to finalize measures leading to the amalgamation of the Ras al-Khaimah Second Brigade (to be known as the Second Badr Brigade) with formations of the UAE Armed Forces.

27 October: Sheikh Zayed performed the *Umra* immediately after his arrival in the Holy City of Makkah before embarking on the rites of pilgrimage. He also had discussions with King Khalid bin Abdulaziz on the current Arab situation and preparations for an Arab Summit Conference to be convened in Tunis on 20 November.

28 October: A report prepared by the Ministry of Planning stated that the average *per capita* share of GDP was 62,200 dirhams for 1978 in comparison to 63,000 in 1977.

8 November: The Holiday Inn Hotel in Khor Fakkan was opened by Sheikh Sultan bin Mohammad Al Qassimi.

10 November: Sheikh Hamad bin Mohammad Al Sharqi opened the new Telephone Exchange in Fujairah, the first of its kind in the country.

14 November: The Supreme Council approved the creation of a Central Bank, after Sheikh Zayed and Sheikh Rashid had agreed to replace UAE Currency Board with a Central Bank.

16 November: Sheikh Hamdan bin Mohammad Al Nahyan opened Zayed Sports City in Abu Dhabi where the qualifying games for the Asian Cup were held.

19 November: Sheikh Zayed arrived in Tunis to participate in the meetings of the tenth Arab Summit Conference.

The Council of Ministers approved the allocation of 92.2 million dirhams as a general reserve for the budget to meet the expansion in medical, information and auditing services.

2 November: Sheikh Zayed returned from Tunis after participating in the tenth Arab Summit during which he held private meetings with a number of Arab leaders concerning the strengthening of the common Arab stance.

24 November: Sheikh Rashid opened the Dubai Cable Company in Jebel Ali.

26 November: The Ministry of Agriculture and Fisheries decided to extend the Zayed glasshouse vegetable production project on a country-wide basis.

28 November: The new session of the Federal National Council was opened by Sheikh Rashid who stressed his determination to support the Federation.

Sheikh Rashid also paid a short visit to Saudi Arabia during which he discussed current Arab developments and a number of matters of mutual concern with the Saudi monarch.

1 December: Sheikh Saqr bin Mohammed Al Qassimi decided to merge Ras al-Khaimah's communications facilities with EMIRTEL.

4 December: ADFAED granted an 80 million dirham loan to finance iron mining in the Jebel al-Ghain area of Mauritania.

5 December: Sheikh Rashid bin Humaid Al Nuaimi opened the First Gulf Bank in Ajman. It was capitalized at 120 million dirhams.

8 December: Sheikh Hamdan bin Rashid Al Maktoum, in a speech at the opening of Dubai Municipality's new 80 million dirham building, commended the UAE President and the members of the Supreme Council of the Federation for making the municipalities the show-case of civic progress.

10 December: The Council of Ministers raised the upper limit on loans to national fishermen from 50,000 to 70,000 dirhams.

Dubai fish market in 1978.

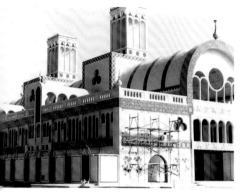

The final murals are painted on Sharjah souk in 1978.

Sheikh Hamdan opens the Dubai World Trade Centre, 29 October 1978.

Bur Dubai and the beginnings of high rise construction in 1978.

Construction of the first Currency Board - Central Bank building, 1978.

Farmers were still living in palm-frond barasti houses in the eastern emirates .

Sharjah overcame an accommodation shortage in 1978 with the Grand Flotel.

Wind towers in Bur Dubai in 1978.

A VIP motorcade inaugurates the DUBAL pot-room in 1978.

Hydroponic cultivation.

HUTCHISON LIBRARY

H.M. Queen Elizabeth II visited the UAE in 1979.

H.H. Sheikh Zayed addressing citizens of the UAE on 19 March 1979 to explain his decision not to stand for a new term as President of the UAE.

With farmers in 1979.

In the Liwa in 1979.

Sheikh Zayed waters recently p

Sheikh Zayed during a visit to the Liwa in 1979.

in 1979.

Sheikh Zayed studies an array of Liwa grown produce in 1979.

HELEN RODGERS

Ras al-Khaimah's cement factory in 1979.

ASPECT

The new port of Jebel Ali in February 1980.

ED MULLIS/ASPECT

Dubai creek in 1979.

The President of Guinea and Sheikh Zayed inspect troops in March 1979.

Sheikh Zayed's visit to Libya in September 1979.

Cargo is piled up on Dubai's creekside harbour in 1980.

Sheikh Zayed talking to students on Delma. 7 September 1980.

Pouring aluminium at Dubal in 1980.

Dubai's new cement works at Jebel Ali industrial zone, in July 1980.

The DUGAS complex in 1980.

Sheikh Zayed with Ali Nasser Mohammad, the then President of the Democratic Republic of South Yemen, on 4 March 1980.

The President of Senegal brought a mission to visit the UAE in September 1980.

Sheikh Zayed meets with other Heads of States at the Arab Summit in Jordan, held during November 1980.

Sheikh Zayed with Siyad Barre, the President of Somalia in 1980.

Sheikh Zayed visits a water irrigation project in the Liwa in 1980.

Exploration for new water resources around Al-Ain led to this discovery, photographed on 17 May 1980.

Abu Dhabi Sheraton Hotel was opened by Sheikh Ahmed bin Hamid.

21 December: Work began on connecting Sharjah and Ajman's electrical grid.

22 December: Sheikh Zayed led a large delegation to Saudi Arabia for discussions with King Khalid bin Abdulaziz covering relations between the two countries and the current Arab and Gulf situation.

24 December: Federal Council of Ministers agreed to contribute 5.9 million dollars to the Arab Fund for Economic and Social Development.

25 December: The ministerial budget committee confirmed a federal budget of approximately 12 billion dirhams for 1980.

29 December: The new Al-Ain Government Hospital was opened by Sheikh Tahnoun bin Mohammad Al Nahyan.

Sheikh Ahmed bin Hamid attended the opening of the Port Sudan highway which was financed by the UAE.

30 December: The UAE condemned Soviet military intervention in Afghanistan which it considered to be a shameful interference in the internal affairs of the Afghani people.

Assistant Judge Ali Abdulla, the first UAE citizen to be appointed a federal judge, took the legal oath of office before Mohammad Abdulrahman Al Bakr, the Minister of Justice, Islamic Affairs and Awqaf.

Nineteen Eighty

3 January: EMIRTEL allocated 300 million dirhams for developing communications services.

Abu Dhabi Marine Areas Operating Company produced its billionth barrel of oil from the Zakum No. 2 offshore field, the second largest offshore oil field in the world after the Al-Safeena field in Saudi Arabia.

7 January: Sheikh Rashid bin Saeed Al Maktoum received Sheikh Surour bin Mohammad Al Nahyan who announced after the meeting that an agreement had been reached on the draft law setting-up the first Central Bank in the Emirates.

Abu Dhabi Executive Council decided to construct the Jebel al-Dhanna hotel.

10 January: The Federation of Chambers of Commerce in the country issued a periodical economic magazine under the name *Afaq Iqtisadiyya* .

12 January: Sheikh Khalifa bin Zayed Al Nahyan ordered the construction of underpasses at heavily populated intersections on Al-Ain-Dubai highway in order to protect pedestrians and facilitate the flow of traffic.

Sheikh Tahnoun bin Mohammad Al Nahyan inspected plans for the new airport at Al-Ain.

13 January: Sheikh Khalifa bin Zayed Al Nahyan and Sheikh Tahnoun paid a fact-finding visit to the suggested site of the new international airport in the Al-Yahar district of Al-Ain.

14 January: The Council of Ministers allocated 2 million dirhams to the budget of the Secretariat General of Municipalities in 1980.

15 January: Sheikh Khalifa bin Zayed Al Nahyan issued an Amiri decree forming the Board of Administration of the National Dredging Company which was capitalized at 60 million dirhams.

19 January: Sheikh Rashid bin Saeed Al Maktoum donated 1 million dollars in aid to the Pakistani Government for assistance to Afghan refugees.

A number of local merchants in Abu Dhabi also donated 1.5 million dirhams in aid to Afghan refugees.

20 January: Palestinian-Japanese dialogue began in Abu Dhabi under the auspices of the UAE.

22 January: The Federal National Council approved a draft law governing the legal profession.

23 January: It was decided to issue new unified drivers licences and car ownership documents country-wide from 1 February.

24 January: Sheikh Doctor Sultan bin Mohammad Al Qassimi issued a new Sharjah law governing the Chamber of Commerce and Industry.

26 January: According to a population estimate by the Ministry of Planning, on 31 December 1979 the UAE population was 891,590, 71 per cent of whom were male and 29 per cent female.

27 January: The Executive Council approved the 1980 development budget for Abu Dhabi amounting to 7.453 billion dirhams.

28 January: Said Ghobash opened the Meridien Hotel in Abu Dhabi.

29 January: During the previous year, 91 nationals graduated from Arab and foreign universities whilst 381 nationals continued graduate studies abroad.

1 February: Three hundred and eighty-one mosques were built in Abu Dhabi between the end of 1974 and the beginning of 1979.

4 February: The Supreme Council of the Federation issued a decree establishing a committee to examine the sites and distribution of public housing units and to lay down a comprehensive housing policy for the Federation.

6 February: The Oil Department in Sharjah announced the discovery of the first gas well in the western offshore waters of the emirate.

8 February: Sheikh Zayed and the Venezuelan President, Louis Hererra, who arrived in the country on an official visit, discussed the international oil market.

9 February: The final communiqué on the results of the meeting between Sheikh Zayed and the visiting Venezuelan President called for joint efforts on the part of the UAE and Venezuela to arrive at a unified system of oil pricing.

Sheikh Zayed held a meeting with officials of the Department of Works in Abu Dhabi, during which he was briefed with models on a number of excavation and reclamation projects, including the Abu al-Abyad Island canal project and reclamation projects on the islands of Umm al-Nar and Al-Salimiyya.

The first issue of the magazine *Diplomacy* was published by the Ministry of External Affairs.

11 February: The Council of Ministers asked for an immediate inquiry into the reasons for a rise in the price of oil derivatives in the Northern Emirates.

In 1979, 1737 public housing units were built in Abu Dhabi at a cost of 201 million dirhams. The sum of 473 million dirhams was allocated for new housing projects in 1980.

Sheikh Humaid bin Rashid Al Nuaimi demanded that petrol marketing operations in the Northern Emirates be taken over by a national company to end shortages and price hikes by foreign companies.

16 February: The Executive Council approved loans to the National Food Company in Abu Dhabi amounting to 40 million dirhams to help control the prices of foodstuffs.

17 February: The First Lady, Sheikha Fatima bint Mubarak, opened the Al-Ain branch of the Abu Dhabi Women's Association.

18 February: Sheikh Zayed, meeting with students at UAE University, announced that he had asked ADNOC to prepare an immediate report on fuel price increases and to find an appropriate solution to the the problem.

19 February: Sheikh Zayed allocated 200 million dirhams to subsidize the price of petroleum products in the Northern Emirates.

20 February: Sheikh Zayed toured Al-Shuwaib region where he inspected the date gardens and public housing. He issued directives to increase the number of houses in the two villages of Al-Heer and Al-Shuwaib.

Sheikh Rashid issued directives to the parties concerned to exempt petroleum products entering the country through Dubai Ports from all taxes.

A huge project to plant 50,000 trees in a green belt encircling the city of Sharjah commenced.

22 February: During an inspection of 90 farms in Al-Wajn district, Sheikh Zayed stressed that: 'Wealth is the tool which is used for achieving comfort and ease for the citizens, and there is no value to money if it is not put to use in the service of the people in order to bring them a high standard of living'.

Mohammad Khalifa Al Kindi announced that 1400 new public housing units would be constructed in 1980 in all parts of the Federation.

23 February: Sheikh Khalifa bin Zayed Al Nahyan issued a decree reserving a number of military air transport planes to transport aid to Iranian flood victims. The first consignment of aid arrived on this date in the Al-Ahwaz area in the Iranian Khuzistan district.

25 February: The Council of Ministers, in addition to assistance to the Northern Emirate, agreed to allocate 450 million dirhams in petroleum product subsidies for the whole country.

26 February: Sheikh Rashid signed a new agreement with the Arco-Dubai Company Ltd to explore for oil onshore in Dubai.

1 March: The foundation stone was laid for the Arab Currency Board building on the Corniche in Abu Dhabi.

2 March: Sheikh Hamad bin Mohammad Al Sharqi opened the Gulf Agency Company Ltd in Fujairah, which will provide marine services to ships and tankers passing through the Arabian Gulf.

Mana Said Al Otaiba said that UAE oil reserves were much bigger than had been previously reported.

5 March: Sheikh Zayed and the Members of the Supreme Council of the Federation, received the French President, Giscard d'Estaing, who arrived in the country on his first official visit. The French President expressed his happiness with Sheikh Zayed who was the first leader in the Arab world to support France's call for a the three way dialogue between Arabs, Europe and Africa.

6 March: Discussions between Sheikh Zayed and President Giscard d'Estaing resulted in the signing of six co-operation agreements between the two countries in the fields of energy, agriculture and health.

Sheikh Khalifa bin Zayed Al Nahyan announced that the Emirates would provide France with all oil requirements in appreciation of the positive role it had played in supporting Arab rights.

9 March: The Executive Council approved a 50 million dirham extension to Abu Dhabi International Airport.

13 March: Following a meeting between Sheikh Zayed and Sheikh Rashid, a number of fundamental decrees were issued which were aimed at reinforcing the Federation. Among the most important of these was that the emirates of Abu Dhabi and Dubai would contribute 50 per cent of their annual oil income to the federal budget and agreement on the Central Bank Law.

Sheikh Humaid bin Rashid Al Nuaimi opened a new unit at the Masfoot Electricity plant.

14 March: Sheikh Rashid issued regulations governing the treatment of nationals outside the country.

15 March: Sheikh Rashid issued a decree separating the Office of Information from the Office of the Municipality which would be directed by Sheikh Hamdan bin Rashid Al Maktoum. Sheikh Hashar Al Maktoum was appointed Director of the Information Office in Dubai.

It was announced that Central Bank reserves would be more than 68 billion dirhams, of which 15 billion dirhams represented 50 per cent of Dubai's oil income as per 1979 estimates. This would be the first time that Dubai's oil revenue had gone into public funds. Abu Dhabi's 50 per cent share was estimated at 45 billion dirhams.

19 March: Sheikh Zayed visited the Ras al-Akhdar region of Abu Dhabi where he observed progress on the breakwater, tourism projects and fishing boat jetties.

20 March: Sheikh Zayed and Sheikh Rashid paid a short visit to Saudi Arabia where they met King Khalid bin Abdulaziz and the Crown Prince, Prince Fahad bin Abdulaziz.

Umm al-Qaiwain lagoon was chosen as headquarters for the regional centre for marine research. The Arab Ministers of Agriculture had recommended the Emirates as the centre's headquarters.

21 March: The Council of Ministers decided that citizens living in public housing units should own their homes and they allocated 50 million dirhams to pay 10,000 dirhams to each citizen for maintenance.

The Currency Board's annual report stated that the Federation's cash surplus stood at 2.5 billion dollars in 1979.

The Ministry of Electricity and Water announced that electrical power increased 28 times during the previous ten years.

22 March: Sheikh Zayed opened the permanent Heritage Exhibition at the Women's Federation in Abu Dhabi.

Sheikh Rashid issued a decree forming a new 33-member Dubai Municipality Council under the chairmanship of Sheikh Hamdan bin Rashid Al Maktoum.

In the 1980 budget, around 1898.3 million dirhams was allocated for investment. During 1979, this figure was 1154 million dirhams.

23 March: Sheikh Zayed, at the first assembly of the country's Secretariat General of Municipalities, stressed that the Federation must support each of the municipalities so that all parts of the Federation would benefit. He issued directives that priority must be given to public housing for citizens.

24 March: The Council of Ministers confirmed the Federation's budget for 1980 amounting to a total of 15.972 billion dirhams.

25 March: The UAE presented ten vehicles to the Lebanese security forces.

28 March: At the end of 1979, there were 31 airlines operating out of Abu Dhabi in comparison with six in 1970. Abu Dhabi International Airport received 60,870 passenger aeroplanes in 1980 in comparison to 9866 in 1970.

29 March: Sheikh Zayed issued a law giving ADNOC responsibility for the operation of ports at Al-Ruwais and Jebel al-Dhanna.

Sheikh Tahnoun bin Mohammad Al Nahyan opened the first exhibition of Islamic books at the UAE University.

It was decided to open an Information Department in the College of Arts of the UAE University during the next academic year.

31 March: The Council of Ministers approved the earmarking of 39 million dirhams as aid to the Federation's municipalities to help them play their role in serving citizens and raising the level of services.

The Executive Council granted ADNOC exploration and exploitation rights for hydrocarbons in both land and sea areas covering 34,547 sq. kms of territory.

2 April: Sheikh Zayed issued a federal law establishing the Secretariat General of Municipalities.

Said Al Ragbani visited Abu Musa Island to determine and fill the needs of the inhabitants, especially as regards marine motors and general fisheries requirements.

3 April: Sheikh Zayed inspected the new extension to the camel race course in Medina Bani Yas in preparation for the huge annual race to be held on 24 April.

4 April: It was decided to raise the maximum loan to fishermen for marine motors from 50,000 dirhams to 70,000 dirhams and for fishing equipment from 10,000 to 20,000. The total maximum loan available to fishermen was 150,000 dirhams, including 60,000 dirhams for fishing boat loans.

7 April: Sheikh Zayed during his visit to the Document and Studies Centre in Al-Husn Palace called for preservation of the heritage and civilization of the country.

Sheikh Zayed announced that he had accepted the resignation of Ahmed Khalifa Al Suweidi from his post as Minister of Foreign Affairs and praised the great role which he had played at local and international levels.

Sheikh Zayed inspected progress on the establishment of a cultural complex in Abu Dhabi.

Sheikh Hamad bin Mohammad Al Sharqi issued a decree forming the new Municipal Council in Fujairah to be composed of 16 members instead of nine. It will be presided over by Sheikh Hamad bin Saif Al Sharqi, the Deputy Governor.

9 April: Sheikh Rashid inaugurated the 266.7 million dollar expansion project at Port Rashid.

12 April: Sheikh Hamad bin Mohammad Al Sharqi opened the 4 million dirham leather and shoe factory in Fujairah, the first of its kind in the Emirates.

13 April: It was decided to expand and support telecommunications in the emirate of Ras al-Khaimah at a cost of 13 million dirhams.

14 April: The Executive Council approved the construction of a two-way highway between Turaif and Jebel al-Dhanna at a cost of 180 million dirhams.

18 April: The number of farms in the Al-Ain area increased from 290 in 1970 to 980 in 1979.

19 April: In 1979, Dubai's revenue was 16.7 billion dirhams, in comparison to 12.7 billion dirhams in 1978.

20 April: Sheikh Sultan bin Mohammad Al Qassimi issued a decree reducing Sharjah's price per kilowatt of electricity to 7.5 fils.

21 April: Sheikh Zayed issued the federal Labour Law.

22 April: Sheikh Rashid inaugurated the $400 million Dubai Natural Gas (DUGAS) liquefaction plant which would produce 55 million cubic feet of residue gas per day to fuel the Dubai Aluminium Company (DUBAL) plant.

25 April: Sheikh Zayed, the Members of the Supreme Council of the Federation, and guests from the Arab Gulf countries attended the first annual pure-bred Arab camel races at the Medina Bani Yas race course.

28 April: The Council of Ministers confirmed the draft Central Bank Law. Dubai Municipal Council allocated 270 million dirhams to build the largest water tank in Dubai in order to supply drinking water to the city, its surrounding areas and the Jebel Ali area.

2 May: It was decided to extend Dubai International Airport at a cost of 361 million dirhams. This would allow it to handle 50 per cent more passengers.

4 May: Sheikh Saqr bin Mohammad Al Qassimi attended ceremonies held in Idhn district to mark the commencement of drilling for oil on-land in the emirate of Ras al-Khaimah.

Two new societies were established, the Teachers Society and the Society of Osteopaths, the first of their kind in the Federation.

5 May: Sheikh Zayed issued a federal law regulating the practise of law in the Federation.

Sheikh Rashid opened the 500 million dirham Hyatt Regency Hotel in Dubai.

6 May: Dubai Municipal Council, for the first time, approved in principle a local partnership participation requirement for granting commercial licences whereby a local partner would have at least a 51 per cent share in a company.

7 May: Sheikh Saqr bin Mohammad Al Qassimi opened the Ras al-Khaimah Chicken and Feed project.

8 May: Sheikh Rashid bin Saeed Al Maktoum issued directives to lower rents by at least 20 per cent for houses managed by the Building Council and owned by Dubai Municipality.

Sheikh Rashid bin Humaid Al Nuaimi issued a decree forming the first municipal council in the emirate of Ajman under the chairmanship of Sheikh Humaid bin Rashid Al Nuaimi.

12 May: The Council of Ministers approved the Supreme Council for Youth and Sports draft law.

Saif Jarwan opened the new Bani Yas Co-operative Society.

14 May: The Council of Ministers decided to raise allocations for housing loans from 1 billion dirhams to 1.6 billion dirhams.

17 May: Sheikh Rashid ordered the building of 1000 public housing units in the Khazan district of Ras al-Khaimah at his private expense.

18 May: Sheikh Sultan bin Mohammad Al Qassimi opened a 10 million dirham chemicals factory for producing insulation materials, considered to be the first of its kind in the Middle East.

Sheikh Tahnoun bin Mohammad Al Nahyan and the French Oil Company for the Middle East signed a contract to establish a company, capitalized at 300 million dollars, for producing and marketing nitrogen fertilizers.

19 May: The Executive Council decided to decrease the cost of electricity in Abu Dhabi from 12 fils to 7 fils per kilowatt, effective from June.

20 May: Sheikh Zayed visited the Abu Dhabi Women's Association in Al-Bateen. He stressed the role of women and their importance in the renaissance of society.

Sheikh Zayed arrived in Falaj al-Mualla at the beginning of a tour of the Northern Emirates.

Sheikh Rashid gave 8 million dirhams to support the organization caring for the families of Palestinian martyrs and fighters.

21 May: Sheikh Zayed, at the beginning of his tour of the Emirates, met with all the Members of the Supreme Council of the Federation and studied with them matters concerning national action and ways for supporting the federal future.

Sheikh Tahnoun bin Mohammad Al Nahyan signed a co-operation agreement between ADNOC and ESSO, whereby ADNOC took over for the first time the supply of fuel to aeroplanes at Abu Dhabi airport.

26 May: The Council of Ministers approved a comprehensive plan for the electrification of all the villages in the Northern Emirates.

A sum of 5 million dirhams was ear-marked for supporting women's societies and handicraft industries.

Forty six demonstrators (male and female) from the UAE were appointed to UAE University.

27 May: Sheikh Zayed and the Kenyan President, Daniel Arap Moi, who arrived in the country on his first official visit, discussed bilateral relations and the situation in the Gulf.

Sheikh Rashid ordered the immediate commencement of construction on the new 300-bed hospital in Fujairah, as well as 100-bed extensions to the Khor Fakkan and Dibba hospitals.

28 May: The Executive Council approved the establishment of a Municipal Council for the city of Abu Dhabi.

29 May: Sheikh Saqr bin Mohammad Al Qassimi signed a second agreement for oil exploration in the offshore area located 5 miles off the coast of Ras al-Khaimah.

31 May: Humaid Nasser Al Nowais signed a contract to import and install 40 water tanks in various parts of the Federation.

1 June: Sheikh Zayed, continuing his tour of the Northern Emirates visited Ajman where he opened the Ajman television production studios.

The Executive Council approved the setting-up of two major centres in Abu Dhabi and Al-Ain for marketing agricultural produce at a cost of 16 million dirhams.

2 June: Sheikh Zayed, during a tour of the emirate of Sharjah, met with the Members of the Supreme Council of the Federation, the Governors of the Emirates. The meeting took place in Government House in Sharjah.

The Armed Forces honoured General Awwad Al Khalidi, Chairman of the Chiefs of Staff in the UAE.

5 June: It was decided to increase the capital of the UAE-Sudanese Investment Company by 50 million dollars.

7 June: Sheikh Zayed, during his inspection trip to Dubai, met with Sheikh Rashid and exchanged points of view regarding affairs concerning the nation and its citizens.

Sheikh Zayed issued an order excusing all farmers and fishermen from repayment of loans which were granted to them by the Ministry of Agriculture up until the current month of June.

9 June: Sheikh Zayed concluded his two-week inspection tour of the Northern Emirates. He expressed great pleasure and pride at his on-going meetings with his brothers, the Members of the Supreme Council of the Federation, and groups of citizens everywhere in the Federation.

The Council of Ministers approved the transformation of EMIRTEL into a 100 per cent national company.

11 June: Sheikh Zayed issued federal decrees accepting the resignation of General Awwad Al Khalidi as Chairman of the Chiefs of Staff of the Armed Forces and appointing him as military adviser to the President with the rank of Minister.

Sheikh Khalifa bin Zayed Al Nahyan opened the petrochemical products and marine services factory on Al-Sadiyyat Island.

12 June: Sheikh Rashid and Sheikh Hamad bin Mohammad Al Sharqi toured the emirate of Fujairah and visited dam sites in Wadi Ham.

15 June: Sheikh Zayed arrived on Sir Bani Yas at the beginning of a tour of the islands.

Sheikh Hamdan bin Rashid Al Maktoum opened the new power and desalination plant in Jebel Ali.

16 June: The Council of Ministers allocated 7.6 million dirhams to import agricultural requirements for this year.

18 June: Sheikh Khalifa bin Zayed Al Nahyan issued a decree reducing the interest owed by the owners of real estate guaranteed by him from 5.5 per cent to 2 per cent, with 20 per cent of the annual rents instead of 10 per cent to be paid to the owners.

Dubai Municipal Council approved a budget of 708.7 million dirhams for the municipality for 1980.

23 June: The Council of Ministers approved the creation of new Ministry of Electricity and Water projects amounting to 231 million dirhams in the Northern Emirates over the following three years.

26 June: Fujairah Municipal Council approved a 25 million dirham budget for the municipality for 1980.

1 July: Sheikh Zayed held official discussions with the Yemeni President, Ali Nasser Mohammad, who was visiting the country. During the meeting, the two Presidents confirmed the necessity of maintaining the security and stability of the Arabian Gulf region and keeping it free from international conflict.

2 July: It was decided to reserve all of the 20 per cent foreign shareholding in EMIRTEL for subscription by UAE nationals.

6 July: Sheikh Tahnoun bin Mohammad Al Nahyan signed a 200 million dollar contract with two Japanese companies to build a petrochemical fertilizer production complex in Al-Ruwais.

7 July: UAE, Saudi Arabia, Kuwait, Bahrain, Qatar, Iraq and Iran agreed to establish a regional organization for Gulf countries to protect the marine environment and combat pollution. The headquarters of the organization (ROPME) will be in Kuwait.

9 July: The UAE University signed a co-operation agreement with the Sorbónne in Paris.

10 July: Sheikh Zayed ended his tour of the Western Region with a visit to the Centre for the Memorization of the Holy Qur'an in Liwa. He encouraged students at the centre to hold fast to the principles of the Islamic religion stressing that knowledge and faith are the path to progress and prosperity.

14 July: Work began on construction of the Al-Ain International Airport which will cost 520 million dirhams.

19 July: A report by the Ministry of Education stated that on average the State paid 13,533 dirhams annually in expenses for each student.

21 July: The Executive Council approved a huge project for building an electricity and desalination plant in Al-Tawila district costing between 30 to 35 billion dirhams.

22 July: Sheikh Zayed opened the second Islamic book exhibition organized by the Abu Dhabi Women's Association.

27 July: Sheikh Saqr bin Mohammad Al Qassimi decreed the creation of a new company in Ras al-Khaimah, Sahil Development and Investment Company, with capitalization of 70 million dollars for intra-emirate and overseas investment and commercial activities.

28 July: The Council of Ministers approved the allocation of 30 million dirhams to support and aid Islamic societies, boards and centres.

29 July: Sheikh Rashid ordered the construction of 40 mosques at his own expense in the emirates of Ras al-Khaimah, Ajman, Umm al-Qaiwain and Fujairah.

31 July: Sheikh Rashid donated 6.6 million dirhams to set up an Arab Gulf region studies centre at Oxford University.

The Executive Council allocated 181.4 million dirhams as compensation for citizens in Abu Dhabi whose homes were affected by development planning projects.

1 August: Sheikh Zayed issued the UAE Central Bank Law.

5 August: Between 1972 and 1979, the UAE extended 6300 million dirhams in aid to Arab and other countries.

7 August: The UAE decided to sever relations with any country responding to Israel's call to transfer its embassy to occupied Jerusalem.

8 August: Since its establishment in 1971, ADFAED loaned 4716 million dirhams for financing 85 economic projects in a number of Arab, African and Asian countries.

16 August: In an official statement, the UAE announced that it was placing all its resources at the disposal of the united Arab Islamic decree for a holy *Jihad*. It called for all Arabs and Muslims to reconsider their relations with powers which supported Zionist aggression in the occupied Arab territories.

17 August: Sheikh Zayed in a statement to the press called for the holding of an Arab summit to unite Arab leadership and an Islamic conference to debate the question of Jerusalem and Zionist settlements.

25 August: The Council of Ministers approved the earmarking of 28 million dirhams to augment the amount allocated to social assistance in the budget. It also endorsed an announcement delimiting the maritime boundaries of the continental shelf and establishing an exclusive economic zone.

The UAE University allocated 20 scholarships for Palestinians for the next academic year.

There were 252 schools in the country at the end of the previous academic year, of which 110 were for boys and 97 for girls, 40 were mixed kindergartens.

29 August: Sheikh Rashid bin Saeed Al Maktoum built 1644 public housing units in Ras al-Khaimah.

During the period 1975 to 1980, the number of farms in Abu Dhabi rose from 744 to 970, covering an area of 42,000 dunams.

30 August: Sheikh Tahnoun bin Mohammed Al Nahyan signed an agreement setting-up a chicken farm in Al-Saad district.

31 August: At the private expense of Sheikh Rashid, work began on the construction of 40 kms of sidewalks on a number of streets in the city of Kalba.

Based on the President's directives, Abu Dhabi Executive Council allocated 26 million dirhams to set up 180 farms in the Northern Emirates.

1 September: The Council of Ministers approved the establishment of a national energy committee and the formation of a public company to take over the distribution of petroleum products.

The 1980 general budget for the city of Al-Ain amounted to 898.6 million dirhams.

3 September: Sheikh Ahmed bin Hamid opened the Juba Sugar Factory in southern Sudan to which the UAE had contributed 78 million dollars.

8 September: The Council of Ministers decided to increase monthly allowances for graduate students studying outside the country, and to increase the item in the budget covering allocations for social assistance to citizens.

9 September: Sheikh Zayed, at the end of his inspection of the Western Region, ordered the allocation of half a million dirhams as a loan to establish a consumers co-operative society and another half a million dirham loan to strengthen the fisheries and transportation company on Delma. During his tour, Zayed inspected the agricultural and development projects underway on the two islands of Sir Bani Yas and Delma and in Al-Dhafra district.

10 September: The UAE extended loans to the Democratic Republic of Yemen consisting of 30 million dollars to finance Aden electricity and 60 million dollars to set up the Nashtoon fishing port.

11 September: Sheikh Rashid bin Ahmad Al Mualla opened the new extension to the Falaj al-Mualla electricity plant.

12 September: ADFAED extended 1345 million dollars in the form of loans and assistance to developing countries, estimated to be nearly 20 per cent of the national product for the year 1978-79.

14 September: Sheikh Rashid visited Ras al-Khaimah during which he inspected the new Saqr Hospital, the Saif bin

Ghobash Hospital and a number of projects which had been established on his orders.

15 September: Sheikh Zayed and the Senegalese President, Leopold Sedar Senghor who was officially visiting the country, discussed Arab-African relations. Zayed also briefed the visitor on the Arabic language educational project in Senegal.

The Council of Ministers affirmed the Publications and Distribution Law.

17 September: Ahmed Al-Madfa attended the first meeting of the founding committee of the Al-Mahd Al-Tayyiba Society.

Heavy rains which fell on the country led to the cutting of telephone connections between Fujairah and the UAE and the outside world.

21 September: Tahnoun bin Mohammad Al Nahyan signed an agreement to expand the Umm al-Nar oil refinery in order to increase its capacity from 15,000 barrels per day to 75,000 barrels per day.

25 September: The Ministry of Labour and Social Affairs issued a decree announcing the formation of the Society of Lawyers.

27 September: Sheikh Zayed and Sheikh Rashid held a meeting attended by Sheikh Mohammad bin Rashid Al Maktoum, during which current regional developments in light of the eruption of war between Iraq and Iran were discussed.

28 September: The Executive Council allocated 26 million dirhams for planting trees and shrubbery on 1500 hectares in the emirate of Abu Dhabi.

29 September: Sheikh Zayed issued a federal law setting-up the first development planning board in the country.

1 October: Sheikh Saqr bin Mohammad Al Qassimi stressed that the question of the Iranian occupation of the three islands was the responsibility of the federal Government and not that of Ras al-Khaimah emirate.

2 October: The commencement of pumping from the Dubai Aluminum Company desalination plant in Jebel Ali to Dubai city water network was celebrated.

Sheikh Saqr bin Mohammad Al Qasimi said that the UAE requested the return of the islands of Greater and Lesser Tunbs and Abu Musa from Iran. 'Our request is simple. The Emirates want to see the islands restored to their rightful owners - in this case the Emirates - as soon as possible ...'.

In August, Minister of State for Foreign Affairs, Rashid bin Abdullah Al Nuaimi, had sent a letter of protest to UN Secretary General Kurt Waldheim that Iran '... continue(s) its occupation of the three Arab islands of Abu Musa, Greater Tunb and Lesser Tunb'. Al Nuaimi also expressed his hope that Iran would correct '... the situation born of the expansionist ambitions of the Shah's regime on the internal and external level'.

5 October: Sheikh Zayed presented to the museum in Al-Ain a rare manuscript of a letter from the Prophet (PBUH) to the Amir of Bahrain, Mundhir bin Sari, calling him to obey the Book of Allah. Zayed received the manuscript as a present from Sheikh Essa bin Salman Al Khalifa, the Amir of Bahrain.

6 October: The Council of Ministers approved the draft law changing the Development Bank to the Real Estate Bank, the first in the country.

7 October: Sheikh Rashid bin Saeed Al Maktoum ordered the construction of 231 public housing units at Al-Gheel and Wadi al-Kafar in Ras al-Khaimah.

12 October: Sheikh Zayed ordered that a medical mission be sent to Algeria to aid earthquake victims in the city of Al-Asnam. He also announced a three-day mourning period in the UAE.

13 October: Sheikh Khalifa bin Zayed Al Nahyan signed two concession agreements for oil exploration, one with a Canadian company and the other with an American company. The two companies will spend 125.5 million dollars during the first ten years of the concession.

14 October: Sheikh Zayed issued the law setting-up the Fertilizer Manufacturing Company in Al-Ruwais with a capital of 75 million dollars.

Sheikh Hamdan bin Rashid Al Maktoum opened the 250 million dirham Chicago Beach Hotel in Dubai.

16 October: Sheikh Sultan bin Mohammad Al Qassimi opened the Golden Tourist Motel in Sharjah.

26 October: The Executive Council approved the purchase of a 40 per cent French shareholding in the Al-Ain Vegetable Production Company to turn it into a 100 percent national company.

27 October: The Council of Ministers allocated 15.19 million dirhams to establish handicapped training in the UAE.

2 November: Abu Dhabi Executive Council approved the 227 million dirham Western Region sewage project in Medinat Zayed.

EMIRTEL made 20 million dirhams profit in 1979.

The Public Housing Committee approved the distribution of 70 houses to citizens in Khor Kalba, Sharjah.

3 November: The Council of Ministers approved the draft law forming the Emirates General Petroleum Corporation (EGPC) with a capital of 400 million dirhams to sell petrol in the Northern Emirates, instead of the foreign companies already present there and to market and sell petroleum products across the Federation.

4 November: Sheikh Zayed issued a law establishing the Gulf Aircraft Maintenance Company in Abu Dhabi.

5 November: ADFAED agreed to loan the Sudan 103 million dollars for construction of Khartoum's International Airport;

6 November: ADFAED agreed to loan Mauritania 6.3 million dollars for an agricultural development project.

9 November: The Executive Council approved the setting-up of the first pedestrian tunnel on Hamdan Street in Abu Dhabi at a cost of 10 million dirhams.

11 November: Sheikh Sultan bin Mohammad Al Qassimi opened the Sanitary Ware Factory in Sharjah.

16 November: Sheikh Zayed issued the Publications and Distribution Law.

17 November: The Council of Ministers raised the capital of the Emirates General Petroleum Corporation from 400 million to 800 million dirhams. It also approved the 30 million dirham electrical energy project in rural areas of the Northern Emirates.

The Currency Board decided to raise interest on dirham deposits by 1 per cent in all the banks in the country.

It was decided to set-up the first blood bank for the Northern Emirates in Dubai.

18 November: ADFAED agreed to loan 1.1 million dollars to Cape Verde Islands off West Africa for a fishing project.

19 November: Sheikh Hamad bin Mohammad laid the foundation stone for the 350 million dirham Fujairah Cement Factory in Dibba.

22 November: Sheikh Zayed, opening the new session of the Supreme Council of the Federation, stressed the importance of supporting the future of the Federation to provide a better life for citizens. He called for the warring parties in Iraq and Iran to stop shedding Muslim blood and to move towards peace and prosperity for all the peoples of the region.

The Civil Aviation Department in Abu Dhabi signed an agreement to install an electronic network for serving passengers and aeroplanes at Abu Dhabi International Airport.

24 November: Sheikh Zayed arrived in Amman at the head of the UAE delegation to the eleventh Arab Summit Conference.

25 November: Sheikh Zayed attended the extended meeting held at the residence of the Iraqi President, Saddam Hussein. Included in the meeting were the leaders of the Arab Gulf States participating in the Arab Summit Conference, King Hussein of Jordan, and the Yemeni President, Ali Abdulla Saleh. They considered developments in the Gulf region and matters being studied by the Summit Conference.

Sheikh Sultan bin Mohammad Al Qassimi signed a new agreement with an Australian company to explore for oil in Sharjah's territorial waters opposite Kalba, Khor Fakkan and Dibba.

27 November: Sheikh Zayed returned to the country after participating in the final session of the eleventh Arab Summit Conference in Amman. He said that Arab differences must be contained and that the greater Arab national interest must be placed above all considerations.

29 November: Sheikh Zayed issued the law setting up the Emirates General Petroleum Corporation.

30 November: Dr Mana Said Al Otaiba attended the ceremonies marking the exporting of the one hundredth shipment of liquid gas from the gas liquefaction factory on Das Island to Japan.

2 December: Sheikh Zayed received the Members of the Supreme Council of the Federation, their Heirs Apparent, and crowds of well-wishers on the occasion of the ninth National Day.

4 December: Sheikh Zayed and Sheikh Saqr bin Mohammad Al Qassimi visited Al-Bureidat and Wadi al-Beeh in Ras al-Khaimah where they chose a suitable site to construct one of the dams in the Wadi al-Beeh area.

7 December: It was announced that oil and gas had been discovered in commercial quantities in the Al-Saja land area in Sharjah emirate.

The Federation's 1980 oil revenues amounted to around 68.25 million dirhams.

8 December: The Council of Ministers fixed the capital of the Real Estate Bank at 2 billion dirhams. The Council also approved the decree appointing Dr Izzedine Ibrahim as the rector of the UAE University, replacing Dr Abdulaziz Al Bassam.

9 December: Sheikh Sultan bin Mohammad Al Qassimi issued a decree appointing Sheikh Ahmed bin Sultan Al Qassimi as Chairman of the Oil and Minerals Department in Sharjah.

11 December: The UAE, in a letter to the General Assembly of the United Nations, called on the international community to take action to return the Greater and Lesser Tunb and Abu Musa islands to complete UAE sovereignty. It also called on the Iranian Government of Iran to enter into serious negotiations to put an end to this problem and return what the former Shah took by force from its original owners.

12 December: Dr Mana Said Al Otaiba signed an agreement to extend the grain silos and flour mills increasing their capacity from 200 to 400 tons per day.

13 December: Saif Al Jarwan issued a decree establishing the first two self-contained accident units in Abu Dhabi and Sharjah.

20 December: Sheikh Rashid bin Saeed Al Maktoum issued a decree forming the Supreme Committee for Combating Illiteracy and Adult Education under the chairmanship of the Minister of Education.

UAE and India agreed to create several joint venture projects including a 12 million tons per year oil refinery - the largest in India - and to increase levels of trade. In addition, UAE agreed to increase levels of oil exports to India by 500,000 tons per year to a total of 1.5 million tons per year. India faced potential oil shortages as a result of the Iran-Iraq War.

22 December: The Council of Ministers approved the formation of the Board of Administration of the Central Bank under the chairmanship of Sheikh Surour bin Mohammad Al Nahyan with Abdulmalik Al Kaz as his deputy. Abdulmalik Al Hamar was appointed Governor.

Work began on establishing the Central Laboratory in the Federation at a cost of 50 million dirhams.

23 December: Sheikh Zayed issued a federal decree creating new projects for the Ministry of Water and Electricity at a cost of 49 million dirhams.

24 December: Sheikh Zayed paid a visit to the Al-Ain office of the Abu Dhabi Women's Association.

28 December: The Board of the Central Bank held its first meeting under the chairmanship of Sheikh Surour bin Mohammad Al Nahyan during which designs for the new 500-dirham bank notes were considered.

31 December: Sheikh Zayed made a tour of the dam region in Ras al-Khaimah.

Nineteen Eighty One

3 January: Sheikh Rashid bin Saeed Al Maktoum inaugurated the oil derivative distribution plant at Jebel Ali as well as the commencement of Emirates General Petroleum Corporation's oil marketing operations in the Northern Emirates.

The Federal Ministry of Petroleum proposed an increase in petrol subsidies to the Northern Emirates from 400 million dirhams to 1.2 billion dirhams.

Sheikh Sultan bin Mohammad Al Qassimi opened the Hilwan Station in Sharjah.

UAE's population at the end of 1980, after the federation's second census, was 1,040,275.

4 January: New stations for the Emirates General Petroleum Corporation were opened in Ras al-Khaimah and Umm al-Qaiwain.

Abu Dhabi Executive Council approved construction of the 5 million dirham municipality building on the island of Delma.

The first public members meeting of the Abu Dhabi Co-operative Society was convened.

6 January: The Supreme Council of the Federation expressed its support for the diplomatic efforts by the Government to confirm the sovereignty and return of the three islands belonging to the UAE, the Greater and Lesser Tunbs and Abu Musa, which Iran had occupied in 1971.

7 January: Fatal traffic accidents claimed the lives of 2379 people in the previous four years (1976-79); 13,987 were also injured in 48,799 traffic accidents.

8 January: Abu Dhabi Executive Council decided to increase the capital of ADNOC from 200 million dirhams to 7500 dirhams. During the previous seven years (1973-79), the company's profits amounted to 16 billion dirhams.

9 January: Sheikh Sultan bin Mohammed Al Qassimi funded the total annual budget of the Al-Samoud Children's House of the Palestinian Tel Al-Zaatar Foundation, amounting to 254,000 Lebanese liras. This will be an annual donation.

12 January: Sheikh Saqr bin Mohammad Al Qassimi, returning to the country after a visit to Bahrain and Qatar, announced that the Iranian occupation of the three islands would be tabled at the Islamic Summit Conference to be held in Saudi Arabia on 25 January.

13 January: Abu Dhabi Executive

Council issued a decree cancelling the supervisory committee for commercial buildings and the Development Loan Establishment. A new organization known as the Commercial Buildings Department will take their place within the Social Services Department.

Sheikh Tahnoun bin Mohammad Al Nahyan signed contracts to build three 27,500-ton oil tankers.

15 January: ADFAED agreed to loan 37.5 million dirhams to North Yemen to assist in an electricity project.

17 January: ADMA-OPCO Company celebrated production of the millionth barrel of oil from the Umm al-Shaif field, the oldest producing field in the Emirates.

19 January: Sheikh Humaid bin Rashid Al Nuaimi ordered the construction of 200 houses in Al-Zahra district which will be distributed to low income families from the islands.

21 January: ADFAED agreed to loan 30 million dollars to South Yemen for a power station project.

24 January: Sheikh Zayed, arriving in Taif at the head of the UAE's delegation to participate in the Islamic Summit Conference, stressed that he was confident that the conference would succeed in arriving at decisions which would serve Islam and Muslims.

28 January: Sheikh Khalifa opened the Arzana offshore oil field.

The UAE declared its support for the establishment of an Islamic world development fund with a proposed capital of 3 billion dollars by donating 500 million dollars to the fund.

29 January: Sheikh Zayed, returning to the country after participating in the Islamic Summit in Taif, announced that the challenges which faced the Islamic *Umma* could not be met unless through Islamic solidarity.

30 January: Sheikh Khalifa ordered the immediate commencement of three new suburbs in Abu Dhabi to solve the housing crisis.

1 February: UAE introduced an oil price increase of 3 dollars a barrel retroactive from 1 January 1981. Price rise followed decisions by Saudi Arabia to raise prices by 2 dollars per barrel and Kuwait and Qatar by 4 dollars per barrel. UAE's increase was seen as a compromise between the two points.

2 February: Abu Dhabi Executive Council allocated 362 million dirhams to construct the first truck route connecting Al-Ain and Musaffah, a distance of 129 kms.

3 February: Sheikh Rashid bin Ahmed Al Mualla signed a street-lighting contract for 16 kms of main streets in Umm al-Qaiwain and Falaj al-Mualla.

4 February: Under the chairmanship of Rashid Abdulla, the UAE participated in meetings of the foreign ministers of Saudi Arabia, the Sultanate of Oman, Bahrain, Kuwait and Qatar in Riyadh, following which the agreement to form a Co-operation Council between the Arab States of the Gulf was announced.

6 February: The Kuwaiti newspaper, *Al-Watn*, stated that Sheikh Zayed would be the first President of the Supreme Committee of the Gulf Co-operation Council at its first meeting to be held in Abu Dhabi.

7 February: The UAE decided to share in strengthening the International Fund for Agricultural Development to the amount of 66.7 million dollars.

8 February: ADFAED extended a 30 million dirham loan to the Niger Republic for a large power plant.

It was decided to open blood banks in all the hospitals in the Federation.

15 February: Sheikh Rashid bin Saeed Al Maktoum issued a decree setting up the Supreme Environment Committee.

16 February: Sheikh Sultan bin Moham-med Al Qassimi established an Islamic *waqf* in Sharjah, the income from which would be spent in support of Jerusalem and its people, to help maintain the city's Arab character and its holy places.

17 February: At the end of January 1981, there was a total of 27,409 employees working in the Federation.

18 February: Sheikh Rashid ordered the immediate construction of a new 300-unit serviced housing district between Al-Rashidiya and Al-Qusais to be called Nadd al-Qusais.

21 February: The death was announced of Sheikh Ahmed bin Rashid Al Mualla, Member of the Supreme Council of the Federation and Ruler of Umm al-Qaiwain. Government offices were closed for one week and a 30-day period of official mourning was announced.

22 February: Sheikh Rashid ordered preparatory studies for a model residen-tial city in Jebel Ali capable of main-taining a population of half a million.

The ruling family in Umm al-Qaiwain pledged their loyalty to Sheikh Rashid bin Ahmed Al Mualla as the successor to his late father.

1 March: Sheikh Zayed returned from a private visit to Pakistan to visit the Islamic Centre Headquarters in Lahore, which was built as a result of his perso-nal contribution of 3.5 million dollars.

Sheikh Hamad bin Mohammad Al Sharqi issued a local law establishing a chamber of commerce and industry in the emirate of Fujairah.

3 March: The Government of Sharjah took over the operation of Port Khalid and the contract of the Port Services Company Ltd, a foreign company which supervised the port administration, was cancelled

4 March: Sheikh Zayed and Sheikh Rashid inspected Jebel Ali Port and the new hotel.

6 March: Sheikh Khalifa bin Zayed Al Nahyan issued directives to complete the 160 million dirham second phase of the Zayed Sports City.

8 March: Sheikh Zayed decreed that the UAE adhere to the international Convention for the Suppression of Unlawful Seizure of Aircraft of 1970, as well as the Convention on Offences and Certain Other Acts Committed on Board Aircraft of 1963.

The Executive Council allocated the necessary sums to open four agricultural marketing centres in Medinat Zayed, Al-Muzaira, Ghiyathi and Al-Ruwais.

9 March: GCC Ministers of Foreign Affairs, during their meeting in Muscat, decided to convene the first Gulf Sum-mit in Abu Dhabi on 26-27 May 1981.

It was decided to increase EMIRTEL's capital from 100 million to 300 million dirhams.

10 March: Sheikh Khalifa ordered the establishment of a complex of services in Al-Ain which would include a central Islamic style market, a vegetable market, a third market for animals and a large bus station, in addition to other services and utilities.

The first air connection between Sharjah

and India was inaugurated at Sharjah International Airport.

15 March: Sheikh Zayed received a letter from US President, Ronald Reagan, delivered by ex-President Gerald Ford, concerning mutual relations and the situation in the Gulf and the Middle East.

Sheikh Zayed, receiving Youth and Sports Ministers who were meeting in Abu Dhabi, spoke of the necessity of uniting efforts to bring-up youth in an intellectual, cultural, and sportsman-like manner since they are the true wealth and most precious potential of the Arab nation.

Sheikh Sultan bin Mohammad Al Qassimi opened the Gulf Industries Company in Sharjah.

17 March: ADFAED agrred to loan 15 million dirhams to Rwanda to finance Kigali International Airport.

20 March: Sheikh Sultan bin Zayed Al Nahyan, during his meeting with Othman Saleh Sebi, Chairman of the Eritrean Liberation Front, was briefed on current developments in Eritrea and the results of efforts being made to unite Eritrean revolutionary factions.

21 March: Sheikh Zayed was shown the plans for the first comprehensive sports city to be built at Al-Hili near Al-Ain at a cost of 100 million dirhams.

22 March: Mana Said Al Otaiba signed an agreement with OAPEC Secretary-General, Dr Ali Attiga, to create an engineering consultancy company - Arab Engineering Consulting Company (AECC) based in Abu Dhabi. Services provided included engineering, design and consulting, to achieve a degree of independent Arab engineering expertise which previously was dominated by foreign engineering companies.

24 March: It was decided to establish an economic department in the emirate of Sharjah under the chairmanship of Sheikh Abdulaziz bin Mohammad Al Qassimi.

27 March: The Council of Ministers approved the allocation of 6.5 million dirhams to bring electricity to 26 schools in the Ras al-Khaimah educational district. It also approved a 100 million dirham project to develop the Fujairah electrical plant.

1 April: Mohammad Said Al Mulla inaugurated the direct telephone line between the UAE and Pakistan.

Abu Dhabi deposited the sum of 20,449,755,000 dirhams into the federal budget for 1981: 50 per cent of the income of the emirate.

2 April: Sheikh Zayed and Sheikh Rashid attended ceremonies for the commencement of work on the development of three oil fields on the island of Delma.

Five hundred million dirhams was allocated in the 1981 federal budget for civil defence requirements in all the emirates of the Federation.

6 April: The value of imports into Dubai during the previous ten years increased from 960 million dirhams in 1970 to 550 million dirhams in 1980, a twenty-fold increase.

7 April: The Sultanate of Oman and the emirate of Ras al-Khaimah signed a border demarcation agreement following successful consultations between Sheikh Rashid bin Saeed Al Maktoum and Sultan Qaboos bin Said aimed at fixing the bases of the agreement and in expediting the re-drawing of the borders.

13 April: The Council of Ministers affirmed the 1981 federal budget: total expenditure was calculated at 24 billion dirhams, an increase of 60 per cent over 1980.

The National Consultative Council approved the draft budget and the annual development schedule for the emirate of Abu Dhabi for 1981. The emirate's income was estimated to be 41.9 billion dirhams, 50 per cent of which had been allocated as Abu Dhabi's contribution to the federal budget.

Minister of Finance & Industry, Sheikh Hamdan bin Rashid Al Maktoum, had a meeting with a representative of the World Bank and revealed that the UAE would not make a contribution to the International Development Agency (IDA) - which deals with soft loans to developing countries - until it was sure that other countries would make their first year contributions in full. UAE's proposed contribution of 79.2 million dollars to IDA formed part of a 792 million dollar package from Arab states - other contributor states being Saudi Arabia and Kuwait.

14 April: Sheikh Zayed received a report from Rashid Abdulla on mediation efforts undertaken by UAE and Kuwait between the Sultanate of Oman and the Democratic Republic of Yemen.

15 April: Sheikh Tahnoun bin Moham-mad Al Nahyan opened the principal sewage treatment plant in Al-Ain.

16 April: A 722 million dirham contract was signed between the Dubai Electri-city Company and an Austrian company to import and operate electrical and water purification plants.

18 April: The Supreme Council of Youth and Sports decided to dispense with foreign players after one season playing handball, basketball and badminton and two seasons of football.

19 April: Abu Dhabi Executive Council approved the opening of ADNOC's liaison office in London.

20 April: The Council of Ministers approved the setting-up of the Emirates Transport and Services Establishment (EMIRTAS) with a provisional capital of 20 million dirhams.

22 April: Sheikh Zayed, in discussions with the British Prime Minster, Mrs Margaret Thatcher, who was on an official visit to the UAE, stressed that Israeli expansion at the expense of Arab countries created a huge danger to the region. He said that the security of the Gulf was the sole responsibility of its people.

First Lady, Sheikha Fatima bint Mubarak, and Mrs Margaret Thatcher discussed the role of women in developing society and the renaissance of women in the UAE, in addition to women's activities in the world.

During Prime Minister Margaret Thatcher's visit, it was announced that UAE had agreed to buy 18 of UK's Hawk trainer aircraft in a package worth 90 million dollars.

OPEC announced that the UAE headed the world-list of donor states since it gave 9 per cent of its GNP in assistance to other countries.

27 April: Sheikh Zayed and the Members of the Supreme Council of the Federation attended graduation ceremo-nies for the new batch of officers from the Zayed Military College in Al-Ain.

The UAE donated 1 million dollars to

the UN Conference on Human Settlements.

29 April: Sheikh Zayed received the West German Chancellor, Helmut Schmidt, who was in the country on his first official visit.

30 April: Discussions took place between a delegation from the UAE, under the chairmanship of Sheikh Zayed, and the West German delegation, under the chairmanship of Helmut Schmidt. International and regional matters which were of mutual concern were dealt with, as were the situations in the Middle East and the Gulf as well as mutual co-operation.

2 May: Rashid Abdulla announced that the first GCC Summit Conference would be convened in Abu Dhabi on 25 May instead of 26 May.

3 May: Sheikh Khalifa bin Zayed Al Nahyan signed an agreement with a group of West German companies, Die Menks, for oil exploration in an area covering 1838 sq kms in the north-west of the island of Abu al-Abyad.

6 May: Sheikh Zayed issued directives to construct 3000 houses in Al-Samha, Sharq al-Ghaba and Medinat al-Dhafra.

11 May: The Council of Ministers approved a 70 million dirham project for establishing a marine workshop in Port Zayed at a cost of 70 million dirhams.

12 May: Sheikh Zayed held talks with Mrs Indira Ghandi, the Prime Minister of India, on the necessity of finding a fair and permanent solution to the Palestinian question, ending the Iran-Iraq war and mutual relations. Sheikh Rashid held similar talks with the Indian Prime Minister.

Mrs Indira Ghandi laid the foundation stone for the Indian Islamic Centre in Abu Dhabi.

17 May: Sheikh Zayed inspected progress on opening the maritime passageway to connect the Musaffah Industrial Port District with Port Zayed.

19 May: Sheikh Zayed held discussions with King Baudoin of Belgium who was on a short visit to the UAE.

20 May: Sheikh Zayed led the UAE delegation at a meeting regarding the first GCC Summit Conference which was to be convened on 26 May. All parties were concerned that it should be conducted in such a way as to ensure its success.

22 May: GCC Ministers of Foreign Affairs held a meeting in Abu Dhabi to prepare for the first Gulf Summit. Abdulla Yacoub Bishara, the former Kuwaiti representative at the United Nations, was nominated as Secretary General of the Council. Rashid Abdulla, who was elected as the Chairman of the conference, stressed that the Gulf Summit would be a visible sign of development and progress in the region. The ministers debated the basic organization of the Council and the structure of the commission for settling disputes.

Humaid bin Nasser Al Nowais signed a Dhs 98.5 million contract to establish the new Qadfa'a electrical plant in Fujairah.

24 May: Sheikh Zayed welcomed the GCC Ministers of Foreign Affairs and wished them success in their preparations for the Gulf Summit. The Ministers held two closed sessions during which they reviewed the economic situation and the possibility of establishing co-operative structures in various economic fields.

25 May: In Abu Dhabi, Sheikh Zayed,

opening the first Gulf Summit Conference in which the rulers of Saudi Arabia, Bahrain, Oman, Kuwait and Qatar participated, expressed his wish that the conference would meet with success. He presented the basic statute of the Council to the leaders who duly signed it, after which it was announced that the Arab Gulf Co-operation Council (AGCC) had come into being.

Humaid bin Rashid Al Nuaimi presided over the first meeting of the Board of Ajman's Chamber of Commerce and Industry in which Hamad Bu Shihab was elected President.

26 May: The leaders of the Arab Gulf Co-operation Council in their final communiqué confirmed that stability in the Gulf region was linked to the realization of peace in the Middle East. They further confirmed their support for Syria and the efforts that were being made to stop the Iraq-Iran War. They stressed that the circumstances of the Gulf region made solidarity a necessity to confront international political ambitions.

Sheikh Zayed stressed to the leaders of the GCC States that they were confronted by a common destiny and that their solid stand together could not be separated from the need to stand shoulder to shoulder with the entire Arab nation. The leaders of the GCC States, in their concluding session, affirmed the joint Gulf working paper, the basic statute of the Supreme Council, the basic statute setting-up a dispute-settlement mechanism, and the appointment of Abdulla Bishara as the Secretary General of the Council. They also decided to hold the second Summit in November in Riyadh at the invitation of the Saudi monarch.

27 May: Sheikh Zayed held a news conference in which he dealt with the current situation, the objectives of the GCC and the importance of keeping the Gulf region free from international conflicts.

Sheikh Sultan bin Mohammad Al Qassimi issued an Amiri decree setting up the Cultural and Guidance Office in Sharjah.

Sheikh Rashid bin Ahmed Al Mualla opened the Emirates Fresh Milk Farm in Umm al-Qaiwain which was established at a cost of 24 million dirhams.

1 June: Sheikh Zayed issued the law governing Abu Dhabi's budget for 1981. Revenue was estimated at 41.8 billion dirhams and expenditure at 36.304 billion dirhams.

2 June: The Ministry of Education confirmed that the right to education was guaranteed to all residents of the UAE and that there was no discrimination between a citizen and a non-citizen in this regard.

3 June: Sheikh Rashid bin Ahmed Al Mualla attended the first meeting of the Umm al-Qaiwain's Chamber of Commerce and Industry, in which the establishment of the Umm al-Qaiwain Insurance Company and the National Bank of Umm al-Qaiwain with a capital of 100 million dirhams was discussed.

5 June: The UAE Central Bank imposed restrictions on offshore trading of UAE dirhams including an imposition of 15 per cent reserve requirement on local banks' dirham lending outside the country, and banning dirham lending to foreign banks.

9 June: Sheikh Zayed concluded his inspection tour of the Western Region including Delma Island, Bia'aya Village, Ghiyathi, Muhadhir Liwa and historic Ghafa island which he visited for the first time in 1945. He inspected development and agricultural projects and ordered the construction of new public housing projects.

The UAE stressed its strong condemnation of Israeli aggression against Iraqi nuclear installations on the 7th of June.

The UAE was the first Gulf country to be elected as a member of the Executive Council of UNICEF.

10 June: The First Lady, Sheikha Fatima bint Mubarak, visited Britain at the invitation of Queen Elizabeth II.

The Japanese company, Udeco, decided to invest an additional 100 million dollars to support its development projects in Abu Dhabi's oil fields.

12 June: Sheikh Zayed issued federal laws establishing the Real Estate Bank with a capital of 2 billion dirhams; the Agricultural Marketing Establishment; and the Institute of Administrative Development.

15 June: Council of Ministers approved the creation of an Industrial Bank to assist in financing industrial projects on a medium and long term basis.

18 June: Sheikh Maktoum bin Rashid Al Maktoum opened new facilities at the Kuwait Hospital in Dubai.

20 June: The Central Bank issued a decree regulating money changing in the UAE which stipulated that a money changer's establishment must have a capital of not less than 500,000 dirhams.

The Ministry of Planning revealed that expatriates from non-Arab countries constituted approximately 71 per cent of the work force in the Federation.

27 June: Sheikh Zayed paid a private visit to Austria where he held discussions with the Austrian Chancellor, Bruno Kreisky, regarding bilateral relations and the situation in the Middle East.

28 June: Sheikh Khalifa allocated the sum of 2516.5 million dirhams to reimburse all citizens whose dwellings were destroyed or damaged in the public interest between 1976 and 1979.

29 June: The representatives of the co-operative societies approved the establishment of the first Co-operative Union in the Federation.

30 June: Sheikh Zayed arrived in Sirte, Libya on an official one-day visit to the Libyan Jamahiriyya.

1 July: Sheikh Zayed held discussions with the Libyan President, Muammar Al Gadhafi covering the international situation and the situation in the Middle East and the Gulf. The two Presidents called for Iraq and Iran to stop the Islamic blood-letting on the occasion of the advent of the Holy Month of Ramadan.

During Sheikh Zayed's visit, UAE and Libya made a joint call for OPEC to implement unified price and production policies following the emergence of a glut on the world oil markets.

5 July: Owing to a saturation of the country with banks, the Central Bank decided to reduce the number of branches of foreign banks in the Federation to seven per bank, the excess branches to be phased out before the end of 1983.

6 July: Abu Dhabi Executive Council approved dredging and reclamation work on the channel between Port Zayed and the Umm al-Nar channel at a cost of 216 million dirhams.

The sum of 85 million dirhams was allocated for undertaking improvements on the Abu Dhabi water distribution network.

10 July: Test production began at the 120,000 barrel per day Ruwais oil refinery in Abu Dhabi

13 July: The Council of Ministers approved salary increases for national employees granting them a social allowance of 300 million dirhams annually.

16 July: Sheikh Sultan bin Mohammad Al Qassimi dedicated the commencement of drilling on Well No. 1 in the Al-Musnad field which is about 30 kms east of Sharjah.

18 July: Sheikh Khalifa bin Zayed Al Nahyan issued a law establishing a complex of cultural and documentary institutions in Abu Dhabi.

19 July: Sheikh Zayed ordered that a medical team, medical supplies and blood be sent to help treat the victims of Israeli aggression against Lebanon.

The Council of Ministers decided to allocate 10 million dirhams to solve the electricity crisis in Ras al-Khaimah.

21 July: Sheikh Zayed issued a social insurance law which stipulated that the minimum social support per person was 800 dirhams a month and the maximum 4000 dirhams.

The National Bank of Abu Dhabi joined the American Express credit card organization.

22 July: The Ministry of Labour and Social Affairs issued a decree proclaiming the first union of consumer co-operative societies in the federation.

25 July: It was decided to provide a monthly allowance of 1000 dirhams for each handicapped student studying either inside or outside the country.

27 July: The Executive Council allocated the sum of 237 million dirhams for a new electricity and water project in Abu Dhabi and Al-Ain.

29 July: Sheikh Sultan bin Mohammad Al Qassimi opened the electricity plant in Layya.

12 August: Sheikh Zayed received the General Commander of the Revolutionary Palestinian Forces, Khalil Al-Wazir (Abu Jihad), who briefed him on latest developments in the Palestinian cause.

17 August: Sheikh Zayed received Sheikh Surour bin Mohammad Al Nahyan and Sheikh Mohammad bin Sultan bin Surour Al Dhahiri, Deputy Governor of the Central Bank, who showed Zayed copies of the new bank notes which would be circulated in 1982.

23 August: Sheikh Zayed received the Libyan President, Muammar Al Gadhafi, who arrived in the country on a short visit. The two leaders held a session of discussions during which they dealt with the current Arab situation and international affairs of mutual concern.

The UAE won the World Youth Chess Championship when Said Ahmed Said triumphed over the Mexican champion.

24 August: The UAE agreed to look after Libyan affairs in the United States of America after the break in diplomatic relations between the two countries.

30 August: The Council of Ministers approved a plan for the general administration of water resources in the Federation, as well as a project for setting-up dams to retain freshwater at a cost of 31.854 million dirhams.

UAE Planning Ministry figures revealed that Fujairah received more federal expenditure than any other emirate - mainly for electricity, communications, water and health projects. Federal Government policy targeted the poorer northern emirates as priorities for expenditure.

1 September: The British company, John Brown Engineering, won a 250 million dollars contract to set-up an electrical plant in Abu Dhabi.

6 September: The death was announced of Sheikh Rashid bin Humaid Al Nuaimi, Ruler of Ajman. A period of 30 days mourning was declared. By acclamation, the ruling family gave their allegiance to Sheikh Humaid bin Rashid Al Nuaimi as successor to his late father.

11 September: The feed factory in Sharjah, with a production capacity of 500 tons per day, became operational.

10 September: Sheikh Ahmed bin Hamid attended graduation ceremonies for the first batch of national film makers who completed their studies in the Cinema Production Unit at the Ministry of Information and Culture.

16 September: Sheikh Zayed issued instructions to construct 3000 housing units in a number of regions of Abu Dhabi.

28 September: The Council of Ministers approved the earmarking of 200 million dirhams as additional payments for public housing in the Northern Emirates.

29 September: The Municipality of Dubai allocated 7 million dirhams to set-up a central market in Al-Hamriyya.

1 October: A contract was signed to construct the Sheikh Khalifa Islamic Technical Secondary School in Mombasa, Kenya.

2 October: The UAE announced its condemnation of and its solidarity with Kuwait over the aggression which three Iranian aircraft perpetrated on oil installations in the Umm al-Eish region.

Forty five million dirhams was allocated for the development of the Abu Dhabi Broadcasting and Television studios and the Emirates News Agency.

3 October: The first air cargo line between the UAE and the USA, via Frankfurt, was inaugurated.

4 October: The Executive Council approved a 86 million dirham project for setting-up a police and security complex at the new Abu Dhabi International Airport.

6 October: Sheikh Khalifa signed an oil concession agreement with the British company Autocal to explore for oil in offshore regions: the company pledged to spend 50 million dollars during the next eight years on the concession.

9 October: The UAE condemned the assassination of the Egyptian President, Mohammad Anwar Sadat, and all political assassinations of any kind whatever differences there might be in policies and points of view regarding national issues, stressing that such methods do not correspond with Islamic values.

19 October: Sheikh Zayed and King Hussein, who had arrived in the country on a short visit, discussed the current Arab situation and the joint efforts of both countries to clear the air in preparation for the Arab Summit Conference to be held in Casablanca.

Sheikh Zayed described the peace initiative which was proposed by the Saudi Crown Prince, Fahad bin

Abdulaziz, as an ideal solution which would solve the Middle East problem.

The Council of Ministers approved the transformation of the General Postal Authority to an independent public institution.

26 October: Direct telephone links with Egyptian cities were opened.

For the first time a forensic medical doctor was appointed to Dubai Police to perform autopsies on homicides and accidental deaths.

28 October: Sheikh Zayed convened a meeting with the Members of the Supreme Council of the Federation in which they studied a number of domestic and foreign issues. They also consulted about the future of the Federation in the next phase of development. It was decided to renew the provisional constitution for another five years, commencing 2 December 1981.

30 October: The emirates of Dubai and Sharjah settled their border dispute.

The Ministry of Public Works awarded a 46 million dollar contract to construct a port in the emirate of Fujairah. A new road was also planned to link Fujairah port with Dubai and Sharjah to save on sea journey times (and risk) through the Straits of Hormuz to reach the remainder of the federation on the Arabian Gulf coast.

2 November: Al-Ain Co-operative Society was established with a capital of 20 million dirhams.

3 November: The Federal National Council, in an extraordinary session, approved the constitutional amendment regarding extension of the provisional constitution for another five years, commencing on 2 December 1981.

6 November: Sheikh Tahnoun bin Mohammad Al Nahyan opened the new 9 km-long camel race course in Al-Ain.

7 November: The Members of the Supreme Council of the Federation elected Sheikh Zayed as President of the Federation for another period of five years, beginning on 2 December 1981. They also re-elected Sheikh Rashid as Vice President and ratified the constitutional amendment extending the provisional constitution.

8 November: Sheikh Zayed received an honorary doctorate awarded by the Argentinean University of Conception from Professor Salvador Liuta, Chancellor of the Argentinean University. Zayed stressed that the UAE, as in the past, would continue to pursue improvements in the standard of living for each individual in the country. He said that a country's size was not the measure of its riches but rather the quality of life it provided for its people.

10 November: Sheikh Zayed led the UAE delegation to the second Gulf Summit in Riyadh. On his arrival, he confirmed his concern for mutual brotherly action.

11 November: The Council of Ministers earmarked 500 million dirhams in support of the electrical capacity of the emirate of Ras Al-Khaimah since fire had destroyed five of the biggest generators at the Al-Nakhil electricity plant.

The UAE paid its 45 million dollar share to the Lebanese Government for reconstruction within the framework of the Arab aid extended to Lebanon at the Summit Conference in Tunis.

13 November: The Ministry of Electricity and Water completed the task of bringing electrical services to 20 villages in the emirate of Fujairah. Work was also underway to bring electricity to 18 more villages during 1982-83.

15 November: Sheikh Zayed issued the Maritime Commerce Law regulating commercial navigation in the Federation.

16 November: The Council of Ministers approved a draft law establishing the National Computer Centre.

Sheikh Hamdan bin Rashid Al Maktoum stated that the UAE would contribute between 750 and 800 million dollars, or 15 to 16 per cent of the total value of the Arab development contract which was affirmed at the last Arab summit in Amman, to finance development projects in less-developed Arab countries.

18 November: Sheikh Zayed presented an electricity generating and water desalination plant to Bahrain.

21 November: The Council of Ministers allocated 69 million dirhams to construct a number of domestic roads in various regions in the emirate of Ras al-Khaimah.

22 November: In Sharjah, Sheikh Sultan bin Mohammad Al Qassimi opened the fifth conference of the Middle East Committee for the Blind.

EMIRTEL's Board of Directors decided to reduce telephone rates inside the Federation by 15 per cent.

23 November: The Council of Ministers approved the creation of the Industrial Bank.

Sheikh Mohammad bin Rashid Al Maktoum opened the 1981 Middle East Airport Exhibition which was held in Dubai with the participation of 60 international companies from Europe and America.

24 November: Sheikh Ahmed bin Hamid signed an agreement setting-up the Popular Heritage Centre of the Arab Gulf States.

25 November: Sheikh Zayed led the UAE delegation at the inaugural session of the twelfth Arab Summit Conference which was held in the Moroccan city of Fez. Hours after it was opened, King Hassan II announced that the conference was indefinitely postponed as a result of differences regarding the matters on the agenda, especially the Saudi peace plan.

Sheikh Surour bin Mohammad Al Nahyan opened the industrial investment conference which was mounted by the Government of Abu Dhabi in co-operation with the United Nations Organization for Industrial Development, UNIDO.

The Emirate Society of the Plastic Arts was accepted as a member in the Arab Plastic Artists Union.

26 November: Sheikh Faisal bin Khalid Al Qassimi opened the Expo centre in Sharjah.

28 November: Sheikh Saqr bin Mohammed Al Qassimi issued a decree setting-up the Economic and Legal Office in Ras al-Khaimah.

Sheikh Humaid bin Rashid Al Nuaimi opened the Ajman Health Complex in Ajman.

ADFAED agreed to loan 30 million dirhams to Mali for a 565 km highway project.

30 November: ADFAED agreed to provide 16 million dirhams to Cameroon for a highway project.

1 December: Sheikh Zayed, in a speech broadcast on French television on the occasion of the UAE's celebration of its tenth National Day, stressed that the constructive work which had been accomplished by the federation was visible for all to see.

5 December: Sheikh Saqr bin Moham-med Al Qassimi opened the Saqr Hospital and the first phase of the Ras al-Khaimah bridge which together cost the federation 162 million dirhams.

6 December: Sheikh Zayed and King Juan Carlos, King of Spain, who was on an official visit to the country, held a closed meeting during which they made a complete review of all current Arab and international matters.

Sheikh Khalifa bin Zayed Al Nahyan approved the the creation of the Cultural Society of the UAE and France under his patronage, to support the development of relations between France and the UAE.

Sheikha Fatima bint Mubarak received Queen Sofia, the wife of the King of Spain, who was briefed during her visit to the headquarters of the Women's Federation on the various aspects of women's renaissance in the country.

7 December: Sheikh Zayed received the Austrian Chancellor, Bruno Kreisky, who arrived in the country on an official visit. Sheikh Rashid bin Ahmad Al Mualla signed an agreement with the American company, Texaco, to prospect for oil in a 650 sq. kms area of Umm al-Qaiwain.

8 December: Sheikh Zayed held discussions with the Austrian Chan-cellor, Bruno Kreisky, during which they made a complete evaluation of Arab and international issues and ways of strengthening relations between the two countries.

9 December: Tripartite talks on the Palestinian question were held in Abu Dhabi between Sheikh Zayed, Bruno Kreisky, the Austrian Chancellor, and the Palestinian leader, Yasser Arafat.

10 December: Sheikh Zayed received OPEC Oil Ministers attending the sixty-second meeting of the organization in Abu Dhabi.

12 December: Humaid bin Nasser Al Nowais signed two contracts amounting to 76 million dirhams for providing water, energy and electrical services to various regions in the Northern Emirates.

13 December: Shareholders in the Abu Dhabi National Bank raised the capital of the bank from 100 million to 1 billion dirhams.

14 December: ADFAED agreed to loan 37 million dirhams to the Congo to assist in redevelopment of a railway line.

15 December: The UAE condemned the Israeli decision to annex the occupied Syrian Golan Heights and considered the move to be contrary to international law.

The UAE also stressed its complete solidarity with Libya in confronting the American escalation against it, and it expressed its readiness to compensate for any shortage occasioned by the withdrawal of American experts from the Libyan oil industry.

16 December: Sheikh Zayed made a complete inspection tour of develop-ment and agricultural projects which were undertaken in remote areas on his orders.

ADFAED agreed to loan 25 million dollars to Pakistan for dam and hydro-electric repairs at Tarbela dam.

21 December: The new hospital in Ghiyathi was opened by Sheikh Zayed.

23 December: The document establish-ing the first Society of Commercial Economists in the country was signed and the statute of the society endorsed.

24 December: The UAE and India signed a 56 million dollar contractfor the laying of a submarine communications cable.

25 December: Sheikh Zayed and the Syrian President, Hafez Al Asad, who was on a short visit to the UAE, discussed ways of strengthening joint Arab action to confront the dangers to the Arab nation.

26 December: Sheikh Khalifa arrived in Algeria on his first official visit.

28 December: Sheikh Zayed convened the new session of the Federal National Council, announcing in the opening address the commencement of a new phase of national action to complete the accomplishments of the Federation in many fields, to decrease the cost of living and to deepen the understanding of democracy. A delegation from the Kuwaiti National Assembly participated in the opening session.

The Council elected Hilal Ahmed Lootah as President, Ahmed Saif Balhassa as first Vice President, and Eid Bakheet Al Mazroui as second Vice President.

31 December: The joint UAE-Libyan commission for the establishment of Islamic centres in Africa decided to build two new centres, one in Mali and the other in Togo, at a cost of 24 million dollars.

Nineteen Eighty Two

2 January: Sheikh Sultan bin Mohammed Al Qassimi received Ahmed ben Bella, the Algerian President and Chairman of the International Human Rights Committee, who had arrived in the country on a short visit.

Ali Khalfan Al Dhahiri, the Director of the Civil Aviation Department, attended the commencement of operations at the new Abu Dhabi International Airport.

3 January: Abu Dhabi Executive Council approved studies for re-organizing the administrative structure and establishing a policy for Arabizing jobs in the local departments.

6 January: ADFAED agreed to loan Bangladesh 85 million dirhams to finance a fertilizer plant in Chittagong.

9 January: At the end of 1981, there were 140,000 telephones in the UAE, or an average of one telephone for every seven persons, the highest average in the world.

10 January: Sheikh Khalifa bin Zayed Al Nahyan ordered a reduction in the bank interest rate charged to real estate owners sponsored by Sheikh Khalifa from 2 per cent to 0.5 per cent in an effort to lighten the burden on citizens.

13 January: Sheikh Khalifa bin Zayed Al Nahyan issued a law establishing the Abu Dhabi National Establishment for Exploration for Hidden Reservoirs, a practical establishment which aims to develop and improve oil extraction techniques.

18 January: Council of Ministers decided to ban companies without a 51 per cent UAE local partnership from carrying out Government projects.

20 January: Abu Dhabi National Oil Company (ADNOC) announced plans to build a 160,000 ton per annum petroleum coke plant in Ruwais Industrial Area to supply Dubai Aluminium Company (DUBAL) and Aluminium Bahrain (ALBA).

24 January: Abu Dhabi Executive Council approved a 7 billion dirham annual development budget for 1982.

The Ministry of Education issued a decree granting a monthly stipend to 152 Eritrean students studying in Egyptian universities. This will become effective at the beginning of this academic year.

30 January: Sheikh Sultan bin Mohammed Al Qassimi issued a decree appointing Sheikh Saud bin Sultan Al Qassimi as Chairman of Sharjah's Survey and Planning Office.

2 February: Sheikh Sultan bin Mohammad Al Qassimi issued a decree appointing Sheikh Saqr bin Rashid Al Qassimi as chairman of Sharjah's Social Services Department.

7 February: The Executive Council approved the appointment of consultants to prepare a plan for centralizing control of traffic lights in Abu Dhabi city.

15 February: Sheikh Zayed and the Members of the Supreme Council of the Federation examined the impact of heavy rain throughout the country. All available equipment was called into action to help those who were stricken, to protect farms and control damage suffered in the Al-Ghiliya region of Ras al-Khaimah as a result of the collapse of the Wadi al-Beeh Dam.

17 February: Sheikh Zayed donated 500,000 dollars to the Islamic Chamber of Commerce and Industry in Karachi.

20 February: Sheikh Zayed, meeting with the French Minister of Foreign Affairs, Claude Cheyson, confirmed that the Palestinian question was the first and central question of the Arab nation and that there would never be a just and lasting peace until the lawful rights of the Palestinian people were reinstated.

21 February: Sheikh Zayed accepted the resignation of Brigadier Sheikh Sultan bin Zayed Al Nahyan from his post as Commander-in-Chief of the Armed Forces.

A security co-operation agreement between Saudi Arabia and the UAE, signed by the Ministers of the Interior of both countries, provided for the exchange of experience and information as well as facilitating extradition of criminals.

22 February: Following discussions with the Yemeni President, Ali Abdulla Saleh, Sheikh Zayed called for action to restore Arab solidarity in order to confront the challenges inherent in this very dangerous stage through which the Arab nation was passing.

UAE Agriculture & Fisheries Minister, Said Mohammad Al Ragabani announced that the Federation became self-sufficient in vegetable production in December 1981, total production at year ending March 1982 being around 126,000 tons.

27 February: Sheikh Zayed presided over the first meeting of the Supreme Board of UAE University. He encouraged the board to study matters connected to the University with frankness and objectivity in order to safeguard the higher interests of the country.

28 February: Sheikh Zayed and the Members of the Supreme Council attended the first graduation ceremonies at UAE University. In a graduation address, Zayed stressed that the true riches of the nation lay in its people and not in its wealth. Stressing that the nation was depending on the youth for the present and the future, Sheikh Zayed granted each graduate the sum of 50,000 dirhams. Sheikh Khalifa bin Zayed Al Nahyan called for the University 'to come up with ideas, opinions and solutions to the problems of society, confirming that university education is a national mission to be achieved by its conjunction with and reaction to the problems of society and its affairs.'

1 March: First Lady, Sheikha Fatima bint Mubarak, Chairwoman of the UAE Women's Federation, delivered a speech to the first female graduates from UAE University, stressing the importance of the role of educated young women in the service of society.

2 March: Sheikh Zayed and the Prime Minister of Malaysia, Dr Mahathir Mohammad, discussed ways of developing relations between the two countries.

3 March: Sheikh Zayed held a closed meeting with the Yemeni President, Ali Nasser Mohammad, who was visiting the country to discuss developments in the Gulf region.

4 March: Sheikh Zayed arrived in Saudi Arabia on a two-day visit to consult with His Majesty King Khalid bin Abdulaziz on ways of strengthening co-operation between the two countries in various fields.

6 March: Sheikh Zayed and the Tunisian Prime Minister, Mohammad Mzali, discussed the strengthening of political and economic relations between the two countries.

7 March: Sheikh Rashid bin Ahmed Al Mualla issued a decree establishing the National Bank of Umm al-Qaiwain as a limited share company. Sheikh Khalifa received the members of the Football Federation and the players of the National Team prior to the hosting by the UAE of the sixth Gulf Championship Games on 19 March.
Sheikh Hamdan bin Mohammad Al Nahyan and the Tunisian Prime Minister, Mohammad Mzali, signed an agreement to form a joint investment bank in Abu Dhabi with a capital of 50 million Tunisian dinars.

8 March: Humaid Al Owais signed a 34.5 million dirham contract to extend electrical services to remote areas in the northern provinces.

Hamad Abdulrahman opened the first cardiac unit and dermatology department in Al-Jazira Hospital .

9 March: Sheikh Khalifa stated that the ceremonies scheduled for the next day to celebrate the opening of the Al-Ruwais Industrial Area heralded the birth of the first comprehensive industrial city in the country, the population of which was expected to reach 50,000. The cost of establishing projects in this area amounted to around 4 billion dollars.

10 March: Sheikh Zayed and the Members of the Supreme Council of the Federation opened projects in Al-Ruwais Industrial Area. Sheikh Tahnoun bin Mohammad Al Nahyan stressed that these projects were a great achievement and represented a victory for the individual in the Federation in the race to achieve progress.
The International Monetary Fund decided to add the UAE dirham to the 25 international currencies which the fund used in granting loans.

11 March: Sheikh Zayed was briefed by Pakistani President Mohammad Zia Al Haq at Abu Dhabi International Airport on efforts being made by the Islamic mediation committee to stop the war between Iraq and Iran.

17 March: A 30 million dollar contract was signed with Japan to set-up a solar desalination plant.

18 March: Sheikh Zayed, receiving the heads of delegations participating in the sixth Gulf Football Games, stressed that the meeting of brothers on UAE territory was an important accomplishment. He said that meetings between leaders of States in the region must continue without interruption because their interests are one and they have a joint destiny.

Sheikh Sultan bin Mohammad Al Qassimi announced at the first meeting of the Society of Petroleum Engineers that the first shipment from Sharjah's land-based oil wells would be exported on 15 May.

19 March: Sheikh Zayed, opening the sixth Championship Games for the Arabian Gulf Football Cup at Zayed Sports City, met with members of the UAE National Team and encouraged them to arm themselves with high moral values and a sporting spirit.

21 March: Sheikh Humaid bin Rashid Al Nuaimi opened the new electricity distribution plant in Ajman.

22 March: Sheikh Rashid bin Ahmed Al Mualla issued a decree establishing the Umm al-Qaiwain Cement Company.

23 March: The Council of Ministers endorsed the 1982 federal budget amounting to 22.559 billion dirhams. Reductions were made to combat inflation in the Federation although utility and staple food subsidies were to remain.

28 March: Sheikh Zayed issued a federal law establishing the Emirates Industrial Bank and stipulated that the bank grant long term loans of 1 billion dirhams to finance industrial projects in the country.

ADFAED agreed to loan 259 million dirhams to the Organization of Senegal River Basin Countries to assist in construction of dams on Senegal river.

30 March: Sheikh Maktoum bin Rashid Al Maktoum approved plans for Dubai's new districts and the construction of 5000 new public housing units.

31 March: Sheikh Tahnoun bin Mohammad Al Nahyan presided over a meeting to examine the feasibility of establishing a tomato paste and vegetable canning factory in order to absorb excess local farm produce.

1 April: Sheikh Saqr bin Mohammad Al Qassimi opened the Arab Animal Production Company in Ras al-Khaimah.

2 April: Sheikh Zayed, receiving the heads of sports delegations participating in the sixth Gulf Football Games, stressed that the purpose of these sports activities was for brothers to get acquainted with each other and to overcome regional sensitivities which undermine the realization of unity between the States of the region.

3 April: Sheikh Khalifa received the members of the Supreme Committee for the sixth Gulf Football Games. He also announced that Sheikh Zayed had decided to present each player on the National Team with a gratuity of 150,000 dirhams in appreciation of the results which the Team achieved in this competition.

4 April: Sheikh Zayed in remarks made to the Kuwaiti newspaper, *Al-Siyasa*, announced that the UAE was prepared to mediate to end the war between Iraq and Iran. He said that he had advised the Iranian leaders that the continuation of the war was not in their or anybody's interest in the region.

5 April: Sheikh Zayed arrived in Kuwait on an official three-day visit.

The Council of Ministers approved the draft federal law regarding judicial authority.

6 April: Sheikh Zayed and His Highness Sheikh Jabir Al Ahmed Al Sabah, Ruler of Kuwait, discussed ways of supporting the future of the GCC and developing relations between the two countries in all fields. They also discussed developments in the Palestinian problem and ways to arrive at a solution to the Iran-Iraq dispute and put an end to the war between them.

Sheikh Tahnoun bin Mohammad Al Nahyan inspected progress on the expansion of Umm al-Nar refinery.

8 April: ADFAED agreed to loan Mauritius 18 million dirhams to assist in a drinking-water supply project.

10 April: Sheikh Zayed, during his helicopter fact-finding tour over Abu Qashi sha and Abu al-Abyad islands observed the agricultural and development projects.

Sheikh Khalifa received the Chairman of the Federal National Council, Hilal Ahmed Lootah, who brought to his attention a number of issues of concern to the nation and its citizens.

The UAE offered urgent aid amounting to 3 million dollars to alleviate the flood damage which had devastated the Yemen Democratic Republic.

Sheikh Hamdan bin Rashid Al Maktoum approved a 3.5 billion dirham, ten-year sewerage and storm water plan in the emirate of Dubai.

Sheikha Fatima bint Mubarak, Chairwoman of the UAE Women's Federation, arrived in Kuwait on an official visit at the invitation of Sheikha Latifa, wife of Saad Al Abdulla Al Sabah, the Kuwaiti Heir Apparent.

11 April: Sheikh Zayed, meeting with Hilal Ahmed Lootah, Chairman of the Federal National Council, discussed a number of matters concerning the country and its citizens, aimed at strengthening the future of the Federation.

12 April: Federal Communications Ministry announced plans to build a 100 million dirham central post office at Zayed City in Abu Dhabi and two in Al-Ain as part of a plan to build ten post offices in Abu Dhabi emirate, four in Dubai and four in Sharjah. Sheikh Khalifa donated a site in Abu Dhabi to the Ministry of Communications for the central post office

13 April: Sheikh Zayed and King Hussein of Jordan, who was on a brief visit to the country, discussed Arab affairs and the situation in the occupied territories.

The Diwan of the President issued a statement regarding the stoppage of work in all Government facilities in solidarity with the Palestinian people in the occupied territories, and in response to the call of King Khalid bin Abdulaziz of Saudi Arabia to the international community to take the required measures to put an end to Israeli terrorist and repressive practices in the occupied territories.

14 April: All local newspapers ceased publication in response to the President's call for solidarity with the Palestinian *intifada* in the occupied territories.

19 April: Sheikh Zayed and the Members of the Supreme Counci attended exercises for the seventh batch of graduates from Zayed the Second Military College.

The UAE and the Yemen Arab Republic signed an agreement to rebuild the Marib Dam with funds provided by Sheikh Zayed.

24 April: Sheikh Rashid bin Saeed al Maktoum approved Dubai Municipality's budget of 1.501 billion dirhams for 1982.

25 April: Sheikh Sultan bin Mohammad Al Qassimi inspected the new 60 million dirham police school in Sharjah.

27 April: Sheikh Zayed and the Senegalese President, Abdou Diouf, who was in the country on an official visit, held discussions on current Arab, African and international situations in addition to mutual co-operative relations between the UAE and Senegal.

29 April: Oliver Tsambo, President of the African National Congress, who was visiting the country, praised the efforts of the UAE in supporting the struggle of the people of South Africa against the racist regime.

Nasser Al Nowais announced that between 1973 and 1982 the UAE gave 35 billion dirhams in aid, assistance and loans to developing countries.

30 April: Sheikh Zayed and the Algerian President, Al Shadhili bin Jadid, who arrived in the country on a short visit, discussed ways of strengthening Arab unity of purpose and achieving solidarity to jointly confront the Zionist enemy.

1 May: Sheikh Zayed presided over an extraordinary meeting of the Council of Ministers during which Arab and Gulf affairs were studied.

The Armed Forces celebrated the sixth anniversary of their unification.

2 May: Sheikh Zayed presided over a meeting of the Supreme Council of the Federation during which the situation in the region and the Arab world in general was discussed. The Council requested Sheikh Zayed to contact Gulf leaders in order to orchestrate attempts to put an end to the blood-letting between Iraq and Iran.

3 May: Sheikh Zayed, meeting with Abdulla Bishara, the GCC Secretary-General, reviewed the steps taken to implement decisions of the GCC Supreme Council concerning the role of the Council in removing Arab differences and unifying efforts to confront the Zionist enemy.

4 May: Sheikh Zayed, arriving in Saudi Arabia on a short visit to King Khalid bin Abdulaziz, discussed current Arab affairs and especially the situation in the Arab Gulf region, as well as efforts being made to contain differences and achieve Arab solidarity.

Sheikh Zayed issued a decree promoting Colonel Mohammad Said Al Badi to the rank of Brigadier along with a federal decree appointing him Chief-of-Staff of the Armed Forces.

5 May: The Central Bank announced that the UAE earned a net 1 billion dollars in 1981 from its foreign investments.

6 May: Sheikh Tahnoun bin Mohammad Al Nahyan opened the Intercontinental Hotel in Al-Ain.

8 May: Sheikh Rashid bin Saeed Al Maktoum inspected the new oil discovery in Dubai's Margham region.

10 May: The Council of Ministers approved a draft law setting-up the first Customs Council to organize, co-ordinate and unify customs in the Emirates.

ADFAED agreed to loan 20 million dirhams to the central African state of Burundi to finance a sugar project. UAE Government had announced in May a doubling of its contribution to ADFAED from 400 million dirhams to 800 million dirhams.

12 May: The UAE and Morocco signed an agreement linking the two countries by air.

16 May: Sheikh Zayed issued federal decrees approving four agreements between the UAE and the International Labour Organization concerning working hours, prohibiting harrassment, obligatory labour, labour inspections, and regulating night work for women.

17 May: Sheikh Zayed met with the Members of the Federal Supreme Council, the Rulers of the Emirates, at the commencement of his annual week-long tour of the Northern Emirates.

28 May: Sheikh Sultan bin Mohammad Al Qassimi who was on an official visit to India met with the President of the Republic of India and Mrs Indira Ghandi, the Prime Minister.

30 May: Said Al Raqbani signed a contract worth 17.5 million dirhams to drill artesian wells throughout the UAE with the aim of discovering and evaluating groundwater sources in the country.

2 June: Sheikh Zayed received Mr David Steele, leader of the British Liberal Party, who was visiting the country.

5 June: UAE and Kenya established diplomatic relations at ambassadorial level and Abu Dhabi Crown Prince and UAE Armed Forces Deputy Commander, Sheikh Khalifa bin Zayed Al Nahyan, donated 20 million dirhams to finance a secondary school in Kenya.

6 June: Sheikh Zayed discussed Eritrean affairs and matters concerning the Horn of Africa with the Secretary General of the Popular Front for the Liberation of Eritrea, Ramadan Mohammad Noor.

Sheikh Tahnoun bin Mohammad Al Nahyan signed an agreement with an Italian company to draw up engineering plans for the Al-Ruwais hydrogen fragmentation complex .

7 June: Sheikh Zayed ordered that a medical mission be sent immediately to Lebanon to extend urgent aid to the victims of the Israeli invasion of Lebanon.

10 June: Sheikh Zayed ordered that sufficient measures be taken to provide transport for volunteers to the battlefield in Lebanon to support the *jihad* of the Palestinian and Lebanese joint forces against the Zionist invasion.

Sheikh Maktoum bin Rashid Al Maktoum donated 20 million dirhams to support the Palestinian/Lebanese struggle in the south of Lebanon.

The first batch of volunteers left Sharjah Airport to support the joint Lebanese/Palestinian forces in confronting the Israeli invasion of Lebanese territory.

10 June: ADFAED agreed to loan 4 million dirhams to Seychelles for highways and water supplies maintenance.

ADFAED announced in June that in the 10 years since its establishment - 1971-1981 - the organization participated in financing 76 projects in 39 different countries, lending a total of 3.478 billion dirhams and technical assistance of 200 million dirhams.

11 June: Sheikh Zayed in a telephone conversation with the Libyan President, Muammar Al Gadhafi, welcomed the convening of an emergency Arab Summit within the framework of the Arab response to the Zionist invasion of Lebanon.

Blood donation centres were opened in all parts of the country to collect blood for those wounded during the Zionist invasion of Lebanon.

13 June: Sheikh Zayed, at the head of a large delegation, attended the funeral of King Khalid bin Abdulaziz. A 40-day period of mourning was declared in the country and Government offices were closed for three days.

Abu Dhabi Executive Council approved the draft law establishing the Emirates Insurance Company.

16 June: The second batch of volunteers left the country on their way to support the Lebanese/Palestinian defence against the Zionist invasion of Lebanon.

19 June: Sheikh Rashid bin Saeed Al Maktoum opened the tunnel at the clock roundabout in Dubai.

29 June: Sheikh Mohammad bin Butti Al Hamid signed a 200 million dirham contract with consultants to supervise the grand international conference hall at the Intercontinental roundabout in Abu Dhabi.

The Supreme Council of UAE University approved the commencement of graduate studies in the university in September. The first phase will be limited to Gulf Studies.

1 July: Sheikh Zayed issued a federal law setting-up the National Computer Centre.

3 July: Sheikh Zayed accepted the resignation of Said Ghobash, Minister of Planning, following his election as the Chairman of the Arab Currency Fund which had it headquarters in Abu Dhabi. Sheikh Zayed issued a decree promoting Brigadier Hamouda bin Ali Al-Dhahiri, Minister of State for the Interior, to the rank of General.

5 July: The Council of Ministers approved the extension of electrical services to public housing units in remote areas of the Northern Emirates.

The Federal National Council, at an extraordinary meeting, called on the UAE to undertake an initiative aimed at repairing the rift in Arab relations.

11 July: The UAE Embassy and five other embassies in Beirut came under sustained fire from Israeli invasion forces in the Lebanese capital.

14 July: Said Al Raqbani signed a 23.5 million dirham agreement to set up and equip an aquaculture research laboratory in Umm al-Qaiwain.

19 July: The Diwan of the President issued a statement cancelling all celebrations for Eid al-Fitr in solidarity with the Palestinian and Lebanese people facing the Zionist invasion of their territory.

20 July: Sheikh Zayed arrived in Geneva on a private visit to Switzerland.

Mohammad Khalifa Al Kindi signed a 152 million dirham contract for the construction of a 220-bed hospital, the largest in Sharjah.

25 July: Sheikh Sultan bin Mohammad Al Qassimi issued a decree appointing Sheikh Saud bin Khalid Al Qassimi as Chairman of the Department of Works in Sharjah.

26 July: In Geneva, Sheikh Zayed received Al-Shadhili bin Jadid, Secretary General of the Arab League. They reviewed the efforts being made to contain the Lebanese crisis.

31 July: Sheikh Humaid bin Rashid Al Nuaimi visited oil drilling operations in Al-Yabisa in the Al-Raqaib district of Ajman.

2 August: The Council of Ministers approved housing regulations for federal employees working on local contracts in Abu Dhabi and Al-Ain.

5 August: Sheikh Khalifa bin Zayed Al Nahyan in a statement on the occasion of the sixteenth anniversary of the coming to power of Sheikh Zayed, stressed that Zayed had taken over the reins of government in the emirate of

Abu Dhabi when there was a call to change the face of life in the emirate and that this was the take-off point for the formation of the United Arab Emirates.

10 August: The Executive Council decided to designate all oil installations in Abu Dhabi as prohibited areas. Police permits will be required for approach or entry to these areas.

14 August: Sheikh Rashid bin Saeed Al Maktoum inspected the industrial area in Jebel Ali.

17 August: Sheikh Saqr bin Mohammad Al Qassimi exempted all factories in the Khor Khwair industrial area from the payment of fees on imports via the Ras al-Khaimah port as an encouragement to local industries.

19 August: The formation of the first higher committee for aid in the country was announced.

22 August: Mohammad Ibrahim Al Juwaid, the Chargé d'Affaires at the UAE Embassy in Kuwait, was wounded when an armed man shot him three times in his office in the Embassy.

24 August: The Executive Council approved the establishment of a free zone at Port Zayed in Abu Dhabi.

26 August: Ibrahim Jawad Rida, the UAE Consul General in Bombay, escaped injury when unidentified attackers opened fire on him a few metres from the Consulate.

1 September: Saif Jarwan issued a decree for the payment of 1.8 million dirhams in annual aid to the Co-operative Union and co-operative societies in the country.

5 September: On his arrival in the city of Fez to attend the Arab Summit Conference, Sheikh Zayed stressed the necessity of unifying Arab ranks in order to regain their rights.

7 September: Sheikh Zayed met with GCC leaders on the periphery of the Fez Summit. Co-ordination of their positions was discussed as was work to make the Summit a success.

10 September: Sheikh Zayed arrived in Rabat on a private visit to Morocco.

14 September: Sheikh Khalifa bin Zayed Al Nahyan, meeting with the British Minister of State for Foreign Affairs, Douglas Hurd, called on the British Government to participate with its partners in the European Community to find a just settlement to the Arab-Israeli conflict.

15 September: ADFAED granted a 26.5 million dollar loan to Morocco to help finance the construction of a dam near Marrakesh.

20 September: Sheikh Zayed sent letters to the presidents of the five permanent members of the Security Council concerning the savage massacres which Israel and its allies were wreaking on the Lebanese and Palestinian people in Sabra and Chatilla. The Foreign Ministry issued a statement blaming America for these massacres.

The Council of Ministers decided to stop work for half an hour in mourning for the victims.

21 September: At his London residence, Sheikh Zayed discussed current developments in the region and the massacres at Sabra and Chatilla with Francis Beam, the British Foreign Secretary. Sheikh Zayed requested that the European countries adopt a decisive position and use their influence on America to avoid a tragedy in the region, since Israeli aggression was supported by America.

22 September: Dubai Civil Aviation (CAA) Director General said Dubai International Airport had received Government approval to build a second runway as one part of six planned extensions. Other proposed modifications included a duty free area.

23 September: The Supreme Council of the UAE University decided to accept all resident students who obtained 85 per cent or more in the Secondary Certificate regardless of their parents period of residency in the country.

24 September: After the Friday worship in all mosques, prayers were said for those who died in the Sabra and Chatilla massacres.

25 September: The President's Diwan issued a statement in which he announced that all Eid al-Adha celebrations would be cancelled because of the circumstances of the Arab nation.

7 October: Sheikh Zayed sent a letter to the Iranian President, Ali Khamenei, in which he called for action to put an end to the blood-letting between Iraq and Iran.

8 October: At the Al-Khazna resthouse, Sheikh Zayed met the members of the National Handball Team on the occasion of their victory in the 14-year-old category in the first Gulf Games Handball Championship held in Riyadh.

11 October: Sheikh Rashid granted a concession to British Petroleum to explore for hydrocarbons in Dubai.

12 October: Sheikh Sultan bin Mohammed Al Qassimi inspected progress on the Layya electricity plant.

16 October: First Lady, Sheikha Fatima bint Mubarak, Chairwoman of the Women's Federation, arrived in Salalah on an official visit to the Sultanate of Oman at the invitation of His Majesty, Sultan Qaboos bin Said' s mother.

19 October: Sheikh Ahmed bin Hamid signed an agreement setting-up a central double-wave (medium and short) transmission station to extend the Voice of the Emirates in Abu Dhabi to all parts of the world.

22 October: Sheikh Rashid bin Ahmed Al Mualla opened the Umm al-Qaiwain National Bank.

25 October: The Council of Ministers approved the construction of a natural gas pipeline to enable gas instead of diesel to be used to operate electrical plants in the Northern Emirates. They also approved raising the capital of the Emirates General Petroleum Corporation to 3 billion dirhams.

26 October: ADFAED agreed to loan 15 million dirhams to North Yemen to assist in a water and drainage project in Taiz province.

30 October: The Executive Council allocated 375 million dirhams to execute a number of new service and development projects in the emirate of Abu Dhabi.

1 November: Emirates General Petroleum Corporation began implementing the first stages of the 700 million dirham project for supplying electrical plants and large factories in the Northern Emirates with liquid gas from Sharjah's Al-Saja field.

3 November: Sheikh Rashid bin Ahmed Al Mualla attended ceremonies mounted by the American company, Texaco, to mark the commencement of oil exploration operations on-land in Umm al-Qaiwain.

4 November: In the first half of 1982, the Federation's surplus trade balance amounted to 20 billion dirhams.

7 November: The Council of Ministers approved the UAE's 40 per cent shareholding in the Arab African Bank which had capitalization of 500 million dirhams. Abu Dhabi Executive Council approved the draft law establishing a new national bank under the name of 'The Bank of Credit and Commerce - Emirates' as a limited shareholding company with a capital of 400 million dirhams.

9 November: Sheikh Zayed, heading the UAE delegation to the third GCC Summit Conference in Manama, stressed that the founding of the GCC confirmed the determination of the region's leaders to provide Gulf citizens with all the fundamentals of a good life.

10 November: Sheikh Hamad bin Mohammad Al Sharqi visited the new Fujairah Port which received its first ship.

14 November: Sheikha Fatima bint Mubarak, Chairwoman of the Women's Federation, called for resistance to the phenomenon of foreign marriages which was creating a dangerous imbalance in the structure of society.

17 November: Sheikh Zayed sent cables of congratulations to Sultan Qaboos bin Said and President Ali Nasser Mohammad on the occasion of their ratification of the Declaration of Principles between the Sultanate of Oman and the Democratic Republic of Yemen which was brought about through the mediation of the UAE and Kuwait.

26 November: Sheikh Sultan bin Mohammad Al Qassimi donated 1 million dollars to establishing the Islamic Centre in Zagreb and to support the centre with an annual payment of 50,000 dollars.

29 November: Sheikh Khalifa bin Zayed Al Nahyan issued the law establishing the Bank of Credit and Commerce - Emirates.

2 December: Sheikh Zayed received the Members of the Supreme Council of the Federation and groups of well-wishers who came to greet him on the occasion of the eleventh National Day. Zayed delivered a speech to the people of the UAE on this occasion in which he stressed the importance of Arab unity in order to achieve well-being, power and victory for the nation.

Sheikha Fatima bint Mubarak, Chairwoman of the UAE Women's Federation, in remarks made to the magazine *Zahrat al-Khaleej*, praised the efforts of the President and his brothers, the Members of the Supreme Council, in supporting the renaissance of women and assisting them to fully participate in life without eroding Islamic Arab traditions.

7 December: Sheikh Saqr bin Mohammed Al Qassimi opened the Wadi al-Beeh Dam in Ras al-Khaimah, one of the largest dams in the country, and the tourist resort in Ain Khat.

8 December: An agreement was signed for the exploitation of Al-Saja gas to fuel the large electricity plants and factories in the Northern Emirates.

10 December: UAE signed the UN Law Of The Sea Treaty in Jamaica.

12 December: It was decided to hold a 'Charity Plate' Festival for the first time on 21 December under the patronage of the President, the proceeds being earmarked for needy orphans in the Arab world.

15 December: Sheikh Zayed ordered that urgent aid amounting to 10 million dirhams be given to help the victims of the earthquake which struck the Dhamar Region in Yemen.

18 December: Sheikh Zayed ordered all the country's hospitals to prepare places for seriously injured cases from the earthquake in Yemen.

19 December: Sheikh Surour bin Mohammad Al Nahyan signed agreements for expansion of the desalination plant on eastern Umm al-Nar, and for constructing a desalination plant in the Al-Taweelah region.

A contract was signed for laying the submarine telecommunications cable between the UAE and Bahrain.

21 December: Sheikh Zayed opened the new session of the Federal National Council.

Sheikh Zayed presided over a meeting of the Supreme Council of the Federation in which Arab and international affairs were discussed.

Sheikh Zayed and the Members of the Supreme Council opened the 'Charity Plate' Festival.

25 December: Sheikh Zayed issued a federal law establishing the country's Supreme Customs Council whose aim was to establish unified customs in the Emirates.

Said Al Raqbani opened the Wadi Idhn Dam in Ras al-Khaimah.

26 December: Pakistan's President, Mohammad Zia Al Haq discussed Islamic and international affairs and the efforts of the Islamic Committee to stop the war between Iraq and Iran with Sheikh Zayed, during a stopover at Abu Dhabi International Airport.

29 December: Sheikh Hamad bin Mohammad Al Sharqi opened the new power station in Qadfa'a and the new offices of the Ministry of Electricity in Fujairah.

Nineteen Eighty Three

1 January: Sheikh Zayed visited a boys and a girls school in Al-Marfa on his tour through the Western Region. He called on the students to seek knowledge at the highest levels because knowledge was the only weapon which would guarantee the future. He also encouraged them to cultivate good manners and be obedient to their teachers. He told them that the State placed its hopes in them and that it provided the school with all requirements. He further stressed that the role of women was not less than that of men because female students are the mothers of the future.

Sheikh Zayed also inspected the new housing units in the city of Al-Marfa and ordered that the streets in the city be paved, that a workshop be built for maintaining fishing boats and that the jetty be lengthened.

Sheikh Rashid bin Ahmed Al Mualla published an order prohibiting the hunting of birds and wild animals in Umm al-Qaiwain.

The Ministry of Public Works and Housing began work on the 320-bed Sharjah Hospital which will cost 160 million dirhams. It also began the 86 million dirham fifth phase of the Umm al-Qaiwain Central Hospital.

3 January: The Council of Ministers decided to require company owners and labour contractors to deposit a bank guarantee when recruiting labour, to ensure their repatriation after the projects for which they were recruited were completed.

The National Bank of Abu Dhabi devalued the dirham by 1 per cent, commencing 1 January. This was the second devaluation in two months, the first (1.5 per cent) took place in November 1982.

The Ministry of Communications commenced implementation of the federal decree which required documents to be deposited with international organizations registering the UAE's adherence to 30 international maritime agreements.

Sheikh Rashid bin Humaid Al Nuaimi opened the electrical expansion project in Ajman, increasing electrical energy to 85.5 megawatts, and laid the foundation stone for the new 2.5 million gallon water reservoir.

5 January: Sheikh Zayed, visiting two schools in Ghiyathi, stressed that knowledge is an essential basis for progress and that it is the basic right of every citizen. He also stated that the Government was exerting all its efforts to develop the country and that investing in the human individual is the best of all investments. He further stated that education should be based on linking the religious and temporal worlds.

The Directorate General of Immigration and Passports decided to terminate the issuing of special recruitment visas for licensed investors without a local partner.

7 January: The UAE donated 500,000 dollars toward the construction of the permanent headquarters for the Islamic Economic Group in Karachi.

Sheikh Zayed issued a decree establishing the Fujairah Quarry Company capitalized at 150 million dirhams.

8 January: Sheikh Zayed opened the first model social centre in the Northern Emirates aimed at reviving traditional arts and crafts and improving social and cultural standards for women.

9 January: Sheikh Zayed signed contracts for the construction of the new municipality offices and the meat market in Umm al-Qaiwain.

10 January: The Council of Ministers granted permission for GCC nationals to operate as contractors in implementation of the Economic Unity Agreement

11 January: Sheikh Sultan bin Mohammed Al Qassimi donated 800,000 dollars to develop the African-Asian Institute in Khartoum and to establish a hall to be named 'Sharjah' at the University of Khartoum.

12 January: The UAE was chosen as a member of the Executive Office of the Council of Arab Ministers of Youth Welfare and Sport.

The first cataract and glaucoma operations were performed at the airborne international teaching hospital at Abu Dhabi Airport.

14 January: Sheikh Sultan bin Mohammad Al Qassimi directed that handicapped children from GCC States be accepted for humanitarian services in Sharjah, commencing in 1984.

Dr Mana Said Al Otaiba stressed that the UAE was eager to maintain the price of oil at 24 dollars per barrel and that Arab Gulf States did not intend to designate the price of their oil, since they believed that the cure for the crisis lay in limiting production and not in reducing oil prices. The Abu Dhabi National Tanker Company expected to take delivery of its first oil tanker in February, the first of seven tankers for which contracts had been signed.

17 January: The Council of Ministers approved a draft law governing the practice of medical practitioners other than doctors and pharmacists.

19 January: Saif Al Jarwan, UAE Minister of Labour and Social Affairs, speaking at the ninth Conference of Asia and Pacific Region Labour Ministers in Tokyo, stressed that the UAE provided its foreign labour force with all the necessary services, most importantly health and education.

20 January: Sheikh Zayed called on Arabs and Muslims to stand firmly and sincerely united against the difficult circumstances facing the Arab Islamic world. He stressed the need to stick together until Islam and Muslims become powerful. During his meeting with a delegation of Moroccan *Ulema* and judges he stated that conflict within the Arab nation was proving very costly:

solidarity, on the other hand, would mean glory and power. Zayed said that if Muslims really practised Islam as a way of life and followed it sincerely that their circumstances would be much changed. He wondered why there was so much tearing apart, why there was so much division, for which there is no basis in *Sharia* law. He expressed the hope that Muslims would stand together and that their world would be one, that Allah would guide them along the high moral path to confront their problems as they exploit the blessings, wealth and potential which Allah had so generously given them and in which there is so much good for the betterment of the Arab Islamic nation.

Sheikh Khalifa bin Zayed Al Nahyan ordered payment of grants totalling 21.6 million dirhams (50,000 dirhams per student) given by Sheikh Zayed to the first male and female graduates of the UAE University.

21 January: Dr Mana Said Al Otaiba, on his departure from the UAE to attend an extaordinary meeting of OPEC, called on all OPEC members to shoulder their responsibilities in dealing with the oil market crisis and to maintain the unity of the organization.

23 January: Sheikh Mohammad bin Rashid Al Maktoum opened the new criminal laboratory at Police Head-quarters in Dubai, the third of its kind in the Arab world.

Dr Mana Said Al Otaiba warned of the dangers which would be posed by an unhealthy oil market if OPEC oil ministers did not solve problems arising from the distribution of production quotas. He described the extraordinary Conference of OPEC Oil Ministers, which was commencing in Geneva, as the most difficult meeting in its history.

Hamad Abdulrahman Al Madfa, Minister of Health, studied a co-operation agreement with Beirut's American University for establishing a College of Medicine at UAE University and a College of Nursing in Abu Dhabi.

25 January: The UAE warned OPEC that the organization was passing through a difficult phase and made it clear that the UAE would reconsider production and pricing in light of its own interests and the interests of its people. It would also review co-ordination with its sister countries, the members of OPEC and the countries which adopted moderate positions. Dr Mana Said Al Otaiba said, following his return from Geneva, that the UAE would produce 1.6 million barrels per day and that Gulf countries would hold consultations in the next few days to co-ordinate their positions *vis-à-vis* prices and production. He stressed that the UAE would endeavour to overcome the differences which appeared during the extraordinary OPEC Conference which resulted in a reduction in OPEC production to 17.5 million barrels per day.

26 January: Sheikh Khalifa bin Zayed Al Nahyan stressed the UAE's concern for OPEC unity and the necessity of maintaining its existence as Dr Mana Said Al Otaiba briefed him on the results of OPEC's Geneva Conference and the circumstances through which the oil market was passing.

The UAE hosted meetings of the technical committee for demarcating borders between the Sultanate of Oman and the Democratic Republic of Yemen.

The UAE joined the International

Organization for Marine Satellites (OGMARSAT).

27 January: Dr Mana Said Al Otaiba warned that an oil war would lead to dangerous problems from which the entire world would suffer, and could lead to the destruction of the international currency system. He said that the UAE exerted its fullest efforts to repair the rift within OPEC but some of the members of the organization violated agreed production quotas.

28 January: Sheikh Khalid bin Saqr Al Qassimi opened the first co-operative society in Ras al-Khaimah.

The Al-Ain Municipality opened five pedestrian underground passageways in the heart of the city.

31 January: The Executive Council approved an aerial photography project and the preparation of tourist maps for Al-Ain.

The UAE Red Crescent Society was registered with its headquarters in Abu Dhabi.

1 February: The Council of Ministers stressed the UAE's concern for OPEC unity, the stability of the European market and the international currency situation, following a briefing on Al Otaiba's comprehensive report of the extraordinary OPEC Conference held in January.

3 February: Sheikh Khalifa presided over a meeting of the ADNOC Board which studied the current situation in the international oil market.

4 February: The first project of its kind in the UAE was opened for transporting five different petroleum products from the principal refinery at Umm al-Nar to giant storage tanks for consumption in the city of Al-Ain. The transport of these products was effected through 105-km pipelines at a cost of 200 million dirhams.

In 1982, the total amount spent on development projects in Abu Dhabi was 5.588 billion dirhams.

7 February: The History and Heritage Committee completed registration and documentation of all information collected in a three year period. These documents were concerned with all aspects of heritage in social political, historical and economic fields.

The oil company, Gulf Ras al-Khaimah (GRAK), announced the discovery of an offshore oifield at Saleh One X test well about 26 miles off Ras al-Khaimah.

8 February: Sheikh Khalifa instructed that 5 million dollars allocated by Sheikh Zayed to the Zayed Centre for Higher Studies attached to the Universities of Karachi and Peshawar be provided.

9 February: The Board of the UAE Institute for Banking Training held its first meeting in which it outlined the steps it would take to provide national cadres in the financial sector.

10 February: Sheikh Tahnoun bin Mohammad Al Nahyan opened Ministry of Agriculture and Fisheries central laboratories established in the Al-Oha district of Al-Ain at a cost of 28 million dirhams.

11 February: The UAE, during the meeting of the joint French-UAE Commission held in Paris, asked that the UAE and other Gulf States be given the necessary know-how to protect their economic infrastructure as well as the equipment and technology for protection against radioactivity.

16 February: Sheikh Hamad bin

Mohammad Al Sharqi opened the 2.8km, 10 million cubic metre capacity dam complex covering Wadi Ham, Wadi Al-Qarfar and Wadi Madook, which will collect rainwater to help in irrigation and replenishment of artesian wells.

17 February: In a speech before the Security Council which was considering Israeli policy in the occupied Arab territories, the UAE stressed that the Israeli policy of expansion threatened the peace of both the Middle East and the world.

An agricultural co-operation agreement was signed in Islamabad between the UAE and Pakistan.

ADFAED agreed to loan 10.3 million dollars to Tunisia to assist in oases development in the south of the country and date production improvements.

22 February: The Riyadh-based micro-wave telecommunications network, connecting the UAE, Saudi Arabia and Qatar, became operational.

24 February: The UAE announced that its share in foreign aid and economic co-operation programmes for developing countries, and especially Arab and Islamic countries, had exceeded 12 per cent of its national income. Sheikh Hamdan bin Rashid Al Maktoum, in line with the Economic Unity Agreement, issued instructions to the directors of customs in the Federation to exempt GCC countries from customs duties on agricultural, animal and natural wealth products, to come into effect on 1 March.

25 February: Sheikh Zayed held discussions in Islamabad with the Pakistani president revolving around the current situation in the Islamic world and on the international scene. Special emphasis was given to developments in the Middle East crisis and the Iran-Iraq war, the two Presidents stressing their concern to put an end to this war by any means.

27 February: Sheikh Saqr bin Mohammed Al Qassimi praised efforts made by the Arab Union for Food Industries to exploit the agricultural wealth and potential of the Arab nation. In the inaugural meetings he welcomed the National Date and Date Palm Committee's choice of Ras al-Khaimah as the site for setting-up a 32 million dirham date factory.

3 March: Sheikh Zayed returned to the UAE from Saudi Arabia where he met with His Majesty King Fahad bin Abdulaziz and attended the ninth annual pure-bred camel races in Janadriya.

4 March: The Ministry of Labour and Social Affairs issued a decree establishing the Al-Ain Co-operative Consumers Society.

6 March: Sheikh Zayed received the Algerian President, Al Shadhili bin Jadid, who arrived in the country on an official visit.

The first session of the eighth round of meetings of the Council of Arab Ministers of Health began in Abu Dhabi.

7 March: Sheikh Zayed held a closed meeting with the Algerian President, Al Shadhili bin Jadid, during which they discussed developments in regional affairs and the Iran-Iraq war. They dealt with on-going developments and initiatives on all levels aimed at ending this war by peaceful means. Sheikh Zayed invoked a blessing on the Algerian President and King Hassan II and hailed the positive change in Algerian-Moroccan relations.

Sheikh Zayed arrived in New Delhi to participate in the seventh Non-aligned Summit of the leaders of the Non-aligned Nations. He called on non-aligned leaders to put an end to differences between the members. He said in his press conference that the world lives in a new cold war athmosphere between the two superpowers but that regional struggles take on a serious international dimension.

8 March: Sheikh Khalifa, during his reception for Arab Ministers of Health, stressed that health and education were the main pillars of the UAE's efforts to develop the individual.

9 March: The Executive Council approved the appointment of an international company to undertake an industrial survey in Abu Dhabi.

The UAE and the Democratic Republic of Yemen signed a cultural and educational co-operation agreement.

UAE Federation of Chambers of Commerce and Industry signed a co-operation agreement with the Omani Chamber of Commerce and Industry in Abu Dhabi. Specific areas covered in the agreement included investment opportunity studies, joint project creation, marketing enhancement in both countries, and creation of a joint committee to meet bi-annually to monitor progress.

10 March: Sheikh Zayed held lengthy consultations with a number of heads of state participating in the Non-aligned Summit in New Delhi.

The UAE expressed its concern over the continuation of the Iraq-Iran war and it called on the two sides to accept a peaceful resolution of the armed conflict, stressing that it was a waste of human resources and a threat to the security and stability of the Gulf region. The UAE also registered its appreciation of Iraq's expressed wish to end the war.

The President, in his speech before the Non-aligned Summit, expressed his belief that the security of the Gulf was the sole responsibility of the States of the area and refused to enter into any military pact since he rejected interference by any foreign state in the UAE's internal affairs.

Sheikh Khalifa bin Zayed Al Nahyan ordered the immediate start of a 2 billion dirham housing complex project for low income citizens, to include 560 apartments for single and married people.

EMIRTEL began installing coin-operated public telephones booths in Al-Ain.

12 March: The UAE hosted the second Arab conference for water purification which was held in the Dubai World Trade Centre.

18 March: The UAE and Iraq signed a two-year cultural, educational and informational co-operation agreement.

20 March: The Ministry of Health reviewed the possibility that the oil spill from Iranian offshore oil fields would reach the UAE's territorial waters.

21 March: The Executive Council approved Abu Dhabi's draft 1983 development programme costing 6.245 billion dirhams.

22 March: Sheikh Zayed attended the secondary-level military schools annual festival mounted in the Medinat Zayed sports stadium in which 25,000 local students took part. He stressed that young people were the country's real treasure and that the country looked to them to build the future.

GCC traffic directors, meeting in Sharjah recommended that each State's driving licence be valid for all GCC States.

24 March: The Council of Ministers in extraordinary session examined the federal budget for 1983.

28 March: The Council of Ministers studied an urgent memorandum from the Higher Committee for the protection of the environment regarding the possibility of pollution resulting from the Iranian Nowruz oil spill reaching the waters of the Gulf.

The twenty-sixth session of the Arab Academic Administration Council for Maritime Transport, in which 16 Arab countries participated, was convened in Sharjah.

29 March: Sheikh Rashid bin Saeed Al Maktoum inspected Jebel Ali Industrial Zone and expressed the hope that the area would become a solid industrial base which would contribute to the UAE's industrial diversification. He described the area as an object of pride for the UAE.

30 March: Sheikh Zayed, and the Members of the Supreme Council of the Federation, witnessed the graduation of the second batch of students from UAE University. He said that the highest achievement of a nation was measured by the level and extent of its education.

Sheikh Zayed and the Members of the Supreme Council of the Federation witnessed the graduation of the new batch of students from the Zayed Military College. Sheikh Khalifa bin Zayed Al Nahyan stated that the UAE was attempting to build its own army to protect the nation, defend its territory, and give its people a sense of security.

Self reliance, he said, would allow the UAE to undertake its responsibilities, participate with others in protecting the Gulf from international strife and face the greed lurking in the region, which was plotting to bleed its wealth dry.

31 March: First Lady, Sheikh Fatima bint Mubarak, attended the graduation of the second batch of female university graduates. She encouraged them to share in the service of society and to bear the responsibility for developing future generations.

1 April: In accordance with the labour agreement concluded by Sudan and Dubai in April 1981, a joint technical committee for labour co-operation between the UAE and the Republic of Sudan met in its first ministerial meeting in Dubai.

The new 4000-line electronic telephone exchange in Sharjah became operational.

5 April: Abu Dhabi Executive Council approved the allocation of 130 million dirhams to construct homes for low income families in the Musaffah region.

7 April: Sheikh Zayed received an invitation from King Hassan II, delivered by his adviser Ahmad bin Souda, to attend the Arab Summit meeting proposed by Morocco. Sheikh Zayed welcomed the holding of the Summit, stressing his support for any Arab movement to consider national issues, the most important of which was the question of Palestine. He also stressed the necessity of on-going meetings between leaders to exchange opinions on matters which are vital to the future.

8 April: The first shipment of protective floating barriers and oil suction pumps arrived in the country as part of a programme to safeguard the UAE's coasts from pollution.

The first Iranian airline connecting Sharjah with Bandar Abbas and Tehran was inaugurated.

9 April: Sheikh Zayed, King Fahad bin Abdulaziz, and the Rulers and Sheikhs attended the grand annual pure-bred Arab camel races in Abu Dhabi.

10 April: Electrical networks in the cities Al-Ain and Abu Dhabi were connected via a 132 kilovolt line in order to deal with emergency situations.

The UAE hosted a UNICEF conference in Abu Dhabi to determine a new strategy for the organization's projects in the Gulf during the next three years.

The Ministry of Education completed the curriculum for the first and second primary grades and the first intermediate grade in preparation for printing in the UAE for the first time.

Twenty eight helicopters from the Abu Dhabi Helicopter Company were mounting surveillance of the oil spill on a continuing basis to make sure that it did not reach the UAE's territorial waters.

The first UAE University holder of a scholarship to study abroad, Hussain Mohammad Hussain Al Mutawa, received his doctorate in Higher Education Administration in the United States and was appointed as a teacher in the College of Education in the University.

11 April: Sheikh Zayed was present at the air base at Al-Dhafra for the graduation of a new batch of pilots. He commended the excellent demonstration mounted by the pilots and said that every citizen could be proud of what he had witnessed.

12 April: Sheikh Zayed was present at the opening ceremonies of Abu Dhabi Women's Association's headquarters in Al-Bateen. He stressed that women not only comprised half of society but that they were the ones who, by and large, had the responsibility of bringing-up future generations in the proper manner.

13 April: First Lady Sheikha Fatima bint Mubarak attended the first Festival of Childhood mounted at the headquarters of the Abu Dhabi Women's Association.

14 April: Sheikh Zayed, visiting the first Festival of Childhood, stressed the necessity of educating the new generations. He remarked that books were both a good means of education and a way of passing the time in a useful and amusing manner.

The Voice of the UAE from Abu Dhabi began transmitting its new broadcasting services, 'The Popular Programme', for two and a half hours per day.

16 April: Sheikh Sultan bin Mohammad Al Qassimi arrived in Islamabad on an official visit to Pakistan, during which he and the Pakistani President, Mohammed Zia Al Haq, discussed co-operation in economic and commercial fields.

In Abu Dhabi the Committee of Information Experts began deliberations in preparation for the eighth round of meetings of the GCC Ministers of Information.

17 April: Sheikh Zayed, having received a report from Hamad Al Midfa, Minister of Health and Chairman of the Environment Committee regarding the steps taken to ensure that the oil spill would not taint territorial waters, stressed the need to continue with protective measures currently underway.

At the first exhibition of GCC municipalities which had opened in Abu Dhabi, Sheikh Khalifa called for an increase in co-operation between GCC municipalities in all fields and the unification of their efforts to provide services to citizens in the States of the region.

The first phase of Dubai Hospital came into operation.

18 April: The Council of Ministers studied results of meetings of the Regional Organization for the Protection of the Marine Environment (ROPME) which was convened in Kuwait with the participation of the UAE.

Sheikh Hamdan bin Rashid Al Maktoum announced that the federal budget for 1983 would be 40 per cent less than that of 1982, in light of the policy of careful spending.

19 April: Sheikh Khalifa stressed at a reception for GCC Ministers of Information, who held their eighth conference in Abu Dhabi, that the conference embodied the existing co-operation between the States of the region and he stressed the importance of joint collective action to develop the Gulf.

20 April: First Lady Sheikha Fatima bint Mubarak witnessed graduation ceremonies for the first batch of female general secondary graduates from the Al-Qadisiyya school in Abu Dhabi.

21 April: Three local graduates of the College of Administrative and Political Sciences were recruited by the Arab Group Insurance Company for the first time.

23 April: The Council of Ministers approved a new draft law governing educational missions abroad, educational assistance and supervision. Sheikha Fatima bint Mubarak, whilst honouring Dr Aisha Al Sayyar who obtained a doctorate, called on young women to increase their knowledge and work for the service of society in developing future generations.

24 April: The first institute in the State for administrative development was inaugurated.

25 April: The Council of Ministers approved the exemption of all farmers and fishermen from debts totalling 7.5 million dirhams until the end of 1983.

26 April: Sheikh Zayed, attending school-closing ceremonies in Abu Dhabi, praised the scientific accomplishments which had been achieved by the students and the originality of experiments in exploiting solar power to desalinate the waters of the Red Sea.

First Lady Sheikha Fatima bint Mubarak attended the graduation of the third batch of female students from the Nursing College in Abu Dhabi.

27 April: Sheikh Sultan bin Mohammad Al Qassimi visited the Institute of Hope in Sharjah which had been supplied with modern equipment for training the handicapped.

28 April: At the request of the UAE, the International Human Settlements Conference at its meeting in Helsinki included the Arabic language in its official work for the first time.

30 April: The Department of Water and Electricity in Abu Dhabi completed the necessary plans to execute the huge long-term project which would produce 180 million gallons of water and 3000 megawatts of electricity.

1 May: Sheikh Zayed received a letter from the Japanese Prime Minister, Yasuhiro Nakasone, delivered by the

Japanese Minister for International Trade and Industry, regarding relations between the two countries and developments in the economic and commercial sectors.

Sheikha Fatima bint Mubarak donated 3 million dirhams from The Charity Plate project to support the Arab Family Organization in Sharjah.

2 May: Sheikh Zayed witnessed naval manoeuvres using live ammunition. He stressed the State's desire to supply the Armed Forces with the latest advanced military technology to increase their fighting ability.

Sheikh Khalifa said that the Navy was equipped with Exocet rockets guided by means of electronic intelligence which were capable of hitting ground targets at a distance of 700 kms.

The first medical operation on a falcon to be undertaken in the UAE was successfully completed.

3 May: The Council of Ministers decided to increase the price of petroleum products in the country, beginning on 4 May 1983.

4 May: A 50 million dollar agreement was signed for setting up a 1000 kms co-axial cable between the UAE and Pakistan to be paid for jointly by the two countries.

5 May: ADGAS's total production for 1982 was 2,331,937 metric tons of natural liquid gas which exceeded the production of energy by DAS by more than 30,000 tons.

6 May: In Manama, Sheikh Zayed and His Highness Sheikh Essa bin Salman Al Khalifa, the Amir of Bahrain, considered the excellent relations between the two countries and ways of developing them, as well as developments in the region

and the current Arab situation. They also attended the annual camel races.

Sheikh Khalid bin Saqr Al Qassimi signed a 62 million dollar agreement to set up a 300,000 ton white cement factory in Ras al-Khaimah.

The Directorate General of Immigration and Nationality decided not to grant residency to labourers until it was confirmed that they were free from infectious and endemic diseases.

7 May: Sheikh Mohammad bin Zayed Al Nahyan and Ahmed Khalifa Al Suweidi inaugurated the first lighted moving sign board in Abu Dhabi and the most modern in the Gulf. It cost 3 million dirhams.

8 May: Abu Dhabi Executive Council approved the setting-up of a solar-powered distillation plant in Al-Wajn at a cost of 2.2 million dirhams.

9 May: Sheikh Rashid bin Ahmed Al Mualla signed a 24 million dirham contract for the second development phase of Umm al-Qaiwain lagoon.

Sheikh Khalifa bin Zayed Al Nahyan had discussions at an official meeting in Abu Dhabi with the French Minister of Defence, Charles Hernu, concerning the strengthening of mutual relations and technical and military co-operation. Sheikh Khalifa stated that the French Minister expressed France's readiness to supply the UAE's Armed Forces with the latest advanced land, sea and air weapons.

12 May: Sheikh Zayed opened the Women's Federation permanent exhibition during his visit to the Environmental Centre for Handicrafts at the Federation's headquarters.

The UAE donated 6 million dollars to the Arab Gulf Fund which gives 56 per cent of its aid to UNICEF.

Two hundred and fifty projects, costing 2914 million dirhams, were completed last year in Abu Dhabi.

13 May: Sheikh Sultan bin Mohammad Al Qassimi returned to the country from Khartoum after participating in the opening of the fourth annual meeting of the Trustees Council of the Islamic Dawa Organization.

14 May: Dr Mana Said Al Otaiba opened the new 32 million dirham Das Island Hospital for workers and residents on the island.

15 May: The Trustees Council of the Complex of Cultural Institutions and Documents in Abu Dhabi studied the setting-up of the National Document Centre.

16 May: The Council of Ministers decided to support local consulting engineering offices in order to encourage nationals.

The first heart operation was performed in Abu Dhabi Central Hospital.

20 May: Sheikh Zayed received a comprehensive report on the results of the GCC mediation mission undertaken by the Foreign Ministers of the UAE and Kuwait to Iran and Iraq in an attempt to limit the Iran-Iraq war.

21 May: Sheikh Zayed held discussions with His Majesty King Fahad bin Abdulaziz in Dhahran. International and Gulf affairs were discussed within the framework of continuing consultations between the two leaders.

22 May: The Council of Ministers approved a draft law regarding pension benefits and retirement payments for some 3000 citizens working for institutions, companies and banks in which the Government is a shareholder.

A Ministry of Health plan for providing blood from local donors to hospitals came into operation after the decision was taken to stop importing blood.

24 May: Sheikh Zayed arrived in Al-Marfa at the beginning of a field tour of agricultural and development projects, as well as public utility services, in the Western Region.

26 May: First Lady Sheikha Fatima bint Mubarak allocated 500,000 dirhams from the proceeds of the festival fund of The Charity Plate for projects organized by the Lebanese government to care for Palestinian and Lebanese orphans, victims of the Sabra and Chatilla slaughter.

27 May: Sheikh Zayed, the Rulers of the Emirates, and Sheikhs attended row and sail boat races in front of the Abu Dhabi Tourist Club.

29 May: Total cost of the Ministry of Electricity and Water projects during 1982 amounted to 4.1 billion dirhams.

30 May: Sheikh Zayed continued his field tour in Liwa where he inspected sand stabilization and land reclamation projects. The reclaimed land will be planted with bushes, palm trees, citrus fruits and vegetables after distribution to local farmers.

31 May: This year the UAE exported its excess production of agricultural crops, such as tomatoes, aubergines and green peppers to Syria and Jordan.

1 June: Sheikh Zayed toured Medinat Zayed during which he inspected the city's development and building projects and the new housing units.

5 June: In Abu Dhabi. Sheikh Zayed and Jordan's, King Hussein discussed developments in the region. Zayed said that Arabs must employ their good offices to achieve Arab solidarity.

11 June: The Central Bank report provided positive indications for the economy of the State. Local liquidity had increased to 43.8 billion dirhams.

13 June: The UAE succeeded in the first division of the individual competition in the fifteenth World Parachute-jumping Championship held in Switzerland.

14 June: Sheikh Khalifa bin Zayed, meeing with the Secretary General of the Arab League, Al Shadhili bin Kulaib, confirmed the UAE's support for efforts being made to unify the ranks, strengthen Arab solidarity and gather Arab energies to meet future challenges.

16 June: The total number of public housing units constructed in Dubai during 1983 stood at 1080. The homes were distributed to low income people, graduates, and families disadvantaged by planning and development projects.

18 June: The total cost of Ministry of Communications projects during 1982 amounted to more than 2.071 billion dirhams.

19 June: Sheikh Khalifa bin Zayed Al Nahyan announced that the UAE would host the first joint manoeuvres of GCC armies to be mounted next October, describing them as a sign of things to come.

21 June: A Ministry of Planning report stated that the UAE national income was 97.611 billion dirhams in 1982; GDP was 113.6 billion dirhams; and wages amounted to 22.1 billion dirhams. The per capita share of GDP was 95,800 dirhams.

24 June: Sheikh Zayed on a private visit to London, reviewed developments in the Middle East with the British Minister of State for Foreign Affairs, Richard Louis.

27 June: The investment programme for the emirate of Abu Dhabi amounted to 3189 million dirhams in 1982.

1 July: In the first three months of this year, 91 per cent of the UAE's industrial exports valued at 2.235 million dirhams, 6 per cent of the UAE's non-industrial products valued at 4 million dirhams, and 3 per cent of the UAE's agricultural produce valued at 725,000 dirhams were exported to GCC countries.

Seven modern dairy farms in the country produced 2500 tons of fresh milk and ten chicken farms produced 102 million eggs and 3473 tons of meat.

2 July: The Board of ADNOC, under the Presidency of Sheikh Khalifa, studied development of the company's operations and international oil policy.

3 July: In 1982, Dubai's investment programmes amounted to 936 million dirhams as compared to 858 million dirhams in 1981.

4 July: Last year, Sharjah's investment programme cost 1.706 billion dirhams.

5 July: Sheikh Rashid bin Humaid Al Nuaimi issued an Amiri decree establishing the Ajman National Company Ltd.

The Executive Council approved Abu Dhabi's budget for 1983 amounting to 24.307 billion dirhams, a deficit of 2.79 billion dirhams.

8 July: Sheikh Zayed issued a federal decree adding seven new ministerial portfolios to the cabinet and releasing two ministers, Ministers of Education and Islamic Affairs and Awqaf, from their posts.

9 July: The new ministers took their oath of office before Sheikh Zayed who asked them to redouble their efforts for the people of the Emirates and in support of the Federation's future progress.

14 July: Sheikh Zayed visited Sheikh Rashid bin Saeed Al Maktoum on the occasion of Eid al-Fitr. He also inspected the dam projects in the Hatta region and observed the progress on the con-struction of two new dams. The Soviet Chess Union decided to hold the semi-final match for the World Chess Championship in the UAE.

16 July: Sheikh Zayed attended the traditional festivities held in Al-Ain public garden on the occasion of Eid al-Fitr as a mark of his concern and care for reviving the old ways and maintaining pure Arab traditions.

18 July: The reshuffled Council of Ministers convened a meeting under the Presidency of Sheikh Rashid bin Saeed Al Maktoum. The Deputy Prime Minister, Sheikh Hamdan bin Mohammad Al Nahyan stated that the Government would exert all its efforts to secure a good and comfortable life for the people of the Emirates and to strengthen the future of the Federation.

19 July: Sheikh Zayed issued a federal decree appointing Sheikh Nahyan bin Mubarak Al Nahyan as President of UAE University.

Sheikh Maktoum bin Rashid Al Maktoum donated 1 million dirhams to construct a new headquarters for the Higher Council for Youth and Sports and the sports Federations in Dubai.

Seven new prosecuting attorneys, the first graduates of UAE University, took the oath of office before the Minister of Justice.

23 July: The National Petroleum Construction Company accepted the handover of the giant barge, DLB, which arrived in Al-Sadiyyat. The sixth in the company's fleet, it is considered to be the largest barge in the Gulf region.

26 July: Sheikh Ahmed bin Hamid presided over the first meeting of Emirates Poets Groups of which there are four. They began a poetry movement and laid down a work plan for the groups for the coming period.

31 July: The Council of Ministers decided to form a ministerial committee to study educational policy and budgetary guidelines in the Ministry of Education.

2 August: The ministerial committee formed by the Council of Ministers studied education policy and educational requirements for the new academic year.

4 August: Sheikha Fatima bint Mubarak sent a cable of congratulations to chess-player, Nadia Mohammad Saleh, who was successful in the second division of the first Arab chess championship for women.

5 August: The Social Service Department financed 2120 buildings, commercial structures and villas amounting to 4 billion dirhams since it was established.

6 August: Sheikh Zayed received the Members of the Supreme Council of the Federation and crowds of well wishers on the seventeenth anniversary of his taking over the reins of government in the emirate of Abu Dhabi.

The Ministry of Foreign Affairs and the Ministry of Communications had deposited documents registering the UAE's adherence to the 1969 International Convention Relating to Intervention on the High Seas in Cases of Oil Pollution Casualties.

7 August: A Ministry of Planning report

stated that the total cost of projects and investment programmes during 1982 was 14.579 billion dirhams.

8 August: Sheikh Zayed, presiding over a meeting of the Council of Ministers, said that the opportunity to serve the nation was open to all citizens. He asked the Ministers to do their best for the good of their country and so that its citizens may achieve their ambitions.

The Council of Ministers approved the Federation's draft budget for 1983 amounting to 18.407 billion dirhams. Revenues were estimated at 12.901 billion dirhams.

The Council decided to exempt citizens from overdue payments for water and electricity amounting to 31 million dirhams.

9 August: Ajman Municipality began construction of the new Industrial Area.

13 August: Sheikh Zayed received a letter from the Iranian President, Ali Khamenei, delivered by Ali Akbar Velayati, the Iranian Foreign Minister, regarding the situation in the region and mutual relations.

There were 139,840 students, both male and female, studying in 347 schools in ten educational districts.

15 August: Sheikh Zayed presided over a meeting of the Council of Ministers which approved the draft law for regulating the hunting of birds and animals in the Federation; the setting-up of a central emergency hospital complex in Abu Dhabi at a cost of 230 million dirhams; and the construction of a new 30 million dirham desalination plant in Umm al-Qaiwain which will produce 2 million gallons of water per day.

Dubai Municipality received the first aerial photographs for their new map which will enable them to mark suitable planning sites and road projects.

19 August: The total value of loans granted by ADFAED to finance development projects in Arab countries was 774 million dirhams.

20 August: Sheikh Zayed inspected agricultural and development projects on the island of Delma, sampling citrus fruit, dates and vegetables from the model farms. He also inspected the dredging work which would increase agricultural and developmental areas. He ordered the setting-up of 30 new farms on Delma and marked the sites for new projects, including the industrial area, dams to control rainwater, the new souk and the electricity and water plant.

23 August: Sheikh Zayed issued a federal decree ratifying the agreement for the Gulf Investment Establishment capitalized at 2100 million dollars, which will be shared by the GCC States.

25 August: Sheikh Zayed, continuing his tour of the Western Region, remote areas and the islands, inspected the agricultural and developmental projects in Ghiyathi and took a look at the 'Green Belt' which includes the afforested area. He ordered an increase in land reclamation in Al-Raga agricultural area, the resulting land to be distributed to citizens for agricultural projects.

27 August: Sheikh Zayed continued his visit to the Western Region by inspecting agricultural and development projects in Liwa. He observed the progress of work in levelling and reclaiming land on which to establish new farms and inspected the new houses which were completed in eastern Mahadhir Al-Mariya and Mahadhir Marwan.

29 August: Sheikh Zayed presided over

a meeting of the Council of Ministers in which a number of domestic affairs were dealt with. These were concerned with the social stability of the citizens and action to improve the work performance of services in all sectors.

The Ajman National Oil Company began oil exploration work in the emirate.

30 August: There were 12,258 farms in the country covering an area of 363,531 dunams; of these 3573, covering an area of 76,902 dunams, were in Abu Dhabi.

1 September: Ahmed Al Tayer, Minister of State for Finance and Industry, announced that the Federation would impose a 4 per cent duty on imported goods following a GCC directive. Imports of foodstuffs, medicines, raw materials for local industries will be exempted from the duty. Whilst not ruling out introduction of income or company taxes in the Federation, Al Tayer said there were no plans to implement such measures at present.

2 September: The value of electrical projects completed during 1982 amounted to 284.8 million dirhams. The value of water projects amounted to 84.821 million dirhams.

10 September: There were 9549 national children registered in kindergartens for the academic year (1981-82), or 48 per cent of the total number of 19,866 four to five year old children registered in kindergartens.

The Council of Ministers decided to allocate 194.9 million dirhams to complete road projects in the country.

14 September: The Central Bank had 106 national employees in 1983, as opposed to 50 in 1980, an increase of 112 per cent.

16 September: The UAE announced its support for United Nations efforts to conclude an agreement prohibiting the use of force in international relations.

22 September: Thirty two million dirhams was allocated in the current budget to set-up 15 new schools throughout the country.

23 September: Sheikh Khalifa announced that joint manoeuvres by the GCC Armies would be conducted in the UAE in the first part of October, an important indication to the world of the determination of the GCC States to preserve their structure and sovereignty, as well as their commitment to the defence of their interests.

The Council of the Secretariat of Municipalities decided to forbid the entry of edible oils and fats into the country until they had undergone analysis.

One hundred and eleven passengers lost their lives in the biggest aircrash in the history of the UAE when a Gulf Air plane coming from Pakistan crashed 20 minutes before it was due to land at Abu Dhabi International Airport.

24 September: Four technical committees were formed to investigate the Gulf Air crash.

28 September: Sheikh Zayed, receiving the King of Nepal, expressed the UAE's support for the proposal designating Nepal as an area of peace, an embodiment of the world desire for the achievement of peace and stability in Asia.

The first phase of the project to lay an underwater communications cable between the UAE, Qatar and Bahrain commenced.

29 September: The Turkish President, Kenan Efren, expressed his pride in his friendly relations with Sheikh Zayed and his great appreciation for the efforts made by Zayed, both internally and on the Arab and Islamic levels. These remarks were made during his reception of Sheikh Ahmed bin Hamid, Minister of Information and Culture, who arrived in Ankara on an official visit.

1 October: Sheikh Rashid bin Mohammed Al Maktoum received a report from American technical experts investigating the air crash near Dubai.

3 October: Sheikh Zayed, presiding over a meeting of the Council of Ministers, directed them to minimize the obstacles facing citizens and to exert the maximum possible efforts to solve the problems connected to these obstacles.

The Council approved the plan to fill posts in the judiciary with nationals and to grant a 30 per cent allowance to encourage nationals to work in the judiciary. It also approved an increase in the children's allowance for national police and security officials from 140 dirhams per child to 300 dirhams per child.

4 October: Hamad Al-Madfa opened two new clinics in Al-Ain within the scope of the ministerial plan to extend health services to all areas in the Federation.

5 October: The UAE called on world powers to respect the sovereignty of the Gulf States and keep them out of the struggle between the big powers, leaving the responsibility for maintaining their security to the States themselves.

In his speech at the thirty-eighth session of the General Assembly of the United Nations, Rashid Abdulla confirmed that the UAE supported the necessary measures to implement the declaration designating the Pacific Region as a nuclear-free zone. He warned that the continuation of the Iran-Iraq war threatened the security and stability of the States in the region.

The UAE called for the the setting-up of an international judiciary to arbitrate in disputes among nations as well as the establishment of an international force to enforce the judgments of this judiciary. These remarks were part of a speech delivered by Hilal Ahmed Lootah, president of the National Council, before the International Parliamentary Union conference in Seoul, South Korea.

6 October: Sheikh Zayed received a letter from the Ruler of Qatar, which included an invitation to attend the fourth Summit Conference of the GCC leaders on 7 November.

Air and naval surveys revealed that the UAE's territorial waters had not been contaminated by oil from Iranian oil spills.

The Omani, Saudi, Qatari and Bahraini military forces arrived in the country to participate in the Al-Jazira Shield manoeuvres.

8 October: Brigadier General Mohammed Said Al Badi, Chief of the General Staff, sated that the manoeuvres by GCC Armies on UAE territory would prove to the world that these Armies were united and that they were entirely prepared to defend the Gulf States without intervention from anyone.

9 October: Sheikh Zayed arrived in Baghdad at the beginning of a tour to Iraq, Syria and Algeria as part of concerted efforts to clear the air before the Arab Summit in Riyadh. He confirmed that the only solution to the dilemma facing the Arab nation was to join in an alliance, co-ordinate their positions and unify their policies because they had common goals and one future. Rashid Abdulla said after the conclusion of discussions with the two leaders, Zayed and Saddam Hussein, that Sheikh Zayed's attempts to bring Arabs together and support Arab solidarity had met with a welcome response from the Iraqi President and that there was a mutual desire to work toward removing obstacles blocking the path of unity.

Sheikh Zayed travelled to Damascus where he was met by Syrian President, Hafez Al Asad.

10 October: Sheikh Zayed arrived in Algeria after important discussions with the Syrian President, Hafez Al Asad concerning joint Arab action. He expressed his complete satisfaction at the results of the talks and it was decided to send a delegation, which included Ahmed Khalifa Al Suweidi and Rashid Abdulla, to Baghdad to apprise the Iraqi President of the results of the Zayed/Al Asad discussions. In Algeria, Zayed announced that he was intending to meet with President Al Shadhili bin Jadid within the framework of supporting and strengthening brotherly relations, exchanging opinions in matters concerning Arab unity and the achievement of solidarity between brothers.

The Council of Ministers approved the institution of express postal services in the country.

The first phase of the GCC Al-Jazira Shield manoeuvres took place.

11 October: Sheikh Zayed held important discussions with President Al-Shadhili bin Jadid after which Zayed confirmed that the Arab nation would never carry much weight unless it acted in concert. Sheikh Zayed said that ... 'it is our duty as brothers not to surrender to despair but to work for the impossible until it achieves what the Arab nation hopes for'.

12 October: Sheikh Zayed, ending his official visit to Algeria, expressed his complete satisfaction with the positive results of his discussions with the Algerian President, which would reflect well on joint Arab action.

A co-operation agreement in judicial affairs was signed between Algeria and the UAE.

15 October: Sheikh Zayed issued a decree awarding the medal of co-operation to the chiefs of staff of the GCC Armed Forces and to the leaders, officers and soldiers who participated in the Al-Jazira Shield manoeuvres. Sheikh Khalifa bin Zayed Al Nahyan attended the conclusion of the manoeuvres and presented the Chiefs of Staff with their decorations. He confirmed that the Al-Jazira Shield manoeuvres were successful and that they achieved all their goals, the first of which was the birth of the GCC rapid movement force and the second was to demonstrate the determination of the Rulers and people of the region to protect their land and wealth without the assistance of foreign intervention, confirming the idea that States had a common destiny.

16 October: First Lady Sheikha Fatima bint Mubarak presided over a meeting of the UAE's Women's Federation, during which the work plan for the coming phase was considered. Preparations were also made to host the third conference of women from the Arabian Peninsula which was to be held in Abu Dhabi in March 1984.

17 October: The Council of Ministers reviewed the results of contacts made by the President of the Federation during his tour of Iraq, Syria and Algeria and commended his efforts in alleviating tensions.

18 October: The UAE Supreme Customs Council approved the draft law imposing customs fees on imports in compliance with the decisions of the GCC finance and economy ministers.

19 October: Sheikh Zayed received a letter from King Hassan of Morocco concerning the good offices which the President was undertaking to improve relations between Algeria and Morocco. Sheikh Khalifa bin Zayed Al Nahyan, in remarks made to *Amman* newspaper, stressed that setting-up a GCC rapid movement force was the first step in a comprehensive strategy aimed at creating a united Gulf military force, capable of confronting any threats or interference to any GCC State and of protecting the security of the Gulf, while defending its Arab and Islamic character. In a speech before the General Assembly of the United Nations, the UAE expressed its complete support for the proposal calling for an signing of an international treaty to forbid the use of force in international relations.

20 October: Sheikh Zayed sent a letter to the Algerian President, Al Shadhili bin Jadid, delivered by Dr Mana Said Al Otaiba, concerning his efforts to bring together Arab points of view and deal with the differences between Algeria and Morocco.

A special 160 million dirham contract was signed between the Ministry of Finance and Industry and the Emirates Public Transportation Establishment for school transport in the current academic year.

21 October: Sheikh Zayed received a reply from the Algerian President and despatched a letter to Morocco's King Hassan regarding his attempts at reconciliation.

22 October: Sheikh Khalifa, in remarks made to the Bahraini newspaper, *Akhbar Al-Khaleej*, said that the Iran-Iraq war was having a huge negative impact on the Gulf region and that its continuation would create great dangers, not only for the belligerents, but also for other countries in the Gulf who have not spared any efforts throughout the last three years to end the bloodshed. He said that the President's journey to Iraq, Syria and Algeria was a step in the continuing efforts of the UAE, Saudi Arabia, Kuwait, Morocco and Algeria to contain the differences between brothers.

The Secretariat General of Municipalities commenced the first programme to comprehensively survey the quality of the UAE's food products and to establish control over them.

The Central Blood Bank began establishment of the first frozen blood unit which will allow the preservation of blood in good condition for more than three years.

23 October: Sheikh Khalifa bin Zayed Al Nahyan announced, in remarks made to the Saudi newspapers, *Okaz* and *Al-Madina al-Munawwara*, that steps toward GCC military co-operation would continue according to a well-planned agenda the final aim of which was to establish a joint military leadership. He said that in the next few days joint air manoeuvres between Saudi Arabia, Kuwait, the UAE and Oman would begin.

It was decided to open 37 new adult education centres as well as centres for eliminating illiteracy in Abu Dhabi, Al-Ain and the Western Region.

24 October: Sheikh Khalifa opened the new General Police Administration building in Abu Dhabi. He stressed that the State was concerned with supporting the police in order to maintain security, and ensure the safety of all citizens and residents in the country.

25 October: The first phase of the 36 million dollar pipeline project which stretched for 250 km from the Al-Saja field in Sharjah to the major electricity plants in Fujairah, Sharjah, Umm al-Qaiwain, Ajman and Ras al-Khaimah was completed.

Some 8349 tourists arrived in Sharjah via 110 air flights during the tourist season of 1982-83, a dramatic increase from the 2500 tourists who arrived on 19 flights during the 1980-81 season.

26 October: Sheikh Mohammad bin Rashid Al Maktoum dedicated one of the largest ships ever built in Dubai on behalf of a national company in co-operation with an international partner. Weighing 450 tons, it cost 4 million dollars to build.

27 October: The UAE demanded that the Middle East and the Pacific region be declared nuclear-free zones. In its speech before the UN General Assembly it called on the great powers to put an end to the arms race and eliminate weapons of mass destruction.

The Minister of Labour and Social Affairs issued two decrees. The first covered the payment of 4.7 million dirhams in financial assistance to public benefit societies. The second covered the payment of 2.8 million dirhams in financial assistance to co-operative societies.

28 October: Sheikh Zayed in remarks to the Emirates New Agency confirmed that work would continue to bring Morocco and Algeria's points of view in respect to pending problems closer together, firm up new ground for relations between the two countries and clear the air in order to create a suitable climate for convening the next Arab Summit in Riyadh. He said that mediation was being conducted in an atmosphere of mutual understanding, and that the UAE would continue to extend its good offices for as long as the two side were ready to accept them. He said that Dr Mana Said Al Otaiba had been commissioned to undertake a new round of visits to deliver letters to King Hassan and President Al Shadhili, stressing that they would never achieve their goals unless they stood shoulder to shoulder for restoration of their rights.

The UAE voted for the UN resolution demanding the withdrawal of all foreign forces from Kampuchea in order to achieve a fair and lasting settlement to the Kampuchean problem and to restore the sovereignty of the country and the right of its people to self-determination.

31 October: GCC Ministers of Foreign Affairs decided to include on the agenda of the next GCC Summit the President of the Federation's efforts at reconciliation between Morocco and Algeria, and between Iraq and Syria.

The Council of Ministers approved the formation of a committee which would include representatives from the ministries of foreign affairs, defence, interior, justice, petroleum and agriculture to prepare maps clarifying the borders of the UAE's economic regions. The decision was also made to commission the Ministry of Agriculture and the Ministry of Finance and Industry to study the country's agricultural policy in respect of production and marketing.

1 November: Sheikh Khalifa expressed the deep concern of the UAE - its people, Government and President - for the Lebanese National Dialogue Conference which commenced in Geneva. He also expressed the hope that the meeting would result in achieving the unity of the Lebanese people, their freedom and the preservation of their independence.

2 November: Sheikh Saqr bin Mohammed Al Qassimi allocated 150,000 dollars for an economic feasibility study to set-up up a 32 million dirham joint Arab project for producing, canning and packaging dates in Ras al-Khaimah.

The Higher Customs Council decided to form a technical committee to prepare a draft unified customs law for the country.

3 November: Sheikh Sultan bin Mohammad Al Qassimi opened the first Arab food industries exhibition in Sharjah. Fifteen Arab countries participated, as did 20 local companies and a number of international companies. Food imports during the first half of 1983 amounted to 405,000 tons, valued at 1037.5 million dirhams.

4 November: Sheikh Ahmed bin Hamid stressed that the good offices undertaken by Sheikh Zayed to achieve true Arab solidarity would continue. He said that the President would brief the GCC leaders on the results of the contacts which he had made last month in this respect.

5 November: Sheikh Khalifa, in remarks to the Qatar News Agency, announced that the people of the Gulf and the Arab peoples were deeply interested in the GCC 'Summit of Responsibilities' to be held in Doha because of the importance of the agenda for the conference; in the forefront of which was the Iraq-Iran war, the situation in Lebanon, correcting the course of Arab relations and firmly securing the future of Gulf co-operation.

7 November: Sheikh Zayed, arriving in Doha to participate in the deliberations of the fourth Summit of the Arab Gulf Co-operation Council (AGCC), began peripheral meetings with the GCC leaders. He announced that: 'We are in great need of well-planned co-ordination and co-operation so we can seriously confront the challenges which are surrounding the region. In this way we can try to achieve the hopes and ambitions of our peoples which will enable them to undertake their role in serving the Arab and Islamic nation and share together in safeguarding the security and peace of the world'.

9 November: Sheikh Zayed stressed that the positive resolutions which were adopted at the fourth Summit of the GCC leaders would promote prosperity and stability in the Gulf region. The President of the Federation vowed to continue his efforts, along with the good offices of the GCC States, to achieve a true and effective solidarity throughout the Arab nation from the Gulf to the Atlantic Ocean.

An agreement was signed for technical co-operation between the UAE and Iraq in the field of labour and social affairs.

12 November: Express mail service was instituted in the UAE as part of its plan to develop mail services in the country.

The UAE University instituted a higher diploma in Gulf Studies.

14 November: Sheikh Zayed, presiding over a meeting of the Council of Ministers, briefed the Council on the results of efforts to muster collective Arab energies to confront current challenges. He confirmed his full intention to continue these efforts in order to achieve a unified Arab stance.

15 November: Sheikh Zayed, arriving in Riyadh on an official visit to the Kingdom of Saudi Arabia, held discussions with His Royal Highness, Prince Sultan bin Abdulaziz, which entailed a minute evaluation of the Arab Gulf situation and their joint attempts to redirect Arab solidarity onto the right track.

16 November: Sheikh Khalifa bin Zayed Al Nahyan participated in the opening ceremonies of the King Khalid International Airport in Riyadh.

17 November: A letter from US President Ronald Reagan about joint co-operation and matters of mutual interest was delivered to Sheikh Zayed by Don Hodell, the American Energy Secretary. Dr Mana Said Al Otaiba and the American Secretary studied conditions in the international oil market and co-operation between the two countries in the field of energy.

19 November: Sheikh Khalifa, returning from his official visit to Saudi Arabia, expressed his great appreciation for the brotherly spirit which distinguished his meetings and discussions with Saudi officials and the joint vision concerning the future of the Arab and Islamic nation which it yielded.

21 November: The technical committee, which was commissioned to prepare maps to clarify the regional economic borders of the country, held its first meeting.

23 November: Sheikh Zayed during his reception of an Eritrean delegation called for unity amongst Eritrean revolutionary factions.

25 November: In the Hague, Holland and the UAE signed a five-year energy, trade, transport, solar energy technology co-operation agreement.

UAE revenue for 1982 was 34.577 billion dirhams.

26 November: The UAE was accepted as a member of the International Dental Union.

29 November: First Lady Sheikha Fatima bint Mubarak donated half a million dirhams to the New Delhi Centre for the Handicapped on behalf of the Women's Federation.

The Ministry of Electricity established a basic electricity grid in Fujairah and electrified 55 villages in the Northern Emirates.

30 November: Sheikh Zayed received a letter from King Hassan II regarding UAE efforts to mediate between Morocco and Algeria.

Sheikh Zayed and the Secretary General of the Arab League, Al Shadhili Al Kulaibi, reviewed current Arab affairs, the situation in Lebanon, developments in the Palestinian problem and preparations for the Arab Summit Conference which was to be convened in Riyadh.

2 December: On National Day, Sheikh Zayed received the Members of the Supreme Council of the Federation, the Rulers of the Emirates, their Heirs

Apparent and crowds of well wishers. The President and the Rulers attended Arab camel races on this occasion.

7 December: Sheikh Zayed received a letter from the Syrian President, Hafez Al Asad, regarding Arab affairs in light of the American air attack on Syrian positions in Lebanon. The UAE stressed that aggression against any Arab country would be considered an aggression against the entire Arab nation. It expressed the hope that efforts would be intensified to stop the military escalation.

Dr Mana Said Al Otaiba said that the UAE would ask OPEC's ministerial council to fulfill its promise to give priority to the UAE for an increase in its production share of 1.1 million barrels per day.

12 December: Sheikh Zayed voiced the UAE's condemnation of acts of sabotage committed in Kuwait. He stressed in his telephone contact with the Ruler of Kuwait that the UAE was in solidarity with the Kuwaiti people in confronting attempts to undermine their security and stability.

13 December: Sheikh Zayed, receiving the US President's envoy, requested that the United States follow a balanced and non-aligned policy in the Middle East and make intense efforts to stabilize the region, especially since America is a great power which bears responsibilities for international security and peace.

In a speech before the United Nations, the UAE strongly condemned the political and military alliance between the United States and Israel. The UAE said that Washington was not prepared to be an honest broker in the Middle East peace process.

Central Bank reserves at the end of last September were 11.875 billion dirhams and the collective reserves of the commercial banks during the same period amounted to 76.901 billion dirhams.

14 December: Dr Mana Said Al Otaiba stressed in a press conference marking the twentieth anniversary of the first export of oil from the UAE that the oil policy of the UAE was based on the premise that the last barrel of oil to be produced in the world would be from its wells. He said that UAE policy, in line with the President's directives, was based on joint efforts within OPEC in the belief that collective bargaining was the best way to achieve the interests of peoples.

16 December: The UAE supported the UN draft resolution condemning Israel for its refusal to do away with its stockpile of nuclear weapons and to put its atomic activities under international supervision.

18 December: Sheikh Zayed issued a federal decree forbidding the hunting of land and sea birds of all kinds inside the UAE. It also prohibited the collection or destruction of their eggs, the Socotra cormorant being an exception to the above law.

19 December: Rashid Abdulla, voicing the UAE's dissatisfaction at the American-Israeli strategic alliance, stressed that the alliance did not serve Arab-American relations and threatened the security of the Middle East.

20 December: Sheikh Zayed convened the fourth Islamic Summit Conference in Morocco, emphasizing his concern to attend and participate in its deliberations.

30 December: At the end of this year, there were 1561 mosques in the UAE.

Nineteen Eighty Four

2 January: Arab Health Ministers from seven Gulf States held meetings in Abu Dhabi.

3 January: The Council of Ministers approved the appointment of UAE graduates with scientific and technical specializations to Grade One, Class Two in the public service. They also approved a special cadre for medical doctors who are nationals, and allocated a 30 per cent allowance to nationals taking up employment as teachers.

5 January: As of October 1983, 241,798 people were employed in the private and public sectors.

7 January: There were 121 night school centres in the UAE, 68 for men and 53 for women.

8 January: The Ministry of Health commenced a regular survey of the Federation's seashores to determine the percentage of crude oil settlement on the beaches.

Sheikh Hamdan bin Zayed Al Nahyan agreed to take over the chairmanship of the Football Federation.

9 January: Sheikh Zayid issued a decree allocating the necessary funds for the Ministry of Education's teaching faculty where 692 new jobs were created, effective from 1 September 1983.

10 January: At the Football Federation Board's first meeting under the chairmanship of Sheikh Hamdan, it was decided to form a national team for the Gulf round to be held in Muscat in March.

11 January: The Ministry of Labour and Social Affairs issued a directive to establishments operating in the Federation stating that it was mandatory to use the Arabic language in all matters and in all instructions directed to company employees, in accordance with Article 2 of the Labour Relations Law.

The Ministry of Planning announced that the number of residents in the Federation was 1.2 million at the end of December 1983.

12 January: Sheikh Zayed issued a federal decree inviting the Supreme Council of the Federation to convene the following day in its first ordinary session of the sixth legislative term.

13 January: Sheikh Zayed, opening the new session of the Federal National Council, declared the UAE's support for efforts to ensure peace and stability among the States of the region. He said that the UAE participated constructively in helping Gulf States achieve their national ambitions. He stressed the importance of supporting the Federation, of focusing on domestic accomplishments and confronting challenges to provide a better life for UAE citizens. He also emphasized Arab solidarity, the determination of the Palestinian people to secure their national rights, and the desirability of a ceasefire in the Iraq-Iran war.

The cost of projects completed by the Ministry of Public Works and Housing during 1983 amounted to 420.608 million dirhams.

15 January: Sheikh Zayed, arriving in Casablanca to participate in the Islamic Summit Conference, called upon Islamic leaders to solve their differences peacefully. He said that the Islamic world required positive united action to confront the full scope of the Zionist danger.

The Council of Ministers approved exemptions for four groups of non-nationals to extend their services after reaching the age of sixty: chief engineers; medical doctors; consultants, specialists, technicians, educational advisers in the teaching faculty; and imams and preachers.

17 January: Sheikh Zayed held substantial meetings with heads of state participating in the Islamic Summit Conference in Casablanca concentrating on unification of the Islamic front and co-ordinating positions to confront the challenges of the future.

Sheikh Rashid bin Humaid Al Nuaimi opened the Ministry of Information and Culture's new cultural centre in Ajman.

Sheikh Khalifa bin Zayed Al Nahyan opened the first National Exhibition of Industries mounted by the Abu Dhabi Chamber of Commerce and Industry, in which 24 local companies participated.

ADFAED agreed to loan 400,000 dollars to Bahrain for a feasibility study on optimizing water resources in the island emirate.

19 January: There were 126 insurance companies with 1381 employees operating in the Federation: 39 national companies, 32 Arab and 55 foreign.

20 January: The Central Bank decided to issue 1 million 5 dirham memorial coins on the occasion of the advent of the fifteenth Hegira century.

The Ministry of the Interior created 25 new civil defence centres in Abu Dhabi, Dubai, Sharjah, Ras al-Khaimah, Fujairah and Al-Ain.

Abu Dhabi International Airport had a passenger throughput of 2,265,946 passengers during 1983, an increase of 2 per cent over the previous year.

21 January: The Ministry of Communications began implementing measures to register ships carrying the UAE flag.

The general shareholders of the Emirates Telecommunications Corporation approved the establishment of the UAE Investment Corporation with a paid-up capital of 1200 million dirhams and a permitted capital of 4800 million dirhams. Recipients of social insurance aid numbered 30,139 in 1983.

Following a visit to Abu Dhabi by Thai Deputy Foreign Affairs Minister, Barbas Howida Baudo, and a delegation of Thai economists, UAE and Thailand concluded an economic agreement.

23 January: Abu Dhabi Executive Council decided to construct a 46.5 billion dirham Immigration/Health/Residence Complex in Sila.

24 January: Sheikh Khalifa attended ceremonies for the Military Medical Services Day, marking the passage of 15 years since it was instituted in the Armed Forces.

25 January: Sheikh Sultan bin Mohammad Al Qassimi, opening two new health clinics in Al-Riqqa and Umm Hatoor, praised the rapid progress of medical services in the Federation.

28 January: The amount of electrical power generated by the electrical plants of the Ministry of Electricity and Water amounted to 1,157,328,059 kilowatts per hour in 1983.

31 January: Sheikh Khalifa bin Zayed Al Nahyan supported the 17 sports clubs in the Northern Emirates to the amount of 4.35 million dirhams.

An agreement for economic co-operation was signed between the UAE and Morocco and a joint committee was formed to supervise its execution.

1 February: Sheikh Khalifa was present at graduation ceremonies for the ninth group of officers in Al-Ain. He expressed satisfaction at the large number of citizens recruited to the ranks of the Armed Forces and he said that joining the Armed Forces was a national duty because a nation must be well-prepared for all eventualities. He stressed that the UAE, as part of its national responsibilities, placed all its capabilities at the service of Arab causes. The Ministry of Labour and Social Affairs issued a decree licensing the first non-governmental institution for the care, rehabilitation and training of the mentally handicapped in Dubai.

2 February: Sheikh Khalifa bin Zayed Al Nahyan received the Al-Ain Club team star-players and the members of its Board of Administration on the occasion of the team's victory in the cup.

4 February: Three Jaguar fighter aeroplanes of the Sultanate of Oman Air Wing arrived to participate in UAE-Oman joint air manoeuvres which were taking place within the scope of strengthening GCC forces.

7 February: The Executive Council approved the allocation of 42.5 million dirhams to administer the new Al-Mafraq Hospital for 1984.

7 February: Sheikh Sultan bin Mohammed Al Qassimi approved the construction of the second phase of the highway connecting Al-Nakheel in Ras al-Khaimah with the International Airport. This 20-km stretch, which was personally funded by Sheikh Sultan, was expected to cost 17 million dirhams.

Dubai Municipal Council decided to allocate 35 million dirhams in its 1984 budget to build an automatic slaughter house, the Al-Jumairah central market and the fish market in Al-Shindagha.

8 February: The UAE Ambassador to France, Khalifa Ahmad Abdulaziz Al Mubarak, was shot dead by an unknown assailant. The UAE denounced the crime as a tragedy and a disgrace both for the perpetrator and for all those who supported such unforgivable deeds. It emphasized that such terrorist acts would not alter the UAE's fundamental position in regard to the Arab cause, but that the effect of such crimes would be to strengthen their determination to oppose all acts of terrorism through faith, good will, respect and honour. General mourning and a lowering of flags for three days was decreed.

9 February: Sheikh Saqr bin Mohammad Al Qassimi attended the ceremonies marking the start of oil production in the emirate of Ras al-Khaimah at Saleh offshore oilfield. Sheikh Khalid bin Saqr Al Qassimi confirmed that oil revenues would help support the federal future and also the emirate's economic advancement.

11 February: Sheikh Rashid bin Saeed Al Maktoum issued an order reducing rents by 15 per cent on real estate owned by the Dubai Government and the Construction Council, in order to help combat inflation and make life easier for citizens and residents coping with the rise in the cost of living.

Sheikh Hamad bin Mohammad Al Sharqi, during his inspection of the new Fujairah hospital, commended Sheikh Zayed's achievements and especially the construction of the hospital from his private purse.

12 February: Abu Dhabi Executive Council approved the allocation of 1300 million dirhams to repair the first 113 kms of the Turaif - Jebel al-Dhanna highway.

13 February: The Council of Ministers, in light of the murderous attack on the UAE Ambassador in France, discussed ways to protect the UAE's diplomats.

19 February: Sheikh Zayed received Abdulmohsin Al Sudairi, Chairman of the International Fund for Agricultural Development, who thanked Zayed for the UAE's continuing support for the Fund which focused on the development of agricultural projects in the Third World. The UAE delegation, led by Rashid Abdulla, returned to the country after participating in the meetings of the joint British/UAE Committee. The delegation confirmed that Britain within the European group would play a more effective role in support of peace. The Committee also stressed the necessity of finding a just solution to the Palestinian cause and a recognition of the rights of the Palestinian people, including their right to establish an independent state on their own soil.

21 February: From 1972 until 1982, the Ministry of Public Works and Housing built 5575 public housing units at a cost of 920 million dirhams.

25 February: Sheikh Rashid bin Saeed Al Maktoum inspected progress at the 30 million dirham water desalination plant in the Al-Sirra area of Umm al-Qaiwain.

26 February: Sheikh Zayed received a letter from the French President, François Mitterand, regarding mutual relations and joint co-operation. The letter was delivered by the French Minister of the Interior, Gaston Defevre, who informed the President of developments in the investigation into the assassination of the UAE Ambassador to France.

29 February: Sheikh Zayed issued two federal laws regarding commercial companies and employees' retirement payments.

1 March: Sheikh Sultan bin Mohammad Al Qassimi opened Sharjah's first arts festival, Expo.

2 March: The Ministry of Planning announced that there were 347 schools with 140,000 students in the Federation during the academic year 1972-73. It was also announced that country-wide electricity production amounted to 8930 kilowatt/hours and that the quantity of water produced reached 55.2 billion gallons during the year.

3 March: Sheikh Zayed returned to the country after a short visit to the Kingdom of Saudi Arabia, during which he met with His Majesty, King Fahad bin Abdulaziz.

They exchanged points of view regarding current problems facing the Arab nation. They also discussed the need to strengthen joint Arab action in the coming phase, within the framework of continuing contacts and consultations between the two leaders regarding matters in the best interests of the Arab and Islamic nation.

4 March: Sheikh Zayed and the Secretary General of the Arab League, Al Shadhili Al Kulaibi, discussed current Arab affairs and developments in the Iraq-Iran war, including possible ways of ending the bloodshed between the two Muslim neighbours.

6 March: Sheikh Zayed received a delegation from the UAE National Football Federation under the chairmanship of Sheikh Hamdan bin Zayed Al Nahyan before they departed for the Gulf Games in Muscat. The President stressed that the Federation provided everything possible to enhance the welfare of youth in various areas. He also expressed his confidence in the ability of youth to advance progress. He declared his appreciation of the role of young people who, he said, are the true treasures of this country, stressing that the stature of any state is measured by its people who bear faith, have high morals and show true decency.

7 March: The Fertilizer Industries Company in Al-Ruwais, Fertile, signed long-term contracts with Indian and Japanese companies for the export of its urea production. The factory which began full production last January produced 1500 tons of ammonia and 1000 tons of urea daily.

8 March: Sheikh Zayed issued a federal decree permitting GCC citizens to engage in economic activities in the Federation.

First Lady Sheikha Fatima bint Mubarak and the wife of Kurt Waldheim, former Secretary General of the United Nations, discussed women's activities in the Federation and co-operation in matters of importance to women at Gulf, Arab and international levels.

10 March: Sheikh Saqr bin Mohammad Al Qassimi announced new discoveries of oil in two onshore sites at Ghalila and Jazirat al-Halili in Ras al-Khaimah.

The UAE National Football Team defeated the Kuwaiti team in the Gulf Games Competition in Muscat.

11 March: The Industrial Bank, established to promote industrial development in the country, financed seven projects amounting to 35 million dirhams during its first year of operation.

12 March: Sheikh Zayed inspected agricultural and building development projects which he had ordered to be executed in Al-Marfa. This was within the scope of his great concern for the development of outlying areas. He also inspected samples of vegetables and citrus fruits produced by farms in the Western Region.

The Council of Ministers examined the Federation's economic situation and decided to form a committee to complete the study of this topic.

Sheikha Fatima bint Mubarak attended the demonstration of girls schools' activities in the Abu Dhabi Educational District. She also inspected the Al-Musahib Exhibition.

The Ministry of Agriculture and Fisheries prepared a five year plan to regulate the use of irrigation water following a depletion of groundwater because of new methods of irrigation such as hydroponics and spraying.

13 March: Sheikh Nahyan bin Mubarak, Chancellor of UAE University, announced that the University's College of Medicine would soon be inaugurated.

14 March: Sheikh Rashid bin Ahmed Al Mualla inspected the 25 million dirham centre for aquaculture studies in Umm al-Qaiwain.

17 March: In Tokyo, Dr Mana Said Al Otaiba and the Japanese Prime Minister, Yasahiro Nakasone, discussed the oil market and the future of energy substitutes. They also discussed co-operation in the fields of oil and gas production and marketing. Dr Al Otaiba also met with the presidents of the Japanese oil companies operating in the Federation who presented him with detailed reports on the activities of their companies during the last year in the fields of earthquake survey, well-drilling and advanced exploration techniques.

21 March: Delegations participating in the third Regional Women's Conference in the Gulf and the Arabian Peninsula, hosted by the UAE, began to arrive in the country. Sheikha Fatima bint Mubarak, President of the General Women's Federation, and Dr Helene Laird, President of the International Guide Organization, discussed the role of that organization in the development of skills and aptitudes of Girl Scouts in the Federation.

22 March: Sheikh Sultan bin Mohammad Al Qassimi signed an agreement establishing the Sharjah Liquid Gas Company Ltd (SHALCO). Sharjah owned 60 per cent of the shares in the company, 25 per cent were owned by Amoco and two Japanese companies each owned 7.5 per cent. The aim of the project was to set up a plant for collecting liquid gas from oil wells in the Al-Saja field and

transporting it via a pipeline to the Al-Hamriya region.

24 March: Sheikh Zayed opened the third Regional Women's Conference in the Gulf and the Arabian Peninsula. He stressed that the UAE had, ever since it was established, worked for the renaissance of women in all fields. It also opened the door to employment and education on an equal basis for women and men. He commended the role which State agencies have played in preparing women to effectively participate in social development and play a leading role in the service of society.

First Lady Sheikha Fatima bint Mubarak, commended the concern which the President of the Federation had shown for the affairs of women in the region and his concern to help them overcome the obstacles they faced in order to occupy a suitable place in society. She extended her thanks to the President for overseeing the conference.

25 March: The Department of Archaeology and Tourism in Al-Ain discovered an important archaeological site near Al-Hili Gardens. The site revealed a major irrigation canal dating from the first half of the first millennium of the present era.

26 March: India and the UAE signed a memorandum of understanding to lay a 100 million dollar submarine cable connecting Abu Dhabi and Bombay.

The National Football Team took fourth place in the seventh Gulf Football Games being held in Muscat.

28 March: Sheikh Maktoum bin Rashid Al Maktoum attended graduation ceremonies for the first batch of pilots, including 20 lieutenants, from the Air School in Dubai.

Sheikh Sultan bin Mohammad Al Qassimi returned to the country after a visit to the Sultanate of Oman where he met His Majesty the Sultan, Qaboos bin Said, and a number of important Omani officials.

First Lady Sheikha Fatima bint Mubarak met the wife of the Pakistani president, Zia Al Haq, on her visit to the headquarters of the UAE Women's Federation and the permanent heritage exhibition.

30 March: Abu Dhabi Municipality completed numbering of districts, streets and houses in the city of Abu Dhabi and its suburbs.

ADFAED agreed to loan 29 million dollars to Oman to assist in road construction.

31 March: Sheikh Zayed asked that European countries play a positive role in bringing about a just and lasting peace in the Middle East during discussions which took place in Abu Dhabi with Dr Alfred Sinowatz, the Austrian Chancellor. The discussions dealt with the current international situation, developments in the Palestinian cause, the Iraq-Iraq war and the situation in the Middle East.

Sheikh Sultan bin Mohammad Al Qassimi inspected progress on the gas pipeline in the Northern Emirates which will supply the electrical plants with gas from Al-Saja oil field.

1 April: Sheikh Khalifa bin Zayed Al Nahyan commended the excellent stand taken by Austria with regard to the Middle East during his meeting with the Austrian Chancellor, Dr Alfred Sinowatz, who stressed that the policy of his country in regard to the Middle East would not change under its new Government.

Official discussions between the UAE and Austria were held under the chairmanship of Sheikh Hamdan bin Mohammad Al Nahyan. It was decided to form a joint committee to meet alternately in Abu Dhabi and Vienna to study the strengthening of co-operation in economic, agricultural, health and electrical fields.

4 April: The statement of the Federal National Council at the meetings of the International Parliamentary Union in Geneva condemned the nuclear arms race between the great powers. It called on the parliaments of the world to participate in the disarmament negotiations now underway for the sake of guaranteeing world peace.

7 April: The National Petroleum Construction Company completed projects worth 250 million dirhams for manufacturing and installing oil-production equipment and installations in Abu Dhabi's and Saudi Aramco's offshore regions.

10 April: Sheikh Zayed attended graduation ceremonies for the third men's graduation class from the UAE University.

11 April: First Lady Sheikha Fatima bint Mubarak attended graduation ceremonies for the third women's graduation class.

16 April: Sheikh Zayed, meeting with Richard Murphy, US Assistant Secretary of State, spoke about the need for the United States to follow a fair unaligned policy and that its current Middle East policy needed a long-awaited fundamental overhaul if the US wished to maintain its friends in the region.

The Council of Ministers approved new computerized systems designed to improve efficiency in federal ministries.

18 April: Sheikh Khalifa bin Zayed Al Nahyan received the Ministers of Finance and Economics and the heads of the Arab economic organizations who were participating in the annual gathering of Arab financial institutions convening in Abu Dhabi.

19 April: Sheikh Zayed planted a date-palm tree in the Al-Khatm area on the Abu Dhabi - Al-Ain highway during ceremonies marking Tree Day in the UAE, as an expression of his interest in agricultural and afforestation projects in the country.

22 April: The Council of Ministers approved the establishment of medical clinics in Abu Dhabi city at a cost of 250 million dirhams.

24 April: A Ministry of Planning report announced that UAE Gross Domestic Product at the end of 1983 was 166.793 billion dirhams, as against 111 billion dirhams at the end of 1982. The average *per capita* income was 22,200 dirhams and the population was 1.2 million. Oil revenues in 1982 amounted to about 35.043, billion dirhams and the revenues from liquid gas amounted to 5 billion dirhams.

25 April: Sheikh Zayed arrived in Nairobi on an official visit to Kenya, during which he held talks with the Kenyan President, Daniel Arap Moi regarding Arab-African relations and mutual co-operation between the two countries.

26 April: On instructions from the President, the Minister of Economy and Commerce issued a decree forbidding the importation of all types of camels to the UAE in order to protect the national herd from disease.

27 April: A joint communiqué issued in Abu Dhabi and Nairobi on the results of discussions between Sheikh Zayed and the Kenyan President, Daniel Arap Moi,

confirmed that the two countries did not believe that a fair and lasting peace in the Middle East could be achieved unless the Palestinian people were granted their rights, including their right to self-determination.

Sheikh Zayed opened the Technical Secondary School in Mombasa and performed the Friday worship in the school mosque.

An economic, technical and cultural agreement was signed between the UAE and Kenya.

During 1984, there were 269 projects completed in the emirate of Abu Dhabi at a cost of 5715 million dirhams.

28 April: Sheikh Zayed paid a visit to the fort and museum of the Islamic city of Mombasa in Kenya where he saw models of antique weapons of war. He said that the great powers studied the history of the Islamic conquest of this region to learn how great empires were made, using the lessons they learned to further their ambitions.

29 April: Sheikh Zayed ordered the establishment of two orphanages in Mombasa at his own expense. He also ordered the creation of a private *waqf*, the income from which would secure the continuation of services for the orphanages.

Sheikh Zayed issued a federal decree affiliating the UAE with the Arab Copyright Agreement.

1 May: UAE and Algeria agreed on the establishment of a joint investment company with a capital of 20 million dollars, each country owning a half interest in the company.

2 May: Sheikh Zayed arrived in Lahore from Nairobi on his way to Dacca to begin an official visit to Bangladesh. He confirmed that his visit to Kenya would result in the strengthening of ties between Arab and African peoples and that it would support the development of mutual relations and joint co-operation.

4 May: Sheikh Khalifa bin Zayed Al Nahyan on the occasion of the anniversary of the unification of the Armed Forces indicated that the Forces had been supplied with the latest weapons technology to increase their firepower.

6 May: Sheikh Zayed met the Pakistani President, Zia Al Haq, in Lahore. They exchanged points of view regarding developments in the Gulf and the Pacific Ocean. They also discussed the need to bring an end to the Iraq-Iran war, the situation in the Middle East, and the necessity of maintaining the Arab-Islamic character of Jerusalem.

7 May: Sheikh Zayed arrived in Dacca at the beginning of an official visit to Bangladesh. He confirmed that the liberation of Islamic holy places, the most important of which is Jerusalem, and the return of dignity to the Islamic nation were the most fundamental Muslim duties. He said that this sacred duty could only be carried out by joining ranks and making a collective effort. Sheikh Zayed held official discussions with the Bangladeshi President, Hussain Irshad, which centred around Islamic solidarity and mutual co-operation.

The Council of Ministers approved the setting-up of a UAE investment body with an allowed capital of 4.8 billion dirhams and a subscribed capital of 102 billion dirhams, in order to support the national economy, the development of capital and investments for citizens.

Sheikh Khalifa bin Zayed Al Nahyan donated 1 million dirhams to the Ajman Sports Club on the occasion of their victory in the President's Football Cup during the 1983-84 season.

The Ministry of Public Works and Housing reported that they had constructed a total of 1150 kms of road throughout the Federation at a cost of 1.450 billion dirhams.

10 May: Sheikh Zayed, the Bangladeshi President, Mohammad Hussain Irshad, and the Palestinian leader, Yasser Arafat, discussed latest developments in the Palestinian cause and means of supporting Islamic solidarity.

11 May: Sheikh Zayed confirmed in his meetings with Arab ambassadors in Dacca that America's ambitions were no less than those of the Soviet Union, and that imperialist greed would not diminish unless Arabs confronted them with their joint forces and stop up the chinks in their armour. He said that they did not seek power in order to be aggressive but to prevent aggression from others and that disputes between Arab countries had lost it the co-operation and confidence of Islamic States.

Sheikh Zayed ordered the drilling of 200 waterwells in Bangladesh, and the construction of two schools and an orphanage in Dacca.

An economic and trade agreement between the UAE and Bangladesh was signed.

12 May: A joint communiqué was broadcast from both Abu Dhabi and Dacca in which the two countries expressed their profound worries about the continuation of the Iraq-Iran war which threatened the security of the region and endangered world peace. They confirmed the right of the Palestinian people to set-up an independent State and they condemned Israeli repressive practices in occupied Arab territories.

14 May: The Council of Ministers affirmed the steps to be taken in implementing the GCC common economic agreement in accordance with the decrees of the Al-Doha summit.

First Lady Sheikha Fatima bint Mubarak called on the young women of the country to join the nursing profession, considered to be the highest of humanitarian professions.

19 May: Ajman cement factory was opened. Costing 26 million dirhams, it had the capacity to produce half a million tons annually.

21 May: Sheikh Zayed opened the new headquarters of the *Sharia* Judiciary in Abu Dhabi. He called on Muslim *Ulema* to pray to Allah, asking that Muslim leaders be successful in rallying together and lessening their differences. He said that Islam tells us how to resolve our differences and how to establish the foundations of peace and sharing.

Sheikh Khalifa bin Zayed Al Nahyan, in remarks to the Lebanese magazine *Al-Sayyad,* called on the Security Council to take action and adopt a clear resolution calling for a ceasefire between Iran and Iraq, as it had done in many other similar disputes which threatened world peace.

22 May: The Executive Council approved the setting-up of a 240 million dirham aircraft maintenance plant in Abu Dhabi. The UAE and Belgium signed an economic and technical co-operation agreement, including commitments on investment and technology transfer.

The Ministry of Foreign Affairs called in the ambassadors of the permanent members of the Security Council to discuss current developments in the Gulf region. The GCC Foreign Ministers decided to take up attacks against Saudi and Kuwait commercial ships with the Security Council.

25 May: Abu Dhabi Municipality reported that it had constructed 1848 kms of surfaced roads during 1983 at a cost of 1600 million dirhams.

26 May: The Supreme Council of the Federation, under the Presidency of Sheikh Zayed, studied a number of local issues and dealt with new Gulf, Arab and international matters.

28 May: The Council of Ministers approved a federal decree setting-up the *Zakat* Council.

30 May: Sheikh Zayed issued a law establishing the International Oil Investments Company with a capital of 500 million dollars. It will look after petroleum and petrochemical industrial projects outside Abu Dhabi.

2 June: The Ministry of Health finished equipping the new Fujairah Hospital which was established at Sheikh Zayed's expense: costs for the equipment and medical requirements amounted to 192 million dirhams.

4 June: Sheikh Zayed issued a federal decree establishing the *Zakat* Council which was charged with the task of receiving *Zakat* contributions and directing them to the *Sharia* banks.

The Central Bank was reported to have assets of 12.597 billion dirhams.

7 June: The Higher Committee for Youth and Sports issued new rules and regulations governing the sports movement and its activities in the country.

9 June: The Ministry of Public Works and Housing began an experiment in the use of heat resistant materials in buildings in order to determine the potential saving in electricity.

10 June: The Supreme Council of the Federation, at its meeting under the Presidency of Sheikh Zayed, debated internal matters and developments in the Gulf. Its previous decree stressed that both Abu Dhabi and Dubai must contribute 50 per cent of their oil revenues to the federal budget.

The Council also renewed the call to stop the Iraq-Iran war.

13 June: Total investments spent on the infrastructure of Dubai during the period 1968 to 1983 amounted to around 13.4 billion dirhams.

14 June: In 1983 there were 12,664 farms in the country with an area of 290,500 hectares. The production of dates and fruit was 68,000 tons which provided 18 per cent of the local market.

15 June: The Abu Dhabi Investment Group confirmed that it had bought 36.5 million shares in the Reuters News Agency for 71.5 million pounds sterling.

16 June: Sheikh Zayed directed the Municipality and City Planning Office to pay attention to the Islamic character, history and civilization of the region in planning public buildings.

18 June: Sheikh Zayed confirmed the decrees passed by the Supreme Council of the Federation which obliged all the emirates to share in the federal budget and to Arabicize the names of establishments.

28 June: The Ministry of Communications celebrated the raising of the flag on the first UAE ship in the Arab Navigation Company.

5 July: Sheikh Faisal bin Mohammad Al Qassimi, Head of the Amiri Diwan in Sharjah, visited the island of Abu Musa where he observed conditions. He inspected the power station, the water desalination plant and the hospital.

It was announced that the combined budget of the Federation's commercial banks stood at 80.997 billion dirhams in March.

6 July: Sheikh Rashid bin Ahmed Al Mualla signed an agreement granting concessions to three oil exploration companies for land areas in Umm al-Qaiwain covering 170,000 hectares.

7 July: Dubai Dry Dock began repair work on three oil tankers which were hit during the tanker war in the Arabian Gulf.

9 July: The Council of Ministers confirmed the federal budget for 1984 amounting to 17.229 billion dirhams with a deficit of 4.3 billion dirhams.

10 July: Sheikh Hamdan bin Rashid Al Maktoum, Chairman of the Board of the Dubai Natural Gas Company (DUGAS), approved renewal of the agreement between the Government of Dubai and two Japanese companies to export natural liquid gas for a period of five years, beginning in July 1985. The Japanese side will recive 600 metric tons of gas.

11 July: Sheikh Zayed received Jalaluddin Hagbani, Deputy Leader of the Afghan *Mujahidin*.

12 July: Sheikh Surour bin Mohammad Al Nahyan signed a 75 million dollar agreement in Sana'a for rebuilding the Marib Dam with financing from the UAE.

15 July: Sheikh Zayed studied practical measures for uniting Eritrean revolutionary factions during his reception of the large Eritrean delegation who thanked Zayed for supporting the struggle of the Eritrean people.

18 July: Sheikh Khalifa began an official visit to Britain during which he met with the Prime Minister, Margaret Thatcher. During his discussions, he stressed the need for finding a just solution to the Palestinian problem and he asked Britain to support Arab rights and to push the wheel of peace forward in the region by working toward the ending of the Iraqi-Iran war.

19 July: Sheikh Zayed examined samples of farm produce from Liwa, Ghiyathi, Medinat Zayed and Abu al-Abyadh island during his visit to the city of Al-Marfa to inspect agricultural development projects. Sheikh Khalifa met with Michael Heseltine, British Minister of Defence. It was decided that the first batch of Hawk aircraft which Britain were supplying to the UAE would be delivered in August. Total aid granted by the UAE to developing countries during the period 1973 to 1981 amounted to 7.5 billion dollars.

25 July: Sheikh Zayed continued his visit to the Western Region where he inspected afforestation projects in Medinat Zayed and Baynunah village, as well as the date palm and vegetable farms in Mahadhir al-Mariya, Al-Muzairah and Liwa and met with citizens in these regions.

30 July: The average cost of education in Government schools during the 1983-84 academic year was 10,000 dirhams per student at primary, intermediate and secondary levels, and 14,000 dirhams per student at technical level.

4 August: Sheikh Zayed received the Libyan Oil Minister and President of OPEC, Kamel Hussain Makhour, and the Indonesian Oil Minister Dr Subruto. Sheikh Zayed stressed the UAE's support for OPEC and the importance of abiding by its resolutions regarding production quotas and prices.

6 August: The UAE celebrated the eighteenth anniversary of Sheikh Zayed's accession as Ruler of Abu Dhabi.

Sheikh Zayed received a letter from the Iraqi President, Saddam Hussein, delivered by Izzet Ibrahim, Vice President of the Leadership Council of the Iraqi Revolution, regarding the latest developments in the region. The President of the Federation expressed his deep understanding of Iraq's position and its sincere response to initiatives aimed at putting a stop to the war and ending the bloodletting between Muslim neighbours.

7 August: The Council of Ministers decided to name the Emirates Telecommunications Corporation 'Etisalat' instead of EMIRTEL in response to the Supreme Council of the Federation's decree regarding the Arabicizing of the names of State establishments.

9 August: Sheikh Zayed arrived in Ankara on an official visit to Turkey, during which he held talks with the Turkish President, Kenan Efren. Zayed stressed that unity and solidarity in the Islamic community would be a source of real self-generated strength, the only way to earn the respect of world powers.

8 August: Sheikh Zayed, during official discussions with the Turkish President, Kanan Efren, called for the ending of all disputes between Islamic states. It was agreed to set up a joint economic committee to strengthen mutual co-operation between the two countries.

10 August: The Turkish and UAE leaders called on Iraq and Iran to find a peaceful solution to the conflict. They renewed their support for the Islamic peace committee and joint efforts aimed at stopping the war, and stressed that a just peace in the Middle East was not viable except on the basis that the Palestinian people be allowed to exercise their right to self-determination.

14 August: Sheikh Zayed, meeting with the OPEC ministerial committee in Istanbul, underlined the UAE's complete support for the steps being taken by OPEC to defend OPEC oil prices and to protect the stability of the oil market in the best interests of producing and consuming countries and the world economy.

15 August: First Lady Sheikha Fatima bint Mubarak opened the Islamic Book Exhibition at the Abu Dhabi Women's Association.

16 August: Sheikh Zayed arrived in Tunis on an official visit. He called for a drawing together of Arab energies and capabilities to create a unified Arab effort for the benefit of all Arabs from the Atlantic Ocean to the Gulf. He said that the UAE made all its capabilities available to help achieve Arab hopes and expectations.

17 August: Sheikh Zayed, following talks with the Tunisian President, Habib Bourguiba, stressed that bringing the Arab nation closer together would ensure that it would become closer to the Islamic world, its natural extension and support for its strength. He called for the economic integration of the Arab nation and said that the goal was to achieve a system which would protect the Arabs from those who covet their wealth.

18 August: In a joint communiqué broadcast from both Abu Dhabi and Tunis, the UAE and Tunisia called on both Iraq and Iran to put an end to the fighting between them and they warned of the dangers of continuing the war. They stressed the importance of Arab solidarity and the right of the Palestinian people to self-determination and the establishment of their own state. They also agreed to strengthen co-operation between the two countries in joint investment and development projects.

In Tunis, Sheikh Zayed discussed current Arab issues and joint Arab efforts with Al Shadhili Al Kulaibi, the Secretary General of the Arab League.

23 August: Sheikh Zayed arrived in Rabat on a visit to Morocco.

25 August: A hijacked Indian airliner landed at Dubai International Airport where the seven hijackers demanded political asylum in the United States of America. After difficult negotiations led by Sheikh Mohammad bin Rashid Al Maktoum which lasted nearly 15 hours, the hijackers surrendered and all the passengers were safely released.

27 August: Sheikh Zayed received a letter from the Indian Prime Minister, Indira Gandhi, containing the thanks and appreciation of the Indian Government for efforts made by the UAE to end the hijack operation on the Indian aircraft.

30 August: Sheikh Saqr bin Mohammad Al Qassimi read the results of the feasibility study for setting-up the first date factory in Ras al-Khaimah based on the recommendation of the Secretariat General of the Union of Arab Food Industries.

31 August: In Rabat, Sheikh Zayed and King Hassan studied the current Arab situation, new developments in the Arab Maghrib and the situation in the Gulf.

2 September: Sheikh Khalifa bin Zayed Al Nahyan approved the general budget for the emirate of Abu Dhabi. Revenue was estimated at 20.83 billion dirhams and expenditure forecast at 21.73 billion dirhams.

The Department of Immigration and Nationality in the Ministry of the Interior decided to grant equal treatment to citizens of GCC States and UAE citizens in respect of sponsorship.

8 September: Sheikh Zayed received an invitation from the Yemeni President, Ali Abdulla Saleh, to lay the foundation stone for the rebuilding of the historic Marib Dam to be funded by Sheikh Zayed.

12 September: Dubai Municipality commenced naming and numbering city districts and streets and installing directional signs in Dubai and Deira.

14 September: Financial liquidity in the Federation at of the end of June stood at 43.7 billion dirhams.

16 September: Dubai Municipality decided to plant 30,000 sq. ft of shrubbery on Jebel Ali's beaches to protect the marine environment.

17 September: The Council of Ministers approved a plan to train and encourage students to join the Arab Maritime Transportation Academy to prepare national cadres qualified for service to the country in this field. It approved the expenditure of a 5000 dollar fee for each student. It also decided to pay each student a 1000-dirham monthly stipend by way of encouragement.

19 September: Central Bank reserves at the end of July 1984 stood at 12.411 billion dirhams.

21 September: ADNOC's 1983 annual report revealed that there was a rise in the daily refining capacity to 195,000 barrels a day and a decrease in the daily production of oil to 747 barrels.

24 September: The International Monetary Fund commended the role of the UAE in supporting the activities of the Fund and the World Bank through their participation in increasing aid extended by these institutions to developing countries.

The UAE were victorious in the Arab Chess Championships. Said Ahmed Said was victorious in the men's first division, Nadia Mohammad Saleh won in the women's first division and Farida Abdulkarim won in the third division.

28 September: Sheikh Khalifa bin Zayid donated 1 million dirhams to the Ras al-Khaimah Club to pay for new facilities.

30 September: A joint committee was formed from officials of the Personnel Offices of the Ministries of Education and Finance to establish a new cadre of teachers in the Federation and grant an allowance of 30 per cent to national teachers.

1 October: Sheikh Zayed began an official visit to Yemen during which he held talks with the Yemeni President, Ali Abdulla Saleh.

The Ministry of Health began applying the rules and regulations governing nationwide health registration.

2 October: Sheikh Zayed and Ali Abdulla Saleh laid the foundation stone for the historic Marib Dam restoration project which Sheikh Zayed was funding. The reconstruction was necessary to avoid the dangers of floods and revive agriculture on 10,000 hectares of agricultural land.

3 October: While in Sana'a, Sheikh Zayed received an invitation from King Hassan II, delivered by Izzedine Al Iraqi, Moroccan Minister of Education, to attend the emergency Arab Summit to study new developments in the Arab world.

4 October: Sheikh Zayed returned to the UAE after his official visit to Yemen. A join communiqué from Abu Dhabi and Sana'a stated that Sheikh Zayed and President Ali Abdulla Saleh were in agreement concerning the necessity of returning to solidarity and Arab unity and called on Arab leaders to support all efforts towards unity for the good of the Arab nation. They stressed the importance of Egypt returning to the Arab camp and welcomed such a move in line with the decrees of the Arab Summit.

6 October: The Air Forces of Kuwait and the UAE began their tenth joint exercises.

7 October: The Zayed Teachers Institute, given by the UAE as a present to the Yemeni people, was handed over to the Yemeni Government in Sana'a.

8 October: The Council of Ministers approved the draft federal law establishing the first Police College in the UAE.

10 October: Sheikh Khalifa bin Zayed Al Nahyan confirmed in a statement to *Al-Sharq al-Awsat* newspaper that the UAE had received the first batch of Hawk training aircraft from Britain. He said that this installment and the delivery of 18 Mirage 2000 aircraft from France fell within the scope of the plan to build an Air Force capable of meeting the UAE's defence requirements.

12 October: The Ministry of Health decided to computerize all their operations.

13 October: The Central Bank undertook measures to support the dirham and regulate payment facilities, including placing an obligation on banks operating in the country to keep 30 per cent of their weekly deposits or loans in dirhams in the Central Bank.

14 October: Sheikh Zayed issued a decree changing the name of the Complex of Cultural and Documentary Establishments in Abu Dhabi to 'The Cultural Complex'.

Work began on the construction of the new 130 million dirham Arrivals Hall at Dubai International Airport. The new hall will accommodate 6 million passengers per year.

16 October: Sheikh Surour bin Mohammad Al Nahyan inspected the 1500 million dollar Tarela Dam project north-west of Islamabad.

ADFAED contributed 95 million dirhams to the financing of the dam.

17 October: Sheikh Zayed received the Prime Minister of Denmark, Paul Sholter. The President of the Federation stressed the necessity of putting an end to the arms race and to exploit resources for the sake of peace.

The European Common Market called for participation in efforts to bring about a permanent and just peace in the Middle East.

Sheikh Hamdan bin Rashid Al Maktoum opened phase two of the 725 million dirham Jebel Ali Commercial Plant.

20 October: An economic, industrial and technical co-operation co-operation agreement between the UAE and the Kingdom of Denmark was signed at the end of the visit of the Danish Prime Minister, Paul Sholter, to the country.

23 October: Participation by the UAE in the International Fund for Agricultural Development was around 42 million dollars.

The Al-Jazira Shield No. 2 GCC manoeuvres in which the Forces of the UAE participated ended in success.

26 October: Mohammad Sultan Al

Suweidi, Vice Consul at the UAE Embassy in Rome, was shot and seriously injured. At the end of 1983 there were 38,445 employees in service in the Federal Ministries, 78 per cent of whom were citizens and Arabs.

27 October: Sheikh Sultan bin Mohammad Al Qassimi laid the foundation stone for the gas liquefaction plant at Sharjah's Al-Saja oil field.

28 October: It was decided to lower the price of telephone communications between GCC countries by 30 per cent during official holidays.

The UAE National Football Team qualified for the finals in the Asian National Cup competition in Singapore, following their defeat over Sri Lanka by five goals to one.

30 October: Sheikh Khalifa bin Zayed Al Nahyan attended graduation ceremonies for the sixth batch of pilots. He commended the willingness of the youth of the nation to join the Air Force and other units of the Armed Forces. He said that the UAE was completing the build-up of its forces for service to Gulf and Arab security. Sheikh Mohammad bin Zayed Al Nahyan, the Commander of the Air School, said that Sheikh Khalifa issued a decree changing the status of the school to the UAE Air College, one of the best military institutes in the Gulf region.

31 October: The Diwan of the President issued a statement regarding the assassination of the Prime Minister of India, Indira Gandhi, expressing the UAE's sorrow at the loss of a true friend who stood for right and justice.

1 November: The UAE and the People's Republic of China decided to establish diplomatic relations at ambassadorial level.

2 November: The first shipment of light crude oil from the Margham land oil field in Dubai was transported by pipeline to the metal storage tanks in Jebel Ali.

4 November: The UAE delegation, led by Sheikh Hamdan bin Mohammad Al Nahyan, returned to the country having attended the funeral of Mrs Indira Gandhi.

6 November: Sheikh Zayed, arriving in Libya on an official visit, said that the Arabs will always demand the right to defend their holy places and that it is the duty of every Arab to follow the path which will achieve the expectations and hopes of the Arab nation. Discussions between Zayed and Al Gadhafi centered on increasing efforts to strengthen Arab solidarity.

The Council of Ministers approved the draft federal law establishing the General Postal Administration with a capital of 200 million dirhams.

8 November: Sheikh Zayed, having arrived in Algeria on an official visit held discussions with the Algerian President Al Shadhili bin Jadid regarding the situation in the Arab world and ways of ensuring Arab collective action.

9 November: UAE banks were reported to have 11,625 employees: 838 UAE nationals, 128 from GCC countries, 2384 from Arab countries and 8279 from other countries.

Of the 1065 nationals sent on training or study missions abroad during the last six years, 22 were from the federal Government.

Afforested areas in the Western Region numbered 412 as of last October: a total of 442,863 trees were planted.

10 November: Local liquidity circulating in the markets increased by 20 per cent during the first half of 1984, rising from

37.4 billion dirhams in December 1983 to 43.6 billion dirhams in June 1984.

11 November: The total value of imports and re-exports in the State during the first six months of 1984 was 28.8 billion dirhams. The value of oil exports stood at 20.9 billion dirhams.

The Central Bank decided to withdraw remaining old banknotes (500, 100 and 1000 denomination) issued by the former Currency Board.

The Secretariat General of the Executive Council of the emirate of Abu Dhabi issued a codification of legislation covering the period 1965 to 1980.

12 November: The Council of Ministers expressed its appreciation for the efforts and good offices of Sheikh Zayed to achieve unity on the Arab and Islamic front. It approved the co-operation, cultural, scientific and technical agreement with Algeria.

13 November: Abu Dhabi Executive Council decreed that the Tawam Hospital in Al-Ain would become a University Hospital.

15 November: A new giant crane capable of lifting 51 tons became operational in Dubai's Port Rashid. Costing 12 million dirhams, the crane was the largest in the ports of the Middle East.

17 November: Sheikh Hamdan bin Rashid Al Maktoum signed a contract for setting-up a new sewage treatment plant in Dubai at a cost of 701 million dirhams. He stressed that the Government of Dubai had earmarked 408 billion dirhams for the execution of seven projects vital to the emirate's infrastructure.

18 November: Sheikh Zayed arrived in Rabat from Algeria continuing his tour of the Arab Maghrib.

19 November: Sheikh Sultan bin Mohammad Al Qassimi opened the International Airport Federation Conference in Sharjah. He stressed that the desire of peoples to move closer together had led to the growth of airports and that the development of their services had become imperative for every country.

20 November: Sheikh Saqr bin Mohammad Al Qassimi ordered the setting-up of a model residential area in the Al-Mamoura district of Ras al-Khaimah.

The total cost of federal investment projects in the current year amounted to approximately 7430.6 million dirhams.

22 November: Sheikh Hamad bin Mohammad Al Sharqi opened the National Bank of Fujairah with a permitted capital of 400 million dirhams and a paid-up capital of 140 million dirhams.

23 November: In the city of Fez, Sheikh Zayed and King Hassan II discussed current Arab affairs and new regional and international developments.

24 November: The Government of Umm al-Qaiwain granted concessions to a number of international companies to explore for oil and gas in offshore areas.

25 November: The UAE had rapidly developed its foreign relations, especially because of its humanitarian activities worldwide: as 1984 came to a close it had 62 diplomatic missions in the UAE and 32 missions abroad: it had also entered into 30 international agreements and 66 regional and Arab agreements.

26 November: In remarks to *Al-Sharq al-Awsat* newspaper, Sheikh Zayed stressed that the GCC acted as a support for Arab brothers in the greater Arab world, because it was part of the Arab nation from which all gathered strength. He said

H.H. Sheikh Zayed accompanies H.M. Queen Elizabeth II, during a visit to Abu Dhabi and the UAE in 1981.

Sheikh Zayed with British Prime Minister, Margaret Thatcher, on 22 April 1981.

An aerial view of Dubai creek and Port Rashid in 1981.

A Book Fair in Abu Dhabi held during 1981.

Heads of State meet at the First Gulf Summit for members of the AGCC on 25 May 1981.

Commemorative coins issued in 1981.

Sheikh Zayed with the King of Spain, Juan Carlos, on 5 December 1981.

At the Al Ruwais Refinery on 10 March 1982.

Navy Day in Abu Dhabi on 2 May 1983.

Sheikh Zayed's visit to Algeria in 1983.

Sheikh Zayed with the Turkish President on 8 August 1984.

Sheikh Zayed with King Khaled of Saudi Arabia on 27 November 1984.

The Fire Brigade at work in 1985.

Making traditional roofing near Al Ain in 1985.

*Road construction
in Abu Dhabi
during 1986.*

Port Zayed, Abu Dhabi, in June 1988.

Coins issued in 1986 and 1987.

Inauguration of the new Marib Dam, in Yemen, in 1986.

Sheikh Zayed made an official visit to Morocco in 1988.

An aerial view of Abu Dhabi city in 1986.

Meeting of AGCC members during the Arab Summit meeting in Casablanca, May 1989.

A friendly meeting with President Hosni Mubarak during the Arab Summit Meeting in Casablanca in May 1989.

Sheikh Zayed greets Benazir Bhutto in 1989.

During Sheikh Zayed's visit to the United Kingdom, seen here with H.M. the Queen Mother, H.M. Queen Elizabeth II and H.H. Prince Philip, the Duke of Edinburgh.

With President Mubarak during Sheikh Zayed's visit to Egypt in February 1990.

With H.M. King Hussein of Jordan on 28 February 1990.

Sheikh Zayed also visited China during May 1990.

A meeting with Saddam Hussein, President of Iraq, during the Arab Summit meeting held in Baghdad on 27 May 1990.

Sheikh Zayed visited Japan during May 1990. He is seen here with Emperor Akahito during the official welcoming ceremony.

Sheikh Zayed with King Hassan of Morocco on 19 July 1990.

UAE troops on parade in 1990.

Gold coins issued in 1990.

that ensuring the future success of the UAE would help to crystallize the idea of the GCC, stressing that the founding of the UAE was an historic departure for the Gulf area and the Arab nation as a whole. Sheikh Hamdan bin Mohammad Al Nahyan announced in his opening address to the new session of the Federal National Council that the Abu Dhabi Government had completed the preparation of a comprehensive industrialization plan until the year 2000, which would meet the requirements of the local market and include export to GCC countries.

28 November: Sheikh Zayed, arriving in Kuwait to participate in the GCC Summit meetings, stressed that GCC unity was at the core of greater Arab unity. He also said that the task of creating an ideal Arab individual in the Gulf and providing the basis on which to build a good life for the people of the region was everyone's responsibility.

Abu Dhabi Municipality began construction of a 36.9 million dirham, 50,400 sq.m. Central Bus Station in Abu Dhabi.

30 November: On the occasion of the World Day of Solidarity with the Cause of Palestine, Sheikh Zayed made a statement in which he stressed that the holding of a world peace conference was the way to solve the Palestinian question and that those opposing the conference supported Israel politically and economically. He called for the UN to bear special responsibility for Palestine because it was responsible for its partition.

2 December: Sheikh Zayed received the Members of the Supreme Council, the Rulers of the Emirates, and crowds of national well-wishers on the occasion of National Day.

Sheikh Zayed accepted a congratulatory letter from Queen Elizabeth delivered by Princess Anne, on the occasion of National Day.

First Lady Sheikha Fatima bint Mubarak received Princess Anne and stressed that UAE women had achieved all their rights according to Zayed's directions.

3 December: Sheikh Zayed and the members of the Supreme Council attended row and sail boat races which were part of the celebrations for National Day.

4 December: Sheikh Zayed, at the opening of the new session of the Federal National Council, called for the formation of a joint committee from the Council of Ministers and the Federal Council to assess ways of tackling problems resulting from declining oil revenues. He said that he strongly believed that there was no alternative to supporting the Federation since it was necessary as a shield to protect the UAE's sovereignty and that aggression against the UAE's embassies would not make it abandon its national obligations. He stressed that positive steps had been taken to protect the security and interests of GCC States. He also referred to the famine which threatened Africa and said that there was no escape from establishing a fair economic system to protect the rights of developing nations.

5 December: Umm al-Qaiwain opened a stock exchange or 'stock centre' to GCC citizens only for trading in UAE and Gulf stocks and shares; and property, currencies, commodities etc. on London, New York and Zurich markets.

8 December: Sheikh Khalifa bin Zayed Al Nahyan, during his meeting with the first

Chinese delegation to visit the UAE, expressed the hope that the visit would create new horizons for mutual co-operation. He also hoped that the new relationship would strengthen development and progress in the world and serve the causes of right, justice and peace.

9 December: Sheikh Zayed received the visiting Chinese delegation who expressed their pleasure at seeing the developments in the country, as well as their appreciation for the establishment of full diplomatic relations with the Peoples Republic of China.

Sheikh Rashid bin Saeed Al Maktoum donated 1 million dirhams to the Al-Nasr Club on the occasion of its victory in the football championship games.

12 December: Sheikh Hamdan bin Rashid Al Maktoum signed an agreement to recruit a team of UN experts to follow-up on the work of the consulting company preparing the master plan for the emirate of Dubai.

15 December: The Civil Service Commission advised all federal ministries and establishments in the State that the Council of Ministers had decided to freeze all appointments and promotions.

16 December: The Diwan of the Ruler's Representative in the Eastern Region completed establishment of the solar energy project for water desalination in Al-Wajn south of Al-Ain, the first of its kind in the region. Initial production in the first experimental stage averaged 80 per cent of a total daily production capacity of 110,000 gallons per day.

It was decided to add 350 new buses to the school bus fleet for the current academic year: the total number of buses in the nation-wide fleet stood at 2150.

17 December: The Council of Ministers decided to strengthen the UAE's Border Guard and provide it with the necessary equipment to enable it to secure the nation's borders. It also decided to exempt national university graduates from the decree, freezing all appointments and promotions in the federal ministries.

The Chief-of-Staff of the Armed Forces opened the Technical Attack Room at Naval Headquarters, the first of its kind in the region.

The UAE University received its new library building costing 21 million dirhams.

By the end of 1984, there were 147 insurance companies operating in the country.

18 December: Sheikh Zayed decreed that the annual income of two of his buildings be allocated to enable handicapped centres to expand their activity, and he transferred two villas in Al-Ain and two in Medinat Zayed to the centres. Sheikha Fatima bint Mubarak donated 1 million dirhams from the Welfare Fund to purchase the necessary equipment and apparatus for these centres.

20 December: Sheikh Zayed and the Palestinian Leader, Yasser Arafat, discussed ways of bringing Arab points of view closer together in an attempt to convene an Arab Summit. They also discussed ways of creating an atmosphere conducive to the success of a summit.

24 December: A letter to Sheikh Zayed from the Libyan President, Muammar Al Gadhafi, delivered by the Libyan Minister of Petroleum, focused on issues relating to the international oil market and the crisis facing OPEC countries. Sheikh Zayed also received a report from Dr Mana Said Al Otaiba regarding the UAE's efforts to maintain OPEC unity and confront the financial crisis.

An agreement was signed in Rome covering economic, industrial and technical co-operation between the UAE and Italy.

Etisalat decided to reduce the cost of domestic telephone calls by between 50 and 53.5 percent.

25 December: Sheikh Zayed held important discussions in Al-Ain with His Majesty Sultan Qaboos bin Said regarding ways to develop co-operation between the two countries in various fields. The talks also covered the current Arab situation.

Work began on the new 145 million dirham Khor Fakkan hospital in Sharjah, which was being built at the expense of Sheikh Rashid bin Saeed Al Maktoum.

28 December: The Emirates National Football Team were victorious in the second division of the West Asian Football competition.

31 December: The Council of Ministers reviewed the international oil market in light of the report presented to it by Dr Mana Said Al Otaiba, Minister of Petroleum and Mineral Resources.

Nineteen Eighty Five

1 January: A Ministry of Planning report stated that Gross National Product rose from 186 million dirhams in 1972 to 9.1 billion dirhams in 1983. The number of workers in the country rose from 288,000 to 572,000 in 1983.

2 January: The General Postal Administration inaugurated an express mail service with three new countries, bringing to 20 the number of countries to which express mail could be sent since 1 November 1983.

3 January: The Council of Ministers approved the draft law computerizing civil service operations in federal ministries and establishments.

4 January: Yasser Arafat unexpectedly arrived in Dubai where he met with the former Austrian Chancellor, Bruno Kreisky, for three hours, during which he listened to details of the Kreisky initiative for settling the Arab-Israeli dispute.

The Documents Centre in Abu Dhabi received 80,000 documents on the history of the Emirates and the Gulf region from the thirteenth century up to the early twentieth century.

The Board of ADNOC decided to raise the capital of the company from 30 to 200 million dirhams to be spent on expanding company projects.

6 January: Sheikh Khalifa received the former Austrian Chancellor, Bruno Kreisky, assuring him that the Arab nation wanted a just and lasting peace and an Israeli withdrawal from all occupied Arab lands. He said that the UAE would support the struggle of the Palestinian people until their usurped rights had been regained.

The UAE gave 8 million dollars to ARABSAT which was to be launched in February.

8 January: The Council of Ministers decreed that priority be given to Ministry of Education projects in preparing the investment programme for the current year.

9 January: A Ministry of Planning report stated that the number of residential units increased from 55,000 in 1972 to 387,000 in 1983.

At the Al-Ain zoo, a golden eagle was hatched in captivity for the first time, an event of international concern and of particular interest to the International Committee for the Protection of Rare Birds and Wildlife.

11 January: According to the Ministry of Planning report, 12 social centres were established since the the Federation was formed, and 683 million dirhams was spent on social assistance and the care of the aged during the period 1973-83.

12 January: Sheikh Hamdan bin Zayed Al Nahyan, President of the Football Federation, was chosen as president of the organizing committee for the finals of the Asian Youth Championship Games, to be hosted by the UAE in March.

A follow-up committee was formed to look after the merger of national banks in order to strengthen the capabilities of the banking sector in the UAE.

14 January: The Council of Ministers allocated 29 million dirhams for the coming year for a new programme to recruit nationals (both male and female) as teachers.

20 January: Documents were exchanged relating to the Economic, Commercial and Technical Co-operation Agreement between the UAE and the European Community following ratification by the Governments concerned.

One hundred and ninety two projects amounting to approximately 3471.2 million dirhams were completed within the annual development programme of the emirate of Abu Dhabi by the end of September 1984.

21 January: The Ministry of Communications issued a decree placing all sea-going vessels in UAE ports under its authority. Offices were opened in Abu Dhabi, Dubai and Sharjah for the registration and control of vessels.

22 January: Al-Ain Dairy Farm achieved an international average production record of 9000 litres of fresh milk daily.

25 January: For the first time, a closed circuit television was used to regulate traffic and monitor traffic violations in the streets of Abu Dhabi. Information on traffic flow was transmitted to a central operations room in the new headquarters of the Traffic Police.

First steps were taken in building the UAE's largest central bus station in Abu Dhabi. Public buses in Abu Dhabi accommodated 9,726,208 passengers in 1984.

27 January: Sheikh Zayed received a letter from Pope John Paul regarding world peace, Islamic/Christian rapprochement and relations with the Vatican.

The joint Iraq-UAE Economic-Commercial Committee held a meeting in Abu Dhabi. Since the signing of the agreement in 1977, trade between the two countries rose from 4.2 million dirhams to 306 million dirhams in 1981 and to 392 million dirhams in 1982.

28 January: The Council of Ministers decided to include computer-studies as an extra-curricular subject in Ministry of Education schools in order to encourage and develop the abilities of the students in working with computers.

Some important archaeological finds were uncovered in Al-Hili in the Al-Ain area, dating back to 2500 B.C.

Dr Mana Said Al Otaiba withdrew from the OPEC meeting in Geneva in protest at the Nigerian position. He said that Nigeria was not honouring price-setting and production quotas agreed by the organization and that it was stabbing OPEC in the back.

29 January: The Executive Council allocated 405 million dirhams to supply Abu Dhabi hospitals with the latest medical equipment in order to provide the best possible medical services.

During a visit to UAE by Iraqi Finance Minister, Hisham Hassan Tawfiq, the Federation signed an economic and trade agreement with Iraq.

30 January: Sheikh Ahmed bin Hamid called for the convening of a joint meeting of Arab Ministers of Information and Communications in order to formulate a unified working plan for utilizing the Arab satellite to be launched in February.

31 January: Dr Mana Said Al Otaiba confirmed that from 1 February the UAE would begin applying the new OPEC agreement which lowered the price of a barrel of oil by 1.5 dollars: the price per barrel was 26.5 dollars.

1 February: In the previous 18 years, Sheikh Zayed distributed 7370 parcels of land in Abu Dhabi and its suburbs to citizens. Some 4878 million dirhams was paid in compensation for lands confiscated for development purposes.

Sheikh Rashid, arriving in Sohar on an official visit to the Sultanate of Oman, met with His Majesty Sultan Qaboos bin Said.

4 February: Sheikh Khalifa announced during graduation ceremonies for the tenth batch of officers from Zayed Military College that the leadership of the country was well aware of the realities and challenges of the times. He also stressed that the determined goal of the leadership was to encourage self-reliance which would protect the nation and ensure peace.

Twenty-six afforestation projects, covering 20,000 hectares of 4 million trees and 200 date palm farms, were executed by Abu Dhabi Municipality in Badii Zayed and Ghiyathi.

5 February: Work began on the first vegetable canning factory in the Abu Samra region near al-Ain. Costing 20.9 million dirhams, it will produce 37 tons of canned vegetables per day.

6 February: First Lady Sheikha Fatima bint Mubarak presided over the first meeting of the Aid Committee for the victims of drought in Africa. The meeting included six women from the diplomatic corps and UNICEF.

Work was completed on the new 20 million dirham municipality building in Umm al-Qaiwain.

Said Ahmed Said from the UAE won the tenth World Chess Championship.

7 February: In Islamabad, Sheikh Zayed and the Pakistani President, Mohammad Zia Al Haq, discussed developments in the Iran-Iraq war and international Islamic affairs. It was agreed that Sheikh Zayed would intercede with the Prime Minister of India, Indira Gandhi, in an effort to mend and improve relations between India and Pakistan.

It was decided to supply Al-Mafraq Hospital with the very latest ultrasonic equipment for shattering kidney stones.

9 February: Sheikh Sultan bin Mohammad Al Qassimi attended the first Children's Cultural Festival in Sharjah.

UAE Central Bank issued a directive requiring all banks in UAE, local or foreign, to disclose their operations in detail. Previously, some banks had only mentioned 'inner reserves' along with the main reserves of the bank in annual reports to shareholders without revealing their size. Central Bank directive required all banks to publish all reserve holdings in the local Arabic press for three days.

10 February: The Information/ Documentation Centre of the Ministry of Information and Culture began collecting all newspapers and periodicals which were issued since the establishment of the Federation in preparation for storage on mocrofiche.

11 February: Sheikh Khalifa bin Zayed Al Nahyan, in Kuwait on an official visit, was received by Sheikh Jabir Al Ahmed Al Sabah, the Amir of Kuwait, who commended the active role of the UAE in regional and Arab affairs.

12 February: Sheikh Khalifa led the UAE delegation and Sheikh Saad Al Abdulla Al Sabah, Heir Apparent of Kuwait, led the Kuwaiti side in official discussions focusing on a comprehensive evaluation of regional and international matters of mutual concern.

The Supreme Council of UAE University approved the draft budget for 1985, amounting to 573 million dirhams.

13 February: The UAE celebrated the sixth Tree Day by planting more than half a million trees.

14 February: For the first time in the courts of Abu Dhabi, it was decided that national judges would preside in criminal cases in the preliminary courts.

15 February: The Electricity and Water Department contracted with Arab administrative consultants to prepare a curriculum and advanced training plan for citizens studying at the technical and vocational training centre of the office in Umm al-Nar in Abu Dhabi.

17 February: Sheikh Faisal bin Khalid Al Qassimi, President of the Amiri Diwan in Sharjah, at the opening of the Arab Co-operative Union, confirmed that the UAE embraced all constructive plans which sought to further the well being of the Arab nation. The President received the delegations from the conference and studied the Arab Co-operative Union work plan for supporting co-operative societies and developing co-operative activity among Arab countries.

18 February: The Council of Ministers decided to change the the name of the Nursing School to the College of Health Sciences.

The Minister of Health said that the first World Cancer Conference in Abu Dhabi represented the beginning of continuing co-operation in all international efforts to uncover the secrets of cancer. He confirmed that the UAE had specialized departments and the necessary qualified and experienced staff to detect the disease in its early stages and the ability to effectively treat it.

19 February: The first steps were taken in building a radio and television studio complex on a 15,000 sq. m site in Abu Dhabi.

20 February: First Lady Sheikha Fatima bint Mubarak arrived in Ankara at the beginning of an official visit to Turkey. She said that the history of this Islamic country was tied to the history of the Arab world and she expressed the hope that her visit would increase the ties of friendship and co-operation between the two countries, especially in the field of women's affairs. During her stay in Turkey, she visited the High Institute for the Development of Heritage in Ankara and the Children's Hospital. She contributed 100,000 dollars to the Turkish Union of Women's Societies, as well as 50,000 dollars to the Society for the Blind and 50,000 dollars to Society of Lovers of the Poor in Ankara.

21 February: Sheikh Zayed visited Oman and had talks on Gulf and international issues with Sultan Qaboos bin Said at Sohar.

22 February: Work began on the construction of the new vegetable, fruit, meat and fish market in Al-Ain. Costing 77.9 million dirhams, it will cover 15.5 hectares.

24 February: Sheikh Ahmed bin Hamid opened two short and medium wave radio stations in Abu Dhabi.

25 February: The Council of Ministers approved a draft federal law limiting the tonnage of trailers on the roads.

The UAE and Iraq signed a technical agreement aimed at developing co-operation in the field of labour and an exchange of experience in labour affairs.

UAE-Turkish commission completed a meeting in Abu Dhabi attended by visiting Turkish Foreign Affairs Minister, Vahit Halefoglu. During the meeting, the creation of a joint investment company, a UAE-Turkish shipping company and opening of Turkish trade centres were proposed.

26 February: Sheikh Zayed, receiving the Yugoslavian Foreign Minister in Abu Dhabi, stressed the important role which the non-aligned nations can play on the international scene. He referred to the necessity for these nations to redouble their efforts to solve their problems, removed from the conflicts of the superpowers.

Sheikh Sultan bin Mohammad Al Qassimi returned to the country after an official visit to Bahrain where he discussed mutual co-operation and Gulf matters with His Highness, Essa bin Salman Al Khalifa.

The Secretariat General of Municipalities decided to Arabicize all commercial names in the country.

27 February: First Lady Sheikha Fatima bint Mubarak, on an official visit to Tunis, donated 200,000 dollars to the Karama Foundation for Tunisian Social Affairs.

She visited the traditional crafts centre in Nabeul and the Wasila Bourguiba Centre for Mothers and Nursing Children. Two newborn babies at the centre were named Zayed and Fatima in her honour. She also visited the National Women's Union.

1 March: Work was completed on the new VIP runway at Abu Dhabi International Airport.

2 March: Etisalat installed an electronic telephone directory as part of its services to customers.

3 March: Sheikh Nahyan bin Mubarak Al Nahyan announced that the UAE University had included the Petroleum Industry as an engineering option in view of its importance to the UAE economy.

4 March: The Council of Ministers debated a comprehensive plan for training national employees in the use of computers, in order to develop their administrative skills.

5 March: The Federal National Council affirmed the first draft law for combating drug abuse in the country.

The Ministry of Health, as directed by the President, completed studies for the creation of the first centre for Public Medicine in the country.

Construction work began on the 40 million dirham first phase of the Central Sharjah Souk which was designed along Islamic architectural lines.

6 March: UAE and Australia signed an economic agreement to support and develop commercial relations and technical co-operation.

7 March: UAE and Pakistan signed a contract to lay a 1174 kms submarine telecommunications cable.

9 March: Sheikh Zayed, in a letter to the President of the Lebanese Chamber of

Deputies, expressed the UAE's support for the Lebanese struggle to free Lebanese soil of invading Zionist forces.

Al-Ain Municipality began work on a 27 million dirham ice skating rink in the Al-Hili Park in Al-Ain.

10 March: The Pakistani President, Mohammad Zia Al Haq, welcomed any mediation by Sheikh Zayed to improve relations between Pakistan and India.

12 March: The first meeting of the Board of Trustees of the International Co-operation Fund for Arab and Islamic Cultural Development was held in Tunis. The UAE, under the leadership of the President, was commended for its support for Arabic language publications and establishing institutes for teaching the Islamic religion in a number of Islamic countries which do not speak Arabic.

16 March: A letter from the Iranian President, containing a request for assistance in bringing about an end to the intensifying war with Iraq was delivered to Sheikh Zayed by Mohammad Arab, Undersecretary of the Foreign Ministry.

17 March: Sheikh Zayed received a letter from King Hussein of Jordan, regarding developments in the Arab world and efforts being made to end the Iraq-Iran war.

18 March: Sheikh Khalifa bin Zayed Al Nahyan and US General Robert Kingston discussed military relations and co-operation between the two countries.

Meetings between the UAE and Morocco were held in Rabat during the sixth session of the Joint Committee for Reviving Islamic Heritage.

19 March: Sheikh Hamdan bin Mohammad Al Nahyan, Deputy Prime Minister, expressed the UAE's regret with regard to the worrisome intensification of the Iraq-Iran war. He called for the international community to undertake its responsibilities to put an end to this war which constituted a serious threat to international security and peace.

21 March: On the occasion of the fortieth anniversary of the founding of the Arab League, the UAE confirmed that the League is an historic symbol of Arab unity and that it is the only way to consolidate unity, preserve independence and protect the nation.

The UAE decided to join the Arab Organization for Education, Science and Culture.

22 March: Sheikh Zayed sent a letter to the UN Committee for Elimination of Racial Discrimination. He renewed the UAE's support and its solidarity with the people of South Africa and their struggle to end apartheid.

The Emirates National Football Team won the bronze medal in the Asian Youth Championship Football Games.

24 March: Rashid Abdulla announced that the GCC States were making concerted moves to end the Iraq-Iran war.

25 March: The first kidney transplant operation in the UAE was successfully completed at Al-Mafraq Hospital in Abu Dhabi.

The shareholders, in a general meeting of the Abu Dhabi Aircraft Company, approved an increase of 30 million dirhams in the company's paid up capital, thus bringing it up to 90 million dirhams, and an increase in the permitted capital to 200 million dirhams. It was also decided to change the name of the company to Abu Dhabi Aviation with three branch companies: Al-Saqr Aviation, Al-Saqr for Supplies and Maintenance, and Al-Saqr International.

26 March: Hilal Ahmed Lootah, Chairman of the Federal National Council, delivered a speech to the conference of the International Parliamentary Union in Lome calling for the international community to bear its responsibilities and continue its efforts to end the Iraq-Iran war to save the lives of victims on both sides, protect the security of the region and safeguard world peace.

The Industrial Bank decided to pay 5 per cent of its paid up capital, i.e. 100 million dirhams, in dividends to shareholders. Profits for 1984 amounted to 38 million dirhams with assets reaching 565 million.

27 March: Sheikh Sultan bin Mohammad Al Qassimi attended the second annual graduation ceremonies for outstanding students in Sharjah Educational District.

30 March: Sheikh Hamdan bin Rashid Al Maktoum and Abdulla Bishara, Secretary General of the GCC Council, studied the provisions of the Economic Unity Agreement between the GCC States.

1 April: Sheikh Ahmed bin Hamid issued a decree establishing a central inspection system in the Ministry of Information and Culture to oversee video shops, cinemas and photographers.

The Office of Planning estimated that the population of Abu Dhabi emirate in 1984 was 509,000 or 43.5 per cent of the total population (1,169,600) of the UAE.

2 April: Sheikh Khalifa decided to raise the rents on commercial buildings owned by nationals which were guaranteed by the Office of Social Services from 30 to 40 per cent, setting aside 10 per cent for maintenance purposes.

The Royal College of Surgeons in London recognized Al-Mafraq Hospital in Abu Dhabi as a teaching hospital for doctors sitting the Royal Internship Examination in Surgery.

4 April: The UAE and Tunis signed an agricultural co-operation agreement.

Daily *per capita* water use in Abu Dhabi emirate increased to 150 gallons per day in 1984, an increase of 18 gallons over 1983.

5 April: Sheikh Zayed and King Hassan II of Morocco conferred in Rabat on the current Arab situation, developments in the Palestinian cause and the situation in the Gulf and the Maghrib. It was agreed to form a joint committee under the chairmanship of the two ministers of foreign affairs to support co-operation and develop relations between the two countries.

8 April: The UAE occupied first place on the list of GCC countries exporting to Bahrain: exports were valued at 7613 million Bahraini dinars.

9 April: There were 100,000 housing units in the emirate of Abu Dhabi in 1984.

13 April: Sheikh Hamdan bin Mohammad opened the first Arab Gulf Social Work Week which was held in Abu Dhabi and distributed certificates of appreciation and shields to the pioneers in this field.

A triple surgical operation for restoring the sight of a 65-year-old woman was performed for the first time in Al-Mafraq Hospital.

19 April: Sheikh Zayed, the Members of the Supreme Council of the Federation and their guests from GCC States attended the grand annual pure-bred Arab camel races.

20 April: First Lady Sheikha Fatima bint Mubarak presided over a meeting of the Council of Mothers of Abu Dhabi educational region. She stressed the importance of co-operation between the school and the home and the participation of mothers in alleviating some of the obstacles which stand in the way of women's education.

21 April: Sheikh Zayed attended graduation ceremonies for the fourth batch of students from UAE University and distributed diplomas to the graduates.

22 April: Sheikha Fatima bint Mubarak attended graduation ceremonies for the fourth batch of female graduates from UAE University. She emphasized that UAE women had achieved the hopes invested in them and had begun to participate fully in building the future.

A delegation of Japanese car manufacturers approved the technical specifications and measurements which the UAE requested for Japanese cars exported to the UAE.

23 April: Sheikh Maktoum bin Rashid Al Maktoum decreed the creation of a a regulatory authority for Jebel Ali port free trade zone.

The Council of Ministers decided to support and encourage national industrial products by giving them purchase priority.

Sheikh Ahmed bin Hamid said that work would begin at the end of the year on the new 400 million dirham broadcasting and television complex which would take three years to complete.

24 April: Sheikh Zayed attended the secondary-level military schools' annual festival mounted at Zayed Sports City.

The UAE and Morocco agreed that national groups from the legal profession would train at the National Institute for Judicial Studies in Rabat.

A session of official discussions was held in the UAE between delegations from the Federal National Council and the Syrian People's Council concerning Arab and international matters of mutual interest.

26 April: The Federal National Council and the Syrian People's Council, in a joint statement on the results of their discussions, stressed the importance of protecting the security and stability of the Gulf region and the necessity of keeping foreign interference at a distance.

27 April: Sheikh Zayed and the Members of the Supreme Council of the Federation attended the third festival concluding school activities. Sheikh Zayed, meeting with some of the students, encouraged them to persevere in their search for knowledge, praised their exhibits and distributed prizes.

Sheikh Mohammad bin Butti opened the new airport bridge and the Said bin Tahnoun bridge in Abu Dhabi. The cost of both bridges was 326 million dirhams.

28 April: Three national commercial banks in Abu Dhabi, Emirates Commercial Bank, Federal Commercial Band Ltd, and the Gulf Commercial Bank Ltd, agreed to the Central Bank proposal to merge to form the Abu Dhabi Commercial Bank.

29 April: The Ministry of Information and Culture signed an information co-operation agreement between the UAE and Tunis providing for the exchange of visits of journalists and technicians, as well as informational and cultural programmes.

30 April: The joint committee composed of members of the Council of Ministers and the Federal National Council completed preparation of the comprehensive report on the UAE's economic situation in preparation for its submission to the Supreme Council of the Federation. Sheikh Hamdan bin Mohammad Al Nahyan, meeting with a delegation of the

Eritrean Revolution, confirmed the UAE's support for the struggle of the Eritrean people and its blessing on their attempt to bring unity to Eritrean revolutionary factions.

Over 3 billion dirhams had been spent in the previous ten years on housing for UAE nationals with limited incomes.

1 May: Sheikh Hamad bin Mohammad Al Sharqi attended ceremonies at the Social Development Centre in Fujairah for the graduation of 14 female students in environmental industries courses. He stressed the necessity of granting women full opportunity for participation in building a better society.

First Lady Sheikha Fatima bint Mubarak opened the Charity Souk in aid of the victims of drought in Africa at the headquarters of Abu Dhabi Women's Society.

The Ministry of Health implemented the first official price list for medicines in all private pharmacies, thereby reducing prices by 50 per cent.

4 May: The UAE and India, in official discussions between their two Ministers of Foreign Affairs in Abu Dhabi, stressed the necessity of finding an urgent solution to the Iran-Iraq war. The UAE commended India's efforts in her capacity as chairman of the non-aligned movement to put a stop to the war.

Dubai Television established a company called 'Dubai Centre for Artistic Productions' to create programmes, including dramas.

6 May: Sheikh Khalifa bin Zayed Al Nahyan ordered that the Federation's Consumers Co-operative Union be given fully-equipped private offices in Abu Dhabi to assist it in supervising and co-ordinating co-operative societies, unifying purchasing, and providing commodities to consumers at reasonable prices.

8 May: Sheikh Zayed began an inspection tour of the Western Region to make certain that services were being provided to citizens in remote areas.

10 May: Sheikh Sultan bin Mohammad Al Qassimi was granted a doctorate in history from Exeter University in England.

12 May: Sheikh Zayed, arriving in Jeddah on an official visit to Saudi Arabia, held discussions with King Fahad bin Abdulaziz regarding Arab and Gulf affairs.

Lighting on the highway between Dubai and Sharjah was switched on.

13 May: A session of discussions was held between Sheikh Zayed and King Fahad, during which the necessity of finding true Arab solidarity, the Palestinian cause, the Iran-Iraq war and the efforts being made to put a peaceful end to it, were discussed.

14 May: Sheikh Zayed, before his return to the UAE, held a second session of discussions with King Fahad bin Abdulaziz centring on developments in the Palestinian cause, in light of the joint Jordanian-Palestinian response to the American initiative.

15 May: Sheikh Zayed held extended talks with King Hussein of Jordan, who briefed the President on the results of his talks with the leaders of the Gulf Countries concerning the joint Jordanian-Palestinian response and the necessity of crystallizing a unified Arab approach to developments in the Arab world.

18 May: Sheikh Hamdan bin Mohammed, Deputy Prime Minister, held official discussions with the Prime Minister of Turkey, Turgut Ozal, covering mutual relations and the situation in the Middle East.

21 May: The Council of Ministers decided to form a committee to alter regulations governing the medical treatment of citizens abroad.

22 May: Sheikh Khalifa praised the Al-Wahda team victory in the season's second division football championship, as well as its promotion to the first division, when he received the team.

25 May: Sheikh Zayed followed news of the cowardly attack on Sheikh Jabir Al Ahmed Al Sabah, the Amir of Kuwait, with great concern. He held a telephone conversation with the Amir to reassure himself about his health and he strongly condemned the terrible crime, stressing that the UAE stood by Kuwait.

27 May: The Council of Ministers condemned terrorism, rejected all acts of terror and sabotage aimed at undermining the security and stability of States in the region, and confirmed the UAE's support for Kuwait's security and stability.

The Federal National Council condemned the criminal act of aggression against the Amir of Kuwait and said that all acts of terrorism are reprehensible and that they only serve the interests of the enemies of the Arab nation.

1 June: The Ministry of Petroleum prepared a comprehensive report regarding the creation of a strategic reserve of oil products for the State.

2 June: Sheikh Dr Sultan bin Mohammad Al Qassimi met with the President of the People's Republic of China, Zhao Ziang, who paid a short visit to the emirate of Sharjah.

5 June: For the first time in Port Rashid Dubai, three steel platforms weighing 60 tons each were loaded onto the Arab Navigation Company ship, *Ibn Al-Nafees*, to be shipped to Japan.

The Governor of the Central Bank signed a 9.5 million dirham contract for setting-up the Institute for Banking Studies and Training in Sharjah.

6 June: Sheikh Hamdan bin Rashid Al Maktoum signed a 1.7 million agreement with the United Nations Development Programme to make use of their experts in supervising a survey of major health engineering stations.

10 June: The Council of Ministers approved a draft agreement setting-up a regional centre for computer-training in the State. It was the first of its kind in the Middle East.

11 June: Sheikh Zayed held discussions with Dr George Habash, Secretary General of the Popular Front for the Liberation of Palestine, who was visiting the country for the first time, concerning the current situation in the Palestinian refugee camps in Lebanon and developments in the Palestinian cause.

17 June: In 1984, the Industrial Bank granted loans amounting to 97 million dirhams to support national industries in the State. The total amount of all loans granted since it was founded was 132 million dirhams.

20 June: Sheikh Zayed ordered that 1 million dollars be given to the Republic of Bangladesh as aid for the victims of the tornadoes and floods which plagued the country. He also ordered that large air and sea shipments of aid and food items be sent to Bangladesh.

22 June: The UAE announced its readiness to attend an emergency Arab Summit to be held in Morocco after the President received a letter from the Moroccan king regarding the Summit.

UAE's non-oil exports rose from 953 million dirhams in 1980 to 1927 million in 1984.

25 June: Sheikh Zayed received a letter from the Iranian President, Ali Khamenei, regarding developments in the region.

26 June: Sheikh Zayed, in a meeting with the Federal National Council, confirmed the need to support the Federation's future development in order to fulfil the hopes and ambitions of its citizens. He stressed that the Emirates had achieved a complete renaissance in a very short time and said that the Rulers must take advice from citizens in order to satisfy their needs.

27 June: Sheikh Humaid bin Rashid Al Nuaimi paid a one-day visit to Sudan during which he met with the Sudanese President, Abdulrahman Sawar Al Dhahab.

30 June: Sheikh Ahmed bin Hamid arrived in Tunis to attend meetings of the Arab Ministers of Information. He stressed the importance of co-ordinating Arab information and unifying its stand in order to serve Arab causes and support Arab solidarity. The Permanent Committee for Arab Information approved the UAE's advice on the importance of using ARABSAT for the exchange of news items and pictures between Arab news agencies.

6 July: Sheikh Zayed sent a letter to the Iraqi President, Saddam Hussein, regarding developments in Arab and regional affairs, to be delivered by Rashid Abdulla, Minister of Foreign Affairs.

7 July: The UAE signed an agreement with the International Governments Information Office to set-up a regional computer-training centre.

8 July: The Council of Ministers approved the application of a heat resistance system for buildings and residences to reduce consumption of electricity by 30 per cent. GCC Foreign Ministers held a meeting in Abha to study the outcome of visits by Rashid Abdulla to Iraq and Prince Saud Al Faisal to Iran, which fell within the framework of GCC efforts to put an end to the Iran-Iraq war.

9 July: Sheikh Zayed gave his blessing to the proposal by the Libyan President, Muammar Al Gadhafi, for the Charter of the Arab Union. He called for an Arab summit to debate the issue and take whatever decisions were required for joint Arab action.

10 July: UAE Women's Federation participated in the UN Women's Conference in Nairobi, the largest gathering of women in the world.

12 July: Sheikh Zayed, continuing his tour of the Western Region, met with crowds of locals from Liwa in Al-Muzaira rest house, in order to assure himself of their well-being as part of his concern for citizens who live in remote areas. He also inspected samples of farm produce such as dates and fruit.

13 July: Sheikh Zayed confirmed UAE support for OPEC in the delicate stage through which it was passing. He made this statement after receiving a report from Dr Mana Said Al Otaiba regarding the outcome of OPEC meetings in Vienna in which it was decided to maintain production levels, quotas and prices.

The President of Djibouti, praised Sheikh Zayed's sustained efforts in establishing Islamic cultural centres, mosques and schools for memorizing the Holy Qur'an and teaching the Arabic language in Africa.

18 July: Sheikha Fatima bint Mubarak received a cable of thanks from the Arab group participating in the World Conference of Women in Nairobi, in appreciation of her half million dollar donation to the United Nations Fund for the Development of Women.

22 July: Sheikh Zayed sent letters to the Libyan President, Muammar Al Gadhafi, regarding developments in Arab affairs; to the Iranian President, Ali Khamenei, regarding the situation in the region and developments in the Iraq-Iran war; and to the Pakistani President, Mohammad Zia Al Haq, concerning the situation in the Gulf.

27 July: Sheikh Saqr bin Mohammad Al Qassimi donated 1 million dirhams to the Saqr Hospital in Ras al-Khaimah to buy modern medical and surgical equipment.

28 July: Sheikh Zayed received a letter from the Kenyan President, Daniel Arap Moi, regarding Arab-African co-operation.

31 July: The UAE's surplus trade balance during 1984 was 33.2 billion dirhams, a 17.3 per cent increase over 1983.

1 August: Sheikh Zayed returned to the UAE following an official three-day visit to the Sultanate of Oman, during which he had discussions with His Majesty Sultan Qaboos bin Said on the necessity of containing Arab disputes, developing mutual co-operation in supporting integration between GCC States, and continuing efforts to end the Iraq-Iran war.

2 August: The Sharjah Port Authority signed an agreement with United States shipping lines to open a corporate container compound in Khor Fakkan.

5 August: Sheikh Hamdan bin Zayed led the UAE delegation to the meeting of Arab Ministers of Foreign Affairs in Casablanca to prepare for the emergency Arab Summit to be held in Morocco.

6 August: Sheikh Zayed received members of the Supreme Council of the Federation and groups of well-wishers on the twentieth anniversary of his rise to power in Abu Dhabi.

Sheikh Zayed arrived in Casablanca to participate in the emergency Arab Summit. He stressed that establishing unity of points of view was the solution to the difficulties in the Arab world.

7 August: Sheikh Zayed led the UAE delegation to the emergency Arab Summit in Casablanca.

The Commander of the Navy confirmed that the territorial waters of the UAE were free of any navigational impediments of any kind and were not affected by floating mines in the Gulf.

The Municipality of Al-Ain began to execute the second five year phase of the 150 million dirham rainwater drainage project in Al-Ain district.

11 August: The Ministry of Education decided to stop importing school books for the intermediate stage from outside the country: the books will be printed locally for the first time, beginning with the next school year.

12 August: Contracts amounting to 180 million dirhams were signed for the construction of a central emergency hospital and a complex of clinics in Abu Dhabi.

The Executive Council approved a 3.2 million dirham aerial photography project for the city of Abu Dhabi and the Western Region.

14 August: The Municipality of Dubai began maintenance and refurbishment of the historic 100-year old house of Sheikh Saeed Al Maktoum.

27 August: Sheikh Zayed, during a meeting with a delegation of Muslim *Ulema*, called on them to beseech Allah to unite the Arab world.

29 August: The National Bank of Dubai paid 550 million dirhams for the Hyatt Regency complex.

4 September: Sheikh Zayed, in a letter to Islamic Ministers of Education, called on them to prepare the universities, schools and cultural centres to spread Islam. He stressed that Islam did not sanction killing and bloodletting, except in a *jihad* for Allah in defence of the faith.

5 September: The UAE, in its speech before the General Assembly of the United Nations, called on the international community to take the necessary measures to bring independence to Namibia and Palestine and to impose sanctions against the racist regimes in South Africa and occupied Palestine.

6 September: Sheikh Hamdan bin Zayed Al Nahyan confirmed that the UAE had completed all the necessary preparations to host the finals for the Ninth Asian Cup in 1988.

18 September: The Executive Council allocated 318 million dirhams to support and develop public utilities and services in the emirate of Abu Dhabi.

22 September: The UAE was elected as Assistant Secretary to the Arab Co-operative Union for a period of four years.

24 September: The Central Laboratory in Abu Dhabi was issued with the latest AIDS-testing equipment.

25 September: Sheikh Zayed meeting the first group of national judges asked them

to be bound by the Book of Allah and to carry-out divine instructions. He told them that it was their duty to oppose those who introduced heretical innovations promoted by the enemies of Islam.

27 September: The cost of school transport during the current academic year amounted to 180 million dirhams.

1 October: The UAE strongly condemned Zionist aggression on the headquarters of the Palestine Liberation Organization in Tunis and it called on the Arab nation to confront Israeli aggression with a firm and decisive stand.

2 October: Sheikh Zayed received a letter from the Tunisian President, Al-Habib Bourgiba, acknowledging his support.

In the Security Council, the UAE condemned Israeli aggression on Tunis and called for a fair solution to the Palestinian problem.

The Council of Ministers decided to form a committee to reconsider the curriculum for Islamic education at all levels, in accordance with the directions of the President of the Federation.

3 October: Sheikh Tahnoun bin Mohammad Al Nahyan opened the new 120 million dirham Al-Ain Amusement Park.

5 October: Sheikh Zayed received a letter from the Iranian President, Ali Khamenei, regarding regional developments and developments in the Arab world.

10 October: Sheikh Sultan bin Mohammed Al Qassimi formally agreed to finance the Oxford Centre for Islamic Studies to teach Islamic *Sharia* and acquaint Europeans with Islam.

15 October: Sheikh Zayed appointed Sheikh Hamdan bin Zayed Al Nahyan as Deputy Minister of Foreign Affairs.

An air transport agreement was signed between UAE Aviation and Indian Aviation.

16 October: Sheikh Khalifa donated 1.5 million dirhams as a reward to the members of the UAE National Football Team.

17 October: The UN General Assembly chose the UAE as a non-permanent member of the Security Council for a two-year period.

Sheikh Humaid bin Rashid Al Nuaimi opened an office complex for judges and the judiciary in the emirate of Ajman.

19 October: UAE exports to Japan during the first half of 1985 amounted to 4.019 billion dirhams, an increase of 12.6 per cent over 1984.

The first bus service between Abu Dhabi and Jebel al-Dhanna became operational, as did the first sea service between Delma and Jebel al-Dhanna.

21 October: Sheikh Mohammad bin Rashid Al Maktoum led the UAE delegation in the GCC Ministers of Defence meeting in which the defence strategy of the member States was confirmed.

UAE Aviation signed an agreement with Pakistan Airlines to lease two Boeing Airbus aeroplanes.

22 October: Sheikh Saqr bin Mohammad Al Qassimi donated 1 million sq. ms of land for an Agricultural Secondary School in Ras al-Khaimah.

23 October: Sheikh Maktoum bin Rashid Al Maktoum inaugurated the UAE Aviation Company, Idhana, as it commenced operations in support of the national economy.

The 34 parks in Al-Ain covered 220 hectares.

25 October: Dubai's airline, Emirates Airline, began operating with services to Pakistan and India and plans to serve European and Gulf destinations.

26 October: Sheikh Zayed sent letters to the Tunisian President, Al Habib Bourgiba, the Iraqi President, Saddam Hussein, and the Libyan President, Muammar Al Gadhafi concerning efforts made by the Arab Reconciliation Committee, comprising UAE, Morocco and Mauritania, which was formed by the Arab Summit Conference in Casablanca. The aim of the Committee was to clear the air as far as Arab affairs were concerned and achieve Arab solidarity.

The UAE requested the United Nations to strengthen co-operation among the nations of the world in fighting terrorism everywhere. It warned of the terrorism undertaken by States and especially by the Government of the Zionist enemy and the racist Government of South Africa.

27 October: In Rabat, Sheikh Zayed and King Hassan of Morocco studied joint efforts being made by the Arab Reconciliation Committee. It also discussed what had been accomplished in removing Arab differences.

28 October: The Council of Ministers affirmed the federal budget for 1985. Expenditure was projected at 16.634 billion dirhams and revenue at 12.997 billion, creating a deficit of 3.637 billion dirhams.

29 October: Sheikh Zayed received a letter from Iraqi President, Saddam Hussein, regarding the current Arab situation and decisions made at the Arab Summit.

Combined budget of the commercial banks in the Federation rose from 29.6 billion dirhams in 1977 to 91.6 billion dirhams in 1984.

30 October: In remarks made at the opening of the Modern Administration

Club, Sheikh Sultan bin Mohammad Al Qassimi stressed that its aim was to raise the competence of the work force.

31 October: Dr Mana Said Al Otaiba announced that henceforth quotas would be abolished because of the failure of OPEC's consultations with non-OPEC oil producing states urging them to abide by the price fixed by the organization.

1 November: Sheikh Zayed stressed in remarks made to the Omani newspaper *Al-Watn,* that relations between GCC States reinforced the ties that bind the Gulf States, and emphasized that the power of the Gulf States strengthened all Arab countries. He also remarked that it was very strange that the Arab nation recognized its mistakes but did not alter its behaviour accordingly.

The UAE presented Al-Azhar University with an English translation of the Holy Qur'an.

UAE imports from the European Community in 1983 totalled nearly 3. 665 billion dollars and exports amounted to 2.9 billion. The trade balance surplus was 290 million dollars in favour of the UAE.

2 November: Sheikh Mohammad bin Rashid Al Maktoum confirmed that co-ordination in defence matters between GCC States had made great strides forward and that a new phase of joint effort had begun.

3 November: Sheikh Zayed arrived in Muscat at the head of the UAE delegation to participate in the GCC Summit. He stated that the GCC was a new shield for the Arab nation and that its establishment was an embodiment of sincere efforts made by the States of the region as a result of their faith in a joint future. Sheikh Zayed held wide-ranging consultations

with the GCC leaders regarding the issues discussed in the Summit for strengthening the future of the GCC.

4 November: The Council of Ministers approved the setting-up of the first institute for teachers in the country.

The assistance of the World Bank and the UAE University was sought in preparing a comprehensive study of the nation's work force requirements.

6 November: Sheikh Zayed, on his return to the country from Muscat after leading the UAE delegation to the GCC meeting, confirmed that Arab solidarity was the basis of Islamic cohesion. He stated that only freedom exercised in a responsible manner could make social reform successful and that the freedom of the press and freedom generally was for those who knew how to protect their country.

Abu Dhabi Executive Council decided to form a committee to organize ways and means of recruiting labour from abroad.

7 November: The UAE supported the invitation to convene an emergency meeting of the Arab Parliamentary Union Council in Baghdad on 16 November.

8 November: Abu Dhabi Municipality accepted the keys to its new 192 million dirham building.

9 November: The first open heart surgery was performed at Al-Mafraq Hospital in Abu Dhabi.

11 November: Sheikh Zayed received the Turkish President, Kenan Efren, who arrived in Abu Dhabi on an official visit to the UAE.

Sheikh Zayed and the Secretary of the Islamic Dawa in Libya studied the work plan for the Joint Islamic Foundation between Libya and the UAE for spreading *dawa* and setting-up Islamic centres in Africa.

12 November: Sheikh Zayed and the Turkish President agreed on the need to put a stop to the Iran -Iraq war by whatever means. They studied developments in the Middle East situation and the necessity of finding a just and comprehensive solution which would guarantee the rights of the Palestinian people.

The UAE requested the Security Council to condemn Israeli practices aimed at obliterating the Arab character of the occupied Arab territories by continuing to build Zionist settlements.

In 1983, UAE's date production was nearly 58,000 tons.

13 November: Sheikh Zayed and the Turkish President, Kenan Efren, visited UAE University and the Umm al-Nar electricity plant. They also attended camel races.

Sheikh Zayed and the Deputy Prime Minister of China, Yau Li Lin, discussed joint co-operation and regional and international affairs.

14 November: Sheikh Zayed, King Hassan of Morocco, and the Mauritanian President, Mukhtar Ould Dada, participated in the meeting convened by the second Arab Reconciliation Committee to study the work done by the committee towards achieving Arab solidarity.

During a visit to UAE by Chinese Vice-President Yau Li Lin, UAE and China signed an economic agreement creating a committee of deputy trade ministers to discuss expansion of economic ties and assess potential joint ventures in oil and tourism.

15 November: The Reconciliation Committee, attended by Sheikh Zayed, King Hassan, President Al Gadhafi, President Mukhtar Ould Dada and representatives from Iraq and Palestine, decided to continue its efforts to eliminate Arab differences. A delegation was despatched to Tripoli and Baghdad in this regard.

The UAE and the USSR established diplomatic relations at ambassadorial level. Sheikh Hamdan bin Zayed announced that this was a confirmation of the UAE's non-aligned policy, an expansion of international activity and a demonstration of friendship with the world.

18 November: Sheikh Zayed arrived in Bamako on an official visit to the Republic of Mali where he met the Malian President, Mousa Tarawari.

At the opening of the Arab Union of Banks in Dubai, Sheikh Hamdan bin Rashid Al Maktoum requested that Arab banks play a role in national development policy by supporting production projects in the Arab nation.

19 November: Sheikh Zayed and the Malian President, Mousa Tarawari, witnessed the ceremonies celebrating the naming of one of the major streets of the Malian capital after Zayed. A joint communiqué was issued at the end of the visit, in which the two presidents stressed their support for Arab and African national liberation movements and for convening an international peace conference for the Middle East. They also condemned the South African and Israeli occupation regimes.

20 November: The Council of Ministers decided to offer educational aid to the children of the Afghani *mujahidin* and *muhajirin*.

Sheikh Ahmed bin Hamid opened the new headquarters of the Al-Ain Society for Popular Arts.

22 November: Since the foundation of the Federation, the Ministry of Public Works and Housing completed 210 schools, at a cost of 1250 million dirhams, and 5747 public housing units costing 1280 million dirhams.

25 November: Sheikh Tahnoun bin Mohammad Al Nahyan opened the 77 million dirham complex of consulting clinics at Al-Ain Hospital.

27 November: Sheikh Khalifa bin Zayed Al Nahyan, in a speech on the occasion of the fourteenth National Day, stressed that the most prominent accomplishment of the UAE Federation was the development of the individual, the most valuable treasure of society and the basic measurement of the wealth of nations.

28 November: Sheikh Khalifa attended ceremonies for the opening of the seventeenth World Military Parachute Jumping Championship hosted by the UAE.

1 December: Crown Prince of Abu Dhabi and UAE Deputy Armed Forces Commander, Sheikh Khalifa bin Zayed Al Nahyan, announced that design work was to begin in 1986 on a new naval base to be built on Taweelah Island off the Abu Dhabi coast for oil installation protection purposes and to '... help ensure sovereignty over our territorial waters, protect our 400 miles of coast ...'

2 December: Sheikh Zayed, receiving the Members of the Supreme Council of the Federation and groups of wellwishers on the occasion of the fourteenth National Day, stressed that the Federation is the citizen and that the individual is the core of all civilized progress. He stated that the individual, through his thinking, his effort and his faith, is capable of achieving any advancement which he may wish.

Sheikh Zayed accepted the Golden Document from the International Organization of Foreigners in appreciation of his efforts in caring for foreign communities working in the country. He said that caring for those who are living away from home is a tradition which can be traced back to the UAE's forefathers and Islamic religion.

3 December: Sheikh Mohammad bin Butti opened the new 203 million dirham tunnel at the Great Mosque roundabout.

4 December: The UAE won the World Military Parachute Jumping Championship which was held in the UAE.

7 December: Sheikh Sultan bin Mohammad Al Qassimi opened the new Khor Fakkan hospital in Sharjah.

8 December: Sheikhs Zayed, Sultan bin Mohammad Al Qassimi and Maktoum bin Rashid discussed various aspects of the national development plan.

9 December: Sheikh Zayed issued a federal decree forming the Board of Administration of the Central Bank under the chairmanship of Sheikh Surour bin Mohammad Al Nahyan.

12 December: In the United Nations, the UAE voted to condemn the relationship between Israel and South Africa.

15 December: Sheikh Zayed presided over a meeting of the Supreme Council of the Federation in which a committee was formed to study recommendations of the joint committee of the Council of Ministers and the Federal National Council. The committee considered the strengthening of the national development plan and approved the federal budget for 1985. Security requirements and each emirate's contribution of 50 per cent of its income to the federal budget were also discussed.

17 December: Sheikh Sultan bin Mohammad Al Qassimi opened the new Chamber of Commerce and Industry building in Sharjah.

18 December: Sheikh Zayed issued a decree forming a committee headed by Sheikh Khalid bin Saqr Al Qassimi to follow-up on Supreme Council meetings. At the Al-Wahda Club in Abu Dhabi, Sheikh Surour bin Mohammad Al Nahyan opened the second Arab Police Badminton Championship in which 11 Arab countries were taking part.

19 December: Sheikh Zayed arrived in Rabat to meet King Hassan in the context of pursuing Arab reconciliation.

21 December: In Rabat, Sheikh Zayed received a letter from the Mauritanian President, Mukhtar Ould Dada, regarding the progress of mediation between Libya and Iraq, on the one hand, and Libya and the Palestine Liberation Organization, on the other. The letter also concerned the Reconciliation Committee's agenda during the next phase.

23 December: The Council of Ministers approved the setting-up of the first regional office for civil aviation information in the country.

24 December: Sheikh Khalifa confirmed whilst meeting with Abdulla Bishara, Secretary General of the GCC, that the UAE had begun preparations to host the seventh GCC Summit Conference in Abu Dhabi.

Six hundred graduates of ADNOC Training and Development Centre were working in the oil fields in technical or administrative capacities.

28 December: The National Drilling Company began measures to complete a comprehensive 50 million dirham survey of groundwater sources in Abu Dhabi.

30 December: The Council of Ministers approved the granting of priority to national industrial products for Government purchasing.

Nineteen Eighty Six

1 January: Abu Dhabi Civil Aviation Department commenced training local personnel to take over the administration and operation of the new Al-Ain International Airport which was scheduled to open in 1988.

6 January: The Council of Ministers approved a list of standardized weights and measures for 47 commodities.

7 January: A major vegetable market was opened in Zayed city in Abu Dhabi.

12 January: In Cairo an agreement was signed to enable Emirates Airlines to service the Dubai to Cairo route.

13 January: The population of the UAE was reported to be 2,622,464 of which 2,052,577 were males and 569,887 females, an increase of 580,000 over the 1980 census.

Abu Dhabi Executive Council decided to pay 388 million dirhams in compensation to 250 Abu Dhabi nationals who were affected by development planning projects.

16 January: The UAE and Morocco, speaking on behalf of Islamic countries, requested the UN Security Council to hold an urgent meeting to look into Israeli violations of the Masjid al-Aqsa Shrine.

17 January: In Marrakech, Sheikh Zayed and King Hassan II of Morocco studied joint efforts at Arab reconciliation. They also discussed the situations in the Arab Maghrib, the Gulf and the Middle East.

18 January: Sheikh Hamdan bin Zayed Al Nahyan, on behalf of the UAE, spoke of the country's concern at the establishment of diplomatic relations between Israel and Spain.

21 January: It was decided to reduce prices at all petrol stations in the country.

24 January: Sheikh Zayed, attending the football finals, presented the Zayed Cup to Al-Nasr Football Club.

26 January: Sheikh Zayed, at the opening of a new session of the Supreme Council of the Federation, stressed that the Federation had been one of the most successful Arab experiments in modern times. He confirmed that the resources were available to build the national economy, strengthen the unity of the Armed Forces, and maintain the security and safety of the country.

27 January: Sheikh Zayed received a letter from the Libyan President, Muammar Al Gadhafi, regarding the American threat to Libya.

The first operation to separate Siamese twins was successfully completed at Al-Mafraq hospital.

30 January: Sheikh Zayed received a report from the Supreme Council's follow-up committee.

The first initialling took place of the air transport agreement between the UAE and the Yemen Arab Republic.

3 February: The UAE rejected American justifications for the use of the veto against the resolution tabled by Morocco in the Security Council to condemn Israeli violations of Al-Aqsa Mosque.

4 February: Sheikh Zayed and the German Federal President, Richard von Weisaker, studied current Arab and international affairs and the international economic situation, in addition to bilateral issues.

Sheikh Tahnoun bin Mohammad Al Nahyan opened the first vegetable canning factory in Al-Ain. With a capacity of 120 tons per day, it can absorb excess agricultural production.

5 February: The UAE strongly condemned Israel's hijacking of a Libyan passenger aircraft. It stressed that it stood firmly by the side of its brother Arab States against such terroristic practices.

Sheikh Hamdan bin Rashid Al Maktoum issued a decree granting locally-produced goods ten per cent preferential pricing for Government purchasing, thereby implementing the Council of Ministers decision on this matter.

7 February: The Security Council, based on a UAE request, in an unusual move voted to allow the Palestine Liberation Organization to participate in debates on the draft resolution condemning Israeli piracy. The UAE warned that the Security Council's repeated inability to condemn Israeli aggression and violations made it clear to Israel that it could continue with its aggression.

8 February: Sheikh Saqr bin Mohammad Al Qassimi issued an Amiri decree setting up a Documents and Studies Centre in Ras al-Khaimah.

9 February: Sheikh Khalifa bin Zayed Al Nahyan presided over a meeting of Abu Dhabi Investments Administrative Council. He commended the role of the organization in developing the wealth of the country to secure the continuation of a good life for future generations.

Sheikh Khalifa presided over a meeting of the Board of ADNOC. During the meeting oil production and marketing policy was studied, as was the efforts of the UAE in following OPEC to re-establish stability and balance in the international oil market.

10 February: Abu Dhabi Executive Council approved the setting-up of a national museum in Al-Ain to protect the national heritage for coming generations. Contracts were signed with four new companies for operations in Jebel Ali Free Zone. There were 70 international companies operating in the Free Zone at this time.

11 February: Ahmed Khalifa Al Suweidi opened the permanent children's centre in the Cultural Complex.

12 February: Sheikh Khalifa attended graduation ceremonies for the new batch of officers from the Armed Forces. He said that this graduation embodied the determination of the leadership to continue building self-reliant forces and he warned of the escalation of the Iraq-Iran war which threatened to open the door to foreign intervention, stressing that the UAE was continuing its efforts to contain the bloodshed.

13 February: Humaid bin Rashid Al Nuaimi inspected archaeological explorations in Ajman after which he announced the discovery of a circular grave site. He called for the establishment of a High Commission for Archaeology in the country.

14 February: The number of co-operative societies increased from 14 principal and branch societies in 1977 to 37 principal and branch societies in 1985, an increase of 164 per cent. The size of their capital increased from 1.6 million dirhams to 182 million dirhams, an increase of 729 per cent.

15 February: In the previous ten years, 31 joint committees were created between the UAE and other countries.

16 February: Sheikh Hamdan bin Mohammad Al Nahyan confirmed the UAE's commitment to abide by OPEC's decisions and he asked for the co-operation of all the producing countries in stabilizing prices. He said that development programmes in the country would not be affected by the decrease in the price of oil.

19 February: Sheikh Sultan bin Mohammad Al Qassimi stressed that the passage of time since the Federation had been established had helped secure the basic foundations of the State.

20 February: A protocol for economic and commercial co-operation was signed between the Federation of Chambers of Commerce in the UAE and the Federation of Chambers of Commerce in South Korea.

24 February: Sheikh Hamdan bin Rashid Al Maktoum stressed that there were no plans to impose income taxes or to decrease salaries of workers. He said that a budgetary review would take place in light of the drop in income because of the fall in the price of oil.

25 February: UAE trade balance surplus was 14.6 billion dirhams during the first half of 1985, with a 10 billion dirham surplus in the balance of payments. The value of oil exports was 19.7 billion dirhams during the period between June 1984 and June 1985.

It was decided to establish a comprehensive first-aid organization in Abu Dhabi with the co-ordination of the Ministry of Health, Civil Defence and the Police. First aid stations were established every 60 kms along the highways outside the cities.

The sixth oil well became operational in Ras al-Khaimah. The amount of oil extracted from the first five wells was 10,000 barrels per day.

27 February: In Islamabad, Sheikh Zayed and the Pakistani President, Zia Al Haq, studied the possibility of making a joint stand to find a peaceful resolution to the Iran-Iraq war.

28 February: Sheikh Zayed opened a medical complex in Lahore which he had personally financed. President Mohammad Zia Al Haq described it as a 'towering edifice of medicine'.

Sheikh Zayed donated a million dollars towards the International Islamic University in Islamabad.

1 March: A 180 million dirham contract was signed to construct the Al-Ain/Dubai highway, a distance of 54 kms.

2 March: Sheikh Sultan bin Mohammad Al Qassimi issued a decree establishing an old peoples home in Sharjah.

First Lady Sheikha Fatima bint Mubarak, presided over a meeting of the Higher Committee of the UAE Women's Federation to review laws affecting working women.

Work was completed in connecting the co-axial cable providing communications between the UAE and 13 other countries.

3 March: The Ministry of Health began to implement measures to change out-patient clinics into comprehensive health centres within the framework of its strategy for achieving health for all by the year 2000.

10 March: During 1984 there were 43,704 births in the country of which 18,656 or 40 per cent were nationals.

12 March: Sheikh Zayed directed UAE University experts to visit King Faisal University in Saudi Arabia to observe scientific developments in date palm agriculture and arrange for the transfer of this technology to the UAE University.

15 March: Sheikh Zayed issued the first federal law in the country to combat drugs.

The first mounted division of the police in Ras al-Khaimah was formed to police the market quarters at night.

17 March: Sheikh Humaid bin Rashid Al Nuaimi approved plans for renovations in the old city of Ajman and the completion of a network of major roads to protect important historical areas.

A 482.8 million dirhams contract was signed to build a gas turbine plant and a water desalination station at Jebel Ali.

19 March: Sheikh Zayed, during his reception of the National Football Team who were participating in the Gulf Games, stressed the country's interest in supporting youth and sports.

20 March: Sheikh Hamad bin Mohammad Al Sharqi announced a plan to expand the establishment of technical schools in Fujairah in order to train the work force required to support national industries. UAE youths between the ages of 15 and 20 accounted for nearly 17.8 per cent (50,000) of the total national population.

23 March: A 65 million dollar contract was signed to set-up an aluminum factory with a capacity of 120,000 tons per annum in Umm al-Qaiwain.

24 March: The Ministry of Health decided to establish a plastic surgery unit in Al-Mafraq hospital.

During 1985, 132 boats were repaired in the Dubai Dry Dock. Total tonnage was 11 million tons.

26 March: The UAE confirmed its support for Libya and condemned American aggression on its territory, which was an obvious violation of its sovereignty and independence.

28 March: Sheikh Hamad bin Mohammad Al Sharqi opened the Arab Chicken Company which had the capacity to produce 4000 tons of chicken meat and 12 million eggs annually.

29 March: It was decided to establish the first College of Nursing in the UAE.

30 March: Sheikh Zayed received a letter from the Libyan President, Muammar Al Gadhafi, regarding American aggression towards Libya.

31 March: Sheikh Zayed was briefed on the recommendations of the national work committee formed by the Supreme Council of the Federation to deal with the economic slump in the country.

1 April: Sheikh Khalifa bin Zayed Al Nahyan, during ceremonies for the seventh batch of graduates from the

Aviation College, confirmed that French Mirage aircraft which had been purchased for the Armed Forces would arrive in UAE in September piloted by UAE nationals.

In the Security Council the UAE condemned American aggression against Libya and described it as constituting a clear violation of the independence, sovereignty and unity of Libyan territory. A human settlement dating back 4000 years was uncovered in the Shamal area of Ras al-Khaimah.

2 April: Sheikh Zayed was briefed on the activities of the UAE's co-operative movement and the economic aims which it was attempting to achieve, especially in putting an end to the rise in the price of basic commodities.

Sheikha Fatima bint Mubarak, in ceremonies marking Handicapped Friends Day, praised the efforts being made for taking care of the handicapped and preparing them to be a productive force in society.

The Ministry of Communications commenced a study of the necessary measures to be taken in planning a policy for regulating the passage of foreign aircraft over UAE airspace and landing rights at UAE airports.

3 April: First Lady Sheikha Fatima bint Mubarak attended the opening of the Abu Dhabi school activities exhibition. She stressed the importance of knowledge as the basis for building a modern progressive society.

4 April: Sheikh Zayed received a letter from US President, Ronald Reagan, delivered by the Assistant Secretary of State, Richard Murphy, regarding developments in the Iraq-Iraq war and the situation in the Middle East.

6 April: Sheikh Zayed opened the Malikite Fiqh conference in Abu Dhabi. He said that the UAE was eager to render assistance to their brothers in the Islamic world, confirming the UAE's commitment to the Book of Allah and its keenness to apply its judgments.

The UAE team were victorious in the second division in the Gulf Games. Sheikh Hamdan bin Zayed Al Nahyan said winning the silver medal was an excellent accomplishment.

April: Sheikh Zayed, during his reception of the German Minister of State for Foreign Affairs, stressed the necessity of reviving Arab-European dialogue and said that Europe should play an active role in solving the Middle East crisis.

In Aden the deeds for 852 new apartments costing 17 milion Yemeni dinars, which were built with financing from the UAE and Kuwait, were distributed.

11 April: Sheikh Hamdan bin Zayed Al Nahyan donated half a million dirhams to the national football players fund which he had suggested be set up to support football players. The fund received over 2 million dirhams in donations from important personalities.

12 April: The combined budget of the commercial banks in the country at the end of January 1986 amounted to 99.3 billion dirhams, compared with 97.8 billion dirhams at the end of December 1985.

13 April: Dubai Police began to use the latest underwater equipment with the aim of rescuing boats in difficulty and combating drug-smuggling.

14 April: The Council of Ministers reviewed the economic situation in the country in light of the drop in oil revenues and the impact on the budget. Sheikh Hamdan bin Rashid Al Maktoum was commissioned to take the necessary steps to deal with the situation.

15 April: Sheikh Zayed and the Members of the Supreme Council of the Federation attended the graduation of the fifth batch of students from UAE University, including the first engineers to graduate from the University.

Sheikh Zayed made telephone contact with the Libyan President, Muammar Al Gadhafi, confirming the UAE's support for Libya, saying that it stood side by side with the Libyan people. These remarks were made following a second bout of US air raids on Libya. Zayed called for a Pan-Arab summit to stimulate much-needed Arab solidarity.

In the United Nations, the UAE condemned American aggression and announced its solidarity with Libya.

The UAE decided to cancel a joint trade and political relations committee meeting with the UK and recalled Foreign Minister Rashid Abdulla from London because of British collusion with America in the bombing raids. It also cancelled a trade show in Britain.

16 April: The Federal National Council condemned American aggression on Libya and called for the Arab and Islamic peoples to shoulder their responsibilities.

17 April: The first initiallings were made on a labour co-operation agreement between the UAE and Jordan.

18 April: Sheikh Zayed received a letter from Libyan President, Muammar Al Gadhafi, in which he commended the UAE's stance regarding American aggression on Libya and he called for an emergency Arab summit conference.

The UAE and other countries prepared a draft resolution which was presented to the Security Council condemning American aggression on Libya.

19 April: The UAE sent an official memorandum to the Arab League in which it called for the convening of an emergency Arab summit to deal with the aggression against Libya and to end the Iraq-Iran war.

24 April: Sheikh Zayed welcomed King Hassan's invitation to convene an emergency Arab summit in the Moroccan city of Fez.

Sheikh Zayed received an invitation from the Yemeni President, Ali Abdulla Saleh, to attend the opening of the renovated Marib Dam which was completed eight months before schedule.

During his reception of Sharif-ed-Din Pirzada, the Secretary General of the Islamic Conference Organization, Sheikh Zayed was briefed on efforts by the Islamic mediation committee to stop the Iran-Iraq war.

25 April: Tawam Hospital in Al-Ain was supplied with the most up-to-date CAT scan equipment in the Middle East.

26 April: The UAE strongly condemned the imposition of economic sanctions on Libya by the European Community and expressed its regret at the EC's submission to American pressure.

The first ready-made clothes factory in the Jebel Ali Free Zone was opened. It had a production capacity of half a million pieces per annum.

28 April: Sheikh Zayed issued instructions for the imposition of taxes on farm imports to protect local farm production.

28 April: The UAE was elected as Vice President of the UN committee overseeing the Security Council arms embargo on the racist regime in South Africa.

Abu Dhabi Executive Council allocated 217 million dirhams to the new Al-Ain International Airport project.

30 April: The First Lady, Sheikha Fatima bint Mubarak, attended the opening of the new headquarters of the Umm al-Qaiwain Women's Society. She commended the great success which had been achieved for women in the country in all fields and their constructive participation in the progress of the country.

1 May The UAE called on Qatar and Bahrain to work toward settling their differences in favour of the higher Arab interests and the principles of brotherhood and good neighbourliness.

5 May: As directed by Sheikh Maktoum bin Rashid Al Maktoum, it was decided to establish a mobile computer training centre to cover training needs in the Northern Emirates. The decision was also made to link all the federal ministries to the National Computer Centre.

6 May: Sheikh Zayed stressed that UAE's election as a member of the Executive of the Asian Football Union was another accomplishment to add to the list of UAE Football Federation achievements.

The Federal National Council issued a statement calling on the federal Government to take steps to alleviate the consequences of the country's recession and urging the Government to diversify the economy away from oil. In May UAE oil prices were between 11 dollars and 12.50 dollars per barrel. 'It has become impossible for us to continue relying on oil as the main source of income,' said the statement. Diversification would help to, '... bring about stability and prosperity.'

7 May: Sheikh Zayed sent a letter to Sheikh Khalifa bin Hamad Al Thani, the Ruler of Qatar and held telephone conversations with King Fahad bin Abdulaziz of Saudi Arabia and the Amir of Qatar within the framework of the UAE's efforts to contain the dispute between Qatar and Bahrain.

A total of 9 billion dirhams was spent on road projects in the emirate of Abu Dhabi during the previous ten years.

8 May: The first initiallings were made on an air transport agreement between the UAE and Switzerland.

9 May: Dubai's non-oil foreign trade in 1985 amounted to 5.617 million tons with a value of 19.731 billion dirhams.

10 May: Dubai's sewerage projects cost 4.25 billion dirhams.

17 May: Based on the directives of Sheikh Khalifa bin Zayed Al Nahyan, equipment was procured for Abu Dhabi Municipality to detect radioactive contamination of imported food items affected by the Chernobyl reactor explosion.

19 May: Sheikh Surour bin Mohammad Al Nahyan issued a decree reducing the interest rate on housing and industrial loans provided by the Emirates Development Bank from 5 per cent to 1.5 per cent, retroactive to 1 January 1986.

21 May: Lloyd's International Insurance Company exempted the UAE from an insurance surcharge of 50 per cent to be imposed on war zones in the Gulf.

25 May: Sheikh Khalifa bin Zayed Al Nahyan issued a decree requesting the Abu Dhabi Finance Office to liquidate the Emirates Development Bank which awarded real estate, industrial and investment loans to citizens.

30 May: The UAE assured the UN General Assembly that development projects in Africa formed one of the basic considerations of its foreign policy and it called on the United Nations to increase their efforts to abolish apartheid in South Africa.

The number of farms in Al-Ain increased eight-fold in 15 years. In 1985 there were 2289 farms covering an area of 10,613 hectares, in comparison to 290 farms in 1970. The production average of the Al-Ain farms surpassed their production capacity, reaching 65 million eggs and 3 million chickens per annum.

1 June: A surgical operation to replace heart valves was performed for the first-time at Al-Mafraq Hospital.

2 June: The Council of Ministers reviewed the UAE's general educational policy in light of the Federal National Council's recommendations on the requirements of the country's development plans.

3 June: Last year, 786,194 people stayed in hotels in the country, spending 2,1147,323 nights, the income from which was over 800 million dirhams.

4 June: Sheikh Zayed issued a decree promoting Major Mohammad bin Zayed Al Nahyan to the rank of Colonel and appointing him as Commander of the Air Force.

Two hundred and thirty four projects costing 4532.7 million dirhams were completed in 1985 as part of the annual development plan for Abu Dhabi emirate. The Emirates Training Institute began a comprehensive programme to train nationals to work in the banking sector.

5 June: The Emirates Gas Company marketed propane liquid gas to be used locally for the first time for industrial purposes.

10 June: At the International Labour Organization in Geneva the UAE demanded resistance to the settlement policies of Israel and support for Arab workers in the occupied territories.

12 June: From 1968 to 1985, 25.78 billion dirhams was spent on development projects in Abu Dhabi emirate.

14 June: The latest highly advanced equipment arrived at Al-Jazira Hospital for the cardiac, x-ray, nuclear medicine and laboratory departments.

15 June: In Abu Dhabi, Sheikh Zayed and the Lebanese President, Amin Jemayyel, discussed bilateral relations and the situation in south Lebanon.

16 June: A joint communiqué was issued in both Abu Dhabi and Beirut on the results of the talks between Sheikh Zayed and the Lebanese President. The UAE confirmed its support for Lebanon's territorial integrity and its sovereignty, while Lebanon announced its support for Zayed's efforts and good offices to restore Arab solidarity.

Sheikh Khalifa bin Zayed Al Nahyan arrived in Rabat on an official visit to Morocco. He said that the visit was aimed at strengthening joint Arab action and firmly securing the ties of co-operation and co-ordination between the two countries.

17 June: Sheikh Khalifa met with King Hassan II of Morocco, who decorated him with the Mohammedi Medal, First Class. The Moroccan monarch confirmed that Zayed's policy was aimed at achieving the best interests of the Arabs.

20 June: A group of professors at UAE University, following the President of the Federation's directives, commenced a study of herbal medicines used in the treatment of diseases in preparation for the establishment of a herbal medicine centre in the country.

21 June: At the conclusion of his visit to Morocco, Sheikh Khalifa and King Hassan discussed strengthening relations between the two countries and supporting joint Arab action. During his visit to Morocco, Sheikh Khalifa visited the military academy in Meknes, the National Defence Centre and a number of other military establishments.

The UAE confirmed its total support for Kuwait's resolute stand against the dangers which it faced. This solidarity was voiced in response to fires lit by incendiaries at Kuwait's oil installations and it called on the Arab nation to take up a united position to confront the dangers and challenges.

23 June: A joint communiqué was broadcast on the results of the discussions which took place between Sheikh Zayed and Sultan Qaboos bin Said at the conclusion of the Sultan's official visit to the UAE. The two leaders confirmed their complete support for joint co-operation and the call for a unified Arab stand. Current international issues were highlighted along with tthe leaders' reflections on all Arab and Islamic affairs.

25 June: Sheikh Rashid bin Ahmed Al Mualla issued a decree establishing the Umm al-Qaiwain Aluminum Company Ltd with a capital of 25 million dollars.

28 June: Abu Dhabi Police College began to admit female applicants from the UAE holding the Secondary School Certificate.

29 June: At an OPEC meeting, the UAE stressed its firm position that its production quota must be raised to 1.5 million barrels per day.

4 July: The UAE condemned American interference in the internal affairs of Nicaragua, describing it as a violation of international norms.

8 July: The country's surplus trade balance last year was 30.7 billion dirhams in comparison to 33.3 billion dirhams in 1984. The value of oil exports declined from 43 billion to 40 billion dirhams.

9 July: The UAE and Belgium made the first initiallings on an air transport agreement between the two countries.

11 July: To meet the needs of public parks until the year 2000, Dubai Municipality completed a new irrigation pipeline network in the city at a cost of 62 million dirhams

14 July: The Council of Ministers discussed the rise in marriages between UAE men and foreign women in light of the recommendations of the Federal National Council on the necessity of combating this phenomenon for social reasons.

The UAE were victorious in the second division of the Gulf and Arabian Peninsula Chess Championship.

23 July: Sheikh Humaid bin Rashid Al Nuaimi donated a plot of land and half a million dirhams to the Ajman Co-operative Society.

24 July: PLO Chairman, Yasser Arafat, announced that Sheikh Zayed had given the PLO 30 million dollars.

27 July: Emirates Airlines decided to purchase three new aircraft to augment its air fleet.

1 August: UAE Ministry of Health began operating the health identity card system to facilitate emergency first aid for patients with chronic conditions

4 August: For the fourth day running, Sheikh Zayed visited the Western Region where he inspected agricultural development projects in Liwa and ordered the establishment of 830 modern houses in 18 of the eastern settlements. He inspected farms in Al-Muzaira and Al-Salimi and gave his attention to date production. He then followed up on the progress of work on development and housing projects in the city of Al-Marfa.

6 August: Sheikh Zayed received the Members of the Supreme Council of the Federation and groups of well-wishers on the twentieth anniversary of his accession as Ruler of Abu Dhabi.

7 August: Dubai Municipality earmarked 667 million dirhams in 1986 for road projects.

8 August: The General Postal Administration installed ten new automatic postage stamp vending machines.

ADFAED, as of mid-1986, had granted nearly 3.994 billion dirhams to finance 86 projects in developing countries.

At this stage there were 86 national and international companies operating in the Jebel Ali Free Zone.

11 August: In Abu Dhabi, Sheikh Zayed and King Hussein of Jordan discussed the current Arab situation, efforts to achieve Arab solidarity and end Arab differences. The latest equipment for providing first aid to victims of traffic accidents was installed in the Central Hospital in Abu Dhabi.

13 August: The underground walkway in Sharjah's Al-Burj Square became operational.

17 August: Work on the second stage of the silos and flour mills project in the Jebel Ali Free Zone began. Three million tons of grain will be supplied to the Arab Gulf States from 1987.

28 August: It was announced that social service and teaching posts at primary level in the emirate of Sharjah were entirely filled by nationals.

1 September: Sheikh Zayed, in a meeting with UAE ambassadors posted abroad, stressed that the individual's true worth lay in his manners, his knowledge and his unblemished reputation. The job of the ambassadors, he said, was to maintain excellent relations and to deal with all in a pleasant way. That true *jihad* is in daily work and not in war and conflict, he said.

3 September: The UAE hosted a meeting of the Governors of the Central Banks of GCC States.

6 September: Sheikh Zayed, who was on a private visit to Germany, and the German President, Richard von Weisaker, discussed the situation in the Middle East, developments in the Palestinian problem and efforts to bring a just and comprehensive peace to the area.

8 September: A technical co-operation agreement in the field of civil aviation was signed between the Ministry of Communications and the United Nations Development Program.

10 September: The Al-Nahda roundabout and underground walkway, costing 45 million dirhams, were opened in Dubai.

14 September: Sheikh Zayed, arriving in Turkey on a private visit, held talks on Islamic affairs with the Turkish President, Kenan Efren. Zayed stressed that Islamic circumstances, now and in the future, call for mutual understanding and assistance and a drawing closer together.

17 September: Sheikh Zayed in his meeting with the Turkish Prime Minister, Turgut Ozal, stressed that the continuation of the Iran-Iraq war was only resulting in greater loss of life and property for the two Muslim countries.

19 September: Sheikh Khalifa bin Zayed Al Nahyan stressed in remarks made to *Amman* newspaper that the UAE was continuing to work on all levels towards a peaceful resolution of the Iran-Iraq war. He said that the imminent GCC Summit would concentrate on building a Gulf defence force and he confirmed that the UAE federal experiment had now exceeded all hopes, ambitions and expectations because of the faith and determination of the people and their leaders.

26 September: Sheikh Zayed sent an invitation to GCC leaders to attend the seventh Summit to be convened in Abu Dhabi on 2 November.

27 September: A 65 million dirham agreement was signed to establish a new anti-static metal pipe factory in Sharjah.

30 September: On behalf of the Palestine Liberation Organization, the UAE submitted a letter to the Security Council regarding Zionist terrorist practices in occupied territories and Israel's aggression against Palestinian refugee camps in south Lebanon.

3 October: The UAE assumed the Presidency of the UN Security Council with Mohammad Hussain Al Sha'ali in the chair. Rashid Abdulla warned of the escalation of the Iran-Iraq war and stressed that the UAE rejected the occupation of any part of Arab territory.

4 October: Study began at Dubai's first medical college for girls.

5 October: Sheikh Zayed held discussions with King Fahad bin Abdulaziz in Riyadh. They agreed to exert their best efforts to unify the Arab position, strengthen the Arab stance and achieve peace between the States of the Gulf and Arab States. They also studied current developments and the necessity of taking action to stop the Iraq-Iran war.

7 October: Dr Mana Said Al Otaiba announced in a press conference in Geneva that the UAE, at the direction of the President of the Federation, had decided to lower its production to 950,000 barrels within the framework of its concern for maintaining OPEC unity. He said that OPEC ministers had sent a special letter of thanks to Sheikh Zayed for his stand.

The UAE warned, in its speech at the International Parliamentary Union in Argentina, that the Middle East was one of the most tense regions in the world because of Israeli occupation of Arab territories and the lack of recognition of the legitimate rights of the Palestinian people. It called for the holding of an international peace conference with the participation of the five great powers in the Security Council.

11 October: Dubai Municipality completed plans for extending and supporting municipal services to rural areas and residential quarters situated at a distance from the city of Dubai, in furtherance of the policy of de-centralizing services.

An up-to-date medical research unit for the diagnosis and treatment of tuberculosis was established at Al-Jazira Hospital.

12 October: Sheikh Zayed presided over a meeting of the Supreme Council of the Federation during which the memorandum of the joint committee of the Council of Ministers and the Federal National Council regarding the consolidation of the Federation was discussed.

The UAE Air Force participated in joint

GCC helicopter exercises held in Muscat.
13 October: The UAE asked the International Atomic Energy Authority, within the scope of the co-operation programme, to make a vital study of the dividing line between seawater and freshwater and the rate at which it would be possible to pump water from wells without increasing salinity. Water consumption in the UAE at this time was 300 million cubic metres per annum, for home and industrial use, and 450 million gallons for agricultural use.

14 October: It was decided to change the Dubai Institute for Police Sciences to the Police College.

15 October: Sheikh Zayed presided over a meeting of the Supreme Council of the Federation in which it was decided by acclamation to re-elect him as President of the Federation for another five years. Sheikh Rashid bin Saeed Al Maktoum was elected as Vice President and President of the Council of Ministers. It was also decided to extend the provisional constitution for another five years and to commission the Ministry of Defence to prepare a study on compulsory national service. The Supreme Council called on Iraq and Iran to respond to peace efforts. Zayed stressed that the Council would continue its efforts to achieve the hopes of the people and strengthen the future of the GCC.

16 October: Eight hundred million dirhams was invested in chicken farms, with an annual production of 13,000 tons of meat and 150 million eggs.

20 October: A Soviet envoy presented Sheikh Zayed with a letter from the Soviet President, Mikhail Gobachev, regarding the results of the US-Soviet Summit. During the meeting, Sheikh Zayed stressed the UAE's concern for developing relations with all countries on the basis of equality.

The Council of Ministers approved the federal budget for 1986. Expenditure was forecast at 14.023 billion dirhams and revenue at 12.837 billion dirhams, leaving a deficit of 1.186 billion dirhams. Seven hundred new jobs for national graduates were included in the budget, along with 350 teacher training posts for national teachers.

21 October: Sheikh Khalifa bin Zayed Al Nahyan, in remarks made to the Emirates New Agency, said that the UAE was using all of its energy to make the seventh GCC Summit, to be held in Abu Dhabi in November, a success. The Summit would look into the development of a defence strategy to secure a real security umbrella for the member States, find ways to redouble efforts to stop the Iraq-Iraq war, support the Palestinian struggle and achieve Arab solidarity, he said.

26 October: GCC Foreign Ministers began meetings in Abu Dhabi to prepare for the Summit. Sheikh Hamdan bin Zayed Al Nahyan stressed that the Abu Dhabi Summit would aim at achieving integration and building a Gulf defence force.

26 October: Sheikh Zayed, receiving GCC Ministers of Foreign Affairs, expressed the hope that the Abu Dhabi Summit would result in fruitful resolutions which would benefit the collective future of the Gulf.

Emirates Airlines signed a contract to purchase two Airbus aircraft. Sheikh Ahmed bin Saeed Al Maktoum confirmed that the company was part of Dubai's contribution towards strengthening the Federation's economy.

28 October: GCC Foreign Ministers concluded their meetings to prepare the agenda for the seventh GCC Summit in Abu Dhabi.

29 October: The UAE supported the United Nations resolution calling on Israel to put its atomic reactors under the supervision of the International Atomic Energy Authority.

1 November: Sheikh Zayed welcomed the imminent arrival of the leaders of the GCC countries. He said that the UAE would continue efforts to achieve good results in the forthcoming summit.

2 November: Sheikh Zayed, opening the seventh GCC Summit, said that the meeting would strengthen mutual assistance among Gulf States.

5 November: The GCC Summit having concluded its deliberations, Sheikh Zayed commended the positive resolutions emanating from the meeting. He said that its success as a result of the efforts made by all its leaders was a major accomplishment.

6 November: The UAE began an intense diplomatic offensive to give effect to the GCC Summit resolutions, especially regarding the necessity of exerting all efforts and utilizing good offices to put an end to the Iraq-Iran war.

The Chinese Maritime Line linking Port Zayed in Abu Dhabi with ports in the Far East was inaugurated.

8 November: An agreement was signed to establish a joint investment company between the UAE and Bangladesh with a capital of 12.5 million dollars.

ADNOC began a new distribution service to supply ships in the territorial waters of the country with fuel.

9 November: Sheikh Zayed received a letter from King Fahad bin Abdulaziz, regarding the situation in the oil market and the efforts being made to stabilize it.

10 November: The Council of Ministers praised the resolutions and recommendations of the GCC Summit. Sheikh Hamdan bin Mohammad Al Nahyan said that GCC efforts would continue to try to put a stop to the Iran-Iraq war.

Investment in the building and construction fields rose from 3.3 billion dirhams in 1978 to 25.5 billion dirhams in 1985, an increase of 673 per cent.

11 November: ADNOC completed a vital project to transform one of its old oil pipelines bringing oil from the Habshan field to Abu Dhabi to a line for transporting drinking water in the opposite direction.

12 November: The number of national graduates working in the federal Ministries increased five times during the previous six years, rising to 1902 graduate employees.

Central Bank reserves at the end of September amounted to 16.835 billion dirhams.

14 November: Sheikh Maktoum bin Rashid Al Maktoum opened the twenty-seventh International Chess Olympiad which was being held in Dubai.

17 November: The Council of Ministers decided to impose annual school fees for children of non-national residents studying in State schools. Annual primary school fees would be 200 dirhams per child; intermediate school-fees would be 400 dirhams; and secondary-school fees, 600 dirhams.

A ship belonging to Ras al-Khaimah's Gulf Cement Company came under attack by two Iranian gunboats.

18 November: Sheikh Zayed, who was

on a private visit to Morocco, met with King Hassan II and together they attended the Sports Festival which was mounted on the occasion of Moroccan Independence Day.

Sheikh Zayed, meeting with UAE students studying in Morocco, stressed that the country was exerting all its efforts to foster personal development and he called on them to hold on to the values and teachings of Islam.

Sheikh Hamdan bin Zayed Al Nahyan held a meeting with the British, French and Chinese Ambassadors within the framework of the UAE's diplomatic campaign to implement GCC Summit resolutions. The UAE encouraged these countries to work toward the execution of the Security Council resolutions regarding the Iran-Iraq war, which called for an immediate cease fire and movement toward a peaceful settlement.

19 November: Abu Dhabi Executive Council approved the second stage of the Umm Al-Nar/Al-Shahama highway at a cost of 61 million dirhams. The Dubai Police Clinics Complex opened to provide advanced health services to policemen and their families.

20 November: Sheikh Zayed accepted the honorary presidency of the Society for the Revival of Popular Heritage in the country. Two headquarters for the society were established, one Abu Dhabi and the other in Al-Ain. Zayed called for the maintenance of pure Arab values, customs and traditions.

21 November: The Computer Centre at UAE University completed the installation of an advanced communications network connecting the centre with all the colleges, in order to provide them with opportunities for training students.

22 November: In a speech before the United Nations, the UAE condemned all attempts aimed at establishing a linkage between the Middle East problem and international terrorism, considering this linkage to be a clear attempt on the part of some countries to escape from their responsibilities with regard to the matter.

24 November: A cultural exchange programme was signed between the UAE and India providing for the strengthening of scientific, educational and informational co-operation.

25 November: UAE oil installations in the offshore Abu al-Bukhoush oil field were attacked resulting in the death of five people and the wounding of 24 others.

The number of consumers co-operative societies in the country increased from four in 1977 to 16 in 1985. Their capital rose from 1.5 million dirhams to 122 million dirhams, an increase in the number of participants from 92 to 5000.

26 November: Sheikh Khalifa bin Zayed Al Nahyan and Sheikh Maktoum bin Rashid Al Maktoum studied the circumstances surrounding the attack on the Abu al-Bukhoush oil field. The Council of Ministers stressed that this aggressive incident increased the threat to the region. The Federal National Council condemned the incident, stressing its complete support for the country's foreign policies.

Sheikh Khalifa bin Zayed Al Nahyan instructed that the UAE's experiences in the field of agriculture and afforestation would be placed at the disposal of its brothers in the region to help further Gulf integration. These directives were issued upon receipt of a letter from Sheikh Saad Al Abdulla Al Sabah, the Heir Apparent of Kuwait, which was delivered by Sheikh Ibrahim Al Duaij, Director of Kuwait's General Board of Agricultural Affairs.

First Lady Sheikha Fatima bint Mubarak was presented with the Shield of the United Nations in appreciation of her participation in the field of development and housing to improve the lot of women and the family.

27 November: Sheikh Sultan bin Mohammad Al Qassimi and Sheikh Khalifa bin Zayed Al Nahyan studied details of the attack on Abu al-Bukhoush oil field. Sheikh Sultan stressed that contacts which the UAE made with world leaders reflected the principles, values and peaceful choices available to the country.

During the previous ten years, 12 million trees were planted on 60,000 hectares in 80 projects in Abu Dhabi emirate alone.

28 November: During the previous ten years (1975-1985), cement production in the country increased 25 times. Production in 1986 stood at 4.8 million tons of which 2.6 tons were used locally and the remainder exported.

29 November: The Kingdom of Saudi Arabia decided to exempt ADNOC products from customs fees.

30 November: Sharjah Police created the first Police Dog Unit to assist in uncovering drugs and explosives and crowd-control.

2 December: Sheikh Zayed received the Members of the Supreme Council of the Federation and groups of well-wishers on the occasion of the fifteenth anniversary of his accession as President of the Federation. He said that the attack on Abu al-Bukhoush oil field would not affect the

UAE's confidence in itself and that what happened did not do more than ruffle a hair on a huge body.

Sheikh Zayed on the occasion of World Solidarity Day with the Palestinian people stressed that the UAE would not hesitate to give aid and support to the Palestinian people to achieve their rightful goals to return to their country and achieve self determination.

3 December: Sheikh Zayed, after a telephone conversation with the Palestinian leader, Yasser Arafat, called on Arab leaders to call for immediate intervention to stop the war on the refugee camps. He said that the UAE was prepared to aid any efforts to stop the brotherly fighting on Lebanese territory.

The Ministry of Health completed the re-registration of 300 pharmaceutical companies in the country and 7000 medical preparations according to new requirements which met the standards of the World Health Organization.

4 December: More than 393 billion dirhams was invested in infrastructure and services since the establishment of the Federation (1971-1985).

First Lady Sheikh Fatima bint Mubarak congratulated the Olympiad Chess Champion, Farida Abdulrahman, who won the gold medal in the International Chess Olympiad held in Dubai.

5 December: The UAE announced that it agreed to attend the emergency meeting of Arab Ministers of Foreign Affairs to study the war in the refugee camps in Lebanon.

The Ministry of Agriculture completed the necessary measures and controls to implement the Council of Ministers decision allowing fishermen to export fish outside the country.

During the previous eight years, 1543 national students (male and female) graduated from Arab and foreign universities and institutes.

7 December: Sheikh Zayed stressed during a meeting with British MP's that the UAE was capable of confronting aggression and that the attack on Abu al-Bukhoush did not hurt the UAE as much as benefit it. He said that the UAE would never ask a friend to confront attacks when it could do so itself. He also remarked: 'I hope that Britain will not do anything so that its promises will not be like the promises of its allies'.

Dr Mana Said Al Otaiba said that the UAE supported the reduction of OPEC production in order to raise the price per barrel of oil to 18 dollars.

Etisalat's budget for 1987 was set at 690 million dirhams.

9 December: Sheikh Khalifa bin Zayed Al Nahyan, in remarks to *Al-Majalla* magazine, stressed that the UAE was working to increase its defence capabilities because weakness incited aggression. He said that the UAE would purchase arms from the Soviet bloc if that served its interest, indicating that the offering of weapons by the United States to Iran placed an additional obstacle in the way of peace.

Sheikh Mohammad bin Rashid Al Maktoum, during a meeting with the Chinese delegation, welcomed constructive co-operation between the UAE and the People's Republic of China. He expressed the UAE's appreciation for China's position on Arab affairs.

12 December: A joint communiqué on the results of the discussions between the Federal National Council and the British House of Commons Committee requested that everyone should refrain from supplying any arms which would assist in the continuation of the Iran-Iraq war. Britain also expressed its deep concern at the shelling of the Abu al-Bukhoush oil field.

13 December: Abu Dhabi Municipality issued an order regulating advertising in Abu Dhabi to become effective from 1 January. The order stipulated that 65 per cent of any advertisement must be in Arabic and that the Arabic text must appear above the foreign language text.

15 December: The first phase of the pipeline network for the distribution of natural gas from the Al-Saja field in Sharjah was completed. The pipeline, which cost 600 million dirhams, had a capacity of 300 million cubic metres.

Five UAE officers earned Masters degrees in military sciences from the Sudanese Staff College.

17 December: Sheikh Nahyan bin Mubarak Al Nahyan issued new regulations governing teaching assistants and students who were sent abroad for graduate studies by UAE University. The new regulations aimed at making the teaching staff entirely national according to a long-term plan.

18 December: It was decided to combine Al-Jazira Hospital and Al-Mafraq Hospital into a unified information organization via the use of computers in the first phase of a plan for the use of computers in curative services.

19 December: Abu Dhabi Municipality spent 18 billion dirhams over the past years in constructing roads, bridges and tunnels.

20 December: Sheikh Zayed arrived in Sana'a to participate in celebrations for the opening of the rebuilt Marib Dam which was funded by him.

21 December: Sheikh Zayed and the Yemeni President, Ali Abdulla Saleh, opened the Marib Dam. Zayed stressed that to support Yemen was to add another force to Arab strength.

22 December: Sheikh Khalifa gave the Bani Yas Sports Club a grant of 55 million dirhams to complete its facilities.

Some 487 million dirhams was expended on projects in the emirate of Sharjah in 1985.

23 December: Sheikh Zayed returned to the country having held discussions with Yemeni President, Ali Abdulla Saleh, which covered efforts to re-establish unity in Arab ranks.

26 December: In 1985 there were 30 plastic factories in the country whereas in 1975 there were only eight such factories. The number of schools in the Sharjah Educational District increased from 90 in 1984-85 to 98 in 1985-86.

29 December: UAE nationals constituted 68.5 per cent of the student body in the Federation.

31 December: Sheikh Zayed opened the new Handicrafts Centre building at the headquarters of the UAE Women's Federation in Abu Dhabi.

Nineteen Eighty Seven

1 January: Sheikh Zayed, accompanied by Sheikh Hamad bin Essa Al Khalifa, Crown Prince of Bahrain, inspected development plans, including extensive tree-planting on the island of Sir Bani Yas. Plans for the island included its designation as the largest natural protected area in the Middle East.

2 January: The Central Bank stressed that the UAE economy had come out of the recession of the previous four years and had entered a new phase of revival. Total local liquidity of between 59 and 62 billion dirhams was forecast for the end of 1987.

3 January: The Ministry of Works installed computers for supervising and planning projects.

4 January: Abu Dhabi Municipality commenced construction of a modern automatic abattoir at a cost of 31 million dirhams.

5 January: Sheikh Zayed received a letter from the Iranian President, Ali Khamenei, regarding developments in the region.

Sheikh Zayed inspected road, housing and farm projects under construction in Al-Marfa for distribution to citizens.

In accordance with Sheikh Zayed's directives, the Department of Electricity and Water increased the water supply to Al-Marfa, Al-Sila'a, Delma and Sir Bani Yas with the help of ten new water distillation plants which raised output by 5 million gallons per day.

The Council of Ministers approved the law governing civil aviation in the country.

Sheikh Hamdan bin Rashid Al Maktoum, based on positive trends in economic and commercial activity, expressed the hope that the financial situation in the country would make greater improvements in 1987 than it did last year.

7 January: Sheikh Zayed decreed that the 1986 budget would operate in 1987 until a new budget was agreed upon for 1987.

Thirty-nine nationals were pursuing science-based Masters and Doctorates in American universities on UAE University scholarships.

Duty-free purchases at Abu Dhabi International Airport amounted to 52 million dirhams.

8 January: Sheikh Zayed received a letter from Sheikh Jabir Al Ahmad Al Sabah, Ruler of Kuwait, which included an invitation to the Islamic Conference Summit to be held in Kuwait on 26

January. Zayed stressed the necessity of unifying Arab and Islamic positions and he called for Arab leaders to play a major role in bringing the different points of view closer together.

The decision was made to train all foreign doctors and nurses in the UAE's hospitals, health centres and out-patient clinics to work through the medium of Arabic.

9 January: The UAE occupied first place among members of the Arab Gulf Educational Bureau in the ratio of females to males enrolled in special education. The ratio of girls to boys was 54:46.

10 January: The UAE and Cyprus initialled an agreement for air transportation between the two countries.

17 January: Sheikh Khalifa bin Zayed Al Nahyan approved outline development plans for Al-Ain up to the year 2000.

20 January: The income from agricultural production in the country increased during the previous seven years (1977-1984) from 984 million dirhams to 1928 million dirhams. Planted areas rose from 2600 hectares to 32,000 hectares and agricultural investments increased from 240 million to 1679 million dirhams.

21 January: Sheikh Zayed donated two Boeing aircraft to Sudan.

23 January: Sheikh Zayed had a meeting in Abu Dhabi with Algeria's President, Chedli Benjadid, who was on a brief visit to the Federation.

UAE nationals comprised 99.2 per cent of students in the State's kindergartens, whereas only 67.4 per cent of students at primary stage were nationals. This figure dropped to 64.4 per cent at intermediate level and 60.9 per cent at secondary level.

26 January: Sheikh Zayed arrived in Kuwait at the head of the UAE delegation to participate in the Islamic Conference Summit. He called for the leaders of the Islamic world to settle their differences by peaceful means and stressed that the unity of the Islamic *Umma* and its solidarity was the only way to command respect. During lengthy meetings with the leaders of Islamic nations, he stressed the importance of joint Islamic efforts.

31 January: Discussions between Sheikh Zayed and the visiting Egyptian President, Mohammad Hosni Mubarak, centred on the necessity of continuing bilateral consultations to support collective efforts towards Arab unity. The two Presidents studied developments in the Arab world and the Iran-Iraq war in light of the results of the Islamic summit.

1 February: Sheikh Zayed and the Palestinian leader, Yasser Arafat, who was visiting Abu Dhabi, discussed current Arab and Islamic affairs and called for the convening of an urgent Arab summit to confront developments in the Arab world. The export of six varieties of *mumtaza* dates was prohibited, thus protecting the national date palm stock.

4 February: Dubai Municipality signed two contacts for storm water drainage in Al-Rashidiya and Al-Karama districts at a cost of 220 million dirhams.

9 February: Sheikh Zayed received GCC Oil Ministers who held an important meeting in Abu Dhabi. He assured them that the UAE was committed to support OPEC and he called for the continuation of policies aimed at stabilizing decisions regarding production and pricing.

10 February: Sheikh Zayed received GCC Youth Ministers who held a meeting in Abu Dhabi to study co-operation and co-ordination in youth and sports affairs.

11 February: Sheikh Maktoum bin Rashid Al Maktoum donated buildings to be used as headquarters for the Institute for Administrative Development and the National Computer Centre in Dubai. He also provided furnishings for the two buildings.

14 February: Sheikh Sultan bin Mohammad Al Qassimi began an official visit to Yemen.

At Dubai International Airport, work was completed on the most modern radar station in the Gulf region at a cost of 22 million dirhams.

15 February: Sheikh Sultan bin Mohammad Al Qassimi, following his visit to the Marib Dam, expressed his pride that history had been repeated because of Sheikh Zayed's assistance in rebuilding the dam.

17 February: The UAE ranked second among GCC States in development spending. Some 54.6 billion dollars was invested in projects during the previous 15 years.

The Civil Aviation Department in Dubai, in co-operation with Police Headquarters, completed the installation of a new closed circuit television network at Dubai International Airport.

18 February: Sultan bin Mohammad Al Qassimi, who was visiting Sudan, opened Sharjah Hall at the University of Khartoum.

19 February: An economic protocol was signed in Ankara between Turkey and the UAE.

20 February: Sheikh Zayed continued his tour of agricultural and municipal development projects in the Western Region, inspecting afforestation projects and farms in Baynunah district. He also ordered the installation of street lighting in Al-Marfa, the creation of new farms and an increase in the acreage of existing farms in the region.

23 February: On the President's directives, the Ministry of Health began work on the construction of a new hospital in Zayed City.

24 February: Sheikh Zayed, at the end of his tour of the Western Region, stressed his concern that a good standard of living be made available to all citizens in the State. He said that knowledge remained while wealth disappeared and that wealth had no value if it was not exploited in the service of the individual.

Sheikh Sultan bin Mohammad Al Qassimi gave 2.5 million dollars to the Islamic Centre in Yugoslavia.

An executive programme for a co-operative cultural and educational agreement was signed in Muscat between the UAE and the Sultanate of Oman.

27 February: The UAE and Morocco signed two co-operation agreements in the fields of air transport, post and telecommunications.

The UAE representative in the United Nations, Mohammad Hussain Al Shamali, was elected for one year as chairman of the UN committee overseeing the embargo on arms exports to South Africa.

28 February: The services sector obtained the largest allocation, amounting to 2.5 billion dirhams, in the UAE's consultative budget programme for 1986.

2 March: Sheikh Hamad bin Mohammad Al Sharqi inspected agricultural projects in Fujairah.

6 March: Sheikh Sultan bin Mohammad Al Qassimi and the Iranian Deputy Minister of Oil, Kadhim Ardabili, discussed a number of petroleum matters, among which was the modality of exploiting new oil explorations on Abu Musa island.

8 March: The UAE signed two agreements with Greece and Tunisia for co-operation in the field of air transportation.

9 March: In 1986, 329.3 million dirhams was given in social aid to deserving citizens in Dubai and the other Northern Emirates.

14 March: Sheikh Sultan bin Mohammad Al Qassimi opened the fourth national arts festival in Sharjah.

The Emirates General Petroleum Corporation began to supply fuel to aircraft at the UAE's airports.

15 March: Sheikh Zayed and the Members of the Supreme Council of the Federation attended the annual festival of school activities. Zayed said that the student demonstration was a joint effort which called for pride and satisfaction. He stressed that the UAE's educational policy and planning had achieved its goals, education being the most important gift which wealth had provided for the nation. Fostering education is a national duty, he said, and the State had made all its resources available to develop the gene-ration of tomorrow and compensate for the deprivations of the past.

17 March: The Executive Council allocated 254 million dirhams to develop service facilities in the emirate of Abu Dhabi.

According to the directives of Sheikh Khalifa bin Zayed al Nahyan, it was decided to supply Al-Mafraq Hospital with the latest ultrasonic equipment for dissolving kidney stones as an alternative to traditional surgery.

18 March: Sheikh Zayed, meeting with GCC Economy and Finance Ministers, called for a concentration on compre-hensive economic and human development, stressing that development was incomplete unless it advanced all groups of society and especially women.

22 March: First Lady Sheikha Fatima bint Mubarak arrived in Riyadh at the beginning of an official visit at the invitation of the wife of King Fahad bin Abdulaziz of Saudi Arabia.

Sheikh Mohammad bin Rashid Al Maktoum opened the new Traffic Office building in Dubai.

23 March: Sheikh Zayed, meeting with GCC Ministers of Education, stressed that the educated individual is the current and future raw material which States have to work with and that he had great confidence in their excellent care of the youth of the region and their nurture of them on the basis of moral excellence.

Sheikh Zayed received a letter from the French Prime Minister which was delivered by the French Minister of Foreign Affairs. Zayed praised France's efforts in bringing about international peace and security and called for stability through the persual of a fair non-aligned policy.

The Council of Ministers decided to form a supreme ministerial energy committee as the highest authority for co-ordinating government bodies dealing with nuclear energy, nuclear safety and protection from nuclear radiation.

Sheikha Fatima bint Mubarak, who was visiting Saudi Arabia, donated 2 million riyals to the Ewa Centre for Handicapped Children and the Women's Society in Riyadh.

24 March: Sheikh Sultan bin Zayed Al Nahyan awarded the Independence

Medal to the Arab Astronaut, Sultan bin Salman bin Abdulaziz, who in turn presented Sheikh Sultan with the medal to commemorate the space journey, *Discovery.*

Sheikh Rashid bin Ahmed Al Mualla issued directives for the Bank of Umm al-Qaiwain to grant citizens long term personal loans for house construction at reduced and easy to pay rates of interest.

25 March: ADNOC won the largest tender in GCC States to supply 3129 million litres of oil annually to the Omani Ministry of Water.

The Bank of Umm al-Qaiwain commenced extending housing loans to citizens. The loans were limited to 300,000 dirhams at 12 per cent interest.

27 March: Sheikh Zayed received a letter from the Libyan President, Muammar Al Gadhafi, regarding current Arab developments and Zayed's efforts to achieve Arab solidarity.

28 March: Sheikh Zayed inspected dams set up in the Falaj al-Mualla region of Umm al-Qaiwain and visited farms in the region.

29 March: Sheikh Zayed, during his reception of the Board of Administration of the Consumers Co-operative Union, called for greater co-operative activity without the creation of monopolies. He confirmed that co-operative societies were free to work without restrictions and that what was requested of them was to supply food and consumer goods to citizens at suitable prices.

31 March: Sheikh Zayed attended graduation ceremonies for the sixth group of students from the UAE University. He stressed that the UAE was gaining the greatest of all riches at each graduation of its young people from the University. He said that it was his great hope that the graduates would achieve the goals of the nation and the citizens' hopes for well-being and progress.

1 April: Sheikh Sultan bin Zayed Al Nahyan inspected Al-Shuwaib Dam after stormwater burst it and destroyed 30 houses. He directed that the remains of the dam in Wadi al-Madam be rebuilt and extended and he expressed his concern for the security of the citizens who suffered damage and made all services available to them. He stressed the necessity of storing rainwater and not allowing it to overflow so that agricultural development projects could benefit.

4 April: Sheikh Saqr bin Mohammad Al Qassimi confirmed that the artifacts discovered in Ras al-Khaimah go back in history some 6000 years and that they reflect the original civilization of the people of the area.

6 April: Sheikh Zayed attended graduation ceremonies for the new group of pilots. He stressed that what he had witnessed gave a good and honourable representation of the UAE's Armed Forces and that each citizen was proud of them. An air transport agreement was signed between the UAE and Turkey.

7 April: The Council of Ministers decided to establish the first Forensic Medicine Office and to reduce the price of telephone calls to a number of countries.

A joint company, capitalized at 2 billion dollars, was formed between the UAE and the People's Republic of China to promote and market Chinese industrial products in Jebel Ali Free Zone.

9 April: Sheikh Zayed and the Malian President, Mousa Tarawari, who was on an official visit to the UAE, gave their attention to Islamic matters. Zayed stressed the necessity of solidarity and the renunciation of disunity between Islamic States. He called for the leaders of the Islamic world to put an end to their dissensions and fulfil the aspirations of their peoples. A joint communiqué broadcast at the end of the visit expressed the two Presidents' concern about the continuation of the Iraq-Iraq war. They also expressed their support for the convening of an international conference to solve the Middle East question and they condemned Israeli aggression against Lebanon.

13 April: Sheikh Khalifa bin Zayed Al Nahyan earmarked 39.35 million dirhams for the recruitment of 300 policemen and supplying them with the latest equipment.

17 April: Sheikh Zayed, the Members of the Supreme Council of the Federation and guests from the GCC attended the annual final races of pure-bred Arab camels.

18 April: In Rabat contracts were signed to construct 600 apartments and 38 villas as low-cost housing, to be funded by a grant from Sheikh Zayed.

20 April: Sheikh Zayed received a letter from the Soviet Leader, Mikhail Gorbachev, delivered by the Soviet Deputy Minister of Foreign Affairs. The President of the Federation called for an immediate end to the Iran-Iraq war. He said that every effort made for peace would go down in history.

21 April: Sheikh Zayed attended the Friends of the Handicapped Festival in Abu Dhabi. He requested that investment be made in exploiting the potential of handicapped persons and that this investment be directed toward production. He said that he was satisfied that there was sufficient technical support available for training the handicapped.

24 April: There were 68 welfare societies in the country in 1986 receiving a total of 55.5 million dirhams in support from the State.

25 April: For the first time a woman, Sheikha Mouza bint Abdulaziz Al Qassimi, was elected to the presidency of the board of administration of a public welfare society, the Emirates Society for the Care and Training of the Handicapped in Sharjah.

26 April: The UAE and the People's Republic of China, following a discussion between Rashid Abdulla and his Chinese counterpart in Beijing, called for a cessation to the Iraq-Iran war. They expressed their concern about the effects of the war on the freedom of navigation in the Gulf.

2 May: In accordance with the President's directives, the Tawam Hospital in Al-Ain became part of the Ministry of Health.

4 May: The first equipment for viral research in the country was supplied to Al-Jazira Hospital in Abu Dhabi.

5 May: The Emirates Central Bank annual report stated that in 1986 total liquidity stood at 57.9 billion dirhams and that the surplus trade balance was 12.2 billion dirhams. Oil exports declined to 25 billion dirhams as against 54.3 billion dirhams in 1985.

6 May: Actual expenditure for all projects in Abu Dhabi's annual development plan for 1986 amounted to 3.798 billion dirhams.

9 May: Sheikh Zayed, meeting with US Assistant Secretary for Near East and South Asian Affairs, Richard Murphy, called on the two great powers to shoulder their responsibilities to stop the Iraq-Iran war. He said that the opportunity was now propitious to achieve a fair and permanent peace in the Middle East and that to lose it would threaten international security.

10 May: Sheikh Dr Sultan bin Mohammad Al Qassimi, opening the Confidence Club for the Handicapped in Sharjah, commended Zayed's concern for the handicapped and his desire to see them integrated into society.

15 May: The consumption of water in Al-Ain increased 35 times in 11 years as a result of developmental, industrial and agricultural activity. Average annual consumption in 1986 was 11,084 million gallons, in comparison to 310 million gallons in 1975.

16 May: An official source categorically denied that the UAE had asked for British protection for its ships in the Gulf. It confirmed the UAE's policy of not hiding facts from the public and that the State saw no justification for requesting foreign protection for its ships.

19 May: Work began in executing the Ministry of Education's plan which required that 40 new schools be constructed nation-wide during the next three years at a cost of 390 million dirhams.

22 May: In 1986, Dubai Petroleum Company dug 28 new development wells and did maintenance work on 17 wells. Eleven per cent of the company's workforce were nationals out of a total workforce of 982 people.

1 June: The paid-out balance in the country last year rose to 4.8 billion dirhams, in comparison to 2.64 billion dirhams in 1985.

3 June: Sheikh Zayed, during his reception of members of the senate of the USA, called for a clear and just policy towards the Middle East. He called for efforts to be made to stop the destructive war between Iraq and Iran and stressed that the security and stability of the Gulf region constituted two basic factors for international peace.

8 June: Sheikh Maktoum bin Rashid Al Maktoum issued a decree setting-up an independent public travel corporation under the name of DNATA. Ownership of the Dubai National Travel Agency will be transferred to this new establishment.

11 June: The UAE, which was presiding over the current GCC session, made a statement regarding ways of ending the Iraq-Iran war, ensuring freedom of navigation in international waters and freedom of navigation and passage for ships to and from GCC ports.

15 June: Sheikh Zayed held important discussions with His Majesty Sultan Qaboos bin Said who paid a short visit to the country. During their discussions, they made a complete evaluation of developments in the region, declaring their support for joint Arab action. They dealt with a number of other affairs of mutual concern in light of the strong fraternal relations between the two countries.

17 June: The Supreme Council of the Federation convened a meeting under the Presidency of Sheikh Zayed. The Council declared that statements issued in the emirate of Sharjah concerning the abdication of Sheikh Sultan bin Mohammad Al Qassimi were null and void. The Council decided to remain in session until the situation had been rectified.

18 June: The Supreme Council of the Federation continued to review the situation in Sharjah. The Council decided to allow time for ongoing consultations between the various parties to reach a successful conclusion, stressing that continuing efforts to pursue all considerations were for the higher good of the nation which the Members of the Council saw as embodying the spirit of one family.

20 June: On the third day of the open session, the Supreme Council of the Federation decided on the reinstatement of Sheikh Sultan bin Mohammad Al Qassimi as the lawful Ruler of the emirate of Sharjah and the appointment of Abdulaziz Al Qassimi as Deputy Ruler and Crown Prince. The Council thanked the President of the Federation, and commended his care and wisdom in directing events in the Council. It also stressed the importance of guaranteeing security and stability while being committed to the constitutional institutions of the State.

21 June: The Supreme Council held a meeting under the Presidency of Sheikh Zayed at which Sheikh Sultan bin Mohammad Al Qassimi was present. The Council adopted a number of decrees for the good of the nation and its citizen and decided to continue its meetings to consider matters of national interest.

22 June: Based on an order from Sheikh Khalifa bin Zayed Al Nahyan, 700 million dirhams was paid to 307 local families as compensation for houses in the Al-Hada'iq and Al-Howamil districts of Abu Dhabi which were destroyed for development purposes.

23 June: Sheikh Zayed bin Sultan Al Nahyan, the Members of the Supreme Council and the Crown Princes attended a brotherly meeting between Sheikh Sultan bin Mohammad Al Qassimi and Sheikh Abdulaziz Al Qassimi. The Members of the Supreme Council issued statements commending the efforts made by Zayed and his wisdom in overcoming the crisis and protecting the Federation. UAE and USSR signed an air transport agreement allowing Gulf Air and Emirates landing rights in USSR and Aeroflot landing rights in the Federation.

26 June: Sheikh Zayed visited Sheikh Sultan bin Mohammad Al Qassimi following the end of the crisis in the emirate of Sharjah. He stressed his concern that the Federation should embody the spirit of one family and that the ties which bind the country would be deepened.

27 June: The Supreme Council of the Federation, under the Presidency of Sheikh Zayed, gave special attention to the situation in the region.

29 June: Sheikh Zayed received letters from King Fahad bin Abdulaziz, Sultan Qaboos bin Said and President Saddam Hussein dealing with developments in the region.

Sheikh Sultan and a group of 17 banks agreed a loan rescheduling 130 million dollars of Sharjah's 900 million dollar debt.

5 July: The Central Bank renewed its request to commercial banks operating in the country to give work opportunities to UAE citizens wishing to engage in bank work and for each bank to employ a percentage of graduates.

6 July: The Council of Ministers decided to form a ministerial committee to study the setting-up of a complex of higher technical colleges to provide trained nationals required by the State in various public utilities.

7 July: Sheikh Zayed sent cables to King Hussein of Jordan, the Iraqi President, Saddam Hussein and the Syrian President, Hafez Al Asad, in which he expressed his deep satisfaction at the meeting of Al Asad and Saddam. He said that reconciliation between brothers was necessary and that all must work to support each other in achieving the hopes of the nation. He said that he was in favour of any initiative which promoted unity and secured the rights of Arab and Muslims.

8 July: Abu Dhabi National Oil Company for Oil Product Distribution (ADNOC-FOD) won, for a second time the Omani National Transportation Company oil supply contract.

9 July: At the end of last year, Abu Dhabi Municipality Traffic Engineering Department had completed the expansion and beautification of 45 kms of major streets and branch roads inside the city of Abu Dhabi at a cost of 881 million dirhams.

13 July: Sheikh Zayed received a letter from the Custodian of the Two Holy Mosques, King Fahad bin Abdulaziz, regarding the Arab Summit to be convened in Amman and developments in the Gulf region.

14 July: Imports into the country decreased by 30 per cent between 1981 and 1985 because of a rise in agricultural production, the development of industrial production and other economic changes. Imports of commodities in 1981 were around 9.585 billion dirhams, decreasing in 1985 to 6.691 billion dirhams.

16 July: The value of the trade via Port Zayed during the first quarter of 1987

amounted to 1215 million dirhams. Some 373 million kilograms of goods were loaded and unloaded at the port.

20 July: Sheikh Zayed met with Sheikh Dr Sultan bin Mohammad Al Qassimi and Sheikh Abdulaziz Al Qassimi to discuss matters concerning the emirate of Sharjah, strengthening the future of the Federation and confirming the recent decisions of the Supreme Council of the Federation.

Sheikh Dr Sultan bin Mohammad Al Qassimi issued a law reorganizing the government structure in the emirate of Sharjah, including the formation of an Executive Council under the chairmanship of Sheikh Abdulaziz Al Qassimi, the Heir Apparent.

23 July: Sheikh Zayed received a letter from the Iraqi President, Saddam Hussein, regarding developments in the region and Iraq's position regarding the Security Council resolution on ending the Iraq-Iraq war.

24 July: The Emirates National Youth Team won the third GCC Handball Championship Cup.

26 July: Dubai International Airport came second among transit hubs behind Japan's Narita Airport.

27 July: Sheikh Hamdan bin Mohammad Al Nahyan arrived in Ankara on an official visit to Turkey. He held discussions with the Turkish Prime Minister, Turgut Ozal, regarding mutual relations, Arab and Islamic affairs and efforts to end the Iran-Iraq war.

Dubai Civil Defence Department began the operation of two new radar systems costing 25 million dirhams at Dubai International Airport.

29 July: Sheikh Dr Sultan bin Mohammad Al Qassimi chaired the first meeting of the Executive Council of the emirate of

Sharjah during which a number of subjects concerning the country were discussed.

30 July: Sheikh Zayed bin Sultan Al Nahyan, the Prime Minister of Tunisia, Rashid Safar, and the Palestinian leader, Yasser Arafat, discussed current developments in the Gulf, the Palestinian proposal to hold an Islamic summit and Tunisian efforts to stop the Iraq-Iraq war.

31 July: Sheikh Zayed concluded his one-week tour of the Western Region during which he inspected agricultural and development projects in Al-Marfa, Sir Bani Yas Island and Mahadhir Liwa where many afforestation, farming, housing and road projects were underway.

2 August: Sheikh Khalifa donated 1 million dirhams to the Sharjah Club on the occasion of its victory in the first and second rounds of the football championship.

3 August: Sheikh Zayed concluded his inspection tour of development and agricultural projects in the Western Region and he ordered the distribution of 30 new farms to citizens in Al-Marfa.

6 August: Sheikh Zayed received groups of well wishers on the twenty-first anniversary of his accession to power in Abu Dhabi. Zayed opened the new Safina Restaurant on the breakwater and attended a dinner with the Members of the Supreme Council to mark the occasion.

10 August: During the first third of this year, trade in Dubai was valued at 8.3 billion dirhams.

12 August: The Armed Forces defused a mine discovered off the coast of Fujairah and continued work to keep the country's sea coasts clear of mines.

14 August: The Ministry of Foreign Affairs confirmed that the territorial waters of the UAE were virtually free of mines thanks to the efforts made by the Armed Forces and the Coast Guard and other authorities.

15 August: Sheikh Zayed, on his arrival in Damascus, conferred with the Syrian President, Hafez Al Asad, on ways to end Arab differences. The two leaders agreed on the necessity of taking immediate action to restore Arab solidarity and to confront imminent dangers.

A state of the art kidney dialysis unit went into operation at Tawam hospital in Al-Ain.

16 August: Sheikh Zayed held two sessions of discussions with Syrian President, Hafez Al Asad. The decision was made to send two envoys to Iraqi President, Saddam Hussein, to acquaint him with the results of the Damascus discussions on mediation efforts to achieve Arab solidarity.

The total value of external loans extended by ADFAED from when it was founded until the end of 1986 amounted to 4.026 billion dirhams. The fund financed 88 projects in 42 developing countries.

19 August: Sheikh Zayed concluded his official five-day visit to Syria during which he held six rounds of working sessions with Syrian President, Hafez Al Asad, regarding ways of furthering reconciliation amongst Arabs. They agreed to continue efforts in this regard.

20 August: Sheikh Tahnoun bin Mohammad Al Nahyan opened the new stadium at the Al-Ain Club.

22 August: Traffic police and Abu Dhabi Municipality began preliminary experiments utilizing cameras to photograph cars which failed to stop at red traffic lights.

25 August: Sheikh Zayed issued an order to construct 909 kms of new branch canals at the Marib Dam in Yemen.

29 August: Sheikh Saqr bin Mohammad Al Qassimi opened the symposium on the history of Portuguese imperialism in the Arabian Gulf convened in Ras al-Khaimah. He confirmed that Arab resistance to Western invasion succeeded in maintaining the Arab character and independence of the Gulf. He stressed that it was important that new generations paid attention to the events of the past and the historic deeds of their fathers and grandfathers.

21 August: Sheikh Zayed arrived in Turkey on a private visit during which he was received by Turkish President, Kenan Efren.

6 September: Sheikh Zayed and the Turkish President, Kenan Efren, discussed the latest upsurge of fighting in the Iran-Iraq war and called on Baghdad and Tehran to save their forces to confront the enemies of Islam.

The UAE condemned the long range rocket attack which struck populated areas of southern Kuwait. It stressed that such operations would lead to a sharp increase in tension in the region and called on the Security Council to take decisive measures to prevent a repetition of such acts of aggression.

7 September: Sheikh Zayed, in talks with the Kuwaiti Minister of Communications in Istanbul, called on Iran to accept the UN Security Council resolution demanding a ceasefire and the opening of negotiations for peace between the belligerents in the Iran-Iraq war.

10 September: Sheikh Zayed, who arrived in Rabat on a visit to Morocco, received a letter from the Ruler of Kuwait regarding developments in the Gulf and ways of strengthening joint Arab action.

11 September: Sheikh Zayed and King Hassan of Morocco studied developments in the Iraq-Iraq war and efforts to promote understanding between Arabs. He stressed that the time was propitious to stop the Iran-Iraq war and that the Arab stand must be united to bring the conflict to an end if the mission of the UN Secretary General, Perez de Cuellar, should fail. He said that Arabs must shoulder their historic responsibilities to achieve unity in their ranks.

14 September: More than 406 million date palm trees of 80 varieties occupied 80 per cent of the land planted with fruit in the UAE.

17 September: The UAE won the GCC Table Tennis Championship and it ranked in the second division in the Volleyball Championship.

18 September: Sheikh Zayed, following discussions with King Hassan of Morocco in Rabat, warned that the Iran-Iraq war was about to widen following an incidence of foreign interference. He said that he had often warned that the continuation of the war would bring the great powers into the region and he called for the two Muslim neighbours to put out the fire today before it consumed them tomorrow.

20 September: A 25 million dirham agreement was signed for the construction of the Jebel Hafit road.

22 September: Sheikh Zayed made a short visit to Riyadh in order to discuss with King Fahad bin Abdulaziz developments in the Gulf and the dangers inherent in the continuation of the Iraq-Iran war, as well as efforts being made to promote Arab reconciliation.

28 September: Sheikh Khalifa bin Zayed Al Nahyan opened the Gulf Air Maintenance Company, considered to be the most modern base for aircraft maintenance in the region.

29 September: Sheikh Zayed and King Hussein of Jordan, who was visiting Abu Dhabi, discussed efforts to end the Iraq-Iran war, the achievement of Arab solidarity and issuance of a call for an emergency Arab Summit.

Two agreements were signed for oil exploration between the government of Ras al-Khaimah and Bermuda International Oil Company.

1 October: The UAE, in its speech at the United Nations, stressed that UN Resolution 598 represented a unique and historic opportunity to settle the Iran-Iraq war. It also stressed its support for the rights of the people of Palestine as demonstrated by its willingness to participate in any efforts aimed at a fair settlement in the Middle East.

4 October: Sheikh Zayed inspected the afforestation south of the city of Al-Ain and ordered that the planted areas be increased.

7 October: Sheikh Zayed, during his reception of the OPEC tripartite committee, stressed the UAE's support for the organization's efforts to maintain unity and stability in the world oil market. The President of the Federation showed his complete appreciation of the committee's mission which was serving the best interests of both producers and consumers. The UAE welcomed the convening of an emergency Arab summit in Amman and expressed the hope that the results of the summit would support joint Arab action.

10 October: Sheikh Zayed, during a private visit to the Sultanate of Oman, discussed with His Majesty Sultan Qaboos bin Said efforts being made to foster joint Arab action in the coming phase. Developments in the region in light of Security Council efforts to end the Iraq-Iran war were also discussed.

11 October: Sheikh Khalifa bin Zayed Al Nahyan meeting with the US Energy Secretary stressed that peace in the Gulf was in the interest of the region and the world. He said that the UAE was attempting firmer co-operation with other countries in the world on the basis of mutual respect and good neighbourliness.

12 October: Sheikh Zayed received GCC Interior Ministers and expressed his hope that their meetings would arrive at positive decisions which would foster security and stability in GCC countries.

13 October: Sheikh Hamdan bin Mohammad Al Nahyan, meeting with American, British and German ambassadors, called for the superpowers to exert all their efforts to put an end to the tension in the Gulf region and find a solution to stop the Iraq-Iraq war.

14 October: Food and clothing donated by Sheikh Zayed for flood victims in Bangladesh were despatched from Abu Dhabi's Mina Zayed.

18 October: The UAE strongly condemned the attack on a ship inside Kuwaiti waters and stressed its solidarity with Kuwait in defence of its sovereignty and territorial integrity.

19 October: A test run took place at the new Fujairah International Airport.

26 October: Sheikh Zayed and the Lebanese President, Amin Jemayyal, who arrived in the country on an official visit, discussed current Arab developments and the situation in

Lebanon, as well as efforts being made to achieve national harmony in Lebanon.

Dr Mana Said Al Otaiba announced that UAE oil reserves were calculated at 200 billion barrels and that the UAE would become the second largest in the world in terms of oil reserves.

27 October: Abu Dhabi Executive Council confirmed a comprehensive plan to renovate school buildings in the emirate of Abu Dhabi at a cost of 455 million dirhams for the first phase.

29 October: In its speech before the United Nations, the UAE supported the holding of an international conference to define the meaning of terrorism. It called for discrimination between the struggle of peoples against imperialism in defence of their rights and terrorism as a criminal act whosoever is the perpetrator.

30 October: Sheikh Zayed began an inspection tour of the Northern Emirates to see how development projects were progressing and to assure himself about the conditions of the citizens.

1 November: Sheikh Ahmed bin Hamid stressed in an interview with the Soviet newspaper, *Pravda*, that the core of the UAE position via-a-vis the Iran-Iraq war was that serious action must be taken to stop the war in the shortest time possible and every effort must be made to enter into a constructive phase to remove the damages caused by war and to achieve security and stability in the region.

In 1986 there was a total of 779 industrial establishments valued at 743,961,000 dirhams in the emirate of Sharjah.

Sheikh Dr Sultan bin Mohammad Al Qassimi inspected the agricultural project in Kalba which was being irrigated directly by brackish water.

The Council of Ministers approved the creation of 600 new jobs for graduates of the educational programme organized by the Ministry of Education to train UAE nationals for teaching posts.

In the first two days following the removal of the ban on fish exports, 7.5 tons of fish were exported.

4 November: In 1986 there was a total of 4344 commercial establishments in the emirate of Sharjah. Investments in these establishments amounted to 13.842 billion dirhams and UAE nationals owned 49 per cent of the establishments.

5 November: Sheikh Rashid bin Ahmad Al Mualla signed a 36 million dirham contract for setting-up a free zone in Port Rashid.

6 November: Sheikh Zayed, in remarks made to the Kuwaiti newspaper, *Al-Rai Al-Aam*, said before the convening of the Arab Summit in Amman that tabling the initiative for conciliation between Iraq and Iran should be done on the basis of empowering Arab leaders and giving them the authority to guarantee the rights of each of the countries after the cessation of conflict and the withdrawal of forces. He said that it was incumbent on the UAE to try to mediate between the warring parties to remove them and their neighbours from the damaging effects of war. He stressed that the return of Egypt to the Arab ranks was just as beneficial for the Arab nation as it was for Egypt.

7 November: Sheikh Zayed arrived in Amman at the head of the UAE delegation to participate in the Arab Summit which was scheduled to begin in the Jordanian capital on the following day. Zayed said that: 'Today we are at the crossroads and the supreme national interest of the Arab nation is not prepared to endure division.

We hope that Arab countries will rise to the occasion, shoulder their responsibilities, and leave their disputes and conflicts behind them'.

8 November: Sheikh Zayed led the UAE delegation at the Arab Summit meetings in Amman. Zayed also headed the meeting of GCC leaders in Amman during which opinions and points of view were exchanged and positions co-ordinated regarding the matters on the Arab Summit agenda.

9 November: The good offices undertaken by Sheikh Zayed and King Hussein succeeded in bringing the Syrian President, Hafez Al Asad, and the Iraqi President, Saddam Hussein, together in the presence of a number of Arab leaders. The athmosphere at the Summit was much relieved as a result of the President of the Federation's efforts and his attempts at reconciliation.

10 November: The Arab Summit Conference formed a six-man committee under the Presidency of Sheikh Zayed to study important issues on the agenda. Zayed continued his consultations with Arab leaders regarding matters under consideration at the Summit. He also met with UAE students studying at Jordanian universities.

Sheikh Hamad bin Mohammad Al Sharqi, during the inauguration of the submarine cable to India, stressed that the UAE through Zayed's leadership focused on comprehensive development and progress in all walks of life in order to achieve the hopes and ambitions of its people.

11 November: Sheikh Zayed led the UAE delegation at the final session of the Arab Summit Conference in Amman after which he left for Morocco on a private visit.

The UAE decided to resume diplomatic relations with Egypt to bring solidarity and strength to Arab ranks.

The Archaeology and Tourism Department in the Ministry of Information and Culture completed the restoration and main-tenance of a number of old castles and watch towers in Mahadhir Liwa in the Western Region.

12 November: Sheikh Zayed received a letter from the Egyptian President, Mohammad Hosni Mubarak, in which he described the decision to restore relations between the UAE and Egypt as an historic decision embodying concern for national interests, and he expressed Egypt's appreciation for the courageous agreement.

14 November: Sheikh Hamdan bin Mohammad Al Nahyan received a letter from the Japanese Prime Minister, Naburo Takashita, regarding mutual co-operation and the Japanese plan to safeguard navigation in the Gulf.

15 November: Sheikh Maktoum bin Rashid Al Maktoum issued a law setting-up the Police College in the emirate of Dubai to train students to become police officers.

16 November: In the city of Fez, Sheikh Zayed and King Hassan of Morocco studied the serious escalation in the Iraq-Iran war. The President of the Federation expressed his hope that implementation of the Arab Summit resolutions in Amman would lead to collective Arab action.

Sheikh Ahmed bin Saeed Al Maktoum opened a motor oil factory in Jebel Ali which would produce 75 types of oil with a capacity of 30 tons per year.

19 November: Sheikh Saqr bin Mohammad Al Qassimi opened the Ras al-Khaimah museum in the old fort which was once the headquarters of the Al Qassimi Rulers.

The UAE in the speech before the United Nations confirmed anew its commitment to the oil embargo imposed on South Africa and the boycott of any form of relations with the racist regime.

21 November: Sheikh Khalifa bin Zayed Al Nahyan, during a reception for the GCC Ministers of Defence who were meeting in Abu Dhabi, confirmed the commitment to collective action in the field of security and defence.

The UAE won the gold medal at the Baghdad International Exhibition.

22 November: The Department of Social Services and Commercial Buildings constructed 400 new houses in the new Musaffah district to accommodate those who were hit by the removal of the housing area in Jarn Yaphour.

23 November: Rashid Abdulla and the Iranian Foreign Minister, Ali Akbar Velayati, studied developments in the Iran-Iraq war. Abdulla confirmed anew the UAE's position which called for an end to the war and he encouraged Iran to respond to UN resolution 598 to stop the war and bring about peace.

24 November: Sheikh Khalifa bin Zayed Al Nahyan, during his meeting with the UK Minister of State for Foreign Affairs, confirmed the need to redouble efforts to stop the Iran-Iraq war and to contain the serious escalation in military operations.

27 November: Sheikh Zayed, meeting with the GCC ambassadors in Rabat, praised the positive results of the Arab Summit in Amman. He said that the Summit concentrated on solidarity as the only way toward collective Arab action. He called for a united Arab Islamic stand to end the Iran-Iraq war.

29 November: Sheikh Khalifa bin Zayed Al Nahyan issued a decree forming a town council in the city of Abu Dhabi.

30 November: The total amount of State assistance to the aged was 189 million dirhams.

The UAE's Shabab Football Club won the cup in the first Sadaka games which were organized by the Sultanate of Oman.

1 December: Before his return to the country, Sheikh Zayed and King Hassan studied efforts being made to contain Arab disputes and developments in the Iraq-Iran war.

Sheikh Zayed, in a speech on the occasion of the UAE's sixteenth National Day, confirmed that the Federation had become as immovable as a high mountain and that through sincere faith, a clear goal and hard work it had lessened difficulties in its way.

2 December: Sheikh Zayed received the Members of the Supreme Council of the Federation and groups of well wishers on the occasion of the sixteenth National Day.

3 December: Since the establishment of the Federation, the Ministry of Public Works and Housing had constructed 13,452 houses at a cost of 1382 million dirhams. The Ministry also established 997 kms of highway outside the cities at a cost of 1355 million dirhams.

The strategic energy reserves of the Federation were reported to be 200 billion barrels of oil and 200 trillion cubic feet of gas.

4 December: Nine cement factories in the Federation were producing 7.4 million tons annually.

6 December: Sheikh Zayed and the Pakistani Prime Minister, Mohammad Khan Junejo, who was visiting the country, studied ways of supporting ties between Islamic countries in a manner which would serve their goals and bring them closer together.

15 December: Al-Ain Municipality required architectural plans for buildings in the city to reflect the Islamic style of design.

20 December: Sheikh Zayed and the Yemeni President, Ali Abdulla Saleh, who was in the UAE on an official visit, discussed efforts being made to achieve Arab solidarity and the dangers resulting from military escalation of the Iran-Iraq war.

An agreement was signed for completing the second stage of the Marib Dam project with a grant from the President of the Federation amounting to 22.445 dollars.

21 December: Council of Ministers approved the 1987 federal budget with a projected deficit of 3.355 million dirhams and total expenditure of 14.421 billion dirhams. Earlier in December, Finance &

Industry Minister, Ahmed Al Tayer had said UAE would maintain a tight control on spending to keep the budget deficit steady.

23 December: Sheikh Zayed donated 1 million dollars to the martyrs of the Palestinian *intifada* and to support the Palestinians against attempts to put an end to their lawful resistance.

26 December: Sheikh Zayed led the UAE delegation to the eighth GCC Summit in Riyadh. He called for a confrontation of the challenges affecting the region.

28 December: The Council of Ministers approved the preparation of the new federal draft Civil Service Law and the granting of a technical allowance to national engineers in the federal government.

31 December: The capital of co-operative societies rose from 1.5 million dirhams to 170 million dirhams over the previous ten years.

Nineteen Eighty Eight

3 January: Sheikh Tahnoun bin Mohammed Al Nahyan announced that in 1987 ADNOC had discovered a large hydrocarbon reserve in the emirate of Abu Dhabi and that explorations revealed an additional reserve of gas the size of which was estimated to be around 3.2 trillion cubic feet.

5 January: Sheikh Zayed, at the new session of the Federal National Council, stressed that a comparison of the past with the present made it abundantly clear how great the UAE's achievements had been. He said that he had high hopes for his people and that the UAE's sons must be proud of their fathers just as his generation were proud of their fathers and grandfathers.

10 January: Sheikh Zayed and Egyptian President Mohammad Hosni Mubarak, who was on an official visit to the UAE, studied the security and political situation in the Gulf and current Arab affairs.

The UAE approved the holding of an emergency meeting of the Arab League to discuss the Palestinian *intifada*.

11 January: Sheikh Zayed held discussions with President Hosni Mubarak before his departure from the country.

President Mubarak praised Zayed's efforts towards Arab unity and he confirmed that the Gulf States were capable of defending themselves.

20 January: Sheikh Hamdan bin Mohammad Al Nahyan stressed the nation's support for the Palestinian cause saying that the *intifada* was the most honourable of *jihad* battles against the Zionist enemy.

23 January: Sheikh Zayed received a letter from Tunisian President, Al Habib Bourguiba, which was delivered to Sheikh Khalifa bin Zayed Al Nahyan during his discussions with the Tunisian Prime Minister, Al Hadi Al Bakkoush. The UAE and Tunisia confirmed their support and backing for the Palestinian *intifada*.

24 January: The number of employees in the ministries and federal institutions at the end of 1987 rose to 14,485, representing 34 per cent of the total workforce.

28 January: An ancient burial site containing 4000 year old archaeological artifacts was discovered in Al-Ain.

29 January: Up until the end of 1987, Abu Dhabi Municipality had built 2035 kms of new roads at a cost of 141 million dirhams.

31 January: Sheikh Maktoum bin Rashid

Al Maktoum donated 1 million sterling pounds to the Gulf Studies Centre at the University of Exeter in the UK.

2 February: ADFAED agreed to loan 36.6 million dirhams to Tunisia to assist in a rural development project.

6 February: Sheikh Zayed received a letter from the Indian Prime Minister, Rajiv Gandhi, regarding developments in the Gulf. The UAE and India confirmed their support for Security Council Resolution 598 to end the Iraq-Iran war.

An agreement was signed with the American Geology Board to undertake a study of groundwater sources in Abu Dhabi.

8 February: In Lahore, Sheikh Zayed held discussions with the Pakistani President, Zia Al Haq. Zayed confirmed that it was up to Washington to play a neutral role to solve the Palestinian problem.

13 February: During the previous seven years, the Government of Dubai constructed 4139 public housing units.

14 February: The First Lady, Sheikha Fatima bint Mubarak, and Princess Alia of Jordan discussed the women's movement in the country and the efforts of Abu Dhabi Women's Association to improve work-opportunities for women.

The National Drilling Company decided to co-operate with the American Geology Board to set up a centre to record groundwater levels at hourly intervals in the emirate of Abu Dhabi.

16 February: Abu Dhabi Executive Council decided to make Al-Bateen Airport a private airport to receive guests of the State.

19 February: Sheikh Zayed directed that all necessary measures be taken to deal with the floods throughout the country,

the result of the heaviest rainfall in 25 years. Branch committees were formed to aid those who suffered damage to property, farms and dwellings from flood waters.

22 February: The Council of Ministers allocated 67 million dirhams for setting-up a complex of higher technical colleges in the country to fill the nation's need for technologically-trained national manpower.

23 February: Sheikh Zayed, for the fifth day in succession, personally supervised operations for repairing Al-Shuwaib dam and expanding Wadi al-Madam so that agricultural projects could benefit from the rainwater. The dam will contain 20 million cubic metres of water. The five dams which were constructed by the Ministry of Agriculture in the Northern Emirates contain more than 9 million cubic metres of rainwater.

24 February: Directions were given by the President to distribute 2000 new farms to citizens in the Western Region.

26 February: Sheikh Zayed inspected the natural grazing area in the Al-Samha region and gave thanks to Allah for the blessings He had bestowed on the country.

27 February: The UAE ratified the international protocol for prevention of violence at civil airports.

A contract was signed to operate the first ice skating rink in Zayed Sports City.

There were 20 dairy producing units in the country with a daily production of 260 litres in which 220 million dirhams was invested.

29 February: Sheikh Zayed received a letter from the Iraqi President, Saddam Hussein, regarding developments in the Iraq-Iran war.

Sheikh Zayed also reviewed regional developments with the Commander of the US Forces in the Gulf who was visiting the Emirates.

Sheikh Zayed, meeting with the Federal National Council, stressed that the citizen was his sole concern and that the Council's responsibility was to safeguard the UAE's achievements. He said that there were those who wished to meddle in the UAE's affairs and that the UAE neither excuses nor pressurises them but will not relinquish its rights.

6 March: Dubai Municipality began to build 400 houses for non-commissioned officers and members of the police force in Dubai.

8 March: Sheikh Maktoum bin Rashid Al Maktoum and the Pakistani President, Mohammad Zia Al Haq, opened the Emirates Golf Club and the sports facilities attached to it.

Dubai Municipality allocated 13 million dirhams to carry-out 22 afforestation projects and plant shrubbery on roads outside the city.

9 March: Sheikh Zayed and the Pakistani President, Mohammad Zia Al Haq, discussed developments in the Iraq-Iran war.

10 March: Sheikh Zayed, during his reception of a delegation from the UK House of Commons, said it was necessary to end the Iraq-Iran war. He further stated that the United States must take a neutral stance and work seriously and fairly for peace.

In 1987, there were 622 industrial establishments in the country with production valued at 6.423 billion dirhams.

11 March: Last year local liquidity in the country was 64.4 billion dirhams, an average growth of 11.2 per cent over 1986.

13 March: Sheikh Zayed arrived in Cairo to an historic popular and official reception. He confirmed that relations between the UAE and Egypt were model relations between two brotherly peoples and stressed that the UAE's goal was to strengthen Arab solidarity and use its energies for the Arab good.

14 March: Sheikh Zayed held discussions with the Egyptian President, Mohammad Hosni Mubarak. They studied the Arab situation and developments in the Palestinian issue. Zayed stressed 'that our hearts, our wealth, and souls support the *intifada.*'

15 March: A trade agreement was signed in Cairo between the UAE and Egypt along with an agreement for strengthening co-operation in labour and social fields.

16 March: Sheikh Zayed, meeting with UAE officers and students in Cairo, stated that the UAE's wealth was visible in a concrete way everywhere in the nation. The wealth, he said, was for the people and not to be held in banks and strong boxes. Sheikh Zayed also issued directions to ADFAED to concentrate on financing food projects in Egypt.

18 March: The Department of Electricity and Water set up the region's largest desalination plant on the island of Sir Bani Yas. Operating on the reverse pumping system, it had a production capacity of 1 million gallons per day.

The UAE National Football Team won in the second division in the Gulf Championship Games.

19 March: Sheikh Zayed, prior to his return to the UAE, attended, along with President Hosni Mubarak, a demonstration of rockets manufactured in Egypt. He said that Egypt should be proud of its military production.

21 March: At Zayed Military College graduation ceremonies, Sheikh Zayed said that the people of the UAE should be following the ways of their fathers on whose structures modern society was created. Sheikh Khalifa bin Zayed Al Nahyan stressed that the UAE's Armed Forces were constantly working toward reinforcing the Federation.

22 March: At the graduation ceremonies for the new batch of students from the UAE University, Sheikh Zayed stressed that the University marked a new phase of readiness to meet the challenges of the twenty-first century.

26 March: In 1987, revenue in the UAE rose to 72.124 billion dirhams, an increase of 13.2 per cent over 1986.

29 March: More than 12 billion dirhams was spent on road networks, bridges and tunnels in Abu Dhabi emirate during the previous ten years.

4 April: Sheikh Khalifa opened an exhibition of Egyptian defence equipment in Abu Dhabi. He stressed that the Arab nation was the largest importer of weapons and that it was not possible to build the Armed Forces while depending on others.

5 April: Sheikh Zayed and the Members of the Supreme Council of the Federation attended graduation ceremonies for the new batch of pilots and a demonstration of live ammunition at Al-Dhafra airbase. He stressed that what he had witnessed should be a source of pride for every citizen. Sheikh Khalifa said that the fruits which had been planted as far as personal development was concerned had resulted

in an excellent harvest for the nation and humanity.

Sheikh Zayed donated 10 million dollars to support the Palestinian *intifada* in the occupied territories.

6 April: At his own expense, Sheikh Khalifa bin Zayed Al Nahyan ordered the construction of a new stadium for the Emirates Club in Ras al-Khaimah.

8 April: Sheikh Zayed visited the Amiri Guard Headquarters in Al-Manhal Palace on the occasion of the passage of 20 years since the Guard was formed. He said that the nation asked of them that they stay on the path of righteousness and that the happy person is the one who follows the example of his grandfathers and forebears with the nobility, honour and self-confidence which Allah granted them.

Sheikh Zayed also attended the annual row and sail boat competition. The prize money for this competition amounted to 3.6 million dirhams.

9 April: ADNOC celebrated the graduation of 110 students from the Training and Development Centre. Over the previous ten years 641 student had graduated from the Centre.

12 April: Sheikh Zayed donated half a million dirhams to improve facilities at the Handicapped Centre in Abu Dhabi.

The Federal National Council recommended the death penalty for drug peddlers and promoters.

An agreement was signed for a 5 million dollar loan to the Bank of the Soviet Union for Foreign Economic Affairs. Participants in the loan were the Abu Dhabi Commercial Bank (65 per cent) and the Abu Dhabi Investment Company (35 per cent).

16 April: The UAE condemned the criminal assassination of the Palestinian leader, Khalil Al-Wazir (Abu Jihad) in Tunis.

17 April: The UAE University, at the direction of Sheikh Khalifa bin Zayed Al Nahyan, examined the feasibility of establishing a unit for research into the captive breeding of hawks and bustards.

19 April: The UAE condemned the attack on one of the oil platforms in the Mubarak field, describing it as without justification and against international norms and customs as well as good neighbourliness. The Ministry of Health purchased ultrasonic equipment for dissolving kidney stones at a cost of 5.4 million dirhams.

24 April: Sheikh Zayed and Sheikh Maktoum bin Rashid Al Maktoum studied various aspects of the national development plan.

30 April: Iran's Deputy Foreign Affairs Minister, Mohammad Besharati, began a visit to UAE, placing emphasis on the good relations between Iran and the Federation. Following the visit, Sheikh Zayed bin Sultan Al Nahyan called for better regional co-operation to protect the Gulf. Sheikh Zayed also called for increased UAE military strengthening 'because there is no room for weak states in world of power.'

3 May: Abu Dhabi Executive Council approved the 1988 development programme for the emirate which amounted to 3.8 billion dirhams.

5 May: Sheikh Zayed, in continuing his efforts towards Arab reconciliation, despatched letters to the Egyptian President, Mohammad Hosni Mubarak, and the Libyan President, Muammar Al Gadhafi, in which he stressed his deep concern for achieving solidarity and mutual assistance in faith and his conviction that Arab power lay in unity.

8 May: Sheikh Zayed was briefed by Rashid Abdulla on the results of the Foreign Minister's visit to Cairo and Tripoli in the context of Zayed's efforts to achieve unity in the Arab rank and file.

10 May: Sheikh Zayed awarded the Sincere Service Decoration to Hamouda bin Ali, Minister of State for Internal Affairs. He awarded similar decorations to high ranking police officers in appreciation of their services to their country in establishing security and stability for all citizens.

13 May: In 1987, the Department of Electricity and Water completed 35 projects at a cost of 83.1 million dirhams. There were 18 government factories valued at 14.699 billion dirhams in the Emirates.

18 May: Sheikh Zayed welcomed the resumption of relations between Morocco and Algeria. He stressed in cables to King Hassan and the Algerian President the importance of this step in reinforcing Arab solidarity.

According to the annual report of the Central Bank, in 1987, GDP rose to 88 billion dirhams, decreasing the federal budget deficit by 21.6 per cent in this new economic phase for the UAE.

22 May: Sheikh Zayed received an invitation from the Algerian President to attend an emergency Arab summit meeting to be held in Algeria in June.

The Council of Ministers allocated 10 million dirhams to purchase radar for the Aviation Information Centre in order to control the UAE's skies.

Fifty eight industrial projects were financed by the Industrial Bank during the previous five years at a total cost of 230 million dirhams.

24 May: Abu Dhabi Executive Council approved a plan to construct an airport on the island of Delma.

25 May: Sheikh Zayed, during his reception of an envoy from the President of the United States, demanded that a firm position be adopted with regard to the Palestinian cause. He said that right and justice must prevail before there can be a solution to the problem. He also stated that if everyone does not obtain their rights, then the Arab countries must confront the enemy.

The Ministry of Economy and Commerce issued a decree forbidding the importation of nylon fishing nets in order to protect the country's fishery resources.

29 May: Sheikh Zayed and the President of Djibouti, Hassan Gouled, who was visiting the country, discussed Arab and international questions which were of mutual concern, as well as Arab-African co-operation.

30 May: Dubai Municipality allocated 46 million dirhams for the design of an automatic roadside shrubbery irrigation project and increased planting of such shrubbery.

1 June: The Department of Electricity and Water commenced operations at the 1 million gallon per day desalination plant on Sir Bani Yas.

2 June: Sheikh Zayed during his meeting in Abu Dhabi with the Palestinian leader, Yasser Arafat, stressed that the *intifada* was the major element in the Palestinian people's struggle. He confirmed his complete concern and support for the continuation of the *intifada* until its aims and ambitions had been realized.

5 June: Sheikh Zayed issued a law establishing the 11-member Supreme Petroleum Council (SPC) under the chairmanship of Sheikh Khalifa bin Zayed Al Nahyan. He issued other decrees which included the appointment of Sheikh Sultan bin Zayed Al Nahyan as President of the Office of Works and Sheikh Said bin Zayed to the Office of Planning, in addition to the appointment of the Board of Directors for the Abu Dhabi Investment Organization.

6 June: Sheikh Zayed led the UAE delegation to the emergency Arab Summit in Algeria. He stressed upon his arrival in Algeria that unity was the only solution to the dilemma facing the Arab nation. He said that the UAE was concerned to end Arab differences and it placed all its capabilities at the disposal of Arab solidarity.

The UAE and Egypt signed an agreement for a 75 million dollar loan from ADFAED for the reclamation of 65,000 feddans of land in Egypt.

7 June: Sheikh Zayed held lengthy meetings and wide-ranging consultations with Arab heads of state at the Summit in Algeria. He asked the Summit to exert all its energies for the liberation of Palestine. He confirmed that the people of the UAE would remain supporters of their brothers in the *intifada* and said that 'the riches within the family surprised the enemy'.

Abu Dhabi Executive Council approved the payment of compensation amounting to 1.5 billion dirhams to 817 families whose homes were affected as a result of development projects.

13 June: Sheikh Zayed received a report from Dr Mana Said Al Otaiba on the OPEC ministers meeting which was held in Geneva. The UAE re-emphasized its concern for the stability of the oil market and its support for OPEC. It also demanded an increase in its production quota.

At the meeting of OPEC ministers, the UAE announced its approval of a six-month extension for the agreement which was arrived at in December 1987, with reservations regarding its share of production.

15 June: The Central Bank requested that banks operating in the country increase their percentage of local employees to 10 per cent of their total workforce.

16 June: Dr Mana Said Al Otaiba announced that the UAE had rejected the 946,000 barrels-per-day quota allotted to it by OPEC. He said that the fair rate should be 1.5 million barrels per day.

17 June: Sheikh Humaid bin Rashid Al Nuaimi issued an Amiri decree establishing the Ajman University College for Science and Technology.

26 June: Sheikh Dr Sultan bin Mohammad Al Qassimi issued a number of decrees in support of the co-operative movement in the emirate of Sharjah: he ordered the payment of compensation to the Sharjah Societies and the Kalba and Khor Fakkan Co-operative Societies and he exempted all of them from the payment of electricity and water bills, municipal registration fees and the fees required by the Chamber of Commerce.

Dubai Municipality endorsed its comprehensive development plan carrying it up to the year 2005 A.D., which included projects costing 11.093 billion dirhams.

27 June: Sheikh Khalifa bin Zayed Al Nahyan approved the payment of 14 million dirhams for school equipment, including laboratories, teaching aids, scientific and research equipment and school libraries, for the next academic year.

The Ministry of Health began a study for setting-up the first centre for dental medicine in Al-Ain at a cost of 6 million dirhams.

ADNOC signed an 1.8 million dollars agreement to distribute its products in Malaysia, which covered the annual export of 3000 tons of various types of oil to the Malaysian markets.

28 June: Sheikh Zayed visited the UAE exhibit at the Casablanca International Exhibition and he expressed his pleasure at the positive level of participation. He stressed the importance of visual impact, saying that 'seeing is believing and better than hearing'.

1 July: Sixty five thousand hectares of land were newly planted in trees and shrubbery in Medinat Zayed, Liwa, Ghiyathi and Al-Wathba, and 261 date palms were planted and given to citizens.

2 July: ADNOC decided to open distribution centres in Sharjah, Ajman, Umm al-Qaiwain, Ras al-Khaimah and Fujairah.

4 July: Sheikh Zayed and Sheikh Khalifa bin Zayed Al Nahyan donated 200,000 dollars as the first payment to Al-Ahli Hospital in Hebron.

The UAE expressed its deep sorrow at the terrible accident which led to the shooting down of an Iranian passenger aeroplane by an American naval unit during engagements in the waters of the Gulf.

The UAE took first place in the second Junior Arab Chess Championship which was held in Baghdad.

5 July: Abu Dhabi Municipality inaugurated a 14.978 million dirham agricultural advice system in Delma and Al-Marfa: they were also offering farmers the necessary agricultural supplies and equipment free of charge by way of encouragement.

12 July: Dubai Municipality completed 22 major local road projects at a cost of 379 million dirhams.

18 July: Sheikh Zayed sent a letter to both the Iraqi President, Saddam Hussein and the Iranian President, Ali Khamenei, after Iran accepted the Security Council resolution calling for an end to the war. The UAE announced that the resolution was an important point of departure for the establishment of security and stability in the region.

Sheikh Khalifa bin Zayed Al Nahyan presided over the first meeting of the Supreme Petroleum Council.

More than 72 million dirhams worth of goods were purchased from the Arab Pharmaceuticals Company in Ras al-Khaimah during the current year.

19 July: Sheikh Zayed sent cables to the Iraqi President, Saddam Hussein, and the Iranian President, Ali Khamenei, in which he stressed that the pinnacle of bravery lay in deciding on mediation in difficult times. He said that he hoped that the response to the Iranian move would be decisive in establishing and supporting security in the region.

28 July: Sheikh Zayed, meeting with OPEC Secretary General Dr Subroto, stressed the UAE's concern to support the organizations' decisions and maintain stability in the oil market.

30 July: Sheikh Zayed received a letter from the Iranian President, Ali Khamenei. Zayed expressed his satisfaction because Iran was tending toward peace in her wish to stop the bloodletting. He said that he hoped that this trend in the progress of events would establish a just and complete peace between two Muslim neighbours.

Dubai Municipality completed arrangements for implementing Sheikh Hamdan bin Rashid Al Maktoum's directives for the establishment of the first statistics and information centre to cover the various activities of Dubai emirate.

31 July: Sheikh Zayed ordered the setting-up of a factory for canning and preserving vegetables in Al-Marfa to utilize the considerable excess in agricultural production.

1 August: Sheikh Zayed received a letter from the Iraqi President, Saddam Hussein, confirming that a comprehensive and fair peace would put out the flames of war forever and that the end of the war between Iraq and Iran would unite the energies and promote the well-being of the people in both countries.

August 6: Sheikh Zayed and the Members of the Supreme Council of the Federation received crowds of well-wishers on the occasion of the twenty-second anniversary of Zayed's accession to power in the emirate of Abu Dhabi.

9 August: Sheikh Zayed began an inspection trip in the Western Region to observe the conditions of the citizens and how their needs were being met, as well as to monitor development projects. He ordered the setting-up of a tourist hotel in Al-Marfa and the construction of new houses and farms.

Two agreements valued at 49 million dirhams were signed for constructing the third phase of the Al-Shuwaib dam project.

14 August: It was decided to supply Abu Dhabi Civil Defence with modern equipment costing 61 million dirhams.

19 August: Sheikh Zayed concluded his tour of the Western Region by inspecting the modern road network, the new farms and soil reclamation operations in Mahadhir Liwa. His tour fell within the scope of his concern for development in remote areas. He also monitored agricultural and afforestation projects, as well as the date palm gardens on the island of Sir Bani Yas and in Ghiyathi.

23 August: A test operation on the 15 million dirham Ajman water desalination plant began. The project was funded by Sheikh Khalifa bin Zayed Al Nahyan.

26 August: Sheikh Zayed sent a letter to the UN Security Council in which he stressed the UAE's support for the efforts being made to free Namibia and to grant it independence so that its people could enjoy their full rights.

29 August: The Council of Ministers approved a draft federal law for establishing and organizing a complex of higher technical colleges in the country. It was decided to set up a fully-equipped centre for vascular surgery at Al-Jazira Hospital in Abu Dhabi.

6 September: The Executive Council allocated 210 million dirhams to upgrade the Abu Dhabi - Al-Ain highway into an expressway.

7 September: First Lady Sheikha Fatima bint Mubarak contributed 6 million dirhams to the building of the Al Hassan the Second mosque in Casablanca.

8 September: Sheikh Zayed and the Palestinian leader, Yasser Arafat, studied developments in the Palestinian issue. Zayed confirmed the UAE's support for any Palestinian decision which would restore the rights of the Palestinian people.

13 September: Abu Dhabi Executive Council approved the devising of a comprehensive 20-year master develop-

ment plan for the emirate and city of Abu Dhabi.

16 September: Sheikh Khalifa bin Zayed Al Nahyan, in a statement on the occasion of the twenty-eighth anniversary of the founding of OPEC, called for the exertion of all possible efforts to prevent a fall in the price of oil. He stressed that the UAE's oil policy was based on the directives of its leader and stressed the necessity of maintaining and protecting OPEC.

23 September: Sheikh Hamdan bin Mohammad Al Nahyan, during his official visit to Egypt, signed an agreement for setting-up a supreme joint committee between the UAE and Egypt. The joint communiqué, which was broadcast at the end of the visit, called for continuing Iran-Iraq negotiations to achieve a fair and comprehensive peace.

25 September: Sheikh Zayed received a letter from the Iraqi President, Saddam Hussein, which was delivered to him by the Minister of Information and Culture, Latif Jassim. Zayed stressed during the meeting that the UAE hoped that true peace could be arrived at between Iraq and Iran. He said that he was watching for the return of the spirit of friendship and Islamic brotherhood between two neighbours and peace for the region as a whole.

11 October: Abu Dhabi Executive Council, implementing Sheikh Zayed's directives, allocated 549 million dirhams for constructing new roads and bridges, planting 100,000 hectares, drilling wells and setting-up water distribution networks in remote areas.

12 October: Sheikh Hamdan bin Zayed Al Nahyan, in remarks made to the Jordanian newspaper, *Al-Dustour*, stressed that the end of the Iran-Iraq war was a point of positive change which would help efforts being made to solve the Palestinian situation.

First Lady Sheikha Fatima bint Mubarak, Chairwoman of the UAE Women's Federation, paid an official visit to Egypt to form an Arab Women's Union. She also donated 1 million dirhams to the 'Right to Life' society.

17 October: Sheikh Zayed launched an initiative to promote immediate action to save Lebanon. He said that it was a duty which the UAE could not leave to its brothers who had been involved in internecine strife for many years.

22 October: The UAE, following the President's initiative, called for the convening of an emergency Arab Summit to save Lebanon. It called on the Arab League to take immediate steps to begin the necessary contacts in this respect.

24 October: Sheikh Khalifa bin Zayed Al Nahyan attended graduation ceremonies for the first batch of graduates from the Police College in Abu Dhabi. He stressed that stability was a blessing in the country and a guarantee of productivity and progress .

25 October: Sheikh Zayed received a letter from the Syrian President, Hafez Al Asad, which was delivered by the Minister of Foreign Affairs, Farouk Al Shara. Zayed stressed that the UAE always called for Arabs to speak with one voice and to unite their ranks, as well as to continue meetings between brothers. He also stressed his concern that the entire Arab nation be blessed with security and stability. He said that the deteriorating situation made it incumbent on him to call for the convening of an emergency Arab summit meeting.

26 October: Sheikh Zayed received the Secretary General of the Arab League, Al Shadhili Al Kulaibi. Zayed requested that the Secretary General contact Arab leaders regarding the convening of an emergency Arab summit meeting to deal with the situation in Lebanon.

31 October: The Council of Ministers approved the 1988 federal budget. Expenditure was estimated at 14.3 billion dirhams whilst the estimate for revenue was 12.4 billion dirhams, leaving a deficit of 1.8 billion dirhams.

12 November: Sheikh Zayed, who was on a private visit to Morocco, and King Hassan of Morocco studied the situation in Lebanon. Zayed stressed that the future of Lebanon could not be separated from the future of the Arab nation as a whole. He called for an end to the heedless stance of the Arabs with regard to a part of the Arab body.

15 November: The UAE announced its support for the decision of the Palestine National Council which announced the setting-up of an independent Palestinian state. The President of the Federation confirmed that he would have no reservations about supporting the decisions of the Council in international circles.

In accordance with the directives of Sheikh Khalifa bin Zayed Al Nahyan, a comprehensive survey of the water sources of the emirate of Abu Dhabi, to be undertaken by remote sensory satellites, commenced.

16 November: The UAE announced its official recognition of the independent State of Palestine with its capital in Jerusalem.

17 November: Some 5.777 billion dirhams were paid to citizens who were affected by developmental planning in Abu Dhabi from 1967 to the end of 1987. This money was distributed to 15,903 local families.

22 November: Sheikh Khalifa bin Zayed Al Nahyan, in a meeting with high ranking leaders and officers of the UAE Armed Forces, announced that a new batch of Crotale air defence missiles had arrived. He also announced that the Navy had obtained modern missile launches supplied with advanced electronic equipment. He confirmed that the UAE nationals in the Armed Forces had shown their ability to work with the most modern weapons technology.

24 November: In Rabat, Sheikh Zayed met with the Secretary General of the Arab League, Al Shadhili Al Kulaibi, who briefed him on the League's efforts to convene an emergency Arab summit meeting to study the situation in Lebanon.

26 November: Sheikh Zayed and the Arab ambassadors in Rabat examined developments in the Arab and international arena.

28 November: The UAE expressed its great regret at the US Government's refusal of an entry visa for the Palestinian leader, Yasser Arafat, to enable him to attend the meetings of General Assembly of the United Nations regarding the Palestinian question.

29 November: Sheikh Zayed in a letter to the United Nations on the occasion of Palestine Solidarity Day stressed that the promised day of liberation for Palestine was near. He stated that the UAE would continue its support and assistance to the Palestinian people until it could celebrate with them in Jerusalem following its liberation.

1 December: UAE GDP rose from 6.5 billion dirhams in 1972 to 87 billion dirhams in 1987.

2 December: Sheikh Zayed received the Members of the Supreme Council of the Federation and groups of well-wishers on the occasion of the seventeenth national day.

5 December: Sheikh Zayed opened the eleventh Arab Conference of Girl Scouts in the Abu Dhabi Cultural Complex. He also opened the exhibition mounted as a part of the conference and he stressed that the UAE welcomed all Arab gatherings at any level in order to deepen Arab ties and bonds.

7 December: Abu Dhabi Executive Council discussed a plan to support national factories and to protect local products.

8 December: Sheikh Sultan bin Zayed Al Nahyan and His Majesty, Sultan Qaboos bin Said, who was visiting the country, inspected the Al-Dhafra Air Base where they saw the workings of the Hawk missile system with various radar equipment.

9 December: In Abu Dhabi, Sheikh Zayed held discussions with His Majesty Qaboos bin Said regarding the Arab and international situation and efforts being made to achieve Arab solidarity and support a joint Arab position.

11 December: The Supreme Petroleum Council, presided over by Sheikh Khalifa bin Zayed Al Nahyan, discussed the situation in the oil market, stressing the importance of solidarity and abiding by the latest OPEC decisions.

Emirates champion, Mohammad Khalifa Al Qubaisi, won the fourth World Bowling Championship held in Mexico.

12 December: Sheikh Zayed, during his

discussions with the Palestinian leader, Yasser Arafat, in Abu Dhabi, stressed that it was vital to continue and intensify the *intifada*. He said that the UAE supported any decision taken by the Palestinian people to achieve their aims and ambitions. He further stated that Arab countries were asking that the *intifada* be supported until the legitimate rights of the Palestinian people were restored.

Sheikh Hamdan bin Zayed Al Nahyan, during a meeting with the American Ambassador to the UAE, called on America to open a dialogue with the Palestinian Liberation Organization, to recognize the legitimate rights of the Palestinian people and to actively participate in convening an international Middle East peace conference.

14 December: Giant transport aeroplanes left Abu Dhabi International Airport carrying the first consignment of medical aid and food to the stricken people of the Republic of Armenia in the Soviet Union, who were suffering from the effects of a tragic earthquake. The President of the Federation had ordered that these shipments be sent immediately in the name of the Government and the people of the United Arab Emirates.

18 December: Sheikh Zayed, meeting with Salah Khalaf (Abu Ayyad), stressed that the UAE supported the Palestinian political movement. He hoped that the *intifada* would continue and increase in intensity until the Palestinian people obtained their rights.

Graduation ceremonies took place for graduates from the first investigative officers training course which was organized by the Criminal Sciences Institute of the Abu Dhabi Directorate General of Police. The course also dealt with the gathering of criminal evidence.

19 December: Sheikh Zayed led the UAE delegation to the meetings of the ninth summit of GCC leaders in Bahrain. He stressed upon his arrival in Manama that the strengthening of co-operation between the States of the region would have a beneficial effect on the Arab and Islamic world.

Sheikh Surour bin Mohammad Al Nahyan opened Al-Bateen Airport in Abu Dhabi which was acquired in 1975. As of December 1988, there were 31 aircraft operating from this airport with 45 pilots and 72 engineers.

20 December: Sheikh Zayed held lengthy talks and consultations with the GCC leaders on the collective work required to support the future of the GCC.

21 December: Sheikh Zayed met with UAE students who were studying in Bahrain. He told them that the UAE's goal was to foster the educated individual. He said that whatever the State spends on knowledge and education is paid back in benefit to the country.

26 December: Sheikh Zayed received the UAE and World Bowling Champion, Mohammad Khalifa Al Qubaisi, and expressed his happiness and pride in his victory.

Nineteen Eighty Nine

2 January: The General Establishment for Industry, implementing the Supreme Petroleum Council's decree, signed a memorandum of understanding to purchase the Abu Dhabi Plastic Pipes Company owned by the Abu Dhabi National Petroleum Company and the Japanese See Eito.

5 January: Sheikh Zayed and the Palestinian leader, Yasser Arafat, laid the foundation stone for the Embassy of Palestine in the UAE. Zayed stressed that the UAE would remain true to its national obligations in regard to the Palestinian people and their just cause.

Sheikh Zayed, during his reception for the British Foreign Secretary, Geoffrey Howe, stressed the necessity of exerting international and regional efforts to bring permanent peace to the Gulf and Middle East regions.

8 January: Sheikh Zayed presided over a meeting of the Supreme Council of the Federation in which he declared that the citizens' happiness and well-being was at the forefront of the Council's priorities. He said that the UAE would continue its progress, making every effort to reach its goals. 'We praise Allah for the accomplishments which have been achieved for the nation and people and for raising our country's banner to wave alongside the flags of all the countries of the world'.

12 January: As of September 1988, cash liquidity amounted to 64.4 billion dirhams, an increase of 10 per cent over 1987.

16 January: Sheikh Khalifa bin Zayed Al Nahyan and the Venezuelan President, Carlos Perez, reviewed the oil market. Sheikh Khalifa stressed that the UAE was still looking for a fair share of oil production and that it was obligated by OPEC accords because of its concern for complete co-operation with the organization and maintainance of unity.

22 January: Sheikh Zayed issued a decree appointing Said Ghobash as Minister of State for Supreme Council Affairs.

Hamad Al Midfa opened the first Islamic medicine and herbal therapy centre in the country.

23 January: Sheikh Zayed, who was visiting Pakistan, held talks with the Prime Minister, Benazir Bhutto, on Islamic and international affairs. Zayed called for more intense efforts to make peace between Iraq and Iran.

26 January: Sheikh Zayed sent a letter to the Custodian of the Two Holy Mosques, King Fahad bin Abdulaziz, regarding the situation in the oil market. He stressed the UAE's commitment to the OPEC accord with regard to production quotas and his great concern to abide by this agreement. Dubai Municipality decided to construct a new bridge parallel to the Maktoum bridge at a cost of 110 million dirhams.

27 January: Sheikh Zayed, during his reception for UAE students studying in Pakistan, called on them to bear their responsibilities capably and worthily. He told them: 'You must become prepared for the tasks which service to the nation will require of you.'

29 January: Sheikh Mohammad bin Rashid Al Maktoum opened the first Dubai International Air Show.

31 January: Sheikh Khalifa bin Zayed Al Nahyan, during his meeting with the Municipalities Council, stressed the right of every citizen to have free access to services. He said that citizens interests was the first axis of concern in the comprehensive development plan and that devoted efforts to serve the citizen was a huge responsibility for all concerned organizations.

2 February: Sheikh Khalifa issued a directive that all facilities be made available to the Ministry of Agriculture and Fish Resources, including aircraft, equipment and insecticides, to ensure the success of operations to contain the invasion of desert locusts and to protect the country's plant resources.

3 February: Aircraft from the Abu Dhabi Aviation Company participated in operations to eradicate desert locusts in the Western Region.

In 1988, exports from the emirate of Fujairah were worth 347 million dirhams, while exports from the national factories in Fujairah amounted to 103 million dirhams.

5 February: ADFAED loaned 40 million dirhams to the Sultanate of Oman to finance the second stage of the Al-Ghabra electricity and water distillation plant expansion project.

In 1988, customs duties collected by Abu Dhabi Customs Department amounted to 33.6 million dirhams.

6 February: Sheikh Zayed, in remarks made at the opening of the eighth session of the Islamic Chambers of Commerce meeting in Abu Dhabi, called for the establishment of an Islamic economic common market. He stressed that the world was moving toward economic consolidation and that small entities would not be viable in the future.

7 February: UAE's foreign trade in 1988 was estimated at around 39 billion dirhams, of which 30.4 billion was imports and 8.5 billion exports and re-exports.

10 February: Sheikh Zayed, at his meeting in Pakistan with UAE female students, stressed that the State required its students to work hard for the country's future. He said that the UAE had accomplished much on its path toward development and progress.

11 February: Sheikh Dr Sultan bin Mohammad Al Qassimi opened the UAE Television Station in Sharjah and asked for co-ordination between responsible officials in the UAE television industry. He also called for the airing of suitable programmes.

Sheikh Zayed's brother Sheikh Shakbut bin Sultan Al Nahyan died at the age of 83. Sheikh Shakbut ruled Abu Dhabi from

1928 until 1966 when he abdicated in favour of Sheikh Zayed. All banks and Government offices in Abu Dhabi and Dubai were closed for three days of mourning.

17 February: The UAE welcomed the establishment of the Arab Co-operation Council which included Egypt, Iraq, Yemen and Jordan. It also welcomed the Arab Maghrib Federation. It stressed that both of these historic events strengthened Arab solidarity and would help eventually to achieve complete unity.

Some 70 thousand hectares in Abu Dhabi had been planted with 14 million trees and shrubs.

19 February: Sheikh Khalifa bin Zayed Al Nahyan issued directives that 30 million dirhams be allocated to establish a new radiation cancer treatment centre at Tawam Hospital in Al-Ain.

20 February: The Council of Ministers endorsed a comprehensive plan to eradicate illiteracy which would be in operation until the end of 1997.

22 February: Sheikh Zayed, during discussions with the Egyptian President, Mohammad Hosni Mubarak, who was visiting the country, stressed that the UAE supported any trend which would lead toward national glory. The discussions covered a general summary of current Arab affairs and a complete evaluation of the future of co-ordinated Arab action.

Sheikh Zayed called on the Lebanese to take on the responsibility for the integrity of their country and territory and the re-building of its institutions. He called on them to forget their differences and rise above their grievances to save their country and restore its unity.

The Federal National Council welcomed the establishment of the Arab Co-operation Council and the Arab Maghrib Federation and congratulated the Arab nation on these great achievements.

28 February: Sheikh Zayed, during his reception for the members of the UAE Students Union, stressed that the Federation would never stint the nation and the citizen. He said that the UAE welcomed all ideas and opinions and hoped that its children would shoulder their national responsibilities now and in the future.

1 March: Sheikh Zayed and the Palestinian leader, Yasser Arafat, discussed efforts which were being pursued to achieve peace in the Middle East. He expressed the hope that the United States was serious about achieving a comprehensive and just settlement.

7 March: In 1987, Central Bank overall profit was 719 million dirhams, in comparison to 977.8 million dirhams in 1986.

9 March: The total amount of commercial exchange in the emirate of Sharjah during the period 1983-1987 was more than 124.5 billion dirhams.

10 March: Sheikh Zayed and the Members of the Supreme Council of the Federation attended the finals in the pure-bred Arab camel races in Dubai.

11 March: Sheikh Zayed issued a decree accepting the resignation of Abdulla Al Mazroui as Minister of Justice. Another decree merged the Ministry of Justice and the Ministry of Islamic Affairs and Awqaf, appointing Sheikh Mohammad bin Ahmed bin Hassan Al Khazraji as the Minister of Justice, Islamic Affairs and Awqaf.

13 March: Sheikh Mohammad bin Butti opened the new 37 million dirham Central Bus Station in Abu Dhabi.

14 March: Sheikh Zayed received Prince Charles, the Crown Prince of Britain, and his wife, the Princess Diana.

The UAE and the USA signed an agreement creating a three-year quota for UAE textile exports to the US.

15 March: Sheikh Surour bin Mohammad Al Nahyan, in the presence of Prince Charles, the Crown Prince of Britain, opened the new 63 million dirham Abu Dhabi Chamber of Commerce and Industry building.

16 March: Sheikh Maktoum bin Rashid Al Maktoum and Prince Charles discussed the status of relations between the two countries and ways of developing them.

The Ministry of Health, following the directives of Sheikh Khalifa bin Zayed Al Nahyan, decided to instigate a complete examination of all handicapped children in the country during the fortcoming visit by a specialized American medical team.

18 March: Sheikh Zayed received a letter from Chinese President Yang Chang, containing an official invitation for him to visit China, which was delivered by the Vice President of the Chinese State Council, Tian Yuan. Discussions held between the UAE, under the leadership of Sheikh Hamdan bin Mohammad Al Nahyan, and the Peoples Republic of China, under Tian Yuan, centred on the development of economic and commercial co-operation and mutual investment between the two countries.

Sheikh Maktoum issued decrees setting-up the Jebel Ali Port Authority and forming the Al-Rawabi Milk Company with an allowed capital of 35 million dirhams.

19 March: Sheikh Zayed received the President of Austria, Dr Kurt Waldheim, who arrived in the country on an official visit. Zayed stressed that people were always looking for a high standard of living under the banner of stability, and that the duty of leaders was to work intensively to achieve security and stability for their countries and to solve international differences by way of dialogue and mutual understanding.

20 March: Sheikh Zayed held a closed meeting with the Austrian President, Dr Kurt Waldheim, during which they agreed on the need for international persuasion to achieve progress in the negotiations between Iraq and Iran and help them reach a lasting peace. Zayed stressed the necessity of holding an international peace conference on the Middle East, as soon as possible, and he requested that the American administration understand the necessity of taking serious and sincere action to shoulder their responsibilities in achieving peace in the region.

21 March: The Executive Council debated the detailed practical study of the electricity and water requirements of the emirate of Abu Dhabi until the year 2000.

22 March: Sheikh Zayed paid a surprise visit to Al-Mafraq Hospital in Abu Dhabi where he ordered that the highest standard of health care be provided for citizens and residents. He said that a good relationship between the patients and those who sacrifice themselves in caring for them was the basis of successful treatment.

25 March: Sheikh Zayed ordered that urgent aid be sent to the Yemen Democratic Republic to repair the damage done by floods.

Sheikh Zayed, during his reception for members of the US Senate, stressed that: 'Peace is the biggest blessing which can be bestowed on a people.' He also said that: 'The strengthening of confidence between America and the Arab countries will come by way of the efforts made to establish peace in the Middle East.'

26 March: Al-Jazira Hospital received 30 high technology intensive care and kidney units.

27 March: During 1988, the Abu Dhabi Hotel Company made a clear profit of 57.5 million dirhams in comparison to 39.6 million dirhams in 1987, an increase of 45 per cent.

28 March: Sheikh Zayed and the Members of the Supreme Council of the Federation attended graduation ceremonies for a new batch of pilots from the Al-Dhafra Air Base. The President stressed that: 'The manliness of our sons which we have witnessed reassured us and gave us confidence in them'.

Sheikh Dr Sultan bin Mohammad Al Qassimi issued a decree setting-up a benevolent society in Sharjah.

General Postal Authority profits in 1988 amounted to 28 million dirhams.

31 March: Sheikh Zayed, the Members of the Supreme Council and the delegations from the GCC countries attended the finals of the annual pure-bred Arab camel races.

1 April: Sheikh Zayed and Sheikh Rashid bin Saeed Al Maktoum attended the opening of Dubai Police College.

2 April: Sheikh Zayed and the Members of the Supreme Council attended the sixth graduation ceremonies at Zayed Military College in Al-Ain.

3 April: Sheikh Saqr bin Mohammad Al Qassimi opened the Asylum for the Aged in the Shaam Region of Ras al-Khaimah. He stressed the necessity of caring for the elderly in appreciation of their past and the role they played in building society.

4 April: Sheikh Zayed and the Members of the Supreme Council attended graduation ceremonies for the eighth batch of students from the UAE University.

9 April: Sheikh Zayed received a letter from Venezuelan President, Carlos Perez, containing a proposal to convene a summit of the leaders of OPEC nations in order to study the international oil situation.

10 April: The Ministry of Communications signed a 1.4 million dirham agreement with the International Radio Services Company to manage aviation meteorological information in the country. A ship loaded with aid left Port Zayed on its way to Aden to help those stricken by floods in the Democratic Republic of Yemen.

11 April: Sheikh Zayed called for Arab intervention to stop the bloodshed in Lebanon. He called for the Arab leaders to shoulder their responsibilities in respect to Lebanon and its people and to take serious action in accordance with the Arab League Charter to restore normality to Lebanon.

The first unit for dissolving kidney stones through the use of ultrasonic waves, located at Al-Mafraq Hospital, began to treat patients.

There were 10.7 million date-palm trees in the country.

16 April: The UAE had signed 34 bilateral air transport agreements between 1982 and 1989.

20 April: As of 1988 there were 250,000 telephone lines in the country, an increase of 150,000 lines over 1987. Over 555 million minutes were spent in local telephone calls and 176 million minutes in long distance calls.

25 April: In 1988 there were 244 large factories in Sharjah with a capital of 836 million dirhams of which 465 million dirhams represented investments by nationals.

26 April: Etisalat earned 838 million dirhams in profits in 1988 and the value of the shares owned by shareholders in the establishment rose to 2033 million dirhams.

29 April: Sheikh Zayed received the Yugoslavian Foreign Minister who briefed him on the agenda for the next Non-aligned Summit. Zayed called for an historic summit which would deal with actual events through which the world was living.

30 April: An experiment carried-out in the physics laboratory of the UAE University College of Sciences achieved cold atomic fission in a similar manner to the experiment conducted in the American University of Utah.

The Department of Social Services and Commercial Buildings stated that during last year 24,204 housing units were completed at a cost of 606 billion dirhams. Abu Dhabi Chamber of Commerce and Industry stated that Abu Dhabi's Gross Domestic Product rose in 1987 to 50.1 billion dirhams, in comparison to 41.4 billion dirhams in 1986.

1 May: Sheikh Zayed received a letter from King Hassan of Morocco regarding the Non-aligned Summit.

An official from the Ministry of Foreign Affairs stated that the UAE welcomed the invitation to an emergency Arab summit conference to deal with matters confronting the Arab nation and to draw the Arab world closer together. The same source confirmed the necessity of convening a regularly scheduled Arab summit because of ongoing events which required such meetings.

10 May: Sheikh Maktoum issued a decree establishing a council for promoting tourism and trade in the emirate of Dubai.

11 May: The combined budget of the commercial banks in the country during last February rose to 114.8 billion dirhams, an increase of 6.9 per cent over the previous year

13 May: Sheikh Khalifa bin Zayed Al Nahyan, arriving in Cairo to an official and popular reception, discussed Arab affairs and bilateral relations with Egyptian President Mohammad Hosni Mubarak.

14 May: Sheikh Zayed, during a meeting with the British Foreign Secretary, William Waldegrave, demanded that Europe play an effective role in solving the Lebanese and Palestinian problems. He praised the Palestinian *intifada* and stressed the necessity of supporting and accelerating it.

Sheikh Khalifa bin Zayed Al Nahyan, during his visit to the heavy arms and rocket factory in Egypt, stated that the Arabs must industrialize arms manufacturing as a national duty, a duty which required the concentrated energies of all the Arab nations. He stressed that the UAE was proud of the international standard of the Egyptian war industries.

15 May: Sheikh Zayed held discussions with Sudanese President Ahmed Al Mirghani, who was paying his first visit to the UAE. Zayed expressed the necessity of taking serious action to solve the Palestinian problem and save Lebanon. He said that the UAE hoped to adopt constructive steps at the emergency Arab Summit which would serve the goals of the Arab nation and strengthen its unity. Sheikh Khalifa, visiting the Bilbis Air Base in Egypt, said that the UAE was proud of the number of UAE pilots who were receiving their training at this excellent base.

16 May: Sheikh Zayed and Naif Hawatameh, the Secretary General of the Democratic Front for the Liberation of Palestine, discussed the progress of the *intifada* in the occupied territories.

Sheikh Dr Sultan bin Mohammad Al Qassimi inspected the agricultural project on saline ground in Khor Kalba. He stressed that the project would increase cultivable land and help control the environment.

17 May: Sheikh Mohammad bin Rashid Al Maktoum received a delegation from GCC municipalities. He emphasized that the President of the Federation was the person who deserved the most credit for the comprehensive renaissance in the Federation and the expansion of planted areas and green belts in the desert.

21 May: Sheikh Zayed said that the emergency Arab Summit, scheduled to begin on the following day in Morocco, should remain open until a solution to Arab problems had been reached. He said that the tragedy in Lebanon was the work of Arabs, but that which befell Palestine was the result of actions by the enemy supported by the great powers.

Agricultural products exported by the State in 1988 amounted to 7400 tons of vegetables, fruit and agricultural seedlings.

22 May: Sheikh Zayed led the UAE delegation to the meetings of the emergency Arab Summit in Casablanca.

He confirmed on his arrival that Arab solidarity was the only solution to the Arab predicament. He said that the Summit would be more positive if there was an agreement among the leaders to keep the meeting open until there was a settlement of all Arab differences.

The Executive Council approved the creation of the first golf club in Abu Dhabi, and it approved the establishment of a hospital in the emirate of Ajman at a cost of 30 million dirhams.

24 May: Sheikh Nahyan bin Mubarak Al Nahyan signed a scientific co-operation agreement between the UAE University and the American University of Beirut.

26 May: The emergency Arab Summit ended its deliberations in Casablanca and, in response to the call of the President of the Federation, it was decided to leave the Summit open until Lebanon had been saved. Zayed praised the Summit and said that it confirmed the Arab leadership's concern for effective Arab action.

28 May: Based on the President's directives, it was decided to create a new medical district to supervise health installations and curative services in the Western Region.

29 May: The Ministry of Health began the fourth stage of the national project to establish the first integrated computer network for health information and patient affairs in co-operation with the National Computer Centre.

31 May: Sheikh Zayed, in an interview with the Egyptian newspaper, *Al-Ahram*, said that the emergency Arab Summit in Casablanca was a frank and reconciliatory meeting and that the return of Egypt to the Arab ranks confounded those who were anxious to divide the nation.

1 June: First Lady Sheikha Fatima bint Mubarak, Chairwoman of the UAE Women's Federation, arrived in Amman on an official visit to Jordan at the invitation of Queen Noor.

During 1988, the major non-oil economic sectors of the country registered a clear growth, with production reaching more than 58.038 billion dirhams.

3 June: Sheikh Zayed issued a decree appointing Hazza bin Zayed Al Nahyan as Deputy Director of the UAE's security services. Another decree altering the structural organization of the service allocated two deputies to the Director.

Queen Noor, on behalf of King Hussein, awarded the highest Jordanian medal to First Lady, Sheikha Fatima bint Mubarak, who had donated 4 million dirhams to Jordanian charities.

There were 200 furniture factories in the country satisfying 20 per cent of local demand.

9 June: Sheikh Maktoum bin Rashid Al Maktoum issued a decree forbidding the use of live ammunition in firearms during celebrations in Dubai.

11 June: Sheikh Zayed issued a law increasing the capital of the Abu Dhabi National Oil Tanker Company from 4 million to 500 million dirhams.

There were 55 installations in operation in the petrochemical industry in the emirate of Sharjah with investments of 327 million dirhams, of which 162.5 million represented investments by nationals. Production was valued at 283.5 million dirhams.

15 June: Sheikh Saqr bin Mohammad Al Qassimi opened the Ras al-Khaimah Ice Skating Rink.

17 June: Sheikh Khalifa bin Zayed Al Nahyan welcomed the holding of the Arab Parliamentary Union conference in Abu Dhabi on 19 June. He said that the Arab Parliamentary Union was a national establishment and a basic pillar of joint Arab action.

The rate of production of the desalination plants on Sir Bani Yas and Delma islands had reached 3 million gallons daily.

18 June: In Rabat, Sheikh Zayed and King Hassan of Morocco discussed developments in Lebanon. Zayed confirmed that the situation in Lebanon was very sad and that it is was not possible to remain silent about it. He said that if the parties in Lebanon could not succeed in solving the problems with the support of Arab leaders, how could the Arab nation hope for salvation?

19 June: Sheikh Khalifa bin Zayed Al Nahyan opened the Arab Parliamentary Union conference in the new Federal National Council building. He said in his inaugural address that their complete faith lay in the principle of consultation and that they were firmly holding on to it. He also said that the return of Egypt to her natural place was one of the prominent results of the Casablanca Summit, and that it was hoped that the efforts of the tripartite Arab committee on Lebanon would be crowned with success.

20 June: Sheikh Zayed, receiving the heads of the Arab parliamentary delegations, stressed that the confident ruler who is content with himself entrusts his sons and brothers, with his assistance, to arrive at a better solution. He said that the positive results of the Casablanca Summit would reflect on joint Arab action in the future and would bring about effective solidarity.

In 1988, Dubai's external trade rose to 5.8 million tons and was valued at 29.2 billion dirhams.

21 June: The Council of Ministers approved the draft law imposing a federal tax of 50 per cent on tobacco and tobacco derivative imports.

Dubai Municipality began a project to set-up seven axial truck weighing stations, each costing 27 million dirhams, along the roads inside and outside the city.

Sharjah's foreign trade during the previous six years (1983-88) amounted to more than 17.329 billion dirhams.

Investments in the emirate of Dubai in transitional industries in 1987 amounted to 954 million dirhams, in comparison to 54 million dirhams in 1970.

26 June: In 1988, UAE commodity imports amounted to 31.563 billion dirhams, an increase of 18 per cent over 1987.

28 June: The Council of Ministers allocated the necessary funds for expanding the teaching of computers. Computer instruction will now begin in the first year in 50 per cent of the secondary schools in the country.

Total actual expenditure in the Federation's investment programmes between 1982 and 1988 was 4.644 billion dirhams.

1 July: Sheikh Zayed met with the Members of the Supreme Council of the Federation in Falaj al-Mualla in Umm al-Qaiwain at the beginning of an inspection tour of the Northern Emirates. He met a delegation of citizens from the Eastern Region and satisfied himself that they were being provided with a decent standard of living.

3 July: Sheikh Zayed visited the headquarters of the Badr Battalion where he inspected the headquarters building and operations room.

There were 840 establishments with a total capital of 3.2 billion dirhams operating in the field of building and construction in the emirate of Sharjah .

4 July: Sheikh Zayed visited the emirate of Sharjah within the scope of his visits with the citizens of the Northern Emirates. He commented: 'We are concerned to provide a better life for all citizens throughout the Federation.' He also said: 'My visits to the Northern Emirates will continue and be repeated so I can be aware of the needs of the citizens and inspect development efforts.'

5 July: Sheikh Zayed continued his inspection tour and his meetings with citizens in the Northern Emirates. He remarked: 'All that I and my fellow Rulers have attended to will, with the help of Allah, be achieved.' He also said: 'I myself have studied and given my attention to all the means of building and progress in the country and it gives me the right to feel pride when it all has been achieved in a short period of time ... We have firmly planted our feet on the way to building the country...and the greatest feat we have achieved is the development of the individual to whom we give priority.'

In 1988, capital invested in trade involving food products in the emirate of Sharjah amounted to 579.9 million dirhams.

8 July: Sheikh Zayed, in remarks made to the Emirates New Agency, called for a new style in work practices in ministries and public institutions. He called for all officials to undertake their duties in such a way as to be an example to their subordinates with whose work they must keep in close touch. He said that a minister or official must understand all work requirements and be familiar with affairs on a minute to minute basis so as to be prepared for any inquiry from a higher authority. He stressed that the industrious would receive recognition for their work but that careless officials did not deserve their position.

10 July: Sheikh Zayed, beginning an inspection tour of the Western Region, asked for a redoubling of efforts in order to achieve a good life and well being for citizens. He said that the coming years would demand untiring work and self-denial from ministers and officials.

12 July: Sheikh Zayed ordered that the island of Sir Bani Yas be opened for tourism.

14 July: Dubai Municipality began construction on the first multi-storey parking lot in Deira at a cost of 30 million dirhams.

15 July: Sheikh Zayed ordered the construction of 400 housing units for citizens in the Northern Emirates. He made this order in the wake of a field tour which he undertook to become acquainted with the needs of the citizens.

ADFAED from the time it was established until the middle of 1988 granted nearly 8 billion dirhams in loans.

18 July: Sheikh Zayed arrived in London on an official visit to Britain. He announced that the UAE was continually aware of Britain's role as a participant in bringing peace to the Middle East and the Gulf.

19 July: Sheikh Zayed held discussions with the British Prime Minister, Margaret Thatcher, on Arab and international political developments. He called on Britain to redouble its efforts to bring a settlement to the Arab Israeli conflict.

The nuclear medicine unit at Al-Jazira Hospital in Abu Dhabi was supplied with diagnostic laser equipment.

21 July: Sheikh Zayed, concluding his official visit to Britain, began a private visit. The combined number of berths in Port Rashid and Port Jebel Ali was 104: goods in Dubai's ports last year amounted to 6 million tons with a value of 29 billion dirhams.

24 July: Sheikh Hamdan bin Zayed Al Nahyan opened the Emirates Week at the International Exhibition in Casablanca.

30 July: Sheikh Zayed sent a letter to the Non-aligned Summit in which he stressed that it was their duty to struggle to put an end to the racist regimes in Palestine and Pretoria. He asked that the gap between developing and developed countries be narrowed through the establishment of fair international economic relations. He stressed that the elimination of weapons of mass destruction was a basic demand in order to achieve harmony and peace among all peoples of the world.

31 July: The Council of Ministers decreed that the sixth of August every year would be an official holiday for the country's federal ministries and institutions.

6 August: Sheikh Zayed received the Members of the Supreme Council of the Federation and groups of well-wishers on the occasion of the twenty-first anniversary of his accession.

9 August: Sheikh Mohammad bin Rashid Al Maktoum ordered the establishment of an Air Navigation College in Dubai to train UAE nationals in the field of aviation.

12 August: Sheikh Zayed, during his reception for the US representative to the United Nations, Thomas Pickering, stressed that the international community blamed the United States for its stand on the Palestinian issue and that the US must intercede to save the dispossessed Palestinian people. He said that the position in the Gulf had become like a smouldering fire under ashes.

14 August: Sheikh Zayed issued a federal decree permitting citizens of GCC countries to undertake wholesale and retail commercial activity in the UAE.

15 August: The Council of Ministers, in an emergency meeting which was convened to deal with the situation in Lebanon, called for an end to the blood letting in Lebanon. It urged all countries to help find a speedy solution to the crisis.

The Federal Civil Service published a list of 450 names of national graduates (male and female), the first batch of graduates to be appointed to the federal ministries and boards in accordance with Sheikh Zayed's directives.

16 August: Sheikh Ahmed bin Hamid announced that the UAE would issue an invitation to Arab countries to organize a co-ordinated information campaign in the United States and Europe to challenge the upsurge of repressive Israeli actions in the occupied Palestinian territories.

19 August: Sheikh Zayed concluded his four-day inspection tour of the Western Region which included Al-Muzairah and Mahadhir Liwa where he met with citizens to get acquainted with their requirements and to inspect the new public housing sites, as well as agricultural and development projects.

There were 22 schools in the Western Region with a student body of 4728, compared with only one school in 1968.

It was decided to establish a number of important medical projects in the Western Region in accordance with Sheikh Zayed's directives. Among the projects was the huge specialist hospital in Medinat Zayed, a highly advanced clinic in Al-Marfa and a mobile unit for traffic accidents on the Abu Dhabi - Sila highway.

20 August: Dubai Municipality began to plant 500 hectares with shrubs and trees in the Badii Al-Mutawa and Medinat Ghiyathi regions.

The first batch of 66 national graduates, both male and female, took up their positions at federal institutions.

22 August: Sheikh Zayed, in remarks made to *Al-Hawadith* magazine, stressed that Arabs themselves would intervene to stop the blood-letting in Lebanon before there was any foreign intervention. He said that the they would never permit the fall of Lebanon because it would effectively mean the fall of the Arabs and the Arab League. He stressed that brotherly dialogue and not information campaigns would solve the differences in the Arab world.

Over 271.2 billion dirhams was invested in projects in both the public and private sectors over the ten years from 1976-85.

23 August: The Works Department prepared a five year plan to establish 85 new schools in the emirate of Abu Dhabi at a cost of 870 million dirhams. Some 65 million dirhams had been allocated to maintain and refurbish existing schools.

27 August: The Council of Ministers endorsed the Charter of Honour put forth by the UAE at the meeting of the Arab Information Ministers in Tunis.

31 August: There were 21 public gardens and playgrounds covering 1.5 million sq. m, along with 2.6 million palm trees, in Abu Dhabi and the Western Region,

1 September: Eight fibreglass factories in the Federation produced 2600 tons annually. In 1988, the factories exported 1500 tons of products to American and Arab markets.

2 September: One hundred and ninety companies registered in the Jebel Ali Free

Zone had invested a total of 600 million dollars.

14 September: The combined budgets of the UAE's commercial banks at the end of last March stood at 113.04 billion dirhams.

19 September: Sheikh Ahmed bin Hamid signed a contract with Etisalat under the terms of which it will operate and maintain the Ministry's microwave networks.

Sheikh Hamdan bin Zayed Al Nahyan signed the Privileges and Immunities Protocol for the conversion programme for Arab trade, the capital for which amounted to 500 million dollars. He stressed the UAE's concern in supporting collective Arab action in the best interests of the Arab nation and its well being.

The value of agricultural production in Sharjah rose, in 1987, to 373 million dirhams and planted areas increased to 87,000 dunams.

21 September: Sheikh Zayed conferred in Rabat with King Hassan on the Lebanese situation. He stressed that the crisis in Lebanon was a true tragedy for Arabs.

Abu Dhabi Municipality began the numbering and naming of streets and buildings in the city of Abu Dhabi and commenced a study to examine the feasibility of establishing the first date factory in Abu Dhabi.

2 October: Sheikh Khalifa bin Zayed Al Nahyan issued a law setting-up the National Avian Research Centre with the aim of breeding bustards and hawks and protecting birds in the region from extinction.

3 October: Eighty-six establishments working in the building materials sector imported 1400 million dirhams worth of materials annually. There were 342 contracting companies in the country with a total investment of 1598 million dirhams.

5 October: Sheikh Khalifa bin Zayed Al Nahyan approved the building and financing of 125 new commercial buildings for citizens in Abu Dhabi and Al-Ain at a cost of 640 million dirhams.

11 October: Sheikh Hamdan bin Mohammad Al Nahyan, Deputy Prime Minister, passed away.

19 October: Sheikh Zayed sent cables to the Egyptian President, Mohammad Hosni Mubarak, and the Libyan President, Muammar Al Gadhafi, in which he expressed his happiness at the meeting between the two Presidents. He said that such Arab meetings were harbingers of good tidings on the road to closer ties and that the meeting between the two Presidents was the beginning of a new stage in Arab co-operation.

21 October: Sheikh Mohammad bin Butti opened the Foodstuffs and Environment Control Centre in Abu Dhabi's Municipality building. Built at a cost of 50 million dirhams, the Centre contained four major laboratories.

25 October: Sheikh Zayed held discussions in the Presidential Diwan with His Majesty Sultan Qaboos bin Said who was on an official visit to the Federation. The discussion covered efforts to achieve Arab solidarity, developments in the region and settlement of the dispute between Iran and Iraq.

Sheikh Zayed sent a letter concerning the situation in the region to Iraqi President Saddam Hussein, which was delivered by Sultan bin Zayed Al Nahyan.

26 October: His Majesty Sultan Qaboos bin Said arrived in Dubai at the beginning of a tour of the Northern Emirates, during which he visited Sharjah, Ras al-Khaimah,

Ajman, Umm al-Qaiwain and Fujairah. He met with the Rulers and donated 1 million dollars to Ajman University College for Science and Technology.

28 October: The Emirates National Football Team made the finals in the World Cup competition in Italy.

30 October: Sheikh Zayed received the National Football Team and told the players that: 'their honourable accomplishment was a source of pride and self-respect for every Arab.'

1 November: Sheikh Dr Sultan bin Mohammad Al Qassimi and Sheikh Maktoum bin Rashid Al Maktoum met the National Football Team. Sheikh Sultan told them that their accomplishment was an honourable one and that it confirmed the ability of the UAE's sons to make achievements for their country.

4 November: Sheikh Zayed sent a letter to the Conference of the Federation of Arab Chambers of Commerce and Industry being convened in Abu Dhabi. In it he stressed that the Arab nation had the potential to form a comprehensive economic block which could provide an honourable future. He said that the common Arab market marked the true beginning of Arab unity.

6 October: Sheikh Zayed received the members of the National Football Team and gave each player half a million dirhams to build a house. He told them that the people of the Emirates expected a great deal from them and that he hoped that they would continue to achieve and that the youth of the Emirates would always be successful in all international gatherings.

In accordance with the directives of Sheikh Khalifa bin Zayed, it was decided to set up the first centre for the handicapped in the city of Al-Ain.

The UAE welcomed the election of Renee Muawad as President of Lebanon and expressed the hope that this would be a step on the path to bringing Lebanon back to its natural state.

14 November: Sheikh Khalifa bin Zayed Al Nahyan issued a decree setting-up a committee to take over the granting of interest- and cost-free loans to citizens for building houses for themselves and their families. The value of the loans was limited to a maximum of 900,000 dirhams to be repaid in equal monthly installments over a period of 25 years. Fifteen per cent of the loan would be deducted in the event of the borrower paying it off in one payment.

20 November: Sheikh Khalifa bin Zayed Al Nahyan attended graduation ceremonies for the new batch of students from the Police College in Abu Dhabi.

21 November: The UAE and Egypt signed an agreement for the reclamation of 155,000 feddans of land at a cost of 1.055 billion dirhams.

The Executive Council approved the allocation of 100 million dirhams to develop and expand the Police College and to bring electricity services to 600 farms in all parts of the emirate of Abu Dhabi.

22 November: The UAE agreed to the convening of an emergency meeting of the Arab League, at the request of Palestine, to deal with developments in the Palestinian question.

23 November: The UAE expressed its great sorrow and sadness at the assassination of the Lebanese President, Renee Muawad, and it called for all Lebanese to be patient and maintain the unity and independence of Lebanon.

27 November: The Council of Ministers endorsed the draft federal budget for 1989. Expenditure was estimated at 14.6 billion dirhams and projected revenues were 12.8 billion dirhams, leaving a deficit of 1.8 billion dirhams.

29 November: Sheikh Zayed renewed his letter to the Palestinian Rights Committee of the United Nations in solidarity with the struggling Palestinian people, offering full assistance to them in their honourable struggle for their freedom and independence. He said that the *intifada* would continue to be a source of pride and esteem.

30 November: Sheikh Khalifa bin Zayed Al Nahyan issued an order for the construction of a new building for the Supreme Council for Youth and Sports in Zayed Sports City.

1 December: Sheikh Zayed, in a speech delivered on the occasion of the eighteenth National Day, said that day by day the Federation was becoming increasingly stable and its progress was worthy of pride. He also stated that the UAE had been able to earn the respect of the nations of the world and establish its place among them even though the international and regional climate had been stormy.

2 December: Sheikh Zayed, the Members of the Federal Supreme Council and guests of the country witnessed an excellent military parade by air, land and sea forces, along with units from other armed forces, on the occasion of the eighteenth National Day. The President declared that: 'Today we are more determined than ever to protect our national destiny.'

3 December: Sheikh Zayed ordered the construction of 500 housing units for citizens in the Northern Emirates to be supplied with all utilities and services.

4 December: Sheikh Zayed held an international press conference in which he stressed that the people were sacrificing themselves for the Federation while defending its future. He praised the committed and sincere role of Sheikh Rashid bin Saeed Al Maktoum in building the Federation. He also called for an amendment to the Charter of the Arab League to allow for a majority vote, explaining that consensus cannot be achieved except in one family.

7 December: Sheikh Dr Sultan bin Mohammad Al Qassimi had undertaken the sponsorship of 100 Palestinian families and he suggested a project of joint social responsibility for families in the occupied territories.

11 December: Sheikh Zayed and the Sudanese President, Omar Bashir, who was on an official visit to the country after he took power in Sudan, discussed bilateral relations and joint Arab action in the coming stage.

12 December: Sheikh Zayed and the Members of the Supreme Council of the Federation, accompanied by the Sudanese President, Omar Al Bashir, attended graduation ceremonies for the new batch of students from the Aviation College. Sheikh Zayed expressed his pride in the high standard of the Air Force and air defence.

18 December: Sheikh Zayed led the UAE delegation to the GCC Summit Conference in Muscat. On his arrival, Zayed said that the Council had made great and important achievements which called for optimism. He further stated that the meetings between brothers would always be a meeting of goodwill which would strengthen co-operation and integration.

19 December: The Muscat Summit honoured 60 prominent Gulf personalities. Sheikh Zayed said that the bestowal of honours was an incentive to other citizens to contribute more to the building and development of the country.

23 December: Sheikh Zayed received the Chinese President, Yang Shangkun, who was paying his first official visit to the UAE. He stressed the UAE's eagerness to develop its relations with China in appreciation of its stand on Arab issues.

24 December: Sheikh Zayed held official discussions with President Yang Shangkun, revolving around efforts being made to solve the Palestinian problem and the exertion of mediation attempts to bring about a just and permanent peace between Iraq and Iran. Mutual relations were also discussed. Zayed called on China to propose more initiatives to bring peace and stability to the world.

30 December: Sheikh Zayed received the heads of delegations to the international conference on salt-water irrigation techniques, being held in Al-Ain. The conference was attended by more than 120 scientists from 35 countries and 50 universities. Zayed said: 'The earth and agriculture are the basis of everything in the life of Man and we are seeking research on non-traditional sources of water for use in the development of the agricultural resources of the country.'

31 December: Sheikh Surour bin Mohammad Al Nahyan opened the first stage of the giant desalination and electricity project at Al-Taweelah. This stage will produce 250 megawatts of electricity.

Nineteen Ninety

2 January: The Al-Ain Department of Agriculture and Animal Production began equipping 600 new farms for distribution to citizens.

10 January: Sheikh Zayed inspected work sites in Al-Dhafra district, along with the afforestation and agricultural projects in Baynunah.

Mediation undertaken by the UAE between India and Morocco brought a successful conclusion to the crisis which erupted between them regarding the export of phosphates and phosphoric acid from Morocco to India.

11 January: Sheikh Zayed, receiving GCC Ministers of Labour and Social Affairs who were jolding their tenth meeting in Abu Dhabi, stressed that responsibility was a trust given to leaders and officials on behalf of the nation. He said that the UAE had become a prominent State which had benefited from the experience of the Arab and Islamic worlds.

14 January: Dubai Municipality began developing 38 kms of the Dubai - Abu Dhabi highway at a cost of 147.5 million dirhams.

15 January: Etisalat decided to initiate several new projects in the Western Region, including car telephone towers and a complete network of fibre optic cables to completely cover the region with advanced services.

16 January: Sheikh Maktoum bin Rashid Al Maktoum issued a decree setting-up an independent legal authority, the Rashid Port Authority, to assume responsibility for the port.

23 January: In 1989, Abu Dhabi Municipality completed the planting of 900 hectares with trees and shrubs in the Western Region.

26 January: During 1989, the Federation's Gross Domestic Product rose to 106 billion dirhams.

28 January: Sheikh Khalifa bin Zayed Al Nahyan, during his reception of Usama Faqih, Director General and Chairman of the Board of Administration of the Arab Currency Fund, welcomed the Fund's choice of Abu Dhabi as the permanent headquarters for the Arab Establishment for Financing Commerce which the Arab countries agreed to set-up with a capital of 500 million dirhams, within the framework of the Arab Currency Fund

29 January: Sheikh Khalifa bin Zayed Al Nahyan, in a meeting of the Supreme

Petroleum Council, stressed that factors in the oil market required that any emergency phenomenon must be contained. He said that the phase through which the market was passing demanded continual planning and delicate study, along with mutual co-operation, to realize the national interests.

30 January: Abu Dhabi Executive Council approved the construction of two bridges on the Al-Ain - Dubai highway at a cost of 37.5 million dirhams. It also approved the establishment of a new factory for canning vegetables and fruits in the Western Region.

5 February: Sheikh Zayed during his reception of John Kelly, the American Assistant Secretary of State, asked that a just and comprehensive solution to the Palestininian problem be found. He also stressed the necessity of putting an end to the shedding of Palestinian blood and an end to Israeli terrorism.

The Council of Ministers issued a statement expressing their great worry over the continuing immigration of Soviet Jews to the occupied territories as part of the Israeli settlement policy.

9 February: Sheikh Zayed and the Members of the Supreme Council of the Federation attended the finals of the annual pure-bred Arab camel races in Al-Ain.

Abu Dhabi Municipality began implementing new agricultural projects, including the setting-up of 21 new public parks both in and outside Abu Dhabi city, covering an area of 1.5 million square metres.

11 February: Sheikh Zayed arrived in Aswan to participate in the international ceremonies for reviving the ancient library of Alexandria.

12 February: At the historic international ceremonies which were mounted in Aswan, Sheikh Zayed donated 20 million dollars to restore the ancient library of Alexandria. He said that the library would become a pinnacle of international culture and a beacon for the continuation of Egyptian civilization.

The Council of Ministers approved the allocation of 20 million dirhams to set-up a meteorological centre for the Federation's Civil Aviation Department.

15 February: Sheikh Zayed, during his visit to Egypt, inspected developmental, agricultural and animal husbandry projects in the Eastern Governate to which the UAE had made financial contributions. At his own expense, Zayed ordered the construction of housing in two villages for the farmers of the region.

17 February: Sheikh Zayed arrived in Manama from Egypt on an official visit to Bahrain.

18 February: Sheikh Zayed and His Highness Essa bin Salman Al Khalifa, the Amir of Bahrain, discussed current Arab affairs. He said that the UAE was concentrating on the continuation of meetings between brothers to study mutual and regional affairs.

Sheikh Sultan bin Zayed Al Nahyan opened the new session of the National Consultative Council. His opening speech said that the Council had played a positive role in looking after the interests of citizens and in achieving their ambitions.

19 February: The Council of Ministers approved the introduction of e-mail exchanges between the ministries.

24 February: Abu Dhabi Municipality began a number of road-improvement projects in the city of Abu Dhabi at a cost of 1.172 billion dirhams.

25 February: Sheikh Khalifa bin Zayed Al Nahyan, in remarks made to the Kuwaiti newspaper, *Al-Siyasa*, said that individual development in the UAE was the greatest accomplishment of the federal experiment and that this remained the present and future goal. He said that the UAE now occupied a respected position in the Gulf, in Arab affairs and internationally, thanks to the dedication of its President. He also said that the national economy was again flourishing with the beginnings of a new round of growth and stability.

26 February: The General Postal Authority began construction of the new 25 million dirham Central Mail Office in Abu Dhabi.

28 February: The Industrial Bank decided to change the percentage requirement for national participation in the projects which it financed from 70 per cent to 51 per cent.

1 March: Sheikh Zayed and King Hussein of Jordan, who was on an official visit to the UAE, discussed ways of supporting Arab action in confronting the challenges to which the Arab nation was exposed. They confirmed the importance of removing all misunderstandings and reviewing developments in the Arab world, including the Palestinian *intifada,* as well as efforts being made to find a fair solution to the Palestinian problem.

2 March: Sheikh Zayed and the Members of the Supreme Council attended the finals in the pure-bred Arab camel races in Dubai.

4 March: Sheikh Zayed, in the presence of its Members, opened the new session of the Supreme Council of the Federation. He stated that the Federation had demonstrated its ability to achieve and provide progress and stability in the country. He said that the people of the UAE, through the Federation, had overcome many obstacles and were able to evaluate the federal experiment as a guiding principle in the Arab nation.

5 March: The Council of Ministers approved the Central Bank decree changing the requirement for national ownership in projects financed by the bank from 70 per cent to 51 per cent.

6 March: Sheikh Surour bin Mohammad Al Nahyan opened the international conference on joint insurance markets which was being held in Abu Dhabi.

7 March: Discussions between Sheikh Zayed and the Tanzanian President, Hassan Mueni, who was visiting the country, centred on the necessity of renewing efforts to bring peace between Iraq and Iran, solidarity with the Palestinian people to help them obtain their fundamental rights, supporting Arab African co-operation and African national freedom movements and resistance to any form of racial discrimination.

10 March: Sheikh Zayed opened the thirty-first session of the permanent Council of the Islamic Solidarity Fund which was convened in the Cultural Complex in Abu Dhabi. It was announced that Zayed had donated 5 million dollars to the Fund to support its benevolent activities.

In 1989, the trade balance achieved a huge surplus: exports were valued at 58.3 billion dirhams and the value of imports was 37.1 billion dirhams.

11 March: Sheikh Zayed, during his reception for Dr Hamid Al Gabid, the Secretary General of the Islamic Conference Organization, called for the formation of an Islamic security council and assembly. He said that it was obligatory that the Book of Allah be the

Muslim constitution and he pointed out that Muslim weakness arose because of division and dispersal as well as the lack of mutual assistance.

14 March: Sheikh Zayed received the Ministers of Finance and the Governors of Arab Funds who were holding their meetings in Abu Dhabi. He said during his meetings that the leaders must not act without consultation with their people and that it is not enough to live in happiness while brothers were miserable. He said that if Arabs helped each other their strength would be even greater than that of the great powers.

The Executive Council approved the undertaking of an intensive study of the water and electricity requirements of the emirate of Abu Dhabi until the year 2010 A.D.

18 March: The Ministry of Health began implementing plans to set-up the first complete micro-surgery unit in Al-Mafraq Hospital.

20 March: Sheikh Zayed and the Members of the Supreme Council of the Federation attended the fifteenth graduation exercises of university-level officer candidates and the seventh graduation exercises mounted by graduates from Zayed Military College in Al-Ain.

26 March: The Council of Ministers approved UAE membership in the International Maritime Organization.

7 April: Work began on the construction of the new Dubai Courts complex at a cost of 557 million dirhams.

10 April: Sheikh Zayed held a meeting on the island of Sir Bani Yas with the Yemeni President, Ali Abdulla Saleh. The President of the Federation stated during the talks that it was necessary to adopt a unified Arab position toward the challenges which face the Arab nation.

The Executive Council decided to set-up ten mobile electrical power generating units, at a cost of 60 million dirhams, to face emergencies in the distant regions of Abu Dhabi emirate.

Sheikh Saeed bin Tahnoun opened the giant 225 million dirhams Al-Shuwaib Dam which can hold 31 million cubic metres of water.

13 April: The UAE confirmed its complete support for Iraq against the tendentious and organized campaigns to which it had been exposed by Zionist circles and for all steps which Iraq would take to defend its people and the security of its territory from attacks because it possessed advanced weapons.

History was made at the Khalifa bin Zayed Laboratory for Genetic Engineering Research by the first ever succesful artificial insemination of camels.

18 April: Sheikh Khalifa bin Zayed Al Nahyan presided over a meeting of ADFAED's Board of Administration, during which the Fund's plan for the coming phase was endorsed. Sheikh Khalifa ordered that special attention to be given to the poorest nations in the Third World.

Sheikh Saeed bin Tahnoun signed an agreement to supply the Al-Hili Amusement Park in Al-Ain with new games at a cost of 12 million dirhams.

23 April: The Executive Council decided to pay 611 million dirhams as compensation to the owners of buildings which were demolished in Abu Dhabi for public development purposes. The total sum paid for compensation to nationals from 1967 until 1990 was more than 80 million dirhams.

30 April: Sheikh Zayed ordered the establishment of a comprehensive psychiatric medicine complex in Abu Dhabi.

In 1989, non-oil sector trading in the Federation amounted to around 49.7 billion dirhams, in comparison to 42.7 billion dirhams in 1988.

1 May: Sheikh Zayed and the Members of the Supreme Council of the Federation attended graduation ceremonies for the ninth batch of students from the UAE University. Zayed said that the university had given the country its most important resource for development and for firmly establishing the foundations of its renaissance.

2 May: Sheikh Zayed, following discussions with the Palestinian leader, Yasser Arafat, stressed that it was necessary to convene an Arab summit as soon as possible, in view of the Arab nation's need for this meeting in the present circumstances.

Sheikh Khalifa bin Zayed Al Nahyan, during discussions with Prince Sidi Mohammad, the Moroccan Crown Prince, who arrived in the country on an official visit, discussed excellent brotherly relations between the two countries and ways of continuing to support co-operation between them.

3 May: Sheikh Zayed met with Prince Sidi Mohammad in Al-Maqam Palace in Al-Ain where they discussed the excellent brotherly relations between the two countries and ways of strengthening mutual co-operation in various fields. Sheikh Khalifa bin Zayed Al Nahyan and Prince Sidi Mohammad inspected the Al-Dhafra Air Base with its permanent exhibition of aircraft and a squadron of Mirage 2000 aeroplanes.

The UAE decided to cut immediately its crude oil production by 200,000 barrels a day, in accordance with the agreement which was reached by OPEC in its meeting in Geneva whereby the UAE quota was reduced from 2.1 million barrels a day to 1.9 million barrels.

7 May: Sheikh Zayed arrived in Beijing at the beginning of tour which included the People's Republic of China, Japan and Indonesia.

9 May: Sheikh Zayed held official discussions with the President of the Chinese State Council, Li Peng, at which the two leaders discussed the development of relations between the two countries and an increase in exchange contacts and visits. The Chinese President praised Zayed's domestic accomplishments and his wise foreign policy.

10 May: Sheikh Zayed met the Secretary of the Chinese Party, Jijang Zimin, to whom he expressed satisfaction at the development of relations between the two countries. He said that the UAE was keen to strengthen friendly relations with China on the basis of mutual respect. Zayed visited the Great Wall of China.

12 May: Sheikh Zayed presented a complete printing press to the Chinese Islamic Society and 30,000 books to the Arabic Language College of the Foreign Language University in Beijing.

13 May: Sheikh Zayed began his official visit to Japan. He stressed the importance of supporting relations between the two countries and said that Japan was the UAE's premier commercial partner.

14 May: Official welcoming ceremonies led by Emperor Akahito were held in Tokyo for Sheikh Zayed. The Japanese Government's reception surpassed the usual traditional ceremonies and the

Japanese Emperor accompanied the President of the Federation on a visit to the Japanese garden at the Emperor's palace for the first time in the history of Japan. Zayed stressed that the UAE was eager to support relations with Japan in order to serve common goals.

Sheikh Zayed held a news conference in Tokyo in which he stressed that the UAE had sacrificed a great deal in order to maintain the unity of the OPEC organization and the stability of the oil market. He said that there was no intention to hold auctions or speculations either in production quotas or prices.

Sheikh Zayed received an invitation to attend the emergency Arab Summit to be held in Baghdad on 29 May. Sheikh Khalifa bin Zayed Al Nahyan, upon receiving the invitation from the Iraqi Minister of the Interior, Samir Abdulwahhab, stressed that the UAE hoped that the Summit would arrive at results to cope with the extent of the challenges.

The Council of Ministers formed a committee to study the comprehensive plan for health services in the country during the coming stage. The committee was formed after a debate on a report presented to the Council by the Ministry of Health.

15 May: Sheikh Zayed, during official discussions with the Prime Minister of Japan, Tosheki Kaifo, called on Japan to participate in solving the Middle East crisis and establish peace in the Gulf. He said that the great powers were the ones who were capable of undertaking this difficult mission, and he stressed the readiness of the UAE to supply the oil and gas requirements of Japan.

16 May: Sheikh Zayed donated half a million dollars to the Japan-UAE Friendship Society.

18 May: Sheikh Zayed, at his meeting with the Indonesian press delegation which visited the country at the beginning of the month, stated that a leader must be true to his people and spend the country's wealth in their service. He said that whoever ignored his past cannot know the value of the present or the future.

Sheikh Zayed, at the conclusion of his visit to Japan, received two Japanese experts on environmental technology who expressed their astonishment at his efforts in planting tress and shrubbery in the desert. They remarked: 'We benefited a great deal from the experience of Your Highness even with all our 40 years experience in environmental sciences.'

19 May: Sheikh Zayed arrived on the Island of Bali preceding his official visit to Indonesia.

21 May: Sheikh Zayed arrived in Jakarta at the beginning of his official visit to Indonesia where the Indonesian President, Suharto, received him. He called for the Islamic countries to exert efforts to meet the fierce challenges which faced them. He said that the leaders of the Islamic countries must give donations as one man to confront their current problems, both big and small.

22 May: Sheikh Zayed, during official discussions with President Suharto, discussed ways of developing relations between the two countries and current Islamic and international affairs.

23 May: Sheikh Zayed, returning to the UAE following his Asian tour, stressed the necessity of strengthening Islamic co-operation to build a better world. He said that whenever someone asks for the UAE's co-operation they will in turn be asked for their views and opinions.

25 May: Sheikh Khalifa, in remarks made

to the Qatari newspaper, *Al-Raya*, confirmed that Zayed's Asian tour achieved important results in Arab affairs. He said that the time had come for America to shoulder its responsibilties regarding the Middle East conflict.

28 May: Sheikh Zayed, arriving in Baghdad to attend the emergency Arab Summit, called for effective Arab solidarity to confront the challenges which surround the present and future. He said that the UAE would exert all its efforts until success at the Summit Conference had been achieved for the sake of rectifying the future of the Arab nation. Total cost to date for developing the liquid gas complex in Dubai was 514 million dirhams, but the estimated expenditure for the project rose to 1615 million dirhams.

29 May: Sheikh Zayed led the UAE delegation to the inaugural session of the emergency Arab Summit in Baghdad. Sheikh Zayed issued a decree promoting Air Colonel Sheikh Mohammad bin Zayed Al Nahyan to the rank of General and appointing him Deputy Chief of Staff. The Council of Ministers allocated 3.5 million dirhams to buy and install a highly advanced marine navigational communications system for the new aviation meteorological centre.

29 May: Sheikh Zayed and the Iraqi President, Saddam Hussein held a meeting during which they evaluated joint Arab action in light of the Summit. Zayed stressed that the Summit had been more positive and useful than had been expected and that it would strengthen Arab progress, especially at this decisive stage of their history.

1 June: Sheikh Hamdan bin Zayed Al Nahyan opened the UAE section at the Polish International Exhibition mounted on the occasion of Italy hosting the finals of the Football World Cup in which the UAE team was competing.

5 June: Sheikh Zayed and the Senegalese President, Abdou Diouf, who was visiting the Emirates, discussed prepa-rations for the coming Islamic Summit Conference and current Islamic affairs.

11 June: The Municipalities of the UAE decided to withdraw all types of British beef from the markets and to forbid further importation because of the incidence of mad cow disease.

13 June: The Supreme Petroleum Council, at its meeting under the chairmanship of Sheikh Khalifa bin Zayed al Nahyan, said that the UAE was obligated to reduce its oil production in accordance with OPEC decrees in order to maintain the unity of the organization and the stability of the oil market.

16 June: Sheikh Zayed issued a decree appointing Sheikh Sultan bin Khalifa as a member of the Executive Council and head of the Office of the Heir Apparent. Sheikh Dr Sultan bin Mohammad Al Qassimi signed a contract to install two 60 megawatt electrical turbines in Sharjah at a cost of 85 million dirhams.

18 June: The Council of Ministers approved the establishment of a central meteorological office.

23 June: Dr Mana Said Al Otaiba stressed at a news conference that the UAE had sacrificed a great deal as a result of its commitments to help Third World nations, because of which it had stopped much work on development projects required by its own people. 'Therefore', he said, 'we must have the second share of OPEC's production because of our vast reserves'.

24 June: Sheikh Mohammad bin Butti Al Hamid signed two contracts for the second stage of the beautification of Abu Dhabi's Corniche and establishing two markets in Al-Shahama and Bani Yas at a cost of 85 million dirhams.

27 June: Sheikh Zayed held discussions with the Lebanese President, Elias Harawi, who was visiting the country. The discussions centred on ways of implementing the Taif Agreement in order to achieve national reconciliation among the Lebanese parties and to support order and stability in Lebanon. He stressed that the UAE would never withhold anything in its power which might be of assistance to Lebanon.

30 June: Sheikh Dr Sultan bin Mohammad Al Qassimi issued a decree appointing Sheikh Ahmed bin Sultan Al Qassimi as deputy ruler of Sharjah and Chairman of the Department of Oil and Minerals.

5 July: Abu Dhabi Department of Electricity and Water decided to establish major energy and water plants in the Western Region costing 700 million dirhams, and to execute a plan for lighting the Abu Dhabi - Dubai highway and adjacent regions, at a cost of 500 million dirhams.

9 July: Sheikh Zayed received the former American President, Jimmy Carter, at the Rodha al-Reef Resthouse. He emphasized that the United States must play an effective role in easing the suffering of the Palestinian people.

12 July: After a telephone call between Sheikh Zayed and King Fahad bin Abdulaziz, the UAE accepted the OPEC quota ceiling of 1.5 million barrels per day instead of 1.9 million barrels.

The total cost of projects executed in the emirate of Sharjah last year amounted to 359 million dirhams.

13 July: Sheikh Zayed received a letter from the Iranian President, Hashemi Rafsanjani, regarding developments in the oil market, conveyed to him by Ghulam Rida Agha Zadeh, the Iranian Minister of Petroleum. Zayed expressed the UAE's concern to support OPEC unity and said that co-operation and solidarity of the member states in the organization would strengthen its power in the oil market.

Dr Mana Said Al Otaiba said that, following Sheikh Zayed's directives, the UAE began an immediate reduction in oil production.

14 July: Sheikh Zayed arrived in Rabat on an official visit where he was received by King Hassan of Morocco. Zayed expressed the UAE's concern to continue meetings between brothers to study all international and regional matters.

15 July: Sheikh Zayed and King Hassan discussed developments in the Arab and Islamic world and joint Arab action. Zayed conferred on King Hassan the UAE's highest decoration, the Sash of the Federation.

The new water plant in the Al-Zawra district of Ajman was opened. Built at Sheikh Zayed's personal expense for the sum of 20 million dirhams, it had the capacity to supply half the drinking-water requirements of the emirate.

20 July: The Ministry of Foreign Affairs sent a memorandum to the Arab League in reply to an Iraqi memorandum which contained accusations against the UAE in respect of the stand it had taken on national issues. The memorandum refuted the Iraqi claims and stressed that they had no basis of truth in them and that the UAE had established its primary concern for the stability of the oil market and the unity of OPEC.

Abu Dhabi Municipality began work on the Sheikh Zayed Park and the planting of 166 hectares with trees and shrubs in Kuwait as Sheikh Zayed's contribution to increasing green areas in Kuwait.

23 July: Saeed bin Tahnoun signed an agree-ment to set-up and maintain various roads in Al-Ain at a cost of 40 million dirhams.

30 July: Sheikh Zayed held discussions with King Hassan of Morocco in Rabat, in which they exchanged points of view regarding the Arab situation and ways of supporting it.

31 July: Sheikh Zayed arrived in Alexandria at the beginning of an official visit to Egypt to discuss current Arab developments.

Sheikh Khalifa bin Zayed Al Nahyan issued the law governing the Housing Loan Board which stiputated the granting of interest-free loans to citizens, ranging between 300,000 to 900,000 dirhams, to be repaid within a period of 25 years.

1 August: Sheikh Zayed held a meeting in Alexandria with Egyptian President, Mohammad Hosni Mubarak, in which they made a comprehensive evaluation of the Arab situation and current develop-ments. The two leaders stressed the necessity of mutual consultations, co-ordination of policies and reduction in the obstacles confronting joint Arab action.

Sheikh Zayed in remarks made to the magazine, *Al-Hawadith*, said that Iraq's memorandum to the Arab League was a summer cloud, a passing thing between brothers. He stressed that UAE production did not exceed its OPEC share because the promise of a Muslim is an oath.

2 August: Sheikh Zayed returned to the UAE following a quick visit to Saudi Arabia where he discussed with King Fahad bin Abdulaziz the necessity of containing the Iraqi-Kuwaiti dispute in the shortest possible time. He said that all honourable means of exchange between brothers must be used and the two leaders agreed on the necessity of holding an urgent Arab summit.

3 August: Sheikh Zayed made important contacts with King Fahad bin Abdulaziz, the Egyptian President, Mohammad Hosni Mubarak, Sultan Qaboos bin Said, Sheikh Jabir Al Ahmed Al Sabah and the Yemeni President, Ali Abdulla Salih, regarding current developments and the holding of an Arab summit.

The GCC condemned the Iraqi invasion of Kuwait.

4 August: Work began on the 55 million dirham project to fix the road between Al-Heer and Sweihan.

5 August: Sheikh Zayed, following a meeting with Sheikh Saqr bin Mohammad Al Qassimi, ordered an end to the electricity crisis in Ras al-Khaimah and the attachment of water and electricity utilities in the emirate to the Federal Ministry of Electricity and Water.

Saeed bin Tahnoun opened the Al-Ain factory for bottling mineral water which will produce 22 million bottles per year.

6 August: The 110 million dirham fruit, vegetable, meat and fish market in Al-Ain was opened.

7 August: In a telephone call with the Turkish President, Turgut Ozal, Sheikh Zayed discussed the recent developments. He received a letter from the Soviet President, Mikhail Gorbachev, delivered by the Soviet Ambassador, on the progress of events. A similar letter from the British Prime Minster, Margaret Thatcher, was delivered by the British Ambassador.

8 August: Sheikh Zayed welcomed the convening of an emergency Arab summit conference in Cairo. Zayed received telephone calls from King Fahad bin Abdulaziz and from US President, George Bush which dealt with recent developments. He also received a letter from the Iranian President, Hashemi Rafsanjani, delivered by the Minister of Foreign Affairs, detailing Iran's reading of the situation.

9 August: Sheikh Zayed presided over a meeting of the Supreme Council of the Federation during which the current political movements to contain the crisis between Iraq and Kuwait were discussed. The Council expressed its confidence in the wisdom of Sheikh Zayed and the Arab leaders and they confirmed the importance of continuing efforts to control events.

Sheikh Zayed arrived in Cairo to attend the emergency Arab Summit Conference where he held wide-ranging consultations with Arab leaders.

10 August: Sheikh Zayed led the UAE delegation at the final session of the emergency Arab Summit Conference in Cairo which decided to send forces to Saudi Arabia and the Gulf States.

Sheikh Sultan bin Surour Al Dhahiri, Chairman of the National Consultative Council, passed away.

11 August: In Cairo before his return to the UAE, Sheikh Zayed and the Syrian President, Hafez Al Asad, discussed the unfolding of events in the region.

Sheikh Zayed ordered that all Kuwaiti families, who had arrived in the country during the previous few days, be received on a brotherly basis. Sheikh Khalifa issued instructions to rent suitable apartments for them and give them immediate cash assistance.

12 August: Sheikh Zayed ordered that Kuwaitis be exempt from medical treatment fees and health card requirements. The young people of the Emirates heeded the call of the nation to fulfill their duty and maintain their honour by coming forth to register their names in the ranks of the military volunteers.

13 August: The Ministry of Economy and Trade confirmed that food items and commodities were available to the mar-kets, that the Government had sufficient stores to last for more than eight months and that, therefore, there was no justification for the hoarding of commodities.

14 August: Sheikh Zayed received a letter from Sheikh Jabir Al Ahmed Al Sabah, the Amir of Kuwait, delivered by the Minister of the Interior, Salim Al Sabah, regarding the development of events in the region. Sheikh Zayed ordered a six-week military training period for national Government employees during which they would be on full pay.

15 August: First Lady, Sheikha Fatima bint Mubarak, Chairwoman of the Women's Federation, ordered the formation of a women's committee to assist in finding suitable living accommodation for Kuwaiti families in the UAE.

Abu Dhabi Municipality announced that it would take strong measures to confront any attempt to raise rents or disturb the stability of the local market.

18 August: Sheikh Zayed received a letter from the Prime Minister of Britain, Margaret Thatcher, conveyed to him by the British Minister of Defence, Alan Clark. The letter was concerned with the impact of the Iraqi occupation of Kuwait on the Gulf region. Sheikh Mohammad bin Rashid Al Maktoum conferred with the British Minister of Defence on relations between the two countries in military fields.

19 August: An official source announced the UAE's approval for the reception of Arab and friendly forces to participate in Arab and international efforts which were being undertaken to defend the region.

20 August: Sheikh Zayed and the US Secretary of Defense, Richard Cheney, conferred on efforts which were being made to end the Iraqi occupation of Kuwait and safeguard the Gulf.

21 August: Sheikh Zayed presided over a meeting of the Council of Ministers to discuss the serious situation in the region. The Council supported the steps being taken by Sheikh Zayed to deal with the developments. It stressed that the Federation's basic and firm policy was that a complete and unconditional withdrawal of Iraqi forces from Kuwaiti territory was a necessity.

22 August: The streets of Abu Dhabi were filled with a large popular parade in support of Kuwaiti legitimacy and condemning the tyrannical Iraqi invasion.

23 August: The UAE, in a letter to the United Nations, confirmed her complete commitment without reservations to the Security Council resolution imposing sanctions against Iraq.

24 August: Sheikh Zayed received a letter from the Turkish President, Turgut Ozal, regarding developments in the region.

25 August: Sheikh Zayed received a letter from the Prime Minister of Japan, Tosheki Kaifo, in which he confirmed his country's support for Sheikh Zayed's efforts to ensure the security and stability of the Gulf.

26 August: The total amount of loans and assistance given by the government of Abu Dhabi and ADFAED at the end of 1989 reached 802 billion dirhams. The Fund financed 91 projects in 42 countries.

27 August: Sheikh Zayed received letters from King Hussein of Jordan and from the Yemeni President, Ali Abdulla Salih, regarding the development of events in the region.

Sheikh Khalifa bin Zayed Al Nahyan donated 1 million dirhams to the Red Crescent Society in the country to enable it undertake its responsibilities toward Kuwaiti families.

29 August: Sheikh Zayed received a letter from President François Mitterand, concerning the crisis in the Gulf. The letter was delivered by Gerard Renaud, the French Minister of State for Defence.

Sheikh Mohammad bin Rashid Al Maktoum and Gerard Renaud discussed military co-operation, training and armaments and the exchange of experience.

2 September: Sheikh Zayed received a letter from the British Prime Minister, Margaret Thatcher, regarding current developments in the region. The letter was delivered by the Foreign Secretary, Douglas Hurd.

Sheikh Saeed bin Tahnoun signed a 32 million dirham agreement for a sewerage project in Al-Khazna district.

2 September: Sheikh Mohammad bin Rashid Al Maktoum, at a press conference with the British Foreign Secretary, Douglas Hurd, expressed the hope that a solution would be found which would guarantee the withdrawal of Iraqi forces from Kuwait and the beginning of a new phase in the region. He said that the foreign forces would leave the region when the reasons for their presence had been removed. He confirmed that the Palestinian problem would remain the basic issue and the prime motivation of the entire Arab nation.

Total loans granted by the Central Bank since it was founded amounted to 345.8 million dirhams, financing 90 industrial projects.

2 September: Sheikh Zayed received an American congressional delegation which was making a tour of the States in the region. He reviewed current developments and stressed that the importance of exerting fullest effort to effect an Iraqi withdrawal and the return of the legitimate Government of Kuwait.

4 September: An official UAE source announced the arrival of military forces from Egypt, Morocco and Syria, which were sent in a spirit of mutual assistance and Arab brotherhood in order to strengthen the UAE's defence capabilities. Sheikh Nahyan bin Mubarak Al Nahyan announced that the University had decided to require that all its students undergo military training.

7 September: Sheikh Zayed and the US Secretary of State, James Baker, reviewed events in the region. The President of the Federation reiterated the UAE's rejection of the Iraqi occupation. He confirmed that the solution would be a complete and unconditional Iraqi withdrawal from Kuwait and a return of the legitimate regime in Kuwait.

8 September: Sheikh Zayed and General Norman Schwartzkopf reviewed the situation. Sheikh Khalifa bin Zayed Al Nahyan and General Norman Schwartzkopf also had discussions on the situation and mutual co-operation.

10 September: Sheikh Zayed received a letter from the Italian Prime Minister, Julio Andreotti, regarding the ongoing crisis.

15 September: Training of volunteers in parachute jumping began in Al-Ain district.

22 September: Sheikh Zayed held discussions with the President of Bangladesh, Mohammad Hussain Irshad. The two Presidents stressed the positions of their two countries, both of which rejected the occupation of Kuwait by Iraqi forces, the necessity of an unconditional Iraqi withdrawal and the return of legitimacy to Kuwait.

Sheikh Khalifa bin Zayed Al Nahyan and the French Minister of Defence, Jean Perrier, discussed co-operation between the two countries and the current situation in the region.

24 September: Sheikh Zayed in a telephone conversation with the Amir of Kuwait confirmed the UAE's solidarity with the people and Government of Kuwait and their insistence on an unconditional and complete Iraqi withdrawal from Kuwait.

Sheikh Mohammad bin Rashid Al Maktoum stressed, after his meeting with the French Minister of Defence, that the peaceful option was the best choice in solving the crisis and guaranteeing the Iraqi withdrawal from Kuwait.

25 September: Sheikh Zayed and the British-European delegation discussed the Iraqi occupation of Kuwait. The President of the Federation stressed the necessity of applying the resolutions of the Security Council and the Arab Summit in their entirety.

28 September: Sheikh Zayed, during his meeting with the parliamentary delegation of the European Union, stressed the necessity of international co-operation to confront the present crisis in the Gulf.

30 September: Sheikh Zayed received a letter from the Italian Prime Minister which was delivered by the Minster of Defence, Virgino Ruginouni.

The air bridge ordered by the President of the Federation began its flights to transport Pakistani and Bangladeshi refugees from Jordan to their home countries. Sheikh Khalifa bin Zayed Al Nahyan and the British Minister of Energy, John Wickham, discussed the situation in the oil market and international efforts to oblige Iraq to withdraw from Kuwait.

Sheikh Mohammad bin Rashid Al Maktoum and the Italian Minister of Defence discussed the development of military co-operation between the two countries.

Last year, the total amount of foreign non-oil trade was 49.7 billion dirhams, in comparison to 30.5 billion dirhams in 1985, an annual increase of 12.6 per cent.

1 October: Sheikh Zayed received letters from King Fahad bin Abdulaziz and Sultan Qaboos bin Said regarding the development of events in the region.

Al-Ain Department of Electricity and Water completed the 90 km overhead electricity line connecting the city of Al-Ain and Al-Wajn district with 220 kilovolts of power.

2 October: Sheikh Zayed attended graduation ceremonies for the first batch of volunteers. He confirmed that UAE youth had inherited the boldness, manliness and bravery of their fathers and grandfathers. He said that the current ordeal in the region would disappear with the help of Allah and that the well-being of the country would remain, as would happiness and stability.

3 October: Sheikh Zayed and the French President, François Mitterand, who arrived in the country on an official visit, discussed developments surrounding the continued Iraqi occupation of Kuwait, the latest events connected with the Gulf crisis and international efforts being made to solve the problem of the Iraqi invasion. In a speech at the United Nations, the UAE called for all the countries of the world to work quickly and decisively to end the Iraqi occupation of Kuwait in order to avert a greater tragedy in the entire region, a tragedy the damage from which could not be predicted nor the results contained.

4 October: The UAE contracted with a Soviet airline to transport refugees from Iraq and Kuwait.

6 October: Sheikh Zayed received a letter from the King of Spain, Juan Carlos regarding events in the region. The letter was delivered by Prince Philip de Bourbon, the Crown Prince.

Sheikh Khalifa bin Zayed Al Nahyan, during his reception of the Spanish Crown Prince, stressed that the opportunity for peace was still available through the resolutions of the international Security Council and that anything other than an Iraqi withdrawal from Kuwait and the return of Kuwaiti legitimacy would not save the area from the woes of war.

7 October: Sheikh Rashid bin Saeed Al Maktoum passed away. Flags flew at half mast, a mourning period of 40 days was announced and Government offices were closed for six days.

8 October: The funeral was held for the late Sheikh Rashid bin Saeed Al Maktoum, Ruler of Dubai. The President of the Federation said that Sheikh Rashid would remain forever in their hearts and that he had been a true pioneer of the nation's unity and of efforts to develop the country.

9 October: Sheikh Zayed received the condolences of the Amir of Qatar. It was acknowledged that Sheikh Rashid had left great works behind him and many enduring accomplishments and that he was at the forefront of those who gave much to their country and people.

The UAE condemned the terrible crime committed by Israel in the courtyard of the Al-Aqsa Mosque against the Palestinian people. It called for the Security Council to oblige Israel to withdraw from the occupied Arab Palestinian territories.

12 October: Sheikh Zayed sent letters to the Prime Ministers of Pakistan, Britain and Italy regarding regional developments.

15 October: Sheikh Zayed held official discussions with the Turkish President, Turgut Ozal, who arrived in the country on a short visit. The two leaders, during the meeting, stressed the necessity of restoring legitimacy to Kuwait and the non-recognition of any results of the Iraqi invasion. Zayed praised the efforts of the international community to maintain security and stability in the region.

ADGAS signed a new 25-year agreement with the Tokyo Electricity Company for the export of liquid gas from 1994. ADGAS produced 3.5 million tons annually.

16 October: Sheikh Zayed and Prince Khalid bin Sultan bin Abdulaziz, the Commander of the Joint Forces, reviewed developments, the current military situation and recent happenings in the Gulf.

21 October: Sheikh Zayed presided over a meeting of the Supreme Council of the Federation during which Sheikh Maktoum bin Rashid Al Maktoum was chosen as Vice President of the Federation. He was also appointed as Prime Minister for the period of five years and was charged with the formation of a new Government. The President gave a full evaluation of developments resulting from the Iraqi occupation of Kuwait and the Council held a wide-ranging debate on the general situation in the Federation. Sheikh Zayed stressed in his talk with the members of the Supreme Council that the late Sheikh Rashid bin Saeed Al Maktoum gave a great deal to the entire country. He said that Kuwait and the UAE were as one, that the Supreme Council was open for debate and discussion and that freedom of opinion was guaranteed for all because of the consultative principle which bound them. He said that there was nothing to fear from opinion and that a matter which does not please any single party does not please everyone.

23 October: Sheikh Zayed received the Egyptian President, Mohammad Hosni Mubarak, who arrived in the country. The two Presidents inspected the Egyptian forces stationed in the country.

24 October: Sheikh Zayed and the Egyptian President, Mohammad Hosni Mubarak, during their discussions, stressed that their two countries rejected the Iraqi occupation and demanded a complete withdrawal from Kuwait.

26 October: The Central Bank said that the economy of the UAE had overcome the negative indications of the Gulf crisis and that next year's economic growth would not be less than 10 per cent.

1 November: Sheikh Zayed received a letter from the Senegalese President, Abdou Diouf, regarding the coming Islamic Conference Summit which was to be held in Dakar in January of the following year.

10 November: Sheikh Zayed received a report from Sheikh Jabir Al Ahmed Al Sabah, the Amir of Kuwait, on the excellent care which was being provided by the UAE to Kuwaitis living in the UAE.

11 November: Sheikh Hamdan bin Zayed Al Nahyan called for an urgent meeting of the heads of the Red Crescent Societies in the GCC States to keep abreast of current events in the region.

12 November: Sheikh Zayed and the British Minister of Defence, Tom King, discussed developments in the region and new events in light of the continued Iraqi occupation of Kuwait.

Sheikh Zayed received letters from the Turkish President, Turgut Ozal, and the Kenyan President, Daniel Arap Moi. Both dealt with developments in the region.

14 November: Sheikh Zayed received letters from King Fahad bin Abdulaziz, delivered by Prince Saud Al Faisal, the Minister of Foreign Affairs, and from the President of Yugoslavia, Dr Borisov Boufik, delivered by the Minister of Foreign Affairs, Bodimir Lunchar. Both letters concerned the course of events in the region. Zayed stressed the importance of the non-aligned movement and the necessity of a resolute stance in the face of aggression. He said that countries which aligned themselves with wrong-doing did not deserve to be in the movement.

20 November: Sheikh Zayed issued a federal decree forming the new 23-member cabinet under the Premiership of Sheikh Maktoum bin Rashid Al Maktoum, with Sheikh Sultan bin Zayed Al Nahyan as Vice Premier.

Sheikh Zayed and Sheikh Maktoum bin Rashid Al Maktoum discussed various aspects of national action during the coming phase.

21 November: The members of the Council of Ministers were sworn in before Sheikh Zayed and he assured them that the people of the Emirates were looking to them with hope and confidence. He told them: 'You are responsible before Allah not just before me or Maktoum, and your duty is to maintain the reputation of the country and its place in the world.'

22 November: Sheikh Hamdan bin Zayed Al Nahyan, in remarks to the magazine, *Al-Hawadith*, stressed that the Emirates did not see any possibility of holding an Arab summit so long as Iraq did not comply with binding international resolutions. He said that Iraq's use of hostages as human shields was inhumane and was condem-ned by the international community.

23 November: Sheikh Zayed in remarks to the German newspaper, *Die Welt*, said that Saddam Hussein was the reason for the stationing of foreign forces in the region. He further stated that there was no historical or legal justification for the occupation of Kuwait and Saddam must not be given any concession for his withdrawal. 'We say to whomever opposes the stationing of foreign forces why did you not oppose the Iraqi occupation of its brother country?', he commented.

24 November: Sheikh Zayed and the Prime Minister of Pakistan, Mohammad Nawaz Sharif, discussed developments in the region and the efforts being made to put Security Council resolutions into effect by the immediate withdrawal of Iraq from Kuwait.

26 November: The Council of Ministers convened its first session after its re-formation under the Premiership of Sheikh Maktoum bin Rashid Al Maktoum. Ahmed Khalifa Al Suweidi attended the session to transmit the directives of the President of the Federation with regard to the coming phase of national action for the new Government and to stress his concern for lessening all the difficulties standing in its way.

Sheikh Khalifa bin Zayed Al Nahyan attended the graduation ceremonies for the two batches of university-level candidates from the Police College in Abu Dhabi.

27 November: Sheikh Khalifa bin Zayed Al Nahyan attended the graduation ceremonies for the new batch of pilot officers from the Aviation College. The UAE, in a speech at the United Nations, strongly condemned the repressive measures taken by the Israeli authorities in the occupied Palestinian and Arab territories, which were crude violations of human rights.

30 November: Between 1971 and 1989, the Ministry of Public Works and Housing constructed 13,554 housing units at a cost of 1400 million dirhams. It also constructed 230 schools at a cost of 1500 million dirhams.

1 December: Sheikh Zayed, on the occasion of the nineteenth National Day, said that the nation's dreams had been turned into reality. He said that a new year in the life of the Federation commenced, a year preceded by nineteen filled with achievements. Sheikh Zayed further stated that the UAE was working for peace and that it was building its Armed Forces to protect the land and its integrity.

3 December: In a speech at the United Nations, the UAE called for speedy action in convening an international peace conference to solve the Palestinian problem.

4 December: Sheikh Khalifa bin Zayed Al Nahyan and the US Energy Secretary, James Watkins, discussed the oil situation and the areas of co-operation between the two countries.

9 December: Sheikh Sultan bin Zayed Al Nahyan opened the international scientific conference which was concerned with the effects of salinity on plants in arid regions. He said that the President of the Federation encouraged the UAE to open itself up to the world's scientific centres in order to strengthen its own capabilities and build up confidence in its own institutions.

10 December: The Council of Ministers approved the draft federal budget for 1990. Expenditure totalled 14.65 billion dirhams.

11 December: Sheikh Maktoum bin Rashid Al Maktoum donated half a million dirhams to UNICEF to aid children who had been adversely affected by the Iraqi invasion of Kuwait.

The heads of GCC Red Crescent Societies met in emergency session at the Intercontinental Hotel in Abu Dhabi, at the request of Sheikh Hamdan bin Zayed Al Nahyan, to study the effects of the Iraqi invasion of Kuwait and the role of the societies.

12 December: Sheikh Zayed held talks with Prince Sultan bin Abdulaziz, the Saudi Second Deputy Prime Minster and Minister of Defence and Aviation, in the presence of Sheikh Khalifa bin Zayed Al Nahyan. During the talks they dealt with the latest happenings in the crisis which had arisen as a result of the continuing Iraqi occupation of Kuwait, as well as the unified stand and consolidated action undertaken by the GCC States.

13 December: Sheikh Maktoum bin Rashid Al Maktoum and Prince Sultan bin Abdulaziz discussed developments in the region.

Sheikh Dr Sultan bin Mohammad Al Qassimi and Prince Sultan bin Abdulaziz discussed the latest happenings in the region in light of the continued Iraqi occupation of Kuwait.

14 December: Sheikh Zayed received 120 scientists from 35 countries and 50 universities who were attending the international conference on salt-tolerant plants growing in arid zones. Zayed told them: 'We have made a prominent experiment in agriculture and we are looking forward to progress.' He said that: 'Some of the experts told us in the past that our land was not suitable for agriculture and they advised us not to try but we tried and we succeeded.' He also commented that: 'Agriculture is the alpha and omega for human beings and that they cannot dispense with plants and the earth which are their origins.'

15 December: Sheikh Zayed, in a statement to the Lebanese newspaper, *Al-Anwar*, called on the Lebanese to employ their wisdom and intellect to prevent all attempts at foreign interference.

16 December: Sheikh Hamad bin Mohammad Al Sharqi opened the desalination plant in the Qadfa'a district in Fujairah, the construction of which was supervised by the Abu Dhabi Electricity and Water Department at a cost of 26 million dirhams. The plant will produce 1 million gallons per day.

The Central Bank confirmed the safety and solidity of the banking system in the country during the crisis in the region. It said that the wave of withdrawals had stopped and that deposits had increased to 59.8 billion dirhams.

17 December: Sheikh Zayed received a letter from the Iranian President, Hashemi Rafsanjani, regarding efforts to end the Iraqi occupation of Kuwait and ways to guarantee security and stability in the region. The letter was delivered by Iranian Foreign Minister Ali Akbar Velayati.

Sheikh Khalifa bin Zayed Al Nahyan donated 1 million dirhams to the Red Crescent Society to support its humanitarian mission.

18 December: Sheikh Zayed received a letter from the Syrian President, Hafez Al Asad, regarding developments in the situation in the region. The letter was delivered by the Foreign Minister, Farouk Al Shara.

Sheikh Maktoum bin Rashid Al Maktoum ordered the construction of 1814 housing units for citizens who had been adversely affected by planning development in the emirate of Dubai.

22 December: Sheikh Zayed headed the UAE delegation to the eleventh GCC Summit in Doha. On his arrival he called for renewed efforts to end the Iraqi occupation of Kuwait. He said that the GCC Summit would arrive at the results it hoped to achieve at these historic meetings which were being held in extraordinary circumstances.

25 December: Sheikh Zayed returned to the country after participating in the final session of the GCC Summit Conference in Doha which called on Iraq to withdraw unconditionally from Kuwait before 15 January and it affirmed that Kuwait must be liberated either through peace or through war.

30 December: Sheikh Zayed issued a decree appointing Dr Mana Said Al Otaiba as his special adviser with the rank of minister.

Nineteen Ninety One

1 January: The Air Force and the Air Defence celebrated the addition of a new squadron of Mirage 2000 aeroplanes.

3 January: In 1990, the Planning Office spent a total of 2519 million dirhams on projects in Abu Dhabi emirate's annual development plan.

5 January: Sheikh Zayed received a letter from Syrian President, Hafez Al Asad, delivered by the Minister of Defence, Mustafa Tlas, regarding international efforts to effect a complete Iraqi withdrawal and the return of sovereignty to Kuwait.

6 January: Sheikh Zayed received a letter from the President of Czechoslovakia, Vaclav Havel, regarding developments in the Gulf in light of the continuing Iraqi occupation of Kuwait.

7 January: The Council of Ministers approved the President's directives to raise social assistance to citizens by 25 per cent to improve living standards.

11 January: Sheikh Zayed and US Secretary of State, James Baker, conferred on developments in the Gulf crisis and international efforts to achieve a complete Iraqi withdrawal from Kuwait.

12 January: Sheikh Zayed and the British Foreign Secretary, Douglas Hurd, conferred on the course of events in the Gulf crisis and international persuasion aimed at ensuring that Security Council resolutions were fulfilled.

16 January: The war to liberate Kuwait began with the participation of the United Arab Emirates.

18 January: The Council of Ministers convened an extraordinary meeting during which they were briefed on the latest report from the Minister of the Interior regarding internal security. The Council called for Government organizations to go about their tasks in the normal fashion.

19 January: The UAE confirmed its resolute stand for right and justice and its complete support for the steps taken to effect resolutions for the liberation of Kuwait after peaceful efforts and intermediaries failed in their attempts.

22 January: The Federal National Council confirmed its confidence and appreciation for Ministry of the Interior efforts to protect society and maintain security and stability in present circumstances.

24 January: In 1990, drinking water production in Dubai amounted to 25.2 billion gallons.

31 January: Sheikh Zayed and Sheikh Maktoum bin Rashid Al Maktoum, in the presence of Sheikh Khalifa bin Zayed Al Nahyan, discussed national affairs, among which was the achievement of a good standard of living for nationals and residents alike in the interests of the country's stability.

3 February: Sheikh Zayed received a letter from UK Prime Minister, John Major, delivered by the Treasury Secretary, John Mellors, regarding operations for the liberation of Kuwait.

6 February: The first test-tube baby to be born in the country was successfully delivered in Tawam Hospital in Al-Ain.

11 February: The Council of Ministers commissioned the Ministry of Public Works and Housing to supervise the construction of 2000 houses in the Northern Emirates.

14 February: Sheikh Zayed was in telephone communication with US President, George Bush, regarding events in the region. Zayed stressed the UAE's commitment to all the Security Council resolutions calling for the liberation of Kuwait.

22 February: In 1990, production of 31,797 tons of varieties of vegetables from national and model farms in the Western Region was valued at 47 million dirhams.

23 February: Land attacks by the coalition for the liberation of Kuwait began with the participation of the United Arab Emirates. Sheikh Zayed issued a decree appointing Yousif bin Umair as a member of the Supreme Petroleum Council.

27 February: Sheikh Zayed congratulated Jabir Al Ahmed Al Sabah, the Amir of Kuwait, by telephone on the restoration of the freedom of Kuwait after it was liberated from Iraqi occupation.

28 February: Sheikh Zayed donated 500,000 dollars to the Maqased Philanthropic Hospital in Jerusalem to enable it to fulfill its medical mission.

Sheikh Khalifa bin Zayed Al Nahyan extended his greetings and expressed his appreciation by telephone to the Commander of the UAE forces in Kuwait. He also extended the greetings and appreciation of the President and the Members of the Supreme Council of the Federation to the UAE land and air fighting units who participated in the battle to liberate Kuwait.

General Mohammad bin Zayed Al Nahyan inspected the UAE's Armed Forces in Kuwait.

1 March: Sheikh Zayed made telephone contact with King Fahad bin Abdulaziz and expressed his happiness at the liberation of Kuwait. He said that what had been achieved through Gulf, Arab, Islamic and international efforts was a victory for both the international community and humanity.

2 March: Sheikh Zayed, in a telephone conversation with Sultan Qaboos bin Said, discussed the political and military situation after the liberation of Kuwait.

Sheikh Zayed received a letter from the French President, François Mitterand, delivered by Michel Charas, Minister of Finance and Terry de Busais, Minister of State for Foreign Affairs, regarding the situation in the region after the liberation of Kuwait.

4 March: The Council of Ministers reviewed political and military developments following the liberation of Kuwait.

The Ministry of Health, at the direction of the President, formed a committee to study Kuwaiti needs for doctors and medical equipment.

Sheikh Mohammad bin Rashid Al Maktoum issued a statement on the occasion of the liberation of Kuwait in which he confirmed that the UAE's Armed Forces participated effectively in the war of liberation, an embodiment of national honour. He said that the United Arab Emirates would remain a cradle of tranquillity and a welcome meeting place for brothers and sons of the Arab nation and the world. He also said that the events which the UAE had passed through would never change the UAE's principles or commitment to Arab national affairs, in the forefront of which was the Palestinian problem.

6 March: Sheikh Maktoum bin Rashid Al Maktoum and Sheikh Khalifa bin Zayed Al Nahyan attended the sixteenth graduation ceremonies for candidates and the eighth for university-level officers from the Zayed Military College in Al-Ain.

8 March: The first of the Red Crescent Society land caravans, carrying 250 tons of aid of various kinds, left for Kuwait.

11 March: Sheikh Zayed presided over a meeting of the Supreme Council of the Federation during which they discussed the political and military situation after the liberation of Kuwait. The Council confirmed that the UAE stood beside Kuwait in re-building their country and praised the heroic performance of the Armed Forces in the battle to free Kuwait.

24 March: Sheikh Zayed received General Hilal Zaid Al Shihhi, the Commander of the UAE forces in Kuwait, and he praised the bravery and the sacrifices of the forces in the battle for right and justice.

1 April: Sheikh Zayed received Dr Hamid Al Gabid, Secretary General of the Islamic Conference. Zayed stressed the power of a united Islamic world and said that the circumstances called for cohesion in the ranks, profiting from the lesson that had been learnt.

2 April: Sheikh Zayed received General Norman Schwartzkopf, the Commander of US Forces and the Coalition Forces in the battle to free Kuwait, and decorated him with the Independence Sash, First Class.

10 April: Abu Dhabi Executive Council endorsed the setting-up of a number of advanced health clinics in the Western Region and Al-Ain at a cost of 100 million dirhams.

16 April: Sheikh Zayed met with a group of officers who participated in the war for the liberation of Kuwait and decorated them with the UAE Military Sash in appreciation of their heroic role.

23 April: Sheikh Zayed arrived in Jeddah at the beginning of a tour of GCC States. He held discussions with King Fahad bin Abdulaziz in which they comprehensively evaluated the political situation and current international and Arab affairs. They expressed their hope that peace would come to the Middle East with a fair and just solution to the Arab-Israeli conflict. Sheikh Maktoum bin Rashid Al Maktoum decreed the creation of Jebel Ali Refinery Corporation (JARC) to own and operate a refinery within Jebel Ali's free zone.

24 April: Sheikh Zayed arrived in Kuwait where he met with Sheikh Jabir Al Ahmed Al Sabah and assured him of the UAE's support in rebuilding a normal life in the country. Zayed also inspected the UAE forces stationed in Kuwait.

Sheikh Zayed arrived in Manama where he met with Sheikh Essa bin Salman Al

Khalifa with whom he discussed regional affairs in the wake of the liberation of Kuwait.

25 April: Sheikh Zayed returned to the country after concluding his tour of a number of GCC states with a visit to Qatar. While in Qatar, he met with Sheikh Khalifa bin Hamad Al Thani and discussed ways of strengthening Gulf co-operation, as well as mediation efforts being conducted to bring peace in the Middle East.

28 April: Humaid bin Nasser Al Nowais signed a contract to import seven turbines costing 375 million dirhams to expand electrical services in the Northern Emirates.

29 April: Sheikh Zayed and the Members of the Supreme Council of the Federation attended the graduation of the tenth group of students from the Emirates University.

30 April: First Lady Sheikha Fatima bint Mubarak attended graduation ceremonies for the tenth group of female graduates from the Emirates University. She said that the tree of knowledge and progress which was planted by Zayed had borne fruit and had given good example in all branches of society, especially in women's affairs.

1 May: Sheikh Zayed, arriving in Muscat on a visit which completed his tour of GCC countries, held discussions with His Majesty Sultan Qaboos bin Said, during which they reviewed important events in the region and ways of developing co-operation. Zayed said that progress and a high standard of living had been given to the people of the region and all the Sultanate's achievements would affect everyone for the better.

2 May: Sheikh Zayed and Sultan Qaboos visited Nizwa, Bahla and the Jibreen Fortress, one of Oman's historical sites.

3 May: Sheikh Zayed and Sultan Qaboos visited Jalali Fort and the city of Muscat. Zayed said that it gave him pleasure to see Qaboos's concern to revitalize the legacy of his ancestors.

4 May: Sheikh Zayed concluded his visit to the Sultan of Oman with a second round of discussions with Sultan Qaboos regarding ways of achieving stability in the region. A joint communiqué was broadcast from both Abu Dhabi and Muscat outlining the results of their talks.

6 May: The Council of Ministers commended the President's GCC tour and stressed that his efforts strengthened the support for the GCC and helped to achieve future security and stability in the region.

7 May: Sheikh Zayed received a letter from US President, George Bush, regarding developments in the region. The letter was presented during a meeting with US Secretary of Defense, Dick Cheney, who discussed security arrangements following the liberation of Kuwait.

The Minister of Electricity announced that in accordance with the directives of Zayed and Maktoum, a five year plan had been prepared and 3.3 billion dirhams allocated to solve all the electricity and water problems in the Northern Emirates.

11 May: Sheikh Zayed received a letter from French President, François Mitterand, delivered by the French Minister of Defence, Pierre Joxe, regarding developments in the region in the wake of the liberation of Kuwait.

14 May: Sheikh Maktoum bin Rashid Al Maktoum decreed the merging of Dubai's two ports - Port Rashid and Jebel Ali. A new company, Dubai Ports Authority

(DPA) was created by decree to take over the two ports. Jebel Ali Free Zone Authority (JAFZA) was not covered in the merging decrees but will be closely involved with the new organization.

15 May: Sheikh Maktoum bin Rashid Al Maktoum issued a law establishing the Dubai Aviation College.

18 May: Sheikh Zayed began a tour of the Northern Emirates during which he met with the Rulers in order to discuss internal affairs and issues related to national action in the days ahead, within the framework of boosting the federal process. He also received citizens to get acquainted with their problems and to assure himself of their well-being and their needs.

22 May: Sheikh Khalifa bin Zayed Al Nahyan returned to the country after a visit to Qatar during which he discussed with Sheikh Khalifa bin Hamad Al Thani ways of developing relations and the firm ties between the two countries.

23 May: Sheikh Zayed received the police chiefs and assured them of his concern for the need to provide security and stability to citizens and residents. He said that the police had an obligation to do their duty in the best possible way and to perform it with honesty and integrity.

24 May: Sheikh Zayed and the Bangladeshi Prime Minister, Khalida Zia, discussed the current situation in the Islamic world and the necessity of action to support Islamic solidarity at the present time.

1 June: In 1990, the value of imported commodities stood at 34.5 billion dirhams, an increase of 5.53 billion dirhams over 1979. The value of non-oil exports stood at 3470 million dirhams.

3 June: Sheikh Zayed and the Italian Prime Minster, Julio Andreotti, who was visiting the country, discussed the latest developments in regional and international affairs, the most important of which was the situation in the Gulf and security arrangements during the period following the war to liberate Kuwait, and the efforts being made to settle the Israeli-Arab conflict.

4 June: Sheikh Khalifa bin Zayed Al Nahyan donated half a million pounds sterling to the International Centre for Islamic Studies at St David's University in Wales.

In 1990, Abu Dhabi Aviation Company made a profit of 36.5 million dirhams of which 26 million dirhams was distributed to its shareholders.

It was confirmed that the UAE had agreed to purchase 20 McDonnell Douglas Apache attack helicopters. The UAE had implemented a new offset policy regarding this and all future defence deals whereby foreign defence companies contracting with the UAE will be required to reinvest some of the proceeds of their contracts back into the UAE.

5 June: Sheikh Zayed received a letter from Soviet President, Mikhail Gorbachev, delivered by General Kotshitov, the First Deputy Minister of the Soviet Ministry of Defence, regarding the current situation in the Gulf following Kuwait's war of liberation.

8 June: Sheikh Hamad bin Mohammad Al Sharqi opened the new water distillation plant in Qadfa'a district, which was financed by Sheikh Maktoum at a cost of 40 million dirhams. The new plant can produce 2 million gallons per day, the total production of sweetwater in the emirate of Fujairah was 5.3 million gallons per day.

9 June: Sheikh Zayed, meeting with Dr Esmat Abdel-Meguid, the Secretary

General of the Arab League, stressed the UAE's support for consolidating Arab unity. He said that Arabs were entering a new era in which the Arab nation would overcome the negative aspects of the Gulf crisis. He stressed the necessity of reviving the effectiveness of the Arab League and changing the Charter to make a resolution valid by a simple majority vote instead of an absolute majority.

14 June: Air Squadron General Sheikh Mohammad bin Zayed Al Nahyan participated in the military and civilian air exhibition at Le Bourget air field in Paris.

16 June: Sheikh Zayed and Sheikh Jallaladeen Haqani, the President of the Consultative Council and leader of the Afghan *Mujahidin*, discussed developments in Afghanistan.

17 June: In Paris, Air Squadron General Sheikh Mohammad bin Zayed Al Nahyan and the French Minister of Defence, Pierre Joxe, discussed military co-operation between the two countries.

18 June: In Cairo, a memorandum of understanding was signed concerning a 85 million dollar grant from ADFAED to the Egyptian Ministry of Works for the reclamation of 188,000 feddans of land in Sinai and the north coast. The grant highlighted Sheikh Zayed's concern for food programmes in Egypt.

19 June: A memorandum of understanding was signed in Cairo between ADFAED and the Sharqiya Governate in Egypt to build 200 dwellings, a mosque and a health clinic for workers on the Al-Qattara agricultural project. The value of the project was 8 million dirhams.

20 June: A 3 billion dirham contract was signed setting-up a huge electricity generating plant and eight water desalination units in Jebel Ali.

23 June: The total cost of economic projects in the annual development schedule for the emirate of Abu Dhabi during 1990 was 3.726 billion dirhams.

27 June: Sheikh Zayed received Mohammed Ali (Cassius Clay), the former boxing champion and Director of the Islamic Centre in Chicago. The President of the Federation was briefed on the activities of the centre in spreading the call to Islam.

28 June: Sheikh Zayed and the President of the Comoros Islands, Said Mohammad Jauhar, discussed the situation in the Gulf, Islamic matters and bilateral relations.

29 June: Sheikh Sultan bin Khalifa Al Nahyan was elected honorary chairman of the Abu Dhabi Chamber of Commerce and Industry. He confirmed the President's concern that the national economy would be self-sustaining and stable, with the potential to move in line with all regional and international economic developments.

2 July: Sheikh Saeed bin Tahnoun signed a 20 million dirham contract setting-up branches of the Al-Ain Co-operative Society.

8 July: The Council of Ministers approved the federal budget for 1991. Expenditure was forecast at 17.413 billion dirhams.

11 July: Sheikh Maktoum bin Rashid Al Maktoum issued directives to Dubai Municipality to set-up a green belt around the city of Dubai to diminish the impact of pollution on the environment.

16 July: Abu Dhabi Executive Council allocated 396 million dirhams to cover the first group of Housing Board loans to nationals, especially those situated in Abu Dhabi and Al-Ain. Sheikh Khalifa bin Zayed al Nahyan stressed that providing suitable housing for each family was one of Sheikh Zayed's vital concerns.

19 July: Abu Dhabi Municipality began the execution of phase 3 of the Eastern Ring Road project in the city of Abu Dhabi.

21 July: The UAE commended the positive and constructive position adopted by Syria under the leadership of Hafez Al Asad whereby he agreed to participate in the proposed Middle East peace conference. The UAE also commended statements by Egyptian President, Mohammad Hosni Mubarak, on the necessity of stopping the building of settlements in the occupied territories as a basic step in the light of which further appropriate measures could be taken to put an end to the Arab boycott of Israel.

24 July: Abu Dhabi Planning Department began executing the comprehensive 20-year regional plan for the emirate.

25 July: Sheikh Zayed received a letter from Sheikh Jabir Al Ahmed Al Sabah about preparations for the coming GCC Summit in Kuwait.

26 July: Abu Dhabi Municipality completed designs for the construction of a 27-hole golf course in Abu Dhabi at a cost of 89 million dirhams.

27 July: Sheikh Zayed and King Hassan of Morocco made a complete evaluation of the circumstances in the Gulf following the liberation of Kuwait during their discussions in Rabat. The two leaders stressed the importance of achieving harmony and erasing differences through mutual understanding in order to maintain unity in the Arab ranks. Zayed expressed his appreciation for the honourable stance taken by Morocco during the Gulf crisis.

30 July: The Department of Works began the construction of 26 schools and 2000 houses in Abu Dhabi at a cost of 795 million dirhams.

3 August: Sheikh Zayed and King Hassan of Morocco discussed new elements in the situation in the Gulf and the Middle East, as well as efforts being made to arrive at a fair and complete settlement of the Palestinian problem. Zayed and King Hassan laid the foundation stone for the Zayed Hospital in Rabat which was being built at Sheikh Zayed's expense.

6 August: Sheikh Zayed received the Members of the Supreme Council of the Federation and groups of well-wishers on the twenty-fifth anniversary of his assumption of power in the emirate of Abu Dhabi.

8 August: Sheikh Zayed, after his visit to the Heritage Village in Abu Dhabi, commented: 'We have begun to taste the fruits of what we planted and youth has come to enjoy culture. The transition of the country from nomadism to a settled existence with a high standard of living has not been achieved easily but rather with much serious effort'. He also said that the UAE would would never stop working to achieve its hopes and ambitions.

10 August: Sheikh Saeed bin Tahnoun signed a number of agreements for implementation of the Wadi Fili project in Al-Ain, an agricultural housing project costing 100 million dirhams.

18 August: Sheikh Zayed toured the Western Region and ordered the building of more houses and farms for citizens.

29 August: The UAE condemned the Iraqi attack on Bubiyan Island and the violation of Kuwait's territorial waters. It stressed that this attack confirmed that there were still aggressive designs in the Iraqi regime and it called for the Arab League and the international community to stand up to the repeated Iraqi attacks on Kuwait.

2 September: Abu Dhabi Marine Areas Oil Company (ADMA) announced that work had begun on developing the Nasr offshore field which would begin production in 1992 with a maximum of 50,000 barrels a day.

8 September: Sheikh Zayed and Sheikh Jabir Al Ahmed Al Sabah, the Amir of Kuwait, who arrived in Abu Dhabi on a short visit discussed developments in the region and the cementing of mutual relations. Zayed stressed that the UAE would help in supporting Kuwait to return to its role of leadership.

9 September: Sheikh Zayed, arriving in Paris on an official visit, held discussions with the French President, François Mitterand. Zayed said that through co-operation the area was trying to erase the after-effects of their recent ordeal and to achieve stability. He said that the UAE wanted France to assume its historic role in bringing a just peace to the Middle East. Sheikh Zayed, in remarks to the French newspaper, *Le Monde*, confirmed his rejection of foreign bases on UAE territory or the granting of facilities to the coalition naval or land forces. He said that the UAE was working to strengthen its Armed Forces and develop them to face an aggressor, and the great loss from the tragedy of the Gulf was not a financial one but the creation of division between Arabs and Muslims.

11 September: Sheikh Zayed, during a meeting with Arab ambassadors to France, stressed that the differences in opinion among Arabs were temporary and that the Arab nation would return to unity of action and effective solidarity. Sheikh Zayed donated 2 million dollars to the Pasteur Cancer Institute.

12 September: Sheikh Zayed arrived in Cairo from Paris where he met with Egyptian President, Mohammad Hosni Mubarak. On his arrival he stressed that history would record Egypt's brave stand and he remarked: 'My visit to Cairo will give a new push to cementing firm relations between the UAE and Egypt.'

14 September: Sheikh Zayed and the Egyptian President, Mohammad Hosni Mubarak, made a complete tour of agricultural developments on the Cairo-Alexandria road. Zayed said that any progress which was achieved for the Egyptian people was for the good of the UAE and the entire Arab nation.

16 September: Sheikh Hamdan bin Rashid al Maktoum earmarked funds for the construction of the first phase of the Dubai - Abu Dhabi road project which was estimated to cost 146 million dirhams.

17 September: Sheikh Zayed arrived in Damascus where he held a closed meeting with Syrian President, Hafez Al Asad, in which they discussed the situation in the Gulf and the Middle East as well as bilateral relations. On arrival, Zayed confirmed his appreciation and pride in the brave stand which Syria took for justice and true brotherhood during the Gulf crisis.

27 September: In 1990, the production of fertilizers reached 880,000 tons or 110 per cent of the entire production capacity of Al-Ruwais Fertilizer Factory.

6 October: Sheikh Khalifa bin Zayed Al Nahyan ordered that one of the major streets in the city of Abu Dhabi, the Airport Street, be renamed in honour of the late Sheikh Rashid bin Saeed Al Maktoum in eternal and grateful memory of the feats and accomplishments of the late departed leader.

7 October: Sheikh Zayed gave a speech at the fifteenth conference of the Society of International Lawyers in Barcelona, in which he called for the laywers who were operating at an international level to exert efforts to ensure that truth may prevail, that supports for justice may be firmly fixed and that peace and freedom may be provided to all nations and peoples in the world, without concern for their colour, sex, creed or religion.

8 October: Sheikh Dr Sultan bin Mohammed Al Qassimi, while presiding over a meeting of the Board of Administration of Sharjah's Chamber of Commerce and Industry, ordered that a piece of land be allocated for a new industrial area.

9 October: Sheikh Zayed issued directives to send urgent food and medical aid to the Soviet Union to help the Soviet people in their difficult economic circumstances.

13 October: Sheikh Zayed received an invitation from the Senegalese President, Abdou Diouf, to attend the Islamic Summit Conference to be convened in Dakar next December.

15 October: Said Al Raqbani said that the UAE had been very successful in expanding the area of land planted in greenery and that there were now 14,279,000 palm trees on 279,000 hectares of forested land.

16 October: The UAE gave 5 million dollars to support the activities of the Islamic Solidarity Fund.

20 October: Sheikh Zayed received a letter from the Soviet President, Mikhail Gorbachev, in which he expressed the appreciation of the Soviet people for the help given to it by the UAE.

Abu Dhabi Municipality completed the construction of a park in Zayed City in the Western Region at a cost of 3.639 million dirhams.

21 October: Sheikh Khalifa bin Zayed Al Nahyan, meeting with the US Assistant Secretary of State, David Lake, stressed that the UAE welcomed the holding of a peace conference on the Middle East in Madrid on 30 October.

28 October: Sheikh Zayed presided over a meeting of the Supreme Council of the Federation, during which he was re-elected as President of the Federation for a period of five years, with Sheikh Maktoum bin Rashid Al Maktoum as Vice President. The provisional constitution was extended for another five years and a committee formed to deal with constitutional changes. Zayed stressed his concern and the concern of his brothers for strengthening the Federation and achieving greater accomplishments for the good of the country. He said that they all had to pay attention to what was going on around them, and that the young people whom they had armed with knowledge must carry the responsibility for national action.

30 October: Sheikh Hamdan bin Rashid Al Maktoum attended the graduation of the first batch of police officers and the second batch of university-level students from the Police College in Dubai.

1 November: A 160 million dirham contract was signed for construction of the largest central vegetable market in the city of Abu Dhabi.

2 November: Sheikh Zayed received Sayyid Fahad bin Mahmoud Al Said, Deputy Prime Minister for Legal Affairs in the Sultanate of Oman, who was visiting the country at the head of a large delegation to attend the first meeting of the joint UAE-Oman Commission.

Sheikh Khalifa bin Zayed Al Nahyan

presided over the UAE portion of the joint Commission's first meeting which was handled on the Omani's behalf by Sayyid Fahad bin Mahmoud Al Said. Sheikh Khalifa stressed that the meeting came within the framework of firm co-operation and strong relations between the two countries. He stressed that there was complete mutual understanding between the two leaders and that the field was open for further development of relations between the two countries.

3 November: The UAE-Oman Commission concluded its meetings with agreement on a number of understandings and concepts which would help to achieve the goals of the two countries as they strive to serve the interests of the two peoples.

Sheikh Mohammad bin Rashid al Maktoum opened the Dubai International Air Show, *Dubai '91,* and he expressed the hope that the Madrid Peace Conference would produce positive results on the way to the achievement of peace and stability in the Middle East.

4 November: The Council of Ministers approved the building of 86 houses in Ajman and Ras al-Khaimah at a cost of 30 million dirhams. The total cost of the State's investment/development projects for 1991 stood at around 3.9 billion dirhams.

7 November: Sheikh Zayed received a delegation from the Kuwait National Assembly under the chairmanship of Abdulaziz Al Masaeed. Zayed assured them that the UAE would support Kuwait until it returned to its usual place among Arabs and the international family. He said that the ordeal had given greater depth to the common destiny of true brothers.

10 November: Sheikh Hamdan bin Zayed Al Nahyan led the UAE delegation to the foreign ministers meeting of the Damascus Declaration States which was held in Cairo. He stressed that the meeting would gain more importance in view of the fact that it was held after the first phase of the Madrid Peace Conference.

13 November: Sheikh Zayed, who was on a private visit to Morocco, received a letter from the Algerian President, Al Shadhili bin Jadid, delivered by the Foreign Minister, Lakhdar Al Ibrahimi, regarding new aspects of Arab affairs.

14 November: The UAE condemned the Israeli decision to declare the occupied Syrian Golan Heights to be non-negotiable territory. The decision was described as null and void and constituting a major obstacle to efforts being made for peace, as well as a contradiction of the principles on which the Peace Conference in Madrid was based.

17 November: ADGAS signed an agreement with the Japanese company, Chiyoda, to construct a third production line for the ADGAS gas factory on Das Island at a cost of 1 billion dollars.

19 November: Sheikh Zayed issued a decree setting up the Staff College for the Armed Forces.

20 November: The first operation of its kind, the insertion of an electronic hearing system, was performed at Al-Mafraq Hospital in Abu Dhabi on deaf children from the UAE.

23 November: Between 1971 and the end of 1990, Dubai Municipality built 4186 houses at a cost of 721 million dirhams.

25 November: Sheikh Khalifa bin Zayed Al Nahyan issued decrees governing the reshuffling of Abu Dhabi's Executive Council, the appointment of chairmen and deputies for local departments and a restructuring of the Board of Administration of the General Industrial Establishment. He also issued a law establishing two new departments for economy and customs.

26 November: In Rabat, Sheikh Zayed received Prince Sultan bin Abdulaziz, the Saudi Second Deputy Chairman of the Council of Ministers and the Minister of Defence and Aviation. They discussed the current situation in Arab regions and bilateral relations.

Sheikh Khalifa bin Zayed Al Nahyan presided over the first meeting of Abu Dhabi's Executive Council after its members took the oath of office. He stressed that the public good came above every other consideration and that wise leadership bound them to the principle of consultation. He called for united action and the intensification of efforts to achieve a good standard of living and prosperity for the country and its citizens.

29 November: In Rabat, Sheikh Zayed and King Hassan of Morocco discussed efforts to achieve Arab harmony and the peace process as well as developments in regional affairs.

30 November: Sheikh Zayed, in a speech given on the occasion of the twentieth National Day, said that the Federation was the product of collective will, fraternal support, family links and faith in the importance of responsibility. He said that it was by the grace of Allah that they had perceived from the beginning that the Federation was not an end in itself but only a means to build the nation and make its citizens happy.

1 December: Sheikh Zayed paid a visit to Prince Abdulla bin Abdulaziz, the Saudi First Deputy Prime Minister and Crown Prince, at Al-Mushrif Palace. Prince Abdulla had arrived in the country on an official visit to attend National Day celebrations.

2 December: Sheikh Zayed, the Members of the Supreme Council of the Federation and guests of the country attended a huge military exhibition mounted on the occasion of the twentieth National Day. Sheikh Zayed said that the Federation had proven its ability to provide and develop and that the leading role of the Members of the Supreme Council and the people of the Emirates in setting-up a modern firmly-grounded State was refelected on with pride and affection. He said that the comprehensive renaissance in the country required an understanding of international changes and a highly aware leadership who appreciated the spirit of the age and how best to proceed. He also stressed that the Armed Forces had been built up to assume the responsibility of maintaining the structure of the State and to participate in the defence of GCC States, and that the UAE's foreign policy commited it to a balanced path based on the principle of protecting its interests and respect for the interests of others.

5 December: Sheikh Zayed visited Abu Dhabi Women's Association exhibition to commemorate National Day. He praised the efforts of the society and its leadership in spreading awareness and culture among the women in the country.

Sheikh Tahnoun bin Mohammad Al Nahyan opened a number of new amusement facilities which were added to the Amusement Park in Al-Hili at a cost of 12 million dirhams.

9 December: Sheikh Hamad bin Mohammed Al Sharqi presided over the meetings of the sixth Islamic Summit in Dakar.

11 December: In a speech before the Islamic Summit Conference in Dakar, the UAE confirmed its concern for security and stability in the Gulf region and the importance of complying with binding international resolutions in their entirety. He stressed the UAE's rejection of attempts by the Iraqi regime to once again draw the region toward the dangers which threatened peace and exposed the Islamic community to the abyss of division.

14 December: Dubai Municipality began work on six huge road and bridge projects costing 900 million dirhams.

16 December: The UAE decided to re-open its embassy in Beirut since the situation in Lebanon had stabilized.

18 December: Sheikh Zayed issued a federal decree forming a new Central Bank Board under the chairmanship of Mohammad Eid Mohammad Jasim Al Mareikhi.

Sheikh Ahmed bin Saeed Al Maktoum signed a letter of intent to purchase 14 Boeing 777 airplanes for Emirates Airlines at a cost of 2 billion dollars.

19 December: Sheikh Sultan bin Mohammad Al Qassimi approved a 62.5 million dirham contract for extending gas pipelines from the Al-Saja field to supply the two electricity plants in Khor Fakkan and Kalba.

22 December: Sheikh Zayed ordered that in Government schools the children of non-national residents should no longer be charged fees.

23 December: Sheikh Zayed led the UAE delegation to the twelfth GCC Summit held in Kuwait. Upon his arrival, he stated that a new period had begun for co-operation in the maintenance of security and stability in the region, and that the convening of the Summit was a clear proof of the UAE's perception of the great importance of joint co-operation.

Sheikh Khalifa bin Zayed Al Nahyan attended flag-raising ceremonies on a number of additions to the naval fleet. He stressed that there could not be confidence in security without the power to protect the nation and its citizens.

24 December: Sheikh Khalifa bin Zayed Al Nahyan attended ceremonies for a new batch of graduates from the Police College in Abu Dhabi.

25 December: Sheikh Zayed, returning to the country after participating in the final session of the GCC Summit in Kuwait, welcomed the holding of the next GCC Summit in Abu Dhabi and he confirmed that the Kuwait Summit achieved good results in the best interests of the citizens of GCC States.

In 1990, the Ministry of Works and Housing completed 470 projects in the emirate of Sharjah at a cost of 470 million dirhams.

26 December: Sheikh Hamdan bin Zayed Al Nahyan announced that the UAE had decided to recognize the new Union of Independent States (CIS) composed of 11 ex-Soviet republics. He affirmed the UAE's desire to establish friendly relations and co-operation with these republics.

Some 400 million barrels of crude oil were refined at Al-Ruwais refinery between 1981 and 1991. The refinery also refined 6 million tons of heavy oil and loaded 3000 ships with oil at its port.

29 December: Sheikh Khalifa bin Zayed Al Nahyan attended graduation ceremonies for the new batch of pilots from Al-Dhafra Air Base.

Nineteen Ninety Two

3 January: Sheikh Surour bin Mohammad Al Nahyan signed a 500 million dirham contract setting-up a new desalination plant at Al-Taweelah.

7 January: Operations for developing the huge Upper Zakum oil field were underway. This field, which is being exploited by ZADCO (owned 88 per cent by ADNOC and 12 per cent by JODCO) is considered to be the fourth largest in the world in the context of underground reserves.

11 January: Sheikh Maktoum bin Rashid Al Maktoum issued a decree setting-up the Dubai Electricity & Water Authority which will take over the ownership, administration and operation of all plants and undertake projects connected with water and electricity in the emirate of Dubai.

12 January: Based on the President of the Federation's directives, Sheikh Maktoum issued a decree ending the effectiveness of the Council of Ministers' 1987 decree concerning the collection of school fees from the children of non-national residents in Government schools.

19 January: Sheikh Zayed issued two federal laws creating the Ministry of Higher Education and Research and Abu Dhabi Police College.

In 1991, the total value of trade in the non-oil sector in Abu Dhabi amounted to 14.4 billion dirhams.

20 January: Sheikh Khalifa bin Zayed Al Nahyan attended opening ceremonies at the Military Staff College in Abu Dhabi. He stressed that the College was a practical, scientific and intellectual addition to the Armed Forces.

21 January: Abu Dhabi Executive Council earmarked 131 million dirhams to build 170 new public housing units in Al-Khazna and Al-Shahama.

26 January: Sheikh Maktoum bin Rashid Al Maktoum allocated 98 million dirhams to construct breakwaters on the Jumeirah beaches.

27 January: Sheikh Maktoum, meeting with the newly-formed Central Bank Board, said that the role of the Bank was to support currency and banking policies in the country and to focus on developing the currency market.

28 January: In accordance with the President's directives, the Ministry of Public Works and Housing formed a working team to list dwellings built by the Government since the establishment of the Federation. It will also list dwellings constructed by local governments in the Northern Emirates and determine the possibility of maintaining them or finding alternate housing.

In Beijing, the foundation stone was laid for the Emirates Centre for Arabic and Islamic Studies which was being financed by Sheikh Zayed.

Sheikh Hamdan bin Zayed Al Nahyan, who was on an official visit to Moscow, stressed that the UAE's participation in the many-sided negotiations between Israel and the Arab countries was dictated by its concern to achieve peace in the Middle East.

1 February: Sheikh Hamdan bin Rashid Al Maktoum approved the establishment of a zoo in Dubai at a cost of 340 million dirhams.

The Ministry of Health completed the final phase of the nation-wide project for establishing an integrated health information network with the installation of a central computerized blood bank in Abu Dhabi.

The UAE's trade surplus in 1991 was 27 billion dirhams and the collective balances of the commercial banks stood at 134 billion dirhams.

2 February: Sheikh Maktoum bin Rashid Al Maktoum issued a decree setting up the Dubai Furnishings Board which will take over the production, collection, transportation, refining, storage, marketing and distribution of natural gas in the emirate of Dubai.

8 February: Sheikh Khalifa bin Zayed Al Nahyan, receiving the Chairman and members of the newly formed Central Bank Board of Directors, stressed the country's support for the bank's efforts to develop and implement currency and credit policies. He said the Government was also keen to ensure that the banking sector was in a position to undertake its responsibilities in the service of the national economy.

An 8 million dollar contract was signed to establish a weaving and spinning factory in the free zone in Fujairah. It will have an annual production capacity of 6 million metres of thread, 15,000 rolls of material of various kinds and 300,000 pieces of ready-made garments.

13 February: Sheikh Maktoum bin Rashid Al Maktoum held official discussions with the Greek Prime Minister, Constantine Mitsotakis. The UAE and Greece, in a joint communiqué, stressed the importance of security and stability in the Gulf and the necessity of finding a just and lasting settlement to the Middle East problem based on the principle of land for peace. They also emphasized the necessity of finding a solution to international problems by peaceful means and their concern to support and develop friendly relations and co-operation between their two countries in various fields.

14 February: In Lahore, Sheikh Zayed and the Pakistani Prime Minister, Mohammad Nawaz Sharif, discussed regional and international affairs, new developments in the Gulf region and the Middle East. Sheikh Dr Sultan bin Mohammad Al Qassimi opened the eight Childrens' Cultural Festival in Sharjah.

17 February: The Council of Ministers allocated 71 million dirhams to import medicines for hospitals and health centres in the country.

18 February: A meeting between Rashid Abdulla and US Assistant Secretary of State, Edward Djerdjian, confirmed that Iraq must comply with all UN resolutions

Women troops of the UAE armed forces.

Sheikh Zayed reviews the UAE troops who helped to liberate Kuwait, during a visit to Kuwait in April 1991.

UAE volunteers are greeted by Sheikh Zayed following the liberation of Kuwait in April 1991.

Sheikh Zayed presented a medal to General Norman Schwartzkopf when he visited the UAE on 2 April 1991.

Mohammad Ali with Sheikh Zayed during the ex-boxing champion's visit to the UAE.

Sheikh Zayed visits a Handicapped Centre in Abu Dhabi.

Sheikh Zayed with some of his grandchildren.

Sheikh Zayed during his visit to Paris 9 September 1991.

Sheikh Zayed on a State visit to France on 9 September 1991.

Sheikh Zayed with French President Mitterand in September 1991.

Sheikh Zayed has always held a close rapport with children.

New water discoveries made in 1996 near Al-Ain.

Sheikh Zayed cruising in the Gulf on 8 June 1991.

A meeting of the Supreme Council.

An official visit to Syria on 18 September 1991.

Coins and currency notes issued in the 1990s.

Retired President George Bush visits Sheikh Zayed.

Secretary General of the Arab League presenting Sheikh Zayed with an award for Man of the Environment and Sustainable Development, in 1993.

relevant to the Gulf crisis, especially those dealing with reparations for damage done as a result of the Iraqi occupation of Kuwait. They also stressed that it was important to support the stability and security of the Gulf region and the Middle East.

21 February: Dubai Municipality began implementing a scheme to plant 8 per cent of the total area of the emirate of Dubai with greenery, including millions of shrubs and trees around the city to protect it from pollution.

Abu Dhabi Municipality commenced construction on the first phase of the 136 hectare golf course in the city of Abu Dhabi.

23 February: Sheikh Zayed held official discussions with Bernardo Fiyara, Chairman of the State Council of Guinea Bissau, who was on his first visit to the country. During the talks there were discussions on ways to develop joint co-operation, developments in the Gulf, efforts being made for peace in the Middle East and Arab-African co-operation.

Sheikh Zayed reviewed the current situation in the Gulf area and the Middle East with General Joseph Hoare of the US Central Command.

Sheikh Zayed was briefed on a plan to organize a comprehensive marine resources development survey by a delegation of Japanese marine experts.

26 February: In Damascus, ADFAED signed agreements with Syria to finance three industrial projects amounting to 911 million dirhams.

29 February: Sheikh Hamdan bin Rashid Al Maktoum opened the Dubai Fertility and Women's Health Centre.

2 March: Sheikh Zayed was briefed on the designs for transforming Lulu Island into a unique international tourist island.

The Council of Ministers approved the federal budget for 1992. Expenditure was forecast at 17.3 billion dirhams while revenue was estimated at 15.9 billion dirhams, leaving a deficit of 1.4 billion dirhams. The Council allocated 963 million dirhams to develop utilities and services for citizens.

3 March: Sheikh Sultan bin Zayed Al Nahyan attended graduation ceremonies for the seventeenth batch of candidates and the ninth batch of university-level officers from the Zayed Military College in Al-Ain.

7 March: Sharjah Municipal Council approved the list of the second group of citizens to qualify for land grants for dwellings in Falah suburb.

8 March: The Ministry of Foreign Affairs paid their share of the 1991 GCC Secretariat General budget, amounting to 12.623 billion Saudi riyals. It also paid 4.302 million dollars as the country's share in a number of Arab, Islamic and international organizations.

12 March: There were 329 million date palm trees in the Western Region planted on farms and along the roadside.

16 March: Sheikh Zayed attended the first marksmanship championships for 1992 which were mounted at the Hunting and Equestrian Club in accordance with Zayed's directives as a way of reviving interest in ancestral sports and channelling the energies of young people.

20 March: Sheikh Sultan bin Mohammad Al Qassimi issued a law protecting pre-1900 A.D. archaeological sites in Sharjah which were considered to be part of the heritage of past generations.

22 March: The UAE and the Sultanate of Oman decided, from 15 April 1993, to permit each others citizens to travel between both countries using identification cards only. This development was published by the two Ministries of the Interior in a communiqué from each country.

24 March: Sheikh Zayed awarded the Independence Sash, First Class, to Dr Michael Elias, Professor of Heart Surgery and Dean of the College of Medicine at Baylor University in America, in appreciation of his prominent role in the service of health institutions in the world. He was decorated with the Sash by Sheikh Hamdan bin Zayed Al Nahyan.

27 March: From 1968 to the end of last year, total expenditure on development projects and Government department programmes in the emirate of Abu Dhabi reached 74 billion dirhams.

28 March: Sharjah Municipal Council approved the list of the first group of citizens who were to be given land to build houses, 156 citizens in Kalba and 124 in Khor Fakkan.

31 March: Sheikh Maktoum issued a law establishing the Economic Office in Dubai. The Works Department in Abu Dhabi began work on a number of new hospital and health clinic projects in Abu Dhabi, Al-Ain and Ajman at a cost of 700 million dirhams.

1 April: Sheikh Zayed granted Abu Dhabi Hunting and Equestrian Club the sum of 1.5 million dirhams to complete the firing range facilities.

Sheikh Sultan bin Mohammad Al Qassimi issued directives to standardize the use of computers in all the offices of the Government of Sharjah and to set-up specialized information centres.

9 April: Central Bank statistics showed that, in 1991, the State's trade surplus was 35 billion dirhams, while the collective balances of the commercial banks up to June 1991 stood at 131.76 billion dirhams.

12 April: Sheikh Zayed, at his reception for a number of newly-appointed UAE ambassadors, stressed that an individual's self-respect obliges others to respect him and that the State appoints men whom it esteems and those in whom it takes pride to these posts.

13 April: ADMA signed an agreement with Bechtel International to develop the Umm al-Shaif gas field to increase the number of gas producing wells.

18 April: Sheikh Zayed attended the horse-racing finals at the Abu Dhabi Equestrian Club race course.

21 April: Sheikh Zayed held official discussions with Syrian President, Hafez Al Asad, who was visiting the country. Talks centred on developments in Arab affairs, the situation in the Gulf and the necessity of strengthening Arab solidarity to serve Arab interests.

27 April: Sheikh Zayed received a letter from Russian President, Boris Yeltsin, regarding mutual co-operation and current international affairs, conveyed to him by the Foreign Minister, Andrei Kozarev.

Sheikh Zayed decorated the former British Prime Minister, Margaret Thatcher, with the Federation Sash in appreciation of her efforts during the Gulf crisis.

28 April: Sheikh Zayed arrived in New Delhi on an official visit to India. He confirmed at a dinner given by the Indian President that the UAE wished to deepen co-operation between the two countries. He said that the UAE attached great importance to the security and stability of its neighbour, India. The Indian President, Rama Swami, commended Zayed's wise policy which was characterized by long-term vision and his efforts for good and for unity in the world.

Sheikh Hamdan bin Zayed Al Nahyan held official discussions with the Russian Foreign Minister, Andrei Kozarev, who announced that his country would stand by the UAE in regard to the unity and security of its territory.

29 April: Sheikh Zayed met with the Indian President, Rama Swami, in the Presidential Palace in New Delhi. The discussions centred on bilateral relations and ways of developing them, especially in economic, commercial and oil areas. There was also an evaluation of the situation in the region and international affairs of mutual concern.

30 April: Before his departure Sheikh Zayed received the heads of the Arab diplomatic missions in India. During the meeting Zayed said that the Arab split will not be healed unless true solidarity prevailed. He said that Arabs needed each other more than they needed their friends, wherever they are, and that the strength of the Arabs is the strength of the Islamic countries.

1 May: In 1991, the total value of the State's foreign trade stood at 76.8 billion dirhams.

2 May: Dubai Municipality completed plans for more than 1560 new houses for distribution to citizens in the emirate.

The Executive Council commissioned a feasibility study to provide Abu Dhabi with a natural gas distribution network.

5 May: The Armed Forces celebrated the sixteenth anniversary of their unification which falls on 6 May.

6 May: The UAE urged Qatar and Bahrain to settle their border disputes in a peaceful manner and expressed the hope that the two countries would be able to overcome the factors which were disturbing brotherly relations between them.

7 May: Sheikh Zayed ordered that educational trips be included in the schools' curriculum. The trips would include visits to the cities, islands and remote areas of the country to acquaint the students with important sites and let them see the accomplishments that had been achieved in these districts.

9 May: Sheikh Zayed was presented with the credentials of Sultan bin Hamad bin Hilal Al Busaidi, the first Ambassador to the UAE from the Sultanate of Oman.

10 May: In Muscat, Sultan Qaboos bin Said received Sheikh Khalifa bin Zayed Al Nahyan and the Emirates' delegation to the UAE-Oman Commission. During their meeting they discussed ways of strengthening relations between the two countries, as well as new developments in regional and Arab affairs.

Sheikh Khalifa announced that he had briefed Sultan Qaboos on the results of the work of the joint Commission which would open the way to more co-operation and constructive action.

11 May: Sheikh Zayed presided over the meeting of the Supreme Council of the Federation. The Council decided to consider agreements between any of the individual emirates and neighbouring states as agreements with the United Arab Emirates. The Council discussed the current situation and internal affairs, as well as ways of supporting national action in the days ahead.

The UAE-Oman Commission met for the second time to discuss ways of improving co-operation between the two countries. The Commission commended the decision to recognize identification cards for the purpose of travel for citizens between the UAE and Oman.

12 May: Sheikh Khalifa bin Zayed Al Nahyan, returning to the country after the conclusion of the UAE-Oman Commission meetings, said that because of the very positive outcome from the second meeting, the UAE had confidence in the future and would continue the joint determination to pursue further the hopes, aspirations and ambitions of the two countries.

Sheikh Sultan bin Zayed Al Nahyan attended graduation ceremonies for the eleventh batch of students from the UAE University and the first batch from the Colleges of Higher Technology.

13 May: First Lady Sheikha Fatima bint Mubarak, at graduation ceremonies for the sixteenth group of female students from the UAE University and the Higher Technical Colleges, expressed her pride and esteem at the role which the daughters of the Emirates were playing in providing knowledge and services to society and the country.

16 May: Sheikh Hamdan bin Zayed Al Nahyan extended an invitation to all the Arab Red Crescent Societies to hold their twenty-second meeting in Abu Dhabi.

17 May: Sheikh Zayed held discussions with the President of the Benin Republic, Nicephor Sugalu, who was visiting the country for the first time. They discussed mutual co-operation and developments in regional and international affairs.

19 May: The Permanent Purchasing Committee approved a number of projects, valued at 51.6 million dirhams, for new services in some of the emirates of the Federation.

21 May: Sheikh Zayed received the Prime Minister of Somalia, Omar Arta, who briefed him on developments in the context of Arab and international efforts to bring peace and stability to Somalia. Zayed expressed his sympathy with the people of Somalia for the ordeal they were enduring and said that he supported efforts to bring stability to their country.

24 May: Sheikh Mohammad bin Rashid Al Maktoum, at his reception for General Joseph Hoare, Supreme Commander of the United States Forces, called for the pressure to be increased on Israel to elicit a new response to Arab and international peace initiatives in an effort to achieve security, stability and a just peace in the Middle East region.

Mohammad Said Al Mulla opened the new 5.5 million dirham tar plant in Jebel Ali which had an annual capacity of 30,000 tons.

25 May: The Council of Ministers approved the draft trademark protection law.

26 May: Abdulhalim Khaddam, Vice President of the Syrian Republic, and Sheikh Sultan bin Zayed Al Nahyan, who arrived in Damascus on an official visit, discussed the latest developments in the Arab - Israeli conflict, the situation in the Gulf and strengthening relations between the two countries.

Sheikh Sultan bin Zayed Al Nahyan and Syrian Prime Minister, Mahmoud Al Zaabi, discussed ways of expanding mutual co-operation between the two countries.

28 May: Syrian President, Hafez Al Asad, met with Sheikh Sultan bin Zayed Al Nahyan to discuss the situation in the region, Arab affairs and mutual relations.

30 May: Sheikh Sultan bin Zayed Al Nahyan, after his return to the UAE, commended the results of his visit to Syria and the firm brotherly relations between the UAE and Syria.

31 May: The UAE condemned ongoing Israeli attacks on Lebanese territory and called for the international community to take the necessary steps to put an immediate end to this unacceptable behavior.

1 June: The Council of Ministers approved draft laws for protecting intellectual property and for establishing a Marriage Fund to encourage marriage between UAE nationals with the aim of combating the phenomenon of foreign marriages: the law stipulated the granting of up to 70,000 dirhams to young men who wished to marry UAE nationals.

2 June: Abu Dhabi Executive Council approved the immediate commencement of the second phase of construction at the Al-Taweelah plant, the aim being to produce 732 megawatts of electricity and 62 million gallons of water daily.

3 June: Sheikh Zayed personally guaranteed payment of the expenses for 250 pilgrims from Guinea Bissau to perform the *Hajj* rites of pilgrimage.

6 June: In 1991, there were 466 light industrial installations in Sharjah worth 19.6 million dirhams with a production valued at 67.4 million dirhams.

7 June: Sheikh Surour bin Mohammad Al Nahyan signed the 6 billion dirham contract to execute phase two of the Al-Taweelah project.

8 June: Sheikh Zayed sent a letter to the International Environment and Development Conference being held in Brazil (the World Summit), in which he stressed that the UAE, in spite of it being a new country, had succeeded in taking wide-ranging steps to protect the environment, combat pollution and conquer the desert. The UAE, he said, had now become an exemplary model for nations who wished to challenge the harsh nature of the desert.

Jebel Ali Free Zone opened the first national meat factory with a production capacity of more than 30 tons daily.

9 June: Rashid Abdulla, in a speech before the World Environment and Development Conference in Brazil, stated that the directives of the President had a huge practical effect on increasing the green areas in the Federation by 1760 per cent during the period 1968-1990.

10 June: Abu Dhabi Water and Electricity Department signed a 141 million dirham contract to install two gas turbines in Medinat Zayed in the Western Region.

15 June: Abu Dhabi Marine Areas Company (ADMA) reported that production during 1991 from two oil fields was as follows:

(1) 280,000 barrels daily from the Umm al-Shaif field and

(2) 330,000 barrels from the Zakum field. A new floating dock has been installed to accommodate giant tankers capable of carrying half a million tons.

19 June: The Ministry of Public Works and Housing began work on 500 new houses for citizens in the Northern Emirates.

20 June: The Ministry of Electricity and Water decided to establish the first reverse osmosis water distillation plant in the emirate of Ajman at a cost of 40 million dirhams and a capacity of 3 million gallons of sweetwater per day.

24 June: During the previous five years, Abu Dhabi Municipality completed 13 road and bridge improvement projects costing 954 million dirhams.

26 June: Sheikh Hamdan bin Zayed Al

Nahyan arrived in Moscow on an official visit at the invitation of the Russian Minister of Foreign Affairs. He announced to *Tass* news agency that the UAE was content with the new Russian foreign policy and stressed the importance of the Russian role in the region. He said that Russia was a friendly state and that the UAE's relations with it were continually evolving and that they would work on strengthening relations.

27 June: Russian President, Boris Yeltsin, received Sheikh Hamdan bin Zayed Al Nahyan in the Kremlin. Sheikh Hamdan conveyed to him a letter from Sheikh Zayed regarding bilateral relations and new events in regional and international affairs. The Russian President praised the UAE President's policy which, he said, was an expression of moderation, openness and wisdom.

Sheikh Surour bin Mohammad Al Nahyan signed a 949 million dirham contract to install rapid gas turbine units in the Abu Dhabi and Al-Ain electricity plants.

Emirates Airlines contracted with three international financial institutions to finance the purchase of two Airbus A310-300 aircraft at a cost of 122 million dirhams.

28 June: In Al-Maqam Palace in Al-Ain, Sheikh Zayed received the President of the Eritrean Provisional Government, Asyas Afwerki. Zayed expressed the hope that in the future Eritrea would be able to flourish as it became more stable. He called for co-operation in the best interests of Eritrea.

Sheikh Hamdan bin Zayed Al Nahyan, returning to the UAE after his official visit to Russia, expressed his satisfaction at the results of his visit. He stressed the UAE's wish to reinforce the ties of friendship and co-operation with all States in which there was mutual interest for everyone concerned.

29 June: Sheikh Sultan bin Zayed Al Nahyan in a meeting with the head of the Eritrean Provisional Government, Asyas Afwerki, stressed the UAE's support for the Eritrean Government and the rebuilding of the country.

An 110 million dirham agreement to install a large factory in the Jebel Ali Free Zone, which would produce 660 million aluminum cans annually, was signed.

2 July: Sheikh Zayed, attending the annual local sail boat races, called on young people to act as a barrier in defence of the nation and to maintain it as it was maintained by their forebears.

4 July: ADMA announced that, between 1972 and 1992, 621 shipments of crude oil were made and that oil reserves stood at 17 billion barrels.

8 July: Dubai Municipality began work on development projects amounting to 4.7 billion dirhams, including public service road and electricity projects, within the comprehensive development plan for the emirate of Dubai.

9 July: Sheikh Zayed received a letter from Lebanese President, Elias Al Harawi, conveyed to him by Lebanese Foreign Minister, Faris Bouez. Zayed stressed that every Arab was obligated to attend to the affairs of his brother Arab and that the UAE, as Arabs, believes that there can be no victory for the Arab nation unless the solidarity of the entire nation is achieved.

10 July: Dubai Municipality began creating and developing three public gardens at a cost of 250 million dirhams.

15 July: Sheikh Zayed sent a letter to students who visited Sir Bani Yas and

Delma islands calling on them to be serious in acquiring knowledge and information on the country and to remember the hardships of their forebears.

18 July: Sheikh Zayed began an inspection tour of the Western Region with a visit to the island of Delma. The tour was part of his great concern for the development and improvement of living conditions in the remote areas of the country and the islands.

21 July: Sheikh Zayed, continuing his tour of the Western Region, inspected soil reclamation projects in Al-Dhafra district. During the tour, he called on responsible officials to advance progress in agricultural development. He said that his tour was to be taken as a letter directed to every minister and responsible official calling on them to work tirelessly to strengthen development and achieve a good standard of living for all citizens.

28 July: Abu Dhabi Executive Council approved the setting-up of a vegetable and date-canning factory in the city of Al-Marfa in the Western Region.

5 August: Sheikh Zayed issued a decree setting-up the Zayed bin Sultan Philantropic Foundation with a capital of 3.671 billion dirhams (1 billion dollars).

7 August: Sheikh Zayed, in remarks made to radio and television on the occasion of the twenty-sixth anniversary of his rise to power in Abu Dhabi emirate, said that the people of the Emirates deserve happiness and well-being, and that whatever the country had provided for them amounts to very little in comparison to the aspirations of the people, a people who had sacrificed a great deal for the sake of the country. He commented: 'What the Rulers and I have done has been for the sake of uplifting the country and enhancing its destiny. The security of the Gulf is the responsibility of its people and Arab action is governed by dialogue and not by aggression.'

7 August: Mohammad Nukhaira Juma Al Dhahiri took the oath of office as the first national to be sworn in as a public deputy. The oath was taken before Sheikh Zayed who encouraged him to adhere to truth, seriousness and sincerity in performing his work and that he must work without fear or partiality in pursuit of justice. He said that the individual in his work and the men who bear responsibility with efficiency and ability are the ones in whom their families and their country can take pride.

9 August: The Ministry of Electricity and Water finished the installation and operation of seven new gas turbines in the Northern Emirates at a cost of 375 dirhams.

18 August: Sheikh Mohammad bin Butti opened the new 37 million dirham fish market in Abu Dhabi.

25 August: The UAE, in a speech before the United Nations, called for action to stop Serb aggression against the people of Bosnia- Hercegovina and for non-recognition of the results of this aggression. The UAE also maintained that the Serb massacres of civilians must not be allowed to pass without putting the perpetrators on trial.

26 August: The UAE's GDP rose to 121.2 billion dirhams in 1991.

27 August: The UAE stressed its continuing concern for the unity and integrity of the territory and people of Iraq. It also called on the regime in Baghdad to implement all international resolutions.

31 August: The Council of Ministers approved the project to industrialize the country's date crop with a capital of 40 million dirhams.

2 September: The Ministry of Foreign Affairs announced that what the Iranian officials have done and are doing on Abu Musa Island was not compatible with relations between the UAE and Iran and reflected negatively on co-operation between the two countries. Iran had prevented more than 100 people who were citizens and employees of the UAE on Abu Musa Island from landing on the island after keeping them at sea for a period of three days from 24 August.

3 September: In remarks made to the Non-aligned Summit in Jakarta, Rashid Abdulla stressed the UAE's keeness to develop economic and commercial relations with all nations and he called for a new world economic order.

6 September: The UAE called on Arab leaders to take immediate and effective action to save Somalia and to assist it in ending its ordeal. An official source said that, as brothers, the UAE must help and not remain mere spectators to the destruction and bloodletting in Somalia.

9 September: At the GCC's Ministerial Council meeting in Jeddah in which Sheikh Hamdan bin Zayed Al Nahyan was participating, the UAE strongly condemned measures undertaken by Iran on Abu Musa Island and it rejected the continuation of the occupation of the Greater and Lesser Tunb Islands. He confirmed the UAE's insistence on maintaining complete sovereignty over Abu Musa island.

10 September: Sheikh Zayed received a letter from US President, George Bush, in which he reaffirmed the American stand against those who threaten their neighbours and challenge the world's determination.

The Foreign Ministers of the Damascus Declaration States, meeting in Doha with the participation of Sheikh Hamdan bin Zayed Al Nahyan, condemned the Iran's actions on Abu Musa Island and said that it was a violation of the sovereignty and unity of UAE territory. They stressed support of their countries for the UAE in exercising its sovereignty over the islands.

11 September: The UAE welcomed the positive stance which the European countries adopted with regard to the tragedy in Bosnia and called for a translation of this stance into practical and decisive steps to put a stop to the outrages which were being committed by the Serbian forces.

12 September: In Rabat, Sheikh Zayed and the Moroccan Minister for Foreign Affairs, Dr Abdulatif Al Filali, discussed the situation in the Gulf and current developments in the Arab world.

13 September: The Council of the Arab League, at its concluding meeting in Cairo in which Sheikh Hamdan bin Zayed Al Nahyan participated, confirmed the UAE's' sovereignty over the three islands of Greater and Lesser Tunbs and Abu Musa. They further confirmed that all the members of the League supported the UAE's entire right to the islands while condemning the illegal Iranian occupation.

The Central Bank annual report revealed that the non-oil sectors had achieved a growth of 5.3 per cent and that there was a rise in GDP to 71.7 billion dirhams in 1991, an increase of 4.2 per cent over 1990. The Central Bank balance rose to 20.42

billion dirhams in 1991, in comparison to 17.285 billion in 1990.

14 September: The UAE Team won first prize for markmanship and were awarded the gold medal in the seventh Arab rifle shooting competition in Syria.

17 September: A ship carrying 2000 tons of various kinds of relief commodities for Somalia departed from Port Zayed.

19 September: The UAE donated 5 million dollars to the American Disaster Relief Fund to aid the victims of the tornado *Andrew* which struck the State of Florida.

21 September: Sheikh Zayed arrived in Alexandria from Rabat where he held discussions with the Egyptian President, Mohammad Hosni Mubarak, about current developments in the Gulf and the achievement of Arab consensus.

24 September: Sheikh Zayed arrived in Damascus where he discussed with the Syrian President, Hafez Al Asad, the current Arab situation, developments in the Gulf and efforts to bring peace to the Middle East.

26 September: Sheikh Zayed arrived in Jeddah from Damascus after holding three rounds of discussions with Syrian President, Hafez Al Asad. Zayed and King Fahad bin Abdulaziz discussed regional developments and bilateral relations.

27 September: The first round of talks between the UAE and Iran concerning settlement of the matter of the three islands (Lesser and Greater Tunb and Abu Musa) was held in the Presidential Office. Points of view were put forth on the subject of the islands.

28 September: The UAE issued a statement in which it laid the responsibility at Iran's door for the lack of progress in the talks on the three islands. It said that the UAE would resort to all peaceful means to assert its sovereignty over the islands after the refusal of Iran to end the occupation of the islands or to raise the case at the International Court of Justice.

29 September: Rashid Abdulla briefed the Council of Arab Foreign Ministers at its meetings in the UN headquarters on the latest developments in steps being taken by the UAE to peacefully resolve the three islands crisis.

30 September: In a speech before the United Nations, Rashid Abdulla again stressed the readiness of the UAE to settle the question of the three islands with Iran by peaceful means in accordance with the Charter of the United Nations, taking into consideration the sovereignty of the UAE over these islands. He warned that the Iranian measures taken on Abu Musa would increase the tension and disturb stability and security in the region and would be incompatible with peaceful co-existence and good-neighbourliness.

1 October: The United States of America expressed its complete support for the United Arab Emirates and the states of the Gulf Co-operation Council in the matter of the three islands occupied by Iran. It announced its rejection of the practices of Iran and its attempt to impose its control by force on Abu Musa Island.
Sheikh Mohammad bin Rashid Al Maktoum opened the new course at the Emirates Golf Club in Dubai.

2 October: Dubai Chamber of Commerce and Industry signed a contract to construct its headquarters building at a cost of 77.5 million dirhams.

5 October: The Council of Ministers approved the allocation of 45 million dirhams to maintain and improve the road between Sharjah and Ras al-Khaimah, and an allocation of 180 million dirhams for student grants in State schools.

6 October: Sheikh Dr Sultan bin Mohammed Al Qassimi signed a contract to import and install two electricity generators in the cities of Khor Fakkan and Kalba at a cost of 100 million French francs.

11 October: Sheikh Zayed held a session of discussions with the Egyptian President, Mohammad Hosni Mubarak, who arrived in the country on a short visit. During the talks, they discussed developments in the situation in the Middle East and the Gulf region and ways to strengthen joint Arab action.

12 October: Sheikh Khalifa bin Zayed Al Nahyan arrived in Islamabad on an official visit to Pakistan where he met Pakistani President, Ghulam Ishaq Khan, and the Prime Minister, Mohammad Nawaz Sharif.

13 October: Sheikh Zayed ordered that 40 million dollars be given to Egypt to repair the damage and aid the victims of the earthquake which struck Egypt.

Sheikh Khalifa bin Zayed Al Nahyan visited the Pakistani industrial complex and military aircraft maintenance set-up where he observed the work being carried out on UAE Air Force aircraft.

14 October: On the instructions of Sheikh Maktoum, Sheikh Mohammad bin Rashid Al Maktoum announced a donation of 10 million dollars to re-house the victims of the earthquake in Egypt.

17 October: Sheikh Zayed received a delegation from the Supreme Executive Committee which was formed by the International Conference on Human Rights in Bosnia-Hercegovina under the chairmanship of Sheikh Mohammad Al Ghazali. The President of the Federation confirmed that the UAE resolutely supported Bosnian resistance. He referred to the fact that the UAE had not, and would never, neglect its duty and called for the international community to stand up to Serbian aggression.

18 October: Sheikh Zayed and Dr Esmat Abdel-Meguid discussed current developments in the region.

20 October: Sheikh Khalifa bin Zayed Al Nahyan ordered that limited income UAE families in Al-Ain be exempted from installment payments on their housing units, apartments and shops in the markets, the value of which amounted to 28 million dirhams and concerned 1454 citizens.

21 October: Sheikh Zayed ordered that 8 million dirhams be set aside for the construction of new buildings for the two branches of Abu Dhabi Women's Association in Al-Marfa and on Delma Island.

26 October: Sheikh Zayed held discussions with King Hassan of Morocco who was on an official visit to the Emirates. During the session, they exchanged points of view about the current situation in the Gulf, ways of re-establishing Arab solidarity on a firm basis and a summary of current developments in Arab affairs. Bosnian President, Ali Izebegovitz, arrived in the UAE on an official visit.

31 October: Sheikh Zayed presided over a meeting of the Supreme Council of the Federation in which he stressed the eagerness of the Rulers, himself included, to achieve the hopes and ambitions of the country and its citizens. He also confirmed that the Federation had their full support and that serious efforts were continuously being made to realize the aims of the Federation. The Council studied developments in the ongoing Iranian occupation of the three islands.

2 November: The Council of Ministers approved the construction of 34 public housing units in Al-Falah district in Sharjah at a cost of 13 million dirhams.

3 November: Abu Dhabi Executive Council approved the construction of 108 public housing units in Al-Marfa and the New Medina Al-Nahdha, and 417 million dirhams was allocated to improve and expand Airport Street and a number of other streets in the city of Abu Dhabi.

5 November: Sheikh Surour bin Mohammad Al Nahyan said that the Al-Taweelah energy and water complex would pipe nearly 40 million gallons of drinking water daily to Al-Ain once stage two of the project was completed.

7 November: In a speech at the United Nations, the United Arab Emirates demanded that the Arab Gulf region be kept free of conflicts and quarrels through efforts to solve existing problems by peaceful means, in accordance with the provisions of the United Nations Charter and the principles of international law.

9 November: Sheikh Zayed received a delegation from the International Lions Club organization which was concerned with good works and humanitarian acts. Zayed received two decorations from the organization in appreciation of the relief he provided for victims of famine and disasters, and in recognition of his efforts and accomplishments in building the United Arab Emirates and supervising its progress.

10 November: Sheikh Khalifa bin Zayed Al Nahyan attended graduation ceremonies for the first batch of students from the Military Staff College at the College headquarters in Abu Dhabi. He confirmed that the United Arab Emirates was a peaceful nation and said 'our keenness to build a modern army depends on high-level scientific capabilities which proceed from our complete faith in the fact that we must have the force necessary to impose peace and that there is no alternative to force in order to bring about peace and then to protect it.'

15 November: Sheikh Khalifa bin Zayed Al Nahyan allocated 2.5 million dirhams to buy computer equipment for Ministry of Education schools, confirming Zayed's support for the future of education. The Ministers of Defence of the Gulf Co-operation Council, at their meeting in Kuwait, condemned Iranian measures being taken on Abu Musa Island. They called on Iran to abide by agreements made between it and the United Arab Emirates with regard to Abu Musa Island.

16 November: The Council of Ministers approved the draft law setting-up a Federal Environment Agency and a draft law regulating the transplant of human organs.

17 November: The Industrial Bank approved the financing of four new programmes valued at 18.7 million dirhams in the paper, carton, glass and building materials sectors.

Sharjah Municipality signed a 32 million dirham contract for the dredging of Al-Khan lagoon as a recreational development, the reclaimed land around the lagoon can also be used for the construction of a business and residential area.

18 November: The UAE, in a speech before the Security Council, called on the international community to shoulder its full responsibilities in maintaining the independence and integrity of the territory of Bosnia-Hercegovina and standing-up to genocidal Serbian aggression.

24 November: The Council of Ministers approved the creation of an institute for judicial training and studies attached to the Ministry of Justice.

25 November: Sheikh Zayed, receiving GCC foreign ministers, told them that the thirteenth Gulf Summit which Abu Dhabi was hosting in December would convene in the shadow of very delicate and important circumstances demanding a shared shouldering of responsibilities. He expressed his hope that the coming Summit would be one of purification and harmony.

The GCC Ministerial Council held a meeting in Abu Dhabi to prepare for the Summit. Rashid Abdulla stressed in his opening speech that the peoples of the region were watching for the results of this summit which would be held while regional and Arab changes of vast importance were taking place. He said that Iran was still refusing to consider the UAE's demand that it end its military occupation of the three islands.

27 November: In Rabat, Sheikh Zayed and King Hassan of Morocco discussed recent developments in the Gulf region. Zayed expressed his appreciation for King Hassan's initiative and his efforts and keenness in bringing the Arab nation together and uniting its ranks.

30 November: Sheikh Zayed, in a speech on the occasion of the twenty-first National Day, stressed that the UAE since its foundation had remained true to its Arab character and had not isolated itself from the Arab nation. It had proved that the Federation was a source of power and that it was striving for complete Arab unity.

1 December: Sheikh Zayed ordered that a complete inventory be taken of the requirements of the UAE's centres for the handicapped, and that they be provided with whatever they needed to enable them to play their role in caring for that special group in society. Zayed donated 1 million dirhams to support the centres.

2 December: Sheikh Zayed received the Members of the Supreme Council of the Federation and groups of well-wishers on the twenty-first anniversary of National Day. He sent a letter of thanks to the Rulers, in which he praised their efforts and their prominent role in setting up the Federation. He said: 'We were able to help each other and work together to achieve a favourable future for the people of the Emirates.'

The UAE donated 500,000 dollars to the United Nations Relief Agency for Palestinian Refugees (UNWRA).

7 December: Sheikh Zayed, in remarks made to the Emirates New Agency on the occasion of the National Day, expressed his esteem and pride in the Federation and in the realization of its benevolent and generous progress. He said that the people of the Emirates had a flourishing future ahead of them and that they would be blessed with a high standard of living and progress under the aegis of the Federation. He called for a sincere Arab and Islamic awakening to confront dangers and said that Arabs must deal with their problems for the sake of reviving glory, esteem and mutual assistance.

5 December: Humaid bin Nasser Al Nowais signed two contracts worth 195 million dirhams to raise high tension electrical power in Fujairah and to deal with brackish water in Ajman.

6 December: Sheikh Zayed ordered that a battalion of the UAE Armed Forces be added to the multinational force which the

Security Council decided to send to Somalia to participate in humanitarian relief.

Sheikh Mohammad bin Rashid Al Maktoum opened the fourth exhibition of the products of companies working in the Jebel Ali Free Zone.

7 December: Sheikh Zayed, in remarks made to the Emirates New Agency, called for the international community to use its power and immediately adopt measures to save the people of Bosnia-Hercegovina, similar to the measures which were agreed upon in the Somali affair. He said that whoever disagrees with putting an end to aggression is a partner to the aggression and oppression.

The UAE, in a statement issued by the Council of Ministers, expressed its sorrow at the actions of an irresponsible group who attacked and destroyed the Babri mosque in the Indian city of Ayodya. He called on the Government of India to put an end to such acts.

8 December: Sheikh Zayed sent an invitation to the leaders of GCC countries to attend the thirteenth GCC Summit to be convened in Abu Dhabi on 21 December. Abu Dhabi Council approved the allocation of 358 million dirhams for Abu Dhabi television and broadcasting development projects, the construction of 100 dwellings in Wadi Al-Fili and doubling the highway to Medinat Zayed.

9 December: Sheikh Zayed issued a federal law with respect to the Marriage Fund which aims at helping and encouraging UAE nationals to marry local women by granting them 70,000 dirhams towards expenses.

Al-Ain Municipality Department signed a contract to erect three water storage tanks in Al-Shuwaib district, each one to store 2 million gallons. The total cost of the tanks is estimated at 89.4 million dirhams.

13 December: Sheikh Maktoum bin Rashid Al Maktoum on the occasion of the convening of the Gulf Summit called for more mutual assistance and support among Gulf Co-operation Council States within the framework of one Gulf family, so that more stability and security can be achieved and that hopes for progress and development can be realized.

14 December: The Council of Ministers welcomed the leaders of the Gulf Co-operation Council States at their summit convened in Abu Dhabi. The Council expressed the hope that the summit would achieve the ambitions of the GCC peoples in the areas of progress and stability.

16 December: The Ministry of the Interior signed a 35 million dirham contact to supply the ministry with computers to store fingerprints.

18 December: Sheikh Zayed spoke to two Egyptian newspapers, *Al-Ahram* and *Akhbar Al-Yom*, and the Lebanese newspaper *Al-Anwar*. He told them that the GCC Summit would be the basis for moulding the Gulf individual into one family and that all efforts would be made to give support and encouragement.

19 December: Sheikh Zayed received GCC Ministers of Foreign Affairs who began their meetings in Abu Dhabi to prepare for the GCC Summit.

20 December: Sheikh Dr Sultan bin Mohammad Al Qassimi opened the Arab Police Conference which was holding its meetings in Sharjah.

21 December: Sheikh Zayed inaugurated the thirteenth Gulf Co-operation Council Summit in Abu Dhabi under the banner of 'Purity'. He expressed his hope that the Summit would achieve the aspirations of the Arab peoples and he held peripheral consultations with the leaders of the Council States to ensure the success of the conference proceedings.

23 December: Sheikh Zayed presided over the final session of the GCC Summit. He stressed that the fruits of the Summit would benefit the peoples of the region and all Arabs and Muslims. He confirmed that the Summit was a decisive rejection of the continuing Iranian occupation of the three islands belonging to the UAE. The Summit endorsed the recommendations for military co-operation among the Council States and it approved the nomination of Sheikh Fahim Al Qassimi as the Secretary General of the Co-operation Council.

28 December: The Council of Ministers praised the results of the GCC Summit

and Sheikh Zayed's efforts to make it a success.

29 December: Sheikh Surour bin Mohammad Al Nahyan signed a 162 million dirham contract for electricity distribution plants in the Western Region.

30 December: Sheikh Zayed decreed the following appointments:

(1) General Hamouda bin Ali was promoted to Major General and was appointed as special adviser to the President with the rank of minister;

(2) General Mohammad Said Al Badi was appointed as Minister of the Interior;

(3) General Sheikh Mohammad bin Zayed Al Nahyan was appointed as Chief of the General Staff and

(4) Sheikh Hazza bin Zayed was appointed as Chief of State Security with the rank of Minister.

Nineteen Ninety Three

5 January: Sheikh Maktoum bin Rashid Al Maktoum issued a law forming an establishment capitalized at 1 million dirhams to finance housing for nationals in the emirate of Dubai. The law governed the granting of property loans on easy terms and without interest.

Sheikh Dr Sultan bin Mohammad Al Qassimi opened the Sharjah Archaeological Museum as part of his concern for the national heritage and his keenness to protect archaeological discoveries in the emirate of Sharjah.

6 January: There were 79 new industrial installations with a combined capital of 99.1 million dirhams created in the emirate of Sharjah during 1992.

9 January: Sheikh Zayed and the Members of the Federal Supreme Council attended the first race meeting where both camels and horses were featured. Zayed expressed his happiness at this festival and said that it was important to continue mounting such races and similar events in order to keep alive traditional sports from the past.

10 January: In 1992, Dubai Municipality distributed 4357 sites to citizens on which they were permitted to construct private dwellings.

11 January: The Council of Ministers approved the draft federal budget for 1993. Expenditure was estimated at 17.631 billion dirhams and revenues projected at 15.911 billion dirhams, creating a deficit of 1.72 billion dirhams.

16 January: Assets of the Central Bank during the first half of 1992 amounted to 19.8 billion dirhams.

18 January: The UAE Armed Forces Battalion arrived in Somalia to participate in the international 'Return of Hope' operation.

22 January: Construction began on the new 310-bed Central Emergency Hospital in Abu Dhabi which will cost 380 million dirhams.

28 January: Sheikh Mohammad bin Rashid Al Maktoum opened the Dubai Creek Golf and Marina Complex

2 February: In reply to the enquiries of the Secretary General of the United Nations regarding Security Council Resolution 778 of 1992 concerning Iraqi oil returns, the UAE advised the UN that there were no Iraqi Government funds in the country.

6 February: Sheikh Zayed, opening the new session of the Federal National

Council, confirmed his desire and the desire of the other Rulers to support Government institutions. He said that the country is one body in which there is collective participation, with opinions voiced and counsel proffered in order to serve the national work programme. He stressed that the principle of consultation is a fixed principle inherited from UAE society before the establishment of the Federal Council. He also said that the occupation by Iran of the three islands is a violation of the sovereignty and territorial integrity of the country, as well as a disturbance to security in the region.

7 February: In Islamabad, Sheikh Maktoum bin Rashid Al Maktoum, who was on an official visit to Pakistan, held talks with the Prime Minister, Mohammad Nawaz Sharif, during which they discussed the situation in the Gulf region and the Indian Ocean as well as bilateral relations between the two countries. During the visit, an agreement was signed forbidding double taxation between the UAE and Pakistan. Sheikh Maktoum donated 1 million dollars to the flood victims in Pakistan.

8 February: In Islamabad, Sheikh Maktoum bin Rashid Al Maktoum and the Pakistani President, Ghulam Ishaq Khan, discussed a number of regional and international matters of mutual concern.

10 February: The UAE settled its share of the Arab League budget for 1993, amounting to 1.8 million dollars.

13 February: Dubai Electricity Board dedicated the new gas turbine at the Jebel Ali Electricity Plant. The turbine which has a capacity of 114 megawatts cost 3 billion dirhams.

As of December 1992, Ministry of Electricity and Water water desalination plants produced 133 million gallons of water per day.

14 February: Sheikh Zayed, in remarks to the Emirates News Agency on the occasion of the opening of the first Defence Exhibition, IDEX '93, stressed that the UAE was keen on strengthening and developing its relations with the nations of the world for the good of its peoples. He said that the country's foreign policy was based on mutual respect between all countries and efforts to win the respect and confidence of the world, as well as to cut off terrorism at its roots.

Sheikh Khalifa bin Zayed Al Nahyan opened the first International Defence Exhibition, IDEX '93, at the exhibition pavilion in Abu Dhabi. He stressed that the UAE, under the leadership of the President of the Federation, did not hesitate for an instant in building-up its forces in order to become one of the Arab supports in the region. He also announced that the UAE would remain true to its pledge to stay at the forefront of the States which build bridges of co-operation and respect good neighbourly relations.

The UAE awarded a French company a contract to supply its Armed Forces with 436 French Leclerc tanks and 46 armoured support vehicles. The 60 per cent offset element required by all defence-related contracts was still to be agreed before final signature on the deal.

15 February: The UAE contracted with an American company to purchase an automated communications, command and control air defence system. The 60 per cent offset element to the contract included provision of a transportation system, aircraft maintenance, power generating, air traffic control systems and possible construction of a radar manufacturing plant.

16 February: The UAE Equestrian Federation won first place in the second GCC championship show-jumping event. The UAE snooker team also won the GCC championship.

20 February: Sheikh Sultan bin Zayed Al Nahyan attended graduation exercises for the fifth batch of officer candidates at the Police College in Abu Dhabi.

1 March: Sheikh Maktoum, after an inspection visit to Dubai Municipality, allocated 200 million dirhams for the intersections project and 250 million dirhams for re-planning the sewerage system.

Sheikh Hamdan bin Rashid Al Maktoum donated 100,000 dollars to the Muslims of Bosnia-Hercegovina.

2 March: The Permanent Committee for Projects allocated 18.7 million dirhams to set up a flight information centre in the country.

4 March: Sheikh Surour bin Mohammad Al Nahyan opened a major electricity line, with a capacity of 120 megawatts, connecting the Al-Ain plant with the northern districts of the city at a cost of 130 million dirhams.

5 March: The Director of Social Services signed contracts worth 287 million dirhams for the construction of 50 new commercial buildings in Abu Dhabi and Al-Ain.

8 March: Abu Dhabi Executive Council approved the granting of loans to citizens to finance the second group of applications which were received by the Housing Loan Board in Abu Dhabi and Al-Ain. Some 423 citizens benefited from the loans at a total cost of 380 million dirhams.

12 March: Sheikh Zayed issued the decree forming the Zayed bin Sultan Al Nahyan Philantropic Foundation under the chairmanship of Sheikh Khalifa bin Zayed Al Nahyan.

15 March: Sheikh Ahmed bin Said Al Maktoum signed a loan for financing the purchase of two Airbus aircraft to augment Emirates Airlines fleet.

17 March: Sheikh Zayed received the learned men and preachers of Islam who had come to the country to enhance the nights of Ramadan. He called for a commitment to the teachings of Islam, stressing that the Book of Allah is the constitution of the Muslims which governs their creed and behaviour. He said that the weakness of the Islamic nation was the reason for divisions, quarrels and deviant religious ideas not found in the Book of Allah or in the guidance of His Prophet. He called for a dialogue to support Islamic action.

21 March: Sheikh Zayed received the judges of the *Sharia* courts and the heads of the country's federal courts. He stressed that 'leniency in judgments is not pleasing to me nor does it please any Muslim. Furthermore, it denigrates the reputation of Islam and the Muslims, contradicts the edicts of Allah and encourages the foolish and ignorant to become insolent and outrageous.' He cautioned that judgments must be based on clear proof and indisputable evidence, while calling on men of religion to resist the phenomenon of religious extremism which Islam rejects. He also stressed that youth must be obedient to the principles of religion and right which encourage people to practise mutual forgiveness and to show human understanding for one another. The killing by a Muslim of his fellow Muslim is rejected, he said.

24 March: Sheikh Mohammad bin Zayed Al Nahyan returned to the country after an inspection visit to the Armed Forces in Somalia.

25 March: The UAE was accepted for membership in the International Federation of Water Sports.

29 March: Sheikh Zayed issued a law setting-up the Federal Environmental Agency.

1 April: Sheikh Zayed held discussions with the Lebanese President, Elias Al Harawi, who was visiting the country. He stressed during the meeting that the UAE would never withhold support for the future development and rebuilding of Lebanon. He emphasized the necessity of achieving Arab solidarity and mutual forgiveness among brothers, and the need to place higher interests above all considerations.

4 April: The meetings of the UAE-Oman Commission began in Al-Ain.

5 April: The UAE-Oman Commission concluded with an agreement to strengthen the ties between the two countries in various fields.

10 April: Sheikh Zayed and the Romanian President, Ian Iliescu, who was visiting the country, discussed political developments in Arab and international arenas and developments in the Gulf.

Sheikh Zayed received former US President, Jimmy Carter, who thanked Zayed for his help in overcoming disasters in Africa by donating 5.7 million dollars in aid.

12 April: Sheikh Sultan bin Zayed Al Nahyan and the President of Bosnia-Hercegovina, Ali Izebegovitch, held a meeting in which Sheikh Sultan stressed the UAE's support for the people of Bosnia in their struggle to maintain the independence of their country and their territorial integrity.

13 April: Sheikh Zayed received the President of Bosnia-Hercegovina, Ali Izetbegovitch. During the meeting Zayed stressed the UAE's support for the Bosnian people in their struggle against tyrannical Serbian aggression, and he called for the international community to assist and support the people of Bosnia in dealing with their ordeal and helping them overcome injustice.

16 April: The UAE, in a speech by the Federal National Council before the International Parliamentary Union in New Delhi, stressed that continuation of the Iranian occupation of the three islands belonging to the Emirates constituted a violation of the sovereignty of the UAE and called on Iran to listen to the voice of peace and put the fundamentals of international legality into effect.

18 April: Work began in setting-up the 22 million dirham computerized control station for the distribution of natural gas to industrial production units in Dubai.

20 April: Sheikh Sultan bin Zayed Al Nahyan attended graduation ceremonies for the two new groups of students from the UAE University and the Higher Technical Colleges.

The second batch of UAE Armed Forces left for Somalia to participate in the international 'Return of Hope' operation.

21 April: Abu Dhabi Executive Council allocated 74 million dirhams to set-up buildings for the Higher Technical Colleges in Abu Dhabi and Al-Ain. ADNOC announced in its annual report for 1992 that it had exported 90 per cent of its oil production. It also said that the development of the Umm al-Nar Refinery project was completed, and that it was producing 2 million barrels a day of crude oil and 10.5 tons of refined products.

24 April: Sheikh Khalifa bin Zayed Al Nahyan donated 3 million dollars to the Islamic Solidarity Fund of the Islamic Conference Organization.

26 April: In Al-Ain, Sheikh Zayed held discussions with Sultan Qaboos bin Said of Oman concerning new developments in Arab, Islamic and international affairs, the situation in the Gulf, ways to strengthen security and stability in the region and supporting the future of the GCC.

The UAE donated 10 million dollars to assist Bosnia-Hercegovina.

28 April: Sheikh Hamdan bin Zayed Al Nahyan stressed in his speech before the meeting of the Islamic Conference Organization in Karachi that the UAE was working with its brother States in the GCC to apply the concepts which came with new international changes based on mutual understanding and dialogue. It was also working to provide security, stability, peaceful coexistence and the settlement of regional disputes by peaceful means. He confirmed anew the readiness of the UAE to continue peaceful dialogue directly with Iran to solve the question of the islands.

28 April: Sheikh Zayed stressed in remarks made to the conference of the heads of youth societies who were meeting in the cultural complex in Abu Dhabi that the UAE was making progress on its way to building a better society and was keen to provide a suitable atmosphere where progress, distinguished advancement and superior performance can be achieved and where there is complete freedom for both the individual and the country.

29 April: In Rabat, the agreement on the Zayed date-planting project, set-up by Sheikh Zayed to plant date trees in Al-Rashidiya district, Morocco, was signed

1 May: Sheikh Sultan bin Khalifa Al Nahyan opened the Abu Dhabi Centre for Commercial Reconciliation and Arbitration which aims at settling disputes through arbitration on the basis of the principles of the Islamic religion and the *Sharia*.

The UAE welcomed the plebiscite conducted under the supervision of the United Nations resulting in the declaration of Eritrean independence.

2 May: Sheikh Zayed received the Lebanese Prime Minister, Omar Al Hariri, and stressed again that the UAE would support the Lebanese people to the best of its abilities as they rebuild their country after the years of destruction and civil war. He called for the Lebanese people to stick together so that the Arabs can stand by their side.

The UAE and the Sultanate of Oman signed a contract establishing the UAE-Oman Investment Company with a capital of 30 million Omani riyals. Each State will own 30 per cent of the company and the remainder of the shares will be offered to the private sector in both countries.

7 May: The *fatwa* section in the office of the *Sharia* Judiciary issued a legal *fatwa* regarding the position of Islam on extremism. It said that in Islam there is no extremism, no terrorism and no fanaticism and that no Muslim has the right to kill anyone who pronounces the two creeds of Islam. Furthermore, the killing of tourists and protected persons is not at all a part of Islam.

Abu Dhabi Municipality created a Heritage Garden on the site of the old bus station in the middle of the city of Abu Dhabi.

9 May: Sheikh Sultan bin Zayed Al Nahyan announced the creation of the UAE Marine Heritage Club which aims at reviving and maintaining traditional water sports.

10 May: Talks were held between the UAE, under the chairmanship of Sheikh Sultan bin Zayed Al Nahyan, and the Belorussian Republic, under the chairmanship of Sviatislav Kabeitsh, the Prime Minister. The peace process in the Middle East and bilateral relations were discussed.

11 May: Sheikh Zayed received the Prime Minister of Belorussia, Sviatislav Kabeitsh, with whom he discussed current international affairs and bilateral relations.

14 May: Sheikh Zayed held a second session of discussions with the Egyptian President, Mohammad Hosni Mubarak, who was visiting the country. During the meeting they discussed Islamic and Arab affairs and support for Arab solidarity on a new and effective basis.

The Social Services Department signed contracts for constructing 32 commercial buildings at a cost of 250 million dirhams.

16 May: Sheikh Khalifa bin Zayed Al Nahyan presided over the first meeting of the Board of Trustees of the Zayed bin Sultan Al Nahyan Philantropic Foundation. He said that setting-up this foundation is a means of undertaking good works, pious deeds and benevolent actions which Zayed has always done and which he will continue to do in following the concepts of the Islamic religion, a religion which encourages co-operation as well as love and respect for one another.

Sheikh Sultan bin Zayed Al Nahyan received UK Energy Minister, Tim Eager.

During their meeting, Sultan confirmed the UAE's opposition to the carbon tax which Europe was attempting to impose on crude oil.

19 May: Sheikh Zayed received the members of the Marriage Fund Board of Administration under the chairmanship of Saif Al Jarwan, Minister of Labour and Social Affairs, who briefed him on the work plan for the Fund. Zayed called for the members to be serious and sincere in their work, in order to achieve the desired goals and to put an end to the phenomenon of the rise in the price of dowries and extravagance in wedding arrangements. He also called for all citizens, and especially the youth, to be aware of and return to the behaviour of their forebears.

22 May: On the island of Sir Bani Yas, Sheikh Zayed met with the Marriage Fund Board of Administration and the members of the Fund's committees in the various emirates, as well as with a number of young people who had decided to get married. He called on youth to take their families into consideration when deciding on dowries and wedding expenses. He asked that serious work be done in following- up on the concerns of youth and their affairs in life, stressing that a girl's honour is not measured by the price of the dowry.

In the Presidential Diwan in Abu Dhabi official discussions took place between the UAE, under the chairmanship of Sheikh Hamdan bin Zayed Al Nahyan, and Iran, under the chairmanship of Ali Akbar Velayati. During the meeting, there were discussions on bilateral relations, ways of strengthening and developing these relations, and a review of current regional and international affairs.

23 May: Sheikh Zayed received a letter from the Iranian President, Hashemi

Rafsanjani, regarding bilateral relations, which was conveyed by the Minister of Foreign Affairs, Ali Akbar Velayati. In a joint press conference, the UAE and Iran expressed their desire and readiness to continue the dialogue between the two countries to resolve questions which were pending, in order to develop and strengthen relations in the service of the security and stability of the region.

Sheikh Sultan bin Khalifa Al Nahyan announced the opening of the Abu Dhabi International Marine Sports Club under his chairmanship and that he will take the responsibility of organizing speed boat racing.

24 May: Sheikh Maktoum bin Rashid Al Maktoum issued directives on the urgency of finding a solution to the problem of electrical cuts in Ras al-Khaimah. He signed a 100 million dirham contract to raise the capacity of the lines bringing electricity to consumers.

28 May: Sheikh Zayed, who was on a visit to Britain, held discussions with UK Foreign Secretary, Douglas Hurd, on developments in the Gulf, international affairs and bilateral relations between the two countries.

2 June: Sheikh Zayed and Sheikh Maktoum attended the British Derby. Zayed expressed his satisfaction at the distinguished participation of the UAE in such horse-racing events.

4 June: In London, Sheikh Zayed and the UK Minister of Defence discussed bilateral relations, the situation in the Gulf and military co-operation between the two countries.

5 June: Sheikh Khalifa bin Zayed Al Nahyan received the Palestinian delegation which was visiting the country under the chairmanship of Mahmoud Abbas (Abu Mazin). Sheikh Khalifa stressed the UAE's support for the right of the Palestinian people to self-determination and he expressed hope that peace negotiations which were being sponsored by the US and Russia would bring about the return of Arab rights and lead to a full, just and permanent settlement of the Arab - Israeli conflict and the Palestinian question. Sheikh Hamdan bin Zayed Al Nahyan then met the Palestinian delegation for official discussions concerning the peace process in the Middle East.

6 June: Sheikh Hamdan bin Zayed Al Nahyan received a letter from the Iranian Foreign Minister, Ali Akbar Velayati, containing an invitation to visit Tehran within the scope of contacts between the two countries.

A 19.4 million dirham contract was signed to construct the first phase of the building for the country's Aviation Meteorology Centre.

12 June: Damascus Declaration Foreign Ministers held their seventh meeting in Abu Dhabi. Rashid Abdulla asked them to translate Sheikh Zayed's call into mutual forgiveness and an end to Arab differences in true solidarity in order to confront the serious challenges which they faced.

13 June: Sheikh Khalifa bin Zayed Al Nahyan received the Foreign Ministers of the Damascus Declaration States who concluded their meeting in Abu Dhabi. He confirmed the support of the President, the people and the Government of the UAE for all the efforts they had made for the higher Arab good. He said that it was a joint responsibility to provide Arab security and that solidarity required a resolution of Arab differences.

17 June: In Geneva, Sheikh Zayed received the Romanian President, Ian Iliescu. They exchanged points of view on a number of regional and international issues.

Rashid Abdulla, in his speech at the International Conference on Human Rights in Vienna, stressed that the UAE had given the subject of human rights and general freedoms special importance because of its heritage, history and traditions of equality, justice, mercy and mutual forgiveness.

19 June: The UAE gave a 1 million dollar fund to the World Health Organization for awarding an annual international prize to organizations or individuals who make outstanding contributions in the field of health.

20 June: During 1993, the Municipality of Dubai distributed 2500 plots of land to citizens on which to build dwellings.

22 June: Sheikh Zayed issued a decree appointing Sheikh Abdulaziz Mohammad Al Qassimi as his special adviser.

Sheikh Khalifa bin Zayed Al Nahyan allocated 265 million dirhams to set up the College of Medicine and Health Sciences with ancillary units in the city of Al-Ain.

25 June: The UAE said that the boycott of Israel was still effective, that the decision to boycott was a united Arab agreement, and that the reasons which brought it into existence were still present.

27 June: Sheikh Khalifa bin Zayed Al Nahyan presided over the second meeting of the Zayed Philantropic Foundation and approved a resolution allocating more than 9 million dirhams for urgent relief and medicines for hospitals in Bosnia-Hercegovinia. It also allocated other assistance for religious, benevolent and educational causes in a number of other countries.

29 June: Abu Dhabi Executive Council approved the setting-up of a complex of out-patient clinics in the city of Al-Ain.

1 July: In Geneva, Sheikh Zayed received Dr Boutros Ghali, the Secretary General of the United Nations. Zayed requested that the United Nations deal in more depth and seriousness with the acute tragedy of the Muslim people of Bosnia. He also called on the United Nations and the international community to put a stop to the fighting and lift the boycott imposed on arms sales to the Muslims of Bosnia.

Discussions were held between the UAE, under the chairmanship of Sheikh Sultan bin Zayed Al Nahyan, and mainland China, under the chairmanship of Li Lan Chang, Deputy Prime Minister. Two agreements were signed for strengthening economic and commercial co-operation between the two countries.

4 July: Sheikh Khalifa bin Zayed Al Nahyan and the French Defence Minister, François Leotard, discussed bilateral relations. Sheikh Khalifa stressed the necessity of advancing the peace process, emphasizing that France and Europe can play an important role in the Middle East.

5 July: In Geneva, Sheikh Zayed and the Eritrean President, Asyas Afwerki, discussed ways of supporting joint co-operation and African-Arab co-operation. The Council of Ministers approved the allocation of 43 million dirhams to install new electricity plants in Ras al-Khaimah.

7 July: Sheikh Surour bin Mohammad Al Nahyan signed an 82 million dirham contract to connect power stations in the two cities of Medinat Zayed and Al-Marfa as part of an on-going electricity development project in the western region of the emirate.

9 July: A 25 million dollar agreement was signed in Beirut for financing a project for re-building dwellings in Lebanon.

12 July: Sheikh Khalifa bin Zayed Al Nahyan granted 2.56 million dirhams to the Al-Ain Football Club following its championship victory.

13 July: Abu Dhabi Executive Council approved the construction of a high-rise bridge on the Abu Dhabi - Dubai highway at a cost of 68 million dirhams. It also approved the construction of 470 new housing units in Al-Shahama district.

14 July: Head of Economics Department at the Ministry of Petroleum, Sheikh Mohammad Al Qassimi, in an interview criticized some oil consuming states who had sought to implement carbon taxes on oil imports, and urged oil exporting states to respond with raised import tarriffs on western manufactured goods and a wellhead tax on oil exports to the benefit of producers.

20 July: Sheikh Hamdan bin Rashid Al Maktoum opened the new 200 million dirham harbour which stretches along Dubai Creek for a distance of 3 km.

21 July: ADFAED extended a 110 million dirham loan to the Algerian Government to finance the Haroun Dam project.

27 July: Abu Dhabi Executive Council approved the setting-up of Al-Marfa central electricity generation and water desalination plant at a cost of 1.8 billion dirhams.

1 August: In Rabat, Sheikh Zayed and King Hassan of Morocco discussed developments in Arab affairs and ways of effecting Arab reconciliation.

13 August: The Social Services Office signed contracts worth 318 million dirhams for the construction of 24 new commercial buildings in Abu Dhabi.

20 August: Sheikh Zayed arranged for the treatment of 50 wounded victims of the armed conflict in Bosnia-Hercegovina in the hospitals of the Federation and special aircraft were despatched to transport the wounded.

22 August: Sheikh Zayed arrived in Alexandria at the beginning of a visit to Egypt. Upon his arrival he met with Egyptian President, Mohammad Hosni Mubarak.

23 August: Sheikh Zayed held discussions with Egyptian President, Mohammad Hosni Mubarak, during which they studied the Arab situation and the peace process, and confirmed the importance of ensuring stability and security in the Gulf.

28 August: ADNOC began the implementation of a huge project to treat and produce gas in the Habshan district, with the aim of expanding and developing the liquid gas factory and the pipelines to raise the production capacity from 540 million cubic feet to 1865 cubic feet daily.

30 August: Sheikh Surour bin Mohammad Al Nahyan signed the 1.8 billion dirham contract implementing the decision to construct a central electricity-generating station and desalination plant in Al-Marfa.

31 August: The UAE called for an international conference in Geneva on war victims. It also called on the international community to shoulder its responsibilities, oblige Israel to respect international law and apply the Geneva Conventions in the occupied territories, and condemned the savage practices of the Serbs and Croats in Bosnia.

5 September: Sheikh Zayed received the Prime Minister of Lebanon, Omar Hariri. He emphasized the UAE's complete support for Lebanon in its efforts to achieve security and stability for the

Lebanese people. He stressed that support for Lebanon was obligatory and that the Lebanese people deserved every assistance in order to achieve a good life. He also said that the UAE would support the Palestinian-Israeli agreement regarding self-rule and that whatever was satisfactory for the Palestinians would satisfy the UAE, because the Palestinians understood their own interests and what was most suitable for them.

7 September: Sheikh Zayed and UK Foreign Secretary, Douglas Hurd, discussed the current situation in the region and the peace agreement between the Palestine Liberation Organization and Israel.

10 September: The Eighth Arab Youth Festival being held in Beirut chose Sheikh Zayed as the 'Man of the Environment ' for 1993 because of the UAE's achievements. Sheikh Zayed has been directly behind moves taken for the protection of the environment.

The decision was made to cancel Sheikh Hamdan bin Zayed Al Nahyan's visit to Tehran because the UAE was not convinced that Iran wished to make a success of the visit. Iran did not accept that a communiqué be issued in which it would be indicated that the visit was aimed at discussing differences over the three islands, Abu Musa, Greater Tunb and Lesser Tunb. These islands belong to the UAE but were occupied by Iran which has officially laid claim to them.

13 September: The UAE welcomed the agreement which was arrived at between the Palestine Liberation Organization and Israel. The Council of Ministers issued a statement saying that the agreement is considered to be the first step on the way to a fair, comprehensive and permanent solution to the Palestinian problem.

16 September: Sheikh Zayed and the Mauritanian President, Muawiya Ould Sayyid Ahmed Al Tayi, who was visiting the country, discussed current Arab affairs, the most important of which was the peace process in the Middle East, and bilateral relations.

20 September: Sheikh Zayed, receiving a delegation from the European Union, renewed his support for the Palestinian-Israeli Agreement. He said that peace meant stability, development and flourishing growth in the world.

27 September: Sheikh Zayed inspected tourist projects in the Al-Jarf and Ghantoot districts.

30 September: At Al-Maqam Palace in Al-Ain, Sheikh Zayed received citizens of Al-Ain and the Eastern Region. He told the young people that it was necessary to shoulder responsibilities and work sincerely in the service of their families and their country with a true dedication. He also called on them to do their duty toward the country and remember their fathers and grandfathers and how they endured their harsh and difficult life.

2 October: Sheikh Zayed continued his meetings with citizens in Al-Ain and the Eastern Region and confirmed his great concern to provide a good life for them. He said that happiness and luxury for citizens is a trust he bears for them and he and his brothers, the Rulers, are keen on exerting all possible efforts for the sake of the good of the citizens and to achieve more progress and advancement for the country.

3 October: General Sheikh Mohammad bin Zayed Al Nahyan attended exercises mounted by the Armed Forces to receive the first shipment of Apache helicopters.

4 October: Sheikh Tahnoun bin Mohammed Al Nahyan opened the latest bottled gas plant in the city of Al-Ain. The plant, with production at 600 bottles per hour, was built at a cost of 17 million dirhams. The UAE confirmed in a speech delivered by Rashid Abdulla before the UN General Assembly that the events in the Gulf region following the liberation of Kuwait embodied a new fundamental stance at two levels, the regional and the international. In this stance there was a conviction of the importance of finding solutions to quarrels through dialogue and peaceful means which accorded with the Charter of the United Nations and international law. These solutions were aimed at confidence building and strengthening peace, security, stability, co-existence and good neighbourliness between the States in the region.

5 October: Sheikh Zayed received groups of citizens and students from UAE University in Al-Ain. He called on young people to arm themselves with knowledge and faith so that they would be prepared to return the favour which their country gave to them and help achieve a complete renaissance in the country. He said: 'I want to see some of you become planters, doers, makers and workers and not be satisfied only with holding down high positions'.

6 October: Sheikh Saqr bin Mohammad Al Qassimi inaugurated drilling for new exploration oil wells in the emirate of Ras al-Khaimah.

9 October: Sheikh Humaid bin Rashid Al Nuaimi issued a decree appointing Sheikh Ammar bin Humaid Al Nuaimi as Heir Apparent in the emirate of Ajman.

10 October: The UAE donated 1 million dollars to help earthquake victims in India.

11 October: Sheikh Zayed met with UAE University faculty-members and asked them to exert their fullest efforts to build a generation which was capable of bearing responsibility, thus realizing the mission of the University.

12 October: Sheikh Khalifa bin Zayed Al Nahyan received the GCC Chiefs of Staff who were meeting in Abu Dhabi. He stressed that it was important to work for strengthening co-operation and co-ordination among GCC States in the military field, in order to achieve security and stability in the region.

Major General Sheikh Mohammad bin Zayed Al Nahyan opened the eleventh meeting of the GCC Chiefs of Staff at the Intercontinental Hotel in Abu Dhabi. He emphasized the importance of the job which had been given to the Armed Forces in the GCC which was the obligation to work quickly for improved co-operation and co-ordination.

13 October: The GCC Chiefs of Staff concluded their meeting in Abu Dhabi. Major General Sheikh Mohammad bin Zayed Al Nahyan stressed that its mission had been accomplished and that there was complete agreement on all matters. He said that the security and stability of the Gulf was the goal.

15 October: The Ministry of Health began to establish and equip new operating theatres for open heart surgery in Al-Mafraq Hospital at a cost of 4 million dirhams.

16 October: UAE Central Bank ruled that, effective from 1994, any bank in the Federation could not make a loan larger than 7 per cent of its capitalization, interbank loans would be limited to 30 per cent of capital, and international bank branches would only be able to loan to a maximum of 20 per cent of capital to their parent institutions. Amendments to the bank loan restrictions were announced later, including limiting the 7 per cent rule to loans, overdrafts or any money the bank lends to a customer, but not to letters of credit, letters of guarantee etc.

17 October: Discussions were held between the UAE, under the chairmanship of Sheikh Sultan bin Zayed Al Nahyan, and Vietnam, under the chairmanship of Nguen Khan, the Prime Minister, who was visiting the country. Their discussions covered efforts being made for peace in the Middle East, mutual affairs and bilateral relations.

Sheikh Sultan bin Khalifa Al Nahyan opened the oil plant established on Umm al-Nar Island by the Abu Dhabi National Oil Products Distribution Company (ADNOC-FOD). The plant has a production capacity of 4000 tons annually.

18 October: Sheikh Zayed received Mahmoud Abbas (Abu Mazin) and told him that the UAE supported the Palestinian-Israeli agreement to achieve long-sought Arab and Palestinian goals and interests. He expressed his hope that this was a true step on the right path.

19 October: Sheikh Zayed held official discussions with Afghani President, Burhanedin Rabbani. He told him that the UAE stood beside the people of Afghanistan and that it supported rebuilding and development to overcome the difficulties and ordeals which they had passed through, in order to arrive at a better future. He condemned the Western conspiracy against the Muslims in Bosnia-Hercegovina and said that he blamed Europe for this situation, as he blamed all humanity for what was happening to the Muslim people of Bosnia.

The Electricity and Water board exempted citizens from late payment of water consumption fees amounting to 120 million dirhams.

20 October: In a speech before the United Nations, the UAE condemned terrorism in all its forms and it called for the punishment of those who commit it. The UAE also announced its readiness to participate in any collective international effort to study this serious crime.

23 October: Sheikh Zayed and Pakistani Prime Minster, Benazir Bhutto, who was visiting the country, discussed current regional and international affairs, the situation in the Gulf, the Middle East and ways of supporting solidarity among Islamic nations.

Sheikh Zayed approved a law governing the Federation's territorial waters, marking their extent in the Arabian Gulf and Gulf of Oman at 12 nautical miles, a contiguous zone of 24 nautical miles, an exclusive economic zone of 200 nautical miles, and a continental shelf of 200 nautical miles. Official maps were to be issued showing all the zones. The new legislation replaced the old maritime boundaries of the individual emirates but recognized oil/economic agreements concluded by emirates with neighbours prior to the Federation of December 1971.

25 October: The Council of Ministers allocated 19.5 million dirhams to buy advanced civil defence equipment.

29 October: The UAE Victory Team won the world speed-boat racing championship staged in Dubai. The races were attended by Sheikh Maktoum bin Rashid Al Maktoum.

3 November: Sheikh Zayed received an invitation from King Fahad bin Abdulaziz to attend the fourteenth GCC Summit to be held in Riyadh in December.

7 November: Sheikh Mohammad bin Rashid Al Maktoum opened the International Air Show - 'Dubai '93' - in which 450 companies, representing 33 countries, participated.

8 November: Sheikh Khalifa bin Zayed Al Nahyan received GCC Defence Ministers who were holding their meetings in Abu Dhabi. He told them that the GCC Summit in Saudi Arabia would study ways of achieving more closely integrated political, strategic, military and security ties among GCC States.

Major General Sheikh Mohammad bin Zayed Al Nahyan presided over the twelfth meeting of GCC Ministers of Defence. He stressed that the Council members had made long-term advancements in the field of constructive military co-operation. He called for a re-doubling of joint efforts and work in security and military co-ordination.

9 November: GCC Ministers of Defence concluded their meetings in Abu Dhabi. An agreement was reached to develop the Al-Jazira deterrent force, set-up a network of unified warning systems, create a unified chiefs of staff leadership and continue military co-operation with Syria and Egypt.

10 November: Sheikh Zayed received the Prince of Wales. They reviewed co-operation and friendly relations between the two countries and current international and regional affairs. Zayed stressed during his visit that Islam is the religion of forgiveness, mercy, pardon, mutual understanding, and togetherness among humankind. Islam does not recognize the violence or force which is practised by terrorists. Zayed praised Prince Charles'

study of the Islamic religion and his deep concern to become familiar and conversant with it in order to obtain precise knowledge.

Sheikh Khalifa bin Zayed Al Nahyan issued a law changing the name of the Abu Dhabi Fund for Arab Economic Development to the Abu Dhabi Development Fund to reflect the broader scope of its financial assistance.

14 November: Sheikh Khalifa bin Zayed Al Nahyan attended graduation ceremonies for the second term of the Military Staff College at the College headquarters in Abu Dhabi.

Sheikh Hamdan bin Rashid Al Maktoum opened DUBAL's new 300 million dirham development and expansion projects.

15 November: The Council of Ministers decided to forbid the importation of bustards into the country in adherence to the provisions of CITES, the international convention governing trade in endangered species.

16 November: Abu Dhabi Executive Council approved the setting-up of a 138-bed general hospital in Medinat Zayed.

17 November: Major General Sheikh Mohammad bin Rashid Al Maktoum attended the second graduation exercises for officer candidates. He also attended graduation exercises for the fourth and fifth batches of university-level graduates from Dubai Police College.

18 November: Sheikh Zayed held a session of official discussions with Sheikh Khalifa bin Hamad Al Thani, the Amir of Qatar, who was visiting the country. During the session, they discussed the current situation in the Gulf, Arab and Islamic affairs and brotherly relations between the two countries.

22 November: Lieutenant General Dr

Mohammad Said Al Badi presided over the twelfth meeting of GCC Interior Ministers which was being held in Abu Dhabi to discuss security co-ordination and facilitate the movement of citizens between GCC countries.

Over 394 billion dirhams was spent by the country in financing various development projects between 1975 and 1990.

23 November: Sheikh Khalifa bin Zayed Al Nahyan received GCC Ministers of the Interior. He stressed that the security of the GCC countries could not and should not be separated from each other because security is a barrier which protects what has been accomplished and on which the hopes of GCC peoples for a good stable life are pinned.

Abu Dhabi Executive Council allocated 996 million dirhams to finance requests for new housing loans.

24 November: The Board of Trustees of the Zayed bin Sultan Al Nahyan Philan-tropic Foundation, under the chairman-ship of Sheikh Khalifa bin Zayed Al Nahyan, decided to donate 36.5 million dirhams in support of the activities of a number of societies and establishments for the public good of the country. It also donated 650,000 dollars for relief of some of the devastated areas in the occupied territories.

Abu Dhabi Development Fund, since its establishment in 1977 until the end of September 1992, granted aid and loans amounting to 10.6 billion dirhams.

26 November: Because of the extent of his political work, Sheikh Hamdan bin Zayed Al Nahyan announced his resignation from the chairmanship of the Football Federation, having taken care of its affairs for nine years.

29 November: Sheikh Zayed, in a letter to the United Nations, again stressed the UAE's solidarity with the Palestinian people and its complete support for them in their struggle for freedom and independence. He also stressed that the UAE supported the agreement between the PLO and Israel as a positive beginning and a step on the way to a permanent and comprehensive solution to the Arab-Israeli conflict.

First Lady, Sheikha Fatima bint Mubarak, Chairwoman of the UAE Women's Federation, opened the Abu Dhabi Centre for Medical Rehabilitation.

30 November: Sheikh Maktoum bin Rashid Al Maktoum ordered that the road beginning at the World Trade Centre roundabout in Dubai and continuing all the way to Abu Dhabi be re-named Sheikh Zayed Highway.

2 December: Sheikh Zayed, the Members of the Supreme Council of the Federation and guests attended the military parade which was mounted on the twenty-second National Day. Sheikh Zayed delivered a comprehensive speech at the ceremonies, in which he spoke about important national affairs, the future of the Federation and current international and Arab issues. Sheikh Zayed called for a peaceful settlement to the dispute with Iran regarding the islands of Abu Musa and Greater and Lesser Tunbs: 'We in the UAE have announced our readiness and true wish for direct dialogue with Iran over its occupation of the three islands that belong to the UAE. We still call for the need to resort to dialogue and peaceful means to end this occupation and return the three islands to the UAE's sovereignty, according to international laws and norms and the principles of neighbourly relations and mutual respect between countries,' he said.

Sheikh Zayed received Dr Esmat Abdel-Meguid, the Secretary General of the Arab League who presented Zayed with the Arab League 'Man of Growth and Development Sash' for 1993.

5 December: Sheikh Faisal bin Khalid Al Qassimi issued a decree forming the new Board of Administration of the Football Federation under the chairmanship of Sheikh Abdulla bin Zayed al Nahyan.

11 December: Sheikh Zayed received the Prime Minister of Bosnia-Hercegovina, Harith Selazdic, and assured him of the UAE's support for the Bosnian people and their struggle in defence of their rights and confronting Serbian aggression.

20 December: Sheikh Zayed led the Federation's delegation to the meetings of the fourteenth GCC Summit in Riyadh. On arrival, he stressed that the GCC had made excellent progress which reflected the interests of the peoples in the GCC States.

22 December: Sheikh Zayed participated in the final session of GCC leaders who stressed in a final communiqué that the security of the GCC States was indivisible. They decided to form a supreme committee to monitor implementation of the resolutions on collective defence and military co-operation. They demanded that Iran reply to the President's invitation to hold a dialogue on the UAE's three islands occupied by Iran. The communiqué also stressed their insistence on the complete Israeli withdrawal from occupied Arab territories and their support for the people of Bosnia.

28 December: Abu Dhabi Executive Council decided to build 470 new housing units in the Al-Khatm and Al-Qoom regions.

Nineteen Ninety Four

3 January: The Department of Works completed the construction of 70 housing units for citizens on the island of Delma, bringing the total number of houses built by the Department on the island to 380.

4 January: Sheikh Zayed received a certificate from the mayor of Elmhurst, Illinois, USA, which designated 2 January 1994, as 'Sheikh Zayed Day' in recognition of Zayed's wise leadership, his success in providing a good life for the people of the United Arab Emirates and in developing the land and people of his country.

5 January: Sheikh Dr Sultan bin Mohammad Al Qassimi contributed to the building of a college of education and a religious institute in Chad, which will serve Muslims and disseminate the Islamic faith and culture.

10 January: The Council of Ministers decided to form a committee to study the establishment of a stock market in the UAE.

17 January: The Council of Ministers approved an application for UAE memebership to the International Agreement on Tariffs and Trade (GATT). It also decided to raise the tariff on electricity for non-nationals from 7.5 to 10 fils. The Minster of Electricity and Water said that the State spent 1.1 billion dirhams annually on the electrical and water sectors.

18 January: The Executive Council approved a project to transport water from the Al-Taweelah plant to Al-Ain at a cost of 900 million dirhams.

19 January: Major General Sheikh Mohammad bin Zayed Al Nahyan attended graduation ceremonies for the new air officer candidates at the Al-Dhafra Air Base.

23 January: The Ministry of Electricity and Water began the execution of projects costing 3 billion dirhams which would bring the Five Year Plan due to end in 1995 to a close. Among the projects was the linking of the Northern Emirates to the integrated electricity network.

24 January: Sheikh Zayed issued a decree promoting Major General Sheikh Mohammad bin Zayed Al Nahyan from Staff General to the rank of Major General.

25 January: Sheikh Zayed, in his concern for heritage, ordered that a major prize be awarded for camel racing. Worth 10 million dirhams, it will be known as the 'Zayed Grand Prize'.

30 January: Sheikh Zayed received Babloo Bawatni, the Vatican envoy of John Paul the Second. Zayed again stressed the tragic nature of events in Bosnia-Hercegovina. He said that unprecedented massacres were taking place and that the efforts of those attempting to put a stop to them amounted to nothing while the rest of the world was standing by, seemingly incapable of helping. He said that it was incomprehensible that nothing was being done to protect this unfortunate country which, at the same time, was unable to obtain weapons for self-defence and the defence of its property. States who were militarily capable of shielding the victims of oppression from their oppressors were not standing up for right and justice, but were giving aid to the wrong doers.

Work on bringing together the fourth stage of the Al-Taweelah A project was completed. Costing 500 million dirhams, the project produces 7.5 million gallons of water daily.

31 January: Sheikh Saqr bin Mohammad Al Qassimi ordered the establishment of a free zone in the emirate of Ras al-Khaimah.

ADCO announced the commencement of work on a huge project to develop gas in the Bab Field. The aim of the project was to increase the production of treated gas by the end of 1995 from 450 cubic feet to more than 2 billion cubic feet daily, in order to meet the increasing demand from consumers up to the year 2005.

2 February: The National Marine Dredging Company announced that during the 17 years since its creation in 1977 it had dredged over 315 million cubic metres on 67 projects.

7 February: The Council of Ministers approved the draft federal budget for 1994. Expenditure was forecast at 17.617 billion dirhams and revenue was estimated at 16.22 billion dirhams.

8 February: The test tube babies unit at the Tawam Hospital was supplied with specialized equipment to treat incurable infertility.

14 February: In a speech at the United Nations, the UAE said that the Serb aggressor must be deterred and that the crimes being committed in Bosnia demand that the entire world take a stand. The speech also called for lifting the arms embargo on the Muslims in Bosnia.

19 February: Sheikh Zayed issued a decree appointing Sheikh Sultan bin Hamdan Al Nahyan as Director of Protocol and Hospitality with the rank of minister.

22 February: Sheikh Zayed received Salim Saleh Mohammad, a member of the Yemeni Presidential Council and Assistant Secretary General of the Yemeni Socialist Party. Zayed expressed his hope that the Yemeni Pledge of Agreement would be implemented to assist in national reconciliation, at the same time stressing his concern for the security and stability of Yemen.

24 February: Sheikh Zayed made an inspection tour of the breakwater and attended a part of the programme 'Competitions on Yesterday's Life'. He called for increased efforts to revive the nation's heritage, at the same time maintaining customs and traditions. He stressed his deep faith in the importance of remembering the past because he who has no past has no present and there is no honour without honour of the family and country.

25 February: The UAE strongly denounced the vile crime committed by

Zionist settlers in the Mosque of Abraham in Hebron, saying that the Israeli Government must take full responsibility for this heinous massacre, and calling on the entire world to take active, decisive and tangible steps to protect Palestinian civilians and especially to disarm the settlers.

27 February: Sheikh Zayed paid a visit to the headquarters of the Amiri Guard on the occasion of the ceremonies marking the twenty-fifth anniversary of its establishment. He expressed his pride at the honourable standard achieved by the Armed Forces in its progress through the various stages of its development. He said that the obvious seriousness, sincerity and manliness of the UAE's sons fulfilled all expectations, adding that these traits were characteristic of their forebears and their fathers.

The Council of Ministers approved the construction of a road between Al-Gariya, Wadi Seeb and Safad in Fujairah at a cost of 16 million dirhams.

Abu Dhabi Municipality completed the 215 dirham eastern Corniche project.

1 March: The Federal National Council denounced the vicious and terrible crime committed by the Zionist settlers in the Mosque of Abraham in Hebron.

11 March: Sheikh Zayed and the Yemeni President, Ali Abdulla Saleh, discussed developments in the situation in Yemen and efforts being made to end the political crisis and address its causes in the context of the Yemeni Pledge of Agreement. He confirmed his great concern for the maintenance of Yemeni unity and the necessity of exerting fullest efforts to put an end to the clash.

General Agreement on Trade and Tariffs (GATT) announced that the UAE had been accepted as its 117th member.

17 March: Sheikh Zayed and the Members of the Supreme Council of the Federation were present at the Arabian horse and camel races. Zayed expressed his wish to maintain the heritage of his forebears and the necessity of keeping this heritage before the public. He asked the youth to become acquainted with their heritage, stressing that a nation without a heritage has no beginning or end.

19 March: Sheikh Zayed, in remarks made to *Hayat* newspaper, stressed that the UAE possesed documented proof of its ownership of the three islands occupied by Iran and it welcomed the arbitration of the International Court of Justice.

An important archaeological find was made on the island of Sir Bani Yas where an ancient monastic settlement was discovered.

26 March: Since it was established, the Abu Dhabi Commercial Building Office had built more than 6500 buildings at a cost of 11 billion dirhams.

28 March: In Rabat, the foundation stone was laid for 140 housing units, a school and a mosque, to be constructed at Zayed's private expense.

31 March: Sheikh Khalifa bin Zayed Al Nahyan opened the new Al-Ain International Airport.

In the city of Mansoura in the Arab Republic of Egypt, the Minister of Health opened the Khalifa Hall in the International Kidney and Bladder Centre. Sheikh Khalifa donated 1 million dollars to develop the centre.

3 April: Sheikh Zayed said in his meeting with the Yemeni Vice President, Ali Salim Al Baydh, 'that we are as concerned about our brothers in Yemen as we are about our own country'.

5 April: The UAE decided to recall its troops from Somalia at the end of their duties in 'Operation Return of Hope' which had been launched by a number of countries under the auspices of the United Nations to assist the Somali people.

12 April: Sheikh Sultan bin Zayed Al Nahyan attended graduation ceremonies for two new groups from the UAE University and the Higher Technical Colleges. Zayed granted a prize of 20,000 dirhams to outstanding students who graduated with distinction from these institutions and to the first group of graduates from the College of Medicine. Sheikh Khalifa issued a rent control law in order to stabilize the market and put an end to arbitrary rent increases. The law stipulated a maximum rent increase of 20 per cent over a two-year period.

13 April: The Executive Council decided to establish new factories in Abu Dhabi for the manufacture of blocks, steel reinforcement rods and electrical cables.

19 April: Total cost of projects undertaken in the country's investment programme during 1993 amounted to more than 5.6 billion dirhams.

20 April: Sheikh Khalifa bin Zayed Al Nahyan attended the first graduation ceremonies for those who received the Bachelor of Military Science degree from the Zayed the Second Military College in Al-Ain. He said that the accomplishment in which the country takes immense pride is development of the human being, assisting him to obtain qualifications in order that he might occupy a distinguished place in the community and participate in the progress of his country. It was decided to establish a distillation plant in Ras al-Khaimah which would operate on the heat principle. Costing 90 million dirhams, it will produce 4 million gallons of water per day.

23 April: Sheikh Zayed held a meeting with the Egyptian President, Mohammad Hosni Mubarak, who was visiting the country, during which they made a general review of bilateral affairs, especially the Gulf situation. They also dealt with new developments in Arab affairs and all matters furthering Arab Islamic causes.

24 April: The joint UAE-Oman Commission held a meeting in Muscat under the chairmanship of Sheikh Khalifa bin Zayed Al Nahyan, on behalf of the UAE, and Sayyid Fahad bin Mahmoud Al Said, on behalf of Oman. Sheikh Khalifa expressed his satisfaction at the results achieved in the meetings.

First Lady Sheikha Fatima bint Mubarak, Chairwoman of the UAE Women's Federation, presided over a meeting of the women's action co-ordination committee in the Gulf and the Arabian Peninsula. Sheikha Fatima donated 50,000 dollars to support the committee's activities.

26 April: The UAE Snooker Team won the third GCC championship. The competition was held in Bahrain for the third consecutive time.

3 May: The Board of Trustees of the Zayed Philantropic Foundation, under the chairmanship of Sheikh Khalifa bin Zayed Al Nahyan, approved the granting of 11 million dirhams in aid to national and Gulf benevolent institutions.

7 May: Sheikh Surour bin Mohammad Al Nahyan signed a contract to construct a dual pipeline for water from the Al-Taweelah plant to Al-Ain at a cost of 1.7 billion dirhams.

9 May: Sheikh Zayed received a telephone call from Yemeni President, Ali Abdulla Saleh regarding developments in the situation in Yemen. He expressed his great worry about the continuation of the fighting in Yemen and said: 'I call on you, the sons of Yemen, to be obedient to Allah and to use your intelligence instead of resorting to arms.' He warned of the spread of fighting and the danger that events would get out of control and said that the leaders of Yemen would bear the responsibility.

10 May: Sheikh Zayed received a telephone call from Yemeni Vice President, Ali Salim Al Baydh. An official source said that Zayed continued to be concerned as he monitored developments in Yemen and that honest and sincere efforts were being made by the Arab world to find a solution to the Yemeni crisis. He stressed the UAE's readiness to continue to mediate in order that stability should return to the Yemen on condition of an immediate ceasefire.

16 May: Sheikh Zayed received a German scientific delegation who were experts in satellite groundwater research. Zayed was briefed on the delegation's plans to make a comprehensive groundwater survey in the country.

The Council of Ministers lauded Sheikh Zayed's efforts to solve the differences between brothers in Yemen. He called on the warring parties to work towards an end to the bloodshed and fighting.

17 May: Sheikh Zayed received a telephone call from Yemeni President, Al Abdulla Saleh, regarding developments in the Yemeni civil war. Zayed expressed his sadness and sorrow at the tragic events unfolding in Yemen and for the Yemeni President's lack of response to the repeated calls for a ceasefire.

26 May: Sheikh Zayed received Sheikh bin Al Ahmar, President of the Yemeni Council of Deputies, assuring him of the UAE's support for the Yemeni people whatever decision they made. He said that the UAE was keen to exert all its efforts to stop the flow of blood in Yemen.

29 May: Ras al-Khaimah and Umm al-Qaiwain reached agreement on demarcating their borders, especially regarding individuals and tribes living near the borders.

5 June: The Electricity & Water Ministry signed an agreement with Amoco Sharjah Oil Company, jointly owned by Sharjah (60 per cent) and US' Amoco Corporation (40 per cent), for supply of natural gas to power stations in the Northern Emirates.

7 June: Sheikh Zayed held a telephone conversation with King Hassan of Morocco, during which they discussed the situation in the Yemen and a number of Arab matters.

Sheikh Zayed reviewed developments in the Yemeni arena with the Prime Minister of Yemen, Haider Abu Bakr Al Attas. Zayed, expressing his sorrow at the serious escalation in the fighting in Yemen, wondered: 'In whose interest is blood being shed between brothers? Whose interest is being served by brother killing brother, and in whose interest is it to destroy the land and the people in one country by the hands of its own sons?'

The Executive Council allocated 252 million dirhams for new installations in the UAE University College of Medicine.

13 June: Sheikh Zayed, receiving the UAE's international referee, Ali Bujassem, who refereed at the World Cup football finals, said that he felt great esteem for the young people of the UAE, their abilities and the effective role they were playing. He said that sincerity, dedication, willpower and respect for work must be the banner of every citizen because jealousy and stupidity will not help the individual accomplish his ambitions.

14 June: Sheikh Zayed received Lakhdar Al Ibrahimi, the UN envoy charged with negotiating a ceasefire in Yemen. Zayed expressed his sorrow at the continuation of the fighting and his readiness to continue his efforts to put an end to the destructive war. He also stressed that a ceasefire was an urgent and necessary requirement.

25 June: A 1.3 million dollar agreement was signed in Beijing for setting-up an Islamic printing press with the aid of a grant from Zayed to support the activities of Chinese Muslims and to spread the Islamic call.

28 June: Sheikh Khalifa bin Zayed Al Nahyan donated 3.5 million dirhams to youth and sports clubs in the Northern Emirates as an expression of his concern and care for youth and sports activities in the country.

4 July: Dubai Municipality distributed plots of land on which to build dwellings to deserving citizens in Al-Mazhar district.

6 July: Sheikh Maktoum bin Rashid Al Maktoum issued a law establishing the Dubai Public Transport Company with a capital of 30 million dirhams.

9 July: Sheikh Zayed received Ahmed Al Saadoun, Chairman of the Kuwait National Council. Zayed stressed that: 'the GCC countries are one family and they are gathered together with one goal and one destiny and that the good which comes to one of them will be for the good and power of all'.

12 July: During the first half of this year, the UAE paid its dues, amounting to 35.1 million dirhams, to a number of international, Arab and Islamic organizations. Sheikh Hamdan bin Rashid Al Maktoum approved the Dubai World Trade Centre project, estimated at 187.3 million dirhams.

14 July: Sheikh Zayed received a delegation from the Yemeni Council of Deputies. He called on them to engage in dialogue and national reconciliation. He again stressed the UAE's concern to bring about peace and stability in Yemen. He said that there must be a period for nursing wounds, but with the passage of time there should be no recriminations.

16 July: Dubai Municipality distributed 1273 sites for building houses in the Nad Shubaib district.

25 July: Sheikh Zayed received a communication from the Yemeni President, Ali Abdulla Saleh, regarding the situation in Yemen and efforts being made to restore security and stability. The call came while Zayed was receiving Abdulaziz Abdulghani, a member of the Presidential Council.

The UAE and the United States of America signed a joint military co-operation programme which came about because of the desire of both countries to develop co-operation in military, economic and commercial fields.

1 August: UAE began enforcing the new customs law passed in May on many imported goods from outside the GCC, in a drive to unify GCC States' import tariffs.

6 August: Sheikh Zayed received the Members of the Supreme Council of the Federation and groups of well-wishers on the occasion of the twenty-eighth anniversary of his accession.

9 August: Sheikh Zayed held a meeting with King Fahad bin Abdulaziz in Jeddah during which they discussed brotherly relations between the two countries and ways of strengthening and developing them in the best interests of the two peoples. They also discussed developments in the Gulf.

10 August: Sheikh Zayed arrived in Alexandria where he praised the positive outcome of his discussions with King Fahad and the congruence of their points of view.

11 August: Sheikh Zayed held a meeting with Egyptian President Mohammad Hosni Mubarak, as part of continuing consultations between the two leaders. They made a complete evaluation of the current Arab situation, new developments and efforts aimed at Arab unity.

12 August: Before leaving Alexandria on his way to Switzerland, Sheikh Zayed donated 7 million dollars to a number of medical and curative centres, as well as scientific and cultural institutions.

20 August: In Geneva, Sheikh Zayed received the Palestinian President, Yasser Arafat. They exchanged points of view regarding the Palestinian question as seen from both Arab and international levels. They also discussed efforts and contacts which were currently being made to bring about a comprehensive peace to the region and to achieve a fair settlement of the Palestinian question.

The Ministry of Education and Water undertook ten new projects valued at 420 million dirhams to augment electricity generation in the Northern Emirates. Included in the projects was the purchase of seven gas turbines which Sheikh Zayed had ordered to be installed at his own expense.

2 September: Sheikh Zayed ordered the creation of additional lakes and reservoirs to be connected via water canals in order to grow more fish of the *Al-Balti* (*Tilapia* sp.) variety as part of Al-Ajbaan district aquaculture project in Abu Dhabi.

6 September: In a speech before the International Population and Development Conference in Cairo delivered by Sheikh Humaid bin Ahmad Al Mualla, the Minister of Planning, the UAE stressed that its development strategy depended on the wise foundations laid down by Sheikh Zayed who, in building the modern country, insists that the individual is the measure of and the purpose for development.

Sheikh Humaid bin Rashid Al Nuaimi ordered that the new hospital in Al-Jarf district in Ajman be named Khalifa bin Zayed Al Nahyan Hospital.

12 September: Abu Dhabi city gave 1 million dollars to equip and furnish the headquarters of the Arab Cities Organization in Kuwait.

13 September: The UAE announced its reservation to the final communiqué of the Housing and Development Conference in Cairo regarding the demand for States to control population increases. The UAE confirmed its reservation in all matters which contravene its religion and *Sharia* Law.

14 September: Sheikh Zayed held a meeting with King Hassan of Morocco in the city of Fez, during which they reviewed Arab affairs.

16 September: In a speech by the Federal National Council before the International Parliamentary Union in Copenhagen, the UAE stressed its strong attachment to all its historic and legal territorial rights. It also expressed its deep concern to pursue peaceful measures as a way of restoring the sovereignty of the three islands, Abu Musa, the Greater Tunb and the Lesser Tunb, from the occupation of Iran.

17 September: Sheikh Hamdan bin Zayed Al Nahyan led the UAE delegation in the GCC Ministerial Council meeting in Riyadh. The Council called on Iran to negotiate the end of the occupation of the three islands. It also called on Iraq to recognize the borders and the sovereignty of Kuwait.

19 September: Sheikh Zayed held discussions with the British Prime Minister, John Major, who was visiting the country. During the meeting, they discussed the situation in the Gulf and the Middle East, as well as the future of peace and bilateral relations. Zayed decorated Major with the Sash of the Federation in appreciation of his efforts to promote good relations.

23 September: Sheikh Zayed received a letter from Libyan President, Muammar Al Gadhafi, containing an invitation to convene an Arab summit with the aim of unifying Arab ranks, and achieving unity and reconciliation.

25 September: The Council of Ministers allocated 20 million dirhams to the Ministry of Agriculture and Fish Resources to purchase fertilizer, seeds and agricultural insecticides for the new planting season.

28 September: The Council of Ministers decided to put a stop to all air and sea transport to and from India to protect the country from the plague which had broken out in India.

29 September: The UAE stressed that the Iranian inauguration of air service to the island of Abu Musa was considered to be a violation of UAE sovereignty over the island and in conflict with the principles of friendship and good neighbourliness. The UAE stressed that the installation of the air link was not an expression of the true status of the island.

2 October: Sheikh Dr Sultan bin Mohammed Al Qassimi, during a visit to Sharjah Television studios spoke of the necessity of concentrating on programmes which promote and inculcate community and family values.

5 October: The UAE, in a speech before the United Nations, stressed its readiness to resort to the International Court of Justice regarding the three islands. It pledged in its speech, which was delivered by Rashid Abdulla, to accept the results of the court's decision.

8 October: Sheikh Zayed in a telephone call with Sheikh Jabir Al Ahmed Al Sabah, Amir of Kuwait, stressed that the UAE supported Kuwait and any GCC country in all matters which threaten its security and stability. It also said it would help protect the State's territory from any outside attack. This statement was made after the massing of large forces on the borders with Kuwait.

10 October: The Council of Ministers commended Sheikh Zayed's pledging of UAE support for Kuwait.

13 October: Units of the UAE Armed Forces arrived in Kuwait to participate with the GCC and other friendly forces in its defence.

15 October: Sheikh Zayed received the Foreign Minister of Russia, Andrei Kozarev, who briefed him on the results of his visit to Iraq within the scope of Russia's attempt to end the crisis resulting from Iraqi threats to Kuwait.

16 October: Sheikh Zayed received a letter

from the French President, François Mitterand, regarding current developments in the region, bilateral relations, new elements resulting from the massing of Iraqi forces on the Kuwait borders and dangers to security, stability and world peace. The letter was conveyed by the Minister of Foreign Affairs, Alan Juppe.

17 October: Sheikh Khalifa bin Zayed Al Nahyan attended the graduation of the third session of the Military Staff College in Abu Dhabi.

18 October: Major General Sheikh Mohammed bin Zayed Al Nahyan attended the graduation exercises of the new batch of officer-pilots from the Air College.

21 October: Al-Marfa canning factory, built at a cost of 114 million dirhams, commenced date-canning as its first phase of operations. Later there will be new lines of production for tomatoes, potatoes and *maloukhiya*.

25 October: The joint UAE-British committee held a meeting in London. The UAE side was led by Sheikh Hamdan bin Zayed Al Nahyan and the British side by Douglas Hogg, the Minister of State for Foreign Affairs. Britain expressed her support for the UAE's proposal to refer the dispute about the islands occupied by Iran to the International Court of Justice.

30 October: First Lady Sheikha Fatima bint Mubarak, Chairwoman of the UAE Women's Federation, called on the women of the UAE to join nursing organizations and involve themselves in this noble humanitarian field, in order to provide better care for the family and society.

1 November: Sheikh Zayed issued a federal decree terminating UAE relations with the Arab Military Industrialization Corporation.

2 November: In Cairo, Sheikh Zayed held discussions with Egyptian President Mohammad Hosni Mubarak which dealt with current Arab matters, developments in the Gulf situation, the peace process in the Middle East and new elements on the international scene.

The Department of Works began a group of development projects costing 1 billion dirhams in Al-Ain and its suburbs. The projects include 891 new housing units, schools, roads, health clinics and mosques.

3 November: Sheikh Zayed arrived in Rabat after completing discussions with Egyptian President, Mohammad Hosni Mubarak, about developments in the situation in the Gulf and donating 13 million sterling pounds to aid flood victims in Egypt.

Sheikh Maktoum opened the twelfth Gulf Football Games in Abu Dhabi.

4 November: It was announced that Sheikh Zayed had donated 1 million dirhams to the National Tumour Institute in Egypt. Sheikh Khalifa bin Zayed Al Nahyan also donated a similar amount to the institute.

5 November: Sheikh Mohammad bin Rashid Al Maktoum ordered that a committee be formed to study the living conditions of citizens occupying rented apartments and houses.

8 November: Sheikh Hamdan bin Rashid Al Maktoum allocated 35.7 million dirhams to set up a sewerage network in Al-Mamzar district.

9 November: The third line of the liquid gas project at the ADGAS factory in Al-Ruwais was opened, raising the capacity of the factory to 5 million tons annually, following an investment of 3 billion dollars.

13 November: Based on Sheikh Zayed's directives, steps were taken to commence construction of 1144 housing units in Al-Ain and its suburbs.

15 November: Sheikh Khalifa bin Zayed Al Nahyan opened the new session of the National Consultative Council. In his opening speech, he stressed that the accomplishments which had been achieved in various fields were considered to be a comprehensive model for national administration and ambitious leadership. He defined three principal areas for Government action in the years ahead:
(i) continued support for economic and social development;
(ii) provision of all facilities to protect national security and
(iii) using the best available resources for encouraging and diversifying national production and income.

20 November: Sheikh Khalifa bin Zayed Al Nahyan attended the flag-raising exercises mounted by the General Staff of the Armed Forces to dedicate the new land weapons which include French tanks and four-line workshops for maintaining and repairing equipment. He stressed that building-up the force and supporting development were in harmony with a balanced future and the growth of the renaissance. He said that the leadership was constantly reviewing military strategy in light of new events.

22 November: Sheikh Khalifa bin Zayed Al Nahyan and the Prime Minister of the Russian Federation, Victor Chernomyrdin, discussed bilateral relations, the situation in the Gulf and the Middle East peace process. Discussions were held between the UAE delegation, headed by Sheikh Sultan bin Zayed al Nahyan, and the Russian Federation delegation headed by the Prime Minister. During the session, they reviewed ways of strengthening bilateral relations, and international and regional affairs.

23 November: Sheikh Khalifa bin Zayed Al Nahyan issued a decree appointing Yousif bin Omair as Director General of ADNOC.

25 November: In Rabat, Sheikh Zayed and the Palestinian delegation under the leadership of Mahmoud Abbas (Abu Mazin) discussed the peace process in the Middle East and ways of supporting Palestinian self-rule.

26 November: In Rabat, Sheikh Zayed and King Hassan of Morocco discussed the Arab situation, new developments and efforts being made toward achieving Arab unity.

27 November: The Central Bank annual report for 1993 stated that Gross Domestic Product had risen to 131.7 billion dirhams: liquidity to 89.3 billion dirhams; and deposits to 89.9 billion dirhams. At the same time, the value of investment and consumer spending in the private sector amounted to 83 billion dirhams.

28 November: In Rabat, Sheikh Zayed received the Secretary General of the United Nations, Dr Boutros Boutros Ghali. He stressed that continuing Serbian aggression in Bosnia was an affront to individual conscience and human rights as well as an ignominious disgrace to mankind. He called for action to stand up to the aggressor.

The Board of Trustees of the Zayed Philanthropic Foundation, under the chairmanship of Sheikh Khalifa bin Zayed al Nahyan, allocated 25 million dirhams to establish religious, educational, local and international projects.

2 December: At the celebrations on the occasion of the twenty-third National Day,

Sheikh Zayed said that the most important achievement made by the Federation since it was established was the firm grounding of a unique national identity and a sense of belonging among the people. He also said that the UAE's success in providing security and stability, as well as a good standard of living for the current generation, had encouraged it to continue the struggle to build a modern country and achieve the best for the country and the citizen.

3 December: Sheikh Zayed received the Members of the Supreme Council of the Federation and groups of well-wishers on the occasion of the twenty-third National Day.

5 December: Sheikh Mohammad bin Zayed Al Nahyan opened the Conference on Work Opportunities in the UAE being held in Abu Dhabi. On the periphery of the conference, he announced that three huge new projects were imminent; the aircraft maintenance centre, the ship-building dock and an international medical centre.

10 December: At the Cultural Centre in Abu Dhabi, Sheikh Abdulla bin Zayed Al Nahyan opened the meeting of a team of experts on the Arab family in a changing society, which was held under the auspices of First Lady, Sheikha Fatima bint Mubarak, the President of the Women's Association and Chairwoman of the UAE Women's Federation.

11 December: Sheikh Zayed paid an inspection visit to the special forces at the Khawla bint Al Azwar School and expressed his pleasure at the high standard achieved by the female recruits.

12 December: Sheikh Zayed, arriving in Casablanca to participate in the Islamic Summit, stressed that Arab and Muslim strength lay in solidarity.

In remarks made to the Lebanese newspaper, *Al-Anwar*, Sheikh Zayed said that the Federation is the UAE's method of operation, the means by which it has become strong and it is also the way it has dealt with its renaissance. The reason why the Federation has endured, he said, is because the citizens are convinced of its feasibility. He expressed the hope that border differences between GCC States would come to an end. He also stated that what was happening in Bosnia represented a loss of hope for the whole world in which human rights were vaunted.

13 December: Sheikh Zayed led the UAE delegation to the opening session of the seventh Islamic Conference Summit in Casablanca.

15 December: Sheikh Zayed praised the results of the seventh Islamic Conference Summit which concluded its meetings in Casablanca. He said that it made significant progress towards mutual assistance and brotherhood among the member States.

17 December: Sheikh Zayed donated 5 million dollars to the Solidarity Fund and a number of other Islamic establishments.

19 December: Sheikh Zayed led the UAE delegation to the meetings of the fifteenth Gulf Summit Conference in Bahrain. On his arrival he stressed that the Co-operation Council was maintaining security and stability in the region.

Sheikh Hamdan bin Zayed Al Nahyan, in remarks to *Ash-Shark Al-Awsat* newspaper, expressed his confidence that the Gulf Conference would achieve better integration and mutual assistance in various fields. He also said that the UAE was following-up on Iran's imminent transformation of the islands of Abu Musa and the Greater and Lesser Tunbs into a military arsenal.

21 December: Sheikh Zayed returned to the UAE having participated in the final session of the fifteenth Gulf Summit in Manama. The Summit's final communiqué called for Iran to agree to refer the question of the islands which it occupies to the International Court of Justice.

27 December: Sheikh Zayed and the Members of the Supreme Council of the Federation attended the 'Federation Shield' exercises which were mounted by the Armed Forces using live ammunition. Zayed, expressing his pleasure at what he witnessed, said: 'What we saw calls for pride and esteem for me, the Rulers and every citizen. It is a great accomplishment for the UAE'.

30 December: The Zayed International Programme for Agricultural Research was successful in propagating new plants which would tolerate irrigation with sea water.

Nineteen Ninety Five

2 January: Sheikh Zayed and the President of Kuwait's National Assembly, Ahmed Al Saadoun, discussed developments in the Gulf and bilateral relations.

Dubai Municipality accepted the handover of eight large road projects costing 67.6 million dirhams.

Al-Ain Municipality signed contracts totalling 200 million dirhams for five new road projects.

3 January: Sheikh Maktoum bin Rashid Al Maktoum issued two decrees appointing General Sheikh Mohammad bin Rashid Al Maktoum as Crown Prince and Sheikh Hamdan bin Rashid Al Maktoum as Deputy Ruler of the emirate of Dubai.

Sheikh Rashid bin Ahmed Al Mualla issued a decree establishing an economic office in Umm al-Qaiwain with Ali bin Rashid Al Mualla as Director General.

9 January: Sheikh Mohammad bin Rashid Al Maktoum, in a newspaper interview, stressed the importance of Arab reconciliation saying that Sheikh Zayed on many Arab and Islamic occasions was the first to call for mutual forgiveness and solidarity between Arab brothers. He went on to say that Sheikh Zayed was the one to raise the flag of reconciliation and open a new page in intra-Arab relations. He stressed that the current Arab situation was unnatural and that the Arab nation was passing under the shadow of a summer cloud.

10 January: Sheikh Zayed received Dr Esmat Abdel-Meguid, the Secretary General of the Arab League. They reviewed Arab affairs and efforts at Arab reconciliation within the framework of the League's mediation attempts.

Sheikh Mohammad bin Rashid, in a newspaper interview, said that the UAE under the leadership of Sheikh Zayed and the directives of Sheikh Maktoum would experience much development, especially in construction. He also said that Kuwait's and Iraq's fate were one and the same and that they were brothers and neighbours in spite of all the tragedies through which they had passed.

Sheikh Sultan bin Zayed, receiving the Norwegian Energy Minister, Jens Stoltenberg, stressed the UAE's concern for the stability of the oil market and the strengthening of co-operative relations with all producers for the good of the market and the producing and consuming states.

12 January: Sheikh Zayed held discussions with the Pakistani Prime Minister, Benazir Bhutto, during which they discussed the development of bilateral relations and regional and international affairs of mutual concern. Zayed stressed that the UAE was most concerned with security and stability on the Indian sub-continent because it is an indivisible part of the security of the Gulf region and the security and peace of the two countries.

14 January: Sheikh Mohammad bin Rashid Al Maktoum, in an interview with the Kuwaiti newspaper, *Al-Siyasa*, spoke about future relations between Iraq and Kuwait. He expressed his love and concern for the interests of Kuwait and its people because, he said, 'I do not want this nation to go on living in an atmosphere of revenge and division.' He also called for the beginning of a Gulf development campaign and the formation of an Arab economic bloc to unify the Arab nation.

18 January: The Government of Dubai donated 1.7 million dollars to complete construction of the Sheikh Rashid bin Saeed Al Maktoum Mosque in Bir Zeit University on the occupied West Bank. The UAE and France signed a defence co-operation agreement.

23 January: Sheikh Khalifa bin Zayed Al Nahyan, receiving Prince Narahito, the Crown Prince of Japan, who was on an official visit to the country, said that this visit was a new strand in co-operation between the two countries, one which would deepen mutual understanding and co-operation.

24 January: Sheikh Humaid bin Ahmad Al Mualla stressed that the UAE succeeded in freeing the market from oil price fluctuations as well as the impact of such fluctuation on all economic activity. One effect was to energize the non-oil sectors of the economy. The country's Gross Domestic Product in 1995 was expected to increase by 3.7 per cent.

25 January: Sheikh Mohammad bin Rashid Al Maktoum received Prince Narahito, the Crown Prince of Japan, who was visiting the Emirates.

27 January: Sheikh Mohammad bin Rashid Al Maktoum and the US Assistant Secretary of State, Robert Pelletreau, exchanged views on the peace process in the Middle East and efforts being made to make the Middle East free of weapons of mass destruction. Zayed considered this to be a basic factor in strengthening peace, security and stability in the Middle East.

30 January: The Council of Ministers endorsed the federal budget for 1995. Expenditure was estimated at 17.949 billion dirhams while revenue was forecast at 16.903 billion dirhams, leaving a deficit of 1.046 billion dirhams.

31 January: The vegetable and date-canning factory in Al-Marfa which produced 54 tons daily, began marketing its products locally.

3 February: In 1994, the cost of projects undertaken by the Ministry of Public Works and Housing amounted to 1.56 billion dirhams.

10 February: The Ministry of Planning commenced a general census of the populations and installations in the State.

11 February: Sheikh Zayed held a closed meeting with the Yemeni President, Ali Abdulla Saleh, in the Al-Wathba guest house, during which they discussed new events in the region and the situation in the Arab world, as well as efforts underway to arrive at reconciliation.

In 1994, the total expenditure for all federal projects in Dubai amounted to 305.8 million dirhams.

12 February: Sheikh Surour bin Mohammed Al Nahyan awarded contracts worth 196.8 million for new electrical power projects in Abu Dhabi, Al-Ain and the Western Region.

Total costs for federal projects in the emirate of Sharjah during 1994 amounted to 710 million dirhams.

13 February: Abu Dhabi Executive Council approved the laying of an 11.6 km water pipe with a diameter of 600 mm from Jebel al-Dhanna to Sir Bani Yas.

15 February: At the directive of the President, Sheikh Khalifa bin Zayed Al Nahyan ordered the allocation of 30.522 million dirhams as the 1995 Ramadan grant to those who qualified for social assistance and to labourers in the fourth grade of the civil service.

16 February: In 1994 the cost of federal projects completed in the emirates of Ras al-Khaimah, Fujairah and Umm al-Qaiwain amounted to 1.3 billion dirhams.

20 February: The UAE welcomed the announcement by Bahrain and Qatar of their desire to solve their border dispute in a friendly manner within the framework of mediation undertaken by Saudi Arabia.

22 February: Abu Dhabi Municipality opened the Heritage Garden in Medinat Zayed in the Western Region. The Garden covers 234,000 square metres and cost 12 million dirhams.

26 February: The UAE welcomed the memorandum of mutual understanding which was arrived at between Saudi Arabia and the Yemeni Republic, in response to the concern of the two countries to solve their differences in a friendly way.

27 February: The Supreme Petroleum Council, under the chairmanship of Sheikh Khalifa bin Zayed Al Nahyan, approved the expansion of the Al-Ruwais refinery, the setting-up of a petrochemical complex and ADNOC's plans to improve its gas and diesel production.

28 February: The Ministry of Electricity and Water, whether from wells or desalination plants, produced 1668 million gallons of water in 1994.

5 March: Sheikh Zayed held a meeting with Filipino President, Fidel Ramos, who was on his first visit to the country. The two Presidents stressed the necessity of maintaining Gulf security and stability and they discussed ways of developing co-operative and friendly relations between the two countries.

6 March: Excavations in the Baynunah area in the Western Region of Abu Dhabi emirate revealed the existence of an ancient river channel with evidence of prehistoric plant and animal life.

10 March: Sheikh Mohammad bin Rashid Al Maktoum stressed, at the preparations for opening the International Defence Show, 'IDEX "95' on 19 March, that the economic policy which the country was pursuing had created great confidence and trust with investors and businessmen on the future of commercial activity in the country.

13 March: The Council of Ministers approved the appointment of Sheikh Abdulla bin Zayed Al Nahyan as Under-Secretary of Information and Culture.

17 March: Sheikh Khalifa bin Zayed Al Nahyan emphasized at the opening of the IDEX - '95 exhibition in Abu Dhabi that the UAE would not hesitate to purchase whatever defence equipment it required for its Armed Forces.

19 March: At the exhibition grounds in Abu Dhabi, Sheikh Khalifa bin Zayed opened the second International Defence Exhibition, 'IDEX '95', in the presence of ministers and military personnel from 55 countries. There were 608 companies from 43 countries participating in the event.

Sheikh Hamdan bin Zayed Al Nahyan opened the naval exhibition at Port Zayed, which formed part of the 'IDEX '95' exhibition.

The UAE paid 1.7 million dollars as its share of the Arab League budget for 1995.

20 March: Sheikh Mohammad bin Rashid Al Maktoum opened the live shooting range in Al-Muqatara district in Abu Dhabi as part of the IDEX '95 exhibition.

21 March: Sheikh Hamdan bin Zayed Al Nahyan, speaking to the Emirates News Agency on the occasion of the fiftieth anniversary of the founding of the Arab League, said that the UAE rejected what was being touted in some Middle East circles as a substitute for the Arab League. He called for a period in which to reflect and review the record of the past in respect to joint Arab action.

The Armed Forces awarded a 435 million dirham contract for a modern communications system to an American company.

22 March: Sheikh Zayed stressed in a talk on the occasion of the fiftieth anniversary of the founding of the Arab League that the experiment has been successful and has given the League much-needed experience. Furthermore, Arabs have been able to absorb much of what has happened, he said. He expressed his hope that some of the articles in the League Charter would be changed to adopt the majority rule system in decision-making, instead of the operation of an absolute majority.

At the end of IDEX '95, the Armed Forces placed orders to buy defence equipment valued at 103 million dirhams.

23 March: The Armed Forces awarded contracts worth 920 million dirhams to a French company for defence equipment, including seven helicopters. The deal was done on the periphery of IDEX '95.

28 March: Sheikh Khalifa bin Zayed Al Nahyan attended the ceremonies surrounding the return of the Arabian oryx and the reem gazelle to their native habitat in a natural protected zone in the Empty Quarter. He praised the efforts being made by Saudi Arabia to protect wildlife and the environment and to provide suitable conditions to conserve endangered species.

29 March: Sheikh Zayed convened a session of discussions with the Hungarian President, Arbad Ghoth, who was making his first visit to the country. They discussed ways of supporting bilateral relations, the situation in the region and the Middle East.

Sheikh Dr Sultan bin Mohammad Al Qassimi issued an Amiri decree setting-up an electricity and water board to take the place of the Department of Electricity and Water in Sharjah.

1 April: At the opening of the Islamic Summit Conference in Abu Dhabi, Sheikh Zayed delivered a speech in which he stressed that the Islamic *Sharia* calls for unity, brotherhood and co-operation in the best interests of worshippers. He called on the learned men of religion to personally guide the Islamic communities in applying a complete and integrated Islamic system.

The National Maritime Dredging Company made 52.1 million dirhams of clear profit last year, or 52 per cent of its capital of 100 million dirhams.

5 April: Sheikh Zayed, accompanied by Sheikh Khalifa bin Zayed Al Nahyan and Sheikh Mohammad bin Rashid Al Maktoum, visited Prince Sultan bin Abdulaziz at the guest house where he was in residence. They discussed firm brotherly relations and matters of mutual concern.

Sheikh Mohammad bin Rashid Al Maktoum opened the Dubai Chamber of Commerce and Industry building. He called for an acceptance of the past, a rising above petty quarrels in order to reach their goal, and the building of an Arab economic bloc to challenge foreign blocs.

Dubai Municipality completed a comprehensive economic survey of the emirate of Dubai which showed that the population was 611,000.

6 April: Prince Sultan bin Abdulaziz visited the island of Sir Bani Yas and stressed that Zayed's gift had made the impossible come true and that any achievement in the Emirates was an asset to all GCC countries.

7 April: Sheikh Zayed and the Members of the Supreme Council of the Federation and guests attended the finals of the pure-bred Arabian camel festival.

8 April: Sheikh Zayed held a meeting with Prince Sultan bin Abdulaziz during which they exchanged points of view about developments in the Gulf.

A session of discussions was convened between the UAE delegation, under the chairmanship of Sheikh Khalifa bin Zayed Al Nahyan, and the Saudi delegation, under the chairmanship of Prince Sultan bin Abdulaziz. At the meeting bilateral relations were reviewed, the two sides stressing their concern for the region's security and their support for joint Arab action.

9 April: The UAE and Saudi Arabia issued a joint communiqué on the departure of Prince Sultan bin Abdulaziz which emphasized their joint concern for supporting and strengthening historical bilateral relations in all fields. The importance of continuing mutual consultations and the exchange of visits between officials to strengthen the ties of brotherhood and friendship were also stressed.

The Ministerial Legislative Committee, on the President's directives, approved a change in the law governing drug offences, which included the death penalty for smugglers and traders and a four-year prison term for drug-users.

Ahmed Al Tayer, Minister of State for Finance and Industry, said that the establishment of the proposed Middle East Development Bank was not in the best interests of Arab economies. He said that the Bank's aims did not stop at the provision of financing but went well beyond this to open Arab markets to Israeli capital and Israeli work forces, in order to tie the Arab economy to Israeli economic outlets.

11 April: Sheikh Zayed held discussions concerning bilateral co-operation with the President of South Africa, Nelson Mandela, who arrived in the country on his first official visit. Zayed decorated Mandela with the Sash of the Federation. Mandela in turn awarded South Africa's highest decoration to Sheikh Zayed.

15 April: Sheikh Zayed, in directives given to the Minister of the Interior, stressed the importance and value of work in building both the individual and society. He said that the country was developed by the strong hands of its people and he praised the skills which the handicapped had accomplished in their training centres in spite of their handicaps. He directed young people who were not handicapped to follow the example of the handicapped in their pursuit of knowledge.

Work began on three new hotels in Al-Jarf, Al-Marfa and Liwa.

16 April: Sheikh Zayed presided over a meeting of the Supreme Council of the Federation in which he stressed his true concern and sincere intentions to support and strengthen progress in the Federation in order to achieve more of the hopes and ambitions of the country and its citizens. The Council also debated recent developments and the Iranian occupation of the three islands (the Greater and Lesser Tunbs and Abu Musa). The Supreme Council directed the Council of Ministers to study the citizens' requirements and to provide them with the necessary services. Sheikh Zayed issued a decree appointing Abdulla bin Zayed Al Nahyan as Under Secretary for Information and Culture.

18 April: Sheikh Zayed and Senator Floyd Spence, Chairman of the National Security Committee in the US Congress, discussed developments in the Gulf and ways of supporting bilateral relations.

Sheikh Zayed attended the graduation exercises of the fourteenth batch of students from the UAE University and the fourth batch from the Higher Colleges of Technology. The fourteenth graduating class from the University included a total of 1403 graduates, 383 male and 1021 female. The fourth graduating class from the Higher Colleges included a total of 115 graduates, of whom 48 were male and 68 female.

23 April: Sheikh Khalifa bin Zayed Al Nahyan attended graduation ceremonies for officers from the Zayed the Second Military College in Al-Ain. He stressed that the ongoing graduations from all the colleges in the country was effective proof that the Federation was continuing its non-stop growth and was further proof of the success of the human development plans for which Sheikh Zayed has been responsible.

24 April: The Council of Ministers praised the President's and the Rulers' sincere determination to support the federal process. They also praised Zayed's directives to the Supreme Council of the Federation to study the needs of the citizens and provide them with the necessary services.

25 April: The National Avian Research Centre succeeded in instituting a programme for tracking the migration patterns of hawks through the use of satellites.

26 April: Sheikh Surour bin Mohammad Al Nahyan signed a 64 million dirham contract to import and install a new 65-km drinking water pipeline in Liwa in the Western Region at a cost of 64 million dirhams.

28 April: Following Sheikh Zayed's directives, the UAE participated in the meeting of donor nations which was held in Washington in October 1994. At the meeting, the UAE pledged to provide the Palestine National Authority with 25 million dirhams over a period of five years beginning in 1994. A total of 15 million dollars had been transferred to the International Bank, constituting all of the UAE's provision for 1995-96, as well as part of its 1994 share.

29 April: Sheikh Maktoum bin Rashid Al Maktoum paid an inspection visit to

Dubai International Airport and Dubai Municipality. He directed that the development plan for Dubai, which will fulfill its needs until the year 2012 A.D., be enacted.

Sheikh Hamdan bin Zayed Al Nahyan, following a meeting held with a Palestinian delegation under the chairmanship of Mahmoud Abbas (Abu Mazin), stated that the UAE condemned the confiscation of land in the Palestinian territory of East Jerusalem. He called on the international community to make urgent moves to contain Israel's violation of the Agreement on Principles.

30 April: Abu Dhabi's Gross Domestic Product rose from 55.827 billion dirhams to 75.119 billion dirhams at the end of 1993, showing a 34 per cent growth.

2 May: During ceremonies in which a number of new judges were sworn in, Sheikh Zayed stressed that the Book of Allah and the traditions of His Prophet are the constitution of the UAE which depends on them without deviation, in the same way that the country's forebears were guided by these teachings. He said that the Islamic *Sharia* is the basis of consultation and that the UAE's democracy proceeds from the Book of Allah.

5 May: Gross Domestic Product for the Emirates during 1994 amounted to 36.3 billion dollars, a growth of 2.2 per cent.

8 May: Sheikh Sultan bin Mohammad Al Qassimi issued a decree setting-up a free trade zone at Sharjah International Airport.

The Council of Ministers formed a ministerial committee to list and classify citizens who apply for work and to institute training programmes to accommodate young people in various fields of employment.

Sheikh Surour bin Mohammad Al Nahyan signed contracts to improve the electricity network in Mahadhir Liwa, including the provision of seven branch stations at a cost of 99 million dirhams.

10 May: The United Arab Emirates called on the US administration to abort the proposal to transfer the US Embassy to Jerusalem because such a move was incompatible with legally-binding international resolutions and pledges given by the American administration in this regard. Sheikh Hamdan bin Zayed, the Minister of State for Foreign Affairs, made the announcement to the Emirates News Agency following his meeting with William Arthur Rugh, US Ambassador to the United Arab Emirates. Sheikh Hamdan said that he had stressed to the American Ambassador that the UAE considered Jerusalem to be the basis of peace in the Middle East and that infringement of this matter was a question of great sensitivity and seriousness for the Islamic and Arab nations. He added that the proposal which some people were determined to bring before the US Senate contradicted the resolutions on the status of Jerusalem passed by the Security Council and the General Assembly of the United Nations. Likewise the proposal was incompatible with the pledges received from the former Secretary of State, James Baker, to the Palestinian side and it was also in contradiction of the trends which were outlined by the Office of the Secretary of State.

12 May: In a speech before the United Nations, the UAE strongly condemned the illegal expansionist measures decided by the Israeli Government, including the confiscation of land in the occupied territory of Palestine in East Jerusalem for the purpose of establishing settlements. The aim of the plan was to uproot Palestinian Arabs and invalidate Palestinian, Arab and Islamic rights in Jerusalem.

15 May: Abu Dhabi Department of Water and Electricity signed a 55 million dirham contract to extend a water pipeline from Jebel al-Dhanna to Sir Bani Yas island with a capacity of 4 to 6 million gallons of water per day.

17 May: The Higher Customs Council decided to exempt all food items, including canned goods, from customs duties, beginning on 1 July.

18 May: Sheikh Hamdan bin Zayed Al Nahyan, during his reception of the Russian Ambassador to the country, expressed the thanks and appreciation of the UAE to the Russian Federation for the position it took in the Security Council regarding the draft resolution governing the Israeli confiscation of Arab land in East Jerusalem. He described the stand as fair, honourable and in harmony with Russia's responsibilities as one of the sponsors of the peace process in the Middle East.

24 May: Sheikh Abdulla bin Zayed Al Nahyan, during the third Conference of Ministers of Information in the Islamic Countries in Damascus, announced that Sheikh Zayed had decided to fund the production of a documentary film about Jerusalem.

26 May: Abu Dhabi Department of Works began work on ten overpass bridge projects on the Al-Ain - Abu Dhabi highway and other areas at a costs of 558 million dirhams.

2 June: Expenditure for general education at all levels throughout the country during the academic year 1993-94 was approximately 3174 million dirhams.

3 June: Sheikh Khalifa bin Zayed Al Nahyan issued directives to set-up at his own expense two centres for the handicapped in Ras al-Khaimah and Fujairah.

5 June: Sheikh Jabir Al Ahmed Al Sabah, the Amir of Kuwait, decorated Sheikh Air Marshal Mohammad bin Zayed Al Nahyan with the Sash of Kuwait, First Class, in appreciation of his role in the victory of Kuwait and the support of its just causes.

6 June: Sheikh Zayed received Dr Esmat Abdel-Meguid, the Secretary General of the Arab League. They discussed the current Arab situation, efforts being made to mediate in Arab affairs and the reinforcement of Arab co-operation in the coming years.

A session of discussions was held between the UAE, under the chairmanship of Sheikh Sultan bin Zayed Al Nahyan, and the Bosnian delegation, under the chairmanship of the Prime Minister, Haris Seladjic. The UAE confirmed its support and aid for the people of Bosnia in confronting repeated Serbian aggression. The UAE also re-affirmed its eagerness to provide political and material support to the Muslim people of Bosnia.

The Ministry of Public Works and Housing completed the construction of 995 housing units at a cost of 365 million dirhams, including the 2000 housing units which Sheikh Zayed had ordered to be built at his own expense in the Northern Emirates.

7 June: Sheikh Zayed and the Bosnian Prime Minister, Haris Seladjic, discussed the situation in Bosnia and the lack of international response to developments in that country. Zayed stressed the need for the international community to adopt a decisive position which would guarantee the ending of aggressive practices against the people of Bosnia and enable them to defend themselves.

13 June: The Ministerial Legislative Committee approved the draft law setting-up the Radio and Television Authority in Abu Dhabi as a governing body for UAE broadcasting.

18 June: Special measures commenced to execute Sheikh Zayed's directives to give jobs to 15,594 unemployed citizens.

19 June: The Council of Ministers approved the establishment of the UAE Radio and Television Authority in Abu Dhabi.

25 June: Sheikh Zayed in remarks made to the British writer, Michael Asher, expressed his great happiness at the country's complete renaissance and remarkable progress. He said that what had been achieved exceeded all imagination and was successfully accomplished with the help and assistance of Allah and with sincere intentions. He stressed that the people's confidence in the Federation proceeded from a translation of words into deeds. He noted that the prevailing international situation where the strong oppressed the weak, the resolutions of the Security Council were not respected, and humanity was devastated, was dangerous.

26 June: The UAE expressed its strong condemnation and outrage over the attempt to assassinate the Egyptian President, Mohammad Hosni Mubarak, in Addis Ababa. The assassination attempt was described as an ugly criminal act. The UAE also condemned international terrorism and said it must be combated.

28 June: Sheikh Zayed held a meeting with the Algerian President, Lamine Zeroual, who was visiting the country for the first time. He stressed that his talks with the Algerian President were in the best interests of the Islamic and Arab nation and he expressed his hope for stability in the Algerian situation and an end to terrorism.

Sheikh Zayed received a letter from Sheikh Hamad bin Khalifa Al Thani who took over the Government in Qatar. The letter was conveyed by the Minister of the Interior, Abdulla bin Khalifa Al Thani. Zayed stressed the UAE's concern for firm fraternal relations and joint co-operation between the two brotherly countries within the framework of the GCC and in the best interests of the peoples of the area and the Islamic and Arab nation.

29 June: Sheikh Zayed and the Algerian President, in a joint communiqué on the results of their talks, stressed the importance of the initiatives aimed at achieving Arab reconciliation based on objective and practical foundations. They said that this would strengthen joint Arab action and the negotiating power of the Arab nation in the best interests of its peoples. They also stressed their condemnation of terrorism in all its shapes and forms as a phenomenon alien to Islamic communities and the teachings of the Islamic religion.

2 July: Dubai Electricity and Water Authority signed a 480 million dirham contract to set-up and operate two new turbines at the Jebel Ali plant.

3 July: Sheikh Abdulla bin Zayed Al Nahyan held separate talks with the Egyptian Minister of Information, Safwat Al Sharif, and the Egyptian Minister of Culture, Farouk Hosni. They discussed ways of supporting cultural and informational co-operation between the two countries.

4 July: Sheikh Zayed inspected the groundwater wells drilled in Jebel Hafit to develop water resources and extend agricultural projects.

5 July: Sheikh Abdulla bin Zayed Al Nahyan presided over the meetings of the Council of Arab Ministers of Information in Cairo.

6 July: Sheikh Abdulla bin Zayed Al Nahyan met with Yasser Abdo Rabbo, the Minister of Culture and Information of the Palestine National Authority, who praised the President's continuing support for the cause of the Palestinian people, and especially the issue of Jerusalem. He said that Sheikh Zayed's initiative in financing the production of an international film on Jerusalem was a confirmation of the resolute path followed by him regarding the rights of the Palestinian people.

7 July: Sheikh Zayed continued his field tour of the groundwater wells project on Jebel Hafit in Al-Ain. He was briefed on the construction of dams to store the water and preserve it.

8 July: The Department of Works began to implement a new 2.7 billion development plan for the emirate of Abu Dhabi.

9 July: In Manama, Sheikh Hamdan bin Zayed Al Nahyan presided over the Damascus Declaration Ministers of Foreign Affairs meetings. In their final communiqué, the ministers expressed their great regret at the lack of an Iranian response to the UAE's repeated calls for a peaceful resolution of their differences, and especially the President of the Federation's initiative in calling for the holding of serious and direct talks in order to end the Iranian occupation of the three

islands in accordance with international law.

Sheikh Khalifa bin Zayed Al Nahyan ordered the granting of financial rewards of 40,000 dirhams to each player on the Al-Ain team as a token of his appreciation for the clubs' victory in the first Super Football Championship for 1994-95.

11 July: The Department of Planning laid down a five year plan for development projects in the emirate of Abu Dhabi, and a 20 year economic stategy for the whole of the Emirates. Abu Dhabi had spent 22.6 billion dirhams on development projects during the previous three years, while total investment in development projects and services over the previous 26 years amounted to 96.6 billion dirhams.

19 July: Sheikh Zayed called on Arab and Islamic countries to adopt a decisive and united stand toward the great powers which were standing by and watching from the sidelines while Serbian massacres were taking place against the innocent. He also called for a lifting of the arms embargo on the Bosnian people so that they could defend themselves. He said that Serbian aggression was an assault on the human conscience, an ignominious disgrace and an affront to humanity.

Air Marshal Sheikh Mohammad bin Zayed Al Nahyan, who was on an official visit to the United States, held a meeting with the US Secretary of Defence, William Perry. He also met with a number of senior officials and members of the Senate.

23 July: The UAE donated 40 million dirhams to help the people of Bosnia.

24 July: During a meeting between Sheikh Hamdan bin Zayed Al Nahyan and the Russian Ambassador, the UAE encouraged Russia to assume its international responsibilities as one of the great powers and work for an end to criminal Serbian attacks against the children, women and old people of Bosnia, especially in areas designated as 'Safe Areas' by the United Nations.

25 July: Sheikh Zayed, during his inspection tour of the Sharia Resort in the city of Al-Rahba, stressed that work is an honour for man and that it is the true path to civilization and a high standard of living. He said that a citizen's work will enable him to play an effective role in society and his country, and gain respect from his family, his Government and his country.

28 July: Sheikh Zayed, in a television interview on Abu Dhabi television conducted by Sheikh Abdulla bin Zayed Al Nahyan, called on citizens and residents to assist the people of Bosnia. He made this call as a national campaign for donation's, organized by the Ministry of Information and Culture in co-operation with the Red Crescent Society, commenced. He said that duty required that we stand against wrongdoing by opposing the miscreant, that the great powers bore the responsibility for the Bosnian tragedy and their silence was a terrible thing behind which lay unclear motives.

Donations in aid of the people of Bosnia reached 158 million dirhams, not counting some donations in kind.

30 July: Sheikh Sultan bin Khalifa Al Nahyan announced that steps had been taken to set-up a UAE international car racing track in Abu Dhabi.

1 August: The UAE strongly condemned Russia's biased support of the Serb aggressors and their many crimes against the people of Bosnia. Sheikh Hamdan bin Zayed Al Nahyan summoned the Russian Ambassador to express his shock at the Russian position which appeared to challenge the world community. He said that Moscow would lose many of its friends and interests in the Arab and Islamic world.

2 August: Sheikh Zayed issued a decree setting-up the Radio and Television Authority for the United Arab Emirates as an independent legal entity based in Abu Dhabi.

7 August: Sheikh Zayed held a meeting in Alexandria with the Egyptian President, Mohammad Hosni Mubarak, during which they discussed means of bolstering the Arab position and removing misunderstandings to facilitate a return to solidarity and unity between brothers.

8 August: In Alexandria, Sheikh Zayed and the Palestinian President, Yasser Arafat, discussed the peace process, Palestinian progress and the Arab situation.

Sheikh Zayed arrived in Damascus and held a meeting with Syrian President, Hafez Al Asad, during which they discussed Arab affairs and the peace process in the Middle East.

In the Syrian capital, Sheikh Zayed received the ambassadors representing the Damascus Declaration States (Bahrain, Kuwait, Oman, Qatar, Saudi Arabia, UAE, Syria and Egypt). He assured them of the UAE's support for whatever strengthened the Arab rank and file, expressing the view that the coming years would see the Arab nations overcoming the negative effects of the Gulf crisis to face new events as they arose. He stressed that Arab solidarity might best be realized if mutual respect could be fostered on a basis of wise, frank and open discussions.

9 August: Sheikh Zayed left Damascus for Switzerland after holding a second meeting with Syrian President, Hafez Al Asad, centring on developments in the peace process.

10 August: In Geneva, Sheikh Zayed met with the Egyptian President, Mohammad Hosni Mubarak, during which they discussed new events in the Arab arena, thereby finalizing their conversations in Alexandria.

21 August: Sheikh Khalifa bin Zayed Al Nahyan received the Prime Minister of Bosnia, Haris Seladjic, stressing the UAE's full support for the Bosnian confrontation of Serbian aggression, a stand which emanated from the UAE's pursuit of right and justice.

4 September: In Geneva, Sheikh Zayed received students studying at American and European universities. He encouraged them to adopt good manners, accept responsibility and be good examples for others. He said that the strength of the country and its development depended on the success of its men.

Sheikh Zayed received a letter from British Prime Minister, John Major, which was conveyed to Sheikh Khalifa bin Zayed Al Nahyan when he received the British Energy Minister, Tim Eager. The President of the Federation stressed the importance of co-operation among the oil producing countries to maintain the stability of oil prices. He emphasized the country's fixed policy with regard to pricing and production.

UAE Gross Domestic Product in 1994 was 134.8 billion dirhams, with a 2.99 per cent growth over 1993 when the GDP was 130 billion dirhams.

10 September: Sheikh Mohammad bin Rashid Al Maktoum, following a visit to Etisalat ordered the establishment of an institute for training nationals.

11 September: Sheikh Khalifa bin Zayed Al Nahyan donated 2 million dollars to establish a training and educational centre for the handicapped in Palestine.

Fujairah established a tourism bureau designed to promote the emirate as a tourist destination.

16 September: In Geneva, Sheikh Zayed and the Yemeni President, Ali Abdulla Saleh, discussed Arab affairs, efforts being made towards uniting the Arab rank and file and achieving Arab solidarity in ways which would serve the goals of the Arab nation and help its causes.

21 September: Rashid Abdulla led the UAE delegation to a meeting of the Arab League in Cairo. The Arab Ministers of Foreign Affairs in their final communiqué emphasized their complete support for the UAE and its policy in regard to the three islands occupied by Iran. They called on Iran to respond positively in order to solve the dispute by peaceful means.

24 September: Sheikh Zayed visited the UAE pavilion at the International Exhibition in Casablanca. He expressed his pleasure at the country's excellent participation in the exhibition. He also said that without the will and the determination these accomplishments would not have been made and that the country would continue on the same path to achieve their hopes and ambitions.

27 September: In Rabat, Sheikh Zayed attended a demonstration of the folkloric arts and mutual heritage of the Emirates and Morocco.

28 September: Sheikh Khalifa bin Zayed Al Nahyan received the Argentinian

President, Carlos Menem, who was on a short visit to the Emirates.

29 September: In Rabat, Sheikh Zayed and King Hassan of Morocco discussed a summary of Arab affairs. Zayed stressed that the situation within the Arab nation called for increased efforts to be made to overcome the divisions which the Arabs were suffering from and for which there was no justification.

30 September: In Rabat, Sheikh Zayed received a delegation from the Society of Moroccan Historians who presented him with the Golden Sash of Arab History, in appreciation of his continuing efforts to serve Arabism and Islam and in recognition of his generosity in the service of knowledge and men of knowledge. Zayed expressed his eagerness to support the activities of the society and said that Arab strength lay in mutual support and assistance. He said that the coming generations must be made aware of the glorious history of their forebears, and he wondered 'why there is silence on the part of Arabs with regard to foreign interventions which disturb the stability of some nations.' He called on the media to bear its responsibility in this regard and to convey the facts to the leaders and the peoples.

2 October: In accordance with Sheikh Zayed's directives, the Council of Ministers decided to form a supreme committee to combat drugs, protect youth and provide security and stability.

3 October: Sheikh Khalifa bin Zayed Al Nahyan attended graduation ceremonies for the fourth session of the Military Staff College at the College headquarters in Abu Dhabi.

4 October: Rashid Abdulla, in his speech before the United Nations, renewed the UAE's call to Iran to participate in direct unconditional negotiations focused on ending the occupation of the three islands. He said that in the event that Iran declined to do so, the UAE would renew its initiative to move the dispute to the International Court of Justice, stressing that the question of building confidence between the states of the region had become fundamental for the Governments of the GCC.

13 October: Sheikh Zayed opened the Al-Shati Recreation Area on the Umm al-Nar - Al-Shahama road. He also ordered the construction of 24 small rest pavilions along the beach.

16 October: Sheikh Zayed, receiving accreditation papers for new ambassadors from Brazil, Sri Lanka, Poland, Holland and Jordan, stressed that the lifting of the sanctions against Iraq to relieve the distress that they were causing the people of Iraq had become a duty. Furthermore, the time for Arab reconciliation had come. He said that Saddam Hussein had erred, but it was the Iraqi people who were paying the price. He stressed that Islam is a religion of love, mutual forgiveness and mercy and Arabs must not remain silent about the distress and hunger of 18 million Arabs, whether or not this pleased the West.

19 October: The UAE, in a speech delivered by Rashid Abdulla before the Non-aligned Conference in Columbia, stressed the importance of treating and containing political and social crises between nations, non-interference in a nation's internal affairs and the peaceful resolution of disputes.

20 October: Sheikh Sultan bin Zayed Al Nahyan arrived in New York to participate in the United Nations celebrations to mark the fiftieth anniversary of its foundation.

22 October: Sheikh Zayed and the Burkino Faso President, Belice Kamaboori, who was on his first visit to the country, discussed Arab-African co-operation and bilateral relations.

23 October: Sheikh Sultan bin Zayed Al Nahyan, delivering the UAE speech before the UN General Assembly of the United Nations on the occasion of the ceremonies marking the fiftieth anniversary of the founding of the international organization, stressed that the Iranian occupation of the three islands in the Gulf was causing a direct threat to the UAE and the security of the region. He said that the peoples of the Arab region were looking to the United Nations to undertake a larger role in dealing with the problems resulting from many wars and conflicts.

Staff General Dr Mohammad Said Al Badi issued a ministerial decree appointing Colonel Sheikh Saif bin Zayed Al Nahyan as Director General of Administration in the Abu Dhabi Police.

25 October: Sheikh Hamdan bin Zayed Al Nahyan and the US Ambassador to the UAE discussed the congressional decision to transfer the US Embassy to Jerusalem. He said that the UAE considered the resolution to be a great blow because it constituted an obvious partiality for Israel, weakened the credibility of America in the Middle East and threatened to wreck the peace process.

26 October: Sheikh Dr Sultan bin Mohammad Al Qassimi secured a loan of 20 million dollars to finance the importation and installation of a new gas turbine at the Layya power station in Sharjah.

31 October: Sheikh Zayed, receiving delegations participating in the Jerusalem Festival, stressed the UAE's continuing support for the people of Palestine until all their national rights on their own territory were restored. He stated: 'We have supported the Palestinian people and we will continue to support them until they have secured their ambition to set up their own independent State in the same way as all their brothers in the Arab nation have done'. Sheikh Zayed expressed his readiness to extend any help requested by the Palestinians in building their country. He further stated that any assistance needed by the City of Jerusalem would be given since Jerusalem was deserving of support. In addition, he strongly emphasized the importance of Arab solidarity and co-operation among the Arabs of the greater Arab nation.

Sheikh Abdulla bin Zayed Al Nahyan opened the Jerusalem Festival which was mounted under the patronage of Sheikh Zayed. In his inaugural speech, he criticized the decision of the US Congress to transfer the American Embassy to Jerusalem and said that Sheikh Zayed ordered the Zayed Philantropic Foundation and the UAE's Red Crescent Society to extend their full support to Jerusalem based on the medical, educational and social needs of the residents of the occupied city. In his speech, Sheikh Abdulla bin Zayed Al Nahyan, Deputy Minister of Information and Culture, emphasized that the City of Jerusalem was always present in the UAE's religious conscience because it was the first direction of prayer and the third of the three holy shrines. 'The UAE's current perception and understanding of the situation in the City of Jerusalem is that its residents are suffering in difficult circumstances. Sheikh Zayed, President of the Federation, ordered that it be announced to you who are present at this Festival that he is very much aware of the difficult circumstances of those Jerusalemites, both Christian and Muslim, who have suffered because of difficult living conditions. Therefore, since there are some housing projects which have been approved but which need financing, the President, in accordance with his customary practice in regard to many Arab and Islamic States and other developing nations, has decided to respond to the calls which have come from the people of Jerusalem to finance a number of housing projects and house repairs in the city of Jerusalem'. Sheikh Abdulla bin Zayed Al Nahyan also reviewed the Arab Islamic history of Jerusalem; Israeli activities backed up by the international Zionist movement; Israel's announcement of a number of illegal measures to falsify the history of Jerusalem; attacks on the holy Islamic and Christian sites in the city; the confiscation of Arab land; the international position which rejects these measures; and Israeli decrees regarding Jerusalem.

1 November: UAE authorities began to co-operate with the Palestine National Authority in studying steps to be taken to implement Sheikh Zayed's decision to finance a number of new housing projects in Jerusalem and to repair some existing buildings.

3 November: The National Victory Club won the 1995 first division championship speed boat races which were held in Dubai.

4 November: According to the census, there were 223,989 buildings in the Emirates.

5 November: In Islamabad, the Prime Minister of Pakistan, Benazir Bhutto, received Hamdan bin Zayed Al Nahyan who was leading the UAE delegation to the meetings of the UAE-Pakistan Commission. Sheikh Hamdan signed four co-operation agreements in various fields with the Pakistani Foreign Minister, Sirdar Assef.

7 November: Sheikh Tahnoun bin Mohammad al Nahyan and Air Staff General Sheikh Mohammad bin Zayed Al Nahyan attended ceremonies for the sixteenth group of pilots to graduate from the Air College in Al-Ain.

8 November: Sheikh Dr Sultan bin Mohammad Al Qassimi donated 800,000 Jordanian dinars to establish a canning factory for agricultural products in Palestine.

Sheikh Dr Sultan bin Mohammad Al Qassimi issued a decree creating Sharjah's Supreme Council for Children during his reception of Arab delegations participating in the first Arab meeting on children.

12 November: Sheikh Hamdan bin Rashid Al Maktoum opened the International Air Show, 'Dubai '95', and expressed his hope that peace and mutual forgiveness would prevail in the region. He confirmed that Dubai would establish an international airport accommodating 15 million passengers annually. Participating in the air show were 500 international companies from 34 countries.

13 November: Dubai revealed its plans to develop the Chicago Beach resort. Development will be in three stages, including construction of a 321 metre tower hotel on a constructed island; a 600 room onshore hotel due to open in 1997; and a 15 acre aqua park to be opened in 1998.

Ajman issued a tender for upgrading of Ajman port which included building a 450 metre quay wall with minimum depth alongside it of 8 metres.

UAE cabinet approved construction of two marine research and salvage centres - one for Abu Dhabi, and one for the remaining emirates.

18 November: At the first meeting of experts from the UAE and Iran held in Doha on the initiative of Qatar, the UAE proposed that four points be included on the agenda for bilateral negotiations:

(i) an end to the occupation of the Greater Tunb and Lesser Tunb islands,

(ii) commitment to the 1971 Memorandum of Understanding regarding the island of Abu Musa and the cancellation of any arrangements which contravene this memorandum,

(iii) settling the question of sovereignty over Abu Musa and

(iv) transferring the dispute to the International Court of Justice if a negotiated solution cannot be arrived at during the allotted time.

21 November: A statement issued by the UAE delegation to the meeting of experts from the UAE and Iran revealed that the meeting failed to reach an agreement on the agenda for negotiations due to the intransigence of the Iranian delegation, thereby negating the purpose for which the meeting had been convened.

25 November: The Supreme Committee between the UAE, under the chairmanship of Sheikh Khalifa bin Zayed Al Nahyan, and the Sultanate of Oman, under the chairmanship of Sayyid Fahad bin Mahmoud Al Said, held its fifth meeting in Abu Dhabi where branch committees were formed to follow-up ways to achieve the mutual interests of the two countries.

26 November: The UAE-Oman Supreme Committee concluded its fifth meeting in Abu Dhabi. The two sides agreed to continue their mutual consultations and co-ordination on bilateral relations and affairs of mutual concern.

28 November: In Rabat, Sheikh Zayed held a meeting with King Hassan of Morocco, during which they reviewed Arab affairs and efforts being made to clear the air in the light of Zayed's initiative and his call for comprehensive Arab reconciliation. Sheikh Zayed confirmed that the situation demanded increased efforts to overcome the division and fragmentation which the Arab world was suffering from and he said that it was necessary to ensure that the Arab destiny is one and the same and to try to establish good Arab relations on the basis of clarity and mutual confidence.

29 November: Sheikh Said bin Zayed Al Nahyan announced the commencement of work on the plan to expand and develop Port Zayed at a cost of 60 million dirhams.

1 December: Sheikh Zayed stressed in remarks made on the occasion of the twenty-fourth National Day that the Federation stood firm because of the strength of its sons, the vision and organization of his brothers, the Rulers, and the efforts of all Government officials.

2 December: Sheikh Zayed met the Members of the Supreme Council of the Federation and groups of well-wishers on the occasion of the twenty-fourth National Day.

4 December: Sheikh Zayed led the UAE delegation to the sixteenth Gulf Co-operation Council Summit in Muscat. He confirmed on his arrival that over the years the Council had achieved some excellent successes which reflected the best interests of the Council and the peoples of its constituent States. He said that, under the circumstances, the Summit would gain in importance.

6 December: Sheikh Zayed returned to the country after participating in the final session of the sixteenth GCC Summit in Muscat. The Summit's final communiqué renewed its support for the UAE's right to restore its sovereignty over the three islands occupied by Iran.

Sheikh Zayed and the President of Tajikstan, Imam Ali Rahmanov, who was visiting the country for the first time, discussed regional and international affairs of mutual concern. The two Presidents confirmed their support for the peace process in the Middle East and the rejection of terrorism.

13 December: World Trade Organization (WTO) approved UAE market access schedules for goods and services.

17 December: In a joint communiqué on the results of their discussions, the President of the Emirates and the President of Tajikstan stressed the necessity of maintaining security and stability in the Gulf region, the principle of non-interference in the internal affairs of States, the rejection of the use of force in international relations and and the necessity for the peaceful settlement of disputes.

18 December: The Council of Ministers discussed the situation of flood victims in some areas of the Northern Emirates and decided to empower the Ministry of Labour and Social affairs to assess the damages and provide the victims with urgent assistance.

20 December: Sheikh Zayed, during discussions which he held with the President of the Palestine National Authority, Yassir Arafat, confirmed the UAE's support for peace on all fronts and efforts being made to achieve a fair settlement of the Palestinian question.

UAE and France signed a defence agreement in Paris following a military accord signed in January 1995.

21 December: Sheikh Zayed received his brother, Sheikh Khalifa bin Hamad Al Thani, on his arrival in the country on a fraternal visit.

Sheikh Zayed received a telephone call from the Yemeni President, Ali Abdulla Saleh, about the latest developments in the situation on the island of Greater Hanish which had been taken over by Eritrean forces. He confirmed the UAE's concern to arrive at a peaceful solution to the dispute between the two countries using the intelligent arbitration to solve the quarrel in peaceful way.

23 December: Sheikh Khalifa bin Zayed Al Nahyan gave 2.5 million dirhams to honour the organizing committees for the Arab Gulf Games hosted by the Emirates in 1994.

24 December: Sheikh Zayed opened the new session of the Federal National Council and said that the Council must participate in all matters involving the achievement of progress, advancement and prosperity of the nation. He called on the Council members to endeavour to raise the standard of the nation and its citizens and to achieve the aspirations of the people.

26 December: The Board of Trustees of the Zayed Philantropic Foundation, under the chairmanship of Sheikh Khalifa bin Zayed Al Nahyan, agreed to allocate 40 million dirhams to support charity projects within the country and abroad.

From its establishment to the end of this

year, the Abu Dhabi Fund for Development granted a total of 12.3 billion dirhams in loans and aid.

29 December: Sheikh Zayed received a telephone call from US President, Bill Clinton, during which they exchanged opinions regarding developments in the region and the Middle East peace process.

Zayed stressed that UAE policies were positive and firm with regard to questions of right and justice and would work toward the stability, security and peace of the two countries.

31 December: UK Defence Secretary, Michael Portillo, visited UAE for talks on a planned defence agreement.

Nineteen Ninety Six

6 January: During a meeting with the Pakistani Prime Minister, Benazir Bhutto, Sheikh Zayed stressed that the international community must exert all possible efforts to bring stability, security and peace to Afghanistan and put an end to the suffering of its people.

Sheikh Abdulla bin Zayed Al Nahyan participated in the Conference on Gulf Security for the Twenty-first Century, organized by the Emirates Center for Strategic Studies and Research.

The Ministry of Public Works and Housing received 27 new public service projects costing more than 158 million dirhams.

In 1995, the Social Services and Commercial Buildings Office constructed 230 commercial buildings costing 202 billion dirhams.

7 January: Sheikh Zayed issued a federal decree promoting Sheikh Hazza bin Zayed Al Nahyan to the rank of General. Sheikh Khalifa bin Zayed Al Nahyan issued an Amiri decree appointing Sheikh Diyab bin Zayed Al Nahyan as Director of the Presidential Office.

Sheikh Sultan bin Zayed Al Nahyan, during his reception of the visiting Eritrean Interior Minister, stressed the importance of peacefully solving the dispute between Yemen and Eritrea regarding the Hanish Islands. Sheikh Humaid bin Ahmad Al Mualla, the Minister of Planning, announced that, according to the 1995 census, there are 2,377,453 residents in the Emirates.

The first shipment of humanitarian aid, donated by the UAE Red Crescent Society to help relieve the suffering of the people of Iraq, reached Baghdad.

8 January: Abu Dhabi Executive Council decided to build 92 popular housing units in the Al-Qoo, district of the Eastern Region. It also approved the Al-Muzairah - Liwa road project and the project for improving and widening the Abu Dhabi - Dubai highway.

The Nationality and Residency Offices in the Emirates began to apply the 1995 resolution of the Council of Ministers establishing the system for granting visas to incoming families and their servants.

The World Health Organization chose Abu Dhabi and Dubai as two of the three most preferable cities in the Middle East, from the point of view of health.

14 January: Humaid bin Nasser Al

Nowais announced that 2 billion dirhams will be spent on water and electricity projects in the Northern Emirates in 1996.

15 January: Sheikh Sultan bin Zayed Al Nahyan, during his reception of Al Haj Abdulla Al Muhairabi and a number of the members of the Federal National Council, stressed the importance of co-operation between the National Council and the Council of Ministers, in order to meet the needs of the public.

16 January: The Federal National Council endorsed the draft law establishing the Civil Aviation Board with a capital of 100 million dirhams.

The vegetable and date canning factory in Al-Marfa commenced production of concentrated tomato paste, with a daily average production of 18 tons.

A ship from the Abu Dhabi Benevolent Society arrived in Mogadishu carrying 24 tons of food and medical supplies in urgent aid for the Somali people.

17 January: Sheikh Hamdan bin Zayed Al Nahyan, during his reception of the Director General of the Arab Labour Organization, Bakr Mahmoud Rasoul, received the 'Labour Shield' which was presented to the President of the Federation by the organization in appreciation of his pioneering role in supporting joint Arab labour.

The new water plant in Al-Hamriyya, Sharjah went on stream. Costing 2.7 million dirhams, it has a capacity of 300,000 gallons of water per day.

19 January: The UAE strongly condemned the terrorism in Bahrain. The Ministry of Foreign Affairs stressed the solidarity of the UAE with the leadership and people of Bahrain.

Abu Dhabi Municipality has been extremely successful in increasing the green area in the emirate and in combating desertification: in 1995, 1800 hectares of greenery were planted in various parts of Abu Dhabi.

20 January: Sheikh Maktoum bin Rashid Al Maktoum issued a law establishing the Judicial Institute of Dubai, and a resolution appointing the Board of Administration and a director for the institute.

The Utilization Committee for Medical Dwellings distributed 65 popular housing units to citizens in Ras al-Khaimah. The committee was headed by the Minister of Public Works.

21 January: In 1995, Abu Dhabi Municipality distributed 524 dwellings to citizens of Abu Dhabi and the Western Region.

22 January: Sheikh Khalifa bin Zayed Al Nahyan ordered the construction of 2118 housing units for citizens in Al-Ain and surrounding areas.

The Executive Director of the World Gold Council announced that the UAE had imported 320 tons of gold through Dubai in 1995.

23 January: Fujairah Municipality distributed 39 houses to citizens, some of the 2000 houses which will be completed in the Northern Emirates by favour of the President of the Federation.

The number of citizens who benefited from the Marriage Fund in 1995 increased 20 per cent over 1994. The Fund approved 3084 grants totalling 209.58 million dirhams during 1995.

24 January: Sheikh Maktoum Bin Rashid Al Maktoum cancelled outstanding repayments of 64 million dirhams on loans from the Development Board in the Al-Safiya and Al-Karama districts in Dubai. Some 300 citizens benefited from these loans.

25 January: Sheikha Fatima bint Mubarak Al Nahyan, Chairwoman of the UAE

Women's Federation, donated 1 million riyals to the Society for Caring for Handicapped Children in Saudi Arabia.

29 January: Abu Dhabi Executive Council decided to build a water distillation plant costing 105 million dirhams in Ras al-Khaimah.

30 January: The National Consultative Council advised against the construction of official Government office buildings in the middle of the capital to prevent overcrowding.

The Jebel Ali Glass Container Factory signed a contact worth 23 million dollars with a banking group to develop its production capacity to an average of 425 million bottles annually.

31 January: Dubai Electricity and Water Board signed an 1082 million dirham contract with a group of Japanese companies to construct an electricity plant in Al-Awir.

1 February: Sheikh Khalifa bin Zayed Al Nahyan issued an order giving 31.4 million dirhams from the Zayed Philantropic Foundation to deserving citizens.

3 February: Sheikh Maktoum bin Rashid Al Maktoum issued a law establishing a new free zone area at Dubai International Airport.

7 February: Sheikh Zayed issued directives to send urgent assistance to Morocco to aid the people who suffered from the floods which hit the country.

The Federal National Council formed a Co-ordination Committee with the Ministry of the Interior to deal with a number of issues, including residential formations, immigration, residence, combating illegal entry into the country and drugs.

The Centre for Security Studies in Abu Dhabi Police Department stressed that a number of attempts to launder illegal money in the UAE had been aborted.

8 February: The World Trade Organization in Geneva approved the membership of the UAE in the organization.

9 February: Sheikh Zayed and the Members of the Supreme Council of the Federation attended the pure-bred Arab horse races staged at the Abu Dhabi Equestrian Club race course.

10 February: General Sheikh Mohammad bin Rashid Al Maktoum announced that the Deira Tower Building in Dubai had become an Islamic trust (*Waqf*) and that the income from the building would henceforth be given to charity. He also donated 5 million dirhams for charity.

The Ministry of Health completed preliminary studies for the establishment of a centre for open heart surgery in Al-Mafraq Hospital and the expansion of the hospital to 200 beds at a cost of 200 million dirhams.

The Sea Ports Authority announced the allocation of 2.4 billion dirhams to carry-out development plans for Port Zayed which are expected to be completed in the year 2000.

Some 300 million dirhams are to be distributed as grants to 7617 junior Government employees and citizens who benefit from social services in Abu Dhabi.

11 February: Sheikh Essa bin Zayed Al Nahyan inaugurated the first Arab Heritage Festival held in Abu Dhabi with the participation of seven Arab countries.

In 1995, expenditure on the construction of road and bridge projects amounted to nearly 1.8 billion dirhams.

14 February: The first air taxi service between Abu Dhabi and Dubai was inaugurated.

15 February: Sheikh Zayed, during his

reception of Al Haj Abdulla Al Muhairibi, instructed the Federal National Council to give priority to citizens' affairs, and he called on youth to bear the responsibility of keeping the country beautiful.

Dubai Shopping Festival '96 began and will continue for 43 days.

18 February: Sheikh Zayed, during his reception of the German Parliamentary Delegation, stressed the UAE's concern to support friendship with the world for the good of its peoples and their mutual benefit as a way of achieving international stability. He said that good will and the happiness of any State is reflected in its relations with other States.

Sheikh Hamdan bin Rashid Al Maktoum issued a decree establishing a systems unit in the Ministry of Finance, to define and distribute technical aid from international development organizations and the World Bank to the UAE.

20 February: Abu Dhabi Municipality completed the new 12 million dirham Heritage Park project which was begun last year in the heart of the city of Abu Dhabi.

26 February: The eastern ring road tunnel connecting Abu Dhabi with the Al-Maqta bridge was opened. Construction costs for the project amounted to 200 million dirhams.

27 February: Sheikh Dr Sultan bin Mohammad Al Qassimi was present at the ceremony honouring the winners of the Arab Gulf States Education Office prize. He stressed that the knowledge disseminated by educated Arabs will generate a reaction and enrich Arab thought and culture.

Khalfan Al Roumi opened a conference on new books which was supervised by UNESCO with the support of the President of the Federation. The Federation of Journalists, Distributors and Publishers have adopted the new books project.

Sheikh Abdulla bin Zayed Al Nahyan crowned the Sharjah team as the football champions for the 1955-96 season.

1 March: The US State Department annual report praised the efforts of the UAE in combating drugs and money laundering.

3 March: Abu Dhabi National Bank made a profit of 214 million dirhams in 1995.

4 March: The Council of Ministers formed a committee to study ways of increasing the number of nationals working in the banking sector. It also approved the formation of the Radio and Television Authority.

Abu Dhabi Municipality completed the construction and equipping of the Handicapped Centre in Fujairah which was established by the largesse of Sheikh Khalifa bin Zayed al Nahyan.

5 March: Sheikh Zayed toured the Western Region where he inspected development and agricultural projects. He received citizens at the Ghiyathi rest house and assured them of the importance of work for the service of the country. He said that seriousness and sincerity are basic principles which a man must demonstrate in his character.

7 March: General Mohammad bin Rashid Al Maktoum issued orders to the security establishments in Dubai to arrest young men who were bothering and embarrassing women in the streets and markets. Their names were to be published in the news media.

The US State Department annual report praised the UAE for its respect for human rights. The report said that the authorities were not responsible for any unlawful deaths and had not passed a death sentence on anyone in the UAE for political reasons.

9 March: Sheikh Zayed and the former British Prime Minister, Edward Heath, discussed the situation in the Middle East region, as well as mutual relations and co-operation between the UAE and Britain.

The UAE paid its share of the Arab League budget of for 1996, amounting to nearly 108 million dollars.

The UAE confirmed that it would participate in the Peace Conference in Sharm al-Shaikh which would focus onways of combating terrorism.

11 March: Sheikh Zayed and the Finnish President, Martti Ahitsari, who was visiting the country for the first time, discussed the situation in the Gulf, peace in the Middle East region and ways of strengthening co-operation between the two countries.

12 March: Sheikh Khalifa bin Zayed Al Nahyan and General Sheikh Mohammad bin Rashid Al Maktoum were present at two graduation ceremonies at the Zayed the Second Military College in Al-Ain.

The UAE and Finland signed two agreements concerning dual taxation and the protection of investments.

The visiting Finnish President and General Sheikh Mohammad bin Rashid Al Maktoum inaugurated the headquarters in Dubai of the Finnish Nesti Company.

13 March: Rashid Abdulla, delivering the UAE's speech to the Sharm al-Shaikh Summit, demanded the maintenance of a fair and balanced approach, as well as peace on the legal basis of 'Land for Peace'.

14 March: Sheikh Ahmed bin Said Al Maktoum accepted the gold prize awarded to the Emirates Airlines by an international tourism magazine as the preferred air carrier in the Middle East.

17 March: The GCC Ministerial Council, at the conclusion of meetings in Riyadh, renewed their support for the UAE in its pursuit of peaceful measures to restore the sovereignty of the Lesser and Greater Tunbs and Abu Musa which are occupied by Iran.

Sheikh Abdulla bin Zayed Al Nahyan attended the ceremonies for the distribution of the Gulf Business Awards for 1995.

18 March: Sheikh Zayed and the former US President, George Bush, discussed efforts being made to establish security and stability in the Gulf region. Zayed decorated the former President with the 'Federation Sash.'

Sheikh Humaid bin Rashid Al Mualla confirmed the stability of the UAE economy and the expectation of a 5.6 per cent increase in Gross Domestic Product during 1996.

19 March: Sheikh Sultan bin Mohammad Al Qassimi approved a new salary scale which will give a pay rise to local Sharjah Government employees.

In a speech delivered in Abu Dhabi, the former US President, George Bush, praised the stance taken by the President of the Federation, and the efforts being made for stability in the Gulf region.

20 March: Sheikh Surour bin Mohammad Al Nahyan signed a contract for the import and installation of two seawater desalination plants for Ras al-Khaimah at a cost of 105 million dirhams. He also signed two contracts to set-up and commission a new electricity plant in the Musaffah area at a cost of 179 million dirhams.

23 March: Sheikh Zayed and the Members

Dubai Creek.

A quiet place to read the Holy Qur'an.

Keen to learn, pupils at Al-Worood
School in Abu Dhabi.

The library of Abu Dhabi Men's Higher College of Technology.

A mechanical model of the camel at
Sharjah Natural History Museum.

At the Documentation Centre in Abu Dhabi.

A student at Abu Dhabi Men's Higher
College of Technology works on a project to
design a "comfortable cow-shed" for a firm
in Al-Ain.

Sharjah's evening sky.

MEDIATEC/WOOLFITT

MEDIATEC/ERIKSEN

MEDIATEC/ERIKSEN

Top left: Camel raised from a frozen embryo. Left: Rheem gazelle. Above left: Ostriches at Sir Bani Yas Island. Top right: White-collared kingfisher. Right: A male houbara bustard displays at the National Avian Research Centre, Abu Dhabi.

Dubai Port and Dry Docks.

The town of Sharjah.

Dubai Museum's recently opened display of traditional life in the UAE.

A motor rally in Abu Dhabi.

Above: Zayed Sports Centre, Abu Dhabi.

Left: An Arabian horse at the 1996 Arabian Horse Show in Abu Dhabi.

Above left: Khor Fakkan, an enclave of Sharjah on the east coast of the Emirates.

Above: Dubai Creek Golf Club main building.

Left: Hatta resort, Dubai.

Abu Dhabi's Port Zayed.

One of Dubai's wharfs.

Abu Dhabi's roads in 1996.

The city of Abu Dhabi in 1996.

of the Supreme Council of the Federation, the Rulers of the Emirates, attended an operetta entitled 'Allah, Oh Nation!' which was put on by the Ministry of Education and presented by 1300 students in the National Theatre in Abu Dhabi.

24 March: The municipalities decided to stop importing beef and all beef products from Ireland to protect the UAE consumer from mad cow disease.

25 March: The Council of Ministers approved an international tender valued at 42 million dirhams for the importation of medicines for the Ministry of Health.

The Sharjah Customs Department destroyed a number of elephant tusks and tiger/leopard skins, valued at more than 2 million dirhams, within the scope of the State's legal obligation to protect animals threatened with extinction and prevent trade and dealings in their products.

26 March: Abu Dhabi Municipality distributed 690 housing units to citizens in Abu Dhabi and the Western Region.

27 March: Sheikh Zayed, during his reception of the Palestinian President, Yasser Arafat, stressed the UAE's stand beside the Palestinian people and its unlimited support for their progress toward peace and stability. For his part, Yasser Arafat stated that Zayed represented the living conscience of the nation. Sheikh Maktoum bin Rashid Al Maktoum attended the Dubai International Cup for horse racing.

28 March: Abu Dhabi's external trade in 1995 was around 18.8. billion dirhams.

30 March: Sheikh Khalifa bin Zayed Al Nahyan issued a law protecting oil installations in the offshore areas.

Staff General Mohammad bin Zayed Al Nahyan stressed the UAE's determintion to restore its three occupied islands from Iranian occupation. In a press interview he said that joint manoeuvres which were being held by the UAE Forces with friendly states were aimed at improving the performance of the Armed Forces and were not directed against any party.

31 March: Sheikh Zayed issued a federal decree promulgating a law limiting the licensing of private health clinics and hospitals to UAE citizens.

Sheikh Nahyan bin Mubarak Al Nahyan opened the sixth International Abu Dhabi Book Exhibition in the Cultural Centre.

Abu Dhabi National Oil Company (ADNOC) announced that it was currently setting-up a unit to deal with toxic waste products. An operation involving a group of its companies in the Al-Ruwais region, it is the first of its kind in Abu Dhabi and a part of the general long term strategy for the protection of the country's environment.

1 April: The meeting between the joint committee of the Federal National Council and the Council of Ministers endorsed the laying-down of a comprehensive strategy to train and employ UAE citizens. The National Council advised the inclusion of workers in the private sector in the draft law on retirement, and it called on the private sector to eliminate obstacles to the employment of national cadres.

Staff General Sheikh Mohammad bin Zayed Al Nahyan arrived in Pretoria on the UAE's first official visit to South Africa.

The Board of Administration of the Television and Radio Authority, at its first meeting under the chairmanship of Khalfan Al Roumi, chose Sheikh Abdulla bin Zayed Al Nahyan as its Deputy Chairman.

2 April: Abu Dhabi Executive Council approved the construction of 105 housing units in the city of Al-Shahama.

The Ministry of Health opened a modern unit for treating addiction as part of the final phase for the establishment of the Psychiatric Medicine Hospital in Abu Dhabi.

3 April: Sheikh Zayed and the German Minister of State for Foreign Affairs, Helmut Schieffer, discussed co-operative relations between the two countries. The German Minister emphasized that the UAE had the full support of his country in their pursuit of a peaceful resolution to the problem of the three islands occupied by Iran.

Sheikh Zayed decorated Sheikh Fahim Al Qassimi with the Zayed the First Sash in appreciation of the efforts he expended as the Secretary General of the GCC.

4 April: Sheikh Essa bin Salman Al Khalifa concluded a three-day visit to the UAE. Before his departure, he announced that Bahrain appreciated the Zayed's support for development in Bahrain.

The Kuwaiti magazine, *Marat al-Umma*, chose the Federation's First Lady, Sheikha Fatima bint Mubarak, Chairwoman of the UAE Women's Federation, as the 'Benevolent Woman' of 1995.

The Social Services and Commercial Buildings Office in Abu Dhabi completed 157 commercial buildings in the Musaffah area at a cost of 347.9 million dirhams.

7 April: The Ministry of Electricity and Water announced that work would commence at the beginning of 1997 on the construction of the electric power grid which will connect all the cities in the country.

8 April: The Council of Ministers endorsed the budget for 1996. Expenditure was estimated at 18.254 billion dirhams and projected revenue at 117.396 billion dirhams, leaving a deficit of 858.2 million dirhams.

9 April: The Federal National Council recommended the setting-up of a supreme board for the appointment of UAE citizens and to follow-up on national manpower. It endorsed the changes in the Immigration and Residence Law to include the imposition of harsh punishments on persons who harbour illegal immigrants, and on those who have helped them enter the country.

10 April: Sheikh Zayed and the Members of the Supreme Council of the Federation, the Rulers of the Emirates, attended the finals of the annual pure-bred Arab camel and horse races in Dubai.

11 April: An 82 million dirham contract was signed to construct the electrical power plant in Al-Awir.

12 April: Sheikh Sultan bin Mohammad Al Qassimi signed two contracts for installing a water desalination plant in Layya and an electrical power plant in Khor Fakkan at a cost of 231 million dirhams.

14 April: Sheikh Zayed ratified the agreement whereby the UAE became a member of the Paris Agreement for the Protection of Industrial Property and the Arab Agreement for Combating Trade in Illegal Drugs.

15 April: General Mohammad bin Rashid Al Maktoum was present at the Khaleej Journalism and Publishing Establishment ceremonies surrounding the publishing of the first issue of the English language daily newspaper, *The Gulf Today*.

16 April: Sheikh Sultan bin Zayed Al Nahyan was present at the graduation ceremonies for students from the UAE

University and the Higher Technical Colleges.

18 April: An official source in the Ministry of Foreign Affairs announced that the Iranian Government was constructing an electrical plant on the island of Greater Tunb which Iran has occupied in 1971. This is considered to be a infraction of the principles of international law and a violation of the UAE's sovereignty over the island. No legal rights can ever accrue to occupiers of territory.

19 April: The Nasr Team won the football championship for 1995-96.

20 April: Sheikh Khalifa bin Zayed Al Nahyan issued a law merging the Abu Dhabi flour and fodder factories and the Al-Ain Mineral Water and Dates Plant. The new project, capitalized at 350 million dirhams, will be known as the 'Abu Dhabi Food Factories'.

21 April: Sheikh Zayed, along with the Members of the Supreme Council of the Federation, the Rulers of the Emirates, and delegations from the GCC States were present at the finals of the seventh annual pure-bred Arab camels races in Al-Wathba.

The International Cable Company announced that, Etisalat, the Emirates telecommunications company, had decided to issue a tender for a satellite, the cost of which will range between 700 million to a billion dirhams.

23 April: Cambridge University gave a reception in celebration of the donation granted to them by the Zayed Philantropic Foundation to finance a chair for Islamic Studies in the University's Divinity College.

Umm Al-Qaiwain Municipality distributed 180 housing units to citizens as part of the project for the construction of 500 dwellings being built at the personal expense of Sheikh Khalifa bin Zayed Al Nahyan.

4 May: Sheikh Zayed and the Chadian president, Idris Dibi, who was on his first visit to the country, discussed Arab and African matters and bilateral relations.

Joint air and sea exercises between the UAE and France, entitled 'Big Fox 2" commenced as part of the military defence and co-operation agreements signed between the two countries in January 1995.

6 May: Sheikh Zayed and His Majesty Sultan Qaboos, the Sultan of Oman, held a session of discussions at Al-Mishrif Palace in Abu Dhabi, during which they reviewed the future of the GCC, the realization of the hopes of its peoples and the strengthening of brotherly ties between the two countries . They also exchanged points of view regarding Arab, regional and international issues.

7 May: The Federal National Council endorsed the 1996 budget and advised that the individual emirates share, as determined, in the percentage of the budget as per their annual income, in accordance with the provisions of the constitution.

8 May: His Majesty Sultan Qaboos bin Said, the Sultan of Oman, ended his three-day visit to the country. He referred to the results of the discussions with Sheikh Zayed and said that their meeting had strengthened warm brotherly relations and had achieved their joint interests.

The four-day joint air and sea exercises between the UAE Armed Forces and French forces came to an end.

11 May: Units of the UAE land forces arrived in Manama to participate in the

'Sword of Glory' exercises with Bahraini forces.

16 May: Sheikh Zayed, during his reception of the Lebanese Prime Minister, Rafiq Al Hariri, stressed that the UAE will stand by the side of Lebanon until it has passed through its troubled times and returned to peace and stability.

20 May: The Supreme Council of the Federation, at its historic meeting under the Presidency of Sheikh Zayed, approved an amendment to the provisional constitution which would delete the term 'provisional' from its clauses. Abu Dhabi will be the capital of the State. The President of the Federation said that the Rulers must work as one to raise standards for the people. He said that, since the income of the UAE citizen was among the highest in the world, no-one in the Emirates should be in need.

21 May: Sheikh Ahmad bin Said Al Maktoum signed an agreement for a 390 million dirham loan to purchase a Boeing aircraft for Emirates Airlines.

24 May: The Educational, Cultural and Scientific Organization (UNESCO) established a prize in the name of Sheikh Zayed bin Sultan Al Nahyan. The prize will be given for the best accomplishment in the field of information. Farid Ricomayder, the Director General of UNESCO, praised the role of the UAE in supporting its activities. He said that UAE participated as a member in the Executive Council and shared in establishing the policies of the organization.

25 May: Sheikh Maktoum bin Rashid Al Maktoum issued a decree increasing the capital of the Dubai Transportation Company to 100 million dirhams. He also issued a decree allowing the proof of lands granted by the Government whether or not they are residential or commercial properties.

2 June: The GCC Ministerial Council, at the end of its meetings in Riyadh, renewed its support for the right of the UAE to restore its three islands from the occupation of Iran. The Secretary General of the Council, Jamil Al Hujailan, said that Iranian activities on the islands are opposed to good neighbourly relations.

4 June: Sheikh Zayed stressed that the UAE continued to stand by Bahrain at all times and in all circumstances. In a telephone conversation with Sheikh Essa bin Salman Al Khalifa, he condemned the interference in the internal affairs of Bahrain and the troubles which some mercenary elements are creating. He said that it was necessary to eliminate this kind of behaviour whether it comes from Iran or elsewhere. He called on the Arab countries to support Bahrain in uncovering revolutionary plots and to arrest members of the terrorist organizations planning to set up a State financed by Iran.

5 June: Rakad bin Salim, the UAE Oil Minister, was chosen as President of OPEC for the next term at the organization's ministerial conference opening meeting in Vienna.

7 June: The first Emirates Boeing 777, one of seven such aeroplanes which Emirates has contracted to purchase, arrived at Dubai International Airport.

9 June: Staff Colonel Sultan Obaid Al-Suweidi, chairman of the organizing committee for exhibitions and conferences, said that 95 per cent of the space for the IDEX 97 exhibition had been taken. The event, in which over 600 companies from 32 countries will participate, will be held in March 1997.

10 June: The Council of Ministers decided that the appointment of UAE citizens to vacant positions in all Government organizations would commence immediately, implementing the directives of the President of the Federation to employ all citizens who are capable of work.

Sheikh Hamdan bin Zayed Al Nahyan and the Foreign Minister of Slovakia, Bawari Shenik, discussed relations between the two countries. The Slovakian minister confirmed his country's support for the right of the UAE to recover the three islands from Iranian occupation by all peaceful means.

11 June: Sheikh Hamad bin Mohammad Al Sharqi signed a contract for constructing an oil storage project, including oil derivatives, in Fujairah, to be completed in 1998. The first phase of the project, which will have a storage capacity of 3 million barrels, will cost 75 million dollars.

The Federal National Council condemned any interference in the internal affairs of Bahrain. In a statement, it praised the stand taken by the President of the Federation in supporting and aiding Bahrain.

12 June: Sheikh Zayed received a letter from the French President, Jacques Chirac, which was conveyed by the French Minister of Foreign Affairs, Herve de Charette. The letter dealt with matters of mutual concern and bilateral relations.

The Supreme Petroleum Council chose the Borealis Company as ADNOC's partner in setting-up the first petrochemical production project in the UAE. It is expected to begin producing in 2000 with an annual production of 45 tons.

15 June: Sheikh Zayed ordered the postponement of celebrations for the thirtieth Accession Day, commemorating the day on which he took over the reins of Government in Abu Dhabi. Celebrations are to be postponed until the 2 December to coincide with the UAE celebrations of its twenty-fifth National Day.

17 June: Sheikh Tahnoun bin Mohammad Al Nahyan inaugurated the production of freshwater from a new well in Al-Ain which is part of a project to discover sources of deep groundwater in Abu Dhabi. This project is being carried-out by the Abu Dhabi Oil Company in co-operation with the National Excavations Company, the German Demilreenz Company and the German Technical Co-operation Establishment.

The Council of Ministers approved the commissioning of the Higher Technical Colleges to replace the American University of Beirut as supervisors of the nursing schools in the Emirates.

18 June: In his meeting with Abdul Karim Al Kabariti, the Prime Minister of Jordan, who was visiting the country, Sheikh Zayed welcomed any Arab meeting aimed at reviving and strengthening the progress of Arab solidarity and supporting the comprehensive and just peace process in the Middle East. He also expressed the hope that the Arab Summit in Cairo would be the beginning of the restoration of Arab solidarity, and he said that there must be a complete review of the Arab situation and that vital and necessary decisions regarding each other must be taken in which all current events are taken into account. Wisdom and awareness must try to make up for what the Arabs have lost in the past.

The Federal National Council endorsed the draft law amending the constitution and cancelling the term 'provisional' from the constitution wherever it is found. It also endorsed Abu Dhabi as the capital of the country.

19 June: Sheikh Zayed received a telephone call from the Egyptian President, Mohammad Hosni Mubarak, during which they conferred regarding the current Arab situation. Sheikh Khalifa bin Zayed Al Nahyan confirmed Zayed's help and support for the efforts of President Mohammad Hosni Mubarak in strengthening Arab solidarity.

The Industrial Bank Administrative Council approved the expenditure of 162 million dirhams on the financing of new industrial projects.

Etisalat stressed that it would cut the Internet service of subscribers who break the regulations and laws and misuse the network.

20 June: Sheikh Khalifa bin Zayed Al Nahyan, before leaving for Cairo at the head of the UAE's delegation to the Arab Summit, called for an end to differences and a strengthening of Arab solidarity. He said that every meeting among Arabs is for the good of the nation and that disputes do not benefit anyone except enemies.

Staff Major Sheikh Sultan bin Khalifa Al Nahyan received his degree from the Higher Military College and he also received a letter from the National Defence College after his graduation from the Nasser Higher Military Academy with an evaluation of 'very good'. He had submitted a research paper on the national security of the UAE as part of his studies.

21 June: The Egyptian President, Mohammad Hosni Mubarak, meeting with Sheikh Khalifa bin Zayid Al Nahyan after his arrival in Cairo, praised the sincere efforts being made by Sheikh Zayed to revive the Arab spirit.

22 June: Sheikh Khalifa bin Zayed Al Nahyan led the UAE delegation to the opening session of the Arab Summit Conference in Cairo. He described the prevailing atmosphere at the Summit as positive and he confirmed anew Sheikh Zayed's support for efforts to revive Arab solidarity.

The Civil Service Council decided to suspend filling vacancies in the Government offices of the emirates and the Federation in preparation for the appointment of nationals who are seeking employment.

23 June: Sheikh Khalifa bin Zayed Al Nahyan headed the UAE delegation in the final session of the Arab Summit Conference in Cairo. He supported the final communiqué of the Summit and all measures which were adopted by the UAE to recover its sovereignty over the three occupied islands. He called on Iran to end the occupation and to stop its illegal imposition of the *status quo.*

24 June: Sheikh Zayed congratulated the Egyptian President, Mohammad Hosni Mubarak, on the success of the Arab Summit. In a telephone call, he expressed his appreciation of President Mubarak's continuing efforts to bring the differing points of view closer together, in an attempt to achieve Arab solidarity and push the just and comprehensive Middle East peace process forward.

25 June: Sheikh Zayed issued a federal decree appointing Sheikh Abdulla bin Zayed Al Nahyan as the Director General of the Radio and Television Authority.

Sheikh Dr Sultan bin Mohammad Al Qassimi signed a contract to establish a branch of the American University of Beirut in Sharjah.

Sheikh Hamdan bin Rashid Al Maktoum,

in his capacity as President of Dubai Municipality, issued a local order regarding the imposition of a road tax on mechanical vehicles in Dubai.

26 June: Sheikh Zayed condemned the criminal explosion in Al-Khobar in Saudi Arabia. In a telephone call to the Custodian of the Two Holy Mosques, King Fahad bin Abdulaziz, Zayed said that the UAE will stand by Saudi Arabia and employ all its capabilities on their behalf, and that criminal aggression is an aggression against everyone in the region and not just against Saudi Arabia.

Yousif Omair bin Yousif , the Secretary General of the Supreme Petroleum Council, and the Director General of the Abu Dhabi Oil Company (ADNOC) opened five new oil projects in the Al-Ruwais industrial zone: the sulphur utilities project; the 'Bab' gas pipeline; the expansion of the shipping port at the Al-Ruwais refinery; and the permanent offices in Al-Ruwais.

Dubai's Office of Health and Health Services budget for 1996 is 800 million dirhams.

29 June: Sheikh Mohammad bin Butti Al Hamid issued a decree organizing the disposal of medical waste from the country's medical establishments, prohibiting its disposal in public garbage bins and fixing the places where it can be disposed.

The second shipment of humanitarian aid from the UAE arrived in Yemen to help those who were afflicted by the floods and rains in the Yemeni provinces. The second shipment consisted of 60 tons of food items while the first contained 38 tons of medicines and food.

30 June: Sheikh Khalifa bin Zayed Al Nahyan, during his reception of Frank Burotera, the French Minister of Industry, Posts and Communications, was given a letter for Sheikh Zayed from the French President, Jacques Chirac, concerning bilateral relations between the two countries. During the reception, aspects of co-operation in various fields between the UAE and France were discussed.

Etisalat's Board of Administration decided to reduce its prices for some of the services it offers, beginning on 1 September. The following fees and charges have been reduced: the quarterly fee of ordinary telephones reduced by 10 per cent; the cost of international telephone calls reduced by up to 15 percent; a 50 per cent reduction of installation fees for an instrument which registers the calling number; reductions of the quarterly subscription fees for mobile telephones (GSM) by 25 per cent; reduction of the price of telephone calls at all times from mobiles telephones by 11 per cent. It was also decided to cancel fees for the installation of faxes.

The Council of Ministers

The Formation of the First Cabinet

His Highness Sheikh Zayed bin Sultan Al Nahyan on 9 December 1971 issued Federal Decree No. 2 for the year 1971 forming the first Federal Cabinet under the prime ministership of His Highness Sheikh Maktoum bin Rashid Al Maktoum. Included in the cabinet were:

Sheikh Hamdan bin Mohammad Al Nahyan, Deputy Prime Minister and Minister of Finance, Economy and Industry

Sheikh Mubarak bin Mohammad Al Nahyan, Minister of the Interior

Sheikh Mohammad bin Rashid Al Maktoum, Minister of Defence

Ahmed Khalifa Al Suweidi, Minister of Foreign Affairs

Sultan bin Ahmed Al Mualla, Minister of Health

Sheikh Mohammad bin Sultan Al Qassimi, Minister of Public Works

Sheikh Sultan bin Mohammad Al Qassimi, Minister of Education

Sheikh Abdulaziz bin Rashid Al Nuaimi, Minister of Communications

Hamad bin Mohammad Al Sharqi, Minister of Agriculture and Fisheries

Ahmed bin Hamid, Minister of Information

Ahmed bin Sultan bin Sulaim, Minister of Finance and Industry

Mohammad Said Al Mulla, Minister of State for Federation and Gulf Affairs and Acting Minister of Electricity

Mohammad Khalifa Al Kindi, Minister of Planning and Acting Minister of Housing

Mohammad Habroush Al Suweidi, Minister of State and Acting Minister of State for Supreme Council Affairs

Otaiba bin Abdulla Al Otaiba, Minister of State for Council of Ministers Affairs

Abdulla Omran Taryam, Minister of Justice

Rashid bin Humaid, Minister of Youth and Sports

Thani bin Essa bin Harib, Minister of Labour and Social Affairs

Hamad bin Saif Al Sharqi, Minister of State

On 19 February 1972 Federal Decree No. 12/19172 was issued which made the following appointments:

Abdulla Humaid Al Qassimi, Minister of Electricity

Said Abdulla Salman, Minister of Housing

Abdulmalik Kayid Al Qassimi, Minister of State for Supreme Council Affairs

On 2 May 1972 Federal Decree No. 42/1972 was issued making the following appointments:

Hammouda bin Ali, Minister of State for Interior Affairs

There was also a reshuffle whereby the following changes were made:

Dr Abdulla Omran Taryam, Minister of Education instead of Justice

Sheikh Ahmed bin Sultan Al Qassimi, Minister of Justice

The Composition of the Cabinet 1973-1977

His Highness Sheikh Zayed bin Sultan Al Nahyan issued Federal Decree No. 43/1973 forming the Council of Ministers under the Prime Ministership of Sheikh Maktoum bin Rashid al Maktoum with the following members:

Sheikh Khalifa bin Zayed Al Nahyan, Deputy Prime Minister of the Council of Ministers

Sheikh Hamdan bin Rashid Al Maktoum, Minister of Finance and Industry

Hamdan bin Mohammad Al Nahyan, Minister of Public Works

Sheikh Mubarak bin Mohammad Al Nahyan, Minister of the Interior

Sheikh Mohammad bin Rashid Al Maktoum, Minister of Defence

Ahmed Khalifa Al Suweidi, Minister of Foreign Affairs

Sultan bin Ahmed Al Mualla, Minister of Economy and Trade

Saif bin Mohammad Al Nahyan, Minister of Health

Mohammad bin Sultan Al Qassimi, Minister of Labour

Abdulla Omran Taryam, Minister of Education

Mana Said At Otaiba, Minister of Petroleum and Mineral Resources

Mohammad Said Al Mulla, Minister of Communications

Abdulaziz Rashid Al Nuaimi, Minister of Social Affairs

Abdulla bin Humaid Al Qassimi, Minister of Electricity and Water

Ahmed bin Sultan Al Qassimi, Minister of Justice

Ahmed bin Hamid, Minister of Information and Tourism

Sheikh Hamad bin Mohammad Al Sharqi, Minister of Agriculture and Fisheries

Said bin Salman, Minister of Housing

Thani bin Essa Harib, Minister of Islamic Affairs and Awqaf

Rashid bin Humaid, Minister of Youth and Sports

Mohammad Khalifa Al Kindi, Minister of Planning

Abdulmalik Kayid Al Qassimi, Minister of State for Supreme Council Affairs

Mohammad Habroush Al Suweidi, Minister of State for Finance and Industry

Hammouda bin Ali, Minister of State for the Interior

Saif Said Ghobash, Minister of State for Foreign Affairs

Said Al Ghaith, Minister of State for Information

Hamad bin Saif Al Sharqi, Minister of State

The Composition of the Cabinet 1977-79

On 3 January 1977, Sheikh Zayed bin Sultan Al Nahyan issued a Federal Decree forming the Council of Ministers under the Prime Ministership of Sheikh Maktoum bin Rashid Al Maktoum with the following members:

Sheikh Hamdan bin Mohammad Al Nahyan, Deputy Prime Minister

Sheikh Hamdan bin Rashid Al Maktoum, Minister of Finance and Industry

Sheikh Mubarak bin Mohammad Al Nahyan, Minister of the Interior

Sheikh Mohammad bin Rashid Al Maktoum, Minister of Defence

Ahmed Khalifa Al Suweidi, Minister of Foreign Affairs

Sultan bin Ahmed Al Mualla, Minister of Economy and Trade

Ahmed bin Hamid, Minister of Information and Culture

Mohammad Said Al Mulla, Minister of Communications

Mohammad Khalifa Al Kindi, Minister of Public Works and Housing

Abdulla Omran Taryam, Minister of Education and Youth

Dr Mana Said Al Otaiba, Minister of Petroleum and Mineral Resources

Thani bin Essa Harib, Minister of Electricity and Water

Hammouda bin Ali, Minister of State for the Interior

Saif bin Ghobash, Minister of State for Foreign Affairs

Ahmed bin Sultan Al Qassimi, Minister of State (without portfolio)

Said Al Ghaith, Minister of State for Cabinet Affairs

Abdulaziz bin Humaid Al Qassimi, Minister of State for Supreme Council Affairs

Mohammad Abdulrahman Al Bakr, Minister of Justice, Islamic Affairs and Awqaf

Khalfan Al Roumi, Minister of Health

Abdulla Al Mazroui, Minister of Labour and Social Affairs

Said Ghobash, Minister of Planning

Said Al Raqbani, Minister of Agriculture and Fisheries

The Composition of the Cabinet 1979-1990

His Highness Sheikh Zayed bin Sultan Al Nahyan issued a Federal Decree on 30 April 1979 forming the Council of Ministers under the Prime Ministership of Sheikh Rashid bin Said Al Maktoum with the following members:

Sheikh Hamdan bin Mohammad Al Nahyan, Deputy Prime Minister

Sheikh Hamdan bin Rashid Al Maktoum, Minister of Finance and Industry

Sheikh Mubarak bin Mohammad Al Nahyan, Minister of the Interior

Sheikh Mohammad bin Rashid Al Maktoum, Minister of Defence

Ahmed Khalifa Al Suweidi, Minister of Foreign Affairs

Dr Mana Said Al Otaiba, Minister of Petroleum and Mineral Resources

Sultan bin Ahmed Al Mualla, Minister of Economy and Trade

Ahmed bin Hamid, Minister of Information and Culture

Mohammad Said Al Mulla, Minister of Communications

Hammouda bin Ali, Minister of State for Interior Affairs

Mohammad Khalifa Al Kindi, Minister of Public Works and Housing

Said Salman, Minister of Education and Youth

Ahmed Sultan Al Qassimi, Minister of State (without portfolio)

Said Ghobash, Minister of Planning

Said Al Ghaith, Minister of State for Cabinet Affairs

Abdulaziz bin Humaid Al Qassimi, Minister of State for Supreme Council Affairs

Abdulrahman Al Bakr, Minister of Justice, Islamic Affairs and Awqaf

Said Al Raqbani, Minister of Agriculture and Fisheries

Rashid Abdulla, Minister of State for Foreign Affairs

Humaid Nasser Al Nowais, Minister of Electricity and Water

Saif Al Jarwan, Minister of Labour and Social Affairs

Hamad Abdulrahman Al Madfa, Minister of Health

This, the fourth cabinet in the life of the federation, continued its work until it was reformed in 1983 when two ministers were relieved of their duties and seven added in their place.

Said Salman, Minister of Education, and Abdulrahman Al Bakr, Minister of Justice, Islamic Affairs and Awqaf were relieved of their duties.

The ministers appointed to the cabinet were:

Saif Al Jarwan, Minister of Economy and Trade

Faraj Fadhil Al Mazroui, Minister of Education

Khalfan Al Roumi, Minister of Labour and Social Affairs

Abdulla Humaid Al Mazroui, Minister of Justice

Sheikh Mohammad bin Hassan Al Khazraji, Minister of Islamic Affairs and Awqaf

Ahmed Humaid Al Tayer, Minister of State for Financial Affairs and Industry

Humaid bin Ahmed Al Mualla, Minister of Planning

The Composition of the Cabinet
8 July 1983

His Highness Sheikh Rashid bin Said Al Maktoum , Prime Minister

Sheikh Maktoum bin Rashid Al Maktoum, Deputy Prime Minister

Sheikh Hamdan bin Mohammad Al Nahyan, Deputy Prime Minister

Sheikh Hamdan bin Rashid Al Maktoum, Minister of Finance and Industry

Sheikh Mohammad bin Rashid, Minister of Defence

Sheikh Mubarak bin Mohammad, Minister of the Interior

Dr Mana Said Al Otaiba, Minister of Petroleum and Mineral Resources

Sheikh Ahmed bin Hamid, Minister of Information and Culture

Rashid Abdulla, Minister of State for Foreign Affairs

Ahmed Sultan Al Qassimi, Minister of State

Abdulaziz bin Humaid Al Qassimi, Minister of State for Supreme Council Affairs

Said Al Ghaith, Minister of State for Cabinet Affairs

Said Al Raqbani, Minister of Agriculture and Fisheries

Mohammad Said Al Mulla, Minister of Communications

Humaid Nasser Al Nowais, Minister of Electricity and Water

General Hammouda bin Ali, Minister of State for Internal Affairs

Saif Al Jarwan, Minister of Economy and Trade

Hamad Al Madfa, Minister of Health

Mohammad Khalifa Al Kindi, Minister of Works and Housing

Faraj Fadhil Al Mazroui, Minister of Education

Khalfan Al Roumi, Minister of Labour and Social Affairs

Abdulla Humaid Al Mazroui, Minister of Justice

Sheikh Mohammad bin Hassan Al Khazraji, Minister of Islamic Affairs and Awqaf

Ahmed Humaid Al Tayer, Minister of State for Financial Affairs and Industry

Humaid bin Ahmed Al Mualla, Minister of Planning

In 1979, the Ministry of Justice and the Ministry of Islamic Affairs and Awqaf became a single Ministry with Sheikh Mohammad bin Hassan Al Khazraji as Minister.

Said Ghobash was appointed Minister of State for Supreme Council Affairs succeeding Abdulaziz Humaid Al Qassimi.

The Minister of Education, Faraj Fadhil Al Mazroui, resigned from his post in 1986 and Ahmed Humaid Al Tayer replaced him.

The Composition of the Cabinet 1990 -

His Highness Sheikh Zayed bin Sultan Al Nahyan issued a Federal Decree on 20 November 1990 forming the new Council of Ministers under the Prime Ministership of Sheikh Maktoum bin Rashid Al Maktoum with the following members:

Sheikh Sultan bin Zayed Al Nahyan, Deputy Prime Minister

Hamdan bin Rashid Al Maktoum, Minister of Finance and Industry

Mohammad bin Rashid Al Maktoum, Minister of Defence

Hammouda bin Ali, Minister of the Interior

Rashid Abdulla, Minister of Foreign Affairs

Mohammad Said Al Mulla, Minister of Communications

Humaid bin Ahmed Al Mualla, Minister of Planning

Mohammad bin Ahmed Al Khazraji, Minister of Islamic Affairs and Awqaf

Humaid bin Nasser Al Nowais, Minister of Electricity and Water

Said Ghobash, Minister of Economy and Commerce

Said Al Raqbani, Minister of Agriculture and Fish Resources

Said Al Jarwan, Minister of Labour and Social Affairs

Said Al Ghaith, Minister of State for Cabinet Affairs

Khalfan Mohammad Al Roumi, Minister of Information and Culture

Hamad Abdulrahman Al Madfa, Minister of Education

Ahmed Humaid Al Tayer, Minister of State for Financial Affairs and Industry

Hamdan bin Zayed Al Nahyan, Minister of State for Foreign Affairs

Mohammad bin Saqr bin Mohammad Al Qassimi, Minister of State for Supreme Council Affairs

Nahyan bin Mubarak Al Nahyan, Minister of Higher Education

Abdulla bin Omran Taryam, Minister of Justice

Ahmed bin Said Al Badi, Minister of Health

Yousif bin Omair bin Yousif, Minister of Petroleum and Mineral Resources

Rakad bin Salim bin Rakad, Minister of Public Works and Housing

Faisal bin Khalid bin Mohammad, Minister of Youth and Sports

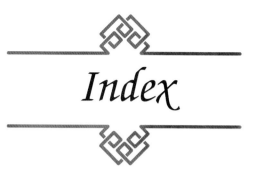

Index